ZOMBIE THEORY

ZOMBIE
THEORY

A Reader

SARAH JULIET LAURO Editor

University of Minnesota Press
Minneapolis
London

Published by the University of Minnesota Press
111 Third Avenue South, Suite 290
Minneapolis, MN 55401-2520
http://www.upress.umn.edu

Printed in the United States of America on acid-free paper

The University of Minnesota is an equal-opportunity educator and employer.

22 21 20 19 18 17   10 9 8 7 6 5 4 3 2 1

Library of Congress Cataloging-in-Publication Data
Names: Lauro, Sarah Juliet, editor.
Title: Zombie theory : a reader / Sarah Juliet Lauro, editor.
Description: Minneapolis : University of Minnesota Press, [2017] | Includes bibliographical references and
    index. |
Identifiers: LCCN 2017001738 (print) | ISBN 978-1-5179-0090-8 (hc) | ISBN 978-1-5179-0091-5 (pb)
Subjects: LCSH: Zombies. | Zombies—Social aspects. | Zombies in popular culture. | BISAC: SOCIAL
    SCIENCE / Popular Culture. | LITERARY CRITICISM / General. | PERFORMING ARTS / Film & Video /
    General.
Classification: LCC GR581 .Z64 2017 (print) | DDC 398.21—dc23
LC record available at https://lccn.loc.gov/2017001738

Contents

Introduction

Wander and Wonder in Zombieland

SARAH JULIET LAURO

For a long time, I've felt as if I were being chased by a horde of zombies—the kind that spring up out of the ground like itinerant mushrooms and swell to insurmountable numbers at your heels. These aren't real zombies, of course, but articles, essays, chapters, short stories, comics, and books *about* zombies, the catalog of which has seemed to grow exponentially over the past decade. Once I felt, working on a dissertation, and then a book, on the figure of the living dead, that I had to read them all. I didn't, I couldn't, I haven't, and I won't. For I soon found that by the time one compiles a reading list and works one's way, methodically, through it, a whole new crop have sprouted that need to have their heads kicked off. It's rather like the way they are never *not* painting the Golden Gate Bridge, or so my grandmother tells me, for as soon as they finish at one end, they have to begin again at the other.

Today, one can find the image of the zombie emblazoned on a wide variety of items, including, but not limited to, lunch boxes, backpacks, pencil cases, wristwatches, iPhone cases, guitar picks and guitar straps, bottles of hand sanitizer, gel pens, key chains, keys and key toppers (Zombikeys), temporary tattoos, lapel pins, and dozens of zombie-themed T-shirts, socks, and even baby onesies. There are novelty items, like a pencil holder in which the writing implement impales a zombie statuette, various zombie pacifiers that give one's infant a grisly gob, zombie garden gnomes, the now infamous Zombie of MontClaire Moors lawn sculpture as seen in the in-flight catalog on various airlines, a zombie front yard flamingo by Forum Novelties Inc., and multiple styles of tin yard signs warning of zombies à la "beware of the dog." There are also zombie items for Fido: a bandana reading "K-9 division zombie hunter," dog tags, and a zombie's severed foot that serves as a chew toy. And, for the kitchen, Undead Fred zombie cookie cutters, a Zombie Brain Jell-O mold, assorted coffee mugs, an Elixir of the Dead wine bottle holder and many zombie-themed wines and craft beers, a cookie jar made out of a zombie's head, Zombie Jerky and Zombie Blood edible snacks, a Zombie Survival energy drink, and Zombie Cajun hot sauce. For the lady in your life, you might buy a zombie cameo necklace by Mobtown Chicago or Zombie for Her spray cologne by Demeter. There are too many games (including bowling pins), toys (including rubber duckies), and other zombie paraphernalia (plush slippers) to mention here. And there are also real weapons and survival kits marketed to the zombie enthusiast, such as the Zombie Apocalypse Survival Kit by Gerber (not the baby food) that includes three knives, two machetes, and an ax in a handy carrying case as well as various other items purportedly for zombie hunting; ammo kits and tin survival kits; zombie target practice sheets; and three-dimensional zombie target dummies that "bleed" when you shoot them. All of this leaves out a myriad of paperbacks, DVDs, video games, comic books, and posters as well as commodities marketed explicitly for Halloween, such as masks, various zombie costumes—including my favorite, Zombie Marie Antoinette—and candy bowls for the porch, seasonal decorations, and zombie makeup kits. Listing all of these items here displays our culture's obsession with zombies and makes visible one of the zombie's most historically legible shibboleths: its gross materialism that is a reflection of our gross materialism.[1] Today, there are many keys in which the zombie narrative plays: there are even appearances of zombies in television commercials advertising cell phones for Sprint, Starburst candy, and Audi cars. Some of these uses of the zombie make for irritating ditties, signifying little and representing a much stripped-down version of the zombie's true complexity, but others transmute our most pressing concerns into haunting and beautiful music.

Though the old adage has it that one ought not judge a book by its cover, one has merely to look at the width of Peter Dendle's two volumes of his *Zombie Movie Encyclopedia*, one devoted to the years 1932–2000 and the second covering only 2000–2010, to see that zombie cinema has lately undergone what Kyle Bishop calls a "renaissance."[2] For Dendle's second volume, spanning only the first decade of the twenty-first century, is longer than the first, which covers the entire history of zombies on film in the twentieth century, by some thirty pages. Fictions produced on the topic in media besides film, such as literature and video games, have kept pace with the number of zombie movies produced. But, as the wide array of zombie commodities—from the bizarre to the banal—indicates, it is also true that the first decades of the twenty-first century witnessed a diversification of zombie demography.

The zombie is not just more present than ever before; it is also more various, and creatures called "zombies" have evolved from their frightening forebears to include comical, romantic, musical, and otherwise anodyne undead. For example, although one expects to find a hefty selection of zombie literature housed in the fantasy or young adult section of the bookstore, and among the graphic novels and comic books, one now finds an increasing diversity of zombies lurking even in the humor section (as mock self-help books or revisions of literary classics "now with violent zombie mayhem") and in the children's section (see, for example, *Zombie in Love* or, a parody of that famously famished caterpillar, *The Very Hungry Zombie*), and they are featured in highly lauded works of contemporary fiction (most notably Colson Whitehead's *Zone One*).[3] Similarly, zombies' digital presence has outgrown the violent first-person shoot-'em-ups and video games that are often credited with the living dead's cultural revitalization and can be found in child-friendly, low-action games like *Plants vs. Zombies*, in educational games like *Math vs. Zombies* (aimed at the K–5 crowd), or in apps to encourage joggers to keep up the pace: Zombies, Run![4]

Because of the zombie's mutability, "What the Zombie Apocalypse Means"—which is incidentally the subtitle of a collection called *Thinking Dead* edited by Murali Balaji— is as roundly metaphysical and complicated a question as the smoking caterpillar's query to Alice: "Who are *you?*" Alice can't answer the question because, having changed sizes, she is no longer sure of herself: "I know who I *was* when I got up this morning, but I think I must have been changed several times since then." Similarly, no one can seem to agree on what the zombie means because, in part, the zombie keeps changing.

Perhaps it remains so captivating to audiences and critics alike because of its fungibility: in one film, its cultural capital is spent representing serious threats like the AIDS panic, fears of racial contamination, and concerns about corruption amid third world development projects, but then one changes the channel and finds zombies on the animated show *SpongeBob SquarePants,* mocking the poor work ethic of a slacker employee in a fast-food joint.

The semiotic "prolixity" of the zombie genre, as Jonathan Eburne writes in *The Year's Work at the Zombie Research Center,*[5] may seem to some the result of the commercial appropriation of the figure (not unlike the way one finds kale in *everything* these days), but the zombie was *never* just one thing. Inherently dual—both living *and* dead—the zombie dwells in contradiction even more than most monsters, which are, as Jeffrey Cohen writes, border crashers by nature, hybrids that "seldom can be contained in a simple, binary dialectic."[6]

As Karen Embry and I first articulated in our article "A Zombie Manifesto: The Nonhuman Condition in the Era of Advanced Capitalism," the zombie's paradoxicality (as living/dead, for example) is the source of its symbolic potential—and for us, this meant specifically its usefulness as a figure that grapples with the fundamental irreconcilability of capitalism and humanism. I now wonder if the zombie's refusal to be just one thing may have translated into its protean nature: that because it operates not on the model of the *either/or* (and neither appropriately *both/and*) but on something closer to the fundamentally pessimistic *neither/nor,* it was thought that it might be made to signify *anything.*

Like poor Alice, then, we have multiple questions at hand. One is, how did we get here? Whence does our cultural fascination with zombies come? Another is, why are we seemingly so surrounded by zombies these days? And, perhaps most central to this volume's purpose, what makes the zombie itself and the zombie's popularity worthy of serious study?

Some may think of this monster as American, but it is deeply global. While I trace the zombie's history in detail in my book *The Transatlantic Zombie,* I'll keep to a thumbnail sketch here, one that is specific to my own assessment of the myth's transmission. I argue in my book that the zombie is an "American" monster only in the sense that it comes directly out of a history of colonialism, enslavement, exploitation, and appropriation. The zombie's lineage can be traced to African soul capture myths that were carried to the New World aboard slave ships bound for the colonial Caribbean. The zombie as we know it today comes from the Haitian *zombi,* a product of sorcery in which a witch doctor enslaves a victim whom he has raised from the dead to do his bidding or work for him for free. Keeping the zombie perpetually in a semiconscious state in between living and dead, the zombie master maintains control (it is said) by means of a powerful narcotic or poison concoction. In its earliest iteration, the *zombi* was read as symbolic of the Caribbean country's past as a plantation economy built on slave labor: drained of its own resources and existing only for the benefit of others. Importantly, the zombie was first brought to Hollywood's attention as a direct result of the neocolonial Occupation of Haiti (1915–34), whereafter the figure was reshaped and rebranded with the mark of a new society's concerns.

In brief, the zombie's uptake in U.S. popular culture was given life by an initial interest in the folkloric Vodou zombie, but the first films exoticized the Caribbean and eroticized racial difference in ways that were deeply problematic. The popularity of the monster, along with the fact that, as a creature derived from folklore, there was no estate to whom one had to pay copyright, as with *Dracula* or *Frankenstein*, ensured the reproduction and revision of the zombie's narrative.[7] As the living dead bore its way deeper into cinema and pulp fiction, it transformed, a pivotal turn that is most commonly identified with the films of George Romero but that really begins with some of the B movies of the 1950s, in which the reanimated were tinged with concerns about atomic power, nuclear waste, and Cold War tensions.[8] Ever since Romero's 1968 film *Night of the Living Dead* presented audiences with a reanimated contagious cannibal and emphasized an apocalyptic breakdown of society as the fallout of the undead epidemic, the zombie has been declared reborn, divested of its origins in the Vodou *zombi*—a myth that was overtly about the enslavement of Africans—and perceived as a more varied signifier capable of incarnating fears of disease and the body's vulnerability, the uncertainty of life after death, the susceptibility of the polis to outside influences, the fragility of law and order in the face of widespread chaos, and—especially with the addition of the zombie's cannibalistic nature—the rapacious hunger of a capitalistic and increasingly corporate society, but also much, much more. However, this whitewashing of the zombie is, to my mind, just as problematic as the grotesque caricatures of the first wave of zombie cinema, for it represents a cultural appropriation of a myth that, ironically or aptly, was *itself* about appropriation—specifically, the appropriation of labor and life under colonial slavery. George Romero's recent passing calls for an account of his central role in the zombie's evolution—most important, to my mind, is the way that his films preserved race as a major theme in zombie films. He is mourned by all who have celebrated the zombie as a valuable figure for meditating on our culture's enduring demons.

In one of its registers, especially in the Western hemisphere, the zombie had signified the powerlessness of the colonial slave who inspired its ancestral mythology, and then the powerlessness manufactured under capitalism, colonialism's heir. Indeed, because of its history, it seemed that the zombie made for a convenient bogeyman in times of economic crisis, such as the great, global recession that marred the first decade of the new millennium. Looking at the surge in zombie cinema and its increasing diversity, many felt the zombie resonated with the occurrences that defined the era: the global economic downturn; the advent of new, anesthetizing pocket technology; the increased sense of terrorist threats in the wake of 9/11; the perpetuation of a state of constant warfare; the looming sense of ecological disaster; a shift in demographics toward an overall aging population.[9] The zombie's symbolic potential seemed profound, and, like the joker in a deck of playing cards, it has been made to take on various suits, signifying a range of conundrums. The zombie's fluidity, what I call in my book its "semiotic fecundity"—its ability to bear a variety of cultural concerns, from environmental anxieties to political critiques—has ensured its continued relevance in diverse contexts.

But, the zombie signifier should not be confused for a whiteboard, onto the face of which we can write whatever we want. As Jennifer Fay writes in the fantastic article "Dead Subjectivity: *White Zombie*, Black Baghdad," on the first ever zombie film and the U.S. Occupation of Haiti, "if today's zombies are the postmodern, timeless creatures of remakes and sequels, it is in part because they have their origins in narratives of erasure."[10] Our modern zombie is a palimpsest. It should not be lost on film audiences that the origin of the zombie is the former colony called Saint-Domingue, the site of the slave revolt that became a revolution for independence, in which an army of insurgent slaves, maroons, free blacks, and mixed-race planters defeated three European armies to declare themselves the citizens of the sovereign republic of Haiti. The zombie is always tinged with this history and represents simultaneously the history of the Atlantic slave trade and also legacies of resistance.

The specter of the African slave remains in the image of the zombie—and cannot be effaced. At times, this changes its meaning. The cannibal zombies that staggered around the shopping mall in Romero's 1978 film *Dawn of the Dead*, for example, were immediately recognized as a critique of consumer capitalism, though the truth is that this follows the lineage of the zombie's folkloric origins in imagery exposing the greed of the colonial oppressor. Thus the zombie may seem to have been pirated: made to bear a new load and to fly a different flag, but I argue in my book that the myth seems, at times, to be following its own course. Even as a symbol, the zombie is unruly and rebellious: just as the monster is never fully living nor entirely dead, it is never wholly terrifying but also pitiable, in between agent and object, master and subject, neither the capable captain nor merely his commanded craft—and this is precisely what makes it worthy of our critical attentions.

In the new millennium, people across all disciplines and from various parts of the globe were swept up by the zombie's increased cultural caché. A special segment on zombies produced by the American outlet Al Jazeera+ in October 2013 reported that the countries with the highest number of Google searches for the word "zombie" were Indonesia, the Philippines, and Vietnam: all, it bears emphasizing, former colonial outposts. Of late, Israel has been having its own zombie renaissance, and Egyptian protest artist Ganzeer has used the zombie to satirize politics in the wake of the Arab Spring.[11] The explosion of interest in the zombie is increasingly interdisciplinary and international, and the monster's pervasiveness right now suggests its legibility as a figure ripe for potential analysis or the (mistaken) assumption that it is an analogic machine that can be reprogrammed to perform a variety of functions.[12]

Zombies on television may be popular internationally, but these serials are not always worthy of extensive dissection. Of course, there is the AMC show *The Walking Dead*, and its new spinoff *Fear the Walking Dead*, but also a pseudo–detective fiction show called *iZombie*, in which an attractive reanimate eats brains to help the police solve murders. The BBC's *In the Flesh* and the French series *Les Revenants*, however, are respectively charming and thoughtful, and cerebral and moody, with narratives that incorporate issues like gay rights and subtly raise the issue of illegal immigration. These European offerings highlight the living dead as a vehicle for dramatizing the way certain types of people are ostracized in contemporary society, or even dehumanized, with representations of the reanimated as speaking, feeling protagonists who make up a feared and oppressed minority. In both shows, the word "zombie" is used as a derogatory term, and the returned or the "partially deceased syndrome sufferers" grapple with their new identity, postmortem. Such examples are in keeping with the zombie's complex history, as the undead characters feel pulled between a desire to retaliate against their monstrous treatment and to be docile, invisible members of society. As relatively new contributions to the zombie mythos, *In the Flesh* and *Les Revenants* also illustrate that to keep pace with the production of new narratives and the evolution of our interest in figures of living death, there will yet be more critical work to do on the "zombie."

The zombie now exists beyond the register of films, fictions, popular nonfiction books (such as Matt Mogk and Max Brooks's *Everything You Ever Wanted to Know about Zombies*), and a variety of live-action zombie events (like walks, runs, pub crawls, proms, and games of tag); it exists also in the academic work that itself purports to explain the monster's significances. Scholarly interest in the zombie myth, which was first made in response to cinema, has risen to the challenge of addressing the rebirth of the zombie and the expansion of the cultural work performed by the living dead, as its presence moved beyond the moving picture to venues as diverse as literature, the visual arts, and public performance. If the zombie underwent a *renaissance* in the late 1990s and the first decade of the new millennium, then a *boom* in zombie scholarship followed swiftly thereafter, a resounding acknowledgment that the increased popularity of the monster had not been lost on cultural critics; that the significances of this surge were worthy of study; and that the many, varied, and historically changing meanings of the monster represented a mostly unmapped territory of the collective unconscious. This collection devotes itself to addressing the horde of zombie scholarship that has been produced as a result of the zombie boom.

Zombies have garnered interest in a variety of academic disciplines in the humanities (for example, in literary, media, cultural, and religious studies) but also beyond them, spreading into sociology, economics, computer science, mathematics, and even epidemiology. Zombies are useful metaphors to discuss diverse phenomena, such as the "zombie categories" first described by sociologist Ulrich Beck, zombie banks, or hacked "zombie" computers, and the zombie narrative has also provided a model for mapping a particular algorithm, or explaining the spread of viruses, and a model for epidemic preparedness put forth by the Centers for Disease Control and Prevention (CDC).[13] A recent book by Timothy Verstynen and Bradley Voytek, for example, called *Do Zombies Dream of Undead Sheep?*, uses comparisons to the zombie to explain the basic principles of neuroscience and some of the complications that arise when the brain doesn't function as one expects. A book by Lisa Desjardins and Richard Emerson, *Zombie Economics*, uses the zombie as a framework for "a guide for personal finance."

Recently, zombies have been useful as we think about the future of academia in a neoliberal economy, when the fate of the university is challenged by things like an increasing(ly) precarious workforce and massive student debt. The editors of the collection *Zombies in the Academy* state in their introduction to the book that it purports "to confront the 'living death' of higher education" and to "do so with the aim of reanimating—or at least 'undeadening'—the current debates about the future of the sector" (3). More broadly, too, the zombie has been a very useful figure for thinking through the workings of neoliberalism in our era. In the collection *Zombies and Sexuality*, edited by Shaka McGlotten and Steve Jones, to take an unlikely example, there are multiple essays highlighting zombies under neoliberalism. And whether the individual authors read the narrative of the zombie apocalypse as a promise "of a clean break and a fresh start," in which the characters are unburdened by the dictates of the American dream and decide for themselves what determines "success," or whether the author finds the persistence of neoliberal ideology in a narrative about a zombie who, through love and hard work, is returned to a human state, it is clear that this myth has an especial relevance today.[14] Under neoliberalism, Jeffrey Nealon explains, "we are at present made to live *and* left to die" in a kind of zombie paradox. In his afterword to Comentale and Jaffe's *The Year's Work at the Zombie Research Center*, titled "Zombie Archive," Nealon writes that "with the neoliberal evisceration of that welfare state capitalism, with the complete unraveling of the liberal state, we in the first world have perhaps jumped the 'or' in Foucault's dual formulation (made to live *or* left to die)."[15] As is evidenced here, zombie scholarship often goes beyond commentary on zombie fictions to read our real world as a landscape peopled with the undead, making manifest latent tensions but also contributing new formulations and figurations of living death to the mythos. It also works to expose and unpack places where real people (like the disabled, the diseased, the drug addicted, or the homeless) are rewritten as the living dead. Both Anna Mae Duane's essay herein and that by Linnemann, Wall, and Green address the complexities inherent in such simile. Indeed, the field of zombie studies has become a constellation in the zombie cosmos, and it is to this corner of the undead universe that this volume provides a guide.

Somewhere along the line, when it finally seemed that the cultural and scholarly interest in the zombie was more than just a passing fad, I started conceptualizing this book. Initially, the objective was to gather together the very best pieces of predecessor zombie scholarship so that future scholars might have a single source to draw from as the zombie's role in popular culture continues to evolve, but given that there is so much diversity of attention given to the zombie, this immediately proved an impossible task. Like water collecting in tide pools, the field of zombie scholarship is scattered across a wide reef, and one could have a single volume of a longer series devoted just to the best scholarship on folkloric zombies (which would include the seminal linguistic and anthropological study by Ackermann and Gautier and excerpts from W. B. Seabrook's *The Magic Island* and Wade Davis's two books), another for early cinematic zombies, yet another on the contagious cannibal after Romero, and others on all manner of subsets within the zombie genus.

Resources on the Internet already exist if, for example, one wants to follow the philosophic zombie down the rabbit hole and visit with work by John Searle, Daniel Dennett, David Chalmers, Robert Kirk, and many others to explore the zombie's uses as a thought experiment addressing the "hard problem" of consciousness.[16] And, if not right now, I think that in a few years' time, we will be able to cull together a whole volume's worth of resources on the zombie in public space: be it performance or protest. In thinking about the field of zombie studies; the academic scholarship that has risen to address this figure's role in cinema, in literature, and, more widely, in popular culture; and the difficulty of producing a volume that would adequately represent it, I thought of George Pfau's monumental *Zombieindex*.

California-based artist George Pfau's Web-based art piece *Zombieindex* concretizes the cultural zombie invasion in a single, albeit multidimensional, multifaceted piece. Originally created as a large watercolor, colored pencil, and ink drawing of a pan-zombie horde, its multidimensionality comes from its multimodal and interactive Internet life. At the live URL Zombieindex.net, the viewer is first greeted by a wide panorama dotted with a panoply of small humanoid forms. Color appears vibrant in certain areas of the visual field, punctuated by deep blues and reds and dark violet; muted in others in a soft, drab yellow, a lilac, or tan; and monochrome in other places, with just a thin gray line, so that at first one's eye struggles to find order within the pattern. The corners, for example, and some of the edges of the frame are brighter: the figures are black lined and jump out immediately to the viewer, recognizable as human bodies. In the bottom left-hand corner, my eye picks out a woman in a blue dress, a man in a winter parka. Across the right side of the space, however, there is less detail to the individual forms—as if a funnel-shaped cloud is obscuring the view of those bodies just behind it. Or else it looks like a page of a coloring book as yet unfinished. Just beneath the image, slightly left of center, there are several buttons, such as one might find on an Internet map page, to toggle left and right, to zoom in on the grid of a city space. Beneath the right side, three words appear in block letters: ZOMBIES, NAMES, INFO. The capital *I*s in the words "zombies" and "info" are in red.

As the cursor floats across the image, the invitation to discover more is signaled by the arrow's transformation into the icon of a small white-gloved hand, index figure extended to indicate an area of interest. If one uses the manicule to click on any given space in the field, that part of the image is enlarged for a closer look. The directional buttons and the three tabs ("Zombies," "Names," and "Info"—to which I'll turn my attention momentarily) remain at the bottom of the screen even when the image is magnified, its tightest focus acquired at three clicks.

The viewer is encouraged to play the image like a keyboard. Scrolling horizontally and vertically, the eye is treated to a diverse array of bodies in a range of different styles and with varying amounts of detail: some are rendered sharply in black and white, others in vivacious color; still others are little more than a series of dots or a smear and only abstractly suggest a human form or a mass of connective tissue. Zooming in, figures that were originally centimeters tall now take up half of a computer screen. Now we see that what appeared as a gray blob at first glance is actually a hooded figure, somewhat like a grim reaper, or it is a gravestone, or it is a man in a gray suit, the top of his head gone. Dragging and pulling the image diagonally, one is given a better glimpse of the horde of zombies, up close in all of its diversity of characters as well as a range of abstraction.

A zombie expert in her own right, Annalee Newitz, author of *Pretend We're Dead: Capitalist Monsters in American Pop Culture*, a text that is required reading in zombie studies, writes of the piece on the popular science website io9.com, "The zombie's plurality is what artist George Pfau has tried to capture in his latest piece of interactive art, Zombie Index. When you go to the site, you'll see an intricate painting of thousands of figures, each standing in for a different kind of zombie. There are orgy zombies and flesh-eating zombies, alongside plague zombies and crap I can't even identify."[17]

The recognition of the zombies is a key element of the piece. For the seasoned zombie fan, this visual text acts like a kind of bizarre "Where's Waldo," or it may call to mind Richie Butcher's cover art for *Dookie*, a 1994 album by Bay Area punk band Green Day that has a similar Easter egg hunt aesthetic. In Pfau's *Zombieindex*, there is pleasure to be derived in the discovery of recognizable zombies amid the mob, such as Michael Jackson in his red leather jacket as a *Thriller* zombie, or the Tarman zombie from *Return of the Living Dead*, or the hoodie-sporting Otto from Bruce LaBruce's *Otto: or, Up with Dead People*. My favorite inclusions are in deference to the Haitian zombie: a man who claimed to have previously been zombified, Clairvius Narcisse; the lord of the cemetery, Baron Samedi; and the skeletal zombies of a 1950 painting by Wilson Bigaud. But the work also includes references to Pfau's other compositions, which far fewer viewers are likely to pinpoint correctly; for example, *Zombie Maison* is miniaturized and included in the *Zombieindex*: this is Pfau's recasting of Louise Bourgeois's *Femme Maison* (1947) with the house from *Night of the Living Dead* perched atop the female body. More importantly, perhaps, the piece challenges us not only to identify the nameable zombies but to think about what a zombie *is* and to question why Pfau includes the imagery that he does. Each figure or abstract figuration that one encounters must be considered, not passed over. Here is the unfortunate hanged man of the child's word game. Here is a group of naked people evacuating a stream of rainbow confetti from various orifices. Is this a reference to Julia Kristeva's theories of the abject, often mentioned in zombie scholarship? Here are several figures holding aloft their own heads; is this an allusion to the Catholic Saint Denis? Here is a stick figure with a blowfish for a head: is this meant to reference merely Wade Davis's research on the puffer fish poison tetrododoxin implicated in Haitian zombie making, or is there also a nod here to the zombie fishmen of Del Tenney's *Horror of Party Beach*? Here is Edvard Munch's screaming figure. Is that the shrunken head man from *Beetlejuice*? Wait, is that the Van Halen symbol, or something that I just can't identify—a zombie or zombie concept that is beyond my recognition?

Zombieindex inundates the viewer with its diverse characters in the two-dimensional plane of the pictorial field. And, in the interactivity of its form, which can be magnified and manipulated to different views, it approximates the oversaturation of our culture with entertainment media. But, more deeply, *Zombieindex* explores what our fascination and seemingly endless reproduction of zombie narratives say about the way our culture both categorizes people and abstracts humanity. It does this most explicitly with its play with visual abstraction.

Pfau has stated, "The visual ideas I've been thinking about involve the amount of information necessary for a figure, or human, or zombie to be recognized. So, I've included a lot of variety in this regard: from stick figures, to blobs, to outlines, to full color renderings."[18] Elsewhere in Pfau's oeuvre, one finds this element developed further.[19] Pfau's Zombiescapes are luscious oil paintings that capture a single frame from a

xviii SARAH JULIET LAURO

zombie film, rendered in a pointillist style. The artist's intentions here are complex, but the stylistic appropriation emphasizes both the blurriness of the zombie identity and the body's breakdown in life as well as death: his use of an impressionist style parallels the physiological diffusion of the decaying body into its environment. Of that series, he says, "The landscapes are rendered in oil on linen allowing for a situation in which figures visibly blend into their environment, and vice versa."[20]

In *Zombieindex*, Pfau's dramatization of the human/zombie form includes shapes that resemble Keith Haring's people, stick figures, blobs, and squiggles that suggest bodies at different levels of being, as if he were trying to see what little economy of pencil strokes can still signify the body. In one place, he makes the word "ZOMBIE" itself suggestive of the human form. This imagistic acrobatics is in keeping with some of the ontological questioning that the zombie raises about being, and the line between life and death, but it is also political and epistemological in nature, as the zombie so often raises questions about who gets recognized as human and who is characterized as a zombie. This is a conversation that is scripted in multiple places in this volume and throughout zombie scholarship, about the dehumanization of others: enemy combatants, for instance; or "illegals," who are depicted as draining national resources; or the faceless underpaid workers in a country far away whose poverty benefits the shareholders and their profit margins; or, as in the zombie's origins in Haitian folklore, the African slave.

Clicking the tab called "Zombies" resets the zombie horde image to its original dimensions. On this page, as I've described, viewers can interact with the digitized image, zooming in for a closer look at the various figures that people the space. Clicking on "Info" raises a small square with the artist's name, his website, the year of production, and the work's copyright signature. On the page titled simply "Names"—which in its pictorial construction might remind one of the Vietnam Memorial in Washington, D.C.—the viewer is invited to click on red lowercase letters in a lexicon of Pfau's influences. Hyperlinks that are seemingly unrelated to the names with which they are connected provide channels to a barrage of articles, book reviews, YouTube clips, websites, and other points of interest for the zombie enthusiast. Just tracing my finger across one vertical line, I open channels to a plethora of references: a *Buzzfeed* article with a slideshow of pictures from a zombie-themed wedding; a scientific article on the tetrododoxin poison; an editorial linking the zombie narrative and mental illness; a PBS piece on what foods would be best to stockpile during a zombie apocalypse; a blog devoted to references to "zombies" in federal court cases; a video from the filmmakers of *Resident Evil* (2002) explaining how they choreographed zombie movement.

Standing (or, more likely, sitting) before it, one is mobbed by this piece: the scope and spectrum of the bodies included in the image and the sheer amount of information provided in the hyperlinks are overwhelming. The zombie jubilee presented in the drawing and the "live" names provide an embarrassment fitting of the typical cinematic zombie mob and of the best films' critiques of capitalist surplus or the excess of consumer culture. And, like most of the essays in this collection, it's about zombies, but it's also about more than just that.

Like the stick figures that pepper *Zombieindex*, the zombie generalizes the specific, rendering the individual into a blank, evacuating it of specific content and rendering it an icon, a floating signifier, rather like the personal pronoun "I," with which Pfau also plays in this work. Of the lowercase letter *i* Pfau has written, "I'm very interested in the anthropomorphic quality of the lowercase and uppercase letter 'I.'"[21] This is something that is highlighted in this expansive work, where the lowercase *i*, turned red, appears like a small human form on the page titled "Names," as if the *i*'s dot were a crown vulnerable to decapitation. Pfau's work is simultaneously about the way we determine what is a body and what is human and what is living, but it is also a commentary on life in the age of the Internet: the paradox of overstimulation, oversaturation, and increasing virtual connection in the face of an intangible, deadening zombification of society. At the same time, it's a visual record of the zombie's rich history, one that uses pictorial texture, in a spectrum ranging from translucent and monochromatic abstraction to dense, colorful detail no part of which should be erased. *Zombieindex* is a vibrant, beautiful, and thought-provoking piece, and I borrowed from it in considering how best to organize this collection. By invoking Pfau's work here, I gesture to the diversity and expansiveness of the field of zombie studies, and at the same time, its methodology informs this book, as I try to emulate the reach and interactivity of *Zombieindex* by providing crowded lists of further reading, bibliographic tours, and indices of references so that the reader can continue to seek information in a variety of areas.

More than a dozen book collections addressing the cultural significance of the zombie were published in the past decade (including one for which I served as an editor), and scores of journals put forth contributions to the zombie enthusiast's growing reading list. Many of these collections, such as my and Deborah Christie's *Better Off Dead: The Evolution of the Zombie as Posthuman* (2011) and Shawn McIntosh and Marc Leverette's *Zombie Culture: Autopsies of the Living Dead* (2008), are useful for tracing the history of the zombie from Haitian folklore to early radio dramas to the first wave of zombie cinema; and the majority of them, such as Stephanie Boluk and Wylie Lenz's *Generation Zombie: Essays on the Living Dead in Modern Culture* (2011) or Christopher Moreman and Cory James Rushton's *Zombies Are Us: Essays on the Humanity of the Walking Dead* (2011), feature highlights from the zombie's development, in the halcyon days of Romero and the splatter cinema it inspired; to the figure's rejuvenation in cinema, pulp fiction, and video games; to the zombie's transversal of traditional boundaries of fiction in zombie walks and survivalist groups; to its Web presence in Internet forums as a means of strategizing survival in dire circumstances. Other collections (like Christopher Moreman and Cory James Ruston's *Race, Oppression, and the Zombie*, 2011, or Cynthia Miller and Bowdoin J. Miller's *Undead in the West*, volumes 1 and 2, 2012–13) take up a particular theme in their investigation of narratives about the living dead. Still others use the figure for a specific pedagogic goal, like Kim Paffenroth and John Morehead's *Undead and Theology* (2012) or Richard Greene and K. Silem Mohammad's *Undead and Philosophy* (2006).[22] There have been single-author volumes devoted to the broader topic (Kyle Bishop's *American Zombie Gothic*, 2010, and Kim Paffenroth's *Gospel of the Living Dead*, 2006) and monographs that use the zombie to understand a particular feature of our contemporary world, such as international relations[23] or economics.[24] There have been books published devoted entirely to one narrative thread, such as Kevin J. Wetmore's *Back from the Dead* (2011), on remakes of Romero's films, and Dawn Keetley's edited collection on *The Walking Dead* show, "*We're All Infected*" (2014).[25] And, of course, there were others that looked at zombies alongside other types of apocalyptic narratives or that compared the zombie to other monsters. At the time of this writing, I personally know of at least six other volumes of new zombie scholarship in production. It is surprising even to me that the zombie's popularity has not diminished.

These volumes, and my own work, draw from foundational texts in horror and monster studies, such as Gregory Waller's *The Living and the Undead* (1986), or Noël Carroll's *The Philosophy of Horror* (1990), or Jeffrey Jerome Cohen's *Monster Theory* (1996), or Marina Warner's *Fantastic Metamorphoses, Other Worlds* (2002). Just as the zombie has a rich and varied history, so too does the legacy of zombie scholarship: the field has its own progenitors in texts like Maya Deren's and Zora Neale Hurston's attentions to the folkloric zombie, a trend that continues in the work of Mimi Sheller, Colin Dayan, Elizabeth McAlister, who is represented in this volume, and others whose work addresses the Haitian zombie in contemporary literature and culture. But it also draws from seminal work by Robin Wood, Steven Shaviro, and Slavoj Žižek's discussion of zombies (in *Looking Awry* and elsewhere) and those who treat zombie cinema classics, such as R. H. W. Dillard's essay on *Night of the Living Dead*, or A. Loudermilk's "Eating *Dawn* in the Dark," or Stephen Harper's "Zombies, Malls, and the Consumerism Debate," or Tony Williams's treatment of the first zombie film, *White Zombie*, in *Jump Cut*, or Gary Rhodes's book *Anatomy of a Horror Film*, not to mention those encyclopedic guides to zombie film by Jaime Russell, Peter Dendle, Glenn Kay, Jay Slater, and others.

Zombie Theory's contribution to the field is that it presents some of the best interdisciplinary scholarship gathered together in one volume. Here are pieces that have already been published and vetted; some of these have stood the test of time and remain culturally relevant, even as the zombie has transformed, such as Steven Shaviro's seminal discussion of Romero's *Living Dead* films from his book *The Cinematic Body*. Others swiftly became instant classics, must-reads for both horror scholars and zombie film fans, such as Gerry Canavan's essay on *The Walking Dead* and the "colonial gaze." The reason that I title this book *Zombie Theory: A Reader* rather than *Zombie Studies: A Reader* is that this collection is not a greatest hits album presenting the best scholarship on zombies in film, literature, comic books, video games, and other narratives; in fact, I guarantee that some of the reader's favorite pieces of zombie scholarship, or the ones he or she may deem the most important to understanding a certain feature of zombie narrative or a particular moment in its cinematic evolution, will be absent. Instead, this book presents a selection of those previously published essays that specifically use the zombie to think through other concepts or issues, presenting the zombie not merely as a monster but as a mode for theoretical work itself.

Zombie Theory is a collection of meditations on the zombie that presents the figure's uses as a theoretical apparatus in a variety of disciplines and methodological approaches. The pieces collected here do not merely *explain* one cinematic figure, but they bring into focus the way the zombie clarifies much larger issues with which we humans, either transhistorically or currently (at the turn of the twenty-first century) grapple—from the death drive and faith in an afterlife, to fears of contagious disease, to the relationship between capitalism and humanism, to the workings of contemporary horror film on the body—and as such, this is not only a book about zombies but is also about much more. The hope is that this volume will be of interest both to aficionados of the undead and to students and scholars of critical theory seeking to examine how we make sense of *being*, and especially of our own human history, of what one of our most circulated metaphors about that existence means to say. Most productively, many of the essays herein present the zombie as a figure of potentiality, expressing that the living deadness of the zombie need not always be read pessimistically but that it can point the way toward a more expansive understanding of our future.

Each of the five sections into which I've grouped the essays is prefaced by a visual detail, an inset from *Zombieindex*, chosen by Pfau himself to correspond to that section, showcasing a grouping of figures that represent the major themes articulated in that part of the book. Pfau's *Zombieindex* therefore not only serves as a backdrop, as scenery before which we stage the main acts of *Zombie Theory*; its imagery acts almost like a kind of chorus. Throughout the book, Pfau's digitized, Web-based art piece *Zombieindex* serves as a reminder of the possibilities one might explore elsewhere in zombie studies: the connections yet to be made between zombie narratives in diverse media and figurations in various disciplines (including art history) that deserve a closer look.

The book's five sections are titled "Old Schools: Classic Zombies," presenting foundational work on the zombie alongside treatment of older depictions, such as the original folkloric zombie; "Capitalist Monsters," providing a slice of what is one of the most common approaches to the subject, investigating the zombie as a critique of capitalism and a commodity itself; "Zombies and Other(ed) People," in which the monster is linked to the oppression and dehumanization of certain types of people; "Zombies in the Street," a look at the zombie's recent upsurge in popularity in performance and protest as well as zombie narratives' commentary on public space; and "New Life for the Undead," a sampling of the way the zombie has been made useful in theoretical work from biopolitics and ecology to postcolonialism and posthumanism. Each section contains four or five essays that fit thematically under that category, and each section is prefaced by some introductory remarks explaining the choice to include these essays, the broader relevance of the themes presented, and suggestions for further reading in that subject area. But, appropriate to the zombie, which is always a liminal figure, the borders here are soggy. Many of the thematics of the zombie, like capitalism, contagion, or, most especially—I would say, because of the zombie's origins as a myth coming from Haiti—*race*, are threaded throughout the volume: such topics cannot be contained in one section of this volume but, like a zombie virus, spread to nearly every page.

Each essay in the collection is followed by its own works cited page, but the book also contains a bibliographic index titled "Further Reading" that lists nonfiction, scholarly articles, books, and book chapters that are worthy of perusal, many of which are mentioned in passing in this introduction and my section prefaces, and many more that are not but are of value. The book's contribution as an aid to scholars exists not solely in the essays included here but also in that extensive list. Though this book only republishes twenty-three essays of zombie theory, this maneuver allows me to reference more than two hundred pieces of scholarship on the zombie, suggesting the wider horde that a piece like George Pfau's *Zombieindex* maps visually, and thereby providing a service

lion, and Living Death (New Brunswick, N.J.: Rutgers University Press, 2015). On Israel's undead pre-*occupation*, see Matthew Rovner, "What's Behind Israel's Zombie Outbreak?," *Forward*, October 17, 2013, http://forward.com/schmooze/185456/whats-behind-israels-zombie-outbreak/.

12. What never varies, it seems to me, is the zombie's dialectical friction as a figure that is simultaneously powerless and powerful, straddling as it does oppositions like living–dead and subject–object: an idea that Karen Embry and I first worked out in our "Zombie Manifesto," *boundary 2* 35, no. 2 (2008): 85–108, which is reprinted in this volume.

13. For a very insightful discussion of Ulrich Beck's use of the term *zombie*, see Michael Drake, "Zombinations: Reading the Undead as Debt and Guilt in the National Imaginary," in *Monster Culture in the 21st Century*, ed. Marina Levina and Diem-My T. Bui, 249–62 (New York: Bloomsbury, 2013). On the CDC's model and zombie risk assessment, see Jordan Carroll, "The Aesthetics of Risk in *Dawn of the Dead* and *28 Days Later*," *Journal of the Fantastic in the Arts* 23, no. 1 (2012): 40–59. For a mathematical modeling of a zombie outbreak, see the article by Philip Munz, Ioan Hudea, Joe Imad, and Robert J. Smith, "When Zombies Attack! Mathematical Modelling of an Outbreak of Zombie Infection," *Infectious Disease Modelling Research Progress* 4 (2009): 133–50. For a definition of zombie banks and consideration of the term's role in defining crisis, see Taylor Nelms, "The Zombie Bank and the Magic of Finance: or, How to Write a History of Crisis," *Journal of Cultural Economy* 5, no. 2 (2012): 231–46.

14. Emma Vossen, "Laid to Rest: Romance, End of the World Sexuality and Apocalyptic Anticipation in Robert Kirkman's *The Walking Dead*," in *Zombies and Sexuality: Essays on Desire and the Living Dead*, ed. Shaka McGlotten and Steve Jones (Jefferson, N.C.: McFarland, 2014), 91; see also Sasha Cocarla, "A Love Worth Un-Undying For: Neoliberalism and Queered Sexuality in *Warm Bodies*," ibid., 52–72.

15. Jeffrey Nealon, afterword to Comentale and Jaffe, *Year's Work at the Zombie Research Center*, 470, 469.

16. See, e.g., David Chalmers, "Zombies on the Web," http://consc.net/zombies.html, or those available on the *Stanford Encyclopedia of Philosophy* at http://plato.stanford.edu/.

17. http://io9.gizmodo.com/5988778/this-interactive-painting-can-explain-why-we-are-still-obsessed-with-zombies.

18. Pfau, artist's statement.

19. My work *The Transatlantic Zombie* discusses Pfau's "textual zombifications," and my chapter "Blurred Lines and Human Objects: The Zombie Art of George Pfau," in *The Walking Med: Zombies and the Medical Image*, ed. Lorenzo Servit and Sherryl Vint, 145–68 (University Park, Pa.: Penn State University Press, 2016), discusses his Zombie Medical Drawings series.

20. Pfau, artist's statement.

21. Ibid.

22. There are also similar offerings on philosophy put forth by Wayne Yuen, *The Walking Dead and Philosophy* (Chicago: Open Court, 2012), and Christopher Robichaud, *The Walking Dead and Philosophy* (Hoboken, N.J.: John Wiley, 2012), focusing especially on the ethics challenged by popular zombie narratives.

23. See, e.g., Daniel Drezner, *Theories of International Politics and Zombies* (Princeton, N.J.: Princeton University Press, 2011).

24. E.g., Henry Giroux, *Zombie Politics and Culture in the Age of Casino Capitalism* (New York: Peter Lang, 2011); Chris Harman, *Zombie Capitalism: Global Crisis and the Relevance of Marx* (Chicago: Haymarket Books, 2009); and David McNally, *Monsters of the Market: Zombies, Vampires, and Global Capitalism* (Chicago: Haymarket Books, 2011).

25. *The Walking Dead*'s multimedia narrative, existing in the graphic novel, the television shows, and a video game, has spawned multiple volumes—one by Travis Langley and John Russo, eds., *"The Walking Dead": Psychology* (New York: Sterling, 2015), and one by James Lowder, *Triumph of "The Walking Dead": Robert Kirkman's Zombie Epic on Page and Screen* (Dallas, Tex.: SmartPop, 2011)—as well as college courses at diverse schools. See Erica Phillips, "Zombie Studies Gain Ground on College Campuses," *Wall Street Journal*, March 3, 2014.

PART I

Old Schools

Classic Zombies

Zombies 101

Recently, I asked my students (about sixty in number, mostly underclass undergraduates) what images the phrase "old school zombies" conjured in their minds' eyes. These were not classes where we had talked about zombies in any detail; rather, I just wanted an informal way to take the temperature of the millennial generation, assess the current state of zombie fever, and measure how much they knew about previous epidemics. Several of them described the visual of a hand reaching up through the soil at a grave site as the first thing that came to mind, perhaps tapping into some latent knowledge of B movies like Lucio Fulci's *City of the Living Dead*, movies that most of them have never seen. Others pictured figures that must be a composite of their own personal repositories of zombie imagery: people in bad makeup with a bluish tint to their skin moaning "braiiiiins" and walking with outstretched arms. Others were specific: Michael Jackson's *Thriller* was the embodiment of the *ancien* zombie. Or it was a childhood memory of cartoon zombies on *Scooby Doo*, or, reaching back further in time, they flagged Egyptian mummies and Frankenstein's monster as fitting examples.

They noted (as I expected them to) that old zombies are slow as opposed to fast and that they are explicitly risen from the dead, whereas the new zombie can just be a victim of a virus who has become "rabid." They said that zombies today are less human, more feral, harder to kill, and, somehow, more realistic. To my delight, one student cited the 1974 Blaxploitation film *Sugar Hill* as representative of his idea of "old school zombies." Raised from the dead by Baron Samedi, lord of the cemetery, these are reanimated African slaves who come back to help the titular character in her quest for revenge.

Through historical study of cinema, literature, anthropology, and folklore, we can pinpoint the first contagious zombies, pointing to George Romero as a kind of Typhoid Mary, or map the transmission of the myth more broadly, charting Haiti as the ground zero from which all other zombies are derived, or we can trace its genealogical similarity to other figures of living death, citing examples from the folklore of other parts of the world or from religious texts. For me, the true "old school" zombie will connect our contemporary mythology to the transatlantic slave trade and remind us that the zombie's origins were implicitly a critique of the inhuman and unnatural peculiar institution. But taking the pulse of my students in this fashion reminded me that our cultural understanding of what constitutes the "classic" zombie is much more varied. Only one student explicitly used the word "Voodoo," though another said "magic," and to my great surprise (and even regret), no one uttered the words "shopping mall," that synecdochal, talismanic phrase that stands for one of the zombie's most biting reflections of American society and such a central part of the figure's cinematic presence that an entire section of this book is specifically devoted to the zombie as a critique of capitalism. This absence prompted me to wonder, is this element of the zombie mythos, which is most often said to originate with Romero's 1978 film *Dawn of the Dead*, forgotten, or is it, rather, still relevant and therefore not yet consigned to the old guard? Regardless—and irrespective of whether his innovations to the figure really merit beatification—one is unlikely to dispute that Romero's renovation of the zombie reset the calendar: zombie taxonomies are often delineated into those "before" and "after" Romero. As we close in on a human half-century since *Night of the Living Dead* was turned in a cemetery on the outskirts of Pittsburgh, this film comes to seem like the modern zombie's year zero, and many scholars measure the distance between our current comprehension of the monster and this *earlier* (but not, I stress, *early*) cinematic zombie.

This first section of the collection pays homage to the variety of types of zombies that might be considered "old school": those that reflect the modern zombie's folkloric origins in tales told in the Caribbean of dead men walking in the moonlight, or those that communicate with key concepts in theology and psychology, or those that look to Romero's canonized films or nonzombie narratives, such as horror films of the midcentury, for the germ from which our contemporary zombie springs. But more than this, the essays included here represent not only classic approaches in zombie scholarship but also classic texts of zombie scholarship.

So much of recent zombie studies (and perhaps all of the best of it) is indebted, in some capacity, to this chapter from Steven Shaviro's book *The Cinematic Body*, and that's why I have put it here, as the first essay of the collection, though, ironically, its relevance to current trends in theory today is such that it might as easily have been placed in our last section, on "New Life for the Undead." Focusing especially on Romero's "trilogy" in his discussion of the effects wrought in the cinematic viewer's flesh, in "Contagious Allegories: George Romero," Shaviro presents ideas that retain importance as central elements of affect theory, showing that these films destabilize "structures of power and domination" on a formal and corporeal level as well as in their content and themes. So many of what today we take to be commonplaces of zombie scholarship were mentioned here first; for example, this essay discusses the creature's defiance of borders, by which I mean both its conflation of the insides and outsides of bodies and its genre-bending capacity for horror–humor hybridity. Nonetheless, Shaviro's attention to the way the films work upon the viewer's body (particularly in their uses of the suspension of action and slowed-down "zombie time") is still unrivaled in the field.

Although the essay by Jeffrey Weinstock included here, "Zombie TV," discusses not only the zombie film classic *Night of the Living Dead* (1968) and, briefly, *Dawn of the*

Dead (1978) but also a movie that doesn't contain any zombies, Tobe Hooper's *Poltergeist* (1982), what is at issue in this piece is the "invasive force of technoculture" represented in both films by the central presence of the television in the plot lines. Written in 1999, this essay anticipates much of the work produced in the last decade within horror studies to address depictions of media and broader issues within media studies. The inclusion of Weinstock's essay here does double-duty: it is a stand-in for much of the classic cinematic excavation of zombie films (like those by Robin Wood, Gregory Waller, Stephen Harper, and many others), but it also points to a very specific nexus within the study of the cinematic zombie: attention to the medium itself, especially when it produces an anesthetizing, or zombifying, effect or affect. This piece is theoretically interesting not only for its engagement with discussions of Avital Ronell's trauma theory, or the role of the television in American society, but also for its use of form: this essays calls to mind Julia Kristeva's use of footnotes in *Stabat Mater,* creating a text pregnant with another text, in her article about the maternal body. Here Weinstock patches into the article (sometimes almost mid-sentence) quotations from hip-hop musicians (Public Enemy, Disposable Heroes of Hiphoprisy), writers (Don DeLillo, Roald Dahl), and popular television shows (*The X-Files*) to create an effect as if someone were changing the channel as we read, highlighting the way consciousness is restructured by media.

In this long excerpt from her book *Contagious: Cultures, Carriers, and the Outbreak Narrative,* Priscilla Wald chronicles the Cold War fascination with contagion and conformity, what became central tropes in zombie fiction and film. Wald reads William S. Burroughs's meditations on conformity, viruses, and communication alongside Jack Finney's serialized novel *The Body Snatchers,* with its pod people replicants, reading in detail its cinematic versions directed by Don Siegel (1956) and Philip Kaufman (1978) as well as drawing connections to Richard Matheson's zombie-like vampires of his novella *I Am Legend.* In many ways, these are the antecedents of today's complex zombies, which signify many things at once, and Wald's essay presages this complexity, hitting upon political, psychological, racial, queer, and even postcolonial significances of these hybrid imposters, the pod people. Fans of the linguistic zombies of *Pontypool* (2008) will benefit from Wald's discussion of Burroughs's work, and students of the latest evolutions of the viral zombie are in need of this lesson in the proto-zombie's epidemiological history.

As I'll continue to stress repeatedly, the zombie's parentage comes directly out of the Caribbean folklore that metaphorized the African population's past slave culture. Here Elizabeth McAlister's essay stands for a much wider field of investigation (one in which I hope my own scholarship is counted) that pays attention to these Afro-Caribbean roots as deeply revelatory of our present-day fascination with the figure. In "Slaves, Cannibals, and Infected Hyper-Whites: The Race and Religion of Zombies," McAlister presents her own ethnographic research on the "zonbi" in Haiti, elucidating the figure's connection to slavery and rebellion, cannibalism, and colonial occupation. McAlister mentions foundational work in this area, such as that of Mimi Sheller, but she also reads this duality's presence in the modern zombie film's depiction of race. Tracing the representation of leading black men in zombie films from Romero's *Night of the Living Dead* to the remake of Richard Matheson's novella *I Am Legend* (2007) starring Will Smith, McAlister considers the black man as zombie killer, a trope she finds—even—in messianic rhetoric surrounding Barack Obama's run for president of the United States that depicted the first African American president as a zombie-slayer.

Ola Sigurdson's contribution, and the final essay of this section, raises a different binary conundrum of the posthuman era than we usually see appear in discussion of zombies in its emphasis on the religious and the secular. Sigurdson questions our oppositional understanding of the terms and emphasizes that (whatever the true nature of the relationship) the tension between these concepts needs to be understood historically. In his deconstruction of the pair, Sigurdson turns to Slavoj Žižek's discussion of the Freudian death drive, to Lacan's application of Freudian psychoanalysis, and, relatedly, to the zombie. As the author here notes, Žižek's direct address of the zombie amounts, surprisingly, to a few scant (but often cited) passages. Working from these, Romero's films, and Augustine's *Confessions*, Sigurdson interprets Žižek's broader philosophy, along the way demonstrating the primary existential crisis of the undead as a mechanism for better understanding the death drive: most strikingly, Sigurdson illustrates where theology and psychoanalysis share common ground, in the naming of an insatiable hunger (for God, or fulfillment of Desire) that is allegorized in the form of the modern undead.

Further Reading

In the introduction, I touched upon what are many of the most useful sources for investigating the cinematic zombie and the Haitian zombie, topics that every essay in this book (but also nearly every essay referenced in these lists) addresses in some capacity. Of course, the bibliographies of the individual essays provide their own accounts of scholarly forebears in these areas and more. Nonetheless, I'll note briefly that Kyle Bishop's essay "The Sub-Subaltern Monster"—in its discussion of early zombie cinema—provides a useful introduction to the important work of Alfred Métraux, Colin Dayan, and others who address the Haitian *zombi*. For their discussion of the zombie film as film, I like Meghan Sutherland's essay "Rigor/Mortis" (on remakes in/as zombies), Adam Lowenstein's "Living Dead" (which applies the theory of "cinematic attractions" to Romero's most recent films), and Steen Christiansen's "Speaking the Undead" (on image and aurality in horror film, with *Pontypool*, 2008, as case study).

As I've already stated, Shaviro's contribution reverberates throughout this volume, but for direct engagement with his argument, see James McFarland's discussion of the "zombie-image," in which the author draws together Shaviro, Benjamin, Žižek, and others, in "Philosophy of the Living Dead: At the Origin of the Zombie Image."

From Weinstock's discussion of the television in *Night of the Living Dead*, we can follow the gaze: cinema's reflection of our evolving relationship to media is chronicled, for example, in Erik Bohman's chapter "Zombie Media" in *The Year's Work* and in Allan Cameron's 2012 essay "Zombie Media: Transmission, Reproduction, and the Digital Dead," a treatment of diverse contemporary zombie films. The opening line of Cameron's article states, "The modern zombie is a media zombie" (66). Indeed, we might also say that the most recent zombie is a *new media* zombie, but this line of inquiry, more accurately filed under "New Approaches to the Undead," can be found in the final section preface.

For work similar to McAlister's offering here, with its attention to the contemporary iteration of the myth in Haitian culture and literature, see the work of Kaiama Glover, especially the essays "Exploiting the Undead" and "New Narratives of Haiti: or, How to Empathize with a Zombie," which is both a meditation on Haiti after the earthquake and an introduction to her book *Haiti Unbound*. Lucy Swanson's two essays "Zombie Nation?" and "Blankness, Alienation, and the Zombie in Recent Francophone Fiction" are also important contributions. Franck Degoul's chapter in *Better Off Dead* is a translated excerpt from his unpublished dissertation "Dos à La Vie, Dos à La Mort," an ethnographic study of the practice of zombification by Vodouists in Haiti in the early twenty-first century. I am listing here only resources for the non-French speaker; the francophone student will find a much vaster list of sources on the Haitian zombie in the index to my book *The Transatlantic Zombie*. For African zombies, see the work of Isak Niehaus (as well as the piece by Jean and John Comaroff in this collection) on "Witches and Zombies of the South African Lowveld."

For more on the zombie narrative's depiction of contagion, the reader should see Jennifer Cooke's book *Legacies of Plague in Literature, Theory, and Film*, in which the final section looks especially at zombies; Stephanie Boluk and Wylie Lenz's article "Infection, Media, and Capitalism: From Early Modern Plagues to Postmodern Zombies"; and Steven Zani and Kevin Meaux's chapter on "Lucio Fulci and the Decaying Definition of Zombie Narratives," which discusses contagion in zombie films at some length. Looking at the Resident Evil franchise and *World War Z* in particular, Steven Pokornowski's excellent essay from the journal *Literature and Medicine*, "Insecure Lives: Zombies, Global Health, and the Totalitarianism of Generalization," reveals how zombie films and narratives "demonstrate and interrogate a generalizing, totalizing, globalized discourse that, preoccupied with contagion and control, demands either assimilation or annihilation" (217). Those looking to go more in depth in terms of characterization of global contagion should see especially Richard Brock's discussion of the now infamous video game Resident Evil 5 in his piece "Of Zombies, AIDS, and 'Africa': Non-Western Disease and the Raciocultural Imagination." Marina Levina's "Cultural Narratives of Blood" also bears some relevance to this topic: it connects the emphasis of blood contagion to racial contamination and underscores the zombie narrative's delineation of certain people as "others." She writes, "A zombie outbreak is portrayed as a war against blood, both individual blood and national blood" (83). One of our contributors whose work appears in another section, Anna Mae Duane, is also working on the topic of "Ebola, Zombies, and Our Viral Past."

For those interested in Wald's treatment of Cold War films, see also Cyndy Hendershot's book *I Was a Cold War Monster: Horror Films, Eroticism, and the Cold War Imagination*. Though there isn't detailed discussion of zombies, many of its examples (like *Invasion of the Body Snatchers* and *I Am Legend*) were integral to the shaping of the modern zombie's mythos.

Related to Sigurdson's offering, there has been a fair amount of work done on the zombie from a theological and religious studies standpoint. In particular, I enjoy Christopher Moreman's essay "Dharma of the Living Dead." In part, it is a critique of Kim Paffenroth's Christian readings of the zombie, in which Moreman asserts that (in its Haitian form especially) the living dead entails "a subversive rejection of Christianity" and resurrection theology (130). Paffenroth has written extensively on the subject. See *Gospel of the Living Dead: George Romero's Visions of Hell on Earth* and the collection *The Undead and Theology*, coedited with John Morehead. Only a handful of the essays in that collection deal with the zombie, but Paffenroth's is of special interest: he interprets the zombie's criticism of materialism and consumerism as a critique of the "prosperity gospel," the idea that those who have material wealth have been blessed by God for good behavior, thereby uniting the subject of the next section, the zombie's long-standing critique of capitalism, with the myth's theological underpinnings.

Many of the zombie-themed essays in Richard Greene and K. Silem Mohammad's edited collection *The Undead and Philosophy*—one of the first of its kind in the new wave of scholarly attention to the zombie—are decidedly old school, with comparisons drawn between the monster and Aristotle, Descartes, and many other diverse philosophers. For example, Simon Clark's chapter "The Undead Martyr: Sex, Death, and Revolution in George Romero's Zombie Films" takes up Freudian theory in relation to the undead. See also contributor Fred Botting's essay "Zombie Death Drive" for another perspective on the psychoanalytic approach and an introduction to some of the key concepts of the philosophical zombie articulated by Robert Kirk, John Searle, and others. See also on this latter point Larry Hauser's chapter in *Undead and Philosophy*. Another essay from before the zombie boom of the early twenty-first century serves as a nice time capsule of the way we used to think about zombies: see Boelderl and Mayr's article "The Undead and the Living Dead: Images of Vampires and Zombies in Popular Culture."

Contagious Allegories

George Romero

STEVEN SHAVIRO

Postmodern Zombies

George Romero's Living Dead trilogy—*Night of the Living Dead, Dawn of the Dead*, and *Day of the Dead*—offers all sorts of pleasures to the willing viewer. These films move effortlessly among sharp visceral shocks, wry satirical humor, and a Grand Guignolesque reveling in showy excesses of gore. They are crass exploitation movies, pop left-wing action cartoons, exercises in cynical nihilism, and sophisticated political allegories of late capitalist America. Their vision of a humanity overrun by flesh-eating zombies is violently apocalyptic; at the same time, they remain disconcertingly close to the habitual surfaces and mundane realities of everyday life. Business as usual bizarrely coexists with extremes of tension and hysteria, in a world on the verge of vertiginous destruction. Everything in these movies is at once grotesque and familiar, banal and exaggerated, ordinary and on the edge. Romero's zombies seem almost natural in a society in which the material comforts of the middle class coexist with repressive conformism, mind-numbing media manipulation, and the more blatant violence of poverty, sexism, racism, and militarism. Romero is at once the pornographer, the anthropologist, the allegorist, and the radical critic of contemporary American culture. He gleefully uncovers the hidden structures of our society in the course of charting the progress of its disintegration.

What can it mean for the dead to walk again? The question is discussed endlessly in the three films, but no firm conclusion is ever reached. Some characters search for scientific explanations; others respond with mystical resignation. Maybe it is an infection brought back from an outer-space probe, or maybe there is no more room in hell. Of course, the whole point is that the sheer exorbitance of the zombies defies causal explanation, or even simple categorization. The living dead don't have an origin or a referent; they have become unmoored from meaning. They figure a social process that no longer serves rationalized ends but has taken on a strange and sinister life of its own.

Deleuze and Guattari aptly remark that "the only modern myth is the myth of zombies—mortified schizos, good for work, brought back to reason."[1] The life-in-death of the zombie is a nearly perfect allegory for the inner logic of capitalism, whether this be taken in the sense of the exploitation of living labor by dead labor, the deathlike regimentation of factories and other social spaces, or the artificial, externally driven stimulation of consumers. Capitalist expropriation involves a putting to death, and a subsequent extraction of movement and value—or simulated life—from the bowels of that death. Whereas precapitalist societies tend to magnify and heroicize death, to derive grandeur from it, capitalism seeks, rather, to rationalize and normalize it, to turn it to economic account. Romero's zombies have none of the old precapitalist sublimity, but they also cannot be controlled and put to work. They mark the rebellion of death against its capitalist appropriation. Their emergence—and this is one of the thrills of watching these films—reminds us of the derisory gratuitousness of death, and of Georges Bataille's equation of death with expenditure and waste. Our society endeavors to transform death into value, but the zombies enact a radical refusal and destruction of value. They come after, and in response to, the capitalist logic of production and transformation; they live off the detritus of industrial society and are perhaps an expression of its ecological waste.

Indeed, Romero has called to life the first postmodern zombies. (There have been many imitations since, in scores of other films: superficial imitation, or proliferating repetition, is the definitive feature of such undefinable not-quite-beings.) These walking corpses are neither majestic and uncanny nor exactly sad and pitiable. They arise out of a new relation to death, and they provoke a new range of affect. They are blank, terrifying, and ludicrous in equal measure, without any of these aspects mitigating the others. Romero's zombies could almost be said to be quintessential media images, since they are vacuous, mimetic replications of the human beings they once were. They are dead people who are not content to remain dead but who have brought their deaths with them back into the realm of the living. They move slowly and affectlessly, as if in a trance, but the danger they represent is real: they kill and consume. They are slower, weaker, and stupider than living humans; their menace lies in numbers, and in the fact that they never give up. Their slow-motion voracity and continual hungry wailing sometimes appear clownish but at other times emerge as an obsessive leitmotif of suspended and ungratified desire.

The zombies' residual, yet all-too-substantial, half-lives reproduce the conditions both of film actors separated from their charismatic presence (which the camera has appropriated) and of film audiences compulsively, vicariously participating in events that they are unable to control or possess. The zombies embody a phenomenological loss that—precisely because it is so viscerally embodied—cannot be figured in terms of "lack." They continue to participate in human, social rituals and processes—but only just enough to drain them of their power and meaning. For instance, they preserve the marks of social function and self-projection in the clothes they wear, which identify them as businessman, housewife, nun, Hare Krishna disciple, and so on. But this becomes one of the films' running jokes: despite such signs of difference, they all act in exactly the same way. The zombies are devoid of personality, yet they continue to allude to personal identity. They are driven by a sort of vestigial memory, but one that has become impersonal and indefinite, a vague solicitation to aimless movement.

The zombies are impelled by a kind of desire, but they are largely devoid of energy and will. Their restless agitation is merely reactive. They totter clumsily about, in a strange state of stupefied and empty fascination, passively drawn to still-living humans and to locations they once occupied and cherished. Only now they arrive to ravage, almost casually, the sites to which their vague memories and attractions lead them. They drift slowly away from identity and meaning, emptying these out in the very process of replicating them. The zombies are in a sense all body: they have brains but not minds. That is to say, they are nonholistic, deorganicized bodies: lumps of flesh that still experience the cravings of the flesh, but without the organic articulation and teleological focus that we are prone to attribute to ourselves and to all living things. They are empty shells of life that scandalously continue to function in the absence of any interiority. All this is particularly evident when active characters, with whom the audience has identified, are killed and monstrously reborn. In their artificial second life, these characters are both the same and not the same. They are still recognizable beneath their gruesome features, but their corpses shamble along or jerk convulsively, graceless and uncoordinated, drained of the tension of purposive activity.

These strange beings, at once alive and dead, grotesquely literal and blatantly artificial, cannot be encompassed by any ordinary logic of representation. In their compulsive, wavering, deorganicized movements, the zombies are *allegorical* and *mimetic* figures. They are allegorical in the sense that allegory always implies the loss or death of its object. An allegory is not a representation but an overt materialization of the unbridgeable distance that representation seeks to cover over and efface. (I am defining allegory here in terms that derive ultimately from Walter Benjamin's *The Origin of German Tragic Drama*;[2] for a discussion of the importance of allegory, so conceived, to postmodernism, see especially Craig Owens[3] and Celeste Olalquiaga.[4]) The "living dead" emerge out of the deathly distance of allegory; their fictive presence allows Romero to anatomize and criticize American society, not by portraying it naturalistically, but by evacuating and eviscerating it. Allegory is, then, not just a mode of depiction but an active means of subversive transformation.

The zombies do not (in the familiar manner of 1950s horror film monsters) stand for a threat to social order from without. Rather, they resonate with, and refigure, the very processes that produce and enforce social order. That is to say, they do not mirror or represent social forces; they are directly animated and possessed, even in their allegorical distance from beyond the grave, by such forces. Thus they are also mimetic figures, in Benjamin's sense of magical participation, perception become tactile, and nonsensuous (nonrepresentational) similarities.[5] The movement from allegory to mimesis is a passage from passive reanimation to active, raging contagion. This progression is the source of the zombies' strange appeal. Forever unequal to themselves, they are figures of affective blockage and intellectual undecidability. They can be regarded both as monstrous symptoms of a violent, manipulative, exploitative society and as potential remedies for its ills—all this by virtue of their apocalyptically destructive, yet oddly innocuous, counterviolence. They frighten us with their categorical rapacity, yet allure us by offering the base, insidious pleasures of ambiguity, complicity, and magical revenge. Romero's films knowingly exploit the ambiguity of their position: they locate themselves both inside and outside the institutions and ideologies—of commercial film production and of American society generally—from which they have evidently arisen.

Survival or Sacrifice?

But what of horror's traditional themes of struggle and survival, of rescuing the possibilities of life and community from an encounter with monstrosity and death? The Living Dead trilogy plays with these themes in a manner that defies conventional expectations. Indeed, it is this aspect of the films that has been most thoroughly discussed by sympathetic commentators, like Robin Wood[6] and Kim Newman.[7] All three films have white women or black men as their chief protagonists, the only characters with whom the audience positively identifies as they struggle to remain alive and to resist and escape the zombies. The black man in *Night* is the sole character in the film who is both sympathetic and capable of reasoned action. The woman protagonist in *Dawn* rejects the subordinate role in which the three men, wrapped up in their male bonding fantasies, initially place her; she becomes more and more active and involved as the film progresses. The woman scientist in *Day* is established right from the start as the strongest, most dedicated, and most perspicacious of the besieged humans. In both *Dawn* and *Day*, the women end up establishing tactical alliances with black men who are not blindly self-centered in the manner of their white counterparts. All these characters are thoughtful, resourceful, and tenacious; they are not always right, but they continually debate possible courses of action and learn from their mistakes. They seem to be groping toward a shared, democratic kind of decision making.

In contrast, white American males come off badly in all three films. The father in *Night* considers it his inherent right to be in control, although he clearly lacks any sense of how to proceed; his behavior is an irritating combination of hysteria and spite. The two white men among the group in *Dawn* both die as a result of their adolescent need to indulge in macho games or to play the hero. The military commanding officer in *Day* is the most obnoxious of all: he is so sexist, authoritarian, cold-blooded, vicious, and contemptuous of others that the audience celebrates when the zombies finally disembowel and devour him. These white males' fear of the zombies seems indistinguishable from the dread and hatred they display toward women. The self-congratulatory attitudes that they continually project are shown to be ineffective at best, and radically counterproductive at worst, in dealing with the actual perils that the zombies represent. The macho, paternalistic traits of typical Hollywood action heroes are repeatedly exposed as stupid and dysfunctional.

Romero dismantles dominant behavior patterns; he gives a subversive, left-wing twist to the usually reactionary ideology and genre of survivalism. To the extent that the films maintain traditional forms of narrative identification, they divert these forms by providing them with a new, politically more progressive content. Carol J. Clover argues that slasher and rape–revenge films of the 1970s and 1980s enact a shift in the gender identification of traditional attributes of heroism and struggle, whereby women take on these attributes instead of men.[8] *Dawn* and *Day* present us with a more self-conscious, radical, and thoroughgoing version of the same shift in cultural sensibilities. But the scope of Clover's argument is limited by the fact that it too easily valorizes heroic triumph. In Romero's trilogy, to the contrary, the success of the sympathetic characters' survival strategy is limited; it does not, and cannot be expected to, resolve all the tensions raised in the course of the three films. Unlike in the slasher and revenge films described by Clover, here the protagonists' survival is not the same as their triumph. The zombies are never defeated; the best that the sympathetic living characters of *Dawn* and *Day* can hope for is the reprieve of a precarious, provisional escape.

And this tenuousness leads us back to the zombies. The Living Dead trilogy does not simply or unequivocally valorize survival; perhaps for that reason, it ultimately does not rely for its effectiveness on mechanisms or spectatorial identification. The zombies exercise too strong a pull, too strange a fascination. The three films progress in the direction of ever-greater contiguities and similarities between the living and the non-living, between seduction and horror, and between desire and dread. In consequence, identities and identifications are increasingly dissolved, even within the framework of conventional, ostensibly sutured narrative.

The first film in the series, *Night of the Living Dead,* is the one most susceptible to conventional psychoanalytic interpretation, for it is focused on the nuclear family. It begins with a neurotic brother and sister quarreling as they pay a visit to their father's grave and moves on to the triangle of blustering father, cringing mother, and (implicitly) abused child hiding from the zombies in a farmhouse basement. Familial relations are shown throughout to be suffused with an anxious negativity, a menacing aura of tension and repressed violence. In this context, the zombies seem a logical outgrowth of, or response to, patriarchal norms. They are the disavowed residues of the ego-producing mechanisms of internalization and identification. They figure the infinite emptiness of desire, insofar as it is shaped by, and made conterminous with, Oedipal repression. The film's high point of shock comes, appropriately, when the little girl, turned into a zombie, cannibalistically consumes her parents. But at the same time, the film's casual ironies undercut this allegory of the return of the repressed. The protagonists not only experience the zombie menace firsthand, they also watch it on TV. Disaster is consumed as a cheesy spectacle, complete with incompetent reporting, useless information bulletins, and inane attempts at commentary. The grotesque, carnivalesque slapstick of these sequences mocks survivalist oppositions. Even as dread pulses to a climax, as plans of action and escape fail, and as characters we expect to survive are eliminated, we are denied the opportunity of imposing redemptive or compensatory meanings. There is no mythology of doomed, heroic resistance, no exalted sense of pure, apocalyptic negativity. The zombies' lack of charisma seems to drain all the surrounding circumstances of their nobility. And for its part, the family is subsumed within a larger network of social control, one as noteworthy for its stupidity as for its exploitativeness.

Romero turns the constraints of his low budget—crudeness of presentation, minimal acting, and tacky special effects—into a powerful means of expression: he foregrounds and hyperbolizes these aspects of his production in order to depsychologize the drama and emphasize the artificiality and gruesome arbitrariness of spectacle. Such a strategy doesn't "alienate" us from the film so much as it insidiously displaces our attention. Our anxieties are focused upon events rather than characters, upon the violent fragmentation of cinematic process (with a deliberate clumsiness that mimes the shuffling movement of the zombies themselves) rather than the supposed integrity of any single protagonist's subjectivity. The zombies come to exemplify, not a hidden structure of individual anxiety and guilt, but an unabashedly overt social process in which the disintegration of all communal bonds goes hand in hand with the callous manipulation of individual response. It is entirely to the point that *Night* ends on a note of utter cynicism: the zombies are apparently defeated, but the one human survivor with whom we have identified throughout the film—a black man—is mistaken for a zombie and shot by an (implicitly racist) sheriff's posse.

The other films in the cycle are made with higher budgets and have a much slicker look to them, but they are even more powerfully disruptive. The second film, *Dawn of the Dead*, deals with consumerism rather than familial tensions. The zombies are irresistibly attracted to a suburban shopping mall, because they dimly remember that "this was an important place in their lives." Indeed, they seem most fully human when they are wandering the aisles and escalators of the mall like dazed but ecstatic shoppers. But the same can be said for the film's living characters. The four protagonists hole up in the mall and try to re-create a sense of "home" there. Much of the film is taken up by what is in effect their delirious shopping spree: after turning on the background music and letting the fountains run, they race through the corridors, ransacking goods that remain sitting in perfect order on store shelves. Once they have eliminated the zombies from the mall, they play games of makeup, acting out the roles of elegance and wealth (and the attendant stereotypes of gender, class, and race) that they dreamed of, but weren't able actually to afford, in their previous middle-class lives. This consumers' utopia comes to an end only when the mall is invaded by a vicious motorcycle gang: a bunch of toughs motivated by a kind of class resentment, a desire to "share the wealth" by grabbing as much of it as possible. They enter by force and then pillage and destroy, enacting yet another mode of commodity consumption run wild. One befuddled gang member can't quite decide whether to run off with an expensive TV set or smash it to bits in frustration over the fact that no programs are being broadcast anymore.

The still alive and the already dead are alike animated by a mimetic urge that causes them to resemble *Dawn*'s third category of humanoid figures: department store mannequins. The zombies are overtly presented as simulacral doubles (equivalents rather than opposites) of living humans; their destructive consumption of flesh—gleefully displayed to the audience by means of lurid special effects—immediately parallels the consumption of useless commodities by the American middle class. Commodity fetishism is a mode of desire that is not grounded in repression; rather, it is directly incited, multiplied, and affirmed by artificial means. As Meaghan Morris remarks, "a Deleuzian account of productive desire . . . is more apt for analyzing the forms of modern greed . . . than the lack-based model assumed by psychoanalytic theories."[9] Want is a function of excess and extravagance, and not of deficiency: the more I consume, the more I demand to consume. In the words of the artist Barbara Kruger, "I shop, therefore I am."

The appearance of the living dead in the shopping mall thus can no longer be interpreted as a return of the repressed. The zombies are not an exception to, but a positive expression of, consumerist desire. They emerge not from the dark, disavowed underside of suburban life but from its tacky, glittering surfaces. They embody and mimetically reproduce those very aspects of contemporary American life that are openly celebrated by the media. The one crucial difference is that the living dead—in contrast to the actually alive—are ultimately not susceptible to advertising suggestions. Their random wandering might seem to belie, but actually serves, a frightening singleness of purpose: their unquenchable craving to consume living flesh. They cannot be controlled, for they are already animated far too directly and unconditionally by the very forces that modern advertising seeks to appropriate, channel, and exploit for its own ends. The infinite, insatiable hunger of the living dead is the complement of their openness to sympathetic participation, their compulsive, unregulated mimetic drive, and their limitless capacity for reiterated shock. The zombies mark the dead end or zero degree of capitalism's logic of endless consumption and ever-expanding accumulation, precisely because they embody this logic so literally and to such excess.

In the third and most complex film of the series, *Day of the Dead*, Romero goes still further. A shot near the beginning shows dollar bills being blown about randomly in the wind: a sign that even commodity fetishism has collapsed as an animating structure of desire. The locale shifts to an isolated underground bunker, where research scientists endeavor to study the zombies under the protection of a platoon of soldiers. All human activity is now as vacant and meaningless as is the zombies' endless shuffling about; the soldiers' abusive, macho posturings and empty assertions of authority clash with the scientists' futile, misguided efforts to discover the cause of the zombie plague and to devise remedies for it. All that remains of postmodern society is the military–scientific complex, its chief mechanism for producing power and knowledge. But the technological infrastructure is now reduced to its most basic expression, locked into a subterranean compound of sterile cubicles, winding corridors, and featureless caverns. Everything in this hellish, underground realm of the living is embattled, restricted, claustrophobically closed off. This microcosm of our culture's dominant rationality tears itself apart as we watch: it teeters on the brink of implosion, destroying itself from within even as it is literally under siege from without. The bunker is like an emotional pressure cooker: fear, fatigue, and anxiety all mount relentlessly, for they cannot find any means of relief or discharge. As the film progresses, tensions grow between the soldiers and the scientists, between the men and the one woman, and ultimately among the irreconcilable imperatives of power, comprehension, survival, and escape. The entire film is a maze of false exits and dead ends, with the zombies themselves providing the only prospect of an outlet.

Day of the Dead is primarily concerned with the politics of insides and outsides: the social production of boundaries, limits, and compartmentalizations, and their subsequent affirmative disruption. The zombies, on the outside, paradoxically manifest a "vitality" that is lacking within the bunker. Their inarticulate moans and cries, heard in the background throughout the film, give voice to a force of desire that is at once nourished and denied, solicited and repulsed, by the military–scientific machine. Inside the bunker, in a sequence that works as a hilarious send-up of both behaviorist disciplinary procedures and 1950s "mad scientist" movies, a researcher tries to "tame" one of the zombies. The dead, he explains, can be "tricked" into obedience, just as we were tricked as children. He eventually turns his pet zombie, Bub, into a pretty good parody of a soldier, miming actions such as reading, shaving, and answering the telephone, and actually capable of saluting and of firing a gun. This success suggests that discipline and training, whether in child rearing or in the military, is itself only a restrictive appropriation of the zombies' mimetic energy. Meanwhile, the zombies mill about outside in increasing numbers, waiting with menacing passivity to break in. From both inside and outside, mimetic resemblances proliferate and threaten to overturn the hierarchy of living and dead. The more rigidly boundaries are drawn between reason and desire, order and anarchy, purpose and randomness, the more irrelevant these distinctions seem, and the more they are prone to violent explosion.

The climax occurs when one of the soldiers—badly wounded (literally dismembered, metaphorically castrated), and motivated by an ambiguous combination of heroic desperation and vicious masculine resentment—opens the gates and lets the zombies into the bunker, offering his own body as the first sacrifice to their voracity. The controlling boundary is ruptured, and the outside ecstatically consumes the inside. Allegory entirely gives way before a wave of contagious expenditure and destruction. The zombies take their revenge; but, as Kim Newman notes, "American society is cast in the role usually given to an individually hatable character."[10] If the zombies are a repressed by-product of dominant American culture in *Night*, and that culture's simulacral double in *Dawn*, then in *Day*, they finally emerge—ironically enough—as its animating source, its revolutionary avenger, and its sole hope of renewal. They are the long-accumulated stock of energy and desire upon which our militarized and technocratic culture vampiristically feeds, which it compulsively manipulates and exploits but cannot forever hope to control.

The Seductiveness of Horror

Everything comes back to the zombies' weird attractiveness: they exercise a perverse, insidious fascination that undermines our nominal involvement with the films' active protagonists. The rising of the dead is frequently described as a plague: it takes the form of a mass contagion, without any discernible point of origin. The zombies proliferate by contiguity, attraction, and imitation and agglomerate into large groups. The uncanny power of Romero's films comes from the fact that these intradiegetic processes of mimetic participation are the same ones that, on another level, serve to bind viewers to the events unfolding on-screen. The Living Dead trilogy achieves an overwhelming affective ambivalence by displacing, exceeding, and intensifying the conventional mechanisms of spectatorial identification, inflecting them in the direction of a dangerous, tactile, mimetic participation. Perception itself becomes infected and is transformed into a kind of magical, contagious contact. The films mobilize forms of visual involvement that tend to interrupt the forward movement of narrative and that cannot be reduced to the ruses of specular dialectics. We cannot in a conventional sense "identify" with the zombies, but we are increasingly seduced by them, drawn into proximity with them. The participatory contact that they promise and exemplify is in a deep sense what we most strongly desire; or, better, we gradually discover that it is *already* the hidden principle of our desire. Romero's trilogy amply justifies Bataille's suggestion that "extreme seductiveness is probably at the boundary of horror."[11]

The first of these modes of seductive implication is a kind of suspension or hesitation. We watch alongside a protagonist who does not see anything—but who is waiting, anxiously, for the zombies to appear, or for dead bodies to rise. Nothing happens; the instant is empty. Of course, such scenes are a classic means of building suspense. But Romero gives the blank time of anticipation a value in its own right, rather than just using it to accentuate, by contrast, the jolt that follows. Sometimes he even sacrifices immediate shock effect, the better to insist upon the clumsy, hallucinatory slowness of the zombies' approach, for even after the zombies have finally appeared, we are still held in suspense—waiting for them to come near enough to devour us, to embrace us with their mortifying, intimate touch. Such a pattern of compulsive, fascinated waiting is especially important in *Dawn*. In one excruciatingly drawn-out scene, one of the barricaded human waits for the moment when his comrade, having just died in bed from zombie-inflicted wounds, will come back to life as one of *them*. There is nothing he can do; he simply sits, gun in hand, taking swigs from a bottle of whiskey. Ever so slowly, the sheets covering the corpse begin to move . . . Again at the very end of the film, the same character is tempted to remain behind and shoot himself in the head, instead of joining the woman survivor in a last-minute departure by helicopter. No true escape is possible; running away now only means accepting the horror of having to fight the zombies again someplace else. One can put an end to this eternal recurrence only by not delaying, by shooting oneself immediately in the head, directly destroying the physical texture of the brain. The man hesitates for a long, unbearable moment, his gun at his temple, as the zombies approach—ravening after his flesh, but still shuffling along at their usual slow pace. Only at the last possible instant is he finally able to tear himself away.

The dread that the zombies occasion is based more on a fear of infection than on one of annihilation. The living characters are concerned less about the prospect of being killed than they are about being swept away by mimesis—returning to existence, after death, transformed into selves. The screams of the dying man in *Dawn* sound very much like (and are equated by montage with) the cries of the zombies. The man is most horrified not by his pain or his impending death but by the prospect of walking again; he promises with his last breath that he will try not to return. Of course, he fails: revivification is not something that can be resisted by mere force of will. To die is precisely to give up one's will, and thus to find oneself drawn, irresistibly, into a passive, zombified state. In these scenes, the protagonist's momentary hesitation is already, implicitly, a partial surrender to temptation. A chain of mimetic transference moves from the zombies, to the man who dies and returns as a zombie, to the other man who watches him die and return, and to the audience fascinated by the whole spectacle. As the moments are drawn out, a character with whom we identify seems on the verge of slipping into a secretly desired incapacity to act, a passionate wavering and paralysis. Living action is subverted by the passivity of waiting for death; indecision debilitates the self-conscious assertion of the will. In *Dawn*, the protagonists end up resisting this temptation and returning to a stance of action and resolve. But it's only a small step from them to the wounded soldier in *Day*, who gives himself over entirely to the zombies.

At such moments in the three films, it is as if perception were slowed down and hollowed out. As I wait for the zombies to arrive, I am uncannily solicited and invested by the vision of something that I endlessly anticipate but that I cannot yet see. Gilles Deleuze argues that the sensorimotor link, the reflex arc from stimulus to response, or from affection to action, is essential to the structure of action narrative.[12] But at such moments of waiting for the zombies' awakening or approach, the link between apprehension and act and action is hollowed out or suspended, in what Deleuze calls a "crisis" in the act of seeing.[13] The stimulating sensation fails to arrive, and the motor reaction is arrested. The slow meanders of zombie time emerge out of the paralysis of the conventional time of progressive narrative. This strangely empty temporality also corresponds to a new way of looking, a vertiginously passive fascination. The usual relation of audience to protagonist is inverted. Instead of the spectator projecting himself or herself into the actions unfolding on the screen, an on-screen character lapses into a quasi-spectatorial position. This is the point at which dread slips into obsession, the moment when unfulfilled threats turn into seductive promises. Fear becomes indistinguishable from an incomprehensible, intense, but objectless craving. This is the zombie state par excellence: an abject vacancy, a passive emptying of the self. But such vacuity is not nothingness, for it is powerfully, physically felt. The allure of zombiehood cannot be represented directly—it is a kind of mimetic transference that exceeds and destroys all structures of representation—but it lurks in all these excruciating, empty moments when seemingly nothing happens. Passively watching and waiting, I am given over to the slow vertigo of aimless, infinite expectation and need. I discover that implication is more basic than opposition; a contagious complicity is more disturbing than any measure of lack, more so even than lack pushed to the point of total extinction. The hardest thing to acknowledge is that the living dead are not radically Other so much as they serve to awaken a passion for Otherness and for vertiginous disidentification that is already latent within our own selves.

A second mode of voyeuristic participation in the Living Dead trilogy comes into play when the zombies finally do arrive. Romero gleefully exploits his viewers' desires to experience and enjoy, vicariously, the rending apart and communal consumption of living flesh. These films literalize obscenity. In their insistence on cannibalism and on the dismemberment of the human body, their lurid display of extruded viscera, they deliberately and directly present to the eye something that should not be seen, that cannot be seen in actuality. Audiences attend these films largely in the hope of being titillated by a violence that is at once safely distant and garishly immediate—extravagantly hyperreal. I'm taken on a wild ride, through a series of thrills and shocks, pulled repeatedly to the brink of an unbearable and impossible consummation. The zombies' almost ritualistic violation of the flesh allows me to regard, for an ephemeral instant, what is normally invisible: the hidden insides of bodies, their mysterious and impenetrable interiority. At the price of such monstrous destructiveness, I am able to participate in a strange exhibition and presentation of physical, bodily affect. These films enact the making evident, the public display, of my most private and inaccessible experiences: those of wrenching pain and of the agonizing extremity of dying. I am fixated upon the terrifying instant of transmogrification: the moment of the tearing apart of limb from limb, the twitching of the extremities, and the bloody, slippery oozing of the internal organs. Fascination resides in the evanescent and yet endlessly drawn-out moment when the victim lives out his own death, an instant before the body is finally reduced to the status of dead meat.

Cheap Thrills

And this is the real reason people flock to see—indeed, why we passionately enjoy—horror films such as Romero's. What is the nature of this fascination, this dread, this enjoyment? In what position does such sensationalistic excess place the spectator, and how does it address him or her? Horror shares with pornography the frankly avowed goal of physically *arousing* the audience. If these "base" genres violate social taboos, this is not so much on account of *what* they represent or depict on the screen as of *how* they go about doing it. Horror and porn are radically desublimating; they make a joke of the pretensions of establishing aesthetic distance and of offering "redeeming social value." They exceed the boundaries usually assigned to mass entertainment by ludicrously hyperbolizing and literalizing what are supposed to be merely the secondary, deferred, compensatory satisfactions of fantasy. More precisely, they short-circuit the mechanism of fantasy altogether: they are not content to leave me with vague, disembodied imaginings but excitedly seek to incise those imaginings in my very flesh. They focus obsessively upon the physical reactions of bodies on-screen, the better to assault and agitate the bodies of the audience. This is precisely why porn and horror films epitomize "bad taste." They do not bring me gratified fulfillment or satiation but insidiously exacerbate and exasperate my least socially acceptable desires.

Romero's films, and the many horror films produced in their wake, do not try to suture the spectator into a seamless world of false plenitude and ideological mystification. Rather, they blithely dispense with the canons of realistic conviction. They indulge themselves in the production of "special effects," in the double sense of grotesque visual effects and of affective and physiological effects upon the viewer. What counts is not the believability of the events depicted but only the immediate response they elicit from the spectator. Whereas the scenes of anticipation previously discussed hollow out the space between stimulus and response, the present scenes of carnage and gore overload this space to the point of explosion. A behaviorist model of discontinuous shock effects replaces the traditional, representational or naturalistic model of apparent depths and plausible causal connections. Indeed, these films go out of their way to call attention to their own irreality, the hilarious and ostentatious artificiality of their spectacular, outrageous special effects.

Romero's movies are filled with marvelously tasteless sight gags reminiscent of 1950s comic books, such as the scene in *Dawn* in which one character is so absorbed in using a machine to test his blood pressure that he virtually fails to notice the zombies tearing him apart (final blood pressure reading: zero), or the shot in *Day* of eyes still fluttering frantically in a head that has been sliced in two. These films do not try to disguise, but openly revel in, their recourse to mechanistic, technological means of manipulation. This cynicism on the plane of expression goes hand in hand with a self-conscious celebration of simulation and monstrosity on the plane of content. Just as the zombies cannot be categorized within the diegesis (they cannot be placed in terms of our usual binary oppositions of life and death, or nature and culture), so on the formal level of presentation, they transgress, or simply ignore, the boundaries between humor and horror, between intense conviction and ludicrous exaggeration.

These films are wildly discontinuous, flamboyantly antinaturalistic, and nonsensically grotesque. Yet the more ridiculously excessive and self-consciously artificial they are, the more literal is their visceral impact. They can't be kept at a distance, for they can't be referred to anything beyond themselves. Their simulations are radically immediate: they no longer pretend to stand in for, or to represent, a previously existing real. Horror thus destroys customary meanings and appearances, ruptures the surfaces of the flesh, and violates the organic integrity of the body. It puts the spectator in direct contact with intensive, unrepresentable fluxes of corporeal sensation. I respond with a heightened tingling of the flesh, with an odd mixture of laughter, anxiety, and disgust. As Romero's films increasingly subvert the pragmatics of survival and slide into a realm of ambivalent, gory fascination, they come to exemplify a base counteraesthetics in shock, hilarity, relentless violence, delirious behaviorism, contagion, tactile participation, and aimless, hysterical frenzy.

I watch these films, finally, with an alarming, ambivalent, and highly charged exhilaration. At the end of *Day* especially, I am seduced and transfixed by the joy and the terror—the disgusting, unspeakable pleasure—of the human body's exposure and destruction. As the flesh of the last few soldiers is deservedly torn to shreds, more and more zombie hands thrust themselves into the frame, grasping, tearing, avidly yet impersonally claiming their gobbets of skin and entrails. The zombie potlatch marks a democratic, communal leveling of all invidious distinctions; it is an ephemeral instant of universal participation and communication. As I witness this cannibal ferment, I enjoy the reactive gratifications of *ressentiment* and revenge, the unavowable delights of exterminating the powerful Others who have abused me. But such intense pleasures are deeply equivocal, ironically compromised from the outset, participatory in a way that implicates my own interiority. For one thing, I can scarcely distinguish the agonies of the victims from the never-satisfied cravings of the avengers, the continuing disquiet of the already dead. What is more, the nervous, exacerbated thrills of destruction, the jolts and spasms that run through my body at the sight of all this gore, threaten to tear me apart as well. I enjoy this sordid spectacle only at the price of being mimetically engulfed by it, uncontrollably, excitedly swept away. I find myself giving in to an insidious, hidden, deeply shameful passion for abject self-disintegration.

On a formal no less than on a thematic level, the Living Dead trilogy destabilizes structures of power and domination. It accomplishes this by being absurdly reactive, by pushing to an outrageous extreme the consequences of manipulation, victimization, and Nietzschean "slave morality." It does not negate, but appropriates and redirects, the simulationist technologies of postmodern control. It does not provide a cathartic release for, but self-consciously channels and intensifies, our aggressive and destructive drives. It abolishes reflective distance and desublimates affective response. It does not propose any utopian vision but overtly imbricates control with the loss of control. These painful ambiguities continue to pursue those few protagonists who do manage to escape. The survivors who reach a tropical island at the end of *Day* have nothing to look forward to but an empty, eventless, nightmare-ridden time—or worse, the eventuality that the zombies will reach them by learning how to swim. There is no possibility of evasion, just as there is none of mastery, and none of firm and stable identification, for the zombies always come in between: they insinuate themselves within the uncanny, interstitial space that separates (but thereby also connects) inside and outside, the private and the public, life and death. In this liminal position, they are the obscene objects of voyeuristic fascination.

In a deeper sense, however, the zombies are the subjects of this fascination as well: their endless desire, their deindividuated subjectivity, infects and usurps my own. They literalize and embody an extremity of agitation, an ecstatic emptying out of the self, a mimetic contagion, in which I can participate, alas, only vicariously. Yet in the long run, this inauthentic, vicarious participation is more than enough. The most intense and disturbing passion is the most factitious. Voyeurism implies a strange complicity, less with the agent of destruction than with the victim. I have survived the vision of hell and apocalypse; I am only sitting in a movie theater after all. My intense enjoyment of this spectacle, my thrilling, pornographic realization that humankind, as Benjamin put it, "can experience its own destruction as an aesthetic pleasure of the first order,"[14] is not something to moralize against but something to be savored. In the postmodern age of manipulative microtechnologies and infectious mass communication, such a pleasure marks the demoralization and collapse of the fascist exaltation Benjamin was warning against, and the birth instead of a politics of mimetic debasement, a subtle and never-completed opening to abjection.

Notes

1. Gilles Deleuze and Félix Guattari, *Anti-Oedipus: Capitalism and Schizophrenia*, trans. Robert Hurley, Mark Seem, and Helen R. Lane (Minneapolis: University of Minnesota Press, 1987), 335.

2. Walter Benjamin, *The Origin of German Tragic Drama*, trans. John Osborne (London: Verso, 1985).

3. Craig Owens, "The Allegorical Impulse: Toward a Theory of Postmodernism," in *Art after Modernism: Rethinking Representation*, ed. Brian Wallis, 203–35 (New York: New Museum of Contemporary Art, in association with David R. Godine, 1984).

4. Celeste Olalquiaga, *Megalopolis: Contemporary Cultural Sensibilities* (Minneapolis: University of Minnesota Press, 1992).

5. Walter Benjamin, *One Way Street and Other Writings*, trans. Edmund Jephcott and Kingsley Shorter (London: Verso, 1985), 160–63. See also Michael Taussig, *The Nervous System* (New York: Routledge, 1992).

6. Robin Wood, *Hollywood from Vietnam to Reagan* (New York: Columbia University Press, 1986), 114–21.

7. Kim Newman, *Nightmare Movies: A Critical Guide to Contemporary Horror Films* (New York: Harmony, 1988), 1–5, 199–201, 208–10.

8. Carol J. Clover, *Men, Women, and Chainsaws: Gender in the Modern Horror Film* (Princeton, N.J.: Princeton University Press, 1992).

9. Meaghan Morris, in Janet Bergstrom and Mary Anne Doane, eds., "The Spectatrix," special issue, *Camera Obscura* 20–21 (May–September 1989), 244.

10. Newman, *Nightmare Movies*, 209.

11. Georges Bataille, *Visions of Excess: Selected Writings, 1927–1939*, trans. and ed. Allan Stoekl (Minneapolis: University of Minnesota Press, 1985), 17.

12. Gilles Deleuze, *Cinema 1: The Movement-Image*, trans. Hugh Tomlinson and Barbara Habberjam (Minneapolis: University of Minnesota Press, 1986), 155–59.

13. Ibid., 197–215.

14. Walter Benjamin, *Illuminations*, ed. Hannah Arendt, trans. Harry Zohn (New York: Schocken Books, 1969), 242.

Zombie TV
Late-Night B Movie Horror Fest

JEFFREY ANDREW WEINSTOCK

The death of God has left us with a lot of appliances.

—Avital Ronell, "Trauma TV"

Channel Surfing Wipeout

"Clear your mind," advises the diminutive psychic (Zelda Rubinstein) in Tobe Hooper's 1982 supernatural thriller *Poltergeist*, "it knows what scares you."[1] The "it" within this context refers to the malevolent entity that has invaded a quiet suburban home via the television and abducted a young child (Carol Anne, played by Heather O'Rourke). The "it," however, also applies to the creative team behind the production of a successful "horror" film such as *Poltergeist*. Bodies are produced to be rended, expended, devoured in a nightmarish parade of violence as the audience munches popcorn, bodies passive, eyes unblinking.

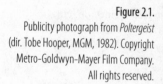

Figure 2.1.
Publicity photograph from *Poltergeist* (dir. Tobe Hooper, MGM, 1982). Copyright Metro-Goldwyn-Mayer Film Company. All rights reserved.

What is "it" that scares the American film-going public? According to George A. Romero's 1968 cult-classic *Night of the Living Dead (NOLD)*[2] and Tobe Hooper's 1982 *Poltergeist*, "it" is technology run amok and the invasion of the American home. What unites these disparate themes in these two films is the emphasis within each upon the destabilizing presence of the television within the American living room. Home as haven, as refuge from the outside world, is shattered by the invasive force of technoculture, embodied by the glow of the TV in the dark living room of the American household—TV as invasion:

> Television exposes that constitutive outside that you have to let into the house of being, inundating and saturating you.[3]

In both *NOLD* and *Poltergeist*, fear of death is coupled with fear of technology, and the locus of supernatural dread is displaced from the graveyard to the living room. In each of these American horror movies, the conduit of supernatural activity is not a Ouija board or other mystical artifact but a technological innovation—the television—a device that occupies a place of central importance within both cinematic homes. Both Romero and Hooper present pictures of American society in which the privileged position of the television within the living room destabilizes the notion of the home as "a place apart" by constantly providing the cinematic character-viewers with "outside" news and information. In essence, the outside world is a space from which escape is no longer perceived as possible because, via the television, the outside has been invited inside:

> the more local it gets, the more uncanny, not at home, it appears.[4]

The space of the living room thus is exploded by the presence of the TV, which dismantles the traditionally perceived public–private boundary of the American living room by allowing outside information (and entities) to invade the space of the home. In each case, this violation of privacy fostered by the technological innovations of the "information age" destabilizes the concept of the home as a comfort zone sheltered from the stress and mayhem of the outside world, ultimately threatening the unity of the American family:

> Moreover, precisely in so far as broadcasting articulates the public and private spheres, it is at the same time a potentially "dangerous" force, in need of regulation; it disrupts or transgresses the boundaries of the family household and its "private universe."[5]

Feature #1

The grainy, black-and-white documentary-style *NOLD* opens in a traditional horror movie location—the graveyard—as brother and sister Barbra (Judith O'Dea) and Johnny (Russell Streiner), generic as their names, arrive to place a wreath on their father's grave.[6] As they exit the car, the radio ominously seems to switch itself on and the announcer explains the prior loss of signal (the radio's "deadness") as the result of "technical problems." Johnny is surprised by the radio's intrusion, having assumed it broken. This early instance of technical difficulties provides the first hint that technology has escaped human control and foreshadows the importance that radio and television news broadcasts will play for the characters within the farmhouse in which Barbra eventually seeks refuge.

The couple's graveside seclusion soon is broken by the intrusion of a third figure in the distance, stumbling among the graves as small American flags wave in the breeze. There is nothing to indicate that the figure approaching them is anything other than another graveyard visitor until the figure unexpectedly attacks Barbra. Johnny intercedes, and as he is thrown to the ground, Barbra flees. Unlike usual horror film conventions, this first appearance of the "undead" is abrupt and undistinguished; the figure approaching from across the graveyard appears in daylight and demonstrates no significantly unusual or "supernatural" characteristics. There is no build in the music or ominous tracking shots of the approaching figure. This first appearance of the undead could easily be misconstrued as an attack by a living, albeit mentally disturbed, person.

Barbra flees from the attack and seeks refuge in the car, only to discover that Johnny has the keys and that she is unable to start the vehicle. She becomes trapped in the automobile—her supposed method of escape—as her undead attacker batters the windows and finally shatters the glass with a rock. In desperation, Barbra releases the emergency brake, and the car rolls down a hill and crashes into a tree. Inability to control specifically transportational technology, as exemplified by Barbra's inability to control the car, is recapitulated again and again throughout *NOLD*: Ben (Duane Jones) recalls witnessing a truck crash through a guardrail; the pickup truck in which Ben arrives is out of fuel and later explodes, killing Tom (Keith Wayne) and Judy (Judith Ridley); the Cooper family recounts how their car was overturned by the undead and how they had to retreat, like Barbra, on foot. From the opening moments of the film, technology not only fails its users but becomes potentially lethal.

Barbra manages to extricate herself from the automobile and flees from her attacker into a secluded farmhouse where technology again fails her—she tries frantically to use the phone only to find it, like the car radio, "dead." Again, she is trapped in a claustrophobic space with no way to communicate her presence to the outside world. The world shrinks to the size of a farmhouse.

Barbra is soon joined within the farmhouse by six other persons seeking refuge from the external mayhem: the intelligent, dynamic, and notably black Ben,[7] the ill-fated teenage lovers Tom and Judy, and the Cooper family—Harry (Karl Hardman), Helen (Marilyn Eastman), and their injured daughter Karen (Kyra Schon). Ben's discovery and utilization of a radio stimulate marital discord between the Coopers as Mrs. Cooper chastises her husband for his decision to remain in the basement, isolated from any source of information:

> In this family [under study] there is a stress on the importance of boundaries and control. Perhaps by way of compensation for his sense of lack of control over the outside world, the man is very concerned to regulate the functions of communications technologies in breaking the boundary between the private and public spheres.[8]

The desire for news from the outside world and the need for authoritative direction force the Coopers to emerge from their basement hiding place to listen to the radio.

What becomes evident, first from radio reports and then from an extended sequence of television news reports and interviews, is that the unburied dead are returning to life and committing acts of murder and cannibalism. As the trapped group gathers around the television in a warped parody of the family, the viewer joins this family, watching as news clips report that the president has called a meeting of the Joint Chiefs of Staff and officials from the CIA, FBI, and NASA to discuss the problem. What follows this report is a series of interviews in which, amid attempts to shift blame and cloud the issue, it becomes evident that the "mutations" of the dead are likely the result of the detonation by NASA of a Venus satellite returning to Earth with a "mysterious, high level of radiation." This revelation confirms the fact that technology has outstripped man's capacity to control it; the "unnatural" return of the dead and the ensuing holocaust of death are revealed to be the direct result of humanity's tampering with the environment and irresponsible use of technology without appropriate safeguards.

The news reports to which the group listens detail an "epidemic of mass murder" that is spreading across the United States. These reports extend the scope and magnitude of the threat from several people trapped in a farmhouse to a large area of the United States. While the farmhouse inhabitants cannot communicate their presence and need of assistance to the outside world, reports of the outside world are communicated via the TV, metonymically linking the local predicament to a situation affecting the nation as a whole:

> What I want to do here is to sketch in some of the ways in which television, as a specific discourse spanning this private/public divide, can be seen to articulate together domestic and national life.[9]

Early reports are only able to identify the assailants as "ordinary looking people" who are part of "a virtual army of unidentified assassins." And indeed, as life begins to approximate the news reports, an army of ordinary (if sickly) looking "people" is what comes to surround the farmhouse. Just as Barbra is unable to identify her assailant in the graveyard as anything other than a normal human being, the rest of the undead are also more or less (depending upon degree of decomposition) indistinguishable from the living. This confusion becomes most evident in the ironic killing of Ben at the end of the movie, during which Ben is mistaken for one of the undead.

The fears of technology and invasion of the American home expressed within the 1968 *NOLD* arise out of the cultural moment of Vietnam, and the televised news accounts of an "army of unidentified assassins" can be read as a striking metaphor for the Viet Cong. Closely paralleling Vietnam news reports, television in *NOLD* brings gruesome reports of the "war" into the farmhouse living room, polarizing group members as child turns against parent and black man confronts white man. Furthermore, government officials are revealed though the television news broadcasts to be incompetent and untruthful, suggesting another Vietnam parallel.

Toward the end of the film, after the night of terror that only Ben has survived, the action of the film moves outside of the farmhouse into the field, as the camera documents the vigilante mob rooting out and gunning down the living dead. As a roving reporter (Lee Hartman) interviews the sheriff (George Kosana) in charge of this "cleanup" operation, the movie itself becomes the news clips earlier reported on the television within the farmhouse; the movie camera becomes the camera filming the interview, providing black-and-white footage comparable to the general in the field indiscriminately eliminating the enemy.

As the story extends beyond the confines of the farmhouse, Romero makes evident that there is little to distinguish the living from the living dead. The members of the sheriff's posse are as vapid and unemotional as the zombies they mercilessly pick off, one by one. And then Romero provides the ultimate irony: the brave and resourceful hero Ben, the sole survivor of the night of terror within the farmhouse, emerges into the light of day and is gunned down, "another one for the fire." There is no happy ending here, and there is no place for the courageous and valiant in a society of zombies.

NOLD, on many levels, is all about television—about dangerous technology that subverts the "laws of nature," about the first war to be broadcast into the American living room, about the erasure of the always-already imaginary line separating the internal world of the home from the external world. We first watch characters watching news clips in the farmhouse and then watch directly as those clips are broadcast from the field, ourselves replacing the now-dead characters of the farmhouse. The black-and-white footage in fact reveals that everything is gray—that the living are as much zombies as the dead—and the viewer, rendered passive by the viewing, is ironically zombified in the process:

> In this peculiar respect, mass communication may be included among the most respectable and efficient social narcotics.[10]

Commercial

One of the interesting things that sometimes happens in electronics departments is that cameras are set up to transmit the image of the consumer to the TV screen. Since the camera and the TV cannot be coterminous, the screen image can never be a mirror reflection—to see one's image on the screen is always to see oneself from an impossible perspective—from above, from the side, even from behind. The effect is uncanny—seeing oneself suddenly through the eyes of another without the possibility of establishing eye contact. More so than a photograph or a videotape, the immediacy of the encounter establishes a hypnotic objectification of the self as other. The uncanniness is heightened by a certain vertigo induced through trying to move one's body for the camera while looking at the screen. Moving for the camera, in essence, one attempts to occupy two spaces at once. Moving for the camera, watching oneself on the screen, one suddenly feels foolish, exposed to the invisible gazes of others. The encounter with the resistant doppelganger is a moment of crisis, of seeing oneself not seeing, and of knowing that one can be seen not seeing. How can one regain control of one's image? By purchasing the camera, of course, and filming others.

Short Subject

Dawn of the Dead, the 1978 sequel to *NOLD*, moves the action from in front of a farmhouse TV to a TV station.[11] The movie opens in medias res, amid panic at a TV studio. The living dead have overrun Philadelphia, and the station is struggling to stay on the air. From *Night* to *Dawn*, the viewer follows the transmission process from the televised footage received by the TV, to the recording of that footage in the field, to the studio—the point of transmission itself. The debate in the studio centers around the ethics of continued transmission—should the studio continue to send out reporters who will be killed? The station boss says yes; his assistant Fran (Gaylen Ross) (one of the four who ultimately will escape from Philadelphia) objects.[12]

From the opening credits, television, capitalism, and zombies are conjoined. Coverage of disaster translates into ratings, which translate into cash. Although the studio debate about whether or not to continue coverage of the disaster focuses primarily on the safety of the reporters and studio crew, the ethics of televised horror is also implicitly raised, ironically interrogating *Dawn of the Dead* and the horror genre itself. Ronell encapsulates the debate surrounding media violence when she asks,

> When [American scenes of violence] pass into the media and graduate into "events" are these scenes already effects of the media?[13]

> T.V., is it the reflector or the director?
> Does it imitate us
> or do we imitate it?

> Because a child watches 1500 murders before he's twelve years old and we wonder how we've created a Jason generation that learns to laugh rather than abhor the horror.[14]

Whereas the farmhouse in *NOLD* functions as a nexus of race, class, and gender conflicts, *Dawn of the Dead* moves the action from rural farmhouse to shopping mall, locating the conflict firmly within the American middle class. Zombie consumption of flesh is paralleled with living consumption of goods in consumer culture. Indeed, Romero's playful sequence of zombies roaming the mall to Muzak is juxtaposed with an extended sequence (reminiscent of DeLillo's *White Noise*) in which the characters Peter and Roger (Scott H. Reiniger) exclaim enthusiastically, "Let's go shopping!" and then joyously proceed to gather consumer goods like children in the proverbial candy store. They return, excited and out of breath, exclaiming, "You should see all the great stuff we've got—this place is terrific!"

In *NOLD*, characters seek refuge in a farmhouse—and the farmhouse is revealed as penetrable, insecure. In *Dawn of the Dead*, television newscasts reveal that a state of martial law has been imposed and that the federal government has decreed that it is unsafe for individuals to occupy private residences. Someplace homier than home must be sought, and the mall is discovered to be this site of comfort and security. In response to the query about why the living dead have congregated at the mall, Roger replies, "Instinct, memory, what they used to do—this was an important place in their lives." Later he adds, "They remember they want to be here." Consumer culture animates both living and dead and renders the distinction uncertain.[15]

Feature #2

> For most people there are only two places in the world—
> where they live and their TV set.[16]

As in *NOLD*, the television within *Poltergeist* also occupies a place of central importance within the American living room. However, within *Poltergeist*, the television not only symbolically dismantles the inside–outside bipolarity but serves as a literal conduit between worlds as well. The film opens with the flashing, disconnected images of a television screen viewed from very close up. As the camera pulls back, the grainy dots resolve, Seurat-like, into a series of patriotic images as scheduled programming draws to a conclusion. The national anthem ends, and the color TV images are replaced by black-and-white static. The recurring juxtaposition of the television screen and the image of the American flag, in light of the television's subsequent invasive function, expresses an ominous sense of distrust toward the government and its alliance with modern technology, a distrust manifested in *NOLD* through NASA's responsibility for the undead. While distrust for the government is only implied in *Poltergeist*, it is obvious that authority structures, while not necessarily malevolent in intent, are insufficient to protect the American citizen; the middle-class family involved in the hauntings at no point resorts to traditional authority structures, such as the police, for protection or to make sense of the bizarre phenomena:

> *X-Files*: After several murders, Mulder and Scully uncover a plot to control minds via television broadcasts. As is usual for the series, the government is suspected of using the American public as guinea pigs for insidious experimentation.[17]

Amid static buzz and the lightning-like flashing of the screen across the living room walls, little Carol Anne, age five, is summoned to the television. She crouches down close to the screen and engages in an interactive dialogue with the set, as her father (Craig T. Nelson) slumbers in the recliner. While the queries put to her by the television are inaudible to the audience, her responses are quite plainly audible, and as she complains that she cannot see to whom she is speaking and that she is having difficulty hearing, her family gathers around her and observes the exchange. Ultimately, Carol Anne places her hands upon the TV screen, as if upon a window, and answers the questions she seemingly is asked.

The image of little Carol Anne in silhouette, lit by the glow of the television in front

of her, is the familiar publicity poster and video box cover for the movie. The viewer sees Carol Anne from behind, watches her interact with the television, which assumes the prominent position in the image. The intriguing aspect of this scene is that the television here no longer serves as a one-way funnel of information into the home but now functions in the exact opposite capacity; the family, with the exception of Carol Anne, can neither see nor hear anything on the television apart from the normal "snow" and static expected from a channel that is no longer carrying a signal. However, some foreign entity at the other end of the transmission process or at some point in between is gathering information about the American family through the living room television set. The TV is now functioning like a camera, allowing an outside entity to observe, through the TV, the family that normally does the watching. The intended technological function of the television has been subverted by the mysterious supernatural third party.

Within *NOLD*, the television performs its "normal" function of providing information to the observers, in the process metaphorically inviting the outside world into the living room. Within *Poltergeist*, the television actually serves as a portal through which another world, the supernatural world, can gain access to the American living room. As the family lies sleeping together in the bedroom during a thunderstorm, the still-operative TV, echoing the movie's opening sequence, plays the national anthem, and the transmitted signal again goes "dead," leaving "snow" and static. It is from this flickering buzz of the television that a green vapor emerges and shoots into the wall above the bed, shaking the house and waking the family in the process. Following this occurrence, Carol Anne utters her now-famous observation, "They're here." In response to her mother's (JoBeth Williams) query, "Who's here?" Carol Anne responds, "The TV people":

> "Mike!" screamed Mrs. Teavee, clasping her head in her hands. "Where are you?"
> "I'll tell you where he is," said Mr. Teavee, "he's whizzing around above our heads in a million tiny pieces!" . . . "We must watch the television set," said Mr. Wonka. "He may come through at any moment."[18]

From start to finish, *Poltergeist* is a movie based around the presence of the television within the American living room. The opening sequence pulls back to reveal a TV, it is through the TV that supernatural forces gain entrance to the household, it is through the TV that the mother can communicate with her daughter,[19] it is with video cameras, televisions, and advanced electronic equipment that "paranormal researchers" investigate the supernatural goings-on (in another case of life approximating TV, the supernatural phenomena ambiguously observed are rendered distinct only by watching the playback of the video), and, in the climax of the film, it is through a portal in the children's closet, whose flashing light and deafening buzz approximate an enlarged version of the living room television flickering in the dark room, that the mother disappears after her daughter. In a comic gesture, the last scene of the movie observes the beleaguered family expelling a television from the depersonalized space of their highway motel room, and the camera lingers on the television as the screen fades to black. Thus, closure is attained—opening image and closing image are unified by a focus upon the television screen. (Since the family now needs to discover someplace more homey than their home, perhaps their next stop will be the mall . . .)

MTV

We have channel-surfed through monster movie features, prime time, commercials, news programs, and the children's station in order to indicate the ways in which television in American culture functions as a locus of fear, as an uncanny presence that undermines one's sense of security. I will now conclude by addressing two images: the front and back cover of Marilyn Manson's 1994 release *Portrait of an American Family*.[20] These two images together nicely encapsulate much of the preceding discussion.

The front cover of *Portrait* (Figure 2.3) creates a disturbing impression of the American family. Surrealistically illuminated by one hanging lightbulb, the scene features four crude papier-mâché figures—a mother, a father, and two sons—all seated facing the viewer. Surrounded by cheap wood paneling, the mother and father sit in an old loveseat, while the two children sprawl on a red carpet. The family is white trash—the tattooed father sits in a dirty undershirt with a beer in his hand and a cigarette in his mouth. His prominent belt buckle reads "nobody ever raped" with a gun pointed at the reader. His pregnant wife sits next to him, cigarette in hand. The youngest child lies naked on the floor, except for socks. A tin of french fries also sits on the red carpet. All the figures feature bulging white eyes and misshapen features. The mother and father sit expressionless, while the older son leers crazily. Each son features an evident wound—the older one on his arm, the younger on his head.

What is missing from this frightening depiction of the white-trash American family is, of course, the television. However, the orientation of the sofa, the fixed gazes of the family, their bulging eyes and zombified stares, make evident that the television is missing from the scene because the viewer is occupying the place of the television, voyeuristically spying on this family through the television. We are now the disembodied entity on the other side of the screen, looking with horror at what the typical American family has become.

And who are we? The back cover (Figure 2.4) makes clear that we are Marilyn Manson

Figure 2.3.
The front cover of
Marilyn Manson's
1994 release *Portrait
of an American Family.*
Released by Nothing
Records/Interscope
Records.

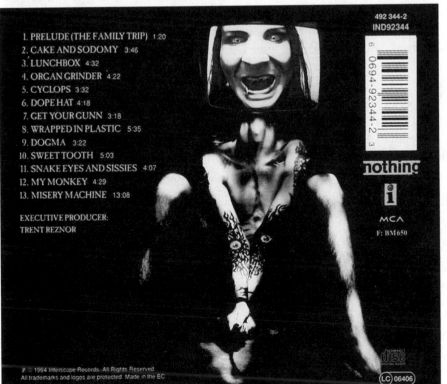

Figure 2.4.
The back cover of
Marilyn Manson's
1994 release *Portrait
of an American Family.*
Released by Nothing
Records/Interscope
Records.

and Marilyn Manson is television. The back cover features a sitting naked man, pale, gaunt, and bathed in shadowy green light, arms outspread in front simultaneously to block the view of his genitals and to display the elaborate tattoos running up and down the arms and converging in eyes at the crux of each inner arm. But the feature of the image that immediately grabs the viewer's attention is the television with an enlarged image of a face in place of where the head of the figure should be. The figure is a nightmarish hybrid of human form and technology. From within the television, Marilyn Manson stares out maniacally, eyes leering, mouth gaping, with pierced lip and decaying teeth.

The inside compact disc packaging reads down the left side "I am you." And, after the credits, Marilyn elaborates on this conflation:

> You spoonfed us Saturday morning mouthfuls of maggots and lies disguised in your sugary breakfast cereals. The plates you made us clean were filled with your fears. These things have hardened in our soft pink bellies. We are what you have made us. We have grown up watching your television. We are a symptom of your Christian America, the biggest satan of all. This is your world in which we grow.
>
> And we will grow to hate you.[21]

The "I am you" designation works in two directions. Marilyn claims to be what "we"—corporate, Christian America—have produced. Marilyn as hatred, Marilyn as freak, is symptomatic of an intolerant, hypocritical, and Puritanical culture. On the other hand, "we" are Marilyn—beneath dark suits, power ties, and pious exteriors lurk the same perversity, hatred, and freakishness that Marilyn incarnates. And the way these characteristics are inculcated in the American family is through consumer culture, with television being its premier medium of imperialism. Thus, Marilyn as zombie TV presents television's true face of capitalist hegemony.

Zombie TV—Don't Touch That Dial!

The death of God may have left us with a lot of appliances, but in horror and certain strands of popular discourse, the appliance begins to assume the vacant place of the Almighty, and humanity's apparent difficulty pulling the plug functions as a source of contemporary anxiety. Both *NOLD* and *Poltergeist*, through the omnipresent insistence of the television, manifest an extreme form of "technoparanoia." The notions that technology can be appropriated and utilized in unintended and dangerous ways and that technology can undermine the privacy and security of the home undergird the premises of both movies. It is only once the television is expelled in *Poltergeist* that a sense of security is reestablished.

However, while the family within *Poltergeist* escapes relatively unscathed, the house itself does not survive. During the (perhaps) unexpected and sexually charged second climax of the movie, the exploded space of the living room violently contracts, and the house, quite literally, implodes. The presence of the television within the living room has compromised the structural integrity of the house, and the weight of the outside world crushes the structure.

What is revealed when the house begins its implosion is that the home is situated atop a graveyard. Whereas *NOLD* opens in a graveyard, which yields up its dead, and ends in a home, which becomes a locus of death, in *Poltergeist*, the home and the graveyard are geographically juxtaposed. Maximal proximity is achieved between the living and the dead as home and graveyard are equated and the porous barrier separating the living from the dead, delineating the natural and the "unnatural," manifests itself in the form of a television screen:

> One of the key functions of broadcasting is the creation of a bridge between the public and the private, the sacred and the profane, the extraordinary and the mundane.[22]

Just as *Dawn of the Dead* suggests a critique of capitalist consumer culture via the conflation of zombie and shopper, *Poltergeist* suggests a similar critique through identifying greed as the moving force behind the supernatural occurrences. Marilyn Manson's white-trash family, TV head, and vitriolic diatribe condense these themes into a forceful articulation of technoparanoia in which television functions as an invasive, imperialist force that colonizes/stupifies the viewer:

> No matter what's on, I daresay, it is emptied of any signified; it is a site of evacuation, the hemorrhaging of meaning, ever disrupting its semantic fields and the phenomenal activities of showing.[23]

In Romero's Living Dead movies, technology gone awry animates the dead, and in *Poltergeist*, the presence of the TV in the living room threatens the American family. Marilyn Manson, however, as monstrous hybrid of human and television who speaks on behalf of the "TV generation," suggests not only that the television compromises the integrity of the home as haven from the outside world but that this invasion zombifies the viewer. *NOLD* and *Poltergeist* manifest anxiety about turning on the TV; Marilyn Manson asks, rather, if it is still possible to turn it off:

> 2, 7, 5, 4, 8 she watched she said
> All added up to zero
> And nothing in her head[24]

Notes

1. *Poltergeist*, directed by Tobe Hooper (MGM, 1982).
2. *Night of the Living Dead*, directed by George A. Romero (Anchor Bay, 1968).
3. Avital Ronell, "Trauma TV: Twelve Steps beyond the Pleasure Principle," in *Finitude's Score: Essays for the End of the Millennium*, ed. Avital Ronell (Lincoln: University of Nebraska Press, 1994), 311.
4. Ibid., 310.
5. David Morley, *Television, Audiences, and Cultural Studies* (London: Routledge, 1992), 257.
6. Timothy Corrigan suggests in *A Cinema without Walls: Movies and Culture after Vietnam* (New Brunswick, N.J.: Rutgers University Press, 1991), 82, that the graininess of the film stock likens it to a home movie. Thus, what is revealed by the destabilizing presence of the television and the disintegration of the family in *NOLD* is precisely the unhomeliness lurking within the home.
7. While the scope of this essay precludes an extended analysis of racial conflict in *Night of the Living*

Dead, NOLD is notable within its Vietnam- and civil rights–era context for its simultaneous foreground-ing and effacement of race. It is Ben, the young, dynamic black man—the only black person, living or dead, in the feature—who first comes to Barbra's rescue. As Barbra, who is blonde and very pale, lies dazed on a sofa, Ben begins to loosen her garments, constructing the historical nightmare/fantasy of the gentile white woman violated by the feral black man. However, although racial conflicts seem imminent, most especially in the interaction between the selfish and intolerant Harry Cooper and Ben, Mr. Cooper surprisingly forbears making the expected racial slurs. Indeed, none of the characters make any reference to race. The issue of race—inescapable on the metafictional level—somehow is effaced from the internal consciousness of the film itself. This erasure becomes most evident when watching the sequel, *Dawn of the Dead*, in which racial conflict is explicit during a police raid on a minority community.

8. Morley, *Television, Audiences, and Cultural Studies*, 241.

9. Ibid., 255.

10. Merton and Lazarsfeld, quoted ibid., 252.

11. *Dawn of the Dead*, directed by George A. Romero (Anchor Bay, 1978).

12. As in *Night of the Living Dead*, in *Dawn*, a masculine active–female passive binary opposition is established. Fran, much like Barbra, remains distant from the mayhem. Indeed, Fran, who, early on, refuses to play homemaker, ends up doing exactly that, remaining in the hideout and nursing the injured Roger. During the course of the movie, the viewer learns that Fran is pregnant. This fact, juxtaposed with her escape from the mall with the black character Peter (Ken Foree), suggests an interesting interracial redefinition of the family.

13. Ronell, "TraumaTV," 309.

14. Disposable Heroes of Hiphoprisy, "Television, the Drug of the Nation," *Hypocrisy Is the Greatest Luxury* (Island Records, 1992).

15. As in *Night of the Living Dead*, where the viewer moves from being situated with the characters in front of the TV to being actually behind the camera filming interviews, life approximates TV in *Dawn of the Dead* as well—all action flows outward from the TV studio. As the movie opens, two events occur: the studio crew debates the ethics of continued coverage of the catastrophe, while a vigorous televised debate between a white scientist and a black commentator airs from the studio. Reports of living dead and volatile race relations are both subsequently instantiated in the movement from the TV studio to a police standoff.

The standoff sequence, eerily proleptic of the 1985 police assault on the MOVE row house in West Philadelphia, introduces explicit racial conflict into *Dawn of the Dead*, conflict absent, as noted earlier, from *NOLD*. In this scene, the Philadelphia police, for reasons that remain unexplained by the movie, surround a hotel and attempt to force out the occupants. Whereas the intolerant Mr. Cooper in *Night of the Living Dead* refrains from racial slurs, the intolerant Philadelphia officer Wooley (James A. Baffico) foregrounds racial tension as he identifies the inhabitants of the building as blacks and Hispanics and confesses his desire to "blow all their low-life little Puerto Rican and nigger asses right off."

16. Don DeLillo, *White Noise* (London: Picador, 1985), 66.

17. "Wetwired," *The X-Files*, season 3, episode 23, directed by Rob Bowman, aired May 10, 1996.

18. Roald Dahl, *Charlie and the Chocolate Factory* (New York: Alfred A. Knopf, 1964), 140.

19. The main dynamic of *Poltergeist* is a mother–daughter relationship. It is the mother who ventures into the limbo-space to retrieve her abandoned daughter. *Poltergeist* thus constitutes a complete reversal from *Night of the Living Dead*—in the former, a mother rescues her daughter; in the latter, a daughter murders (and devours!) her mother.

20. Marilyn Manson, *Portrait of an American Family* (Interscope Records, 1994).

21. Ibid.

22. Morley, *Television, Audiences, and Cultural Studies*, 283.

23. Ronell, "Trauma TV," 311.

24. Public Enemy, "She Watch Channel Zero?!," *It Takes a Nation of Millions to Hold Us Back* (Def Jam Records, 1987).

Viral Cultures

Microbes and Politics in the Cold War

PRISCILLA WALD

A magnified photograph of the human immunodeficiency virus (HIV) entering a helper T cell offered the readers of the November 3, 1986, issue of *Time* magazine a visual representation of what scientists and journalists were calling "the disease of the century."[1] Since such images have long been a staple of popular science writing, the photograph does not seem remarkable. The caption explains: "Viruses (blue dots) attack a helper T cell, a crucial part of the immune system. Invading the cell, the virus commandeers its machinery, making it begin producing viruses. This eventually destroys the cell, weakening the immune system."[2] The article is typical of the media coverage of the epidemic, which, especially in its first decade, tended to fall within the science beat.[3] In the 1980s the HIV/AIDS epidemic provided occasion for a range of science lessons for the general public.

The *Time* article is entitled "Viruses," and the subtitle explains that "AIDS research" has spurred "new interest in some ancient enemies." The title and caption interpret the photograph for readers, explaining that what they are witnessing is an invasion. The language is familiar: viruses as enemies and invaders insidiously commandeer the machinery of the cell to reproduce themselves and, in so doing, damage or destroy the host. The article develops the metaphor as the stealthy viral marauder "single-mindedly" eludes "scouts" and "evades . . . rapidly advancing defenders." The virus is a "diminutive foreigner" that, taking "over part of the cellular machinery," directs the cell "to produce more AIDS virus [*sic*]," an "alien product" that eventually overwhelms the entire system (67). This remarkably unremarkable language of the viral foe subtly turns a photograph of macrophages into a story of an invasion; it is the result of conventions that consolidated through a conjunction of science and politics in the 1950s. Inviting the reader to look through the scientist's microscope, the photograph confers the authority of science on the article and on the story of viral invasion.[4]

A microscopic gaze turned with new intensity on human beings in the decade following the Second World War. While viruses first became visible to scientists in the early 1930s, it was not until the 1950s that new technologies of visualization let researchers peer with new eyes into the mysterious workings of viruses, where they marveled at how viruses differed from any entity they had studied before.[5] Unlike their bacterial counterparts, viral microbes existed on—and seemed to define—the border between the living and the nonliving. Viruses showed how the circulation of "information" allowed an organism to function, promising the imminent cracking, as one piece in the *Science News Letter* put it, of the "code for the organization of life from a microscopic egg to a human being."[6] In so doing, they helped to change scientific understanding of the gene—and of life itself. The new insights they provided as well as the media campaign around the mid-century polio epidemics and the widespread trials of a polio vaccine made virology good copy and introduced a general readership to one of science's newest discoveries.

Accounts of viruses frequently shared the page with another topic of particular interest: the allegedly emerging global threat of Communism and the politics of the Cold War.[7] The rise of two superpowers competing for world domination and the decolonization movements rippling across continents led to the breakdown of familiar social, economic, and political hierarchies. The inevitable uncertainty attendant on such rapid change fueled the infamous paranoia of Cold War politics. Circulating information animated collective as well as individual organisms, as governments classified "information" on which the integrity and security of the state depended, making its theft a capital crime. Conceptual changes in science and politics commingled, as the possibility of stealing or corrupting information was imagined in the labs of cutting-edge scientists and debated in the highest echelons of government. It was the subject of speculation in the mainstream media and of fascination in popular fiction and film. It generated whispered promises of the creation or preservation of life and of terrifying images of "brainwashing" and nuclear devastation, depersonalization escalating into collective annihilation.

In this chapter I document a gradual change in the language through which the media depicted viral contagion and the changing Cold War world that suggests a conceptual exchange between virology and Cold War politics. As viruses became increasingly sinister and wily, sneaking into cells and assuming control of their mechanisms, external agents, such as Communists, became viral, threatening to corrupt the dissemination of information as they infiltrated the nerve center of the state. The exchange crystallized vague and often conflicting anxieties about the changes of the postwar world. The new affiliations that came with political realignments brought the need for new stories of group origins and the triumph of human values shaped in the crucible of possible devastation: the histories and mythologies that accompany profound social change. The insights of virology were central to those stories, as the vocabulary that permeated the newspapers and science journals of the period found extended expression in the plots of novels and films. Those works dramatized the new scientific concepts, and like the media, they acted as a kind of reservoir host—to borrow a metaphor from science—in which scientific and political theories recombined, informing the mythology of the new age.[8] The elusive "diminutive foreigner" that comes from without and assumes control of cellular mechanisms in the *Time* magazine piece is a legacy of the conceptual exchange.

The avant-garde William Burroughs was especially prescient about the conceptual centrality of virology to the fashioning of a mid-century mythology. He followed developments in virology with fascination, finding them useful in his efforts to depict the mechanisms of what he saw as the dangerous, mindless conformity of the Cold War world. The "word virus" was a key feature in his witty and arcane novels, in which he offered his own creation story, "a mythology for the space age," to explain and revivify a world he found increasingly devoid of spirit and creativity.[9] Burroughs's critical insights and experimental writing, not surprisingly, earned him a cult following rather than a mass readership, but his analyses elucidate the broader appeal, and the virological features, of a story that would achieve paradigmatic status in Cold War America: Jack Finney's *The Body Snatchers*. Finney's best-selling 1955 novel generated numerous novelistic and cinematic spin-offs and quickly became a reference point in discussions of social and political behavior. His monstrous pod people infused as they embodied the science and politics of their moment, and the many retellings of their story attest to its continuing explanatory power.

Finney's story captured the imagination of a generation that had witnessed the transformation of the promise of atomic energy into a weapon more destructive than most could have imagined and that had heard accounts of the perversion of medical research in the service of torture in the Nazi death camps. Science for them was full of danger as well as promise, and no genre grappled with both in this period more than science-fiction horror. The big screen reveled in monstrous creations resulting from radiation or the encounter with dangerous aliens in the course of space travel and treated audiences to the thrilling horror of an apocalyptic loss of humanity emanating from a variety of sources. Finney's story brought monstrous aliens to medical science and the language of virology into a battle for the survival of the human race. His eerily memorable pod people worked like viruses, stealing the essential information from human beings and producing the mindless conformity that troubled Burroughs, who confessed, in the introduction to his novel *Queer*, that he lived "with the constant threat of possession, and a constant need to escape from possession, from Control."[10]

The Body Snatchers arguably produced a subgenre, epidemiological horror, that depicted the transformative power of disease and groups. With the pod people, Finney captured the horror of a protagonist's dawning awareness that the humanity of his or her closest associates is being drained from them and the terrifying estrangement that results as they try to maintain their human connections. The terror of their estrangement marks the deferred recognition of commonalities, the uncanny familiarity, that heralds new social configurations.

The monster–alien invasion works of this period have sparked numerous allegorical readings, especially among film critics, who have seen in them anxious depictions of Communism, McCarthyism, homosexuality, race, or gender.[11] Those issues represent the pressure points of changing social hierarchies and political realignments worldwide, and the novels and films invite those readings. Yet the underlying concerns of the moment come into sharper focus when the issues are considered together, even (perhaps especially) when they seem contradictory. It is not surprising to find contagion anxieties surfacing with the profound transformations of the moment, and Kirsten Ostherr brings public health into the mix when she argues that the mingling of anti-Communism and homophobia with "the imagery and anxieties of world health" manifests their shared concerns with a distrust of appearances, a fear of border crossings, and a lack of faith in the possibilities of detection.[12] Andrew Ross links "the Cold War culture of germo-phobia" more broadly to "the demonology of the 'alien,' especially in the genre of science fiction film, where a pan-social fear of the other—Communism, feminism, and other egalitarianisms foreign to the American social body—is reproduced through images drawn from the popular fringe of biological or genetic engineering gone wrong."[13] But the connection between that pan-social fear and the object of contagion that most in-trigued scientific medicine—the virus—allows for more specificity. The microscopic entities that fascinated scientists (atoms and genes as well as viral microbes) threatened potential catastrophe, but they also offered dramatic insights into the nature of life itself. The novels and films reveal a deep concern with the possible loss of humanity conceived as the theft of mind and body, a horrifying metamorphosis that is at once apocalyptic and ecstatic. The power of the viral image came from its simultaneous invocation of disgust and fascination, the mundane and the mystical. It permeated the cultural imagi-nation and imported its power when summoned, consciously or not, by writers and di-rectors. Finney's story offered a winning formula with its viral inflection of the threat of dehumanization and its epidemiological response. Epidemiology, after all, was a science that had not lost its humanitarian promise. William Burroughs urged his readers to keep their eyes open; Finney's story and its offshoots conceded the difficulty, perhaps impos-sibility, and certainly the urgency of doing so. Yet, ultimately, even at its most hopelessly apocalyptic, it affirmed the worth of humanity and carried the promise of its survival.

The successive versions of *Invasion of the Body Snatchers* illustrate the evolution of the epidemiological horror story and its conventions, notably, in the pod people, the sinister, crafty incarnated virus that could be identified and fought in a mythic battle between Science and Nature, a battle that harnessed apocalyptic energy as an antidote to estrangement and malaise. Philip Kaufman's 1978 film uncannily foreshadowed the early years of the HIV/AIDS epidemic, and epidemiological horror served as a shadow tale, supplying the conventions of horror to the outbreak narrative, as its contours were coming into focus. The pod people forecast and would soon metamorphose into the malevolent, willful viral–human carriers who are featured in the story of disease emer-gence. Kaufman's 1978 film and its forerunners suggest the importance of the conven-tions of the epidemiological horror story, and its Cold War roots, to the conceptual landscape in which the epidemic surfaced.[14]

A Mythology for the Space Age

No one more insightfully chronicled the anxieties of the age than William S. Burroughs, who was disturbed by the mindless conformity, creeping numbness, and hypocrisy of his native land. A canny observer, Burroughs put viruses at the center of his analysis and of his "mythology for the space age," a wild saga about viral space invaders, designed primarily to challenge his readers to become more critical observers of what he thought of as a deepening cultural pathology that he sought to diagnose and treat in his work. The social contagion that the Chicago sociologists set out to study was, for Burroughs, a sign of a dangerous pathology that was not limited to one side of the Cold War but was intrinsic to most forms of communication in the postwar world. His barometric writing was an artistic measure of the preoccupations of his moment, into which his status as an expatriate American living in Tangier afforded him a unique perspective.

Burroughs understood any communication that produced group thinking as a kind of contagion, and, like them, he meant the term literally. His contagion was explicitly viral, the expression of an invariably corrupting social control, especially pernicious at the level of the state. "The virus power manifests itself in many ways," he told an interviewer in 1964. "In the construction of nuclear weapons, in practically all the existing political systems which are aimed at curtailing inner freedom, that is, at control. It manifests itself in the extreme drabness of everyday life in Western countries. It manifests itself in the ugliness and vulgarity we see on every hand, and of course, it manifests itself in the actual virus illnesses."[15]

The scion whose family name was associated with the late-nineteenth-century invention of the adding machine came of age as a writer against the backdrop of cybernetics, and his work registers the centrality of information to his understanding of all social interactions. Anything that affected that information did not just act *like* a virus but actually *was* viral and, in his work, involved a sort of genetic alteration. Viral illnesses were no less material, for him, for being metaphors through which social dynamics manifested themselves. Metaphors produced material conditions, and he set out to demonstrate the material consequences of language. As Oliver Harris insightfully puts it, "to say the word is a communicative sickness was not, for Burroughs, metaphoric analysis of poststructuralist platitude but an awareness integral and material to the act of writing, and this is what the toxicity of Burroughs' textual politics insists upon, *ad nauseam*."[16] The viral, as it develops in his work, is anything that usurps creative agency, from addiction and the corporate interests that sustain the "junk business" to the official policies and customs and habits that enforce unthinking conformity, a species of mind control. In the introduction to his most widely read novel, *Naked Lunch* (1959), Burroughs explains the circumstances of its composition—his own drug addiction—and he offers an analysis that situates addiction in literal as well as metaphorical relationship to capitalism: drugs are "big business."[17] The danger of addiction shades gradually into contagion, beginning with his comparison of addicts, who "can be cured or quarantined," to "typhoid carriers" (xii) and grotesquely exemplified by the especially dedicated narcotics agent turned junky Bradley the Buyer, who literally "assimilates" (liquefies and absorbs) his district supervisor when he attempts to terminate his employment and, as Bradley explains, his "lifeline" (16). Bradley exemplifies the transformative and destructive power not only of addiction but also of bureaucracy and (literally) corporatism. Language was the instrument of the transformation.

Burroughs prided himself on understanding the science he used in his work, and in his novels from the 1960s, explanations from virology grew increasingly elaborate. In his 1962 work *The Ticket That Exploded*, he introduced the concept of "criminal controllers" who "occupy human bodies" but are not visible. "'Can you see a virus?' he asks. 'Well, the criminal controllers operate in very much the same manner as a virus—Now a virus in order to invade, damage and occupy the human organism must have a gimmick to get in—Once in the virus invades damages and occupies a certain area or organ in the body—known as the tissue of predilection—Hepatitis, for example, attacks the liver—Influenza the respiratory tract—Polio and rabies the central nervous system—In the same way a controller invades, damages and occupies some pattern or configuration of the human organism.'"[18] Burroughs imagines the controllers as space invaders who humorously but distinctly repeat the familiar history of conquest. Specialized, like viruses, in their means of infection, they summon that past through a tangled mythologized history of viral and political invasion and colonization. A controller who operates "through addicts [does so] because he himself is an addict—A heavy metal addict from Uranus—What we call opium or junk is a very much diluted form of heavy metal addiction—Venusians usually operate through sexual practices—In short these controllers brought their vices and diseases from their planet of origin and infected the human hosts very much in the same way that the early colonizers infected so-called 'primitive populations'" (59).

The distinction between mind and body made no sense to Burroughs for understanding addiction, language, or physical illness. Daily existence demonstrated the physical impact and consequences, the transformative power, of communication, and viruses explained as they exemplified how such processes became corrupted. As one character observes in *The Ticket That Exploded*, "Anyone who keeps his bloody eyes open doesn't need a Harly St. psychiatrist to tell him that destructive elements enter into so-called normal sex relations: the desire to dominate, to kill, to take over and eat the partner . . . these impulses are normally held in check by counter impulses . . . what the virus puts out of action is the *regulatory centers in the nervous system*" (20, ellipses original). The social analysis is an explicit feature of Burroughs's confrontational aesthetic: he was determined to teach his readers to see the means of infection.

The virus represents communication gone awry: the sources of connection turned into the terms of corruption. In a section of *The Ticket That Exploded* entitled "Operation Rewrite," Burroughs describes the "short step" from "symbiosis to parasitism": "The word is now a virus. The flu virus may once have been a healthy lung cell. It is now a parasitic organism that invades and damages the lungs" (49). The solution, as the title of the section suggests, arises out of the problem. If the word *virus* not only manifests but is actually generated by the corruption of language, a different approach to words can also supply the antidote: *"Communication must become total and conscious before we can stop it"* (51). In the 1985 introduction to *Queer* (published more than three decades after its composition), he would describe writing itself as "inoculation. As soon as something is written, it loses the power of surprise, just as a virus loses its advantage when a weakened virus has created alerted antibodies. So I achieved some immunity from further perilous ventures along these lines by writing my experience down."[19]

The strategy of inoculation became an explicit aesthetic with a new technique in composition that Burroughs developed with his poet and painter friend Brion Gysin following the publication of *Naked Lunch*. In what became known as his "cut-up" trilogy—*The Soft Machine* (1961–67), *The Ticket That Exploded* (1962), and *Nova Express* (1964)—he cut, pasted, folded, and patched his own work as well as that of other writers into the middle of works in progress to develop a compositional technique that would disrupt even a loose structure and force readers to focus on the elements of composition and the practices of reading that typically escaped attention. Burroughs shared that goal with other experimental writers; Gertrude Stein, for example, is an acknowledged presence in his work. He was involved in filmmaking while he was writing his trilogy in the early 1960s, and, like Stein, he understood the importance of the visual features of the cultural dynamics that he sought to bring to consciousness. "Most people don't see what's going on around them," he complained. "That's my principal message to writers: for God's sake, keep your *eyes* open."[20] As it did for Stein, cinematography offered him a conceptual analog for the easy manipulation of the perceptual field, and they shared the goal of wanting their readers to become aware of how they are made to see (perceive, understand, and envision) as they do: of how, that is, meaning is produced. Burroughs specifically evokes Stein and the writing experiments for which she was known—with an allusion to the title of her coauthored *Four Saints in Three Acts*—to mark his move into the cut-up technique in a passage from *The Ticket That Exploded*:

> He had been meaning Sexexcellency Sally Rand cunning Navy pilot Alan B. Weld two acts for three saints in outer space proudly registered in Phoenix was it are you sure that's right infectious night biter Mo. 18 I'm going to answer the doorbell definitely definitely the first time in thirty years Houston's outbreak the first time in who said Atlantic City? I was supposed to have done the sets for it and B. was supposed to acquire the virus from birds yeah then I think they paid a dollar for infectious disease processing the actual film but the disease quietly spread to all West Texas beauty unscheduled in outer space . . . "You mean you did it yourself you didn't have your assistant do it?" . . . "Nope just spreading epidemic of St Vacine maybe we should." . . . "How long did it take you to process this photo to squirt at anything that flew dyeing and all that it's all part of the city's sudden healthy people infectious beauty disease spreading epidemic of immune humans." (11, ellipses original)

The passage comes near the beginning of a work in which it is already difficult to distinguish between espionage and moviemaking. It interlaces what appears to be the making of a film and the acquisition of a virus (from birds); it is, for example, impossible to tell whether "they paid a dollar for" an "infectious disease" or for "processing the actual film." The "outbreak"—"disease quietly spread to all West Texas beauty unscheduled in outer space"—attests to the lack of control in both cases. The dissemination of information follows its own course and logic. With the cut-up technique, Burroughs, like Stein, conspicuously displayed his relinquishing of control, which was essential to mental liberation and creativity. Even free association was not sufficient for him—"one's mind can't cover it that way," he once remarked.[21] The cut-ups disrupted conventional reading practices and forced readers to think about plot and composition, about how they received and processed information. Cut-ups, as he explained in an interview in 1965, "make explicit a psycho-sensory process that is going on all the time anyway."[22] His determination to envision that process led to the connections Burroughs perceptively emphasized among viruses, mind control, and information. With the added narrative structure of interplanetary commerce, and the space invasions it engendered, he configured these themes into the critical perspective of his new mythology for the space age. If his artistic technique was unusual, however, this configuration was not.

Of Pods and People

By the time he penned his trilogy, the cultural myths that intrigued Burroughs had already found more popular appeal (albeit with less theoretical self-consciousness) in the hybrid genre of science-fiction horror and its offshoot, epidemiological horror, epitomized by Jack Finney's pod people. Finney originally published the 1955 novel as a serial in *Collier's* in 1954, and the first film version was based on the serial. The film was remade in 1978 (in turn prompting a revised edition of the novel) and again in 1993 and 2007, and the story continues to be retold in spin-off versions, such as Robin Cook's 1997 *Invasion*, which was also made into a film.[23] Burroughs's critical perspective and thematic choices, the cultural preoccupations that he captured so insightfully, explain the broad appeal of this story, which is evident not only in its many retellings but also in its widespread and continuing use as a cultural point of reference and in the appearance in other stories of its central features: the snatched bodies and the conversion of one's most intimate associates into something other than human.

Interest in a presumed political allegory has dominated critical response to the story, as in Harry M. Benshoff's observation that the "human-looking monsters have been thought to reflect a paranoid fear of both mindless U.S. conformity and Communist infiltration, wherein a poisonous ideology spreads through small-town USA like a virus, silently turning one's friends and relatives into monsters."[24] No specific ideology fits the story exactly. Rather, the snatched bodies of an American small town register the uncertainties raised by social and political transformation and scientific and medical discoveries in the postwar world. Benshoff's metaphor picks up on the viral features of the pods that run subtly from Finney's novel through the films, becoming explicit in Cook's version, in which the human beings succumb to an aggressive alien virus implanted in primordial DNA. In all versions, *Body Snatchers* recounts the story of an ecological invasion that turns willful and even malicious with the incarnation of the pod people. The pods' viral features fleshed out the viral agency emerging in the medical literature and mainstream media and helped to develop the conventions of the incarnated virus and the epidemiological struggle over the fate of humanity that characterized the outbreak narrative.[25] *The Body Snatchers* offered a mythology for the moment: a story about the uncertain nature of human being conceived as a struggle for the future of humanity. Finney's protagonists experience the terror of utter estrangement when they find themselves suddenly certain that everything is different despite the evidence of their senses, which tells them that nothing has changed. It is a story about carriers, spawning one of the few films of the genre, as Benshoff notes, in which the monsters physically resemble human beings. While Burroughs encourages inspection of the nature of human beings, Finney forestalls any such inquiry. "Humanity," in his novel, is at risk, but never in question, and although it seems precarious, it proves finally indestructible.

The novel chronicles the gradual discovery by the doctor narrator, Miles Bennell, of the source of his patients' disturbing insistence that close relatives are not who they claim to be in the personality theft perpetrated by the intergalactic pods. Of the uncle who raised her, one woman puzzles, "He looks, sounds, acts, and remembers exactly like Ira. On the outside. But *inside* he's different. His responses . . . aren't *emotionally* right. . . . There's something *missing*."[26] The difficulty of detecting the pod people's subtle loss of humanity makes those who notice it seem delusional. Naturally, the experts consulted in this case assume that they are witnessing a psychological phenomenon, what Miles's psychiatrist friend Mannie Kaufman calls "the first contagious neurosis" he has ever seen, "a real epidemic" (23) of an imagined disease, panic spreading "like a contagion" (98).

The problem, of course, turns out not to be in the minds but in the snatched bodies of the residents. Having isolated Santa Mira from the rest of the world, they are invasive and colonizing: actively determined to spread. Miles and his girlfriend, Becky Driscoll, watch in horror from Miles's office while three farm trucks loaded with pods drive up to the town center and begin to distribute the pods to townspeople with "families or contacts" in surrounding towns (147). They are also transformative, leaving no one "what he had been, or what he seemed still, to the naked eye. The men, women, and children in the street below . . . were something else now," Miles explains, "every last one of them. They were each our enemies, including those with the eyes, faces, gestures, and walks of old friends. There was no help for us here except from each other, and even now the communities around us were being invaded" (149).

Humanity is negatively defined by the pod transformation: they become automatons, lacking passion, compassion, and emotions of any sort. They also lose their uniqueness in the display of a hive mentality. Depictions of mass hypnosis and mental control had long preceded Cold War science fiction. David Seed identifies a gothic tradition that associates a horrifying loss of humanity with the state's aggressive manipulation of its citizens.[27] Through the conventions of horror, the loss of humanity becomes a loss of individuality and is configured through features designed to provoke disgust, such as the decaying body and oozing innards of the zombie. By the 1950s, horror and disgust were implicit in the idea of mind control. Finney's novel conjoined these associations with contemporary technological innovations and scientific theories to dramatize the possibility of a transformational loss of humanity and the threat that imperceptibly changed human beings could in turn pose to the state. While Richard Condon's 1959 novel *The Manchurian Candidate* pointedly showed how mind control could turn a human being into an assassin, Finney's novel depicted the disturbing biological mechanisms of mental contagion, and virology supplied the vocabulary through which Finney explained the metamorphosis.

When Miles, Becky, and their friends Jack and Theodora Belicec begin to piece together the phenomenon, the pod people become viral. Following an odd clue in a daily newspaper, Jack, an author and attentive reader, has led them to the index case, the former botany professor Bernard Budlong, who explains the pod phenomenon in language that might have been lifted from a virology textbook: the pods are a life-form, although not in a conventional sense, and they have arrived on earth "by pure chance, but having arrived, they have a function to perform. . . . The function of all life, everywhere—to survive" (152). Stressing their lack of malevolence, he concedes that "the pods are a parasite on whatever life they encounter. . . . But they are the perfect parasite, capable of far more than clinging to the host. They are completely evolved life; they have the ability to re-form and reconstitute themselves into perfect duplication, cell for living cell, of any life form they may encounter in whatever conditions that life has suited itself for" (153).

Understanding how the pods work entails coming to terms with a new conception of human being, Budlong explains, as he cautions Miles not to be trapped by his limited assumptions about life. Noting that Miles's grandfather would have been dubious about radio waves, Budlong anticipates that Miles will be similarly skeptical of the insights that the human body "contains a pattern" that "is the very foundation of cellular life" (155), that "every cell of [an entire body] emanates waves as individual as fingerprints" (155), and that "during sleep . . . that pattern can be taken from [the sleeper], absorbed like static electricity, from one body to another" (155–56), which is precisely what the pods do. This description recasts individuality: every human being is unique, but also predictable, conforming to a pattern. Every individual can be reducible to patterns of "information" and can therefore be "snatched."

Budlong's explanation rehearses the version of information theory that Norbert Wiener had popularized in *The Human Use of Human Beings*.[28] Wiener had declared a "pattern . . . the touchstone of our personal identity. Our tissues change as we live: the food we eat and the air we breathe become flesh of our flesh and bone of our bone, and the momentary elements of our flesh and bone pass out of our body every day with our excreta. . . . We are not stuff that abides, but patterns that perpetuate themselves."[29] Noting that a "pattern is a message, and may be transmitted as a message," and drawing, like Budlong, on the patterns of sound and light that make radio and television work, he contemplates "what would happen if we were to transmit the whole pattern of the human body, of the human brain with its memories and cross connections, so that a hypothetical receiving instrument could re-embody these messages in appropriate matter, capable of continuing the processes already in the body and the mind, and of maintaining the integrity needed for this continuation by a process of homeostasis" (96). If Wiener suggests that the human body is information that could conceivably be transmitted (a sort of human fax), *The Body Snatchers* represents the potential abuse of that information—the alienability of the human personality. In response, Finney's story insists that humanity consists of something at once intangible and physiological that cannot be reduced to information.

The pods in *The Body Snatchers* do not exactly reproduce the human beings whose information they steal. Like viruses, they replace that alienable information with themselves, something distinctly not human. While their initial introduction into the earth's ecosystem was accidental—an "invasion" in the ecological sense—their mandate to survive turns them into willful carriers: "From the moment the first effective changeover occurred, chance was no longer a factor" (160). Family members and service providers, "delivery men, plumbers, carpenters, effected others" (160). The *effected* changes seem initially passive, brought about with the least sense of conscious agency it is possible to convey. *Effected*, however, invokes the more expected *infected*, which implies the deliberate spread of a disease. When the pods take human shape, they evolve into unmistakably sinister, cunning, and conniving beings, a conspiratorial race of carriers.[30] The concept of an invasion, which was added to the title with the 1956 film, *Invasion of the Body Snatchers*, becomes more pronounced with each version. Like any viral invasion, it comes from without and proceeds to take over the host's bodily functions and mechanisms to reproduce itself. The animation of this viral agent is a stock feature of outbreak narratives, and it shows how and why they readily generate narratives of bioterrorism.

The scale of the danger escalates rapidly to a species-threatening event. Budlong explains that the pods have used up the resources of every planet on which they have landed and will use up the earth's within about five years and then move on. Miles and Becky are not convinced by his justification that human beings similarly have used up many of the earth's resources. "You're going to spread over the world?" Miles asks in disbelief. And Budlong maps out the conquest of "this county, then the next ones; and presently northern California, Oregon, Washington, the West Coast, finally; it's an accelerating process, ever faster, always more of us, fewer of you. Presently, fairly quickly, the continent. And then—yes, of course, the world" (163). Budlong's five-year forecast resembles the Soviet's Five Year Plan, summoning the predictions made in the United States about the industrializing Soviet state and explaining readers' temptation to read the novel as a simple political allegory, despite Finney's demurrals. The wasted police state that Finney describes offers readers a glimpse into the effects of Communist infiltration on prosperous small-town USA. But the pods are more generally colonizers, and the apocalyptic vision of world conquest and rapidly expended resources expresses colonizing anxieties in environmental terms, linking a global exhaustion of resources to a terrifying loss of humanity; social and political transformation becomes a threat to "humanity" that shades into an ecological catastrophe.

Mimicry and Hybridity

The danger of the dehumanized pods—and what distinguishes them from most other 1950s science fiction monsters—lies in their mimicry. They can spread because their human appearance enables them to mask their conversion and communicate normally with human beings. Among themselves, the emotionless pod people manifest their hive mentality as an alternative means of communication, which replaces constructive information with unhealthy information and reproduces an absorptive collective at the expense of its individual hosts. Despite Budlong's insistence that the pod invasion is accidental and that the pods are exclusively concerned with their survival, their subterfuge eventually metamorphoses into malice. Miles experiences the malice while eavesdropping on one of his patients, Becky's cousin Wilma, as she recounts a conversation she had had with Miles, retracting her initial report of her uncle's strange behavior. Listening at the window of Becky's house, where her relatives are waiting to infect the couple, Miles hears Wilma describe their interchange in a way that, he recalls, "made my hair on the back of my neck prickle and stand erect. 'Oh, Miles,' Wilma suddenly said, in a cruel imitation of her last talk with me—and the venom in her caricature of herself made me shiver—'I've been meaning to stop in and see you about—what happened.' Then she laughed falsely, in a hideous burlesque of embarrassment."[31] The laughter that follows forces Miles to acknowledge that those former acquaintances were not only no longer themselves but "not human beings at all," and he is sickened by the thought of their inhumanity.

In the *Collier's* version and in Siegel's film, the scene dramatizes the protagonists' full appreciation of their danger, as they learn that even their family members have become dangerous hybrids determined to convert them as well. Finney revises and significantly expands on the incident in the novel, however, where it marks his effort to turn the pod invasion into broad social critique. In the novel Miles prefaces his account of Wilma's comment with a memory of an experience that had similarly disturbed him. He had been awakened, he recalls, after having slept off the effects of a party in his car, by a conversation between two men, "Billy, . . . a middle-aged black man [who] had a shoe-shine stand," whom Miles describes as "a town character" (118), and one of his friends. Billy had always given Miles "the feeling of being with that rarest of persons, a happy man," someone who "obviously took contentment in one of the simpler occupations of the world" (118), and he can barely recognize the "suddenly strange and altered tone," the "queer, twisted heartiness" (119), with which the disembodied voice mimics his usual pleasantries. Miles remembers that "the voice was Billy's, the words and tone those the town knew with affection, but—parodied, and a shade off key. . . . The pent-up bitterness of years tainted every word and syllable he spoke . . . and never before in [his] life had [he] heard such ugly, bitter, and vicious contempt in a voice, contempt for the people taken in by his daily antics, but even more for himself, the man who sup-plied the servility they bought from him" (119). Bill (as his friend calls him) disrupts the performance of his expected role—white America's stereotype—and thereby puts the terms of that performance on display. Miles is horrified to see, and see through, the forced performance of a cultural stereotype. As "Billy," Bill performs servility for white America, while as "Bill," he seethes with a resentment that turns him "bitter," "queer," and "twisted." Hearing this act of mimicry makes Miles aware not only of having been duped by a performance but also of the transformative resentment that is its cost.

Miles's memory establishes the disturbing experience of overhearing an act of verbal mimicry as the connection between Wilma and Bill. "Mimicry," for the postcolonial theorist Homi Bhabha, names the uncanny expression of colonized subjectivity. It in-heres in the colonized subject's performance of the terms of colonial identity. Bhabha marks the performance as racialized and racializing, describing the colonized subject as "almost the same, but not quite," which is to say, "almost the same, but not white."[32] Mimicry is disturbing because it exposes the performative dimensions of the coloniz-er's identity as well as the racialized hierarchies that exclude the colonized from the full terms of personhood. Finney's two mimics, by contrast, deliberately mock their conscious performances of their expected roles. Although they occupy different social positions and stand in different relations to Miles, Wilma and Bill come together for him—and for Finney—because they are similarly unsettling. The disjunctive digression reveals the nature of Miles's discomfort, and the key to the pod people's uncanniness, to be their hybridity.

Finney wrote *The Body Snatchers* against the backdrop of desegregation and de-colonization and the breakdown of familiar racialized hierarchies worldwide that they promoted. His story appeared in the wake of the 1954 Supreme Court desegregation decision of *Brown v. Board of Education* and the numerous essays in mainstream news-papers and periodicals about race relations in the United States that the case had gen-erated. In two consecutive issues in October 1954, roughly a month before the first serialized installment of *The Body Snatchers* appeared, *Collier's* had run a piece by the celebrated South African author Alan Paton entitled "The Negro in America Today." The author of *Cry, the Beloved Country* had journeyed to the United States, heartened by the progress represented by the *Brown* decision that declared segregated schools discriminatory. He hoped to find in the United States lessons that he could bring home to South Africa, and the piece documents both the hopeful signs of progress and the persistent racism—exclusion of black Americans from full and equal citizenship—that he discovered. Everywhere he turned, especially in housing (for which legislation was pending in the Supreme Court) and, most disappointing to him, in the churches, segregation remained a fact of life throughout the country. He quotes the "powerful words" of the Bishop of Raleigh, who believes that "the virus of prejudice will not die out of itself; it has to be killed by being exposed to the light of Faith," and, hopeful that "Christians" will eventually "cease thinking in categories of race," he nonetheless echoes the Bishop's conviction that "there are times when the virus has to be *killed*; one does not wait for it to die."[33] The memory of "Billy" was the only significant addition Finney made when he turned the 1954 *Collier's* serial into the novel, and it draws out the implicit racialization of the pod people, who, like Bhabha's mimics (colonial hybrids), register the disturbing exposure of racial hierarchies.

The pod people bring to Finney's story the long history of *hybridity*, beginning in botany and zoology, where it referred to the offspring produced by parents of different species.[34] The term moved quickly to the human species, where, with "mixed-blood," it described the offspring of parents from different races and registered the confusion of social and biological classifications that characterizes racism. The term became increasingly common in the nineteenth century, and fiction as well as science and law from that period document the attraction and repulsion, the fear and fascination of social and sexual intermingling. The legacies of mercantilism and migration, of slavery and colonization, are written in the tragic fates and criminal dispositions of literary depictions of "mixed-blooded" products of sexual unions across "races."

A striking metaphor in one of Freud's most influential essays demonstrates the uncanny power of this figure. In "The Unconscious" Freud defines his theory of the mechanisms of repression and human psychology generally, and he reaches for the figure of the mixed-race hybrid to ground an abstract point: why certain ideas that appear as though they should be admissible to consciousness (and would therefore belong to the system preconscious) have characteristics that make them more appropriately assigned to the system unconscious. Freud compares these ideas "with individuals of mixed race who, taken all round, resemble white men, but who betray their coloured descent by some striking feature or other, and on that account are excluded from society and enjoy none of the privileges of white people."[35] Ideas are refused—cannot come to consciousness— because they represent insights that are too disturbing for an individual to acknowledge. By analogy, the figure of the human hybrid, the result of heterosexual reproduction across racial classifications, evokes similarly disturbing insights.[36]

The exclusion of some individuals from "the privileges of white people" shows that hierarchies of power and prestige are racialized and defined by their exclusions. Human hybridity threatens to undermine the racial logic of those hierarchies. It attests to the permeability of social boundaries and the impermanence of racial classifications; it also puts heterosexual reproduction on display as the mechanism of that intermixture, biology confounding rather than reproducing social categories. Those insights are refused, and the biology of classifications reinforced, when the individuals "betray their coloured descent by some striking feature or other" and are thereby excluded from the privileges of whiteness. The visual processes by which such features are produced as indelible difference (the language of "descent") prioritize the biology of the classifications and obscure their social construction. The figure that Freud invokes to illustrate the workings of consciousness and the mechanisms of repression implies a broad social analysis as well. The betrayal and exclusion to which Freud refers depict both the racialization of power and the potential disruption of racialized power posed by sexuality. Freud's analogy also implies that both racialized power and the challenge posed by sexuality are ideas that are sufficiently disturbing to generate mechanisms of collective repression and are therefore formative for social psychology.[37]

The hybrid was a key figure for the early-twentieth-century sociologist Robert Park as well. While Park insisted, following an ecological model, that worldwide interconnections would lead inevitably to the dissolution of cultural boundaries (universal hybridity), he also conceded that the process slowed down when differences between groups found expression in distinctive physical traits. His own hybrid—marginal man—displayed the processes of cultural amalgamation, but Park also underscored the anguish experienced by this involuntary herald as he was sacrificed on the altar of social transformation.[38] The role of the hybrid in nineteenth- and twentieth-century social thought explains its imaginative power as a figure of danger, transformation, and sacrifice.

The (viral) strategies of pod reproduction uncannily disrupt—and thereby highlight—the taxonomies on which humanity relies for its distinction. Unlike black Americans, pod people are colonizers, but Miles links Wilma and Bill in the acts of mimicry through which both disturb the social surface. The word "queer" appears several times in the novel to mark that disturbance. The protagonists were originally alerted to the pod presence because Jack Belicec habitually collected newspaper stories that told of the "queer little happenings . . . that simply don't fit in with the great body of knowledge that the human race has gradually acquired over thousands of years" (72). At the end of the novel, Miles establishes his own account of the pod invasion as one of the "occasional queer little stories, humorously written, tongue-in-cheek, most of the time," (191) that circulate in the media or through rumors. The "queerness" of Jack's cut-outs, he explains, alerts the writer to new information that conditioning—Burroughs's "psychosensory process"—keeps people from noticing. Miles's "queer little stories," Jack's "queer little happenings," and the "queer, twisted heartiness" of Bill's mimicry all signal a tear in the fabric of received wisdom that catches the attention of Jack, the author—and Miles, the reluctant listener—and leads them, in different ways, to the dark underside of Santa Mira.

Queer most obviously has its conventional meaning—"odd" or "unusual"—but in the 1950s it was also already a slang term for "homosexual," as in Burroughs's *Queer*. Anticipating queer theory, Burroughs viewed homosexuality as a disruption of normative institutions, and he linked it to other such disturbances that could lead to a questioning of the blind spots of convention. Anxiety surrounding homosexuality in the period—expressed, for example, in the purging of gay men and lesbians from jobs in the government, the media, and education (the "nerve center" of U.S. society)—was evidence for him of the threat alternative sexualities posed to habits of thought. Pod reproduction, a feature on which the films graphically dwelled, called attention to the taxonomies that not only reproduced social hierarchies but also defined humanity itself. Neither Wilma nor Bill reproduces the social relations that Miles expects and on which his understanding of humanity rests. Nothing in the novel suggests that Finney was aware of the history summoned by his human–vegetable hybrids or the insights they engendered, and the resolution of the novel affirms the most conventional definition of humanity and the superficiality of Finney's race critique. Although Miles is on the verge of telling a queer story that could expose the racialized and gendered logic of biological classifications and social hierarchies, that is not finally the story Finney tells. Where Burroughs depicted habits of thought as viral, with racism, homophobia, and other biases as signs of illness, Finney saw the problems themselves as viral. Racism had corrupted and transformed Billy, turning him into Bill. The happy shoeshine boy of Miles's fantasy is, for him, the real (uninfected) person. Despite hearing his interlocutor call him "Bill," Miles continues to refer to him as "Billy." He responds to the conversation by feeling "ashamed of [Bill's unsuspecting patron], of Billy, of [himself], and of the whole human race" (120). Racism, Paton noted, was both viral and un-American. Finney seems to have concurred. Like the virus Wilma hosts, it comes from without and corrupts, creating an enemy within. This externalization of racism deflects Burroughs's more difficult and controversial structural analysis of the viral nature of practices and institutions, including such basic unquestioned institutions as marriage and the family. Finney forecloses on any potentially critical insights with his novel's triumphant conclusion.

Studies of brainwashing in the 1950s continually stressed an inalienable humanity that could be heroically maintained by the strongest and most courageous. Edward Hunter, for example, describes the subject of one case study as having "something in him they [the Communists] couldn't take away without destroying his mind or body."[39] Finney similarly insists on the defiant spirit of humanity that expresses itself in Miles's and Becky's final heroic resistance of the pods. Having escaped from their captors, they head for the freeway, only to confront the hopelessness of their situation: a field of pods with hundreds of pod people waiting to intercept them. Although "it made capture an absolute certainty," they decide "to use [themselves] against the pods" (185). Setting the fields on fire, they are quickly surrounded "by hundreds of advancing figures" who hardly touch them—"there was no anger, no emotion in them" (187)—but are nonetheless too numerous to resist. Almost immediately, however, the crowd stops, and "the great pods" ascend into the sky (187). In the original serial version, the Belicecs appear with the FBI, but the pods are already airborne. Finney omitted that detail from the novel, underscoring the triumphant individualism of Miles's and Becky's heroic decision. "Quite simply," Miles recounts,

the great pods were leaving a fierce and inhospitable planet. I knew it utterly and a wave of exultation so violent it left me trembling swept through my body; because I knew Becky and I had played our part in what was now happening. We hadn't, and couldn't possibly have been—I saw this now—the only souls who had stumbled and blundered into what had been happening in Santa Mira. There'd been others, of course, individuals, and little groups, who had done what we had—who had simply refused to give up. Many had lost, but some of us who had not been caught and trapped without a chance had fought implacably, and a fragment of a wartime speech moved through my mind: *We shall fight them in the fields, and in the streets, we shall fight in the hills; we shall never surrender.* True then for one people, it was true always for the whole human race, and now I felt that nothing in the whole vast universe could ever defeat us. (188–89)

Miles doubts that the pods *thought* or *knew* so much as "sensed . . . that this planet, this little race, would never receive them, would never yield" (189).

Against the aliens, "this little race"—the human race—is united, the emotionless Wilma implicitly replacing the embittered Bill as a threat. The triumph of the human spirit is a victory for a white America—free from disturbance—that, as signified by Churchill's familiar words, has moved beyond racial and national distinctions and contained the potentially global outbreak. The end of the novel returns to the Allied victory during the Second World War, substituting a hot war for a cold war. The solution to the pod invasion, as to racism, is to confront the *external* threat directly and fight heroically to defeat it. Humanity is preserved through the affirmation of threatened institutions. Miles and Becky, both divorced at the beginning of the novel, get married and raise a family in a town and a nation that they helped to save.

The good doctor defeats the pods because he knows how to fashion the "queer little happenings" into an explanatory narrative that allows him to identify and address the pod problem. The defeat of the pods depends on his ability to tell the right story about them. His most important medical act is therefore the fashioning of the "queer little stories" into this—patriotic—outbreak story in which a man of science does apocalyptic battle with a global threat that emanates not from science or the state but from a space invasion.

The films rejected Finney's conclusion in favor of increasingly ominous endings. Even Cook, who similarly ends *Invasion* victoriously, substituted the more interesting conclusion of *War of the Worlds* for Finney's deus ex machina. Yet Finney's novel underscores an important feature that is contained in the plot of the story itself and retained even in the more ambiguous endings of the films: the appeal of an epidemiological model that would turn all problems (including racism) into sinister embodied viruses that came from elsewhere and could be seen and at least potentially rooted out. It is a deflection from another story that he might have told and that haunts *The Body Snatchers* and its subsequent incarnations.

Visualizing the Contagion of Conformity

When the independent producer Walter Wanger read Finney's story in *Collier's*, he immediately recognized its cinematic potential, and he contacted director Don Siegel, with whom he had recently worked. Siegel, in turn, brought in scriptwriter Daniel Mainwaring, with whom he had also successfully worked on a previous project.[40] Since *The Body Snatchers* was a visual story—a story that connected the deceptiveness of appearances to a horrifying loss of humanity—it was an ideal vehicle for cinematic adaptation. Where *The Body Snatchers* described a mental contagion that turned out to be the result of physical possession, the 1956 film showed what that looked like. *Invasion of the Body Snatchers* promoted the iconic status of the story and helped to develop visual conventions for depicting carriers, outbreaks, and mental possession in the performance of affectlessness and as threats to "humanity."

Critics have disagreed about the politics of the film as well as the allegorical meaning of the pods, reading the hope that the FBI will be able to defeat the pods with which the film ends (departing from Finney's story) as a faith in government institutions that marks a shift either to the Left or to the Right. The confused politics is in the film itself, a result both of the differing politics of the many people involved in its production—from Finney to Mainwaring, Siegel, Wanger, and the studio executives, who insisted that Siegel and Mainwaring change their original ending—and of the pressures placed on everyone involved by the House Un-American Activities Committee's notorious presence in Hollywood in the 1950s. Siegel sidestepped the question of political allegory by emphasizing the social dimension of a mindless conformity to fashion, especially among his Hollywood colleagues. "Many of my associates are certainly pods," he asserted in an interview. "They have no feelings. They exist, breathe, sleep. To be a pod means that you have no passion, no anger, the spark has left you."[41]

It is one thing to read about the pod conversion and another actually to witness it. Point-of-view shots encourage the viewer's identification with the characters' frustration as they try to draw attention to the changes and with their sense of estrangement as their allies are converted. The pod people are more uncanny than the undead creations that populated the 1950s screen, since their difference is barely perceptible, if at all.

Richard Matheson's 1954 novella *I Am Legend*, and its 1964 film adaptation, *The Last Man on Earth*, similarly distinguish between the zombielike "vampires" that weakly threaten the protagonist, the sole human survivor of a bacterial infection, and the hybrids, the intermediate creatures who have found a partial antidote that keeps them from full conversion and who can therefore "pass" as human. While the undead vampires taunt the protagonist, they are not sufficiently organized to present an insurmountable threat; the hybrids, however, plan to build a new society. The film makes their racial inflection particularly apparent in their preternatural pallor. These whiter-than-white beings harbor a particular antipathy for the former society and eagerly purge the last remaining human being. Siegel marks the hybridity of his pod people by their featureless protohumanity as they emerge encased in slime from the giant (womblike, of course) pods. He ensures the disgust factor by showing the crushed and bloody faces of the protagonists' would-be pod incarnations as Miles smashes them with a shovel in his greenhouse.

Pod uncanniness inspires a unique spectatorial experience. While grotesque creatures tempt the viewer to look away from the screen, the pod people compel intense scrutiny. Vivian Sobchack describes how Siegel's direction twists "the secure and familiar . . . into something subtly dangerous and slyly perverted. . . . The subject matter is familiar, ordinary, but one experiences a tension which seems to spring from no readily discernable cause, a distortion of angle so slight as to seem almost nonexistent, but so great as to set the teeth intolerably on edge." The viewer is "seduced by the minimal activity and novelty of what's on the screen into an attentive paranoia which makes us lean forward to scan what seem like the most intentionally and deceitfully flat images for signs of aberrant alien behavior from the most improbable of suspects."[42] That attentive paranoia becomes the experience of an invisible threat.

Where Sobchack distinguishes the pod people by their "*negative* behavior, . . . [their] not doing something: a gasp not gasped, a kiss not returned," however, there are also distinct visual and aural cues of commission: an uncanny deadening of the eyes and tone (automatism) that can readily turn into contempt, which is troubling in a stranger but devastating in an intimate.[43] *Invasion of the Body Snatchers* helped to create a visual and aural vocabulary of possession, establishing these cues as signs of a pathological loss of humanity resulting from an infectious mental possession that turned human beings into sinister hybrid automatons.

Siegel complements the subtle distortions to which Sobchack refers with extreme close-up shots of the eyes of the pod people that make perception thematic. The protagonists know they cannot fully trust their senses in this disturbing new world, but the eyes can subtly betray the pod people with a lack of focus that suggests the absence of emotion. The extreme close-ups convey the anguish produced by the experience of looking into eyes that should register recognition, fondness, and love and instead show indifference, disdain, and contempt. If the eyes are indeed the window into the soul, the film depicts what soullessness looks like and seeks to produce what it feels like to inhabit a soulless world.

Indifference proves harder to fathom for the protagonists than malice. Miles's first response on witnessing pod reproduction is to look for a plot. "Somebody or something wants this duplication to take place," he tells Becky. With a moment of reflection, he begins to think more like a scientist, summoning in the process dominant themes of 1950s science fiction cinema. "So much has been discovered these past few years," he speculates, "anything's possible. Maybe the results of atomic radiation on plant life or animal life. Some weird alien organism, a mutation of some kind." In the absence of

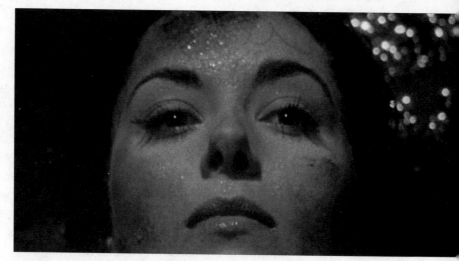

Figure 3.1.
Unable to resist sleep, Becky turns from passionate lover to "inhuman enemy bent on [Miles's] destruction." Her conversion is evident in her eyes. Still from *Invasion of the Body Snatchers* (dir. Don Siegel, Allied Artists Pictures, 1956).

an explanation, he settles on a description that mediates between accident and design. "Whatever it is . . . that it can govern the forming of human flesh and blood out of thin air is fantastically powerful, beyond any comprehension, malignant."[44] When Miles and Becky witness the dissemination of pods in the town square, Miles elaborates on this explanation, calling it "a malignant disease spreading over the whole country." In science-fiction horror, science frequently proves to be a limiting framework, obscuring a problem until it is too late to solve it. Robert Neville, the protagonist of *I Am Legend*, discovers the bacteria that cause vampirism only after an epidemic turns him into the last surviving human being. He survives because of the immunity he develops after having been bitten by a bat in South America.[45] Matheson's vampires, like Finney's pods, are not the result of atomic fallout or state-sponsored experimentation gone awry, as in much science fiction, or supernatural, as in many horror stories. They are part of the "natural" world, but no less horrifying for their "natural" origins. Not only does "nature" have no special regard for human welfare but an ecological worldview makes the eventual extinction of human beings a foregone conclusion. Facing execution at the hands of the new hybrid race, Robert Neville accepts that from their perspective the last unevolved human being is indeed an anachronism: extinction is the flip side of evolution.

Finney's (and Siegel's) heroic doctor never concedes that point, and the film, like the novel, ultimately asserts the malice of the pod–human hybrids. *Invasion of the Body Snatchers* draws on the conventions of film noir to depict the sinister shadows that are gradually darkening the sunny Northern California town. In an opening voice-over, Miles explains that the town has been "possessed by something evil." When Miles, Becky, and the Belicecs see their first pods, a low-angle shot of Miles suggests the pods' looking back. Although the pod invasion starts out as a chance meeting of alien ecologies, they evolve. Becky's conversion near the end of the film creates, as Miles explains, "an inhuman enemy bent on [his] destruction."

Humanity becomes the unquestioned object of Miles's heroism. "Only when we have to fight to stay human," Miles tells Becky, "do we realize how precious it is." The pod people, in the form of his most trusted friends and colleagues, Mannie Kaufman and Jack Belicec, offer Miles the profound temptation to be "reborn," as Mannie promises, "into an untroubled world." The film insists on the difficulty of Miles's struggle through the temptations of the visual medium itself. Active viewing is stressful. Cultural observers such as Joost Merloo cautioned against the "hypnotizing, seductive action of any all-penetrating form of communication," especially television; he worried in particular about "the passive peeping contagion of the television screen," which intruded "into family life and cut off the more subtle interfamilial communication" that kept minds alert and alive.[46] *Invasion of the Body Snatchers* reproduces Miles's challenge in the audience's own active viewing experience, which the film depicts as heroic and associated with humanity. Merloo similarly praises the "heroes of the mind" who bravely "fight their inner battle against rigidity, cowardice, and the wish to surrender conviction for the sake of ease" by "remaining awake when others want to soothe themselves with sleep and oblivion."[47] Burroughs, too, urges his readers to "stay awake," and *Invasion of the Body Snatchers* dramatizes the metaphor, casting the effort to remain awake and alert as a heroic battle for humanity.

Siegel and Mainwaring had intended to end the film with a close-up of Miles's anguished face as he screams, "They're after all of us. Our wives, our children, everybody. They're here already. You're next." Finding that conclusion too bleak, however, the studio insisted on adding the frame story, in which Miles tells his story to a psychiatrist in a hospital emergency room; the psychiatrist assumes he is crazy until external evidence persuades him of the existence of the pods. The revised film ends with the psychiatrist's frantic command to summon help from national law enforcement agencies and with restored faith in the authority of experts, from the psychiatrist to the military. The emphatic insistence of the film that emotions should fully replace appearance in defining the terms of humanity suggested the role of these experts in establishing and facilitating access to those terms. The position is consistent with a liberal assimilationist recasting of political protest in psychoanalytic terms that characterized the decade, finding expression in such films as *Rebel without a Cause* (1955).

Siegel's and Mainwaring's preferred ending challenges viewers to assume responsibility for the preservation of humanity, to respond to Miles's invitation to join his heroic struggle. The studio either missed or dismissed the point of Siegel's and Mainwaring's visual and emotional call to arms. The film nonetheless registers both points of view, simultaneously affirming expertise and advocating personal responsibility and active, engaged viewing in its epidemiological instruction: its visual and narrative lessons about how to recognize a contagious dehumanization and its willful disseminators. The contradiction between personal responsibility and deferral to experts did not diminish— and might even have enhanced—the contribution of the film to the development of the mythic features of Finney's story: the heroic struggle to preserve nothing less than humanity itself against both external threats and the personal inattention that operates unwittingly in their service.

The Myth Updated

Philip Kaufman chose to remake *Invasion of the Body Snatchers* in the late 1970s, at the height of what Christopher Lasch called "the culture of narcissism" and Tom Wolfe dubbed "the me decade."[48] The generation that came of age in that decade was routinely denounced in the media as self-absorbed and disconnected compared to their socially and politically conscious predecessors of the 1960s, but, as the cultural critic Jonathan Schell noted in his widely read book *The Time of Illusion*, "if the new generation was absorbed in pleasures of the moment and tended to be uninterested in thought or in culture or in anything else that was meant to endure beyond a single generation, it might well be because they were the first generation to doubt that the human species had a future."[49] The 1970s generation lived not only with the possibility of nuclear annihilation but also with the threat to the species posed by environmental devastation on a global scale. A 1969 report from the United Nations Economic and Social Council warned that "for the first time in the history of mankind, there is arising a crisis of world-wide proportions involving developed and developing countries alike—the crisis of the human environment" and that "if current trends continue, the future of life on earth could be endangered."[50] The threat was collective and (often explicitly) racialized.

People coming of age in the 1970s had witnessed the Cold War turn hot repeatedly as the superpowers used the decolonizing world as a battleground. The war in Vietnam catalyzed discontents and ignited a social and cultural revolution domestically, as it galvanized opposition to what Harold R. Isaacs, writing in *Foreign Affairs*, called the "common whitism" of the United States and the Soviet Union. Isaacs wrote of the racial tensions of a new world order in which "the entire cluster of some 70 new states carved out of the old empires since 1945 is made up of nonwhite peoples newly out from under the political, economic and psychological domination of white rulers" and of people "stumbling blindly around trying to discern the new images, the new shapes and perspectives these changes have brought, to adjust to the painful rearrangement of identities and relationships which the new circumstances compel."[51] Official political leadership in the United States had fallen notoriously short, as the televised Watergate hearings made clear in 1973, and faith in government and expertise generally waned.[52] Amid accounts of social, cultural, political, economic, and environmental instability worldwide, the "me generation" of white middle-class Americans produced the culture of "self-help" and "New Age" theology against the alienation of a society that was, paradoxically, increasingly connected and atomized.[53]

That generation could see itself reflected in the 1978 remake of *Invasion of the Body Snatchers*. More than two decades after the pods invaded the idyllic town of Santa Mira, Kaufman's pods found root in the gritty, urbane world of San Francisco. His appropriately transformed cast of characters featured the morphing of the earnest small-town physician Miles Bennell into the ironic San Francisco public health officer Matthew Bennell and of perky Becky Driscoll into his sophisticated coworker, Elizabeth. The metamorphoses include Jack Belicec's reincarnation as an unappreciated writer who runs a mud bath with his New Age wife, Nancy, and Mannie/Dan Kaufman's replacement by Leonard Nimoy's brilliantly executed, best-selling pop psychologist David Kibner. Reviewing this hip, campy, and self-referential film in the *New Yorker*, Pauline Kael proclaimed, "For its undiluted pleasure and excitement, it is . . . the American movie of the year—a new classic," possibly "the best movie of its kind ever made."[54] Commenting on Kaufman's brilliant direction, she describes his capture of a zeitgeist as well as a genre and a style. The success of this late-1970s renovation of the story of the body snatchers updated the mythic features of the apocalyptic battle for the survival of humanity as it incorporated them into the concerns of their moment. Kaufman drew out the medicalization of the pods and the epidemiological features of the story at a time when the World Health Organization's conquest of communicable disease promised to be one successful global initiative in an age of massive transition, unrest, and uncertainty. Audiences who filed into theaters across the country to see Kaufman's renovated pods, however, could not have imagined how much the film forecast another mysterious epidemiological crisis—an invasion of sorts—that would soon hit San Francisco (along with New York and Los Angeles). Kaufman could not have predicted how uncannily his film would illuminate the assumptions that colored early accounts of the HIV/AIDS epidemic.

The opening shots create visual associations among several images, lingering on what Kael calls "diaphanous gelatinous spores" (48) against the backdrop of what emerges as a barren, uninhabited planet. The initial shot combines images of scientific expertise, resembling the view through an electron microscope of macrophages and viruses, which accounts of HIV would soon make all too familiar, and summoning the photographs that documented space exploration. The shot widens to chronicle the cosmic journey of the spores as they are blown from the barren landscape to drift through the universe, with a brief pause on an iconic shot of the earth from space: the blue planet, symbol of global interdependence. Disorienting cuts to the point of view of the spores shot at oblique angles mark their entrance into the earth's atmosphere. Time-lapse nature photography, such as was featured in *National Geographic* television specials, captures the pods' taking root amid the earth's flora. The dizzying crosscutting between these close-ups of nature scenes and extreme long shots of the San Francisco skyline in this opening sequence establishes the "invasion" of the title in ecological terms—a chance introduction of alien vegetation into an ecosystem—as it conditions the viewer to attend to subtle visual details. The immediacy and aggression with which they take root suggests the dangerous hybridity of the intergalactic pods; lovely, pink blossoms emerge that quickly sprout bright red, thrusting, podlike centers. Despite the visual invocations of scientific expertise, science will prove useless at best in the disorienting world of Kaufman's film.

Similarly disorienting crosscuts and oblique angles show how the human world echoes the cosmic one. While pod conversions turn the warm relationships of Santa Mira sinister, there is already an ominous quality to the relationships in Kaufman's San Francisco, making it even harder to recognize the pod conversions than in Siegel's film. A close-up introduces Elizabeth as she picks one of the pod flowers; she is in a playground, and her attention is first drawn to the flowers by a group of schoolchildren whose teacher encourages them to pick them and take them home to their families. Rapid cuts place Elizabeth in a triangular relationship with the grimacing teacher and a smirking priest on a swing set (Robert Duval in a cameo appearance). Something has turned these trusted figures sinister, and the canted shot that slants the houses on Elizabeth's block as she returns home with the flower depicts a skewed world. Kaufman's direction, like that of his predecessor, emphasizes a visual vocabulary of paranoia, which is augmented by the dissonant, edgy electronic musical score.[55]

The pods take root in a receptive environment. Elizabeth is intrigued to discover that the strange plant may be a "grex," a hybrid produced by the cross-pollination of two different species. Characterized by "rapid and widespread growth" and often observed in the large war-torn cities of Europe, these adventitious botanical survivors seem to "thrive on devastated ground."[56] If these hybrids were first observed in the postwar landscape of Europe, the violence and excessive growth of the vegetative oddities suggest a war-torn jungle landscape in the 1970s. They are certainly out of place in San Francisco.

Neither Elizabeth nor her live-in boyfriend, Geoffrey, is distinctly visible during the conversation in which she shows him her discovery. The scene is shot through several doorways, and they appear primarily through the reflection on a French door. Geoffrey barely disguises his lack of interest in Elizabeth's "grex," as she explains that such plants are often "epilobic, from the Greek 'epi,' 'upon,' and 'lobos,' 'a pod.' . . . Many of the species are dangerous weeds and should be avoided." The couple appears habituated to their disconnection, and it is not surprising that Elizabeth inadvertently brings the

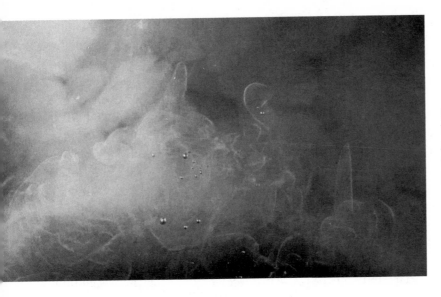

Figure 3.2.
The opening shot of Philip Kaufman's 1978
Invasion of the Body Snatchers suggests
the view through an electron microscope
(dir. Philip Kaufman, United Artists, 1978).

strange plant home—grex are dangerous only in a garden, she assures Geoffrey—where she produces the conditions that will convert her boorish, disheveled dentist boyfriend into a well-groomed, unemotional pod person who will indeed become dangerous in his hybridity.

The disturbing interactions of the public health officer Matthew Bennell (Donald Sutherland) complement Elizabeth's alienating domestic relations in their display of urban anomie. Bennell is introduced through a distorting fish lens (a peephole) as he engages in a surprise visit to a high-end restaurant, entering a hostile, duplicitous environment that presages his subsequent interactions in a changed world. The restaurant staff communicate among themselves wordlessly as Matthew argues with the manager about whether an "ingredient" of one of the dishes is a caper or, as Matthew insists, a "rat turd." Matthew returns to find his car window smashed by a wine bottle, and the scene heralds the pod world he will enter, first in the cold and menacing glare of two members of the kitchen staff and then in a quick cut to a shadier figure watching through a dark window. Human relations are already in crisis in Kaufman's San Francisco.

Kaufman revels in the noir aesthetic, with relentless shots of darkened hallways, stairways, and alleys and cross-hatched shadows supplemented with even more sinister and visually taunting shots of distorted reflections in windows and mirrors and shadows falling at impossible angles. But powerfully informing this sinister world is a sense of exhaustion, which Kaufman conveys through cinematic mania. As Elizabeth and Matthew talk in Matthew's car, her efforts to persuade him that something has changed are punctuated by rapid crosscutting between her memories of the meetings between Geoffrey and strangers that she had witnessed as she followed him throughout the day and the images of people staring out of windows and doorways. The urbanity and wit of Matthew's banter and Kaufman's visual excesses are overlaid by a creepy sense of claustrophobia and conspiracy produced by tightly framed shots and the film's conspicuous acknowledgment of the iconic status of the story. In his attempt to comfort Elizabeth, Matthew begins to tell her a joke that he has told her before, but he is interrupted by a fleeting shot of Kevin McCarthy, the actor who had played Miles in Siegel's film, screaming the words with which the 1956 film was supposed to have ended: "They're coming! Help! Help! They're coming! Listen to me! Please! You're next! We're in danger! You're next! Please, listen to me! Something terrible—please! You're next! Here they are! They're already here! You're next! They're coming!" Fleeing a crowd like the one that had chased him onto the highway in the earlier film, McCarthy is hit and killed by a car. Shocked by the (non)reaction of the crowd, Matthew is drawn into the pod conspiracy. Later, when he and Elizabeth attempt unsuccessfully to flee San Francisco, Don Siegel is their cabdriver. These references create the sense of enclosed emplotment, of living within an unfolding story that has somehow already been told (like Matthew's joke, which he never finishes retelling).

They are also, however, in-jokes, and the retold, iconic story simultaneously expresses and offers an antidote for exhaustion. The film oscillates between wit and terror, which effectively keeps the audience off-balance; it is hard to know if we are in on the joke or the object of it. The shifting perspective involves scientific expertise and cultural authority and turns on the contrast between the quirky Belicecs, with their combination of New Age philosophy and conspiracy theories, and Nimoy's hyperrational Kibner. Jeff

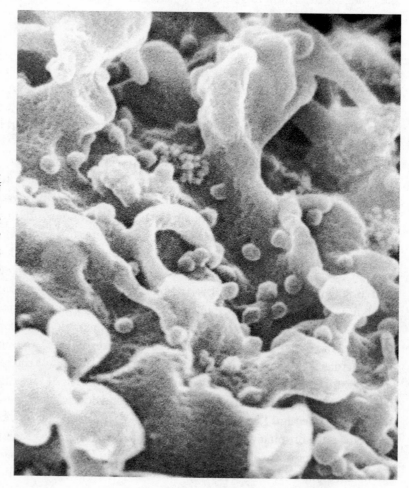

Figure 3.3.
A scanning electron micrograph of HIV grown in cultured lymphocytes. The image resembles the spores in the opening of Kaufman's *Invasion of the Body Snatchers*. Courtesy of the Centers for Disease Control and Prevention's Public Health Image Library, #1842. Cynthia Goldsmith, P. Feorino, E. L. Palmer, W. R. McManus, 1984.

Goldblum plays Jack with his characteristic comic mania, and Veronica Cartwright plays his wife with a charming warmth and earnest compassion, both of which contrast dramatically with Nimoy's emotional deadpan. The man of science's insistence that "people are changing. Becoming less human . . . all around us" deflects attention from the pod invasion. Dismissing any possibility of a literal explanation, he diagnoses the problem as cultural malaise: "People are stepping in and out of relationships too fast," he maintains, "because they don't want the responsibility. That's why marriages are going to hell. The whole family unit is shot to hell." When Elizabeth and others protest that their loved ones really have changed, Kibner diagnoses a "hallucinatory flu" that seems to be going around, and Matthew wonders if it is a public health problem, asking the question that circulates throughout the film: is it contagious? To a late-1970s audience, an illness that confounded physical and psychological distinctions might invoke such strange ailments as chronic fatigue syndrome, similarly and controversially attributed to cultural (and generational) anomie. Again, the audience gets a wink, since Nimoy is best known for his role as Mr. Spock, the emotionless human–alien hybrid of the television drama *Star Trek*.[57] But the Belicecs get the last word—if not the last laugh. Even the Belicecs are surprised when their over-the-top paranoia turns out to be not nearly paranoid enough. It is Nancy who actually identifies the source of the pod infection when she suggests that it could be the "space flowers" and worries that they "could start getting into our systems and screwing up our genes, like DNA, recombining us, changing us, . . . just the same way those rocket ships landed thousands of years ago so spacemen could mate with monkeys and apes and create the human race." Such is the cosmic joke of evolution.

Kaufman underscores the joke when the creepy Mr. Giannelli, who leaves the pod that almost steals Jack in the mud bath, conspicuously displays a copy of *Worlds in Collision*, a book he tells Nancy he knows she would enjoy. Published by Macmillan in 1950, the book, by Immanuel Velikovsky, a psychiatrist, argued that the repetition of ancient myths across cultures—especially about cosmic invasion—suggested that those myths were in fact repressed memories of catastrophic events that had been obscured by the assumptions of physics and astronomy. Velikovsky's intergalactic ecological analysis found a popular audience in the 1950s, including the "New York literati," concerned about the creeping scientism of their moment.[58] Maybe science did not have all the answers; maybe the urgency of catastrophe needed a fresh perspective. And maybe the almost compulsive retelling of the story of snatched bodies offered new insight into the problems, if not the solutions, of environmental exhaustion and cultural anomie.

Simultaneously spoofed and respected by the film, New Age Nancy directs the audience to that insight. Only she remains wakeful while the other protagonists sleep and is therefore able to alert Matthew to the process of pod reproduction. And only she is sufficiently attuned to her surroundings to figure out how to move among the pods undetected. Nancy alone remains unconverted at the end of the film, when, hailing Matthew, she (and the audience) learns that he, too, has succumbed. The film ends as Nancy adds her human scream to the piercing, inhuman one that identifies Matthew as a pod person. Unlike Miles, Matthew does not hail the viewer, but the film itself does. The pod invasion turns the malaise in the film into an apocalyptic threat, setting the terms of a battle for humanity that, as Nancy resiliently demonstrates, is at least worth waging.[59]

In all of its incarnations, *Body Snatchers* is a story about alienation and dehumanization. By insisting on its epidemiological features, I do not mean to suggest that it is any more "about" viruses than it is "about" Communists or McCarthy conformists—or, as Matthew Bennell quips in Kaufman's version, "Republicans." It is, however, a story about a threat conceived as a public health concern with medical and/or public health personnel responsible for solving the mystery: an outbreak in search of a narrative. Epidemiological horror tells the story of that outbreak as the threat of an ecological "invasion" that produces dangerous hybrids and generates an apocalyptic battle for the fate of humanity. That framework, and the simultaneous terror and reaffirmation that it generates, heralds the conventions of the outbreak narrative.

More than the San Francisco setting of Kaufman's *Invasion of the Body Snatchers* forecasts the climate of the earliest years of the HIV/AIDS epidemic. Kibner's smug dismissal of the actual threat posed by the pod people echoed the sanguinity of epidemiologists who had already begun to herald the end of communicable disease as a serious problem and turn their attention to social epidemics. With the increasing shift of epidemiology away from the exclusive study of outbreaks of physical ailments and toward widespread behavioral patterns, such as alcoholism and other drug abuse, domestic violence, and teenage suicide, epidemiologists lost their heroic edge; sociology did not make for risky, exciting disease detection.

The mysteries and terrors of the new epidemic would invigorate both the field of epidemiology and the evolving outbreak narrative, inflected by the conventions of epidemiological horror, which *Invasion of the Body Snatchers* helped to produce. The "disease" is spread in the story of *Body Snatchers* in all of its incarnations by carriers who do not appear as such. The story line stresses simultaneously the lack of intentionality or malice involved in the initial introduction of the pods and the sense that the carriers *become* the infection, which they then transmit willfully. Through these deliberate disseminators, the pod infection becomes an "invasion," which inaugurates a struggle for the fate of humanity. The resonance between the conventions of epidemiological horror and those of scientific and mainstream accounts of the epidemic demonstrates not so much the influence of a particular story as how the circulation of the conventional features through epidemiological narratives of all kinds shapes the outbreak narrative.[60] The familiarity of the genre of horror could recast the uncertainty of the ending of a movie such as *Invasion of the Body Snatchers* as a mythic struggle for humanity. The grim realities of a devastating communicable disease in the late-twentieth-century United States that genuinely challenged the authority of medical science offered no similar promise. Yet scientists and journalists striving to write the outbreak narrative of this elusive disease drew on the conventions. The social, scientific, and medical consequences of their efforts are an important part of the history of the epidemic and the emergence of the outbreak narrative.

Notes

1. Claudia Wallis, "AIDS: A Growing Threat: Now That the Disease Has Come Out of the Closet, How Far Will It Spread?," *Time*, August 12, 1985, 40.

2. Joe Levine, "Viruses: AIDS Research Spurs New Interest in Some Ancient Enemies," *Time*, November 3, 1986, 66. The image described resembles the image from *Scientific American* reproduced in Figure 3.3.

3. See Randy Shilts, *And the Band Played On: Politics, People, and the AIDS Epidemic* (New York: St. Martin's Press, 1987), and Cindy Patton, *Fatal Advice: How Safe-Sex Education Went Wrong* (Durham, N.C.: Duke University Press, 1996).

4. Cindy Patton, among others, traces the authority of science to "its ability to 'see' what ordinary people cannot." Patton, *Inventing AIDS* (New York: Routledge, 1990), 57.

5. On the importance of visualization technologies in medicine, see especially Lisa Cartwright, *Screening the Body: Tracing Medicine's Visual Culture* (Minneapolis: University of Minnesota Press, 1995), and Kirsten Ostherr, *Cinematic Prophylaxis: Globalization and Contagion in the Discourse of World Health* (Durham, N.C.: Duke University Press, 2005).

6. *Science News Letter* 69, no. 18 (1956): 275.

7. My conclusions in this chapter are based on my reading of numerous articles on McCarthy, Communism, viruses, and the polio vaccine from the following news and science periodicals between 1949 and 1960: *New York Times, Ladies' Home Journal, Saturday Evening Post, Saturday Review, Today's Health, Vital Speeches, Commonweal, Scientific American, Science Digest, Science News Letter, Time, New Republic, American Mercury, Scholastic, Reader's Digest, Newsweek, New Yorker, Harper, Commentary, New Statesman, Nature, Science, Esquire, Christian Century,* and *Look*.

8. The reservoir host is the organism in which an infectious agent lies dormant or multiplies; in some cases, the organism can host two infectious agents at once, allowing them to recombine. Unstable viruses such as influenza are especially susceptible to such processes.

9. Eric Mottram, "Rencontre avec William Burroughs," in *Conversations with William Burroughs*, ed. Allen Hibbard (Jackson: University Press of Mississippi, 1999), 11.

10. William S. Burroughs, *Queer* (New York: Viking Press, 1985), xxii.

11. On alien invasion and 1950s science fiction cinema, see especially Ostherr, *Cinematic Prophylaxis*; Vivian Sobchack, *Screening Space: The American Science Fiction Film*, 2nd ed. (New Brunswick, N.J.: Rutgers University Press, 2001); Harry M. Benshoff, *Monsters in the Closet: Homosexuality and the Horror Film* (Manchester, U.K.: Manchester University Press, 1997); Peter Biskind, *Seeing Is Believing: How Hollywood Taught Us to Stop Worrying and Love the Fifties* (New York: Pantheon Books, 1983); Charles Derry, *Dark Dreams: A Psychological History of the Modern Horror Film* (South Brunswick, N.J.: A. S. Barnes, 1977); Cyndy Hendershot, *I Was a Cold War Monster: Horror Films, Eroticism, and the Cold War Imagination* (Bowling Green, Ohio: Bowling Green State University Popular Press, 2001); Nora Sayre, *Running Time: Films of the Cold War* (New York: Dial Press, 1982); David J. Skal, *The Monster Show: A Cultural History of Horror* (New York: W. W. Norton, 1993); Jacqueline Foertsch, *Enemies Within: The Cold War and the AIDS Crisis in Literature, Film, and Culture* (Urbana-Champaign: University of Illinois Press, 2001); Ernesto G. Laura, "Invasion of the Body Snatchers," in *Focus on the Science Fiction Film*, ed. William Johnson (Englewood Cliffs, N.J.: Prentice Hall, 1972), 71–73; Rick Worland, *The Horror Film: An Introduction* (Malden, Mass.: Blackwell, 2007), esp. Chapter 8, "'Horror in the Age of Anxiety': *Invasion of the Body Snatchers* (1956)," 193–207; and Stuart Samuels, "The Age of Conspiracy and Conformity: 'Invasion of the Body Snatchers,'" in *American History/American Film: Interpreting the Hollywood Image*, 203–17 (New York: Ungar, 1980). Foertsch was especially helpful in my thinking about the connections between the Cold War and the HIV/AIDS epidemic, as was Daryl Ogden, who formulates the link in terms of virology and immunology. See Ogden, "Cold War Science and the Body Politic: An Immuno/Virological Approach to *Angels in America*," *Literature and Medicine* 19, no. 2 (2000): 241–61. Susan Sontag's "The Imagination of Disaster" has been influential on critical thinking about science fiction and Cold War anxieties. See Sontag, "The Imagination of Disaster," in *Against Interpretation and Other Essays* (New York: Farrar, Straus, and Giroux, 1966).

12. Ostherr, *Cinematic Prophylaxis*, 139.

13. Andrew Ross, *No Respect: Intellectuals and Popular Culture* (New York: Routledge, 1989), 45.

14. [Editor's note: Three sections of Wald's original book chapter were excised for the sake of length in this reprint and to bring forward the work's attention to zombielike figures in science fiction and film.]

15. Mottram, "Rencontre avec William Burroughs," 12. The original interview was conducted in 1964 and published in *Les Langues Modernes* (January–February 1965): 79–83.

16. Oliver Harris, "Can You See a Virus? The Queer Cold War of William Burroughs," *Journal of American Studies* 33, no. 2 (1999): 247. Literary critical engagements with Burroughs tend in general to stress the nonmetaphorical nature of his idea of contagion. Robin Lydenberg, for example, explains that the "'evil virus' . . . travels from one host to another along mathematical lines of extension or along biological circuits of need—it proceeds by literal metonymic juxtaposition and contagion rather than by metaphorical resemblance." Lydenberg, *Word Cultures: Radical Theory and Practice in William S. Burroughs' Fiction* (Urbana-Champaign: University of Illinois Press, 1987), 13. On the virus imagery in Burroughs, see also Barry Miles, *William Burroughs: El Hombre Invisible*, rev. ed. (London: Virgin Books, 2002).

17. William S. Burroughs, "Deposition: Testimony Concerning a Sickness," in *Naked Lunch: The Restored Text*, ed. James Grauerholz and Barry Miles (1959; repr., New York: Grove Press, 2001), 205.

18. William S. Burroughs, *The Ticket That Exploded* (New York: Grove Press, 1962), 58–59.

19. William S. Burroughs, introduction to *Queer* (New York: Viking Press, 1985), xiv.

20. Conrad Knickerbocker, "White Junk" (interview with William Burroughs), in *Burroughs Live: The Collected Interviews of William S. Burroughs 1960–1997*, ed. Sylvere Lotringer (Los Angeles: Semiotext(e) Double Agents Series, 2001), 68.

21. Ibid., 67.

22. Ibid.

23. The 1993 film, which takes place on a military base, is an exception; it did not have a significant following, and I do not discuss it in this chapter. It is interesting that in the most recent version, *The Invasion*, directed by Oliver Hirschbiegel (Warner Pictures, 2007), the pods are replaced by a virus that is transmitted through direct contact with bodily fluids. The alien invasion is understood and described throughout the film as a spreading epidemic. Investigators from the Centers for Disease Control and Prevention are among the first infected, and the infection is contained by the U.S. Army Medical Research Institute of Infectious Diseases. The alien virus ultimately proves weak enough to destroy.

24. Benshoff, *Monsters in the Closet*, 128.

25. "The outbreak narrative" is the name I give to the formulaic plot that begins an outbreak of a devastating communicable disease, tracks it through the global networks through which it travels, and chronicles the scientific and epidemiological work that ends with its containment.

26. Jack Finney, *The Body Snatchers* (New York: Dell, 1955), 18–19.

27. David Seed, *Brainwashing: The Fictions of Mind Control: A Study of Novels and Films since World War II* (Kent, Ohio: Kent State University Press, 2004). Seed frames his reading of *Body Snatchers* with a discussion of Hunter and Merloo. See also his chapter on William Burroughs.

28. The mind control literature focused on the work of the Russian scientist Ivan Petrovich Pavlov, who won a Nobel Prize for his research on behavioral conditioning, and Pavlovian conditioning was central to works such as Condon's. Finney's novel, however, was more concerned with the biological features of the human personality that would allow the alienation—or literal theft—of human identity.

29. Norbert Wiener, *Human Use of Human Beings: Cybernetic and Society* (New York: Da Capo Press, 1988), 96.

30. On conspiracy theories, see Peter Knight, ed., *Conspiracy Culture, Conspiracy Nation: The Politics of Paranoia in Postwar America* (New York: New York University Press, 2002), and Timothy Melley, *Empire of Conspiracy: The Culture of Paranoia in Postwar America* (Ithaca, N.Y.: Cornell University Press, 2000).

31. Jack Finney, "The Body Snatchers," *Collier's*, December 19, 1954, 121. This piece is the second in a three-part series published between November 26 and December 24, 1954.

32. Homi Bhabha, "Of Mimicry and Man: The Ambivalence of Colonial Discourse," *October* 28 (Spring 1984): 126.

33. Alan Paton, "The Negro in America Today," *Collier's*, October 15, 1954, 62. The piece was continued the following week. See Alan Paton, "The Negro in the North," *Collier's*, October 22, 1954, 70–80.

34. Much has been written on hybridity and "mixed-bloodedness" in postcolonial and U.S. race and ethnic theory. For a history of the concept of hybridity, see esp. Robert J. C. Young, *Colonial Desire: Hybridity in Culture, Theory, and Race* (London: Routledge, 1995). In addition, see the discussions of hybridity in Homi Bhabha, *The Location of Culture* (London: Routledge, 1994); Tariq Modood and Pnina Werbner, eds., *Debating Cultural Hybridity* (London: Zed Books, 1997); and esp. Lisa Lowe's brilliant essay

"The Intimacies of Four Continents," in *Haunted by Empire: Geographies of Intimacy in North American History*, ed. Ann Laura Stoler, 191–212 (Durham, N.C.: Duke University Press, 2006).

The "intimacies" of Lowe's title are the expression of the multiple contacts of continental interdependence in the early nineteenth century. Lowe shows how Chinese immigrant figures ("the Chinese coolie"; "the Chinese woman")—often associated in the colonial imagination with racially mixed figures—serve as cultural hybrids that help to produce "a hierarchy of racial classifications" (197) that underpins liberal humanism and the political economy of modernity. I find in these figures an intriguing lineage for the carrier.

For a variety of discussions of mixed race in the U.S. context, see Werner Sollors, *Neither Black, nor White, Yet Both: Thematic Explorations of Interracial Literature* (New York: Oxford University Press, 1997); Ronald Takaki, *A Different Mirror: A History of Multiculturalism in America* (New York: Back Bay Books, 1993); Eva Saks, "Representing Miscegenation Law," *Raritan* 8, no. 2 (1988): 39–69; Walter Benn Michaels, *Our America: Nativism, Modernism, and Pluralism* (Durham, N.C.: Duke University Press, 1995); David Palumbo-Liu, *Asian/American: Historical Crossings of a Racial Frontier* (Stanford, Calif.: Stanford University Press, 1999); and Alys Eve Weinbaum, *Wayward Reproductions: Genealogies of Race and Nation in Transatlantic Modern Thought* (Durham, N.C.: Duke University Press, 2004).

35. Sigmund Freud, "The Unconscious," *Standard Edition* 14 (1957): 191. Freud wrote "The Unconscious" in 1915.

36. See Young, *Colonial Desire*.

37. On the interarticulation of race and sexuality (specifically, reproduction) in Freud, see Alys Weinbaum, *Wayward Reproductions*. It is interesting that Freud's strongest justification for group psychology turns on a racial metaphor.

38. For more on Robert Park, see Chapter 3, "Communicable Americanism: Social Contagion and Urban Spaces," of the book from which this chapter is excerpted: Priscilla Wald, *Contagious: Cultures, Carriers, and the Outbreak Narrative* (Durham, N.C.: Duke University Press, 2008).

39. Edward Hunter, *Brainwashing: The Story of Men Who Defied It* (New York: Farrar, Straus, and Cudahy, 1956), 65.

40. See Al LaValley, "Invasion of the Body Snatchers: Politics, Psychology, Sociology," in *Invasion of the Body Snatchers: Don Siegel, Director*, ed. Al LaValley, 3–17 (New Brunswick, N.J.: Rutgers University Press, 1989). See also Stuart M. Kaminsky, "Pods," in *Don Siegel: Director*, 99–108 (New York: Curtis Books, 1974).

41. Stuart M. Kaminsky, "Don Siegel on the Pod Society," in LaValley, *Invasion of the Body Snatchers*, 154.

42. Sobchack, *Screening Space*, 124.

43. Ibid., 125.

44. *Invasion of the Body Snatchers*, directed by Don Siegel (Allied Artists Pictures, 1956).

45. Matheson's novella has spawned three film versions, *The Last Man on Earth* (dir. Ubaldo Ragona, 1964), *Omega Man* (dir. Boris Sagal, 1971), and *I Am Legend* (dir. Francis Lawrence, 2007). None of the films retains the bat explanation, and in *Omega Man*, the epidemic is the result of government research.

46. Merloo, *Rape of the Mind*, 209.

47. Ibid., 292.

48. Christopher Lasch, *The Culture of Narcissism: American Life in an Age of Diminishing Expectations* (New York: Warner Books, 1979); Tom Wolfe, "The 'Me Decade' and the Third Great Awakening," *New York*, August 23, 1976, 26–40.

49. Jonathan Schell, *The Time of Illusion* (1975; repr., New York: Vintage Books, 1976), 14. Most of the book had appeared in a series of *New Yorker* articles, which were also widely read.

50. United Nations Economic and Social Council, "Crisis of Human Environment," *Problems of the Human Environment: Report of the Secretary General*, 47th Session, Agenda Item 10, May 26, 1969, 4.

51. Harold R. Isaacs, "Color in World Affairs," *Foreign Affairs* 47, no. 2 (1969): 235.

52. According to Douglas T. Miller, public trust in the medical profession dropped from 73 percent to 42 percent from the mid-1960s to the mid-1970s, and in 1976, faith in the legal profession had dropped to 12 percent. See Douglas T. Miller, "Sixties Activism in the 'Me Decade,'" in *The Lost Decade: America in the Seventies*, ed. Elsebeth Hurup, 133–43 (Aarhus, Denmark: Aarhus University Press, 1996).

53. Douglas T. Miller's "Sixties Activism in the 'Me Decade'" documents both the nostalgia and the

social and political activism that, contrary to dominant representation of the decade, was prevalent in the 1970s.

54. Pauline Kael, "Pods," *New Yorker,* December 25, 1978, 48, 51.

55. Denny Zeitlin, a jazz musician and practicing psychiatrist, did the musical score for the film.

56. *Invasion of the Body Snatchers,* directed by Philip Kaufman (Metro-Goldwyn-Mayer, 1978).

57. He was also subsequently Martin Dysart, the psychiatrist in a 1977 Broadway production of *Equus.* Kibner's role as family counselor might also coyly invoke Spock's nominal predecessor, Dr. Benjamin Spock, on whose advice parents reared the generation that includes Matthew and Elizabeth.

58. See Carl Sagan, *Broca's Brain* (New York: Random House, 1979). The scientific response to Velikovsky was not favorable.

59. It is interesting that the most recent films, *Omega Man* and *I Am Legend,* differ from earlier incarnations of that story in positing a small band of human beings dedicated to the survival of the species.

60. On the shaping of the epidemic through epidemiological narratives, see esp. Gerald M. Oppenheimer, "In the Eye of the Storm: The Epidemiological Construction of AIDS," in *AIDS: The Burdens of History,* ed. Elizabeth Fee and Daniel M. Fox, 267–300 (Berkeley: University of California Press, 1988).

Slaves, Cannibals, and Infected Hyper-Whites

The Race and Religion of Zombies

ELIZABETH McALISTER

"Cool Obama" and "Zombie McCain"

After shaking hands with Barack Obama at the conclusion of the last U.S. presidential debate, John McCain started to head the wrong way off the stage before realizing his mistake and reversing course. As he fell in step behind his opponent, he acknowledged his error with an extravagant full-body grimace. His grotesque pose was frozen by photographers and instantly uploaded onto the Internet with the caption "Zombie McCain." Other zombie-themed captions for the image proliferated, including one on PoliticalHumor.com that read, "Obama: cool enough to just ignore zombies" (see Figure 4.1).[1]

The fact that McCain's clumsiness figured him as a zombie in contradistinction to Barack Obama's unflappable "cool" reflects the widespread fascination with zombies in U.S. media and culture—consider the recent success of the book *Pride and Prejudice and Zombies* or the sudden currency of the term *zombie bank*.[2] It also indexes markers in U.S. popular culture of racial whiteness and blackness. As Robert Farris Thompson points out in his classic essay "An Aesthetic of the Cool," the concept of "cool" in many African-derived cultures is a metaphor for the aesthetic and moral value of remaining composed under pressure and is ultimately a marker of "transcendental balance."[3] The juxtaposition of this "cool" black presidential candidate—lithe and poised—with a stumbling and staggering white "zombie" candidate is emblematic, I will suggest, of a wider form of mythmaking about race currently at work in U.S. culture.[4]

This essay shows that a "comparative analysis of nightmares" can be a productive method for analyzing salient themes in the imaginative products and practices of cultures in close contact.[5] I pair ethnographic interpretation of work on the *zonbi* in Haitian religious thought and art with a religious studies reading of key films about zombies made in the United States.[6] I run a finger along several conceptual strands from Haitian religious arts that remain to haunt zombie representations in U.S. popular culture. Like the Haitian zonbi, the U.S. film zombie must be understood as being embedded in a set

Figure 4.1.
Cool Obama and
Zombie McCain meme.
Origin unknown.

of deeply symbolic structures that are a matter of religious thought. In both contexts, zombie narratives and rituals interrogate the boundary between life and death, elucidate the complex relations between freedom and slavery, and highlight the overlap between capitalism and cannibalism. What I want to stress especially is that in each context, race is the pivot on which these dynamics articulate themselves.

Zombies: A Brief History

What intrigues me as a scholar of Afro-Caribbean religion is that the mythmaking comprising and surrounding the zombie in America originates from sensationalized descriptions of a set of Afro-Caribbean mystical arts. The word *zonbi* appears in writing as far back as colonial Saint-Domingue, glossed by travel writer Moreau de Saint-Méry as the slaves' belief in a returned soul, a *revenant*.[7] Twentieth-century reports describe not a returned soul but a returned body—a person bodily raised from the grave and turned into a slave worker. As a spirit or a slave, complex spiritual formulae separate body and soul and compel one or the other to work. These entities—especially the invisible *zonbi astral* (astral zombies)—continue to be fairly common inhabitants of the unseen mystical world of Haitian Vodouists.

A very different kind of zombie populates U.S. film and television: a ghoul who lumbers around trying to eat people. George Romero's Living Dead films exemplify this concept of the zombie in the popular imagination. The idea refers, of course, to dead people who are still alive and driven to kill and cannibalize the living. These monsters made an appearance in Michael Jackson's smash hit music video *Thriller* and now star in the more recent *I Am Legend, 28 Days Later,* and other films. In this first decade of the new millennium, the walking dead and their cannibalistic appetites seem to be everywhere. We hear a lot lately about "zombie banks"—banks whose debts are greater than their assets—which drain bailout money from the government but don't facilitate more lending in turn.[8] Zombies show up in pop songs and are stock characters in comic books and graphic novels. They appear in video games, such as in the Resident Evil series, and in the Resident Evil movie spin-offs. Since 2000, about one hundred movies and scores of video games have featured undead, cannibal zombies. Zombielike creatures called *inferi* make an appearance in the sixth book of the Harry Potter series. Zombies have even earned a special place in the academy: the philosopher David Chalmers, in order to elaborate various ethical questions, has posited the "philosophical zombie," or p-zombie, a human body without consciousness that behaves like a human with consciousness.[9]

Mel Brooks's son, Max Brooks, wrote the best-selling *Zombie Survival Guide* (2003), a tongue-in-cheek manual for surviving a widespread zombie attack, and he packs lecture halls when he speaks about the impending zombie apocalypse.[10] Especially intriguing are the "zombie walks" in many U.S. cities, where ordinary people dress up like zombies from all walks of life—construction workers, doctors, nuns—and lumber through the parks and streets. Zombie flash mobs move through downtown spaces, having read rules for play on the Internet. In 2007, a zombie flash mob invaded a San Francisco Apple store to stage an anticonsumerist performance piece where zombies pretended to eat the computers on display. *Pride and Prejudice and Zombies*—the Jane Austen novel "mashed up" with a zombie plotline—soared to the top of numerous best-seller lists. The 2010 television series *The Walking Dead*, on the cable channel AMC, is set in a zombie postapocalypse and won a Golden Globe Award for Best Drama. Zombies are all around us. Americans have brought to life—or death, if you prefer—a proliferation of monsters who are doing a fair amount of cultural work.

What if we highlight this fact about zombies: the zombie is the one stock horror character that does not have a genealogy in European tradition or much presence in gothic fiction, as do the ghost, vampire, werewolf, and Frankenstein.[11] Rather, the zombie originates in Afro-Haitian religious thought and practice and is traceable (in part) to colonial-era Kongo religion from Central Africa. Deleuze and Guattari assert that "the only modern myth is the myth of zombies," and this is quite true in any number of ways.[12] The zombie came into being (as it were) in the plantation society of colonial Saint-Domingue, and I will argue here that its figure, its story, its mythology, are at once part of the mystical arts that have developed since that time *and* compose a form of mythmaking that effects the mystification of slavery and ongoing political repression. That is, the zombie represents, responds to, and mystifies fear of slavery, collusion with it, and rebellion against it. The zombie was born (so to speak) in what Michael Taussig terms the colonial "space of death" and is inextricable from the "culture of terror" of the plantation.[13] This modern monster is a complex and polyvalent Other that points us to art and thought produced out of the nightmarish aspects of modernity. In particular, this monster refers and responds to the nexus of capitalism, race, and religion.

There are many kinds of zombies, and many levels, if you will, of the representation and meaning of zombies. Working from the gothic, sensationalized travel writers' accounts of black West Indian "superstition," early Hollywood produced several "zombie" films, such as *White Zombie* (1932) and *I Walked with a Zombie* (1943). As a constellation of misunderstood and distorted elements in early Hollywood films, these Caribbean zombie representations might be described as a profound example of what Toni Morrison calls "American Africanism," that is, "the denotative and connotative blackness that African peoples have come to signify, as well as the entire range of views, assumptions, readings, and misreadings that accompany Eurocentric learning about these people. As a trope, little restraint has been attached to its uses."[14] The films invariably cast black sorcerers (or quack sorcerers) plotting for conquest of and control over white women, and blackness is unmistakably linked with primitive menace, superstition, and the diabolical.

Contemporary American zombie films have diverged quite a bit from their Caribbean beginnings. Most zombies now are figured as racially white, and most of the films that portray them are set in the United States. As an American horror film genre character, the zombie has come to make certain statements about *whiteness* in America. Yet this inversion or inside-outness of earlier racial associations also presents a meta-commentary on the same subjects as do Haitian zonbi: the intersections of capitalism and consumption, slavery and cannibalism, bodily excess and race. Whether in Haitian religious practices, art, and cultural mythology or in U.S. films, the zombie serves to index the excessive extremes of capitalism, the overlap of capitalism and cannibalism, and the interplay between capitalism and race in the history of the Americas.[15]

Capturing, Enslaving, Feeding, and Dressing Zonbis in Haiti

I accidentally bought two zonbis in Haiti. My zonbis are not the walking dead but rather the common, everyday spirits of the recently dead, zonbi astral. The spirits were captured from a cemetery in a mystical ritual and then contained in an empty rum bottle. I did not do the capturing and containing; this feat was achieved by a man named St. Jean, who made his living (in the face of chronically high unemployment) as a *bòkò*, or sorcerer, in a neighborhood near the cemetery in downtown Port-au-Prince.[16] I had gone to interview the bòkò, and when I complimented a colorfully decorated bottle that sat on his altar, he asked if I would like to have one like it. In agreeing, I got much more than a decorated bottle. My encounter with the sorcerer turned into something far more complex than the commission of what I took to be an art object. When I returned to pick up the bottle, St. Jean performed a complex ritual that infused human life into the bottle and transformed the container into a living grave, housing a human–spirit hybrid entity.

The essence of the zonbis' spirit life emanates from shaved bits of bone from two human skulls. The zonbis in the bottle cannot properly be understood as souls but rather as fragments of human soul, or spirit. In Afro-Haitian religious thought, part of the spirit goes immediately to God after death, while another part lingers near the grave for a time. It is this portion of the spirit that can be captured and made to work; let's say, a form of "raw spirit life." The bòkò performed a spontaneous ritual, which began when he popped a cassette tape into a player. Our soundscape was a secret society ceremony to which he said he belonged.

He put these skull shavings into the bottle, along with the ashes from a burned American dollar and a variety of herbs, perfumes, alcohols, and powders. Robert Farris

Thompson spelled out the logic of this sort of "charm" in his work on *minkisi* (containers of spirit) from the Kongo culture, which are surely one of the cultural sources of the zonbi:

> The nkisi is believed to live with an inner life of its own. The basis of that life was a captured soul. . . . The owner of the charm could direct the spirit in the object to accomplish mystically certain things for him, either to enhance his luck or to sharpen his business sense. This miracle was achieved through two basic classes of medicine within the charm, *spirit-embedding medicine* (earths, often from a grave site, for cemetery earth is considered at one with the spirit of the dead) and *spirit-admonishing objects* (seeds, claws, miniature knives, stones, crystals, and so forth).[17]

In my bottle, the spirit-embedding medicine includes cemetery earth, but also more to the point, the skull shavings. At some previous time, St. Jean had most likely prepared the skulls in a sort of spirit-extracting ritual, treating them with baths of dew, rain, and sunshine. The skulls had been given food (which they absorb mystically, as spirits in the

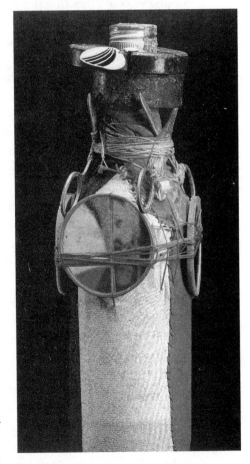

invisible world generally do) and had been baptized with new, ritual names. Their names would have been cryptic phrases, such as *je m'engage* (I'm trying) or *al chache* (go look). Each skull would have been charged with a specific strength, job, or problem to treat. Presumably, these skulls were activated with the ability to enhance luck, wealth, and health.

"Spirit-admonishing medicines" instruct the zonbis in the work that they are being commanded to do on my behalf. Ingeniously, this technology of good luck zonbi-making involves dressing the zonbis in the very instructions and work directions the maker intends them to perform. The mirrors around the center of the bottle are its "eyes for seeing" and will identify any force coming at me with malevolent intent (see Figure 4.2). The scissors lashed open under the bottleneck are like arms crossed in self-defense. The dollar bill in the bottle instructs the zonbi spirits to attract wealth. The herbs are for the zonbis to heal me of sickness and disease, while the perfumes are to make me attractive and desirable. St. Jean created for them a magnetic force field by placing two industrial magnets as a kind of collar on the neck of the bottle. This object is now swirling with polarity, intention, and life.[18] It is what Stephan Palmié has called "a life form constituted through ritual action."[19]

Figure 4.2.
A bottle containing spirits of the dead. Courtesy of the Fowler Museum, University of California, Los Angeles.

This zonbi bottle refuses the Western ontological distinction between people and things, and between life and death, as it is a hybrid of human and spirit, living and dead, individual and generic. In Afro-Creole thought, spirit can inhabit both natural and human-made things, and what is more, this force can be manipulated and used, often for healing and protection, sometimes for aggression or attack. When I later interviewed the bòkò, I learned about the deep moral ambiguity of the zonbi astral. St. Jean told me that the zonbis were trapped in the bottle until the time when, as with every person, their spirits would go on to God. The bòkò instructed me to ask the zonbis for anything I wanted, because, captured and ritually transformed, they were working for him, and now, as if subcontracted, for me.

I realized that I was effectively in the position of a spiritual slave owner. Besides being dismayed and upset, I found it puzzling that people would practice the enslavement of this "raw spirit life" considering that their ancestors suffered extreme brutality during colonial slavery in Haiti, where the life expectancy of an enslaved person on a plantation was only seven years. Planters fed and inaugurated the modern system of Atlantic capitalism through dehumanization, starvation, and torture; these were the routine ways of extracting production value to fund the obscenely lucrative sugar trade.

But, then again, the living *take charge* of their history when they mimetically perform master–slave relationships with spirits of the dead. The production of spiritual (and bodily) zonbis shows us how groups remember history and enact its consequences in embodied ritual arts. The slave trade and colonial slavery—whose modus operandus was to cast living humans as commodities—are quite literally encoded and reenacted in *this* living object. Just as slavery depended on capturing, containing, and forcing the labor of thousands of people, so does this form of mystical work reenact the same process in local terms. It is, as Taussig famously put it, history as sorcery.[20]

Under slavery, Afro-Caribbeans were rendered nonhuman by being legally transposed into commodities. Now, the enslaved dead hold a *respected place* within the religion. In what might seem counterintuitive, Randy Matory recently argued that in Afro-Latin religions, "instead of being the opposite of the desired personal or social state, the image and mimesis of slavery become highly flexible instruments of legally free people's aspirations for themselves and for their loved ones."[21] He notes that in these religions, the slave is often considered the most efficacious spiritual actor. The relationship between spirit worker and the dead is inherently unequal and exploitative, yet it is nuanced in fascinating ways that give the spirits of the dead some agency. Usually the dealings between people and the zonbis are just that—economic affairs, caught up in a system revolving around money, work, captivity, predation, and coercion.

I did feed the zonbis a ritual meal of unsalted rice and beans, feeling somewhat sheepish the entire while. But I was determined to operate in as ethical a manner as I could toward this bottle, which its maker understood to be a living thing. Who was I not to take care of my obligations to the zonbis? I was haunted by a comment made by the scholar Luminisa Bunseki Fu-Kiau at a conference. "When you put our 'charms' and 'fetishes' in your museums," he said, "you are incarcerating our ancestors." I did not want to get in trouble in any way, either with the living or the dead.

I had been privy to a case of sorcery involving a malevolent zonbi. I watched while

Papa Mondy, an expert healer in spirit work, diagnosed a teenager who had taken sick and was acting strange. After extensive consultation and divination, Papa Mondy informed the boy's mother that someone with bad intentions had *voye zonbi* (sent a zonbi) against the teen and had "sold" the boy mystically to a secret society. The teen had been captured mystically in the unseen world, and his life force was being "eaten." In a family drama of sickness and healing, once again the transactions of slavery were at play. This diagnosis reenacted the capture, sale, and exploitation of the life of a person, here in the unseen world of everyday Haitian life.

The cure—and the teen was cured, at least in the semipublic neighborhood narrative—involved a complex process of ritual freeing, negotiating, and buying back: an unraveling and undoing of the spiritual enslavement. The director of this healing ceremony was Papa Gede Loray, himself a spirit of a former colonial slave—considered the best "worker" among the spirits—who came to possess the priest Mondy for most of the proceedings. The teen was ritually buried, lying down (up to his neck) beneath a light layer of earth in a symbolic grave, and the zonbi was tricked and forced to remain in the grave when the boy was lifted out. The zonbi was quickly covered up with earth then bound and tied to the spot with a rock and a rope. These Haitian spirit workers once again performed some of the actions famously used against the African enslaved—tricking, capturing, binding, and shackling—but this time the ritual actors were the present-day descendants of slaves, enacting the commodification and traffic in humans through the ritual vocabulary most salient to their history, in what Connerton called "the capacity to reproduce a certain performance."[22]

The boy was freed of the zonbi, but he still needed to be "bought back" from the secret society. Since it was unclear (as it often is) who sent this misfortune, the crucial redeeming deal had to be made with Bawon Samdi, the spirit-in-chief of the recently dead and the ultimate authority over the cemetery. We were going to buy the boy back from the cemetery, before the cemetery swallowed him up. We went, quite late at night by now, to an intersection of two roads where diplomatic spiritual protocol necessitated that the family make a payment to Met Kalfou, the spirit of the crossroads. *Si kalfou pa bay, simitye pa pran*, goes this important principle: "If the crossroads won't give (way), the cemetery won't take (accept)." When we got to the cemetery, Papa Mondy set up shop next to the tomb of Bawon. An elaborate series of ritual exchanges ensued. Mondy gently ripped the boy's clothes from his body until he wore only his underthings and then laid the boy on top of the tomb. To the accompaniment of prayers and prayer-songs, Mondy swept the boy with a broom to remove any remaining negativity. He entreated Bawon to buy back this boy from those who wanted to steal him and stood pleading with two arms outstretched while the rest of the small group sang behind him. First he spoke to the afflicted boy, but really to us, to the dead, and to the evil-doer. "Now you are known by the cemetery. Now you are like one of the dead. How can you kill a dead man, *mon cher*? They can do nothing to you." Next he addressed Bawon: "You are the one with power over death. *You* are the only one who can kill him," said Mondy. "I sell this boy to you, and you alone are buying him. It is you who will determine the day he will die." Papa Mondy knelt down and threw down a small package wrapped in brown paper, held together with pins. He deftly poured rum over the whole thing and lit a match. A hungry blue flame engulfed the clothes, the brown paper, and the precious four hundred and twelve dollars that were inside.

With this monetary sacrifice, Bawon was paid and the boy was bought. Mondy stood the boy atop the tomb and dressed him in clean white clothes. He told the boy he would no longer be under the influence of other humans or spirits who wished to harm him—only Bawon "owned" him. That night in the cemetery, the teen boy was literally, and with Haitian currency, sold to a moral and powerful guardian, in order to escape being owned by a malevolent and exploitative one.

In this case, selling a person was an act of redemption, a far cry from—and yet also an echo of—the Atlantic slave trade. One cannot help but notice the various profound ways that layers of historical events and conditions are remembered and mimetically enacted through ritual, from the slave trade to the current patronage system of politically powerful "big men" and their more vulnerable followers. This religious logic also bears a parallel to the Christian notion that Jesus pays the debt of sin for the believer, whose soul is bought and paid for through the blood of the crucifixion. In both cases, a supernatural entity can buy the spirit (or soul) of a human and become that person's mediator with the unseen world and the afterlife.

Some Vodouists understand Jesus as the first zonbi. This myth holds that Jesus's tomb was guarded by two Haitian soldiers, who unscrupulously stole the password God gave when He resurrected Jesus. The soldiers stole the password, sold it, and the stolen secret is now part of the secrets of sorcerers. If we examine the story carefully, we see that the buyer of people (Jesus) is victimized by people rebelling against him. The ordinary folk—the soldiers—are stealing from God, who after all set the terms of all negotiations. In this story, the sorcerer acknowledges his opposition to (Roman Catholic) Christianity, which, in its affiliation with landowning elites, has not always served the interests of everyday Haitians. Yet insofar as being made a zonbi is a terrifying form of victimization, this story also sympathizes with Jesus. In a beautiful ironwork sculpture by Gabriel Bien-Aimé, cut and hammered from a recycled oil drum, Jesus with his crown of thorns is being taken down from the cross with a chain around his neck. At the other end is the sorcerer controlling him.[23]

Like the colonial slave, or the oppressed worker, zonbis also possess the potential for out-and-out rebellion. There are plenty of stories of people who ask these "bought spirits" for wealth, land, or political promotion and who cannot provide the food demanded in return. Then the zonbis are said to rise up to attack their owners, consuming *their* life force as payment. Eating them through magic, the zonbi becomes more and more powerful as its master wastes away through sickness. St. Jean himself was said to have been "eaten" in this manner, consumed by his own enslaved zonbi, turned cannibal in response to St. Jean's voracious greed. Perhaps that process is what is described in this mural, painted on the interior wall of a Vodou temple (see Figure 4.3). Here, a sorcerer (indicated as such by his red shirt and by the whip in his hand, a tool used to "heat up" ritual and activate spiritual energy) is attacked by hundreds of skeletal figures while facing a tomb.

Taussig, the Comaroffs, and others have written about the ways such sorcery narra-

Figure 4.3.
Mural near Jacmel, Haiti, 2005. Photograph by Katherine M. Smith.

tives are provoked by, and are a rendering of, the basic mechanisms of capitalist production, that is, the creation of value for some through appropriating and consuming the energies of others.[24] Haitian spirit workers have redescribed this aspect of capitalism in religious ritual. Seen this way, zonbi-making is an example of a non-Western form of thought that diagnoses, theorizes, and responds mimetically to the long history of violently consumptive and dehumanizing capitalism in the Americas from the colonial period until the present.[25] Zonbis can be understood as a religious, philosophical, and artistic response to the cannibalistic dynamics within capitalism and a harnessing of these principles through ritual.

Human Trafficking in the Walking Dead

In order to understand the appropriation of zombie mythology by filmmakers, we must rehearse in the broadest possible strokes the controversial mythology of the *zonbi kò kadav*, or walking corpse, which is the reverse of the astral zonbi. The idea is this: in the absence of a strong national government, traditional, male-headed secret societies operate as quasi-governments, as mafias controlling markets, and as juridical systems in the Haitian countryside. One extreme and rare form of punishment these societies can hand down to an accused criminal (who has, say, sold the family land without permission) is to be made into a zonbi kò kadav, whereby his spirit is extracted from his body and his body is sold into modern-day slavery to cut cane on a sugar plantation. Underneath the cultural process of becoming a zonbi kò kadav, the ethnobotonist Wade Davis famously claimed, lies a scientific one. He argued that the would-be zonbi is surreptitiously given tetrodotoxin from the puffer fish, which lowers his metabolism to the point where he appears dead. His family buries him, usually in an aboveground tomb as is typical in

Haiti. That evening, the society's sorcerer returns to the cemetery, opens the tomb, and gives the victim datura plant, a hallucinogen, and mystically separates out parts of the spirit from the body.[26]

In this scenario, mystical technology much like that applied to the zonbi astral separates the spirit from the body, except that the separation takes place before rather than after the body's death. The body then is left, visible, as a religious and social corpse. In the final phase of punishment, this body—which we might redescribe as a traumatized, bound, socially stigmatized, ensorcelled, and possibly brain-damaged person—is said to be trafficked to a labor camp cum sugar plantation, with the secret society collecting a procurement fee. But before being disappeared, the bound victim is forced to pass by his family's home and call out to someone he knows, "Se mwen-menm!" (It's me!).

In this mural on the wall of a Vodou temple, a sorcerer uses a whip to drive a shrouded figure whose hands are bound behind the back with a length of rope held by the sorcerer (see Figure 4.4). The bottle under the sorcerer's arm signals that the victim's spirit has been captured inside. It is striking that the process of capturing slaves and leading them, bound and whipped, to be sold for labor is represented in religious terms. Here the moment of punishment-by-zombification throughout Haitian history replicates and reproduces the crucial transformative moment in the lives of West and Central Africans and the slaves in the colonies, where Africans were seized, kidnapped, bound, whipped, sold, and forced to labor. Insofar as this form of mythmaking (and, it is said, actual practice) reenacts this primal moment, the zonbi phenomenon in Haiti can be said to continue the inflicting of terror through the bodily reenactment of historical memory.[27]

My husband—an avowed religious nonbeliever—swears that as a youth, he was tapped on the shoulder while walking down a country road one evening by a man from his home village who had been buried just that afternoon and was being hurried past by two other men. The two friends with my husband—who looked and witnessed the "zonbi," became sick with high fevers for several days. They were traumatized themselves, or were victims of a poison powder spray administered by the passing sorcerers. This form of psychic and political terror is broadcast to the community and made known as a kind of "semipublic secret." The secret is broadcast in satire during carnival, when small bands of "zonbi" dress in white sheets behind a sorcerer and parade the myth: the walking living performing the walking dead (see Figure 4.5).

The important point here is that the walking zonbi these maskers are playing is rendered a monstrous form of "raw life" through a mystical technology that is also a political punishment. Edwidge Danticat, in her book on Jacmel carnival, recalls that as a girl, she once heard a radio broadcaster announce that a few dozen zonbis had been discovered wandering in the hills. Danticat's aunt had no doubt that those "zonbis" were actually political prisoners "who were so mentally damaged by dictatorship-sponsored torture that they had become either crazy or slow."[28] The announcers' plea for family members to reclaim these "zonbis" was a trap. Danticat's story highlights the ways in which mythmaking about zonbis can serve the interests of dictatorship and other male-dominated secret societies. Highlighting its use as a mythology of liberation, Kaiama Glover discusses how Haitian writers used the zonbi as a metaphor in their writings about dictatorship and its dilemmas, often stressing the potential for the zonbi

Figure 4.4.
Mural of sorcerer leading zonbi on the wall of a Vodou temple. Photograph by Elizabeth McAlister.

Figure 4.5.
Troupe of zonbis at carnival in Jacmel, Haiti, 2008. Photograph by Katherine M. Smith.

to awaken and rebel.[29] A living nightmare of modern capitalism, this kind of zonbi, with all the secrecy, rumors, and mystification of power that surround it, remembers and re-performs the history of enslavement, as well as the capitalist consumption and cannibalism of human bodies and spirits in contemporary Haiti.

Apocalypse and the Religion of American Zombies

Now we're going to move from the question of the zonbi in the Haitian context to a question of a different order: by what means did the zombie become a U.S. American, as it were? Others have written helpfully about zombie mythology as it's taken up by early Hollywood in Caribbean settings, such as in *White Zombie* and *I Walked with a Zombie*. The horror of the Haitian zombie, for white Americans, was the image of the disfigured body dispossessed of its soul, will, agency, and hence its interiority and its very humanity. When set against Christian dualisms of body and soul that placed theological priority on the soul, these religious differences were terrifying. White Americans became fascinated with zombie mythology and reproduced it in writings on Haiti during the Marine Occupation between 1915 and 1934, usually overlooking its obvious articulations with slavery, capitalism, and political control.[30] Instead, the zombie myth authorized military intervention. Laënnec Hurbon writes about how the zombie, along with the cannibal practices that were imputed to be part of Haitian culture, become the image of the Other through which barbarism comes to be the sign for the Haitian.[31]

So early Hollywood invited the New World walking corpse to take its place in the monstrous pantheon alongside Old World figures such as the vampire, werewolf, and ghost. From the 1930s until the 1960s, and still today, the zombie is synonymous with a kind of barbaric racial blackness. But zombie images also spin off in a totally different and fascinating direction.

From the 1940s to the 1960s, Hollywood produced a slew of "trash films" featuring a variety of mutated, radioactive, or hybrid monsters that were termed "zombies" but had fairly little formulaic coherence.[32] Then came George Romero's 1968 film *Night of the Living Dead*, which he soon followed with *Dawn of the Dead* (1978) and *Day of the Dead* (1985). His independent, low-budget trilogy of Dead films set the terms for the American zombie horror flick and most pop culture zombie images since. Consistent with the historical pattern of the horror genre, Romero lifted the monstrous from its exotic setting in the Caribbean and set it down squarely in everyday America, to lurch and rampage its way into the popular imagination. Although Romero reportedly did not think of his creatures as zombies, and the word is rarely used in other films about the ravenous walking dead, from *Night* on, the critics and the public pronounced the label.[33]

Stephen King writes that horror "arises from a pervasive sense of disestablishment, that things are in the unmaking."[34] As other commentators have noted, Romero's films are *anti*-establishment parables about the corruption and decay of the American way of life. *Night of the Living Dead* attacks the nuclear American family, patriarchy, and racism; *Dawn of the Dead* fastens its attention on the deadening effects of rampant consumerism; and *Day of the Dead* offers an indictment of militarism and American misuse of science and technology. Virtually all scholars writing on zombie films either take a Marxian economic and consumer studies approach or they spin out in Lacanian terms the films' abject-monstrous psychoanalytic operations. I want to insist that the U.S. film zombie cannot be fully understood apart from its meanings against a set of deeply embedded symbolic structures that, like the Haitian zonbi, are a matter of religious thought.

Now, within the narrative, Romero's zombie films are set in a secular frame, with no reference to an otherworld or to a superhuman force. Zombies that had been created by a sorcerer in Haiti now had an indeterminate, usually scientific cause—dust from Venus, radiation, or an inexplicable virus. Romero visually rendered the metaphors of eating another's life force. That which was religious about the spirit zonbi in Haiti— the fact that human spirit lives on beyond death in an invisible part of the cosmos and has dealings with the living—was turned inside out, like the Haitian corpse zonbi. The film zombie is a former human with a body, but no soul, spirit, consciousness, interiority, or identity. This above all has become the common understanding of zombies in contemporary culture. Zombies are autonomous, but incapable of autonomy. They are a representation of a stripped-down form of "raw life," if you will, animating a body, plus an animalistic drive to consume human flesh. They are not commodified, but they consume; they are hyperconsuming. The most horrifying and excessive aspect of film zombies is their violent cannibal drive, as they lumber and lunge toward the living protagonists and take enormous, gory bites out of their necks, arms, and torsos. What is more, the American zombie is almost always a sign and a symptom of an apocalyptic undoing of the social order.

As secular apocalypse film, the zombie film is postmodern in that it has undermined the opposition of God and human.[35] But a religious logic inflects and infects American zombie monsters, and—in the way of so many narratives of secular popular culture—a biblical blueprint underlies and informs them. Romero's zombies are monstrous, but not demonic, precisely because no evil animates them. However, they always refer implicitly to the biblical apocalyptic tradition, and it is through this referencing that meaning is created. In this sense, zombie films are residually religious—articulated with religious themes to create secular ones.

In classical examples of religious monstrosity, we find a consistent pattern (from the ancient Near East until today) in which a chaos god or chaos monster threatens to undo creation and must be defeated by another god—or hero—to maintain cosmic order.[36] From the etymology of *monster*, the Latin *monstere*, we find "to demonstrate, or to warn." The monster gestures, inherently, to a sort of prophetic revelation. Like the uncanny "danger within," many ancient monsters are not antidivinities or "evil," as such, but rather are "part of a divinity that is deeply divided within itself about the future viability of the cosmos."[37] Timothy Beal notes that in some places in the Bible, the monstrous is against God, but at other times, God lays claim to monsters, such as Leviathan, who is an aspect of God's power. God and monsters are intertwined in a complicated dialectic that often confuses humankind.

The monstrosity and horror of film zombies revolve precisely around the uncanny familiarity of the zombie as a dispossessed monster in human form. Yet zombies are anonymous and pose a counterexample to the more common Western monster narrative centered on a single figure, to whom the characters are forced to relate, such as Leviathan, Dracula, and Frankenstein. Zombies are human sized and human shaped and have no supernatural attributes. They are neither sexually attractive nor sexually attracting. Like slaves in rebellion, they are most dangerous as a collective horde. Zombies (like Hobbes's Leviathan) are formed of many strands of society and unleash themselves on the world to release chaos from within the logic of society itself.

Film zombies are a collective of chaos monsters threatening to destroy civilization and order in a secular scenario of world destruction. However, the zombie apocalypse resists ancient chaos monster mythmaking—where the hero or god saves the world by fighting the chaos god and thus restores order to the cosmos. In the zombie films, order is not restored at all. Rather, a small band—or couple—of survivors comes to relative, contingent, and uneasy safety in a postapocalyptic enclave. The films work around the classic end-time paradox that the world must be destroyed in order for it to be reborn, and time must end in order for there to be a future.[38] The films all close with a gesture— but nothing like a full realization—toward a new beginning.

In biblical apocalyptics, a prophetic seer reveals a future rupture in time and space, which is preordained by God. Apocalypse, etymologically linked to the word *unveiling*, is a process of revealing in the Books of Ezekiel, Daniel, Revelation, and others; the revelation conveys both the fact of and the details about the future divine order. In the Christian apocalypse of John of Patmos, the entire earth is destroyed in order to bring about God's new heaven and new earth. But the survivors of zombie films certainly don't manage such feats of new creation. The films point back to the viewers' future, as it were, as a future of violent and chaotic degradation. Since no transcendent figure has predetermined the apocalypse, it is humans alone who have caused the end and humans alone who must survive it. There is no judgment day in these apocalypses; judgment is not internal to the film but rather relies on the viewer's pronouncement, based on interpretation.[39] Film zombies are good postmodern monsters, which emerge as "self-fulfilling prophecies of modernity."[40]

Yet the "revealing" or "warning" that zombie monsters occasion is not divine revelation but rather a politics cloaked in pseudo-religious form. Especially in the Romero films, the revelation is a confrontation with the insight that the film viewers are all zombies in the making. We are all in mortal danger of being made inhuman by virtue of being conformists, empty consumers, automatons, and cannibals. One clear message of most post-Romero zombie films is that the zombies are a logical result of the racism, corruption, greed, violence, and other flaws that already characterize Americans. Especially in *Dawn of the Dead*, in which the survivors shelter in a shopping mall, the parallel is drawn that hell is being damned to repeat endlessly the mistakes Americans have made as hyperconsumers, effecting our own "shopocalypse."[41]

Whereas zombies were often cast as black workers in the early Hollywood films, the vast majority of Romero-forward zombies are figured as white Americans, and zombie film heroes, interestingly, include black men often of West Indian descent. It is interesting that Peter, the black survivor/hero in *Dawn of the Dead*, offers a theological explanation for the ghoulish uprising that refers back to Vodou in the Caribbean. It comes in the form of wisdom from his Trinidadian grandfather, who was "into all that Obeah and Vodou." About the zombies, Peter says, "They're us, that's all. When there's no more room in hell, the dead will walk the earth." This idea transposes Vodou to deliver a prophetic vision of Christian apocalypse. In a reversal of the promise presented by the Book of Revelation—of the bodily resurrection of the saints, who will be given perfect bodies free of disease, sin, and death—*Dawn* offers the idea that the zombies are sinners inhabiting hell, which has backed up and overflowed like a sewer through some kind of divine abdication of biblical promise.

True to the classic patterns of religious monstrosity, the band of survivors who fight the chaos monsters are by definition doing battle with "otherness." Here the "other" is a monstrous version of the human, and so like the Christian binary between good and evil, the zombie monster is in binary opposition—or at least in tension—with what is human. If zombies are not demonic and therefore not evil, what precisely makes them monstrous and not-human? Certainly their mindless, catatonic quality renders them suspect. Gretchen Bakke argues that one index of what counts as human in film is a character's capacity to carry narrative weight, to be "seething with story."[42] All we know about most zombies is that they were bitten and/or they died. One thing that marks zombies' status as inhuman is precisely their lack of narrative freight as individuals. Zombies are generic; they are nothing except not alive—remnants, remainders.

The main way that we know zombies are not human is their cannibalism, and this is an interesting way the Romero zombies rhyme with the Haitian case. The genius of Romero was to figure the zombies as both catatonic and cannibals. Romero evokes a kind of spectral remainder of the Caribbean zonbi by reaching back to this iconic historical figure of barbaric otherness during the age of conquest and colonialism. Recent scholarship addresses the recurring theme of cannibalism in early African and American colonialism, beginning with the term's first use by Columbus in writing about natives of Hispaniola, now Haiti. Postcolonial scholars redescribe how the Europeans convinced themselves of the twin facts of native cannibalism and native inhumanity. Linked across representations of Africans, Natives, and Jews, the cannibal was a linchpin Other in the European imagination. The cannibal, writes Elspeth Probyn, "reminds us of that which cannot be included in the *polis*, the social life of man. Yet its very exclusion serves to define humanity."[43] The cannibal functions in the necessary place of the monstrous other in the quasi-religious paradigm of zombie films. Perfectly uncanny, the cannibal is the perfect "something human" outside humanity.

Zombies, Messiahs, and Race

Of course, any secular apocalypse film requires a human messiah hero who will do battle with the death-seeking "other" that threatens to destroy the world. Zombie films' plots center on the survivors, who form a kind of militaristic counterinsurgency but who are weakened by conflicts and power struggles from within. By virtue of being the ultimate survivors, one, two, or a trinity of survivors emerge. Insofar as they occupy the symbolic place of messiah in the narrative of apocalypse, what is interesting here is that from the hero Ben in *Night,* to Peter in *Dawn* (see Figure 4.6) and John in *Day,* to Robert Neville in *I Am Legend,* a central male hero is black, two of whom are West Indian.

The trend begins with Ben in *Night,* who, as Steven Shaviro writes, is "the sole character in the film who is both sympathetic and capable of reasoned action."[44] Self-possessed, direct, logical, capable, Ben understands the zombie threat and takes decisive action to preserve himself and the group that forms by happenstance around him in an abandoned farmhouse. His role is striking, coming in 1968 as it does, in its portrayal of black male leadership and calm authority, at a time when most black males in film were peripheral at best, viciously stereotyped at worst. A white man in the film challenges Ben's authority, but Ben prevails and ends up the lone survivor of the zombie attack (up to a point). Peter and John in the next two Romero films are likewise solid, dependable,

Figure 4.6.
Peter with a gun in *Dawn of the Dead*
(dir. George Romero, United Film
Distribution Company, 1978).

capable black men who strategize and fight their way to survive the zombie outbreak. All three make alliances with the one white woman in each group, who also makes it to the postapocalypse.

Will Smith's character Robert Neville in *Legend* is a striking example of the black male secular messiah.[45] Neville is a consummate hero who has everything: he's a loving husband and father, a dog owner, a U.S. Army colonel, and a PhD in virobiology who is in perfect physical, intellectual, psychological, and moral condition. He has chosen to stay behind in Manhattan, shouting, "I am not going to let this happen," not only to become the lone survivor of an infectious pandemic but to fight off attacking zombies, shelter any remaining survivors he can find, *and* find the cure of the infection to save humanity.

What can we make of the interesting trend that establishes zombies as the monsters black men are to vanquish? In the successful zombie films I am considering, black men are, like the spirits of former slaves in Vodou, once again most efficacious. More than the whites in these films, black men are exemplars of moral personhood. They all work cooperatively with the survivors, they fight capably and ethically, and they are nice to the women. Unlike the trend in action films where the black characters are among the first to be killed, these black men survive by virtue of their own character strengths to see a fragile postapocalyptic future.

A problem here is that black characters in mainstream cinema have always been made to signify both less and more than themselves. On one hand, we get what legal theorist Thomas Ross calls "black abstraction," "the refusal to depict blacks in any real and vividly drawn social context."[46] On the other, black characters often carry *more* meaning than the typical individual character when they are made to signify blackness in general, in addition to its related associations with looseness, aggression, sexuality, and other stereotypes. Related to this, black people have long been deployed "as mirrors that help construct whiteness" in Hollywood films, as Judith Weisenfeld helpfully notes.[47]

So we might wonder, in turn, what it is about *whiteness* in zombie films that the black male messiah characters point to. Here, Richard Dyer makes a fascinating argument. Blacks in film are often depicted as lively, musical, religious, as "having more life" than the whites around them. Whiteness, which appears in mainstream society as "nothing in particular," is "revealed in emptiness, absence, denial, even a kind of death."[48] Examining the Romero films—and I think we might extend his argument to other works as well—Dyer argues that blacks in pop culture are often depicted as "having more life," and "whiteness represents not only rigidity but death."[49]

Dyer goes on to say that "in all three [Romero] films, it is significant that the hero is a black man, and not just because this makes him 'different,' but because it makes it possible to see that *whites are the living dead.*"[50] Zombies are overwhelmingly white in Romero's films, and the small minority of African American zombies have powdered whiteface. Just as whites in society are "ordinary looking," and therefore unmarked as white, as "nothing in particular," so too are the zombies. "If whiteness and death are equated, both are further associated with the USA."[51] In all of these films, the violence of the zombie catastrophe has killed the majority of the population, toppled the government as well as the media, and caused society to cease functioning altogether. Dyer argues that "what finally forces home the specifically white dimension of these zombie–US links are the ways in which the zombies can be destroyed. The first recalls the liberal critique of whites as ruled by their heads; as the radio announcer says, 'Kill the brain and you kill the ghoul' since, it seems, zombies/whites are nothing but their brains."[52]

Romero and post-Romero zombies are cannibals, and white people and zombies are both insatiably destructive consumers. Bakke writes that the fact that zombies eat in order to reproduce—since in most zombie films, the zombie bite is what spreads infection—means that eating is "formally and racially transformative."[53] Eating and consumption are also what make zombies reproductive and monstrous. Allegorically, excessive, rampant consumption is what makes white people white and dead.

A new racial logic seems to be unfolding in action films produced since the turn of the millennium. Bakke identifies the emergence of a new category of whites in these films: "zombies, vampires, the virus-infected and other sorts of *hyperwhites*—that is, whites over-endowed with traditionally white characteristics (cultural as well as racial)—have, since the late 1990s, swarmed the big screen."[54] Zombies, as a subcategory of hyperwhites, are exemplified by the virus infected in *I Am Legend* and in *28 Days Later*. As Bakke notes, they have blue eyes, white skin so translucent that blue veins show through, are hairless, and—like earlier film zombies—have little or no culture or language. It is the hyperwhiteness, and the death they both embody and spread, that is destroying human civilization. And it is this hyperwhite apocalypse that the black male messiah is called upon to destroy. Bakke points out that Neville in *Legend* is actually a black man inherently immune to the virus, immune to whiteness, and that "in making [the black man] into the civilizing agent the filmmakers turn an old story about colonization, savagery, and skin color on its head."[55] In these films, the black male messiah must save humanity from the affliction of *whiteness* (see Figure 4.7).

Figure 4.7.
An "infected" with Robert Neville
(Will Smith) in a still from *I Am Legend*
(dir. Francis Lawrence, Warner Bros.
Pictures, 2007).

This reading raises a number of critical questions. Is this subtrend of black male hero protagonists a progressive one, as these roles feature positive and sympathetic men who fight to (contingent) victory at the end? Or are these black male heroes in white-produced films a new way for white culture to "eat the other," in bell hooks's terms, where whites "spice up" white culture by consuming racial difference?[56] Is it, as Hazel Carby reads multiculturalism, a way to focus once again "on the complexity of response in the (white) reader/student's construction of self in relation to a (black) perceived 'other'"?[57] Is white filmmakers' casting of black men in the role of the messiah just racialization in a new form, one in which blacks, as part of having "more life," are figured as "more religious"? We might compare the black messiah to the postmodern stock character Spike Lee has termed "the super-duper magical negro" in such films as *The Green Mile* (1999) and *The Legend of Bagger Vance* (2000).[58] In these films and others, a black man with magical qualities appears out of nowhere to help a down-and-out white person realize his full humanity or attain a goal.[59] Zombie-fighting heroes possess no magic, but they do function as capable helpmates of their white allies. Instead of redeeming one single broken white person, the zombie-fighting heroes save (what's left of) all of corrupt or infected humanity. It is possible to read the black messiah as an exaggeration of the Magical Negro, insofar as, in zombie films, blackness is figured as a personified antidote to the problem of whiteness, and black individuals are the planet's remediator, rectifier, and redeemer. Yet, arguably, the black male messiah zombie killer is more fully human than the Magical Negro. These black zombie killers are not magical but are ordinary, imperfect, and just as interested in saving themselves as in assisting their white compatriots. What is more, the white man does not end up with the (white) woman in the zombie apocalypse. In all the films I consider here, the black male is paired with the white female in the final scenes of the film. Still, just as the Haitian zonbi myth mystifies the terrorism of slavery and political violence, zombie films displace and mystify the real threats to human survival. Neither nuclear war nor climate change but rather the walking dead will trigger the apocalypse. The films foreclose the possibility of organized, cooperative resistance (since the majority of the population is dead or infected); instead, only a small band of individuals survives.

An interesting feature of these zombie films is that, for better or for worse, the zombie postapocalypse is not only black. By the end of the films (with the exception of *Night*), the remaining survivors are the white woman and the black man, and sometimes others. Whether surviving to stay human by not succumbing to the excessive consumption of whiteness, as in the Romero films and *28 Days Later*, or going so far as to save the future of humanity by finding the cure to the vicious virus of hyperwhiteness in *Legend*, these films all point to a postapocalyptic future that is multiracial. Such a future may not bring us new bodies free of disease and death, as in the Christian story. But the future society will consist of nonwhite and multiraced bodies and, presumably, culture.

Leader of the Zonbis for Obama

Two weeks after the final presidential debate that took place on October 15, 2008, it was time to observe the feast of the Day of the Dead in Haiti. Every November 1 and 2, the cemetery in downtown Port-au-Prince fills with people who come to honor their departed loved ones. Decorated with candles and stacked with plates bearing food offerings, the aboveground cement tombs are beehives of activity. The deity Bawon presides over the spiritual affairs of this necropolis, and the cross that stakes out his presence is ringed with people beseeching him for health, food, and relief from suffering. In 2008, many Haitians added another prayer to their long list: "We pray for Obama," they said. "Give Obama health, bring Obama strength, and let Obama become president." The head of state of the nation of the dead—and the spiritual leader in charge of zonbis— was being petitioned to support the election of the popular young candidate who would become the first black U.S. president.[60]

A common trope in many commentaries during the presidential campaign was that the American psyche, wounded by and guilt-ridden over slavery and racism, longed for the health and wholeness that would be signified by the election of a black president. In other words, President Obama would be a Magical Negro to the entire nation; he would rectify the nation's many problems, assuage white guilt over racism, and simultaneously recast black men as reasoned leaders in place of stereotypes of hypersexuality and criminality. Obama was also referenced in a messianic idiom; scores of journalists, commentators, and artists either likened his campaign to the second coming of Christ or noted the instances where he was described in an exalted, prophetic vocabulary.[61] Elected in the teeth of an economic supercrisis, Obama was figured as the zombie killer who would slay the zombie banks threatening to cannibalize the nation's funds. As the offspring of a white mother and black father, Obama has also been seen both as a symbol of America's multiracial future and as someone with special power and authority to make it a reality. In quickly casting the stumbling, white John McCain as a zombie, the maker of the "cool Obama–zombie McCain" image brought American zombie films into conversation with the dramatically unfolding presidential campaign. McCain was associated with the dead and corrupt cannibalistic policies of the Bush administration, which Obama possessed the natural "cool" to slay—or just ignore, until they go away.

Zombie mythmaking began in Haitian colonialism as a complicated engagement with slavery and death-dealing capitalist formations. In white American books and films, zombie mythmaking became articulated through, and into, a sign for black barbarism, only to reemerge recently as a cipher whose meaning has to do with the death-dealing qualities of whiteness itself. The zombie has been part human, inhuman, slave, revolutionary, cannibal, monster, destroyer, and that which it is moral to destroy. Insofar as the zombie is a cipher, it can be cast to form any number of meaning sets; it is always shifting signification, and yet it can be said to hint at something of the original. After all, we all know what a zombie is.

Notes

1. Image from http://cheezburger.com/View/1184086272. Use of images in this article is by permission, or they are reproduced under fair use as stipulated by section 107 of the U.S. Copyright Act. See the Society for Cinema and Media Studies's statement of fair use best practices for media studies publishing, http://www.cmstudies.org/?page=positions_policies.

2. Seth Grahame-Smith and Jane Austen, *Pride and Prejudice and Zombies: The Classic Regency Romance—Now with Ultraviolent Zombie Mayhem* (Philadelphia: Quirk Books, 2009).

3. Robert Farris Thompson, "An Aesthetic of the Cool," *African Arts* 7, no. 1 (1973): 40–43, 64–67, 89–91. Scores of news articles referred to the "cool" of Barack Obama and his even temperament throughout the campaign and into his presidency.

4. This discussion revisits and expands upon an earlier article, Elizabeth McAlister, "A Sorcerer's Bottle: The Art of Magic in Haiti," in *Sacred Arts of Haitian Vodou*, ed. Donald J. Cosentino, 302–21 (Los Angeles: UCLA Fowler Museum of Cultural History, 1995). For their comments and encouragement, I would like to thank Jill Morowski and Wesleyan Center for Humanities Fellows Gretchen Bakke, Andrew Curran, Joe Fitzpatrick, Peter Gottschalk, Jason Craige Harris, and Letia Perta, as well as Erol Josue, Christina Klein, Nick Marshall, Pierre Minn, Robin Nagle, Katherine M. Smith, and Gina Athena Ulysse and discussants following its presentation at the Society for the Anthropology of Religion, including Paul C. Johnson, Patrick Polk, Kate Ramsey, Karen Richman, and all the students in my course Zombies as Other.

5. Monica Hunter Wilson, "Witch Beliefs and Social Structure," *American Journal of Sociology* 56, no. 4 (1951): 313.

6. I will use the Kreyòl spelling, "zonbi," when discussing the ethnographic practice or thought about it in Haiti, and "zombie" when speaking of ideas and appropriations of the figure.

7. M. L. E. Moreau de Saint-Méry and American Imprint Collection (Library of Congress), *Description Topographique, Physique, Civile, Politique Et Historique De La Partie Francaise De L'isle Saint-Domingue*, 2 vols. (Philadelphia: Chez l'auteur, 1797).

8. http://www.npr.org/templates/story/story.php?storyId=100762999.

9. David John Chalmers, *The Conscious Mind: In Search of a Fundamental Theory* (New York: Oxford University Press, 1996). And it goes on . . . the University of London hosted a conference in September 2009 on "Zombomodernism."

10. Max Brooks, *The Zombie Survival Guide: Complete Protection from the Living Dead* (New York: Three Rivers Press, 2003).

11. Markman Ellis, *The History of Gothic Fiction* (Edinburgh: Edinburgh University Press, 2000).

12. Gilles Deleuze and Félix Guattari, *Anti-Oedipus: Capitalism and Schizophrenia* (Minneapolis: University of Minnesota Press, 1983), 335.

13. Michael Taussig, *Shamanism, Colonialism, and the Wild Man: A Study in Terror and Healing* (Chicago: University of Chicago Press, 1987).

14. Toni Morrison, *Playing in the Dark: Whiteness and the Literary Imagination*, 1st Vintage Books ed. (New York: Vintage Books, 1993), 6–7.

15. See also Mimi Sheller, *Consuming the Caribbean: From Arawaks to Zombies* (London: Routledge, 2003).

16. Even the employed are not making a living wage; in August 2009, the minimum wage in Haiti was *raised* to $3.72 *per day*, from just $1.75. It is against this background of abject poverty and exploitation

that one must understand the religious arts in Haiti. Positioned apart from the societies of "servants of the spirits" in Haitian religion, and working alone for clients, sorcerers like St. Jean function through their exclusion from the normative practices of Vodou.

17. Robert Farris Thompson, Joseph Cornet, and National Gallery of Art (U.S.), *The Four Moments of the Sun: Kongo Art in Two Worlds* (Washington, DC: National Gallery of Art, 1981), 37. This living object surely evolved from both the contained spirits called *minkisi*, in Kongo religion, and *bocio* carvings or *bo* bottles, "empowered cadavers" associated with the spirits of the dead, in Benin and Togo Vodun practice. For the latter, see Suzanne Preston Blier, "Vodun: West African Roots of Vodou," in Cosentino, *Sacred Arts of Haitian Vodou*, 61–87.

18. McAlister, "A Sorcerer's Bottle."

19. Stephan Palmié, "Thinking with Ngangas: Reflections on Embodiment and the Limits of Objectively Necessary Appearances," *Comparative Studies in Society and History* 48, no. 4 (2006): 861.

20. Michael Taussig, "History as Sorcery," *Representations* 7 (Summer 1984): 366.

21. J. Lorand Matory, "Free to Be a Slave: Slavery as Metaphor in the Afro-Atlantic Religions," *Journal of Religion in Africa* 37, no. 3 (2007): 400.

22. Paul Connerton, *How Societies Remember* (Cambridge: Cambridge University Press, 1989), 22. Cited in Rosalind Shaw, *Memories of the Slave Trade: Ritual and the Historical Imagination in Sierra Leone* (Chicago: University of Chicago Press, 2002), 6.

23. Karen McCarthy Brown, *Tracing the Spirit: Ethnographic Essays on Haitian Art: From the Collection of the Davenport Museum of Art* (Davenport, Iowa: The Davenport Museum, distributed by the University of Washington Press, 1995).

24. Taussig, *Shamanism, Colonialism, and the Wild Man*; Jean Comaroff and John Comaroff, "Alien-Nation: Zombies, Immigrants, and Millennial Capitalism," *The South Atlantic Quarterly* 101, no. 4 (2002): 1–25.

25. For helpful descriptions and analyses of history and Cubans' dealings with spirits of the dead, see Stephan Palmié, *Wizards and Scientists: Explorations in Afro-Cuban Modernity and Tradition* (Durham, N.C.: Duke University Press, 2002); Kenneth Routon, "Conjuring the Past: Slavery and the Historical Imagination in Cuba," *American Ethnologist* 35, no. 4 (2008): 632–49; Todd Ramon Ochoa, *Society of the Dead: Quita Manaquita and Palo Praise in Cuba* (Berkeley: University of California Press, 2010).

26. Wade Davis, *Passage of Darkness: The Ethnobiology of the Haitian Zombie* (Chapel Hill: University of North Carolina Press, 1988). Davis's research sparked great controversy, and his hypothesis has not been conclusively validated to my knowledge, although the high-profile traditional priest Max Beauvoir, and others, have supported it. I am not in a position to evaluate the science at issue; my interest lies in examining the social narratives surrounding people who are claimed to be zombies, which often follow the pattern Davis and Beauvoir outline.

27. Shaw, *Memories of the Slave Trade*.

28. Edwidge Danticat, *After the Dance: A Walk through Carnival in Jacmel, Haiti*, 1st ed. (New York: Crown Journeys, 2002), 69–70.

29. Kaiama L. Glover, "Exploiting the Undead: The Usefulness of the Zombie in Haitian Literature," *Journal of Haitian Studies* 11, no. 2 (2005): 105–21.

30. An exception to this is Seabrook, who describes Haitian workers as "zombies" who work like slaves in a description consistent with capitalism. William Seabrook, *The Magic Island* (New York: Literary Guild of America, 1929).

31. Laënnec Hurbon, *Le Barbare Imaginaire* (Port-au-Prince, Haiti: H. Deschamps, 1987).

32. Jamie Russell, *Book of the Dead: The Complete History of Zombie Cinema* (Surrey, U.K.: FAB Press, 2007).

33. http://tvtropes.org/pmwiki/pmwiki.php/Main/NotUsingtheZWord.

34. As cited in Timothy K. Beal, *Religion and Its Monsters* (New York: Routledge, 2002), 54.

35. Conrad Ostwalt, "Armageddon at the Millennial Dawn," *Journal of Religion and Film* 4, no. 1 (2000), http://digitalcommons.unomaha.edu/jrf/vol4/iss1/4.

36. Beal, *Religion and Its Monsters*, 15.

37. Ibid., 22.

38. David Pagano, "The Space of Apocalypse in Zombie Cinema," in *Zombie Culture: Autopsies of the Living Dead*, ed. Shawn and Marc Leverette McIntosh (Lanham, Md.: Scarecrow Press, 2008), 71.

39. Ibid.

40. Richard Kearney, *Strangers, Gods, and Monsters: Interpreting Otherness* (New York: Routledge, 2003), 97.

41. This term is coined in the context of anticonsumer activism by performance-artist-activist Reverend Billy, whose website is http://www.revbilly.com/.

42. Gretchen Bakke, "Continuum of the Human," *Camera Obscura* 22, no. 3 (2007): 64.

43. Elspeth Probyn, *Carnal Appetites: Foodsexidentities* (London: Routledge, 2000), 88.

44. Steven Shaviro, *The Cinematic Body*, vol. 2 of *Theory Out of Bounds* (Minneapolis: University of Minnesota Press, 1993), 87.

45. This film is a remake of *The Omega Man* (1971), in which the "nightseekers" are more like vampires than zombies, and in which the protagonist was not black; the screenplay of *Legend* apparently did not specify the race of its hero. Also, the film's "second ending" (on DVD only) might change my analysis here. Nevertheless, the version of the film as released to theaters is what concerns us.

46. Thomas Ross, "The Rhetorical Tapestry of Race: White Innocence and Black Abstraction," *William and Mary Law Review* 32, no. 1 (1990): 2.

47. Judith Weisenfeld, "Projecting Blackness," in *Race, Nation, and Religion in the Americas*, ed. Henry and Elizabeth McAlister Goldschmidt (Oxford: Oxford University Press, 2004), 308.

48. Richard Dyer, "White," *Screen* 29, no. 4 (1988): 44.

49. Ibid., 59.

50. Ibid., emphasis added.

51. Ibid., 60.

52. Ibid., 61.

53. Gretchen Bakke, "Dead White Men: An Essay on the Changing Dynamics of Race in American Action Cinema," *Anthropological Quarterly* 83, no. 2 (2010): 414.

54. Ibid., 407–8.

55. Ibid., 424.

56. bell hooks, *Black Looks: Race and Representation* (Boston: South End Press, 1992).

57. Hazel Carby, "The Multicultural Wars," *Radical History Review* 54, no. 7 (1992): 3.

58. Susan Gonzales, "Director Spike Lee Slams 'Same Old Stereotypes in Today's Films,'" *Yale Bulletin and Calendar*, March 2, 2001.

59. Audrey Colombe, "White Hollywood's New Black Boogeyman," *Jump Cut: A Review of Contemporary Media* 45 (2002), https://www.ejumpcut.org/archive/jc45.2002/colombe/blackmentxt.html.

60. Thanks for this observation go to Katherine M. Smith, personal communication, August 2009.

61. David Ehrenstein, "Obama the 'Magical Negro,'" *LA Times*, March 19, 2007. See more than one hundred examples of commentators using messianic language in reference to Obama at http://obamamessiah.blogspot.com/.

Slavoj Žižek, the Death Drive, and Zombies
A Theological Account

OLA SIGURDSON

Something uncanny is haunting the West—the specter of religion. The talk of the "return of religion" or its "new visibility" is now ubiquitous in academia, after the demise of any strong form of the sociological thesis of the death of religion as an inevitable aspect of modernization. How best to interpret these changed circumstances may well be a matter of argument, but I would suggest that one of the philosophically and theologically more interesting aspects of our so-called postsecular condition is the way it undermines some of the categories through which at least Western modernity has come to understand its own cultural and social context. One binary category that recently has come under critical scrutiny is the oppositional understanding of religion and secularity. Rather than regarding these binary designations as a part of the structure of reality itself, it has been increasingly obvious that both religion and secularity, as concepts, need to be understood historically. This could be the occasion for a long conceptual and cultural analysis of the histories of these concepts, but suffice it to say for now that "secularization" was from the beginning a theological concept, meaning that something—a thing, a territory, an institution, or a person—passes over from an ecclesiastically defined condition to a worldly defined condition, as when a Roman Catholic priest no longer lives in his religious community but in the "secular" world or when a piece of land passes over from ecclesial to worldly possession.[1] And even when the concept is used in a more polemical way, as a characterization of a nation-state no longer ruled by a particular church, it still belongs to the effective history of theology, so that a (purportedly) secularized nation such as Sweden still is a recognizably Lutheran secularized nation. There have been a number of fine analyses of the mutual dependence of the European process of secularization on religion, and vice versa, and I will not repeat them here.[2] They all suggest that the current configuration of the relationship between religion and secularity—whatever it happens to be—is a contingent, historical development rather than a lawlike historical necessity. As all contingent, historical developments, it can change. One result of the historical deconstruction of the binary opposition between religion and secularity is that both of these concepts become more ambiguous. I would suggest that if there is any academic mileage to be had from such a concept as the "postsecular," it is when it is used as recognition of the ambiguity of our current situation: it is neither religious nor secular but may be more aware of its hybridity than in previous decades.[3] This is why any talk of the "return of religion" could be misleading, as it suggests that something called religion once was here, then went away, but now is back—a little like my colleagues at the University of Gothenburg remarked about my ten-month hiatus in Princeton before I returned to Sweden. But this would be a misinterpretation of religion, I would suggest, because, among other things, it is not a "thing" or an "essence" that keeps its form intact throughout its movements in history. The deconstruction of the binary opposition between religion and secularity means, perhaps, that religion never did go away but was transformed and now is transformed to a more visible state again. This is why any shift in the perception of today often is accompanied or even brought about by a reinterpretation of history. If yesterday was like that, today cannot be like this.

One sign of this emerging hybridity between religion and secularity in philosophy is the interest in theology that could be found in contemporary politically radical philosophy. Unpersuaded by the thesis of the "end of history" or by the virtues of liberal capitalism, some of today's most prominent Marxists have turned to religion and theology for inspiration. This, to be sure, should not be understood as a religious conversion; for the most part, as far as I can understand, most of these political philosophers are as unbelieving as ever, and in no way do they disregard religion as a source of oppression in the world today, even though they might be inclined not to pose religion as the sole cause of human misery, but rather, in line with Karl Marx himself, as "the sigh of the oppressed creature, the heart of a heartless world, and the soul of soulless conditions."[4] As long as people live in oppressive conditions, religion will be around, according to this Marxist interpretation, and the only way of bringing about the end of religion is to end self-inflicted human misery. In the meantime, theology, as the theoretical reflection on religion, is a powerful instrument for both analysis and critique, as it has always suggested that another world is, in fact, possible.

One of the more famous representatives of this trend of using theology for his own critical theory without being committed to any religious belief in the traditional sense is the Slovenian philosopher and psychoanalyst Slavoj Žižek, whose use of theology will be the topic of this article. Žižek is the author of more than twenty books (and that is counting only those in English) and is regarded as a contemporary reviver (not uncontroversially) of both the Marxist and the psychoanalytic legacies, as well as an astute political and social commentator and cultural critic. He has coauthored several collaborations with British Radical Orthodoxy theologian John Milbank, *The Monstrosity of Christ* and *Paul's New Moment*, as well as with Croatian theologian Boris Gunjević in *God in Pain: Inversions of Apocalypse*. Theology has a marked presence throughout his work, especially since his interpretation of the German Idealist philosopher F. W. J. Schelling in 1996.[5] Besides incorporating in his theoretical work interpretations of popular movies, Žižek has himself been the subject of at least three films, including *The Pervert's Guide to Cinema* (2006). And finally, despite unambiguously describing himself as an atheist,

Žižek believes that "the Christian legacy is worth fighting for" and that "to become a true dialectical materialist, one should go through the Christian experience."[6] Žižek is, in other words, a decidedly Protestant atheist and continually draws upon the Christian theological tradition, but all the while suggesting that it is only through a materialistic, Marxist interpretation of its legacy that its emancipatory potential is truly released.[7]

There are, of course, many ways that lead into Žižek's use of theology, but in this article I have chosen to focus upon his understanding of the Freudian death drive as well as the figure of the zombie retrieved from popular culture. The reason for this perspective is a comment by Žižek that the reason for his holding on to the term *theology*, even for his own project, is that theology "is a name for what is, in a revolutionary subject, beyond a mere collection of individual humans acting together."[8] There is, then, in Žižek's philosophy a concept of transcendence, although a wholly immanent understanding of transcendence. This notion of something within human beings that is more than human beings themselves is what Žižek calls, in more psychoanalytical terminology, the *death drive*. The death drive is, for a Freudian interpretation, the immortal principle within human beings; in Žižek's words, it is "an uncanny excess of life, . . . an 'undead' urge which persists beyond the (biological) cycle of life and death, of generation and corruption."[9] And what is the "undead" if not a zombie? This is an interpretation of the undead that Žižek himself has advanced, but, curiously enough, given his interest in popular culture, including horror movies, he is relatively silent on the topic, except for some significant passages to which I will come in due time. In this article I will take my cue from Žižek's suggestion that it is the awareness of the "undead" dimension of human existence that earns the nomination "theology" for his philosophy, moving from an exposition of the Freudian death drive to a discussion of zombies in contemporary media toward a critical assessment of Žižek's use of theology.

The Death Drive

What is the death drive? It is a psychoanalytic concept that Sigmund Freud minted in his 1920 publication *Beyond the Pleasure Principle*. Although put forward more as a hypothesis than as a fact, it broke with, modified, or developed his previous psychoanalytic theory (depending upon your interpretation), which was more or less centered upon the pleasure principle, or *eros*, as the main principle governing the human psyche.[10] To Freud in *Beyond the Pleasure Principle*, however, the striving for pleasure is not enough to explain some phenomena that he encountered in his psychoanalytic practice, for example, in his treatment of war neurosis and the experience of trauma (what we nowadays call posttraumatic stress disorder, PTSD); the "compulsion to repeat" was now seen as the symptom of quite another principle, namely, the death drive. Human beings are not solely governed by the pursuit of pleasure but also, perhaps, by a principle that seems to be almost its opposite, the principle of death. This principle was not an aspect of the pleasure principle but something more primitive, and it suggested to Freud that dreams could be about something else than the mere fulfillment of wishes. In this publication, where he first put forward this hypothesis, Freud explained this drive in a biological fashion, suggesting that it is to be seen as an inherent trait of all organic life to return to inertia.[11] This might be the reason that the original German *Trieb* in Freud's text was translated as "instinct" rather than as the more direct and also more active "drive."[12] The *Todestrieb*, however, is more uncanny than an instinct, as it seems to run counter to the interest of self-preservation that is essential to a biological organism, and the preferred translation would, then, be "death drive."

This death drive is occasionally experienced by the subject as the possession of a "demonic power" in that it, contrary to the subject's conscious wish, seemingly forces her or him to destructive behaviors, as when a person constantly experiences that she is betrayed by her friends or repeatedly ends his love affairs in the same disastrous way.[13] These are, of course, to Freud not at all the effects of an external power but the workings of the unconscious psyche that finds expression in compulsive behavior. It is because of the death drive's unconscious nature that it is experienced by the subject as an external power over which he or she has no conscious control, and because it works against the conscious wishes and the explicit well-being of the subject, it is experienced by the person as a malign power. Recurring dreams about the original occurrence of a trauma, and children's games such as the famous Fort-Da game of Freud's grandson, as well as compulsive behavior, are the psyche's ways of trying to master a trauma retrospectively.[14]

There has been a lot of discussion of the death drive in Freud, one central issue of which concerns, among other things, where he derived the idea in the first place. It has a striking similarity to Friedrich Nietzsche's contrast between Apollo and Dionysus in *The Birth of Tragedy* from 1872, but Freud denied having read Nietzsche at the time of the conception of his ideas. Arthur Schopenhauer's essay "Über die anscheinende Absichtlichkeit im Schicksale des Einzelnen" (1851), however, is mentioned by Freud in *Beyond the Pleasure Principle* as a parallel account of how death is really the purpose of life.[15] But Freud's intellectual debts are of little importance here, except to note, perhaps, that Freud's publication *Beyond the Pleasure Principle* reflects a more general postwar emphasis on the persistent irrationality at the heart of human existence. The parallelism to both Nietzsche and Schopenhauer can be compelling without suggesting any direct influence on Freud's text.

To Žižek, the death drive is central to his philosophical project, but his understanding of it is indebted to the reinterpretation of Freudian psychoanalysis by Jacques Lacan, so we need to say something about Lacan and the death drive before we come to Žižek. Lacan also valued the death drive concept as central to psychoanalysis, but his interpretation of it changed during his career. Most importantly for us, in his later works, Lacan did, contrary to Freud, dissociate the drive from biology, locating it instead in culture rather than nature, and he also saw it as an aspect of every drive, not as a drive separate from *eros*. This is exploited by Žižek, who regards the death drive as what biological instinct becomes once it enters language as a differential structure.

The death drive, in Žižek's Lacanian understanding, is also, as mentioned in the beginning, the way that "immortality" gets our attention according to psychoanalysis. This might be a somewhat surprising claim, but I will try to make clear what Žižek means by this. Immortality, to begin with, should not here be understood as some kind of belief in the immortality of the soul or as a resurrection of the body, or indeed as any other traditional religious or philosophical rendering. His concept of immortality, rather, lies more closely to what Søren Kierkegaard suggests in his *The Concept of Anxiety* from 1844, that anxiety is what reveals our innermost freedom to us, a freedom that is in excess of any particular realization of this freedom, so that our possibilities never are in accord with our actuality; our existence is always "out of joint" with itself.[16] Our anxiety is not caused by the fact that we are limited, finite creatures, but quite the opposite, because we are, in a certain way, unlimited, infinite creatures. By reducing our existence to finite factors—genes, biology, social determination—we try to escape, in vain, the vertigo of being free creatures, never fully determined by our biology or our circumstances. Žižek's preferred term for this immortality is *excess of life* or *undeadness*, and especially the last term should direct our associations toward zombies. But before we enter zombieland, we should linger for a while around his understanding of the death drive.

Even in Žižek, the death drive is a principle that works against the self-preservation of the ego, but this does not mean that it unambiguously should be understood as opposed to life.[17] In a helpful gloss on Freud's concept, the philosopher Jonathan Lear has pointed out that we need to beware of thinking about the death drive as a "thing" or as something we really understand, and I shall follow Lear here, as I think he has accomplished one of the clearest expositions of the concept, even for our understanding of Žižek.[18] The importance of not interpreting the death drive as a "thing," according to Lear, is that we run the risk of understanding it as a teleological principle that is somehow contrary to the teleological principle that is directed toward human flourishing as its goal, when, in reality, it is the suspension of any teleology as such. The death drive is not ordered toward death as its *telos* but is, rather, just a disruption—it is devoid of purpose; it is not *for* anything. The "compulsion to repeat" is the psyche's way of defending itself against such traumatic disruptions. It is an epiphenomenon of the failure of giving meaning to the original trauma, "the stillborn attempt to heal the wound by dreaming a meaning," to use Lear's helpful phrasing.[19] This is where, I believe, it is important to recognize the difference between an instinct and the drive, because where the instinct is teleologically ordered to the preservation of biological life, and therefore serves some purpose, the drive is purposeless and has no direction. Lear is, to be sure, critical of what he believes is Freud's reintroduction of a hidden teleological principle, but as "death," in Freud's text, functions as an enigmatic signifier, Freud should really have seen through his own move, not complementing one principle, pleasure, with another, death, thus giving the impression that the death drive was a "thing," when it really is an insight into how the human psyche works.[20] This disruption that is the death drive is neither good nor bad, but just how the psyche works; whether it is for good or bad really depends upon what happens next. The principle of the death drive—if we do not take the term "principle" literally as something that we claim to know—is a metapsychological principle of how the psyche is disrupted by itself from within in a kind of pure creativity that simply is the presupposition of there being conscious life at all. "Freud's deepest insight," Lear suspects, "is that, appearances to the contrary, life can never be lived without remainder"—or, to put it differently, life never coincides with mere biological existence but presupposes some initial impulse without which it would never get going.[21] This impulse always threatens any established order as the moment of madness always presupposed by but never exhausted in any kind of sense and order. The death drive is the way life always exceeds itself, the sheer pressure to be alive, and so its disruptions are not equal to any particular possibility but "a possibility for new possibilities."[22]

Although Lear does not mention the theological connotations of this language, there is a certain structural affinity with the understanding of God as the transcendent yet still immanent source of our human freedom and creativity, a source that could never be fully thematized without remainder without compromising this transcendence. The parallel is pointed out, however, from a psychoanalytic perspective by Eric L. Santner, who writes of "an enigmatic density of desire calling for response beyond any rule-governed reciprocity" in the midst of human life and suggests that "God is above all the name for the pressure of being alive in the world, to open to the too much of pressure generated in large measure by the uncanny presence of my neighbor."[23] Thus, Žižek assigns the term *theology* to this "more" that is active in revolutionary subjects. Indeed, the association of the death drive with Christian theology is a recurring theme in Žižek, up to the point where he suggests that Christ is the embodiment of this "excessive" or "undead" dimension of human existence, also quoting the Gospel of John: "I am come that they might have life, and that they might have it more abundantly."[24] Through Christ we can assume this abundant life as our own, thereby avoiding its projection on some other. But to do this, to assume the excess of life, we must, paradoxically, die to the world and be born again (to use a Pauline terminology), shedding our defenses against this excess of life. Only thus can we "traverse the fantasies" with which we try to heal the wound or cover up the abyss of our existence. Only through dying to the world, undergoing what Žižek calls a "subjective destitution" where we recognize the horrible fact that any redemption is totally up to ourselves, do we tap into the excess of life, which changes the very coordinates with the help of which we make sense of our lives—which is why Žižek calls it a "revolution." It is through our identification with Christ on the cross—as the incarnation of the excess that forever prevents us from attaining identity with ourselves—that we come to recognize this "undead" dimension of ourselves, what in us is more than ourselves. Please note here that Žižek's use of theology is in service to his psychoanalytic theory, which does not discount its authenticity, to be sure, but only signifies that its meaning should not necessarily be associated with traditional Christian theology.

Žižek does not deny, of course, that in a sense we are limited, finite creatures, determined by our cultural, social, and religious contexts, and so forth. But what he suggests is that through a materialist version of grace, we could avoid being defined by our circumstances. Even if we never can undo these circumstances, we can nevertheless transcend them in a radical act—and this is "what Freud called 'death drive' and what German Idealism called 'radical negativity.'"[25] In other words, the negative force of the death drive is at the same time a positive force. It is, to Žižek, the possibility of a radical act of renewal or, with Lear's words, "a possibility for new possibilities." But why Žižek's predilection for talking about it in terms of "undeadness"? It is high time that we turn to the zombies.

Zombies: The Return of the Undead

Despite the attractiveness of zombies in contemporary popular culture, severe misunderstandings remain that need to be cleared up before any serious discussion of the undead can be achieved. The most important of these is the confusion of zombies with vampires. Owing to the simultaneous popularity of vampires and zombies in contemporary popular culture, they are sometimes seen as different species of the same genus. Nothing could be further from the truth. To begin with, zombies do not attend high school, like the vampire in Stephenie Meyer's Twilight series. In fact, they could not, as they hardly communicate at all in the ordinary sense of the word, aside from a grunt here and there (which, one might argue, still seems to be a requirement for attending any kind of high school). Neither do they engage in amorous or erotic relationships with human beings, as is the case in the Southern Vampire Mysteries by Charlaine Harris, also known through the TV series *True Blood*. Unlike vampires, zombies are not desirous creatures; as will shortly become clear, zombies are in most cases characterized by drive rather than desire—as desire, from a psychoanalytic standpoint, presupposes some kind of symbolic structure that seems to be absent from most of the canonical stories about zombies. Their craving for human flesh is thus utterly different from the vampiric thirst for blood, as it never becomes or is part of some elaborate network of signification that encompasses both human beings and their inhuman counterparts. Finally, in terms of class, there is a distinct difference between the two, as vampires often are rendered as culturally, economically, intellectually, and sometimes even hereditarily aristocratic, whereas zombies are most decidedly a part of the proletariat, as is shown by the marked sensitivity to power issues in many of the classic zombie movies.

A preliminary characterization of zombies will suffice for the moment. Before I elaborate a bit further on this theme, however, it is important to establish what I regard as the canonical exploration of zombies in popular culture, namely, the zombie films by the American director, screenwriter, and editor George A. Romero, especially his first feature film *Night of the Living Dead* from 1968.[26] I would like to emphasize that by no means am I here expressing some idiosyncratic view of my own. Rather, I merely follow what seems to me to be a unanimous view among zombie scholars. For example, the religious studies scholar Kim Paffenroth, in his *Gospel of the Living Dead* (2006), suggests that "when one speaks of zombie movies today, one is really speaking of movies that are either made by or directly influenced by one man, director George A. Romero," and he goes on to claim that "Romero's landmark film, *Night of the Living Dead* (1968), has defined the zombie genre since its release, and has even spilled over into the depiction of zombies in any medium, including books, comic books, video and board games, and action figures."[27] Other scholars have suggested that *Night of the Living Dead* "defined the modern horror movie" or that "all modern works in the zombie canon are rooted in the kind of ghoul that first appeared in George Romero's *Night of the Living Dead*."[28] Even if there is an abundance of references to the flesh-hungry, undead ghouls we call zombies both before Romero—for example, in romantic authors such as Mary Shelley or H. P. Lovecraft—and beyond him, in TV series like *Walking Dead* (2010), I take it that we can rely on Romero for the distinctively *contemporary* understanding of zombies.

What does Žižek make of the zombies? Surprisingly little, given Žižek's interest in popular culture, especially horror movies, as well as the centrality of the death drive for his theory. As far as I have been able to discern, Romero's *Night of the Living Dead* is mentioned only once, in one of Žižek's introductions to Lacan, *Looking Awry* from 1991, where the return of the dead is crowned the "fundamental fantasy of contemporary mass culture."[29] Žižek also recognizes the seminal influence of Romero's movie, as the "unattained archetype of a long series." The zombies or "undead" in this movie "are not portrayed as embodiments of pure evil, or a simple drive to kill or revenge, but as sufferers, pursuing their victims with an awkward persistence, colored by a kind of infinite sadness."[30] But then Žižek goes on to ask the perhaps naive but still pertinent question why the dead return at all. The answer we get from Lacan is the same as we get from popular culture, namely, because they are not properly buried (I am not sure that this is the answer we get from Romero's movies, but be that as it may). In more psychoanalytical terms, the dead return because their deaths are not properly inscribed in the text of the tradition, and because of this, they have to haunt us instead of living on in our memory. Another of the few occasions when the zombies get mentioned in Žižek's oeuvre is apropos to the alleged incommensurability between human existence as objective embodiment and subjective consciousness, where Žižek suggests that "we all *are* zombies who are not aware of it, who are self-deceived into perceiving themselves as self-aware."[31] Even if this indeed is not unrelated to Žižek's theory of the death drive, in this article, I have to focus more directly on this theory itself. If we are to find Žižek's more pronounced view on zombies, we have to look elsewhere than to direct engagement with them, to Žižek's returning discussions of the "undead." But to get the right angle on these discussions from the perspective of this article, I shall interweave Žižek's theory with Romero's films to let the zombies enlighten us about how Žižek understands the "undead."

According to the Zombie Research Society, a zombie is "a biologically definable, animated being occupying a human corpse."[32] This is a minimal but apt definition that is consistent with the way zombies are portrayed in Romero's zombie movies, but a few things need to be added.[33] What is horrifying about Romero's zombie movies, except for the fact that the dead return to life, is their monomaniacal persistence in hunting for and devouring human flesh. This craving to eat the living does not seem to be for purposes of nourishment, however, as zombies seemingly can go on forever without actually eating. To eat the living seems to be their sole purpose, and this is a purpose they follow mindlessly, without any regard whatsoever to their own self-preservation. This is why zombies could and should be associated with the death drive beyond any conscious desire; they are the embodiment of an imbecile drive outside of any conscious plan or goal, but also beyond any animal instinct for the preservation of the individual or the species. Along with the zombie movies, then, "undeadness" in Žižek is really what distinguishes us as human beings. Thus what is "inhuman" about zombies is that in us which at the same time makes us into human beings and not just animals. Let me show this through an illustrative example from one of Žižek's commentators, the theologian Marcus Pound, who turns our attention to an episode of *The Simpsons* where Lisa wishes to investigate whether her brother Bart is dumber than a hamster.[34] She devises a booby trap with either some food for the hamster or a cupcake for her brother, where the one that tries to obtain it is exposed to an electric shock. After repeated attempts, the hamster learns to avoid the food, whereas Bart persists in reaching for the cupcake until his synapses are burned out. It is this persistence of pleasure beyond anything remotely beneficial for one's own well-being that distinguishes human life from mere instinctual life, and this is why zombies are not just something different from human beings but the terrifying "inhuman" or "undead" core of our innermost being.

That zombie movies really are about an aspect of ourselves rather than just a figuration of some monster, entirely different from human beings, should be clear. This has surely not been lost to most commentators on the genre, whether influenced by psychoanalysis or not, but still needs to be pointed out, as zombies sometimes merely are pictured as an alien threat, as for instance in the political scientist Daniel W. Drezner's interesting but ultimately unsuccessful book *Theories of International Politics and Zombies* (2011). To understand this is essential to coming to grips with what is a defining characteristic of Romero's zombie movies: their cultural criticism. Indeed, zombie movies, as well as most or perhaps even all other movies, belong to a voyeuristic art form that also caters to our desire to be mesmerized and seduced. As all movies are polysemic, open to many interpretations rather than just one, to watch a zombie movie, accordingly, must not necessarily be seen as a kind of social critique; with all its violence, the zombie movie is susceptible to the kind of escapist pleasure–pain typical of the voyeuristic experience of horror movies. But that being said, and given that a movie can be simultaneously both parody and prophecy, the continuing appeal of Romero's zombie movies lies in their ability to address a number of political issues relevant to the times of their original screenings as well as our own time. An exhaustive discussion of this is well beyond the scope of this article, but let me briefly state a few of these issues.[35]

In *Night of the Living Dead*, for instance, the predatory nature of the zombies is reciprocated by the small band of human beings who have taken refuge from the zombies in a small farmhouse; despite the external threat of the zombies, their constant bickering and self-assuming pride prevent them from forming any consistent resistance to the threat. Even in the face of an imminent threat to their lives, they find it possible to pursue their own selfish agendas. But the film is not only an allegory of human depravity; it also addresses more concrete social vices, such as sexism and racism. To exemplify the latter, one of the leading characters in the movie is Ben, a black man, who, despite the strife, makes it to the final scene. There, suddenly, while looking at the approaching zombie-killing posse that finally has come to his rescue, he is shot at point-blank range, mistaken for one of the zombies by the posse (portrayed in the all too familiar American lynch mob genre). Not accidentally, this movie was released in 1968, three years after the killing of Malcolm X and the same year as the killing of Martin Luther King Jr.—in other words, at a time of intense racial tension in American society.

Dawn of the Dead, the sequel from 1978 (with an interesting remake by Zack Snyder in 2004), covers slightly different ground in its critique of society; its main focus is the sin of consumerism. The setting of its story is for the most part a shopping mall at a time when these were not as omnipresent in America as they are today. "What the hell is it?" one of the characters in the movie asks when they are approaching this huge building in a helicopter, searching for a place to land on its roof. Despite their precarious situation, the small group of human beings on the run from the zombies cannot resist the temptation of indulging in the goods on display in the shopping mall, now up for grabs given that all shops are abandoned in light of the encroaching zombies. The most telling scenes of this movies are, perhaps, two: first, right after landing on the roof of the shopping mall and seeing all the zombies occupying it, Fran asks Steve, "Why do they come here?" to which she receives the reply: "Some kind of instinct. Memory. What they used to do. This was an important place in their lives." The second notable scene is the very last scene, where, during the roll of the end credits, the zombies have fully overtaken the mall and are happily shopping to the sound of the Muzak in the background. Both scenes emphasize, comically, how there is a faint, remaining echo of the undead's humanity in their habit of going shopping. Paffenroth comments: "This is the first of several points on which Romero will equate zombies and humans in the film, and it is the most important: both zombies and humans are insane and insatiable consumers."[36] This is another example of how Romero's zombie movies capture the political issues of the day, potentially offering a critique of contemporary society.

What Romero's zombie movies show us, then, is not that zombies are aliens that need to be defeated so that human life can continue but that zombies represent the alien *within* us. Indeed, zombie movies are almost always apocalyptic in the sense that they confront us with a scenario where human life is threatened, but the apocalypse should not be understood as a vision of a dystopic future but instead as an apocalypse of the here-and-now. Zombies are liminal creatures, and what Romero's movies do, in their best moments, is start out with an oppositional relation between human beings and zombies that is subsequently, in the diegetic progress of the movie, undermined. What should be disturbing to us in watching a zombie movie is not (or perhaps not only) that zombies devour human beings but that human beings feed on human beings. As Paffenroth puts it, "what makes zombies more terrifying than other monsters is that this confusing resemblance of zombies to normal people never goes away."[37]

After this brief excursion into Romero's popular zombie movies, we can return to Žižek by noting that, for my purposes, the point is not that the "undead" or excessive aspect of our existence is the drive to consumption. Rather, the point of the zombies is that they embody this inhuman kernel in human existence to the effect that they confront us with it. Zombies are not a fantasy; quite the contrary, they stand for the overcoming of fantasies about our identity, fantasies that soothe us into thinking that deep down there is some positive attribute, some sublime factor that defines me as a human being, my experience of myself. Paradoxically, at our most intimate, we encounter what Lacan termed the "ex-timate" kernel of our being, that is, something other, an opaque density that is not me but is what makes me me—a zombie or, in other words, the death drive. This ex-timate kernel is not something that exists, according to Žižek, but something that *insists*.[38] It is as a kind of indestructible life force that the zombies insist, which, in the words of British philosopher Stephen Mulhall, becomes "a nightmare embodiment of the natural realm understood as utterly subordinate to, utterly exhausted by, the twinned Darwinian drives to survive and reproduce."[39] Again, we should heed the warning of Jonathan Lear of turning this death drive into a "thing"; for Žižek, it is most decidedly a "no-thing," a force of negativity; it is the abyssal freedom of human subjectivity that opens up when we traverse our fantasies. The aim of analysis, says Žižek, is "to deprive the subject of the very fundamental fantasy that regulates the universe of his (self-)experience," and to this end, the zombie movie can be complicit.[40] It is not by accident that it is through cinema that we are confronted with this death drive in the form of zombies; as says the passage by Lacan that Žižek is fond of quoting, "truth has the structure of fiction."[41] Because of the nature of the truth we are exposed to, the only access to it is an indirect road, because what we need to wake up from is not sleep as such but the fantasy that structures our reality while we are awake.[42]

A Return to/of Theology

It is now time to draw this article to a close and return to the question from where I began, namely, what do the "undead" have to do with theology? As we have seen, for Žižek, "undeadness" is another name for the Freudian death drive. This death drive could never be understood in a direct way, first because it is not a "thing," and second— and perhaps more important—because normally it remains hidden to us, unconscious, covered by fantasies that structure our perception of ourselves so that we will not be confronted with the madness that is the presupposition of our ordered existence. We only notice its presence indirectly, through its effects upon us; and to trace the origin of these symptoms, we have to look elsewhere, to fiction. Zombies are a fictional embodiment of this "undead" aspect of ourselves, which, according to Žižek, is that which is in us that is more than ourselves: immortality or freedom. Noticeable is that Žižek's understanding of this death drive is rhetorically cloaked in quite radical language, which I have gone along with here, in the example with the zombies. To Lear and Santner, who come quite close to what Žižek is saying in substance, even if not in terminology, the death drive presents itself in less dystopic terms as "a possibility for new possibilities" or "the pressure of being alive in the world." But Žižek has a reason for the extremity of his language, and that is his political ambition, as he thinks that a radical, and not only piecemeal, renewal of society is necessary for any serious alternative to capitalism. Quite like the zombie movies, there is in Žižek's latest work a positive use of apocalyptic imagery, as is evident, for example, in the title of his 2010 book *Living in the End Times*. Along with Christianity, Žižek believes that change is, in fact, possible and that the future does not necessarily need to imply just more of the same. This is because "at the very core of Christianity there is a . . . destructive negativity which ends not in a chaotic Void but reverts (organizes itself) into a new Order, imposing itself on reality."[43] But that does not mean that Žižek himself subscribes to any traditional form of Christianity; on the contrary, he believes that it is only his version of atheistic materialism that truly realizes the emancipatory potential inherent in it, and so with the help of psychoanalysis and German Idealism, he has embarked upon an ambitious project of reinterpretation. His use of theology is thus decidedly untraditional, compared to most historical and contemporary theology. I have elsewhere argued for a characterization of his theory as a version of Protestant atheism, and although he wants to emphasize the importance of institutions (which, typologically at least, is more Catholic in emphasis), this means that however atheistic his theory might be, it is still recognizably Christian.

One way of evaluating Žižek's use of theology would be to embark in a direct discussion of the lack of a transcendent transcendence in favor of an immanent transcendence. A reason for Žižek's rejection of a transcendent transcendence is because such an endeavor always runs the risk of a reification of God; that most traditional theology is strategically aware of this risk is unfortunately not discussed by Žižek and might be a point of critique, as this highlights Žižek's somewhat limited theological repertoire. Nevertheless, instead of pursuing this line of critique, I shall stick to the theme of this article and instead reflect further on the features of undeadness, comparing it with Augustine's understanding of human subjectivity in *Confessions*, and then conclude by posing a critical question to Žižek's political philosophy regarding human alienation.

What occurs to me from Žižek's discussion of the death drive is that it offers, in contemporary terms, a protest against any too facile or one-dimensional view of the human psyche that does not recognize its entanglement in all sorts of conflicting projects, often unrecognized by its own conscious will and often also in direct conflict with the most obvious form of well-being of a subject. It has been suggested by contemporary biblical scholarship that when Paul in Romans 7:15 says, "I do not understand my own actions. For I do not do what I want, but I do the very thing I hate," this is not an example of Western introspective consciousness but rather of living before or after the reception of the Good News. I certainly think there is something to be said for this interpretation, especially as it has brought forward new and less supersessionistic ways of conceiving the relationship between Judaism and Christianity. Nevertheless, no matter its historical origin, the split and troubled interiority have not gone away as such, which might still constitute an essential trait of character for unredeemed human existence.

A major turning point in the interpretation of the troubled consciousness is Augustine's *Confessions*. Even if I would not suggest that we read Augustine as a proto-Cartesian, but rather that we understand his (mature) interpretation of self as more "liturgical," that is, as constituted by practices that configure its desire in a certain way, entanglement in sin and alienation of self still characterizes its description of the psyche. Žižek is quite dismissive of all premodern philosophies and theologies, suggesting that they merely externalize transcendence, in contrast to Kantian and post-Kantian philosophy, which places it at the core of the human being, thus interpreting transcendence as immanent.[44] But such a characterization of Augustine is surely too facile. Moreover, this also goes against the spirit of his constant interlocutor, Lacan, who, according to Erin Felicia Labbie in her book aptly titled *Lacan's Medievalism*, developed his theories of the structure of desire in response to an interpretation of medieval texts and followed them along in much of what he had to say on the matter.[45] Maybe Žižek, too, could have learned something from Augustine and later premodern theologians for whom desire most decidedly defined human existence. Let me briefly turn to Augustine to elucidate from a decidedly theological perspective some of the questions under consideration in this article.

When Augustine famously says to God that God is "more inward than my most inward part and higher than the highest element within me," this is certainly a more complex view of the relationship between immanence and transcendence than a mere positing of a transcendent object somehow influencing Augustine's innermost self.[46] The self that Augustine is is indeed not a form of self-possession in any transparent way; on the contrary, it is the confrontation with God that occasions the questioning of the subject by itself: "In your eyes I have become a problem to myself, and that is my sickness."[47] The introspection of Augustine before the eyes of God does not end in the discovery of a simple, clear, and stable identity but rather the opposite, in an increase of its mysteriousness: "What then am I, my God? What is my nature? It is characterized by diversity, by life of many forms, utterly immeasurable."[48] Especially the "utter immeasurability" of the self is interesting here, as it tells of a self that cannot be contained by any external measure. At the same time, we understand, from the first quotation from Augustine above, that the innermost being of the self is not the self itself but something other than the self: God. To be sure, to a human person narcissistically curved in on himself, God is experienced as an alien force, but this is because the traumatic encounter with God forces the human subject out of himself; as the innermost of the human person, the traumatic encounter with God is at the same time a (re)turn to a more original standing. In Žižek's Lacanian terminology, Augustine's concept of God could in some ways be characterized productively as "ex-timate," that is, as "a nonassimilable foreign body in the very kernel of the subject."[49] God is present, according to Augustine, as the enabling source of human knowledge and freedom.

Even if *Confessions* is a discourse on the fantasy through which human beings hide from this immeasurability in the midst of self—referred to as "sin" in more traditional theological terms—there is a sense in which it is the sinful self rather than the redeemed self that is unaware of its own complexity, thus taking itself for a simple, clear, and stable identity. The excess of the self over itself becomes visible only to the eyes of faith, as for Žižek. But unlike Žižek, the ground of this excess is for Augustine ultimately benign to human concerns; for Augustine, alienation is not by essence tragic. Put another way: it is possible to distinguish between the immeasurability of the self that makes it impossible for the self transparently to contain itself and the form of alienation that is the effect of sin. Undoubtedly, for a self used to being the master of its own house, the experience of this excess in the midst of self could well be endured as unbearable, horrific, and zombie-like. In this sense, there is something perhaps unavoidable in Žižek's language of excess, as when he claims that any attempt to break through the ideological edifice always will be understood as evil, which does not mean that it is bad in the sense of wishing others to fare ill.[50] To Augustine, however, there is a hope, not that the fundamental immeasurability of the self will go away, as this would be the destruction of what is most human in humanity, but that this alienation at the core of the self is not tragic in the sense that we are forever doomed to an existence of discord and violence; the "lust of domination" will be turned into a love free from all greed.

A central passage for Augustine's account of greed in *Confessions* is the famous episode in book 2, where Augustine tells how he, as a young boy, together with some friends, steals pears from a garden. The reason for Augustine's account of his theft is most likely not to suggest that stealing pears is a serious crime but to show how senseless this theft really was. Augustine steals the pears primarily out of a lust for stealing. The action was, in other words, perverse; he enjoyed it because it was forbidden. He did not even eat the pears but threw them to the pigs; for someone suffering from a spiritual hunger, the pears only produce depletion and a feeling of meaninglessness. Such is the account of all other desires that Augustine exemplifies from his own life in *Confessions*: finite things, although created by God, never suffice to satisfy the hunger for the infinite with which they are irreducibly intertwined; the only way out is a radical reordering of the desires through a traumatic encounter with God. Structurally at least, Augustine's account of the desires is parallel to Žižek's psychoanalytical account: there is no possibility of actually getting what we think we want, because every possible concretization of what I think I want (a new car, a new home, a new TV set) will never be *it*; it will just lead me to relocate the object for my desire to something else (another car, another home, another TV set). The motor that keeps our desire going is in reality not any particular thing at all but the eternity of desire as such. As long as we can go on thinking that it is a particular object that we really want, we are basically fine (or so we tell ourselves), but exposed to the eternity of desire, we lose our bearings. This is also the aim of psychoanalysis, according to Žižek, namely, to remove the ground from under our feet by dissolving the fantasy that structures our desire and exposes us to the drive. Of course, for Žižek, this eternal hunger that cannot be satisfied—the drive—is ultimately not understood in theological terms but as sheer negativity. Nevertheless, the parallel between these two accounts is striking and should give pause to any suggestion that, despite the (admittedly important) question of God, there is a stark contrast between Augustine and Žižek. Even if there is a sense in which we will ultimately find rest in God, according to Augustine, since God is not a thing, this longed-for rest cannot be incompatible with an infinite, erotic seeking.[51]

Here, exemplified by Augustine's account of human subjectivity, we get some idea of what theology potentially has to offer Žižek, namely, an account of hope that can earn some legitimacy in the face of hopelessness. There is a sense in which the suspicion lingers that Žižek hides a message of despair through his upbeat style. His use of theology—a kind of Lutheran "theology of the cross," if there ever was one—takes him very close to abandonment, despair, and nihilism, insofar as alienation almost turns out to be our destiny. In terms of his overall political purpose, the crucial question is whether there really is an alternative to the cynicism that he so emphatically rejects. To be sure, Žižek might regard most of the "Hallelujahs" through history to be dangerously premature, exchanging hope for fantasy. Nevertheless, might it not be too much to ask for some kind of reason, whatever that would mean in this context, for the hope that utter alienation is not the end of the story? And might not one press the matter even on Žižek's own political terms; namely, what are the grounds from which Žižek's own political perspective might gain any kind of plausibility or even—if I dare to use the word—desirability? From the perspective of Augustine or any similar theologian, Žižek's theology is a prematurely aborted theology, not because it insists on the need for a radical reconstitution of the self (which in a sense is also the sacrifice of the self as Christians know it), but because it does not have the hope of getting it all back again, in a moment of grace. To Žižek, such a hope probably seems wildly implausible. But surely we could ask, perhaps, is not any expression of hope, as distinct from mere optimism, bound to invoke some ultimate horizon of goodness without which we remain forever stuck with the zombies (as depicted in Romero's dystopic movies)? In the explanation of the death drive provided here, I have shown how both Lear and Santner have hinted at the possibility of a nontragic interpretation of the death drive, but one has to look very hard to find anything similar in Žižek. What Žižek offers theology—at least as a reminder, but possibly also as a critique—is an account of human subjectivity that does not shy away from its profound alienation. It is only through passing through the acceptance of the death drive within ourselves—"traversing the fantasy" in psychoanalytic parlance—that we can lose all narcissistic pretentions of being in charge of our actions and their consequences or of having a given place in the symbolic edifice, paradoxically gaining our true subjectivity and our ultimate freedom. True, theology has, as shown, had something to say about sin and alienation even before Žižek and the psychoanalytic tradition. But there still is a sense in which a psychoanalytic account of the death drive can potentially liberate theology from a too opportunistic or even bourgeois understanding of our predicament, or even throw up a warning against turning sin into a "thing" that then can more or less easily be avoided. As I have already suggested, there is also a sense in which Žižek can remind theology of not exchanging hope for fantasy in some version of "cheap eschatology." Žižek's Hegelian perspective would warn us theologians against making the crucifixion and death of Christ merely a stepping-stone on the way to resurrection and glory; this is actually a way of cheating in that it does not take death—including the devastating conditions of human life in history and today—seriously. It is only through taking death seriously, including its finality, that resurrection will not be confused with mere optimism.

Through this staging of a mutually critical dialogue between Žižek and Augustine, I hope I have illuminated some ways in which Žižek's account of undeadness may have something to offer theology, both in terms of a reminder of some of its own central themes and as a theoretical resource through which these themes could, perhaps, find a contemporary expression. If nothing else, I hope that it will have given a glimpse of one context within which Žižek's psychoanalytic discussion of the death drive makes theological sense. If so, then it will also have illustrated my thesis of the hybridity that characterizes our current situation: the return of historical theological discussions under the guise of psychoanalysis or Marxism or German Idealism. By putting the dialogue in this reciprocal way, I am not suggesting that there is a symmetrical relationship between Žižek and theology. What I have tried to show is that even if a philosopher like Žižek would want to claim that his theory surpasses traditional theology in that it and it only has the power to claim theology's emancipatory legacy, it is always possible to turn the tables in suggesting, especially in the light of Žižek's rather superficial treatment of theological traditions apart from their reception in German Idealism, that it is precisely because of its unacknowledged dependence on theology that his philosophy is able to hope for some kind of emancipation at all. And maybe it is not within the power of mere theory to propose which version ultimately is right—Žižek himself certainly suggests this—but only to acknowledge this ambiguity in the moment before any of us is claimed by one or the other interpretation. Suffice it to say that they are united in rejecting any shallow and transparent understanding of self, be it religious or secular.

Notes

1. Hermann Lübbe, *Säkularisierung: Geschichte eines ideenpolitischen Begriffs,* 3rd ed. (Freiburg: Karl Alber, 2003), 23–27.

2. See, e.g., Charles Taylor, *A Secular Age* (Cambridge, Mass.: Belknap Press, 2007), and Michael Allen Gillespie, *The Theological Origins of Modernity* (Chicago: University of Chicago Press, 2008).

3. See here my book *Det postsekulära tillståndet: Religion, modernitet, politik* (Göteborg: Glänta, 2009), 322–34.

4. Karl Marx, *Critique of Hegel's "Philosophy of Right,"* ed. Joseph O'Malley (Cambridge: Cambridge University Press, 1970), 131.

5. Slavoj Žižek, John Milbank, and Creston Davis, eds., *The Monstrosity of Christ: Paradox or Dialectic* (Cambridge, Mass.: MIT Press, 2009); John Milbank, Slavoj Žižek, and Creston Davis, eds., *Paul's New Moment: Continental Philosophy and the Future of Christian Theology* (Grand Rapids, Mich.: Brazos Press, 2010); Slavoj Žižek and Boris Gunjević, *God in Pain: Inversions of Apocalypse,* trans. Ellen Elias-Bursać (New York: Seven Stories Press, 2012); Slavoj Žižek, *The Indivisible Remainder: An Essay on Schelling and Related Matters* (London: Verso, 1996).

6. Slavoj Žižek, *The Fragile Absolute or, Why Is the Christian Legacy Worth Fighting For?* (London: Verso, 2000); Žižek, *The Puppet and the Dwarf: The Perverse Core of Christianity* (Cambridge, Mass.: MIT Press, 2003), 6.

7. Why Žižek is a Protestant rather than a Catholic atheist (or any other variety of atheism) is explained in detail in my book *Theology and Marxism in Eagleton and Žižek: A Conspiracy of Hope* (New York: Palgrave Macmillan, 2012), and the argument will not be repeated here.

8. Slavoj Žižek, "Dialectical Clarity versus the Misty Conceit of Paradox," in Žižek et al., *Monstrosity of Christ,* 290.

9. Slavoj Žižek, *In Defence of Lost Causes* (London: Verso, 2008), 54.

10. Sigmund Freud, "Beyond the Pleasure Principle," *Standard Edition* 18 (1920): 7–65.

11. Ibid., 43, 72–73.

12. Ibid., 53.

13. Ibid., 23, 41.

14. Ibid., 36–37.

15. Ibid., 59–60.

16. Søren Kierkegaard, *The Concept of Anxiety,* trans. Reidar Thomte (Princeton, N.J.: Princeton University Press, 1981).

17. See, e.g., Slavoj Žižek, *Living in the End Times* (London: Verso, 2010), 77.

18. Jonathan Lear, *Happiness, Death, and the Remainder of Life* (Cambridge, Mass.: Harvard University Press, 2000), 2. Lear's critical interpretation of the death drive is "sanctioned" by Žižek in *On Belief* (London: Routledge, 2001), 100.

19. Lear, *Happiness,* 78.

20. Ibid., 87–88.

21. Ibid., 96.

22. Ibid., 112.

23. Eric L. Santner, *On the Psychotheology of Everyday Life: Reflections on Freud and Rosenzweig* (Chicago: University of Chicago Press, 2001), 9.

24. Žižek, *On Belief,* 104; John 10:10 (KJV).

25. Slavoj Žižek, "Neighbors and Other Monsters: A Plea for Ethical Violence," in *The Neighbor: Three Inquiries in Political Theology,* ed. Slavoj Žižek, Eric L. Santner, and Kenneth Reinhard (Chicago: University of Chicago Press, 2005), 140.

26. Of course, the notion of the zombie has its roots in Haitian Vodou, but my interest here is strictly their presence in popular culture. In other words, I am interested in the cliché of the zombie in con-

temporary Western culture, not the admittedly more complex phenomenon of the zombie in religious cultures around the world.

27. Kim Paffenroth, *Gospel of the Living Dead: George Romero's Visions of Hell on Earth* (Waco, Tex.: Baylor University Press, 2006), 1. For more about the context of Romero's film as well as an analysis of it, see Ben Hervey, *Night of the Living Dead* (Basingstoke, U.K.: Palgrave Macmillan, 2008).

28. Stephen Harper, "*Night of the Living Dead*: Reappraising an Undead Classic," in *Bright Lights Film Journal* 50 (November 2005), http://www.brightlightsfilm.com/50/night.htm; Daniel W. Drezner, *Theories of International Politics and Zombies* (Princeton, N.J.: Princeton University Press, 2011), 21.

29. Slavoj Žižek, *Looking Awry: An Introduction to Lacan through Popular Culture* (Cambridge, Mass.: MIT Press, 1992), 22–23.

30. Ibid.

31. Slavoj Žižek, *Organs without Bodies: On Deleuze and Consequences* (New York: Routledge, 2004), 136.

32. Zombie Research Society, http://www.zombieresearch.org/.

33. See Paffenroth's list of zombie characteristics in *Gospel of the Living Dead*, 2–6, for a comprehensive overview.

34. Marcus Pound, *Žižek: A (Very) Critical Investigation* (Grand Rapids, Mich.: William B. Eerdmans, 2008), 31n19. Cf. Žižek, *On Belief*, 103–4.

35. Here I rely on the excellent analyses of each of Romero's zombie movies in Paffenroth's *Gospel of the Living Dead*. However, unlike Paffenroth, who also relates zombies to theology, my interest in zombies from a theological perspective goes via the death drive.

36. Ibid., 57.

37. Ibid., 9.

38. Slavoj Žižek, *How to Read Lacan* (London: Granta Books, 2006), 62.

39. Stephen Mulhall, *On Film* (London: Routledge, 2001), 19. Mulhall here analyzes the Alien movies, but I would suggest that Romero's zombie movies are even better instantiations of this, as their liminality is even more emphasized than that of the nonhuman aliens.

40. Žižek, *How to Read Lacan*, 53.

41. The quote by Lacan can be found in Jacques Lacan, *The Ethics of Psychoanalysis 1959–1960: The Seminar of Jacques Lacan*, book 7, ed. Jacques-Alain Miller (New York: W. W. Norton, 1997), 12. Žižek's use of it is ubiquitous, often without referring to its source. See, e.g., Slavoj Žižek, *The Ticklish Subject: The Absent Centre of Political Ontology* (London: Verso, 1999), 167.

42. Žižek, *How to Read Lacan*, 60.

43. Slavoj Žižek, *Living in the End Times* (London: Verso, 2010), 116.

44. Cf. Žižek, *How to Read Lacan*, 47.

45. Erin Felicia Labbie, *Lacan's Medievalism* (Minneapolis: University of Minnesota Press, 2006), 3.

46. Augustine, *Confessions*, trans. Henry Chadwick (Oxford: Oxford University Press, 1992), III. vi, 11.

47. Ibid., X. xxxiii, 50.

48. Ibid., X. xvii, 26.

49. Slavoj Žižek, "The Abyss of Freedom," in *The Abyss of Freedom/Ages of the World*, by Slavoj Žižek and Friedrich Schelling (Ann Arbor: University of Michigan Press, 1997), 45.

50. Slavoj Žižek, *The Indivisible Remainder: An Essay on Schelling and Related Matters* (London: Verso, 1996), 92.

51. Augustine, *Confessions*, I. i, 1.

PART II
Capitalist Monsters

In a Supermarket at the End of the World

In zombie films, scenes of plunder are recognizable as bittersweet fantasies in which the viewer is invited to celebrate the end of capitalism: sweet in that everything is now free, and bitter in that everyone you know is dead. Such scenes evoke the looting of the riotous mob, they make visible our society's gross materialism, and they call into question the worldview of those outside the frame of the camera shot. Maybe, in some instances, such scenes raise the specter of the piracy of imperialism (as Dan Hassler-Forrest argues: the typical contemporary zombie narrative follows a formula torn from *Robinson Crusoe*, of survivors foraging for supplies, that thus preserves a colonial ethos) or predatory lending and its resultant evictions, as we see the survivors as squatters occupying spaces as diverse as airports (*Warm Bodies*, dir. Jonathan Levine, 2013), prisons (*The Walking Dead*), pubs (*Shaun of the Dead*, dir. Edgar Wright, 2004), and, of course, shopping malls. This trope begins, most would say, with Romero's 1978 film *Dawn of the Dead*, with its survivors barricaded in a shopping mall, and yet the trend is visible even earlier, for example, in 1971's *Omega Man*, starring Charlton Heston—in a reprisal of the role of Robert Neville, the protagonist of Richard Matheson's novel *I Am Legend*—which depicts Neville "shopping" in an abandoned department store. Indeed, one could trace the motif of postcapitalist consumerism in apocalyptic narratives from the 1964 film *Last Man on Earth*, starring Vincent Price (the earlier cinematic rendition of Matheson's novel) to the contemporary television comedy of the same name, starring Will Forte, in which the titular character loots not only grocery stores and shopping malls for necessities but the world's museums and historical monuments for household objets d'art. But this would be a book project in and of itself. Instead, I want to say just a few words about the depiction of the supermarket at the end of the world.

I've always had a strange relationship with the supermarket. I'd like to think it comes from a childhood spent in West Africa, where my father had taken a job in the field of public health in the 1980s, when AIDS was ravaging the continent. Each summer, when we came "home" to the United States, it became a kind of ritual that we'd wander the fluorescent-lit aisles of the local supermarket, marveling, in both wonder and disgust, at the overwhelming abundance. "Thirty kinds of mustard," I remember my mother saying, shaking her head. But I know there isn't anything special about my musings on the *hypermarché*: it's clear from its depictions in art—like its treatment in Don DeLillo's novel *White Noise,* or Allen Ginsberg's poem "A Supermarket at Night," or photographer Andreas Gursky's panoramic image of the 99 cent store—that the supermarket is an icon of capitalist plenty irradiated by an aura of the postmodern sublime that falls somewhere between harrowing and holy, a dichotomy that is stressed in representations of the supermarket in zombie films.

In a film that, for all of its dark beauty, seems overwhelmingly joyless (especially since the few, brief scenes of levity are punctuated by disaster), the supermarket scene stands out in Danny Boyle's 2002 film *28 Days Later.* For starters, it may be the only scene in the film that is accompanied by music other than the brooding score; it is also one of the most colorful scenes in the film, in an otherwise dimly lit picture that (except for a few scenes in the green countryside) has a fairly drab color palate. After a narrow escape from the "infected" (the film's brand of fleet-footed, viral "Rage" zombies) in a London tunnel, the four human characters pull over to investigate a large grocery. It's pristine: miraculously untouched, mysteriously unlocked, and, most importantly, unoccupied by the infected. And in this, it is different from the depictions of grocery stores in other zombie films, which are fraught with danger and often the setting for battles with the undead, as in *Zombieland,* in which Tallahassee (Woody Harrelson) dispatches a "redneck" zombie with a banjo, or the BBC series *In the Flesh,* wherein the grocery store is a site of trauma for one of the main characters, who encounters her zombified brother eating her patrol partner. It seems odd, then, that there's no initial investigation by the four characters in *28 Days Later* of the space of Budgens' grocery, especially these four (Jim, Selena, Hannah, and Frank), who are so cautious, and who do come across the odd infected in a church or a gas station restaurant. Upon entering its doors, they seem to sense that this is some kind of safe zone, a return to the prelapsarian garden, complete with incorruptible (likely genetically modified) apples.

The opening shot begins on the ceiling and then tilts downward to reveal Selena on the other side of the glass door, looking curiously into the spacious, well-lit shop. A long establishing shot shows the characters surveying the colorful aisles from afar before a high-angle shot of them from behind shows Selena smiling in profile as she beckons to the group: "Let's shop." Tinkling electronic music begins as we see trolley carts put to actual use here, rather than serving as barricades against the undead. Each character careens around the shop piling luxuries and foodstuffs into his or her own cart. The patriarch of the group, Frank, muses over sixteen-year-old single-malt scotch and, after deliberating, pulls down four bottles into his arms. Even the movements of the camera in this scene are joyful and distinct from the rest of the film's reliance on quick cuts, shaky handheld action, and still long shots depicting the isolation of the characters in desolate city space. Tracking shots zig and zag across the space of the store and are coordinated with or counter the characters' movements, emulating the smooth motion of the shopping carts as the characters hungrily fill them with tins of food—having been reliant for so long on candy and soda, the scavengings of the many vending machines shown in the early scenes of the film. A low-angle shot from Selena's basket puts the viewer in the place of the commodities she drops in her cart after lovingly plucking them from the shelves. The final dolly shot cuts horizontally across the characters' forward motion as each rides his or her cart through the checkout aisle; the tracking camera bisects the characters' transversal of the space, as if in a choreographed dance that ends as Frank sardonically places a credit card on the checkout stand's empty countertop.

One might, at first, attribute the playfulness of this scene to a kind of nostalgia for the banal, everyday workings of life as usual under capitalist society, but Frank's final gesture makes clear that this is something else. It's doubtful that this working man, a cab driver in the time before, it is intimated, would have been able to afford four bottles of Lagavulin scotch (about a hundred dollars a bottle) on his salary. But this credit card bill will never come due. And that's something worth celebrating, though the world be at its end.

We begin here because this section of the book considers depictions of capitalism in the zombie mythos and traces the way that our figuration of the zombie has changed as our economic system morphed from an emphasis on production and labor to one of consumption and service-based industries. The essays included here tell a story with and through our zombie narratives about how capitalism has changed in the twentieth and twenty-first centuries, highlighting the rise of neoliberalism, the reach of immaterial labor, and the role of the postcolony in the global economy.

Despite the title's emphasis on the viral aspect of the modern zombie myth, "Some Kind of Virus: The Zombie as Body and as Trope," what this oft-cited and enjoyably written piece by Jen Webb and Sam Byrnand offers the reader is explicitly "useful ways of thinking 'zombie'" (112), which is the larger goal of this assemblage of articles. Along the way to the essay's discussion of the zombie as "capitalist analogue" (116), the authors gesture to the figure's importance for psychoanalysis and philosophy, specifically referencing the p-zombie described by David Chalmers and Daniel Dennett. The authors divide the essay into three parts, psychoanalytic, capitalist, and cognitive analogues— the middle treatment being, perhaps, the most valuable part of the essay for our purposes in this section, offering eminently quotable lines and deep engagement with Karl Marx, Michel de Certeau, and Hardt and Negri—but the article also reaches beyond accepted zombie narratives to illustrate the way that texts as diverse as Ursula K. Le Guin's *A Wizard of Earthsea* (1968), Ridley Scott's *Alien* (1979), and Joseph Conrad's *Heart of Darkness* (1899) do similar work as do the living dead. The authors illustrate that global capitalism appears like a zombie-making virus and that consumerism renders individuals into zombies without empathy, for instance, for those who labor in sweatshops to produce the cheap goods we consume. This essay relates the fundamental sense of loss at the heart of the consuming zombie to the psychoanalytic lack and to an ontological "darkness inside."

Next, the excerpt included from David McNally's *Monsters of the Market*, "Ugly Beauty: Monstrous Dreams of Utopia," is the conclusion to his book on figurations of the zombie and the vampire as they metaphorize global capitalism. Reprising many of the central claims of his argument, McNally illustrates the twinned images of the zombie-laborer (directly related, genealogically, to our own Hollywood zombie, coming to the United States via the Occupation of Haiti) and the vampiric siphoning of surplus profit from labor, arguing that the combination of these figures provides a dialectical image of global capitalism. Providing rich and terrifically useful readings of Marx, Hegel, Fanon, and others, McNally's conclusion focuses especially on the zombie and the zombie in revolt, with detours into the Baktinian grotesque, Shelley's *Frankenstein*, and Thelonious Monk's "zombie music." It is also a beautifully written piece, with its own musicality, as seen in phrases, like "festive zombie riot," that liltingly infect one's brain. Many of the notes sounded here are developed more fully in other essays within this collection: Comentale on zombie music, Orpana on the grotesque, and the Comaroffs in the next essay, on the sub-Saharan living dead. In the main, McNally's essay presents the dark magic of capitalism that makes objects of people and illustrates the capacity for a zombie awakening in a reconstruction of the collective identity as a Frankensteinian composite; this is paralleled to what we've seen happen to the zombie myth itself, appropriated from Haitian folklore and reified in cinema, transformed from an iconic laborer into a consumer, but McNally suggests that the image's deradicalization can be reversed. The posthuman potential of the zombie is a subject that is sketched out more fully in this book's final section, "New Life for the Undead."

Anthropologists Jean and John Comaroff's important 2002 article "Alien-Nation: Zombies, Immigrants, and Millennial Capitalism" addresses the spectral labor of rural South Africans. They profile herein contemporary fears of being made into a "zombie" by means of sorcery or witchcraft and forced to labor against one's will; in this essay, the reader encounters diverse types of enchantment, phantom laborers, and half-time zombies, which represent a range of social ills plaguing South Africa, including xenophobic tensions, anxiety surrounding unemployment, and the encroachment on available jobs by migrant workers in the postapartheid era. In its characterization of various types of "ghost workers," this essay gives a glimpse of the continued relevance of imagery of living death for an articulation of the postcolony's experience of globalized capitalism, particularly where it serves as a repository for cheap, outsourced labor. Importantly, this essay cautions us not to ignore the producer in the "neoliberal stress on consumption."

Lars Bang Larsen's "Zombies of Immaterial Labor," which he updates for this collection, reminds us that the zombie "straddles the divide between industrial and immaterial labor, from mass to multitude, from the brawn of industrialism to the dispersed brains of cognitive capitalism."[1] Like many before him, Larsen considers the zombie as a figure of alienation, putting George Romero in conversation with Julia Kristeva, Franco Moretti, Slavoj Žižek, and others, but he goes further in this revision, arguing that the zombie is also an image of our self-commoditization, our self-consumption under late capitalism and its "experience economy." This essay has changed the way that I view my own relationship to social media in its portrayal of a zombielike production/consumption of self. I inadvertently perform immaterial labor, for example, when I produce myself as a consumer, as in those food pics posted so often to Instagram or in showing off a new pair of shoes. Most strikingly, Larsen reads the World Wide Web as an extended network enabling zombie infection (or undergirding capitalism's reach), like the alien plants in Philip Kaufman's *Invasion of the Body Snatchers*. Yet, for all his skepticism, Larsen does not foreclose the potential for an aesthetic reconceptualization of the zombie—as in his field, art—after all, as he notes, "what is helpful about the monster is that it is immediately recognizable as strange. In this respect, it is, in fact, nonalienating."

Finally, Sherryl Vint's essay, "Abject Posthumanism: Neoliberalism, Biopolitics, and Zombies," provides a useful summation of some of the key work in zombie studies that seeks to make sense of the figure's commentary on capitalism, both by authors who are included in this volume (Canavan, Wald, McNally, and Jean and John Comaroff) and by those who aren't but are crucial to a full understanding of the issues in play: Slavoj Žižek, K. Silem Mohammad, and Achille Mbembe. In contrast to some of the work that views the zombie as a figure of posthuman potential, Vint here articulates a particular category of the "abject posthuman" zombie: an apt figuration of the dehumanization of the other that is a key component of "the logic of neoliberalism [which] fragments subjects" across different lines. If Vint seems less convinced of the usefulness of reading the zombie as posthuman (à la Haraway's cyborg), she sees more value in its resemblance to Agamben's *Homo Sacer* for what it reveals about the crises of our current world. Just as McNally illustrated how the cinematic zombie morphed from a representation of the capitalist laborer to the consumer, Vint traces here the zombie's transformation (within Romero's oeuvre but also in works like the AMC series *The Walking Dead*), in which the figure becomes less monstrous and more pitiable, as revelatory of the relationship between neoliberalism and biopolitics. Finally, the author argues that we can make such narratives into cautionary tales (as with an Argentinean film called *Fase 7* that dramatizes the tension between humans in survival narratives) and reimagine the future without such societal, economic, and political structures, but as one of "new beginnings."

In their essay included herein, Jean and John Comaroff write that zombies tend to be associated with "rapidly changing conditions of work under capitalism," and each different type of zombie "congeals the predicament of human labor at its most concrete." I agree that zombies seem always to speak about labor or consumption, about colonialism or capitalism, and that is precisely what makes this topic important, but it also makes a list of further reading difficult to compile: when we talk about zombies, we are never *not* talking about capitalism. The list of suggestions that follows expands upon subcategories elucidated by the authors included in this section and, at the same time, refers to many essential and foundational (but, for many, already well-known) works in the field.

Further Reading

Many of the most obviously important resources in this area were signaled out in the introduction of the book, including Annalee Newitz's book *Pretend We're Dead: Capitalist Monsters in American Pop Culture*, economic studies like Chris Harman's *Zombie Capitalism*, and Henry Giroux's investigation of *Zombie Politics and Culture in the Age of Casino Capitalism*. Jaime Peck's article "Zombie Neoliberalism and the Ambidextrous State" succinctly summarizes the relevance of the imagery to the neoliberal economy, applying Neil Smith's phrase "dead but dominant" to a defunct ideology: "the living dead of the free-market revolution continue to walk the earth, though with each resurrection their decidedly uncoordinated gait becomes even more erratic" (109). Though not about zombies directly, Rob Latham's book *Consuming Youth: Vampires, Cyborgs, and the Culture of Consumption* may be of interest to those just delving into this subject of capitalism's monsters. So many other essays included in different sections of this book, or works listed in the suggestions for further reading, might be cross-listed and appear here as well, like Sasha Cocarla's reading of *Warm Bodies* and neoliberalism or Jennifer Rutherford's discussion of the "collective zombie" in her slim book.

Definitionally in this subject area, Steven Shaviro's essay "Capitalist Monsters" is foundational and so central to this discussion that I wish I could have included both this article from *Historical Materialism* and his offering from *The Cinematic Body*, which is included in the first section of this book. I also like Joshua Clover's discussion of John Quiggin's study of *Zombie Economics* in *The Nation*, "Swans and Zombies: Neoliberalism's Permanent Contradiction," and selections of Evan Calder Williams's volume *Combined and Uneven Apocalypse*, which includes musings like the following: "zombie films are not about the living dead. . . . They are about the undying living. They are about *surplus-life*" (92), as opposed to surplus labor. I'll repeat here the good advice given me long ago by Joshua Clover that investigation of the zombie and capitalism begins with Franco Moretti's discussion of *Frankenstein* in *Signs Taken for Wonders*. See the chapter "Dialectic of Fear" in that book.

Work in this area spans discussions of films where a critique of capitalism is particularly pronounced, like the slacker ethos of *Shaun of the Dead* (see Lynn Pifer on this topic) or corporate takeover in *Fido* (see Michele Braun's essay) to investigation of the zombie broadly as a metaphor or allegory for our lived condition. Related discussions of utopia and dystopia, apocalypse and revolution, in zombie films are often relevant, like David Pagano's "The Space of Apocalypse in Zombie Cinema" in *Zombie Culture*; Tyson Lewis's "Ztopia" in *Generation Zombie*; R. Colin Tait's essay "(Zombie) Revolution at the Gates" in *Cinephile*; or Chris Boehm's chapter "Apocalyptic Utopia: The Zombie and the r(Evolution) of Subjectivity" in *We're All Infected*, which, with its attention to the work of Slavoj Žižek and Alain Badiou, is sure to be of interest to some of the readers of *Zombie Theory*.

Naturally, it becomes difficult to separate the zombie's caricature of the political economy from other aspects of politics (as seen in Daniel Drezner's book *Theories of International Politics and Zombies* or the entire collection devoted to zombies and the future of higher education, *Zombies in the Academy*) or biopolitics, as is seen in Vint's essay included in this section. Jennifer M. Proffitt and Rich Templin's "'Fight the Dead, Fear the Living': Zombie Apocalypse, Libertarian Paradise?" looks at a fundamental conundrum in American politics between individualism and distrust of government at the same time that people expect to be able to count on emergency services and infrastructure. Focusing on Romero's films, their essay looks at the zombie narrative's depiction of this paradox.

In regard to Romero's oeuvre, work seems to concentrate on consumerism in *Dawn of the Dead* and on revolution in *Land of the Dead*. For the former, Kyle Bishop provides a nice synthesis of this field of study in his essay "The Idle Proletariat: *Dawn of the Dead*, Consumer, Ideology, and the Loss of Productive Labor." See Steven Harper's and A. Loudermilk's essays and, for a different take, Matthew Walker's offering in *The Undead and Philosophy*, which connects zombie consumerism in Romero's films to

Aristotle's *Nicomachean Ethics*. For the latter, see June Pulliam's excellent discussion of class consciousness in *Land of the Dead*, "Our Zombies, Ourselves," or (in a different approach) Outi Hakola's reading of individualism and community in *Undead in the West*.

Those interested in Larsen's attention to the zombie, immaterial labor, and art should also consider Joshua Gunn and Shaun Treat's essay on the zombie's metaphorization of ideology in rhetoric and communication studies, "Zombie Trouble: A Propaedeutic on Ideological Subjectification and the Unconscious." I have a chapter on zombie art and its revolutionary potential in *The Transatlantic Zombie*, as well.

Finally, Jeffrey W. Mantz's "On the Frontlines of the Zombie War in the Congo: Digital Technology, the Trade in Conflict Minerals, and Zombification" should be required reading for those interested in contemporary zombies in Africa. In brief, this article presents the horrors of mineral mining in the Congo and the territorial wars surrounding control of natural resources, which have been fostered by global demand for the minerals used in cell phone technology. The author draws a parallel between the consumer's willful ignorance and lack of empathy for the far-away producers as zombie-like (not to mention the anesthetizing and social paralysis of the technology itself) and addresses the terrors of living in such war zones as creating conditions akin to what is experienced by the survivors in zombie apocalypse narratives.

Note

1. Lars Bang Larsen, "Zombies of Immaterial Labor: The Modern Monster and the Death of Death," *e-flux Journal* 15 (2010), http://www.e-flux.com/journal/15/61295/zombies-of-immaterial-labor-the-modern-monster-and-the-death-of-death/.

6

Some Kind of Virus

The Zombie as Body and as Trope

JEN WEBB and SAMUEL BYRNAND

Zombie as Trope

"Zombies are cool," said a graduate student at a recent seminar. "Zombies are vile," said a film studies lecturer. "Zombies are whitey's way of expressing the terror of alterity," said a presenter at a recent conference.

All true, perhaps. There are many points of attraction in the zombie character, and in a period when zombies seem to be permeating popular culture and emerging in scholarly literature, there are perhaps as many ways of approaching and evaluating zombies as there are people who approach and evaluate. Those people include novelists, moviemakers, cultural theorists, adolescents, philosophers, and the mass of fans, each of whom has a solid idea about what constitutes a zombie, what constitutes a seminal zombie text, and why it is worth researching zombies. Because the idea of zombie travels so widely, and across so many fields, it has become a very familiar character, one that participates in narratives of the body, of life and death, of good and evil; one that gestures to alterity, racism, speciesism, the inescapable, the immutable. Thus it takes us to the "other side"—alienation, death, and what is worse than death: the state of being undead.

But what is this thing called "zombie"? Although they are, of course, a fantasy, we know enormous amounts about them—their tastes, appearance, biology, reasons for their emergence, how to neutralize them, why we should despise and fear them. This knowledge comes in large part from the armies of fans who, driven by some sort of anthropological urge, have studied and recorded their ontology and behavior. Thus we know, for instance, that zombies are unrelentingly, unquenchably, and indiscriminately hungry. When they see their environment, they see a place whose only observable features are food. They are also utterly implacable because they are, in David Chalmers's term, "all dark inside,"[1] lacking ethical or affective judgments. Yet they are disturbingly like us, and as such can act as springboards into ways of understanding the ontology of the subject.

Like humans, zombies aren't social isolates—they seem to prefer to live in groups, within built environments; like us, they actively colonize spaces for themselves; like us—at least in the West—they seek to spread well beyond their local region and to dominate people and places. Consequently, though we do not know their points of origin, we typically come across them in the most ordinary and safe of environments—our own home ground. Indeed, there is always something "nearly me" about the monster. This is evident in how easily we are infected with "zombieness": a mere bite from one of them, or a drop of their bodily fluid into my eye, and I too become zombie. The transmission of the "virus" between us and them indicates our closeness: viruses (mostly) travel between like species, and the job of the average zombie seems to be to (1) eat as many people as possible and (2) infect as many people as possible. So, the story goes, once they have arrived among us, carrying "some kind of virus," they metastasize rapidly, devastating cities, decimating populations.

The idea of zombie has similarly ramified, or metastasized, infiltrating society at a number of levels; and given that Western (and especially U.S.) media products now permeate the global media, and hence inf(l)ect global audiences, zombies are also traveling more widely than in previous times. Because of their long history—especially in the West—and because of the rhetorical turns associated with their use in different periods and different cultural fields, we take the perspective that zombies are as much trope as character or effect and hence are available to be reworked and reframed in any number of ways. In this article, we attempt to contribute to the debate and suggest what we see as useful ways of thinking "zombie."

The philosopher David Chalmers has identified a number of "turns"—or categories—of zombie, the better known being the Hollywood form, of reanimated flesh-eating corpses; the Haitian form, of living people deprived through magic or medicine of soul and free will; and philosophical or p-zombies, which look like humans but lack consciousness. We do not, in this article, take up the two latter forms but focus rather on the Hollywood form and some of what we consider its immediate progenitors. And we are particularly interested in what the narrative suggests about what it means to be a human being in the contemporary world: a world dominated by neoliberal economics, by globalization, and by the work of capitalist production that simultaneously enchants and disenchants peoples in the interest of pursuing a dream of radical, hegemonic capital.

We take this position because the zombie trope is so often associated with power and its exploitation, as is exemplified by the Shadow in Ursula K. Le Guin's *A Wizard of Earthsea* or the golem in Cynthia Ozick's *The Puttermesser Papers*. A precursor to this type is the *shletl* golem/zombie on which Ozick's was based; this "zombie" was created to relieve people of heavy or dirty work and to protect its maker, most particularly from pogroms. The zombies in this category have a fantastical–theological point of origin because they were made by invoking the holy words of creation or powerful words of magic. But they are not safe creatures: in each golem narrative, they exceed the control of their creators, running amok and threatening rather than serving them. In this respect, they can be read as metaphors of our own shadow selves, the part that always returns to bite us and which we can never keep fully repressed.

We see this notion that there is a "zombie" within each of us in a novel like Joseph Conrad's *Heart of Darkness* and its movie spin-off, Francis Ford Coppola's *Apocalypse Now* (1979). Here the zombie trope is mobilized as a critique of colonialism and as a warning: the mindless brutality of the colonizers and soldiers ends only in horror, in terror. Indeed, it is instructive that the zombie trope always generates fear. In the stories where their provenance is a military event or scientific accident—Boris Sagal's 1971 film *The Omega Man*, for instance—it is fear of the self. In those that locate the origin of zombiedom in an alien attack—the Alien film series, for instance—it is fear of the other. In either case, the zombie character also draws attention to social alienation and to the drive that catches people up in a maelstrom of ceaseless consumption, ceaseless destruction.

The Psychoanalytical Analogue

Psychoanalysis provides one point of entry to the trope of zombie—particularly as it allows readings that focus on identity and loss—because of zombies' likeness to human beings. This is well established in the academic literature and in popular narratives too. Think *Day of the Dead*, where the crazy scientist, Dr. Logan, insists of his zombies, "They are us, they are extensions of us, they are the same animals." The same, yet not identical: zombies are "people without minds"; the undead; and thus are both us and not us. In this respect, they are like the dead themselves, and so must be exiled from the community of the living. Michel de Certeau writes:

> The dying are outcasts because they are deviants in an institution organized by and for the conservation of life. An "anticipated mourning," a phenomenon of institutional rejection, puts them away in advance in "the dead man's room"; it surrounds them with silence or, worse yet, with lives that protect the living against the voice that would break out of this enclosure to cry: "I am going to die."[2]

Only in finding a way to ignore, overlook, or eradicate them can we forget the fact that as they are, so too I will be. And yet, and yet. What is remarkable about so many zombie movies is that the survivors of the plague/accident/alien invasion that caused the infection do so little to distinguish themselves from zombies; it's very much a case of *as you are, so too am I*. The death of Charlton Heston's Robert Neville in *Omega Man*, for instance, is no real loss: it is difficult to empathize fully with him and his grim, unrelenting performance of isolated, violent, and angry male, particularly when he is set against his "zombie" bête noir, the charismatic Matthias (Anthony Zerbe). In story after story, there seems to be no limit to the survivors' rage or their incapacity to empathize with one another; in the horror of their changed world, they become like zombies, "all dark inside."

This manifests sometimes in the terrible violence shown in movies like *Day of the Dead*, where the soldiers turn on citizens and on themselves, or in *28 Days Later*, where the hero, Jim, takes on many of the physical and emotional characteristics of the "infected" so that he might survive the horror being dealt out by his own kind. The zombies in this film have been infected with a viral rage; Jim avoids the infection but can't avoid or control his innate, personal rage. The effect in either case is practically identical: for all intents and purposes, in the moments of his rage, Jim is zombie. In fact, the deleted scenes show Jim running unmolested among a pack of the infected to gain entry into the soldiers' house: he sides with the zombies in order to kill his human tormentors, and even the zombies can't tell that he's not one of them.

This zombification manifests also in the dampening of affect, seen in movies like Kurt Wimmer's *Equilibrium* (2002), where the government has identified as society's main enemy the sensate realm. In this society, everyone knows the danger of feeling, and the related need to "destroy the ability to feel"; sense criminals are summarily executed; books, art, and music are destroyed (indeed, the movie opens with the destruction of the *Mona Lisa*); and the community is kept numb, or neutralized (zombified), by taking a drug called Prozium, a kind of mirthless soma that makes it impossible for them to care for others. In either case, what we have is people who, like zombies, have no capacity for subjective phenomenal experiences or for ethical or affective judgment—and this alone is cause for the fear they generate in audiences for such films. As Shaviro writes, "the hardest thing to acknowledge is that the living dead are not radically Other so much as they serve to awaken a passion for otherness and for vertiginous disidentification that is already latent within our own selves."[3]

They may lack empathy, but even the numbed residents of Libria, the dystopic community in *Equilibrium*, experience hunger, another characteristic shared by zombies and people. What is interesting about zombies' hunger, though, is that unlike us, they don't need to eat to maintain (their version of) life. They eat because they crave, not because they need; they are motivated—in Freudian terms—by drive, which is, Freud writes, "so to say our mythology. Drives are mythical entities, magnificent in their indefiniteness."[4] Drive, that is, lacks an obvious generative structure—it is not desire; it is not need.

Let us diverge, briefly, to mark the differences between drive and the other forces that motivate us. One important force is desire, a term adopted by scholars from across the spectrum. We do not intend to engage in a long discussion on the complexities of this issue but only to note that generally in the literature, desires are on one hand culturally constituted (so that, for instance, the consumer society generates in its subjects a longing for commodity objects) and are on the other hand the fundamental aspect of identity and its vicissitudes. Subjects *are* because they desire; and yet desire is also the point at which we are separated from ourselves, made aware that we lack. In desiring, we search for the self, the idea of a unified and intrinsic individual self, which of course does not exist, and which is why desire can never be satisfied.

A second motivating force is need. Need is generally seen as based in the body: as a matter of physiological requirement. Where desire is mediated by culture, need is usually regarded as unmediated: as the raw urgency of the body to eat, drink, rest, and seek shelter. But it is not quite as simple as that: need is not just a phenomenological effect, and desire is not just a cultural effect; they are part of the same operation. Deleuze and Guattari write, "Desire is not bolstered by needs, but rather the contrary; needs are derived from desire."[5] Think, for instance, of the *need* for vehicular transport, something that emerged out of a *desire* for faster, more comfortable travel and is now a necessity for people in much of the world. Thus need, for humans, seems to be mediated just as desire is; and like desire, it can never be satisfied because, as long as we are alive, we must attend to the body and its needs.

So here is a point at which humans and zombies diverge. *We desire*, constantly seeking that which we do not have in order to fill the empty place of the self; zombies show no signs of independent identity or understanding of the lack at the heart of the self.[6] *We need*, constantly searching out what the body requires to maintain physical life; zombies seem not to respond to the normal requirements of the body for rest, nourishment, and shelter. So when it comes to both need and desire, humans operate according to a different economy from that of zombies.

Drive is another matter, because here humans and zombies do seem to have something in common. And drive, of course, is neither need nor desire but is the unthinking response of the subject to what Lacan, following Freud, has called "the Thing"—the "little a."[7] The "little a"—the other—is what emerges in the primordial void created when a person leaves the world of sensation for the realm of language, the symbolic order. The Thing—the object a—created in the moment we are inscribed as subjects of the symbolic order, remains as a hollow in the self, what we can call the "dark inside," which renders us always Other to ourselves. From this point, we can never be fully "at home," because there's always something else in there with us, lurking.

This notion that there is an absence–presence within—something uncanny or "beyond our ken" about ourselves—is not just a truism of cultural theory; it is also a physiological principle. Freud alludes to this in his essay "Instincts and Their Vicissitudes,"[8] where he writes that the source of the drive is somatic—located in the body. Neurologist Richard Cytowic develops this, writing that we are never free agents because there is, buried in our brains and our cognitive functioning, the inexpressible, the unconnectable, the thing that makes us work as beings, yet which we cannot access. "Part(s) of us," he writes, "are *inaccessible to self-awareness,* the latter being only the tip of the iceberg of who and what we really are. The 'I' is a superficial self-awareness constructed by our unfathomable part."[9] The "unfathomable part," the unacknowledged yet frightening and obscene Thing within, may well have the capacity to *zombie* us from the start of our career as subject but also exists as something alluring. The object a fascinates because it gestures toward who and what we might be: someone with the capacity to reject the symbolic order and return to the wildness of the id. It fascinates too because it recalls the essential knowledge that death, the ultimate unfathomable, is the only way to regain what we have lost, to fill the void. The problem is, of course, that at the point of death, when the subject is returned to the void, it's too late to know or articulate this recovered fullness, so the Thing, the inner zombie, remains just out of reach. Hence, very like death, it always haunts us, reminding us of the risk that we could end up trapped—like Antigone[10]—between physical and symbolic deaths.

Just as anxious self-aware humans try to suture the gap between the self and its unfathomable parts, and between those two deaths, so too producers of zombie-type narratives often attempt to reconcile the two sides. In *A Wizard of Earthsea*, for instance, Ged acknowledges and embraces his shadow, transforming it from his threat to his strength. In the Alien series, Ripley becomes both human and monster and only in that capacity is able to manage the horror. In *Day of the Dead*, Dr. Logan turns zombie Bub into a kind of pet by means of behavioral treatment—and Bub later avenges his death as only a human would do. Their "like-us-ness" manifests; something is reconciled; the horror is put back into the closet, out of sight—until the next relapse.

The Capitalist Analogue

So that is one way of looking at the zombie trope: as a way of illuminating something about the constitution and functioning of the self—and particularly of the inaccessibility of (much of) the self to the laws of language, culture, and society. And it's one that segues smoothly into a second reading, one that involves a critique of the capitalist system, because of the central issue, those motivating forces of drive, desire, and need that can all be termed aspects of hunger, of appetite.

Capitalism, we suggest, works as an analogue of zombiedom because it too is predicated on insatiable appetite and the drive to consume. But it is not necessarily the mindless consumption of the zombie. Marx and Engels point out that the satisfying of basic hungers/needs/desires is

> the first premise of all human existence and, therefore, of all history. . . . Men must be in a . . . position to live in order to "make history." . . . Life involves before everything else eating and drinking, a habitation, clothing and many other things. The first historical act is thus the production of the means to satisfy these needs, the production of material life itself.[11]

Unless we satisfy the basic hungers, we cannot live. Without life, we cannot "make history." Zombies seem to operate purely on the basis of drive and have no obvious concern with "the production of material life" (all they do is consume and destroy). Taking Marx and Engels's point, we can say that being human is about more than basic hungers; it is about individuals organizing to achieve aims, and thus all our needs and hungers are peculiarly social and cultural, and hence peculiarly mediated. There is something unthinking, unthought, about zombie consumption; there is something organized, systematic, about capitalist consumption. The latter is, indeed, a system, one that works to produce history, one every bit as teleological as any religion or, indeed, as classical Marxism. And like many religions, and like Marxism, it has global aspirations and a global reach. What seems to be happening on a global scale is the production not just of history but of hunger in people around the world, and the production of a way of thinking that posits capitalism as the only viable system for social organization and geopolitical relations as well as for economic exchange. It is, indeed, all-encompassing in scale and overwhelming in scope. And it is predicated on a wanting, on what works sometimes according to drive, sometimes according to desire, sometimes according to need, that can be seen as another manifestation of the virus that renders us zombies, or zombielike. We know, for instance, that our needs/desires motivate us to seek their satisfaction but that we are never really satisfied. The fabulous dinner, the new car, the cool drink, the attractive companion: none fill our desire; all are mere stepping-stones leading us, continually, to more and more wants. As Zygmunt Bauman observes, "for good consumers it is not the satisfaction of the needs one is tormented by, but the torments of desires never yet sensed or suspected."[12] We want more, and more, and more; and we want, for the most part, unreflectively.

Such unrelenting desire has in common with the economy a ceaseless flow, as Baudrillard writes:

The compulsion toward liquidity, flow, and an accelerated circulation of what is psychic, sexual, or pertaining to the body is the exact replica of the force which rules
market value.[13]

The "force" he mentions can, we suggest, be identified with what is the dominant ideology, or form of reason, in the contemporary era. This is neoliberalism, the current
form of what, following Immanuel Wallerstein,[14] we can call the world-system—which
comprises the global civil society, the globalized economy, and the increasingly globalized polity.

Perhaps the most important aspect of globalization-as-neoliberalism is the way it has
combined the retreat of the state with the advance of global capitalism—often in the
face of resistance from local, regional, and national interests. It operates according to the
same logic of capitalism: the idea of freedom. But the freedom of neoliberalist capitalism
is one that aims to liberate us from everything, even, as philosopher Michael Polanyi
writes, "from obligations toward truth and justice, reducing reason to its own caricature."[15] Freedom, for neoliberalism, for capitalism, equals free trade: an unbounded
economy and the unfettered circulation of people, capital, and goods. Its founding
principle is the pursuit of self-interest through competition between producers and producers, consumers and consumers. Now, across the world, the profit motive overrules
virtually all other motives, including religious, nationalist, and environmental ones, in a
system that comprises tentacles of trade and exchange crisscrossing the globe, promising
rewards to those who serve the capitalist system and setting in place a blurring of need
and desire that turns us all into mindless consumers.

Capitalist competition is visible in its roughest, rawest form in depictions of the average zombie, who spends all his or her energies in struggling to gain more and more—
the perfect consumer, the perfect exemplar of the search for personal advance through
self-interest. George Romero's 1968 movie *Night of the Living Dead* and its sequels are
particularly good examples of zombie films that lay down the terms by which the
zombie trope "reads" capitalism. Like their predecessor, Sidney Salkow's *Last Man on
Earth* (1964), and any number of films up to, say, Danny Boyle's *28 Days Later* (2002),
Romero's films point to the ways in which major social institutions become the site for
zombification. Set in shopping malls, churches, schools, laboratories, prisons, or army
barracks, they show the horror at the heart of the everyday; they show the terrible inevitability of infection in what should be safe environments; they show how easily the
protectors of society turn into a threat or become its jailers. In this they are allegories for,
or analogies of, American capital that, in terms of geopolitics, globalized economy, and
geoentertainment, is the perfect hegemon: provider and protector that is also the ultimate infection. They show, too, what is perhaps the most devastating aspect of zombie as
metaphor for the current economy: there is no (evident) way out. Your only option, when
faced with the zombie menace, is to kill or be killed. Either way you're screwed, because
you are dead or you have become what you fear. The act of violence that removes the
horror and threat of the zombie reconstructs me, the human, as zombie—a being that is
only body, without empathy, without respect for life: very like the marketplace, in fact.

Capitalism is nothing like the state of being-zombie, of course, because it is not the living dead but a system of economic and social organization based on individualism and private ownership of the means of production. Yet like zombies, it is all-absorbing with respect to its environment: Hardt and Negri point out that "today nearly all of humanity is to some degree absorbed within or subordinated to the networks of capitalist exploitation."[16] In other words, global capitalism is boundless and insatiable. It depends entirely upon consumption—after all, why produce something no one will buy?—and must generate hunger, or desire, in people who may have no practical need for the object or service being marketed. To advance this mission, capitalism also, and again like zombiedom, depends on excess or a surplus. Just as we rarely see a solitary zombie, but usually a mob, an extraordinary surfeit of them—far more than should be necessary to consume a city—so too capitalism produces far too much because it works through the operation of surplus value, and surplus value is realized most effectively when there is excessive consumption. So we can read capitalism as a self-replicating endemic virus, as Marx might have but didn't quite put it, when he wrote,

> The bourgeoisie, by the rapid improvement of all instruments of production, by the immensely facilitated means of communication, draws all, even the most barbarian, nations into civilization. . . . It compels all nations, on pain of extinction, to adopt the bourgeois mode of production; it compels them to introduce what it calls civilization into their midst, i.e., to become bourgeois themselves. In one word, it creates a world after its own image.[17]

Once a capitalist bites you, in other words, you've had it—you've caught the bug. And we capitalists do in fact infect others, despite our best intentions.

The issue is not that we all begin to buy the same kinds of jeans and eat the same potato chips but that this apparently most democratic system of economic management leads not to a democracy of wealth but to a divided society in both global and local terms: the few-too-few who have nearly everything and the many-too-many who are reduced to little or nothing. Those multitudes comprise what Heidegger termed the "standing army" of workers, crowds of shoppers at the mall, the couch potatoes on a million sofas across the nation, all reduced to unthinking obedience and/or consumption—to zombies. The obesity crisis to which the media is currently paying so much attention is in this respect connected to capitalism-as-zombie: mindless consumption of the unnecessary by the unneedy. Consider the endless advertising and promotion of unhealthy fattening food, and alongside this the plethora of health promotions, pharmaceutical advertisements, and diet products, all of which suggests that we, the people, are being zombied. Our consciousness of self and control of self have been seized by a bottomless hunger to consume no matter what, and no matter that it doesn't nourish us.

However, the imposition of a market logic on the world-system has not been entirely successful—or rather, has not occurred without resistance—and it would be wrong to argue that even Western society has been completely given over to capitalism. Despite the most positive statements issued by mouthpieces for the market and despite its necessary teleology, there have always been gaps in its practice. John Frow points to a number of areas in which society has gone against market interests, as it did with respect to the abolition of slavery or the setting of other limits on capitalism during the Victorian era in Britain when, despite the apparent giving over of everything to the capitalist dream, the state invested enormously in roads, rail, libraries, schools, and hospitals.[18] Indeed, "every extension of the commodity form," Frow writes, "has been met with resistance and often with reversal."[19] The zombie trope may well buy in to this countercapitalism as part of the generalized assault it seems to make on global capital. So many of the examples—the Dead series, *Last Man on Earth*, *The Omega Man*, or *28 Days Later*—show the heart of capitalist settlement littered with the detritus of modern civilization: paper and old clothes drifting among the bodies on pavements, cars uselessly lining the streets, and looted stores opening wistfully out onto the emptiness beyond. Perhaps what we can suggest about this use of the trope is that the zombie is the worm that turned. Capitalism produced and overproduced it, and now it is eating capitalism.

Jean-Paul Sartre pointed out the same sort of issue in his critique of the colonial mission. Colonialism manifestly worked as a kind of zombie-ing practice, in a *Heart of Darkness* kind of way: colonial administrators and the colonists who came with them typically treated locals not as people but as exploitable objects, commodities, mute things, things without affect. But as Hegel might have argued, and as Sartre thunders at the colonizers in his preface to Franz Fanon's *The Wretched of the Earth*, this relationship is precariously balanced. Just as the colonizers had zombied, or dehumanized, the locals, Sartre wrote, so too the locals will come to see them not as humans but as things, and to zombie them in turn. "Turn and turn about," he warns; "in these shadows from whence a new dawn will break, it is you who are the zombies."[20]

In de Certeau's terms, we might call this a "re-bite": writing about the "uncanniness" of a repressed history, he pointed out that we can never destroy without the destroyed thing returning to take its own vengeance, in its own way: "The dead haunt the living. The past: it 're-bites' [*il re-mord*] (it is a secret and repeated biting)."[21] Fredric Jameson picks up on similar concerns in *The Geopolitical Aesthetic* (1992),[22] particularly when he points out the way in which films like *Alien* represent a world of capitalist-driven, technological totalization, where every part of life is alienated and infiltrated by institutions and agents operating within the global machine of capitalism. Worse than the alien monsters in the first film of the Alien series is, first, the affectless android, a zombie-type who will destroy his fellow crew without batting an eye, and second, the company man, who will alienate every value, and every living thing, for the sake of the company's profits. Their violent ends, as well as their previous actions, recall Kurtz and what he said in the appalling coda to *Heart of Darkness* and *Apocalypse Now*: "The horror! The horror!" This is surely the only response to the realization that everyone and every value has been consumed—and that now it's his turn to go to the wall.

Capitalism has the same heartless all-consuming character, particularly in its pure form, in which the "invisible hand" of the market is supposed to bring about a dynamic equilibrium between supply and demand. This has had devastating outcomes: though the invisible hand may even out imbalances between supply and demand over time, this often comes about at great human cost, requiring the "surplus" people in a community to die or flee; viz. the Irish Potato Famine of 1846–50. The problem is that capital doesn't care and doesn't weigh human costs. It is simply zombie—hungry, and hence focused on feeding and expanding regardless of the consequences.

The Cognitive Analogue

This is rather demoralizing material that says very little about the capacity of human beings to resist the slide into zombiedom or to inoculate ourselves against twin viruses of all-consuming drive or heartless emptiness. A third—and more optimistic—perspective that we can bring to the zombie trope is an analogy between thinking and being that might function as a mode of resistance to the trend toward becoming zombie. Richard Cytowic points out the inadequacy of using an android logic to approach the workings of the mind, writing, "All analogues of the mind to a machine are inadequate because it is *emotion, much more than reason, that makes us human.*"[23] And intimately associated with emotion is qualia—or phenomenological life, the feeling of being.

We do not intend, in this final section, to engage with the p-zombie debate, except to gesture toward the way in which it has been picked up by philosophers of cognition. For some of them, the zombie trope expressed as p-zombie has been a very alluring site because of the potential it seems to offer for reflection about what it means to be human. Not all agree about the value of zombies as an analogue for humans. Daniel Dennett, for instance, is the poster boy for those philosophers who reject the idea of p-zombie as a logical absurdity: to be human, he argues/they argue, is to have consciousness; if zombies have consciousness, whether or not they also have a soul, then they must, Dennett argues, be human and not zombies. He writes,

> Sometimes philosophers clutch an insupportable hypothesis to their bosoms and run headlong over the cliff edge. Then, like cartoon characters, they hang there in mid-air, until they notice what they have done and gravity takes over. Just such a boon is the philosophers' concept of a zombie.[24]

This is a perfectly reasonable position, but it does miss the opportunity to take on board something very interesting about cognition: Dennett's fellow philosophers, poised on the cliff, may have used language clumsily to argue their point, but perhaps he was just a touch too serious and has himself fallen into a category error by reading a metaphor as an actuality. While we agree with Dennett about the incongruity of deploying a creature of fiction, a rhetorical device, as a serious research tool, we do argue that zombies as trope, not actuality, remain valuable springboards into consideration of human ontology. Principally, we take the fantasy of zombie morphology as a way of considering what it means to be a human, living in a community of humans, and what it means to be a cognitive being.

"Living systems," biologist Humberto Maturana writes, "are cognitive systems, and living as a process is a process of cognition."[25] While zombies are not precisely living—in the human sense—they're not dead either, or inanimate. Instead, they seem to fulfill some of the main requirements of a cognitive organism, specifically the aspect biologists call autopoiesis: "a way of establishing and maintaining a system's boundary by select-ing meaningful elements—or distinctions the system can use—out of an otherwise in-distinct, 'noisy,' environment."[26] This is a model for the emergence of the self, any sort of self, as the result of a combination of circularity and complexity on the part of systems. From amoeba through freshwater prawns to Einstein, Maturana insists, we exist and form ourselves by interacting with our environments and adjusting to the conditions in which we find ourselves. In this definition, zombies are also living, cognitive entities. They are biological phenomena because their brains clearly undertake at least some information-processing activities; after all, they generally retain some memory of their prezombie lives, and this capacity is surely found only in the functioning brain. Zombies have discrimination too, in the sense that they respond to their environment; and they are capable of some quality of interaction, whether to seek out and eat human beings or to huddle together in their dismal spaces. They might have pus for brains, and yet their remarkable similarity to us can be used to turn our attention to *embodied* knowledge, *embodied* cognition, *embodied* identity, and in this way move us closer to an aesthetics in our human as well as our professional identity: a resensitizing of ourselves as subjects to the world of human intercourse, and against zombie practices.

In this respect, it is worth pointing out zombies' relation to art, which is either to ignore it or destroy it. Despite our many similarities, one thing that is distinctly dif-ferent between (most) humans and zombies is their level of adroitness. Zombies are clumsy, and insensitive, with words and objects, and do not respond aesthetically or empathically to cultural products. In Libria, the postulated society in *Equilibrium*, art was destroyed without hesitation; and even the very smooth Matthias in *The Omega Man* cries out at Charlton Heston, "Your art, your science, it was all a nightmare, and now it's done!" And this is a point at which humans and zombies part company, and at which the conditions for cognitive being run up against some limits. Zombies are incapable of nuance, of sensitivity, and so while they might have been able to fit the older definition of cognition—which distinguished emotion from reason—they don't fit the current definition which incorporates "all information-processing activities of the brain, ranging from the analysis of immediate stimuli to the organisation of subjec-tive experience."[27]

In this reading, *pace* Maturana, cognition must include emotional and aesthetic capacity. Melanie Swalwell describes the importance of embodied sensory experiences in bringing the processes of cognition to light, and hence of aesthetic factors in how we perceive and conceive our world.[28] The zombie aspect of the self and of society may reject the aesthetic domain, but it is here, in the world of creative production, that the foundations for cognitive function can be found; as Barbara Stafford points out,

> in the widespread postmodern denigration of the aesthetic, what is forgotten is that from Leibniz to Schiller, the term connoted the integration of mental activity with feeling. Aisthesis, as perception or sensation, has in post-Cartesian and especially post-Kantian thought become separated from cognition. Rediscovering its pragmatic capacity to bridge experience and rationality, emotion and logic, seems all the more important in the era of virtual reality and seemingly nonmediated media.[29]

We rediscover its capacity when we start with the premise that cognition generally involves the creative shaping of our conceptions of the world. We rediscover its capacity in considering how metaphors drive the cognitive process—laying down fresh pathways for thought and practice. We rediscover its capacity when we recognize that art, by reinforcing ways of looking at the world, is necessarily a cognitive process and that therefore the zombie heart of all of us and of society, with its devotion to consumption and its incapacity to interact, is not the way to be human.

Conclusion: Some Kind of Analogue

The homology between humans and zombies is, we argue, one very solid reason for their enduring appeal and fascination: we humans are arrested by ourselves and by that of which we are capable. The likeness between zombies and humans, along with the terrifying otherness of zombies, is pitched—in our reading—at the unendurable, unending story of otherness, the underside of our symbolic order that is posed by the three weird sisters: death, the Sublime, and the Real. Zombies analogize the Other in these forms and bring our attention to the limit and the boundary of life and meaning in part because they themselves have escaped this Other, Freud's "Thing." For us it is the limit, but not for them, because they have already identified with the "other" side and been separated from the order of humanity. We have not been, however hungry or heartless we may be. Like Jim in *28 Days Later*, we may perform as zombie at times, yet we can always pull back and return to the human condition because we have not yet crossed the boundary that marks the end of self-awareness, removes the human subject from the symbolic order, and returns it to the Real.

So why look to zombies, or the zombie trope, to discuss this? Because, given the internal pressures described so richly by psychologists and psychiatrists, and even more so the external pressures of globalized capital, the easier thing to do would be to collapse into zombie status: mindlessly consume, and/or exile from ourselves the capacity to feel, and thus to be. Mikhail Bakhtin writes, "The better a person understands the degree to which he is externally determined, the closer he comes to understanding and exercising his own freedom."[30] Bringing zombieness, the hidden aspects of the self and society, into light may allow us to consider more reflectively what it means to be a "me."

Notes

1. David J. Chalmers, *The Conscious Mind: In Search of a Fundamental Theory* (New York: Oxford University Press, 1996).

2. Michel de Certeau, *The Practice of Everyday Life*, trans. Steven Rendall (Berkeley: University of California Press, 1984), 190–91.

3. Steven Shaviro, *The Cinematic Body* (Minneapolis: University of Minnesota Press, 1993), 98.

4. Sigmund Freud, "New Introductory Lectures on Psychoanalysis," *Standard Edition* 22 (1933): 22.

5. Gilles Deleuze and Félix Guattari, *Anti-Oedipus: Capitalism and Schizophrenia*, trans. R. Hurley, Seem Mark, and Helen R. Lane (Minneapolis: University of Minnesota Press, 1983), 27.

6. Indeed, zombies cannot be subjects, strictly speaking, because they are outside the symbolic order, the domain of language: they utter, but don't articulate, cannot speak. At the point of zombification, they exited the symbolic order and thus cannot desire in the psychoanalytic sense.

7. Jacques Lacan, *The Ethics of Psychoanalysis: The Seminar of Jacques Lacan*, book 7, trans. Dennis Porter (London: Routledge, 1992), 51–52.

8. Sigmund Freud, "Instincts and Their Vicissitudes," *Standard Edition* 14 (1915): 111–40.

9. Richard Cytowic, *The Man Who Tasted Shapes* (London: Abacus, 1993), 170–71.

10. As described by Lacan, *Ethics of Psychoanalysis*, Seminar 7. In this respect, we might say, Antigone is the first of this form of zombie.

11. Karl Marx and Friedrich Engels, *The German Ideology*, ed. C. J. Arthur (New York: International, 1970), 48.

12. Zygmunt Bauman, *Globalization: The Human Consequence* (Cambridge: Polity Press, 1998), 82.

13. Jean Baudrillard, *Forget Foucault*, trans. Nicole Dufresne (New York: Semiotext(e), 1987), 25.

14. Immanuel Wallerstein, "The Rise and Future Demise of the Capitalist World System," in *Globalization: The Reader*, ed. John Beynon and David Dunkerley, 233–38 (London: Athlone, 2000).

15. Michael Polanyi and Harry Prosch, *Meaning* (Chicago: University of Chicago Press, 1975), 14.

16. Michael Hardt and Antonio Negri, *Empire* (Cambridge, Mass.: Harvard University Press, 2000), 43.

17. Karl Marx, *Selected Writings*, ed. David McLellan (Oxford: Oxford University Press, 1977), 225.

18. John Frow, "Res Publica," *Australian Book Review* 208 (February–March 1999): 23–27.

19. John Frow, *Time and Commodity Culture: Essays in Cultural Theory and Postmodernity* (Oxford: Clarendon Press, 1997), 135.

20. Jean-Paul Sartre, preface to *The Wretched of the Earth*, by Frantz Fanon (New York: Grove Press, 1963), 33.

21. Michel de Certeau, *Heterologies: Discourse on the Other*, trans. Brian Massumi (Minneapolis: University of Minnesota Press, 1986), 3.

22. Fredric Jameson, *The Geopolitical Aesthetic: Cinema and Space in the World System* (Bloomington: Indiana University Press, 1992).

23. Cytowic, *Man Who Tasted Shapes*, 156, emphasis original.

24. Daniel Dennett, "The Unimagined Preposterousness of Zombies: Commentary on T. Moody, O. Flanagan and T. Polger," *Journal of Consciousness Studies* 2, no. 4 (1995): 323.

25. Humberto Maturana and Francisco Varela, *Autopoiesis and Cognition: The Realization of the Living* (Dordrecht, Netherlands: D. Reidel, 1980), 13.

26. Joseph Tabbi, *Cognitive Fictions* (Minneapolis: University of Minnesota Press, 2002), xxiii.

27. Reuven Tsur, "Aspects of Cognitive Poetics," in *Cognitive Stylistics—Language and Cognition in Text Analysis*, ed. Elena Semino and Jonathan Culpeper, 279–318 (Amsterdam: John Benjamins, 2002).

28. Melanie Swalwell, "The Senses and Memory in Intercultural Cinema," *Film-Philosophy* 6, no. 32 (2002), http://www.film-philosophy.com/vol6–2002/n32swalwell.

29. Barbara Stafford, *Good Looking: Essays on the Virtue of Images* (Cambridge, Mass.: MIT Press, 1998), 52.

30. Mikhail Bakhtin, *The Dialogic Imagination* (Austin: University of Texas Press, 1981), 139.

CHAPTER 7

Ugly Beauty
Monstrous Dreams of Utopia

DAVID McNALLY

Capitalist market-society overflows with monsters. But no grotesque species so command the modern imagination as the vampire and the zombie. In fact, these two creatures need to be thought conjointly, as interconnected moments of the monstrous dialectic of modernity. Like Victor Frankenstein and his Creature, the vampire and the zombie are doubles, linked poles of the split society. If vampires are the dreaded beings who might possess us and turn us into their docile servants, zombies represent our haunted self-image, warning us that we might already be lifeless, disempowered agents of alien powers. "Under the hegemony of the spirit world of capital," writes Chris Arthur, "we exist for each other only as capital's zombies, its 'personifications,' 'masks,' 'supports,' to use Marx's terms."[1] In the image of the zombie lurks a troubled apprehension that capitalist society really is a night of the living dead.

Arthur's insight returns us to the salient image that proliferates throughout sub-Saharan Africa today: the zombie-laborer. Having emerged in Haiti in the early twentieth century, the earliest zombies were indeed "dead men working," unthinking body-machines, lacking identity, memory, and consciousness—possessing only the physical capacity for labor. Unlike flesh-eating ghouls, who have come to stand in for them in the culture industries of late capitalism, these zombies harbor the hidden secret of capitalism, its dependence on the bondage and exploitation of human laborers. However, because they are the *living* dead, zombies possess the capacity to awaken, to throw off their bonds, to reclaim life amid the morbid ruins of late capitalism. As much as they move slowly and clumsily through the routinized motions of deadened life, zombies also possess startling capacities for revelry and revolt, latent energies that can erupt in riotous nights of the living dead. Bursting across movie screens and the pages of pulp fiction, such zombie festivals contain moments of carnivalesque insurgency, horrifying disruptions of the ordered and predictable patterns of everyday life. Without warning, a rupture in the fabric of the normal transforms the living dead into hyperactive marauders. The maimed and disfigured seize the streets and invade shopping malls; authority collapses; anarchy is unleashed. Part of the attraction of such displays, and of much of the horror genre generally, resides, of course, in its capacity to gratify as much as to frighten. As viewers, we (or at least many of us) derive a deep pleasure from images of fantastic beings wreaking havoc upon polite citizens of well-ordered society. And, here, we can locate part of the utopian charge animating zombie rebellions.

As Mikhail Bakhtin reminds us, utopia often comes bathed in the grotesque. It does so in reaction to the antisensuous, anticorporeal striving of official cultures to tame bodies and desires, enclose property and personality, regulate labor and recreation, control festivity and sexuality. Against the dreary and anticorporeal seriousness of sanctioned modes of life, oppositional cultures engage in parody by way of inversion. They elevate the degraded and debased—outcasts, freaks, the simple-minded, and the hideously deformed. And they often do so by celebrating the bizarre, fractured, and oversized human body, deploying a *grotesque realism* that mocks dreary officialdom and inverts its values and symbolic orders. The utopian register of grotesque realism moves via a dialectic of inversion; the degraded now do the degrading, bringing low that which official culture has elevated, uplifting what has been suppressed. Yet, the utopian impulse highlights rebirth as much as degradation. "To degrade is to bury, to sow and to kill simultaneously, in order to bring forth something more and better," writes Bakhtin. "To degrade also means to concern oneself with the lower stratum of the body, the life of the belly and the reproductive organs." Contrary to the defined and enclosed heroic body of the bourgeois/ aristocratic male, then, the grotesque body "is unfinished, outgrows itself, transgresses its own limits. The stress is laid on those parts of the body that are open to the outside world . . . the open mouth, the genital organs, the breast, the phallus, the potbelly, the nose."[2] And, with respect to the zombie genre, we should add: the cut, the sore, the dangling limb, all of them reminders of the corporeal fragmentation at the heart of capitalism, and of the open wounds that join wage laborers into a monstrous collectivity.

To be sure, the culture industries seize on, sanitize, and repackage these carnivalesque images, endeavoring to cathect riotous energies into the consumption of commodities. Such commodification of the carnivalesque proceeds by reifying its elements, replacing regenerating laughter with mere irony.[3] And yet, the process of taming subversive impulses is never total; something always exceeds and resists its grasp. After all, the very deradicalizing effects of mass culture are achieved only by awakening precisely the desires meant to be sublimated. It follows that "a process of compensatory exchange must be involved here," as Fredric Jameson observes:

> If the ideological function of mass culture is understood as a process whereby otherwise dangerous and protopolitical impulses are "managed" and defused, rechanneled and offered spurious objects, then some preliminary step must be theorized in which these same impulses—the raw material upon which the process works—are awakened within the very texts that seek to still them.[4]

And it is these utopian energies that animate the nightmares of the ruling classes, the bad dreams that surface in characters like Jack Cade, the homeless rebel in Shakespeare's *Henry VI*, Part 2; in the father of young Azaro, the protagonist of Ben Okri's *The Famished Road*, as he grows monstrously large and vanquishes the thugs of the Party of the Rich; in the many-headed hydra of the rebellious mob; in the riotous women of Okri's *Infinite*

Riches; in Frankenstein's Creature, as imagined by author Mary Shelley; in Marx's image of the insurgent global proletariat.

One of the decisive things about the many-headed monster and Frankenstein's Creature is that they are multiplicities that compose a unity. The hydra-mob's many heads connect to a common body, just as the corporeal bits of Frankenstein's Creature, made up of animal and human parts, cohere into a living, breathing, speaking colossus. The ascription of the latter attribute—speech—is, as we have seen, among the most subversive aspects of Mary Shelley's story, perhaps why it is omitted in most film adaptations. It is bad enough, after all, that a creature assembled from fragmented parts might actually assume a human form, however distorted. But, with speech, it becomes exponentially more threatening, capable of association with others of its ilk. In Shelley's tale, of course, the Creature is isolated and forlorn, desperately seeking a companion. It speaks only to its oppressors and tormenters. But traversing her novel lurks the anxiety that the Creature might not forever be alone, that it might acquire a companion, reproduce, and form a monstrous social collectivity—and this prospect is hinted at in the sailors' rebellion that hurries the novel to its close.

Collective rebellion by laborers signals the course imagined by Marx, who is said to have enjoyed the story of *Frankenstein*.[5] In his call for associated action and organization, Marx imagines that the "crippled monstrosity"[6] of the working class might reassemble itself, find its voice, and begin to move to a new rhythm, not that of capital's machines but one of its own making. In this dance of the grave diggers, Marx identifies monstrous forces of redemption and regeneration. He envisions the multiplicity that is the collective worker acquiring a new consciousness and identity, a new praxis. There is no loss of individuality here; on the contrary, a new mode of individuality is generated in the act of revolutionary reassemblage. In this spirit, Marx projects the emancipation of the collective worker in terms of the creation of a new "organic social body wherein people reproduce themselves as individuals, but as social individuals."[7] In so doing, he envisions proletarian liberation as a dance of the *concrete universal*, to borrow a term from Hegel, a dynamic totalization that affirms identity and difference, or what Marx calls elsewhere a "unity of the diverse."[8] While Marx himself may not always have envisioned this collective agent in all its potential diversity, this is the direction in which the logic of his position tends.[9]

It is suggestive in this regard that Britain's sailors, the group responsible for collective revolt in *Frankenstein*, were just such a unity of the diverse, "multiracial—Irish, English, African," as two historians note. So much was this the case that "by the end of the Napoleonic wars, roughly one-quarter of the Royal Navy was black."[10] Assembled from multiple groups of the dispossessed, the deep-sea proletariat rose to moments of exceptional militancy and solidarity. It seized ships in mutinous insurgencies; it challenged the rule of state and capital; and it transgressed the enclosures among nationalities and ethnoracial groups, acquiring a heightened grotesquerie in its violations of the emerging categories of race.

Proletarian monsters are, by definition, monsters of the body. Not only do their corporeal powers become the life force of capital, enabling the latter's vampirelike expansion; more than this, their emancipatory struggles entail monstrous claims of the body against the abstracting powers of capital. Marx's dance of the grave diggers—a festive zombie-riot—involves a victory of the sensuous over the nonsensuous, the material over the abstractly ideal. Bodies loom large, grotesquely so, in this narrative of liberation, and their monstrous presence reverberates across stories of zombies on the march.

This is the point at which Marx's communist vision rejoins the great plebeian tradition excavated by Bakhtin, in which "the immortal labouring people constitute the world's body," in the words of one commentator.[11] It is also the point at which it converges with that *anthropological materialism*, to use Walter Benjamin's designation, whose pivot is the emancipation of the flesh.[12] In affirming its concrete embodiment as a living collectivity, the insurgent working class rescues laboring bodies from their near-death, their function as mere automata that enable capital's valorization.

This moment of rebellion is also one of recuperation. The zombies awake and, in doing so, reclaim their very corporeality from the abstracting powers of capital, establishing the ontological precondition for the recovery of memory, identity, and history. So shattering is a zombie awakening, so disruptive of the molecular structure of bourgeois life, that it is typically figured as a frenzied upheaval of nature itself. After all, the monstrous collective body of labor inevitably appears as an elementally natural force in a society that has abstracted it from history and the social. In his *Famished Road* cycle, Ben Okri grasps precisely this naturalization of the laboring body when, in portraying Azaro's father at work, he tells us that "his blood trickled from his back and mixed with the rubbish of the earth."[13] The idiom of horror remains the only genre for registering the insurgency of a monstrous body joined to the very earth itself. Take Dickens's description from *Barnaby Rudge.* He begins with three ringleaders of the 1780 Gordon Riots in London, whom he describes as "covered with soot and dirt, and dust, and lime; their garments torn to rags; their hair hanging wildly about them; their hands and faces jagged and bleeding with the wounds of rusty nails." Behind them is "a dense throng" of insurgents, offering "a vision of coarse faces . . . a dream of demon heads and savage eyes, and sticks and iron bars uplifted in the air." This "bewildering horror," Dickens writes, pulsed with "many phantoms, not to be forgotten all through life."[14]

There is a horrified poetics of class and gender at work here. The mob is simultaneously animalized and feminized. Its femininity does not, of course, partake of genteel passivity; rather, it consists of crazed, transgressive, plebeian womanhood. The riotous rabble is defined by blood and dirt, by huge, all-consuming passions, by the life-swallowing powers of "mother earth." The female grotesque thus features centrally in the construction of the monstrous.[15]

The extent to which the European working classes were "racialized" in the discourse of emergent industrial capitalism is rarely appreciated today. Yet, during the epoch in which scientific racism emerged in order to rationalize the oppression of Africans and colonized peoples, its categories were sufficiently pliable to racialize the laboring poor of Europe as well. Granier de Cassagnac, for instance, in his *Histoire des classes ouvrières et des classes bourgeoises* (1838), asserted that proletarians were a subhuman race formed through the interbreeding of prostitutes and thieves. In a similar register, Henry Mayhew's *London Labour and the London Poor* (1861) divided humanity into two distinct races: the civilized and the wanderers. The latter, including the laboring poor of Britain, were defined by their ostensible incapacity to transcend the body and its desires.[16] Similar processes can be observed in Sweden, where proletarians were represented as "another race," as "crude" and "coarse," as "a seething mass, a formless . . . rabble," partaking in the realm of "the primitive, the animal."[17] Central to this racialization and feminization of the working classes was the attribution of a grotesque corporeality.

It is this stuff of hyperembodiment that is frequently celebrated in popular culture, including the horror genre. When the zombies strike back, it is their huge, awkward, oozing bodies that appear most prominently. As in Marx or Bakhtin, there is a plebeian poetics at work here, an ugly beauty of the grotesque body of the oppressed.

There is something lacking, however, in the zombie revolts that emerge in popular culture today. And that something is what has been lost in the transition from Haitian to Hollywood zombies—and the very thing that has been recuperated in zombie tales emanating today from sub-Saharan Africa. Haitian zombies, as we have seen, are mindless laborers, people reanimated from the dead who lack everything—identity, consciousness, memory, language—save the brute capacity for labor. They are physical bearers of labor-power and nothing more. This feature figured prominently in American popular appropriations of zombies in the era of the Great Depression. In William Seabrook's *The Magic Island* (1929), zombies are portrayed as "dead men working in the cane fields," as "automatons . . . bent expressionless over their work."[18] And, throughout the Depression era, the image of the zombie as a living-dead laborer was never lost in Hollywood horror. In the film *White Zombie* (1932), for instance, Bela Lugosi plays Murder Legendre, bewitched sinister factory owner in Haiti who raises the dead to toil in his sugar mill. As one critic of the film remarks, "the gaunt, sinewy workers with sunken eyes shuffle in production assembly lines and around the large, central milling vat. They are reifications of despair and hopelessness, no more than cogs in the mighty machine themselves."[19] This image of alienated, crushing, mindless labor in capitalist society resonated powerfully in a United States wracked by unemployment, poverty, and class resentment. But it was largely lost with the revival of the zombie in American culture during the radical upsurges of the 1960s, a revival that owes much to George Romero's pioneering films beginning with *Night of the Living Dead* (1968). For Hollywood's rediscovery of the zombie was, in fact, a revision, one that short-circuited the figure of the zombie-laborer. Interestingly, as previously noted, although he used the term "living dead," Romero initially imagined his monsters as flesh-eating ghouls, not zombies, and it is that construction—as flesh-eating monsters—that now defines "zombies" within mass culture in North America and Europe.[20] This emphasis on consumption, on eating flesh, was central to the displacement of the zombie-laborer. By repositioning zombies as crazed consumers, rather than producers, recent Hollywood horror films tend to offer biting criticism of the hyperconsumptionist ethos of an American capitalism characterized by excess. But this deployment comes at the cost of invisibilizing the hidden world of labor and the disparities of class that make all this consumption possible. As a result, contemporary zombie films, at their best, tend to offer a critique of consumerism, not capitalism—one that fails to probe the life- destroying, zombifying processes of work in bourgeois society.

The occlusion of the zombie-laborer also deradicalizes images of zombie revolt. During World War II, a period of race, gender, and class upheaval in America, zombies emerged as figures of rebellion. A whole series of 1940s zombie movies, in fact, "denied the possibility of complete containment,"[21] locating horror in zombie *awakening* rather than in their passive, controlled state. Rarely, however, was the zombie idiom used as subversively as it was in Jacques Tourneur's haunting film *I Walked with a Zombie* (1943). Celebrated as "one of the finest of all American horror films,"[22] *I Walked with a Zombie* depicts the decline of colonial capitalism in the form of a dysfunctional white family, descended from slave owners, as it sinks slowly into decay and self-destruction on a small Caribbean island. Deploying a problematically gendered trope, a white woman comes to stand in for a dying colonialism. Characters in the film remark of her, as of her class as a whole, that "she was dead in her own life" and "dead in the selfishness of her spirit."[23] In a dramatic reversal, zombies now take shape as creatures from the imperial metropole, not the colonial hinterland, as the living dead of a morbid colonialism, passively waiting to be washed away by the tides of history. Fittingly, the film ends with the deceased "white zombie" and her lover disappearing into the sea, as the voice of a black character intones, "Forgive them who are dead and give peace and happiness to the living."

At the historical moment *I Walked with a Zombie* was offering its cultural critique of empire, a new and innovative "zombie music" was emerging to give expression to rebellious countercurrents among African Americans. The very year the film appeared (1943), the so-called Harlem Riot erupted following the shooting of a black soldier by a white cop.[24] The Harlem uprising came amid a growing radicalization of African Americans in unions, the military, and burgeoning civil rights organizations. As new practices and cultures of resistance formed, music became a key register for expressing discontent with racism, menial jobs, unemployment, poor wages, and military conscription.[25] In after-hours clubs and apartments, a young, defiant generation of jazz musicians forged a radically new musical language, soon known as *bebop*, as an aesthetic idiom for new structures of feeling—anger, pride, nonconformity with white America, hostility to racism and privilege.[26] Bebop was a complex, musically sophisticated, emotionally expressive protest music. It required exceptional musicianship and creativity and enormous facility at improvisation. In and through it, the new jazz revolutionaries produced a music of dissonance, of jarring contrasts and polyrhythms, as they turned chord progressions around, played against a tune's underlying harmony, and shifted tempos—all in an effort to create a visionary African American aesthetic that spoke to a world in disarray while pulsating with the rhythms of zombie rebellion.

One of the geniuses at the heart of this artistic revolution was pianist Thelonious Monk (1917–82), who created a series of remarkable jazz compositions built around his singularly angular phrasing, highlighted by unusual intervals, dissonance, and displaced notes.[27] Among fellow jazz artists, Monk's musical language was sometimes known as *zombie music*. Pianist Mary Lou Williams explains: "Why 'Zombie music'? Because the screwy chords reminded us of music from *Frankenstein* or any horror film."[28] In Monk's music, "screwy chords" express the rhythms of a world out of joint, a space of reification in which people are reduced to things—and in which they violently awaken from their frozen state. This is an aesthetic of disharmony, of a broken world whose bits can never be entirely reassembled. There is a stark and unsettling beauty here, one comprising "frozen sounds," as Williams puts it. Monk's tunes insert us into a world in which things come to life—in which, to reprise Marx, tables begin to dance and evolve "grotesque ideas" out of their wooden brains.[29] But, in Monk's compositions, we hear not only the jarring sounds of things coming to life; more than this, we heed the rhythms of zombie movement, the ferocious sounds of the dance of the living dead. It is now widely recognized that the entire African American experience is bathed in living death, in the "double consciousness" of being both person and thing.[30] And Monk's music captures this in the monstrously beautiful cadences of the banging, smashing, crashing chords of an emerging African American protest music, one that gave a new urban cadence to "the rhythmic cry of the slave," to use Du Bois's apt expression.[31]

The music of the enslaved—both song of sorrow and cry of freedom—is, like all horror idioms, a language of doubling. Across these musical landscapes, freedom and bondage clash, producing that jarring dissonance in which pursued and pursuer reverse positions, each chasing and fleeing the other. Only a music of polyrhythms, shifting tempos, and displaced notes could begin to capture the "ugly beauty" of this experience, to invoke the title of one of Monk's compositions.[32] After all, enunciating the wounds and scars of oppression, the beauty of zombie music can only be ugly. In giving voice to bodies in pain, it howls these wounds, names them, explores them, accents them. For this reason, horror must remain one of its idioms. And yet, in its very artistic production, it defiantly asserts the enduring beauty of survival and resistance—and of the pursuit of freedom. For, as Monk's preeminent biographer states, "Thelonious Monk's music is essentially about freedom," and this contributes to its haunting beauty.[33] Like Frankenstein's Creature, the crippled monsters of labor, the descendants of African slaves, speak—and sing, dance, and create world-moving art. Through this zombie music, the living dead come to life, dance across a landscape of corpses and ruin, and affirm the irreducible beauty of their freedom song.

Today, modern jazz no longer occupies its central position as protest music, even if its influences can be detected in genres as diverse as hip-hop and Afrobeat. Interestingly, a new zombie music of sorts, carrying a jazz influence, emerged in Nigeria during the 1970s, just as neoliberal globalization was setting in and provoking the spate of vampire and zombie tales we have explored. In Fela Kuti's hit album *Zombie* (1977), the image of the living dead is redeployed in a searing attack on the Nigerian army, whose members (and their political masters) figure as zombified monsters preying on the people. A churning mix of black power, socialism, and pan-Africanism, Kuti's Afrobeat music both reflected and inspired social protest and opposition (including riots in Accra during a 1978 performance of "Zombie").[34] As in *I Walked with a Zombie*, Kuti's famous tune reverses the metaphor, portraying the ruling classes and their troops as the true zombies, not those who labor for capital.

Like the gothic novel, Kuti's tune rehearses a dialectical reversal whose classic formulation is to be found in Hegel's drama of master and slave. In his *Phenomenology of*

Spirit, Hegel takes us through a role reversal in which the master, in his dependence on the labor of the slave, becomes a passive, lifeless being, bereft of historical initiative, while the slave discovers in labor her life-generating, world-building capacities.[35] The dialectic thus undergoes a boomerang effect, zombifying society's rulers and awakening the oppressed to their historical capacity to extend the realm of human freedom. If, in the Hegelian dialectic, "progress in the realization of Freedom can be carried out only by the slave,"[36] historical reversal toward freedom comes for Marx by way of the insurgence of the global proletariat. But, here, Marx's knowledge was deficient, as he too did not grasp the extent to which an actual revolution made by African slaves—the Haitian Revolution (1794–1805)—figured directly in Hegel's view that the freedom of slaves must be won through their own emancipatory struggle in a revolutionary "trial by death." But Susan Buck-Morss's pathbreaking research in this area suggests persuasively not only that Hegel followed Haitian events but that "he used the sensational events of Haiti as the linchpin in his argument in the *Phenomenology of Spirit.*"[37] In so doing, she reinstates the dialectic of race and class that is constitutive of capitalist modernity, while demonstrating that a revolutionary movement of black slaves was the high point of freedom struggles in the "age of revolution."[38]

Rethinking the history of bourgeois modernity in this way requires that we read the post-Hegelian treatment of the master–slave relation through Frantz Fanon as much as through Karl Marx.[39] Indeed, doing so renders more powerful Marx's reversal of the zombie dialectic. After all, Marx depicts capitalists too as prisoners of reification, as systematically zombified. "The capitalist," he writes, "functions only as *personified* capital, capital as person, just as the worker is no more than *labour* personified." In strictly economic terms, it is capital that rules, not capitalists; the latter are mere bearers of capital's imperatives. Because they are merely things personified, "the rule of the capitalist over the worker is the rule of things over man, of dead labour over the living." As a result, capitalists too function as the living dead. Colonized and directed by things, they live hollowed out lives, spiritually poor for all their plenty. Yet, reified though they are, capitalists do not have an interest in or capacity for dereification. Instead, they "find absolute satisfaction" in this "process of alienation," whereas the worker "confronts it as a rebel and experiences it as a process of enslavement."[40] While capitalists can only remain in their zombie state, workers are impelled toward a dialectical awakening.[41]

And yet, there are blockages here, which perpetuate the sleeplike state and postpone the moment of awakening. And the danger is that the moment of awakening might be missed, to paraphrase Theodor Adorno.[42] Put differently, there is a danger that the proletariat might not be monstrous enough, that its internal separations, the ultimate key to capital's power over it,[43] might leave it too uncoordinated to perform its zombie dance. Because internal division is the secret to the zombie sleep in labor's relation to capital, to its submissiveness and subordination to an alien will, Marx saw the key to unions and workers' organization not in their strictly material achievements but rather in the spirit of opposition they cultivated. Without struggle, resistance, and international organization, he argued, workers risked becoming "apathetic, thoughtless, more or less well-fed instruments of production"[44]—in short, zombies who cannot awaken. Until that awakening, monstrous utopia lives on in stories, dreams, music, art, and moments of resistance that prefigure the grotesque movements through which the collective laborer throws off its zombified state in favor of something new, frightening, and beautiful.

And this returns us to the emancipation of the body, to the liberation of monstrous corporeality and sensuous existence from the abstracting circuits of capital. But it should also serve to remind us that there is no emancipation of the body short of a radical transformation of the relations between persons and things, short of the liberation of all our "relations to the world—seeing, hearing, tasting, feeling, thinking, contemplating, sensing, wanting, acting, loving."[45] It is the essence of any materialist phenomenology that humans are enmeshed in an object-world shaped in and through their practical activity—clothes, dwellings, beds, chairs, tables, cups, plates, tools, toys, books, and more compose the social–material and meaningful nexus of all lived experience. Yet capitalism inserts the market as forced mediator in our relations to such things. It wraps objects in the straitjacket of the capitalist value-form. And, in so doing, it empties them of their concrete, sensible features, turning them into mere repositories of exchange-value. "Warmth is ebbing from things," observed Walter Benjamin, in a reflection on the hollowing out of things into mere vessels of phantom objectivity (value).[46] As Peter Stallybrass brilliantly reminds us, these dynamics of reification and abstraction touched so personal an item for Marx as his own overcoat, whose circuits in and out of the pawnshop he gloomily tracked. Ironically, an overcoat figured crucially in the actual life and death of Aris Kindt, the anatomized subject of Rembrandt's *The Anatomy of Dr. Nicolaas Tulp*. Unable to procure the money with which to buy one, Kindt resorted to a nonmarket solution: theft. For that, he was convicted, executed, and dissected. It is such struggles between life and death, bound up with our relations to things, that Marx tracks throughout *Capital*. The overcoming of the rule of the market thus also means a restoration of the world of concrete objectivity, so that objects might become things "that are touched and loved and worn."[47] The liberation of people from the dictates of the market entails, for Marx, their reconnection with things in their concrete, sensuous, textured particularities. Dialectical reversal means not only the political victory of the oppressed; it also means dereification, the reanimation of the relations among things and persons via the liberation of things, as well as persons, from circuits of abstraction.

It seems particularly significant that such a drama of reconnection with things appears prominently in a series of stories that Marx created for his daughter Eleanor. Centered on a down-on-his-luck magician named Hans Rockle, who kept a toy shop, Marx spun these stories for his daughter over several months. Rockle, explained Eleanor Marx,

> was always "hard up." His shop was full of the most wonderful things—of wooden men and women, giants and dwarfs, kings and queens, workmen and masters, animals and birds as numerous as Noah got into the Arc, tables and chairs, carriages, boxes of all sorts and sizes. And though he was a magician, Hans could never meet his obligations either to the devil or the butcher, and was therefore—much against the grain—constantly obliged to sell his toys to the devil. These then went through wonderful adventures—always ending in a return to Hans Rockle's shop.[48]

Here, we observe the dialectic of loss and recovery, as Hans Rockle's toys are alienated (in payment to the devil) and disappear into commodity circuits where they undergo great adventures, only to return to his shop. And, in this return, resides the dream of utopia. In their reversion to use-value and their disalienation, in their exit from the circuits of market exchange, things are recuperated, their ebbing warmth restored.

There is a magic at work in liberation, then, one that brings persons and things back to life and breaks the spell of zombieism. That magic resides often in stories today, just as it did in Marx's tales for his daughter. Lurking in such stories, observes Leslie Marmon Silko, are "relentless forces, powerful spirits, vengeful, restlessly seeking justice." In *Almanac of the Dead*, she thus imagines "Marx as a storyteller who worked feverishly to gather together a magical assembly of stories to cure the suffering and evils of the world."[49] Ultimately, as Marx well knew, magical stories press to be taken up by "magic hands," to borrow Fanon's term. Rather than the detached "hands" to which capital tries to reduce them, the world proletariat needs to become a many-headed and many-handed monster, like Shelley's Demogorgon (the people-monster), capable of shaking the very planets and upending Jupiter's throne. We glimpse something of these possibilities in Jack Cade's ramblings, in the battles of Black Tiger, in the mobs that smash the locks and burn down the prisons in *Barnaby Rudge*, in the "industrious women of the city" who storm government offices and police stations in *Infinite Riches*. Too often, however, these insurgent crowds stop short, seeking liberation at the hands of others. This is why everything rests, as Fanon saw, on the oppressed realizing

> that everything depends on them . . . that there is no such thing as a demiurge, that there is no famous man who will take the responsibility for everything, but that the demiurge is the people themselves and the magic hands are finally only the hands of the people.[50]

It is those magic hands that possess the power to slay the monsters of the market. Until such time, the endless toilers of the earth will continue to nurture monstrous desires for utopia as they walk the "endless dream of their roads."

Notes

1. Chris Arthur, *The New Dialectic and Marx's Capital* (Leiden, Netherlands: Brill 2004), 172.

2. Mikhail Bakhtin, *Rabelais and His World*, trans. Helene Iswolsky (Bloomington: Indiana University Press, 1984), 21, 26. Bakhtin's brilliant study is not without its limitations. I address some of these in *Bodies of Meaning: Studies on Language, Labor, and Liberation* (Albany: State University of New York Press, 2001), chapter 4. For one particularly interesting attempt to rework Bakhtin in terms of gender and race, see Mary O'Connor, "Subject, Voice and Women in Some Contemporary Black American Women's Writing," in *Feminism, Bakhtin, and the Dialogic*, edited by Dale M. Bauer and S. Jaret McKinstry, 199–217 (Albany: State University of New York Press, 1991).

3. See Bakhtin, *Rabelais and His World*, 386–88, on Lucian. The culture industries, I contend, merely exacerbate these same tendencies.

4. Fredric Jameson, *The Political Unconscious: Narrative as a Socially Symbolic Act* (Ithaca, N.Y.: Cornell University Press, 1981), 287.

5. See Wheen, *Karl Marx* (London: Fourth Estate, 1999), 72.

6. Karl Marx, *Capital, Volume 1,* trans. Ben Fowkes (Harmondsworth, U.K.: Penguin Books, 1976), 481.

7. Karl Marx, *Grundrisse* (Harmondsworth, U.K.: Penguin Books, 1973), 832.

8. Ibid., 101.

9. See my article "The Dialectics of Unity and Difference in the Constitution of Wage-Labour: On Internal Relations and Working Class Formation," *Capital and Class* 39, no. 1 (2015): 131–46. It is also worth noting that the late Marx returned to some of these questions, writing tens of thousands of words on ethnicity and gender. See David Norman Smith, "Accumulation and the Clash of Cultures," *Rethinking Marxism* 14, no. 4 (2002): 73–84, and Kevin B. Anderson, "Marx's Writings on Non-Western Societies," *Rethinking Marxism* 14, no. 4 (2002): 84–96. But, as Susan Buck-Morss has powerfully and provocatively noted, recording the true diversity of plebeian insurgence also means rewriting the story of freedom (and slavery) in terms of the suppressed record of the world-historical Haitian Revolution. See Buck-Morss, *Hegel, Haiti, and Universal History* (Pittsburgh, Pa.: University of Pittsburgh Press, 2009).

10. Peter Linebaugh and Marcus Rediker, *The Many-Headed Hydra: Sailors, Slaves, Commoners, and the Hidden History of the Revolutionary Atlantic* (Boston: Beacon Press, 2000), 132, 311.

11. Darko Suvin, "Transubstantiation of Production and Creation: Metamorphic Imagery in the *Grundrisse*," *Minnesota Review* 18 (1982): 113.

12. Walter Benjamin, *The Arcades Project,* trans. Howard Eiland and Kevin McLaughlin (Cambridge, Mass.: Belknap Press of Harvard University Press, 1999), 591, 633.

13. Ben Okri, *The Famished Road* (London: Vintage 1992), 149.

14. Charles Dickens, *Barnaby Rudge* (Harmondsworth, U.K.: Penguin Books, 2003), 419.

15. See generally Mary Russo, *The Female Grotesque: Risk, Excess, Modernity* (New York: Routledge, 1994). The postmodernist tenor of this text means, unfortunately, that the thematics of class are largely eclipsed. See also Susan Sipple, "'Witness to the Suffering of Women': Poverty and Sexual Transgression in Meridel Le Sueur's *Women on the Breadlines*," in *Feminism, Bakhtin, and the Dialogic,* edited by Dale M. Bauer and S. Jaret McKinstry, 135–54 (Albany: State University of New York Press, 1991), where internal relations of class and gender are perceptively posed. An outstanding historical treatment of these dialectics of class, race, and gender is presented by Anne McClintock, *Imperial Leather* (New York: Routledge, 1995).

16. See David McNally, *Bodies of Meaning: Studies on Language, Labor, and Liberation* (Albany: State University of New York Press, 2001), 4. On the construction of scientific racism, see McNally, *Another World Is Possible: Globalization and Anti-Capitalism* (Winnipeg, Canada: Arbeiter Ring, 2002), chapter 4.

17. J. Frykman and O. Lofgren, *Culture Builders: A Historical Anthropology of Middle Class Life* (New Brunswick, N.J.: Rutgers University Press, 1987), 129.

18. William Seabrook, *The Magic Island* (New York: Blue Ribbon Books, 1929), 94, 101.

19. Peter Dendle, "*Night of the Living Dead*," in *The Zombie Movie Encyclopedia* (Jefferson, N.C.: McFarland, 2007), 47. *White Zombie* has produced a wide range of reactions among critics. Its racist stereotypes of Haitians have been rightly deplored. At the same time, some critics have seen in the film a (perhaps unconscious) critique of U.S. imperialism in Haiti. For a sampling of positions, see Gary Rhodes, *White Zombie: Anatomy of a Horror Film* (Jefferson, N.C.: McFarland, 2001); Tony Williams, "*White Zombie*: Haitian Horror," *Jump Cut: A Review of Contemporary Media* 28 (1983): 18–20; Edward Lowry and Richard deCordova, "Enunciation and the Production of Horror in *White Zombie*," in *Planks of Reason: Essays on the Horror Film,* rev. ed., ed. Barry Keith Grant and Christopher Sharrett, 173–211 (Lanham, Md.: Scarecrow Press, 2004); and Kyle Bishop, "The Sub-Subaltern Monster: Imperialist Hegemony and the Cinematic Voodoo Zombie," *The Journal of American Culture* 31, no. 2 (2008): 141–52. As Dendle, "*Night of the Living Dead*," 48–49, notes, *White Zombie* also registers deep gender anxieties about the growing independence of American women during the war.

20. See Dendle, "*Night of the Living Dead*," 121, who points out that the word "zombie" never appears in the film, only "ghoul" and "flesh-eating ghoul." On the remaking of the zombie as ghoul over the past forty years, see Kevin Alexander Boon, "Ontological Anxiety Made Flesh: The Zombie in Literature, Film and Culture," in *Monsters and the Monstrous: Myths and Metaphors of Enduring Evil,* ed. Niall Scott (Amsterdam, N.Y.: Rodopi, 2007), 38.

21. Dendle, "*Night of the Living Dead*," 49.

22. Ellen Meiksins Wood, "The Question of Market Dependence," *Journal of Agrarian Change* 2 (2004): 126.

23. A clear gender theme runs through *I Walked with a Zombie*, suggesting that anxiety about female independence functions as a trope for exploring anxieties about the death of colonialism.

24. See "The Harlem Outbreak" in C. L. R. James et al., *Fighting Racism in World War II*, 281–87 (New York: Monad Press, 1980), and Dominic J. Capeci Jr., *The Harlem Riot of 1943* (Philadelphia: Temple University Press, 1977).

25. For a treatment of the overall social and cultural context, see also Robin D. G. Kelley, *Race Rebels: Culture, Politics and the Black Working Class* (New York: Free Press, 1996), chapter 7.

26. Leroi Jones [Amiri Baraka], *Blues People* (New York: Morrow Quill, 1963), 171–211, remains among the best treatments of the social and musical foundations of the bebop revolution. Also worth consulting, even if less insightful, are Ted Giola, *The History of Jazz* (New York: Oxford University Press, 1977), chapter 6; Ira Gitler, *Swing to Bop: An Oral History of the Transition in Jazz in the 1940s* (New York: Oxford University Press, 1985); Eric Hobsbawm, *The Jazz Scene* (London: Weidenfeld and Nicolson, 1989), 54, 82–84. Ross Russell, *Bird Lives! The High Life and Hard Times of Charlie "Yardbird" Parker* (London: Quartet Books, 1973), has intimations of the political content of many of the bebop rebel's musical innovations. Scott Saul, *Freedom Is, Freedom Ain't: Jazz and the Making of the Sixties* (Cambridge, Mass.: Harvard University Press, 2003), part 1, is also helpful. I should add here that my claim for bebop as an African American protest music does not mean that it is an exclusively black cultural phenomenon. Like all great aesthetic movements, it has a universalizing dynamic, a capacity to express a wide range of cultural experiences; but its social, cultural, and political roots are African American.

27. At long last, we now have the biography Monk deserves in Robin D. G. Kelley's outstanding work *Thelonious Monk: The Life and Times of an American Original* (New York: Free Press, 2009). Appendix A, "A Technical Note on Monk's Music," outlines Monk's signature musical innovations.

28. Mary Lou Williams, "In Her Own Words . . . Mary Lou Williams Interview," *Melody Maker*, April–June 1954. See also Marshall Stearns, *The Story of Jazz* (London: Oxford University Press, 1958), 222.

29. Marx, *Capital*, 163–64.

30. The foundational text here is W. E. B. Du Bois, *The Souls of Black Folk* (1903; repr., New York: Dover, 1994). On the history of this pioneering text, see David Levering Lewis, *W. E. B. Du Bois: Biography of a Race, 1868–1919* (New York: Henry Holt, 1993), 277–96. Du Bois's concept of "double consciousness" has influenced generations of social theorists. For important discussions, see Ernest Allen Jr., "On the Reading of Riddles: Rethinking Du Boisian 'Double Consciousness,'" in *Existence in Black: An Anthology of Black Existential Philosophy*, ed. Lewis R. Gordon (New York: Routledge, 1997), 49–67, and Lewis R. Gordon, "Existential Dynamics of Theorizing Black Invisibility," ibid., 69–79. A crucial text in extending the range of application of Du Bois's concept is Paul Gilroy, *The Black Atlantic: Modernity and Double Consciousness* (Cambridge, Mass.: Harvard University Press, 1993). For an important critical response to Gilroy's text, see Laura Chrisman, "Journeying to Death: Gilroy's *Black Atlantic*," *Race and Class* 39, no. 2 (1997): 51–64.

31. Du Bois, *Souls of Black Folk*, 156.

32. Monk's tune "Ugly Beauty" first appeared on his album *Underground* (Columbia Records, 1968).

33. Kelley, *Thelonious Monk*, 2.

34. It must be acknowledged, however, that Fela Kuti's music and life also embody elements of misogyny in his efforts to uphold "traditional" practices of male polygamy.

35. G. W. F. Hegel, *Phenomenology of Spirit*, trans. A. V. Miller (Oxford: Oxford University Press, 1977), 117–18.

36. Alexandre Kojève, *An Introduction to the Reading of Hegel*, trans. James H. Nichols (New York: Basic Books, 1969), 50.

37. Buck-Morss, *Hegel, Haiti, and Universal History*, 59.

38. Eric Hobsbawm's *The Age of Revolution 1789–1848* (New York: New American Library, 1962) barely registers the Haitian Revolution. For a key historical study that corrected the record, see the classic work by C. L. R. James, *The Black Jacobins*, 2nd ed. (New York: Random House, 1963). See also Robin Blackburn, *The Overthrow of Colonial Slavery 1776–1848* (London: Verso Books, 1988), chapter 6, and Laurent Dubois, *Avengers of the New World: The Story of the Haitian Revolution* (Cambridge, Mass.: Harvard University Press, 2004).

39. The key text here is Frantz Fanon, *The Wretched of the Earth* (New York: Grove Books, 1968). Fanon's dialogue with Hegel is well known, though often poorly theorized. Fortunately, Ato Sekyi-Otu's

powerful work *Fanon's Dialectic of Experience* (Cambridge, Mass.: Harvard University Press, 1996) provides us with a philosophically rich reading of Fanon in this regard. Feminist deployments of the master–slave dialectic have often operated within a psychoanalytical frame in which slavery is treated as a metaphor for domination rather than an actual social–historical relation. See, e.g., Jessica Benjamin's important work *The Bonds of Love: Psychoanalysis, Feminism, and the Problem of Recognition* (New York: Pantheon Books, 1988).

40. Karl Marx, "Results of the Immediate Process of Production," in *Capital*, 989–90.

41. On dialectics of awakening in Walter Benjamin, see McNally, *Bodies of Meaning*, 211–19.

42. Theodor Adorno, *Minima Moralia*, trans. E. F. N. Jepcott (London: Verso Books, 1973), 3. While the profundity of Adorno's point ought never to be understated, he comes perilously close to de-dialecticizing the historical moment of working-class failure. See McNally, *Bodies of Meaning*, 216–19.

43. A point made powerfully by Michael Lebowitz, *Beyond Capital: Marx's Political Economy of the Working Class* (New York: St. Martin's Press, 1992), 66–83.

44. Karl Marx, "'Chartism,' July 1, 1853," in Karl Marx and Frederick Engels, *Collected Works of Marx and Engels*, vol. 12 (New York: International, 1979), 169.

45. Karl Marx, "Economic and Philosophic Manuscripts," in Marx, *Early Writings* (Harmondsworth, U.K.: Penguin Books, 1975), 351.

46. Walter Benjamin, "One-Way Street," in *Selected Writings: Vol. 1. 1913–1926*, ed. Marcus Bullock and Michael W. Jennings (Cambridge, Mass.: Belknap Press, 1996), 453.

47. Peter Stallybrass, "Marx's Coat," in *Border Fetishisms: Material Objects in Unstable Spaces*, ed. Patricia Spyer (New York: Routledge, 1998), 186.

48. Eleanor Marx, "Recollections of Mohr," in *Marx and Engels on Literature: A Selection of Writings*, ed. Lee Baxandall and Stefan Morawski (St. Louis: Telos Press, 1973), 147.

49. Leslie Marmon Silko, *Almanac of the Dead* (New York: Penguin Books, 1992), 316.

50. Fanon, *Wretched of the Earth*, 197.

Alien-Nation

Zombies, Immigrants, and Millennial Capitalism

JEAN COMAROFF and JOHN COMAROFF

Productive labor—or even production in general—no longer appears as the pillar that defines and sustains capitalist social organization. Production is given an objective quality, as if the capitalist system were a machine that marched forward of its own accord, without labor, a capitalist automaton.

—**Michael Hardt, "The Withering of Civil Society"**

Automaton, n. Thing imbued with spontaneous motion; living being viewed materially; piece of machinery with concealed motive power; living being whose actions are involuntary or without active intelligence.

—*Oxford English Dictionary*

Prolegomenon

What might zombies have to do with the implosion of neoliberal capitalism at the end of the twentieth century? What might they have to do with postcolonial, postrevolutionary nationalism? With labor history? With the "crisis" of the modernist nation-state? Why are these spectral, floating signifiers making an appearance in epic, epidemic proportions in several parts of Africa just now? And why have immigrants—those wanderers in pursuit of work, whose proper place is always elsewhere—become pariah citizens of a global order in which, paradoxically, old borders are said everywhere to be dissolving? What, if anything, do they have to do with the living dead? What, indeed, do any of these things, which bear the distinct taint of exoticism, tell us about the hard-edged material, cultural, epistemic realities of our times? Indeed, why pose such apparently perverse questions at all when our social world abounds with practical problems of immediate, unremitting gravitas?

So much for the questions. We shall cycle slowly back toward their answers. Let us move, first, from the interrogative to the indicative, from the conundrums with which we shall be concerned to the circumstances whence they arise.

Spectral Capital, Capitalist Speculation: From Production to Consumption

In the eighteenth and nineteenth centuries, consumption was the hallmark illness of the First Coming of Capitalism, of the industrial age in which the ecological conditions of production, its consuming passions, ate up the bodies of producers.[1] By the end of the twentieth, semantically transposed into another key, it had become, in the words of Wim van Binsbergen and Peter Geschiere, the "hallmark of modernity."[2] Of its wealth, health, and vitality. Too vast a generalization? Maybe. But the claim captures popular imaginings, and their mass media representation, from across the planet. It also resonates with the growing Eurocultural truism that the (post)modern person is a subject made by means of objects. Nor is this surprising. Consumption, in its ideological guise—as consumer*ism*—refers to a material sensibility actively cultivated, ostensibly for the common good, by Western states and commercial interests, particularly since World War II.[3] In social theory, as well, it has become a prime mover, the force that determines definitions of value, the construction of identities, even the shape of the global ecumene.[4] As such, tellingly, it is the invisible hand that animates the political and material imperatives, and the social forms, of the Second Coming of Capitalism—of capitalism in its neoliberal, global manifestation. Note the image: the *invisible hand*. It recalls a moving spirit of older vintage, a numinous force that dates back to the Time of Adam. Adam Smith, that is. Gone is the deus ex machina, a figure too mechanistic, too industrial for the post-Fordist era.

As consumption has become the moving spirit of the late twentieth century, so there has been a concomitant eclipse of production—an eclipse, at least, of its *perceived* salience for the wealth of nations. With this has come a widespread shift, across the world, in ordinary understandings of the nature of capitalism. The workplace and honest labor, especially work-and-place securely rooted in local community, are no longer prime sites for the creation of value. On the contrary, the factory and the workshop, far from secure centers of fabrication and family income, are increasingly experienced by virtue of their closure: either by their removal to somewhere else—where labor is cheaper, less assertive, less taxed, more feminized, less protected by states and unions—or by their replacement by nonhuman means of manufacture. Which, in turn, has left behind forever more people, a legacy of part-time piecework, menial make-work, relatively insecure, gainless occupation. For many populations, in the upshot, production appears to have been replaced, as the *fons et origo* of capital, by the provision of services and the capacity to control space, time, and the flow of money. In short, by the market and by speculation.

Symptomatic, in this respect, are the changing historical fortunes of gambling. Until very recently, living off its proceeds was, normatively speaking, the epitome of immoral accumulation; the wager stood to the wage, the bet to personal betterment, as did sin to virtue. Now it is routinized in a widespread infatuation with, and popular participation in, financial "investments" that take the form of vast, high-risk dealings in stocks and bonds and funds whose rise and fall appear to be governed purely by chance. It also expresses itself in a fascination with "futures" and with their down-market counterpart, the lottery; banal, if symbolically saturated fantasies these of abundance without effort, of beating capitalism on its own terms by drawing a winning number at the behest of unseen forces.[5] Once again that invisible hand. At a time when taxes are anathema to the majoritarian political center, gambling has become a favored means of raising revenues, of generating cultural and social assets, in what were once welfare states. Some even talk of the ascendance of "casino capitalism." Argues Susan Strange, who likens the entire Western fiscal order to an immense game of luck, undignified even by probability "theory":

> Something rather radical has happened to the international financial system to make it so much like a gambling hall. What that change has been, and how it has come about, are not clear. What is certain is that it has affected everyone. . . . [It] has made inveterate, and largely involuntary, gamblers of us all.[6]

The gaming room, in other words, has become iconic of the central impetus of capital: its capacity to make its own vitality and increase seem independent of all human labor, to seem like the natural yield of exchange and consumption.[7]

And yet crisis after crisis in the global economy, and growing income disparities on a planetary scale, make it painfully plain that there is no such thing as capitalism sans production; that the neoliberal stress on consumption as the *ur*-source of value is palpably problematic. At once in perception, in theory, in practice. Indeed, if scholars have been slow to reflect on the fact, people all over the world—not least those in places where there have been sudden infusions of commodities, of wealth without work—have not. Many have been quick to give voice, albeit in different registers, to their perplexity at the enigma of this wealth. Of its origin and the capriciousness of its distribution. Of the opaque, even occult, relation between means and ends embodied in it.[8] Our concern in this essay grows directly out of these perplexities, these imaginings: out of worldwide speculation, in both senses of the term, at the specters conjured up by real or imagined changes in the conditions of material existence at the end of the twentieth century.

We seek here, in a nutshell, to interrogate the *experiential* contradiction at the core of neoliberal capitalism in its global manifestation: the fact that it appears to offer up vast, almost instantaneous riches to those who control its technologies, and, simultaneously, to threaten the very livelihood of those who do not. More specifically, our objective is to explore the ways in which this conundrum is resolved, the ways in which the enchantments of capital are addressed, through efforts to plumb the mysterious relation of consumption to production; efforts that take a wide variety of local, culturally modulated forms; efforts that reveal much about the nature of economy and society, culture and politics, in the postcolonial, postrevolutionary present. As anthropologists are wont to do, we ground our excursion in a set of preoccupations and practices both concrete and historically particular: the obsession, in rural postapartheid South Africa, with a rush of new commodities, currencies, and cash; with things whose acquisition is tantalizingly close yet always just out of reach to all but those who understand their perverse secrets; with the disquieting figure of the zombie, an embodied, dispirited phantasm widely associated with the production, the possibility and impossibility, of these new forms of wealth. Although they are creatures of the moment, zombies have ghostly forebears who have arisen in periods of social disruption, periods characterized by sharp shifts in control over the fabrication and circulation of value, periods that also serve to illuminate the here and now.

We argue that the half-life of zombies in South Africa, past and present, is linked to that of compromised workers of another kind: immigrants from elsewhere on the continent, whose demonization is an equally prominent feature of the postcolonial scene. Together, these proletarian pariahs make visible a phantom history, a local chapter in a global story of changing relations of labor to capital, of production to consumption— indeed, of the very pro and con of capitalism—on the cusp of the millennium. Their manifestation here also allows us to ponder a paradox in the scholarly literature: given that the factory model of capitalist manufacture is said now to infuse all forms of social production,[9] why does labor appear less and less to undergird the social order of the present epoch?[10]

Thus we bring you the case of the Zombie and the (Im)Migrant, this being the sequel to an earlier inquiry into work, labor, and the nature of historical consciousness in South Africa.[11] But first a brief excursion into the problematic status of production in the age of global capital.

Labor's Lost

The emergence of consumption as a privileged site for the fashioning of society and identity, it may be argued, is integrally connected to the changing status of work under contemporary conditions. For some, the economic order of our times represents a completion of the intrinsic "project" of capital, namely, the evolution of a social formation that, as Mario Tronti puts it,[12] "does not look to labor as its dynamic foundation."[13] Others see the present moment in radically different terms. Scott Lasch and John Urry, for instance, declare that we are witnessing not the denouement but the demise of organized capitalism, of a system in which corporate institutions could secure compromises between employers and employees by making appeal to the national interest.[14] The internationalization of market forces, they claim, has not merely dislocated national economies and state sovereignties; it has led to a decline in the importance of domestic production in many once industrialized countries. All of which, along with the worldwide rise of the service sector and the feminization of the workforce in many places, has dramatically eroded the bases of proletarian identity and its politics—dispersing class relations, alliances, and antinomies across the four corners of the earth. The globalization of the division of labor reduces workers everywhere to the lowest common denominator, to a disposable cost, compelling them to compete with sweatshop and family manufacture.[15] It has also put such a distance between sites of production and consumption that their relationship becomes all but unfathomable, save in fantasy.

Not that Fordist fabrication has disappeared. Neither is the mutation of the labor market altogether unprecedented. For one thing, as Marx observed, the development of capitalism has always conduced to the cumulative replacement of "skilled laborers by less skilled, mature laborers by immature, male by female."[16] For another, David Harvey reminds us, the devaluation of labor power has been a traditional response to falling profits and periodic crises of commodity production.[17] What is more, the growth of a global free market in commodities and services has *not* been accompanied by a correspondingly free flow of workers; most nation-states still regulate their movement to a greater or lesser extent. Yet the likes of Harvey insist, nonetheless, that the current moment is different, that it evinces significant features that set it apart, rupturing the continuing history of capital—a history that "remain[s] the same and yet [is] constantly changing."[18] Above all else, the explosion of new monetary instruments and markets, aided by ever-more-sophisticated means of planetary coordination and space-time compression, have allowed the financial order to achieve a degree of autonomy from "real production" unmatched in the annals of modern political economy. Indeed, the increasingly virtual qualities of fiscal circulation enable the speculative side of capitalism to seem more independent of manufacture, less constrained by either the exigencies or the moral values of virtuous labor.

How might any of this be connected to conditions in contemporary South Africa, to the widespread preoccupation there with reserve armies of spectral workers? What might we learn about the historical implications of the global age by eavesdropping on popular anxieties at this coordinate on the postcolonial map? How do we interpret mounting local fears about the preternatural production of wealth, about its fitful flow and occult accumulation, about the destruction of the labor market by technicians of the arcane? The end of apartheid might have fired utopian imaginations around the world with a uniquely telegenic vision of rights restored and history redeemed. But South Africa has also been remarkable for the speed with which it has run up against problems common to societies—especially to postrevolutionary societies—abruptly confronted with the prospect of liberation under neoliberal conditions.[19] Not only has the miraculously peaceful passage to democracy been marred by a disconcerting upsurge of violence and crime, both organized and everyday, but the exemplary quest for truth and reconciliation threatens to dissolve into recrimination and strife, even political chaos. There is widespread evidence of an uneasy fusion of enfranchisement and exclusion, hope and hopelessness; of a radically widening chasm between rich and poor; of the effort to realize modern utopias by decidedly postmodern means. Gone is any official-speak of an egalitarian socialist future, of work-for-all, of the welfare state envisioned in the Freedom Charter that, famously, mandated the struggle against the ancien régime.[20] Gone, too, are the critiques of the free market and of bourgeois ideology once voiced by the antiapartheid movements, their idealism reframed by the perceived reality of global economic forces.[21] Elsewhere, we have suggested that these conditions, and similar ones in other places, have conduced to a form of "millennial capitalism."[22] By this we mean not just capitalism at the millennium but capitalism invested with salvific force—with intense faith in its capacity, if rightly harnessed, wholly to transform the universe of the marginalized and disempowered. At its most extreme, this faith is epitomized by forms of money magic, ranging from pyramid schemes to prosperity gospels, that pledge to deliver immense, immediate wealth by largely inscrutable means; in its more mundane manifestation, it accords the market itself an almost mystical capacity to produce and deliver cash and commodities.

Of course, as we intimated in speaking of consumption and speculation, market redemption is now a worldwide creed. Yet its millennial character is decidedly more prominent in contexts—like South Africa and central Europe—where there has been an abrupt conversion to laissez-faire capitalism from tightly regulated material and moral economies; where evocative calls for entrepreneurialism confront the realities of marginalization in the planetary distribution of resources; where totalizing ideologies have suddenly given way to a spirit of deregulation, with its taunting mix of desire and dis-appointment, liberation and limitation. Individual citizens, many of them marooned by a rudderless ship of state, attempt to clamber aboard the good ship Enterprise by whatever they have at their disposal. But, in so doing, they find themselves battling the eccentric currents of the "new" world order, which forge expansive connections between the local and the translocal; short-circuit established ways and means; disarticulate conventional relations of wealth and power; and render porous received borders, both within and between nation-states. In the vacuum left by retreating national ideologies—or, more accurately, by ideologies increasingly contested in the name of identity politics—people in these societies are washed over by a flood of mass media from across the earth, media depicting a cargo of animated objects and lifestyles that affirm the neoliberal message of freedom and self-realization through consumption.

Under such conditions, where images of desire are as pervasive as they are inacces-sible, it is only to be expected that there would be an intensification of efforts to make sense of the hidden logic of supply and demand, to restore some transparency to the relation between production and value, work and wealth. Also to multiply modes of accumulation, both fair and foul. The occult economies of many postcolonial societies, and the spectacular rise within them of organized crime, are alike features of millen-nial capitalism, disturbing caricatures of market enterprise in motion, of the impetus to acquire vast fortunes without ordinary labor costs.[23] Yet, distinctive as they are, the con-ditions we speak of here are not unprecedented. In Africa at least, they recall an earlier moment of global expansion, of dramatic articulations of the local and the translocal, of the circulation of new goods and images, of the displacement of indigenous orders of production and power. We refer to the onset of colonialism. It, too, occasioned world-transforming, millennial aspirations.[24]

With this parallel in mind, we turn to contemporary South Africa.

Alien-Nation—the Nightshift: Workers in the Alternative Economy

No job; no sense. Tell him, Joe, go kill. Attention, quick march . . .
Open your hat, fall in, fall out, fall down . . . Order: dismiss.

—"Zombie," Fela and Africa

There can be no denying the latter-day preoccupation with zombies in rural South Africa.[25] Their existence, far from being the subject of elusive tales from the backwoods, of fantastic fables from the *veld*, is widely taken for granted. As a simple matter of fact. In recent times, respectable local newspapers have carried banner headlines like "'Zombie' Back from the Dead," illustrating their stories with conventional, high-realist photographs;[26] similarly, defense lawyers in provincial courts have sought, by forensic means, to have clients acquitted of murder on grounds of having been driven to their deadly deeds by the zombification of their kin,[27] and illicit zombie workers have become an issue in large-scale labor disputes.[28] Public culture is replete with invocations of the living dead, from popular songs and prime-time documentaries to national theatrical productions.[29] Not even the state has remained aloof. The Commission of Inquiry into

Witchcraft, Violence, and Ritual Murders, appointed in 1995 by the Northern Province administration to investigate an "epidemic" of occult violence, reported widespread fear of the figure of the zombie.[30] The latter, it notes in a tone of ethnographic neutrality,

> is a person who is believed to have died, but because of the power of a witch, he is resurrected . . . [and] works for the person who has turned him into a zombie. To make it impossible for him to communicate with other people, the front part of his tongue is cut off so that he cannot speak. It is believed that he works at night only . . . [and] that he can leave his rural area and work in an urban area, often far from his home. Whenever he meets people he knows, he vanishes.[31]

Speechless and unspeakable, this apparition fades away as soon as it becomes visible and knowable. It is a mutation of humanity made mute. The observations of the commission are amply confirmed by our own experience in the Northwest Province since the early 1990s; although our informants added that zombies (*dithotsela*; also *diphoko*)[32] were not merely the dead-brought-back-to-life, that they could be killed first for the purpose. Here, too, reference to them permeates everyday talk on the street, in private backyards, on the pages of the local press, in courts of law. Long-standing notions of witchcraft (*boloi*) have come to embrace zombie making, the brutal reduction of others—in South Africa, largely unrelated neighbors—to instruments of production, to insensible beings stored, like tools, in sheds, cupboards, or oil drums at the homes of their creators.[33] In a world of flex-time employment, it is even said that some people are made into "part-time zombies," whose exhaustion in the morning speaks of an unwitting nocturnal mission, of involuntary toil on the night shift.[34]

Thus do some build fortunes with the lifeblood of others. And, as they do, they are held to destroy the job market—even more, the very essence of self-possessed labor—in the process. Those typically said to conjure up the living dead tend, unsurprisingly, to be persons of conspicuous wealth, especially new wealth, whose source is neither visible nor readily explicable. Such things, of course, are highly relative: in very poor rural communities, where (almost) all things are relative, it does not take a great deal to be seen to be affluent. In point of fact, those actually accused of the mystical manufacture of night workers, and assaulted or killed as a result, are not always the same as those suspected: much like peoples assailed elsewhere as witches and sorcerers, they are often elderly, relict individuals, mostly female. Note: Mostly, not all, although there is a penchant in much of northerly South Africa to refer to anyone alleged to engage in this kind of magical evil as "old women."[35] Conversely, their primary accusers and attackers, more often than not, are young, unemployed men.[36]

Zombie makers, moreover, are semiotically saturated, visually charged figures. In contrast to their victims, who are neutered by being reduced to pure labor power, they are stereotypically described as sexual perverts whose deformed genitalia and poisonous secretions make them unable to reproduce—worse yet, to make them likely to spoil the fertility of others. Also, by extension, of the collectivity at large, be it a clan, a village, a town. Which is why they have become iconic of a perceived crisis of household and community in rural South Africa.³⁷ In this respect, they fuse, in a single grotesque, the very essence of negative value: the simultaneous, reciprocal destruction of *both* production and reproduction.³⁸ On one hand, by manufacturing spectral workers, they annihilate the very possibility of productive employment, imaginatively if not manifestly; on the other, by taking jobs away from young people, they prevent them from securing the wherewithal to establish families and to reproduce—and so make it impossible for any community to ensure its future. No wonder that, in one of the most poignant witch killings of the 1990s, the old woman set alight by morally outraged youths—determined to save their community by removing all evildoers—was to hear in her final agony the words, "Die, die, you witch. We can't get work because of you!"³⁹

Discourse in a range of overlapping public spheres, from "customary" tribunals and provincial courts through local religious and political assemblies to the print and broadcast media, makes it clear that, for many, the threat of a spectral workforce is all too concrete. And urgent. On more than one occasion, large crowds have gathered in towns in the region to watch the epic effort of healers to "liberate" zombies from their captors—in vernacular parlance, to "return them home." Here the spectral becomes spectacle. The fantasy of forcing underground evil into public visibility, of reversing the arcane alienation that creates phantom workers, is a palpable feature of the domestic cultural scene. The media, widely Africanized since the fall of apartheid, have been crucial in all this. They have taken the conventions of investigative reporting far beyond their orthodox rationalist frame in order to plumb the enigma of new social realities—harsh realities whose magicality, in the prevailing historical circumstances, does not permit the literary conceit of magical realism, demanding instead a deadly serious engagement with the actuality of enchantment.⁴⁰

Thus a long-running saga in 1993 on the pages of *Mail* (formerly the *Mafeking Mail,* a small, town newspaper, now a Northwest provincial weekly with large circulation in the region) in which a pair of journalists sought to verify the claims of a healer, one Mokalaka Kwinda. Kwinda had claimed that he had revived a man who had been living for four years as the "slave" of witches in the nearby Swartruggens district, and this before the "eyes of his," the zombie's, "weeping mother."⁴¹ Likewise a quest that same year to cover the efforts of four diviners to "retrieve" a "zombie woman" from the clutches of a malevolent in the nearby Luhurutshe district.⁴² These stories marry the surreal to the banal, the mystical to the mundane: in the former case, the healer told the reporters that his elusive patient was undergoing "preliminary" treatment, so that he might be "able to speak and return to normal life."⁴³ Such events are not confined to the outback. In Mabopane, in the eastern part of the Northwest Province, "hundreds of students and workers" reportedly filled the streets one weekday in May 1994 eager to witness a "zombie hunt."⁴⁴

The fear of being reduced to ghost labor, of being abducted to feed the fortunes of a depraved stranger, occurs alongside another kind of specter: a growing mass, a shadowy alien-nation, of immigrant black workers from elsewhere on the continent. So overt is the xenophobic sentiment that these workers are disrupting local relations of production and reproduction—that they usurp scarce jobs and resources, foster prostitution, and spread AIDS—that they have been openly harassed on South African streets. Like zombies, they are nightmare citizens, their rootlessness threatening to siphon off the remaining, rapidly diminishing prosperity of the indigenous population. Interestingly, like zombies too, they are characterized by their impaired speech: the common term for immigrant, *makwerekwere*, is a Sesotho word implying limited competence in the vernacular. Suggesting a compromised capacity to engage in intercourse with autochthonous society, this usage explains why migrants live in terror that their accents might be detected in public.[45]

Their apprehension is well founded. In September 1998, for example, a crowd returning by train from a march in Pretoria—held, significantly, to protest mass unemployment—threw three *makwerekwere* to their deaths, purportedly for stealing scarce jobs; two were Senegalese, one was from Mozambique.[46] Three months later, in December, there came alarming reports of a band of hoodlums in Johannesburg who seemed bent on the "systematic elimination" of foreign nationals.[47] Immigrants from neighboring countries, and from farther abroad, have worked in industry, on farms, and across the service sector in South Africa for more than a century. But, in the 1990s, the tight regulation of these labor flows has given way to less controlled, often subcontracted sources of supply.[48] Employers are ever more attracted by the potential of this cheap labor; it is said that as many as 80 percent of them use casual, "nonstandard" workers.[49] A recent investigation shows that, while the preponderance of immigrants in the past decade have actually been male entrepreneurs plying their trade in large cities, a great number do find their way into other areas of the economy, often in provincial towns;[50] some, especially those lacking legal documentation (frequently, women and children), land in the highly exploitable reaches of rural agriculture—in places like the Northwest Province.

Wherever they land up in South Africa, immigrants take their place on a fraught historical terrain. Anxieties about unemployment have reached unprecedented levels: by common agreement, the rate is much higher than the unofficial 38 percent to which the state admits. According to one estimate, five hundred thousand jobs, virtually all of them held by blacks, have evaporated over the last five years.[51] And this is probably a conservative reckoning, based primarily on shrinkage in the formal sector. "No jobs means our youth are destroyed," a resident of Soweto told a reporter from the *Chicago Tribune* in February 1999.[52] Even that eternal optimist Nelson Mandela, his retirement imminent, once quipped, "In a few months, I'll be standing by the road with a sign: Please Help. Unemployed with a new wife and a big family."[53] In the northerly provinces, which are among the poorest in the country, there has been scant evidence of the prosperity and redistribution that were expected to follow the fall of apartheid. True, the newly deregulated economy has granted some blacks a larger share of the spoils: postcolonial South Africa has seen a raised standard of living for sections of the African middle class, most notably for the "liberation aristocracy," a few of whom have become instant millionaires—and living personifications of the triumph of nonracial, neoliberal capitalism.[54] Despite all this, or perhaps because of it, the so-called transition has, as we noted earlier, kindled a millennial faith in the opportunities of "free" market enterprise, now ostensibly open to all. "I want every black person to feel that he or she has the opportunity to become rich and only has himself to blame if he fails," declared Dan Mkhwanazi, launching the National Economic Trust.[55]

But, for the vast majority, millennial hope jostles material impossibility. The much-vaunted Reconstruction and Development Plan, designed to root out endemic poverty, has thus far had minimal impact. Indeed, its broad reformist objectives, which harked back to the age of the welfare state, soon hardened into GEAR, the government's Growth, Employment, and Reconstruction strategy, which privileges development understood in terms of privatization, wage flexibility, and massive public service cutbacks.[56] Little of the positive effects of these policies, or of recent post-Fordist expansion in domains like tourism, find their way into the arid rural landscapes of the North or the Northwest Provinces. Here a living has to be eked out from pitifully small-scale subsistence farming and (very) petty commerce, from such things as brewing, sex work, and the refashioning of used commodities, classically the pursuits of women. Such assets as pensions, paltry though they may be, have become the subject of fierce competition; their beneficiaries, mainly widows and surviving old men, are prime targets of bitter jealousy and allegations of avarice. Meanwhile, the regular migrant labor wages that had long subsidized agrarian endeavors, and had given young men a degree of independence, are noticeably diminishing; this, in turn, has exacerbated their sense of threatened masculinity and has underscored the gendered, generational conflicts of the countryside. Which is why the overwhelming proportion of those accused of witchcraft and zombie making are older and female. And why their accusers are overwhelmingly out-of-work young adult males.

At the same time, provincial towns in these northerly provinces are home to small but bustling black elites, many of them spawned originally by the late homelands, into which the apartheid regime pumped endless resources over several decades. Well positioned to soak up novel business opportunities and to engage in behind-the-scenes dealings, they have quickly taken charge of a sizable proportion of retail marketing and the provision of services in the countryside. For them, increasingly, the conspicuous consumption of prized commodities—houses, cars, TVs, cell phones—does more than just signal accomplishment. It also serves to assuage the inequities of the colonial past. But, as it does, it also marks the growing inequities of the postcolonial present. These distinctions, to those who gaze upon them from below, also seem to be a product of enchantment: given that they have appeared with indecent speed and with little visible exertion, their material provenance remains mysterious. So, even more, does the cause of joblessness amid such obvious prosperity. In the upshot, the two sides of millennial capitalism, postapartheid style, come together: on one is the ever-more-distressing awareness of the absence of work, itself measured by the looming presence of the figure of the immigrant; on the other is the constantly reiterated suspicion, embodied in the zombie, that it is only by magical means, by consuming others, that people may enrich themselves in these perplexing times.

The symbolic apotheosis of this syllogism is to be found in a commercial advertisement run by a "traditional healer" in Mmabatho, capital of the Northwest Province. It appears in, of all places, the *Mafikeng Business Advertiser,* a local trade weekly. Top among the occult skills on offer is a treatment that promises clients "to get a job early if un-employed." The healer in question, Dr. S. M. Banda, should know. He is an immigrant.[57]

Precursors: The Ghosts of Workers Past

Phantasmagoria comes into being when, under the constraints of its own limitations, modernity's latest products come close to the archaic.

—Theodor Adorno, *In Search of Wagner*

On the face of it, much of this is new. When we did research in the Northwest in the late 1960s and mid-1970s—it was then the Tswana ethnic homeland—most males were, or had been, away as migrants in the industrial centers. There was barely a black middle class to speak of and no manifest anxieties about immigrants. Laborers had long come from elsewhere to seek employment in local towns and on the farms of the neighboring Western Transvaal, and there were "foreigners"—Zimbabweans and Xhosa descendants of those who had built the railroad at the turn of the century, for instance—who lived quite amicably with Tswana-speaking populations. There was also no mention of zombies at the time. True, many people spoke of their concern about witchcraft, understood as an unnatural means of garnering wealth by "eating" others and absorbing their capacity to create value. On occasion, moreover, malevolents would cause young migrants to lose their moorings, to forsake their kin at home and eschew the demands of domestic reproduction.[58] But there was nothing like the current preoccupation with the danger of humans being made into toiling automatons, nor with the sense that a spectral economy, founded on the labor of these and other aliens, might be draining the productive or reproductive potential of the community at large.

Yet these late-twentieth-century preoccupations are not entirely unprecedented either. In disinterring vernacular conceptions of work, labor, and consciousness during the high years of apartheid, we noted that Tswana regarded certain modes of migrant toil (*mmèrèkò*) as alienating—that they spoke of the way in which its disciplined routines reduced humans to draft animals, even to "tinned fish."[59] These tropes implied a contrasting notion of self-possessed work (*tiro*), typically work at home, which created social value. By contrast to selfish activity, this form of exertion constructed personhood in a positive key through the simultaneous building up of others. And, concomitantly, of a centered collective world. But the historical record indicates that Tswana ideas of estranged labor are not limited to the experience of proletarianization alone. Accounts from earlier this century tell of a condition linked to the eclipse, typically by witches, of self-possession and, with it, the capacity to accumulate wealth and social power. An individual afflicted in this manner was "alienated from fellowship with his kith and kin," noted J. Tom Brown, a missionary-ethnographer with a well-developed grasp of Setswana.[60] He goes on, in the real-time ethnographic present:

> They apply to him a name (*sebibi or sehihi*), which signifies that though the body lives and moves it is only a grave, a place where something has died or been killed. The essential manhood is dead. It is no uncommon thing to hear a person spoken of as

being dead when he stands before you visibly alive. When this takes place it always means that there has been an overshadowing of the true relationships of life.

Here, patently, we have a precursor of the zombie. But, whereas the latter is conjured from a corpse, either killed for the purpose or already deceased, *sehihi* is a state of eclipse effected by the appropriation of the essential selfhood of a living person, leaving behind a sentient shell as mute witness to the erasure of the social being it once housed. Moreover, where *sehihi* entailed the loss of all human creativity—often said to have been eaten whole by witches to enhance their own physical, political, and material potency—the zombie is transformed purely into alienated labor power, abducted from home or workplace and made to serve as someone else's privatized means of production.[61]

Evidence from elsewhere in southern Africa fills out this phantasmagoric history of labor, enabling us to track its fitful figurings, its continuities and breaks. Thus Harries's study of the world of Mozambican migrants to South Africa between 1860 and 1910 shows that witches (*baloyi*), held to be prevalent in the mines, were said to seize the "life essence" of others, forcing them to toil for days as zombies (*dlukula*) in closed-off subterranean galleries, where they lived on a diet of mud.[62] The poetic particularity of phantom workers—here, as elsewhere—is a sensitive register of shifting experiences of labor and its value. The introduction of compensation pay for miner's phthisis, for example, quickly led to a notion that zombies returned from below ground with numbers—potential payouts, blood money—chalked on their backs. Henri Junod, classic ethnographer of early southeastern Africa, remarked on similar fears in the southern Mozambique countryside around 1910.[63] "Modernized" witches there, anticipating their latter-day South African counterparts, were thought capable of reducing their fellows to a nocturnal agrarian workforce, masquerading by day as innocent children.[64] Some could even induce young men to wander off to the Witwatersrand mines, never to return. Once more we see the zombie as a "walking spectre," an object of collective terror and desire, to use E. J. Clery's description of the "terrorist genre" of haunted gothic fiction in late-eighteenth-century England, where industrialization was similarly restructuring the nature of work-and-place.[65] Like these "Horrid Mysteries," zombie tales dramatize the strangeness of what had become real; in this instance, the problematic relation of work to the production of social being, secured in time and place.

Other instances of ghost workers in Africa underline the point. Take Edwin Ardener's piquant narrative of zombie beliefs among the Bakweri of West Cameroon.[66] These beliefs—an intensification, it appears, of older ideas about witchcraft—arose at the time of the Great War, with the relatively sudden penetration of German colonizers into this fertile agricultural region. Their land expropriated for the establishment of plantations manned largely by foreigners, the Bakweri found themselves crowded into inhospitable reserves; as a result, they entered a period of impoverishment and reduced fertility. It was then that the zombie labor force (*vekongi*) first made itself felt, sheltering in tin houses built by those locals who had somehow managed to profit from the unpromising circumstances.[67] The living dead, many of them children, were said to be victims of the murderous greed of their own close kin; they were sent away to work in distant plantations, where witchmasters had built a town overflowing with modern consumer goods.

Here, as in newly colonized Mozambique, we see the sudden conjuncture of a local world—in which production is closely tied to kin groups—with forces that arrogate the capacity to create value and redirect its flow. Above all, these forces fracture the meaning of work and its received relation to place. Under such conditions, zombies become the stuff of "estranged recognition": recognition not merely of the commodification of labor, or its subjection to deadly competition, but of the invisible predations that seem to congeal beneath the banal surfaces of new forms of wealth.[68] In their iconography of forced migration and wandering exile, of children abused and relatives violated, the living dead comment on the disruption of an economy in which productive energies were once visibly invested in the reproduction of a situated order of domestic and communal relations—an order through which the present was, literally, kept in place. And the future was secured. Ardener notes the complex continuities and innovations at play in these constructions, which have, as their imaginative precondition, ideas of the occult widely distributed across Africa and the new world, in particular, the idea that witches, by their very nature, consume the generative force of others.[69] Zombies themselves seem to be born, at least in the first instance, of colonial encounters, of the precipitous engagement of local worlds with imperial economies that seek to exert control over the essential means of producing value, means like land and labor, space and time. It is in this abstract, metaphorical sense that René Depestre declares colonialism to be "a process of man's general zombification."[70] In purely historical terms, the affinity between colonization and zombification is less direct: colonialism does not always call forth zombies, and zombies are not always associated with colonialism. What they *do* tend to be associated with, however, are rapidly changing conditions of work under capitalism in its various guises, conditions that rupture not just established relations of production and reproduction but also received connections of persons to place, the material to the moral, private to public, the individual to the communal, past to future. In this respect, the living dead join a host of other spectral figures—vampires, monsters, creatures of gothic "supernaturalism"—who have been vectors of an affective engagement with the visceral implications of the factory, the plantation, the market, the mine.[71]

However abstract a set of ideas may be embodied in the living dead sui generis, any particular zombie congeals the predicament of human labor at its most concrete, its most historically specific. How, then, might those we have encountered in rural South Africa be linked, in more precise terms, to the late-twentieth-century transformations with which we began? Or to the impact of millennial capitalism in this postcolony?

Conclusion

These questions have been anticipated, their answers foreshadowed, elsewhere. Thus Harries has argued that, among early-twentieth-century Mozambican miners in the Transvaal, zombie-making magic was a practical response to the unfamiliar: specifically, to the physical depredations of underground work and to the explosion of new forms of wealth amid abject poverty.[72] Witchcraft, in a virulently mutated strain, he says, became a proxy for capitalist exploitation; witch hunting, a displacement of class struggle. Isak Niehaus, writing of the rural Northern Province at the other end of the century, arrives at a similar conclusion: mystical evil is a "cultural fantasy" manipulated by the dominant to defend their positions of privilege.[73] Explanations of this sort belong to a species of interpretation that brings a critical understanding of ideology to Edward Evans-Pritchard's classic conception of witchcraft as a "socially relevant" theory of cause.[74] Many would agree with their underlying premise that witches and zombies are to be read as etiological principles that translate structural contradictions, experiential anomalies, and aporias—force fields of greater complexity than is normally implied by "class struggle"— into the argot of human agency, of interpersonal kinship, of morality and passion.

But herein lies the rub. How does this very general truism, as valid for early colonial witchcraft as it is for latter-day zombies, relate to the implosive, shifting histories of which we have spoken? If the living dead are merely walking specters of class struggle, why have they not been a permanent fixture of the modern South African scene? What accounts for their comings and goings—and, to return to our opening conundrums, for the dramatic intensification of their appeal in the postcolony? How, furthermore, do we make sense of the particular poetics of these fantasies, whose symbolic excess and expressive exuberance gesture toward an imaginative play infinitely more elaborate than is allowed by a purely pragmatic, functionalist explication?

We have tried, in the course of this narrative, to show that the mounting preoccupation with zombies and immigrants here is owed to a precise, if large-scale, set of historical conditions—that these conditions underlie a postcolonial moment experienced, by all but the most affluent, as an unprecedented mix of hope and hopelessness, promise and impossibility, the new and the continuing. They have their source in social and material transformations sparked by the rapid rise of neoliberal capitalism on a global scale, a process that has intensified market competition; translocalized the division of labor; rendered national polities and economies increasingly porous, less sovereign; set many people in motion and disrupted their sense of place; dispersed class relations across international borders; and widened the gulf between flows of fiscal circulation and sites of concrete production, thus permitting speculative capital to appear to determine the fate of postrevolutionary societies. What is more, because industrial capital chases cheap, tractable labor all over the earth, searching out optimally (de)regulated environments, it often erodes the social infrastructure of working communities, adding yet further to the stream of immigrants in pursuit of employment—and to the likelihood that they will be despised, demonized, even done to death.

The backwash of this process, as we have seen, is readily evident in contemporary South Africa, where rapid deregulation, increasingly labile employment arrangements, and the gross shrinkage of the job market have altered the generic meaning of labor, the specific relationship of production to reproduction, and the connection of work to place. Where, also, labor migration—which had become a rite of passage to social manhood—has all but vanished. In the void left behind, especially in the countryside, there have risen new, unaccountable manifestations of wealth—wealth not derived from any discernible or conventional source. In this void, too, jobs seem available only for "nonstandard" workers: those, like immigrants, who will take anything they can get. Zombies, the ultimate nonstandard workers, take shape in the collective imaginary as figurations of these conditions. In their silence they give voice to a sense of dread about the human costs of intensified capitalist production; about the loss of control over the terms in which people alienate their labor power; about the demise of a moral economy in which wage employment, however distant and exploitative, had "always" been there to support both the founding of families and the well-being of communities. This bears its own measure of historical irony. In the colonial epoch, the migrant contract system was regarded as a social, moral, and political travesty, breaking up black households and forcing men to toil under exacting conditions for pitiable earnings; then a frequent object of protest, it is seen, in retrospect, as having been one of the secure foundations of the social landscape. Shades, here, of earlier revolutions, earlier metamorphoses in the articulation of capital and labor.

Here, then, is what is unique about the moment in the South African postcolony—what it is that has called forth an alien-nation of pariah proletarians, dead and alive. It is a historical moment that, in bringing together force fields at once global and local, has conduced to a seismic mutation in the ontological experience of work, selfhood, gender, community, and place. Because the terms of reference for this experience are those of modernist capitalism—indeed, these are the only terms in which the present may be reduced to semiotic sense and sensibility—it is framed in the language of labor lost, factories foreclosed, communities crumbling. Which is why the concern with zombies in the northerly reaches of the country, while in many ways a novel confection, replays enduring images of alienated production. In Adorno's phrase, "it sounded so old, and yet was so new."[75] Much like the story of labor itself, which, in an abstract sense, is still subject to the familiar "laws" of capitalism, yet, as concrete reality, has been substantially altered by the reorganization of the world economy as we know it. To reiterate: it all "remain[s] the same and yet [is] constantly changing."

One final point. Although we have tried to subdue the fantasy of spectral labor by recourse to historical reason, its key animus still eludes us. What, finally, are we to make of its symbolic excess? What does the intricate discourse about alien workers tell us of the subterranean workings of terror, of the life of standardized nightmares in a world of "daylight reason"?[76] There is little question that this discourse gives motive and moral valence to disturbing events—that, in the classic manner of ideologies everywhere, it links etiology to existing orders of power and value. But zombie-speak seems to do much more: its productive figurations feed a process of fervent speculation, poetic elaboration, forensic quest. The menacing dangers of zombification—the disoriented wanderings, the loss of speech, sense, and will, the perverted practices that erase all ties to kith and kin—serve to conjure with inchoate fears, allowing free play to anger and anguish and desire. Also to the effort to make some sense of them. Like gothic horror, the elaboration of these images "encourage[s] an experience of estranged recognition."[77] And not only at the immiserated edges of polite society. The hard-boiled social analyst might insist that the obsession with the living dead misrecognizes the systemic roots of deprivation and distress. But its eruption onto the fertile planes of postapartheid public culture—via sober press reports, TV documentaries, and agitprop theater—has had a tangible impact. It has forced a recognition of the crisis in the countryside, of the plight of displaced youth, of an alien-nation within the postcolony itself. As the very conditions that call forth zombies erode the basis of a conventional politics of labor and place and public interest, we would do well to keep an open mind about the pragmatic possibilities of these creatures of collective dread—about the provocative manner in which they, perhaps more than anything or anybody else, are compelling the state to take note. Even to act.

Notes

We would like to thank Patrick Harries for both his insightful comments on an earlier presentation of some of this material and his very useful bibliographic suggestions. Hylton White, whose insightful ethnographic research in KwaZulu-Natal has made an important contribution to Africanist anthropology, was kind enough to share some of his comparative knowledge with us. We also owe a major debt of gratitude to Maureen Anderson, our research assistant, for her help in preparing this essay for publication.

1. Susan Sontag, *Illness as Metaphor* (New York: Farrar, Straus, and Giroux, 1978); compare Jean Comaroff, "Consuming Passions: Nightmares of the Global Village," *Culture* 17 (1997): 7–19.

2. [Editor's note: This text was listed as unpublished in the original article publication. It has since been produced: Wim van Binsbergen and Peter Geschiere, *Commodification: Objects and Identities (The Social Life of Things Revisited)* (Münster: LIT, 2005).]

3. Not only by Western capitalist states. By the early 1990s, even Deng Xiaoping was calling for "consumption as a motor force of production." Arif Dirlik, "Looking Backwards in an Age of Global Capital: Thoughts on History in Third World Cultural Criticism," in *Pursuit of Contemporary East Asian Culture*, ed. X. Tang and S. Snyder (Boulder, Colo.: Westview Press, 1996), 194.

4. Ecumene refers to a region of "persistent cultural interaction and exchange." Igor Kopytoff, "The Internal African Frontier: The Making of African Culture," in *The African Frontier*, ed. Igor Kopytoff (Bloomington: Indiana University Press, 1987), 10. Compare Ulf Hannerz, "Notes on the Global Ecumene," *Public Culture* 1, no. 2 (1989): 66.

5. The mounting, increasingly millennial allure of lotteries is evident across the globe, from mass-mediated images originating in the West to reports of "lottery mania" in Asia. Note, in respect to the former, the film *Waking Ned Divine* (dir. Kirk Jones, 1998), which replays the ideology of the national lottery in Britain, fantasizing about the way in which a large win might enable communal regeneration in a peripheral, impoverished village. The latter appears to have occasioned suicides and mobilized state government in India; see "Lottery Mania Grips Madhya Pradesh, Many Commit Suicide," *India Tribune* (Chicago ed.), January 2, 1999, 23 (I), 8.

6. Susan Strange, *Casino Capitalism* (Oxford: Oxford University Press, 1986), 1–3; compare David Harvey, *The Condition of Postmodernity: An Enquiry into the Origins of Cultural Change* (Oxford: Oxford University Press, 1989), 332; Roman Tomasic, *Casino Capitalism: Insider Trading in Australia* (Canberra: Australian Institute of Criminology, 1991).

7. Michael Hardt, "The Withering of Civil Society," *Social Text* 45 (1995): 39.

8. John Comaroff and Jean Comaroff, "Occult Economies and the Violence of Abstraction: Notes from the South African Postcolony," *American Ethnologist* 26 (1999): 279–301; van Binsbergen and Geschiere, *Commodification*.

9. Gilles Deleuze, *Foucault* (Paris: Editions de Minuit, 1986).

10. Hardt, "Withering of Civil Society," 39.

11. John Comaroff and Jean Comaroff, "The Madman and the Migrant: Work and Labor in the Historical Consciousness of a South African People," *American Ethnologist* 14 (1987): 191–209.

12. Mario Tronti, "The Strategy of Refusal," *Semiotext(e)* 3 (1980): 32.

13. Hardt, "Withering of Civil Society," 39.

14. Scott Lasch and John Urry, *The End of Organized Capitalism* (Madison: University of Wisconsin Press, 1987), 232.

15. Terence Turner has argued, in this respect, that the globalization of the division of labor has elevated class conflicts to the level of international relations. Terence Turner, "Globalization, the State and Social Consciousness in the Late Twentieth Century" (Walnut Creek, Calif.: AltaMira Press, 2003).

16. Karl Marx, *Capital, Volume 1* (New York: International, 1967), 1:635.

17. Harvey, *Condition of Postmodernity*, 92.

18. Engels, as cited by Andre Gunder Frank, *Capitalism and Underdevelopment in Latin America: Historical Studies of Chile and Brazil* (Harmondsworth, U.K.: Penguin, 1971), 36.

19. By postrevolutionary societies, we mean societies—such as those of the former Soviet Union—that have recently witnessed a metamorphosis of their political, material, social, and cultural structures, largely under the impact of the growth of the global, neoliberal market economy.

20. The Freedom Charter was, for all practical purposes, the founding document in the populist fight against the apartheid state. Signed in 1956 by all the protest organizations in the so-called Congress Alliance, it made a commitment, among other things, to nationalize major industries and to mandate a heavily state-run, welfare-freighted political economy. See, e.g., Peter Walshe, *The Rise of African Nationalism in South Africa: The African National Congress, 1912–1952* (Berkeley: University of California Press, 1971); Tom Lodge, *Black Politics in South Africa since 1945* (London: Longman, 1983); Francis Meli, *A History of the ANC: South Africa Belongs to Us* (Bloomington: Indiana University Press, 1989); Heidi Holland, *The Struggle: A History of the African National Congress* (New York: G. Braziller, 1989).

21. Compare John Sharp, "'Non-racialism' and Its Discontents: A Post-Apartheid Paradox," *International Social Science Journal* 156 (1998): 243–52; Steven Robins makes the point cogently in noting how quick the ANC government was to disparage John Pilger's film *Apartheid Did Not Die*, which provides harsh evidence of the continuing contrast between white opulence and black poverty: "Whereas critiques of racial capitalism were once accepted as truth within the liberation movements, they are now dismissed by the new ruling class as pure polemic and/or naive utopian socialist rhetoric." Robins, "The Truth Shall Make You Free? Reflection on the TRC," *Southern Africa Report*, August 1998, 13.

22. Comaroff and Comaroff, "Occult Economies and the Violence of Abstraction."

23. Ibid.

24. Compare Karen E. Fields, *Revival and Rebellion in Colonial Central Africa* (Princeton, N.J.: Princeton University Press, 1985).

25. We are grateful to Nathan Sayre for alerting us to the song, a portion of whose lyrics appear at the opening of this section; also to Josh Comaroff for transcribing it and, more generally, for availing us of his creative imagination. In our discussion of rural South Africa, we focus primarily on two provinces, the North and the Northwest. These have been the sites of the most concentrated occult activity in the country over the past decade or so. See Comaroff and Comaroff, "Occult Economies and the Violence of Abstraction." The Northwest is also the region in which we have done most of our ethnographic and historical research since 1969.

26. Sonnyboy Mokgadi and Moopelwa Letanke, "'Zombie' Back from the Dead," *Mail* (Mafikeng), June 11, 1993, 1, 7. See also Sonnyboy Mokgadi and Moopelwa Letanke, "Zombie Missing," *Mail* (Mafikeng), December 17, 1993, 1, 4; Joe Davidson, "Apartheid Is Over, but Other Old Evils Haunt South Africa: Witch-Burning Is on the Rise as Superstitious Villagers Sweep House of Spirits," *Wall Street Journal*, June 20, 1994, A1, A10. Sonnyboy Mokgadi, coauthor of the first two stories and many others on the topic, was killed some two years later, in mysterious circumstances involving a "township fight"; rumors soon spread that his violent death was due to his investigation of zombies.

27. See, e.g., "Petrol Murder Denial," *Mail* (Mafikeng), June 2, 1995, 2; Nat Molomo, "Bizarre Zombie Claim in Court," *Mail* (Mafikeng), March 31, 1995, 2.

28. In 1995, for example, striking workers on an Eastern Transvaal coffee plantation demanded the dismissal of three supervisors accused of killing employees to gain control of their jobs and, even worse, of keeping zombies for their private enrichment. See "Spirits Strike at Labour Relations," *Weekly Mail and Guardian*, December 27, 1995.

29. See Ntokozo Gwamanda, "Disturbing Insight into Kokstad Zombie Killings," *Sowetan*, July 15, 1998, 17; also the SABC2 documentary series *Issues of Faith*, whose program on July 12, 1998, dealt with the topic. The program made reference to *Zombie*, a play by Brett Bailey featured at the popular and prestigious Standard Bank National Arts Festival in Grahamstown from July 4 to 14, 1996. The events on which it was based began with a taxi van accident in Kokstad in which twelve schoolboys were killed and ended with the murder of two elderly "witches" by comrades of the deceased. The appearance of this play on such a prominent stage suggests that the phenomenon itself is entering into the mainstream of public consciousness. We are grateful to Loren Kruger, of the Department of English at the University of Chicago, for sharing with us a review of the production.

30. N. V. Ralushai et al., *Report of the Commission of Inquiry into Witchcraft Violence and Ritual Murders in the Northern Province of the Republic of South Africa* (To: His Excellency the Honorable Member of the Executive Council for Safety and Security, Northern Province) (1996).

31. Ibid., 5. As we note elsewhere, the report of this commission, chaired by a retired professor of anthropology, N. V. Ralushai, speaks in two different registers; see Comaroff and Comaroff, "Occult Economies and the Violence of Abstraction." It gives an orthodox ethnographic account, couched in cultural relativist terms, of African beliefs; it also offers a stark condemnation, phrased in Western legal language, of the evils of occult violence. What is more, it speaks explicitly of the contradiction between European law, which criminalizes witchcraft, and its African counterpart, which accepts it as a pervasive, mundane reality. Ralushai et al., *Report of the Commission*, 61. For their own part, the commissioners do not call the actuality of witchcraft itself into doubt.

32. The use of *diphoko* for zombie—*diphoko* being from the Afrikaans "spook" (earlier, from the Dutch; see note 64 in this article)—points to the existence here of a cultural interplay, across lines of race and language, of ideas of haunting and enchantment.

33. Ralushai et al., *Report of the Commission of Inquiry*, 50.

34. Ibid., 224–25.

35. Our own collection of narratives about zombies and ritual murder in the Northwest, where we elicited both descriptive accounts of the phenomena and specific case histories, evinced a sharp gender distinction. Ritual murder—that is, the killing of people to harvest their body parts for medicine—could be perpetrated by either men or women, with or without the help of a "traditional" healer. But zombie conjurers were, more often than not, said to have been female.

36. Comaroff and Comaroff, "Occult Economies and the Violence of Abstraction."

37. For an unusually fine analysis of the crisis of domestic reproduction in South Africa, centered in northern KwaZulu-Natal, see Hylton J. White, "Value, Crisis, and Custom: The Politics of Sacrifice in a Post-Apartheid Countryside" (PhD diss., University of Chicago, 2001). Of course, the connection between a shrinking labor market and the threat to community is not purely a South African phenomenon. Several recent films from Britain, a few of them popular successes, like *Brassed Off* (dir. Mark Herman, 1996) and *The Full Monty* (dir. Peter Cattaneo, 1997), make it clear that the north of England is suffering precisely the same unhappy conjuncture, ushered in by the Thatcherite attempt to force a neoliberal revolution.

38. Compare Nancy D. Munn, *The Fame of Gawa: A Symbolic Study of Value Transformation in a Massim Society (Papua New Guinea)* (Cambridge: Cambridge University Press, 1986).

39. Ralushai et al., *Report of the Commission*, 193; Comaroff and Comaroff, "Occult Economies and the Violence of Abstraction."

40. Lesley Fordred, "Narrative, Conflict, and Change: Journalism in the New South Africa" (PhD diss., University of Cape Town, 1998).

41. See Mokgadi and Letanke, "'Zombie' Back from the Dead," 1, 7; Sonnyboy Mokgadi, "Healer Vows to Expose Those behind Zombie Man," *Mail* (Mafikeng), June 18, 1993, 7; Mokgadi, "Death and Revival of 'Zombie' Man Still a Mystery," *Mail* (Mafikeng), June 25, 1993, 2; Mokgadi and Letanke, "Zombie Missing," 1, 4.

42. Sonnyboy Mokgadi and Moopelwa Letanke, "New 'Zombie' Claims, but Now about a Woman," *Mail* (Mafikeng), August 13, 1993, 1, 5.

43. Mokgadi, "Healer Vows to Expose Those," 7.

44. See Mthake Nakedi, "Witch-Hunt Sets Town Ablaze," *Mail* (Mafikeng), May 27, 1994, 2; see also "Petrol Murder Denial," *Mail* (Mafikeng), June 2, 1995, 2, which describes a similar exorcism, this time in a village in the Molopo district.

45. See, e.g., Chris Barron, "Meet SA's Strange New 'Racists,'" *Sunday Times* (South Africa), September 13, 1998, 19. The connection between immigrants and zombies is visible in other domains as well; in rural Zimbabwe, for instance, stories abound about figures termed *ntogelochi* (from *thokoloshe*, the Nguni term now universally used for witch familiars in South Africa). Said to be brought from South Africa, they are purchased as general factotums to do all manner of work. But they come to haunt their possessors, following them everywhere—onto planes, into church—like unruly shadows. Or the alienated essence of their own labor (Dana Bilsky and Thomas Asher, pers. comm.).

46. "Jobless Mob Goes on Death Rampage," *Cape Argus*, September 4, 1998, 9.

47. Tangenu Amupadhi, "African Foreigners Terrorized," *Mail and Guardian*, December 18–23, 1998, 3.

48. A refugee bill was tabled by the South African Parliament in fall 1998, aiming to bring the country into line with international and constitutional obligations in respect to migrants and refugees (previously regulated under the provisions of the Aliens Control Act). The move was also seen to be related to growing national concerns about immigration and other threatening forms of cross-border traffic, in particular, those involving gun running, drug trading, money laundering, and organized crime syndicates. See Chiara Carter, "New Bill for Asylum Applications," *Mail and Guardian*, September 11–17, 1998, 6.

49. Horwitz, cited in Herbert Adam et al., *Comrades in Business: Post-Liberation Politics in South Africa* (Cape Town: Tafelberg, 1998), 209.

50. See the findings of the South African Migration Project, reported in Chiara Carter and Ferial Haffajee, "Immigrants Are Creating Work—Not Taking Our Jobs," *Mail and Guardian*, September 11–17, 1998, 6, 7.

51. Paul Salopek, "Mandela Stresses Success, Struggle," *Chicago Tribune*, February 6, 1999, 3.

52. Paul Salopek, "S. Africa's Uncertain Future," *Chicago Tribune*, January 31, 1999, 1, 14.

53. Salopek, "Mandela Stresses Success, Struggle," 3.

54. Adam et al., *Comrades in Business*, 203.

55. Ibid., 217. In a telling irony that speaks volumes about the Midas touch of neoliberalism, Adam et al., ibid., 207, note that even the South African Communist Party is considering establishing an investment arm in order to "trade its way out of the red."

56. Ibid., 206.

57. Dr. S. M. Banda claims to be "one of the best traditional healers from Malawi." His special expertise, he says, includes a knowledge of the means "to get promoted" and "to help your business be successful." *Mafikeng Business Advertiser*, December 1998, 2(1), 11.

58. This point is made in a divination sequence in the film *Heal the Whole Man* (Chigfield Films, 1973), based on our research in the Mafikeng District.

59. John and Jean Comaroff, *Ethnography and the Historical Imagination* (Boulder, Colo.: Westview Press, 1992), 169; see also Hoyt Alverson, *Mind in the Heart of Darkness: Value and Self-Identity among the Tswana of Southern Africa* (New Haven, Conn.: Yale University Press, 1978), 225. The reference to tinned fish captures the spatial congestion of the notorious mine hostels in which workers' bunks were stacked above each other in tight rows.

60. Tom J. Brown, *Among the Bantu Nomads: A Record of Forty Years Spent among the Bechuan* (London: Seeley Service, 1926), 137–38.

61. Geschiere, writing of the rise of similar beliefs about zombies in Cameroon, observes that "witches see their fellow men no longer as meat to be eaten . . . as life to feed upon in order to strengthen one's own life force—but rather as laborers that have to be exploited." See Peter Geschiere, "Globalization and the Power of Indeterminate Meaning," in *Globalization and Identity: Dialectics of Flow and Closure*, ed. Birgit Meyer and Peter Geschiere (Oxford: Blackwell, 2003), 232.

62. Patrick Harries, *Work, Culture, and Identity: Migrant Laborers in Mozambique and South Africa, c. 1860–1910* (Portsmouth, N.H.: Heinemann, 1999), 221.

63. Henri Junod, *Life of a South African Tribe* (London: Macmillan, 1927), 298–99; compare Harries, *Work, Culture, and Identity*, 221.

64. These unfortunates were termed *shipoko* (from the Dutch or Fanagalo "spook, ghost"), a word borrowed, Junod notes, from European animism; Junod, *Life of a South African Tribe*, 488; see also note 32.

65. E. J. Clery, *The Rise of Supernatural Fiction, 1762–1800* (Cambridge: Cambridge University Press, 1995), 174.

66. Edwin Ardener, "Witchcraft, Economics, and the Continuity of Belief," in *Witchcraft Confessions and Accusations*, ed. M. Douglas, 141–60 (London: Tavistock, 1970).

67. Ardener's account—he also describes a resurgence of the phenomenon in the 1950s—makes it necessary to complicate Geschiere's claim that zombie witchcraft (*nyongo, ekong*, and the like) is a "new" phenomenon in Africa. Ardener, "Witchcraft, Economics, and the Continuity of Belief"; van Binsbergen and Geschiere, *Commodification*.

68. Clery, *Rise of Supernatural Fiction*, 114.

69. Ardener, "Witchcraft, Economics, and the Continuity of Belief," 148.

70. René Depestre, "Déclaration à la Havane," *Violence II*, no. 9 of *Change* (Paris: du Seuil, 1971), 20. This phrase is also cited by Wade Davis, *Passage of Darkness: The Ethno-biology of the Haitian Zombie* (Chapel Hill: University of North Carolina Press, 1988), 75.

71. Compare Ardener, "Witchcraft, Economics, and the Continuity of Belief," 156; Clery, *Rise of Supernatural Fiction*, 9.

72. Harries, *Work, Culture, and Identity*, 221.

73. Isak Niehaus, *Witchcraft, Power, and Politics: Exploring the Occult in the South African Lowveld* (Cape Town: David Philip, 2001); Isak Niehaus, "Witches of the Transvaal Lowveld and Their Familiars: Conceptions of Duality, Power, and Desire," *Cahiers d'Etudes Africaines* 35, no. 2 (1995): 138–39, and 35, no. 3 (1995): 513–40; Isak Niehaus, "Witch-Hunting and Political Legitimacy: Continuity and Change in Green Valley, Lebowa, 1930–93," *Africa* 53 (1993): 498–530; Isak Niehaus, "Witchcraft in the New South Africa: From Colonial Superstition to Postcolonial Reality?," in *Magical Interpretations, Material Realities: Modernity, Witchcraft, and the Occult in Postcolonial Africa*, ed. Henrietta Moore and Todd Sanders, 184–205 (New York: Routledge, 2001).

74. Edward Evans-Pritchard, *Witchcraft, Oracles, and Magic among the Azande* (Oxford: Oxford University Press, 1937); Geschiere, "Globalization and the Power of Indeterminate Meaning"; James Ferguson, "Demoralizing Economies: African Socialism, Scientific Capitalism, and the Moral Politics of 'Structural Adjustment,'" in *Moralizing States and the Ethnography of the Present*, ed. S. F. Moore, American Ethnological Society Monograph Series 5 (New York: American Ethnological Society, 1993); John Comaroff and Jean Comaroff, eds., introduction to *Modernity and Its Malcontents: Ritual and Power in Postcolonial Africa* (Chicago: University of Chicago Press, 1993).

75. Adorno, *In Search of Wagner*, 96.

76. Ian Duncan, *Modern Romance and Transformations of the Novel: The Gothic, Scott, Dickens* (Cambridge: Cambridge University Press, 1992), 143. It was Monica Wilson who first spoke of witch beliefs as the "standardized nightmares of a group." Wilson, "Witch Beliefs and Social Structure," *American Journal of Sociology* 56 (1951): 307–13.

77. Clery, *Rise of Supernatural Fiction*, 114.

Zombies of Immaterial Labor
The Modern Monster and the Consumption of the Self

LARS BANG LARSEN

Undead and abject, the zombie is uncontrollable ambiguity. Slouching across the earth, restlessly but with hallucinatory slowness, it is a thing with a soul, a body that is rotten but reactive, oblivious to itself yet driven by unforgiving instinct.

It follows that if the zombie is defined by ambiguity, it cannot be reduced to a negative presence. In fact, it could be a friend. So why does it lend itself so easily as a metaphor for alienation, rolling readily off our tongues? Resorting to the zombie as a sign for mindless persistence is unfair to this particular monster. When it obstinately refuses the division of biopower into those who can live and those who must die, this identification is as apathetic and unthinking as what we have made out the zombie to be.

My proposal is that the zombie begs a materialist analysis with a view to contemporary culture. Such an analysis—that may be perverse or brain-dead insofar as it is aided and inspired by the zombie—will necessarily be double bound. Incarnating pure need without morality, the zombie counterintuitively promises a measure of objectivity: we know exactly what it wants—brains, flesh—because this is what it always wants. And at the same time as abject monstrosity is impossible to render transparent or luxurious, abjectness itself promises something constitutive—of a blunt and limited kind, admittedly, but at least it negatively outlines limits to norm, order, law, hygiene, and sovereignty.

In twentieth-century pop culture, the zombie was related to mass phenomena: mass production, mass consumption, mass death. It is not an aristocrat like Dracula or a star freak like Frankenstein but the everywoman and everyman monster in whose world panic coexists with business as usual. However, historically, the zombie traces a wide arc from the enslaved, non-Western, colonial subject to the dispersed brains of a cognitive capitalism. With zombies—or so I claim—we can address contemporary relations of social reproduction, too, in which it can be seen no longer to represent a mass ontology in the modern sense but instead the multitude's dispersed and humiliated forms of being. A key issue in this regard is what I call the consumption of the self: when processes of subjectivization—online, in work, in cultural participation—are hooked up to incessant self-representation and to calls for turning individual experience into a commodity, self-consumption is the order of the day. In its eloquent muteness, the zombie may be able to speak of this, too.

The following, then, is an attempt at a sociological reading with (and of) the zombie. More than that, the text considers the monster as a critically empowering figure that has rarely received its due as such due to its aesthetic and political opacity. If we are to free the zombie and its full historical significance as an abject subject from instrumental bondage, in the end the subversion of the premises of the sociological analysis is inevitable, as we begin to resist knowledge production and subject formation with aesthetic exacerbation of the status quo.

Marxploitation of the Gothic

As a figure of alienation, the zombie is the entranced consumer suggested by Marxian theory. It is Guy Debord's description of Brigitte Bardot as a rotten corpse and Fredric Jameson's "death of affect"—and of course what media utopianist Marshall McLuhan called the "zombie stance of the technological idiot."[1] Zombification is easily applied to the notion that capital eats up the body and mind of the worker and that the living are exploited through dead labor.

And when Adam Smith invoked the moral operations of the "invisible hand of the market," he had something else in mind than an integrated world economy that recalls Freud's *unheimlich*: "Severed limbs, a severed head, a hand detached from the arm, feet that dance by themselves—all of those have something highly uncanny about them, especially when they are credited with independent activity."[2] Under the globalized reinforcement of capitalism, the independent activity of spectral limbs is increasingly apparent, yet no less gratuitous and unsettling.

Political theory has in this way often dressed up economy and production in gothic styles. It is doubtful, of course, whether Karl Marx would have endorsed the zombie as a figure of alienation, inasmuch as the living dead incarnate a collapsed dialectics (between life and death, thinking and doing, productivity and apathy, freedom and contingency) that cannot be recaptured. Leafing through *The Communist Manifesto* of 1848, however, one finds rousing gothic metaphors. The power of class struggle is famously likened to a ghost that is haunting Europe—the "specter of Communism." We are also told that with the proletariat, the bourgeoisie has produced "its own gravediggers," and that modern bourgeois society "has conjured up such gigantic means of production and of exchange" that it is like "the sorcerer, who is no longer able to control the powers of the netherworld whom he has called up by his spells."[3]

The gothic, understood as the revival of medieval styles in the seventeenth century and since, is the theatrical representation of negative affect that emanates from a drama staged around power—a dialectic of enlightenment that shows how rationality flips into barbarism and human bondage. Thus it is in bad faith that Marx and Engels employ gothic metaphors related to the Middle Ages that, in their own words, "reactionists so much admire."[4] If the gothic is the notion that fear can be sublime and pleasurable, it makes for affective contraband in the self-professed rational and progressive political text. It seems that the authors of the manifesto, after all, didn't dare to rely on the "sober senses" of their readers but spiked their text with a little extra something to compel them to face their "real conditions in life."[5] How did the excess and grimacing of morbid rhetorical tropes come to prominence in the revolutionary project?

"Marx does not like ghosts any more than his adversaries do," Derrida writes in *Specters of Marx*. "He does not want to believe in them. But he thinks of nothing else. . . . He believes he can oppose them, like life to death, like vain appearances of the simulacrum to real presence."[6] Once it becomes clear that Marxist ghost hunting is already corrupted by a gothic impulse, it allows for a reconstruction of Marxist critique—a new "spirit of Marx," as discussed by Derrida. In terms of traditional aesthetic hierarchies, the gothic definitely belongs among the underdogs of genres, to an aesthetic proletariat. Maybe this is what spoke through Marx, like spirits inhabiting a medium, and helped shape his literary intuition?

There is no political or aesthetic reason to exclude the gothic, then. The New York artists collective Group Material were among the first to establish a link between the gothic and a Marxist line of cultural critique.[7] The flyer for their 1980 show *Alienation* mimicked advertising for *Alien*, and the film program included James Whale's *Frankenstein* (1931). In their installation *Democracy* (1988), a zombie film was continuously screened throughout the exhibition: *Dawn of the Dead*, "George Romero's 1978 paean to the suburban shopping mall and its implicit effects on people." The film was "an especially significant presence . . . one which indicated the pertinence of consumer culture to democracy and to electoral politics."[8]

Franco Moretti, too, makes it clear that you can't sympathize with those who hunt the monsters. In his brilliant 1978 essay "Dialectic of Fear," he notes that in classic shockers such as Bram Stoker's *Dracula* and Mary Shelley's *Frankenstein*, "we accept the vices of the monster's destroyers without a murmur."[9] The antagonist of the monster is a representative of all that is "complacent, stupid, philistine, and impotent" about existing society. To Moretti, this indicates false consciousness in the literature of fear; it makes us side with the bourgeoisie. But by passing judgment on the literature of fear through a dialectic of reason and affect (Stoker "doesn't need a thinking reader, but a

Figure 9.1.
Film still from *Dawn of the Dead* (dir. George Romero, United Film Distribution Company, 1978).

Figure 9.2.
Film still from *Night of the Living Dead*
(dir. George Romero, The Walter
Reade Organization, 1968).

frightened one"), Moretti's ideology critique ultimately joins the ranks of the destroyers of the monster and thereby of those fictitious characters he criticizes. In fact, Moretti kills the monster twice: he ultimately doesn't question its killing in the text, and he has no need for it outside the text.

George Romero analyzes the conflict between the monster and its adversaries in a similar vein. Crucially, however, his trilogy *Night of the Living Dead* (1968), *Dawn of the Dead* (1978), and *Day of the Dead* (1985) reverses Moretti's conclusion and turns cultural space inside out. In Romero, antagonism and horror are not pushed to the outside of society but double back on society qua a certain nonhuman innocence of the monster. The real issue isn't the zombies but the "heroes"—the police, the army, the good old boys with their guns and male-bonding fantasies. If they win, racism has a future, capitalism has a future, sexism has a future, militarism has a future. Romero also implements this critique structurally. As Steven Shaviro observes, discomfort is not only located in the films' graphic, genocidal cannibalism: the low-budget aesthetics makes us see "the violent fragmentation of the cinematic process itself."[10] The zombie in such a representation may be uncanny and repulsive, but it is the imperfection of the zombie's face—the bad makeup, the failure to hide the actor behind the monster's mask—that breaks the screen of the spectacle.

Brian Holmes writes in "The Affectivist Manifesto" (2009) that activism today faces "not so much soldiers with guns as cognitive capital: the knowledge society, an excruciatingly complex order. The striking thing . . . is the zombie-like character of this society, its fallback to automatic pilot, its cybernetic governance."[11] Holmes's diagnosis gets its punch from the counterintuitive tension between the notion of control and the zombie's sleepwalking mindlessness: even our present culture's schizophrenic scenario of a free-wheeling neoliberal economy and postdemocratic reinforcement of the state apparatus cannot be reduced to something as simple as pure evil. But if Holmes uses the monster trope to define a condition of critical ambiguity, he follows Marxist orthodoxy by setting this definition to work dialectically vis-à-vis his affirmative use of the manifesto format. The manifesto is haunted by its modernist codification as a mobilization of a collective *We* in a revolutionary *Now*. This code—the desire it represents and the collectivity it expects and constructs—is invariably transparent to itself and to its instrumentalization of the aesthetic. Once more, the zombie is condemned, its opacity gotten rid of.

Monster of Mass and Multitude

Metaphorical uses of the zombie are lent functionality from its abjectness. According to Julia Kristeva's definition, the abject is what I must get rid of in order to be a self.[12] It is a fantasmatic substance that must be expelled—from the body, from society—in order to satisfy a psychic economy, because it is imagined to have such a likeness or proximity to the subject that it produces panic or repulsion. This, Hal Foster writes, echoing critical preoccupations in the art of the 1980s (the abject) and of the 1990s (the "return of the real"), qualifies the abject as "a regulatory operation."[13] The obverse of the abject is a hygienic operation that promises a blunt instrumentality of getting rid of—of expulsing, excluding, severing, repressing. As we have seen, things are not so clear. The abject tends to sneak back in as an opaque supplement that subverts hygienic operations.

I will hypothesize that the zombie's potential lies in "exacerbating" it as a cliché of alienation with the power to "dramatize the strangeness of what has become real," as anthropologists Jean and John L. Comaroff sum up the zombie's cultural dramaturgy.[14] Why would one want to exacerbate anything? One way to reply is that as schizoanalysis had it, the problem with capitalism is not that it breaks up reality; the problem with capitalism is that it isn't schizophrenic and proliferating *enough*.[15] In other words, it frees desire from traditional libidinal patterns (of family and religion), but it will always want to recapture these liberated energies through profit. According to this conclusion, one way to circumnavigate capitalism would be to encourage its semiotic excess and its speculation in affect to block or clog up its apparatuses of capture. Capitalism is not a totalitarian or tyrannical form of domination. That is, it primarily spreads its effects through *indifference* (which can be compared to the zombie's essential lack of protagonism): it is not what capital is but what it doesn't do and what it allows to come into being. The fact that it does not have a concept of society or what it means to be a citizen; that it does not counteract exploitation of nature; that it has no concept of rights, whether animal or human; that it doesn't care about intelligence and love. It is a slave morality that makes us cling to capital as though it were our salvation. The logic of capital is to always withdraw, parasitically; it creeps back into the shadows and lets people and proxies act on its behalf. Dramatization of capital through exacerbation and excess can perhaps help call it out, distill this state of affairs.

Now, the zombie isn't just any monster but one with a pedigree of social critique. As already mentioned, alienation—a Marxian term that today is in as bad taste and comically undead as the zombie itself—is central to this genealogy. To Marx, the loss of control over one's labor is a kind of viral effect that spreads throughout social space and results in estrangement from oneself, from other people, and from the "species-being" of humanity as such. This disruption of the connection between life and activity has "monstrous effects."[16] Today, in the era of immaterial labor, whose forms turn affect, creativity, and language into economical offerings, alienation from our productive capacities results in estrangement from these faculties and, by extension, from artistic production as well as from processes that shape subjectivity. What is helpful about the monster is that it is immediately recognizable as strange. In this respect, it is, in fact, nonalienating. Second, with the monster, we may address alienation without a concept of nature—a good thing, since the humanism in the notion of "the natural state of man"—which for Marx is the positive parameter against which we can measure our alienation—has today been irreversibly deconstructed.

Franco "Bifo" Berardi describes how Italian Workerist thought of the 1960s overturned the dominant vision of Marxism. The working class was no longer conceived as "a passive object of alienation, but instead the active subject of a refusal capable of building a community starting out from its estrangement from the interests of capitalistic society."[17] For the estranged worker, acknowledged alienation became productive, a motif for struggle. Deleuze and Guattari were part of the same generation of thinkers who went against the grain and overturned a traditional view of alienation by considering schizophrenia as a multiple and nomadic form of consciousness and not as a passive clinical effect or loss of self. They were, exceptionally, intellectuals who gave the zombie its due: "The only modern myth is the myth of zombies—mortified schizos, good for work, brought back to reason."[18]

The origin of the zombie in Haitian Vodou has an explicit relationship to labor, as a repetition or reenactment of slavery. The person who receives the zombie spell "dies," is buried, is excavated, and is put to work, usually as a field hand. In his book *The Serpent and the Rainbow*, ethnobotanist Wade Davis tells the story of a man called Narcisse, a former zombie:

Figure 9.3.
Still from *I Walked with a Zombie* (dir. Jacques Tourneur, RKO Radio Pictures, 1943).

Figure 9.4.
Still from *I Walked with a Zombie*
(dir. Jacques Tourneur, RKO Radio
Pictures, 1943).

[Narcisse] remembered being aware of his predicament, of missing his family and friends and his land, of wanting to return. But his life had the quality of a strange dream, with events, objects, and perceptions interacting in slow motion, and with everything completely out of his control. In fact there was no control at all. Decision had no meaning, and conscious action was an impossibility.[19]

The zombie can move around and carry out tasks but does not speak, cannot fend for itself, cannot formulate thoughts, and doesn't even know its own name: its fate is enslavement. "Given the colonial history"—including occupation by France and the United States—Davis continues:

the concept of enslavement implies that the peasant fears and the zombie suffers a fate that is literally worse than death—the loss of physical liberty that is slavery, and the sacrifice of personal autonomy implied by the loss of identity.[20]

More than any inexplicable physiological change, victims of Vodou suffer a social and mental death, in a process initiated by fear and embodied (because racialized) cultural memory. The zombie considered as a subaltern born of colonial encounters is a figure that has arisen, then, out of a new relationship to death: not the fear of being taken by the anonymous hordes in the zombie apocalypse, as in the movies, but the fear of losing autonomy, being submitted to a master, becoming a slave. It can be added that with his concept of necropolitics, Achille Mbembe addresses the historical continuity from colonial-era slavery to contemporary forms of sovereignty that develop "in the interest of maximum destruction of persons and the creating of *death-worlds*, new and unique forms of social existence in which vast populations are subjected to conditions of life conferring upon them the status of *living dead*."[21] Whenever forms of racism and apartheid reduce life for the other, the abject subject must be represented and fought for.

With its highly ambiguous relationship to subjectivity, consciousness, and life itself, we may hence consider the zombie a paradigm of immaterial labor. Both the zombie and immaterial labor are celebrations of logistics and the colonization of the brain and the nervous system. The living dead roam the world and have a genetic relationship with restlessness: they are "pure motoric instinct," as it is put in Romero's *Dawn of the Dead*; or they represent a danger "as long as they got a working thinker and some mobility," as one zombie hunter puts it in Max Brooks's novel *World War Z*.[22] The counterintuitive reference to the zombie's intellectual capacity may be brought to bear on the terms "intellectual labor" and "cognitive capitalism," used to denote brain-dead industries such as advertising and mass media. Or the "working thinker" in the zombie's dead flesh might be an indication of the Marxist truth that *matter thinks*. As Lenin asked, what does the car know—of its own relations of production? In the same way, the zombie may prompt the question, what does my rotting flesh know—of the soul? As Spinoza said, what the body can do, that is its soul. And zombies can do quite a lot.

In Philip Kaufman's 1978 film *Invasion of the Body Snatchers*, a space plant that duplicates people as empty versions of themselves spreads its fibers across the earth as if it were a premonition of the Internet. The bodies snatched don't just mindlessly roam the cities in search of flesh and brains but have occupied the networks of communication and start a planetary operation to circulate bodies in a buzzing regime of mediation and reproduction. Things on the move are valorized *because* they are physically in motion and are visually proliferating virally. More than ever, the exchange of information in itself determines communicative form and content: what is exchanged recedes in favor of the significance of dissemination.

Exigencies of social adaptation, by now familiar to us, also appear in *Invasion of the*

Figure 9.5.
Still from *Invasion of the Body Snatchers* (dir. Philip Kaufman, United Artists, 1978).

Body Snatchers. Somebody who has clearly been body snatched tells the main character (Donald Sutherland, trying to escape his destiny) not to be afraid of "new concepts"—imperatives to socialize and to reinvent oneself, shot through with all the accompanying tropes of self-cannibalization: self-realization, self-management, self-valuation, self-regulation, self-exploitation, the self-extinction of our species, and so on; self-gratification in front of screens . . . the list can be continued. Incarnating mobility without nervousness, zombies and body snatchers are caricatures of ideal being in a logistical world.[23]

"Solipsistic, Asocial Horror" and Auto-consumption

If social life today tells us something, it is this: you are your own resource and limit, your dream and your impossibility. In a culture of self-realization, you are your own weakest link. Instrumentalized evocations of your affects and desires introduce new distances in the subject—inner distances across which one is expected to consume one's self. At the same time, one is expected to forget the "process of history's destruction of the body," as Foucault puts it, how the body is always "totally imprinted by history."[24]

The rather obvious sociological explanation is that the contemporary subject consumes itself because it lives flexibly, precariously, and lacks (or doesn't want) a coherent, stable life narrative that develops predictably and progressively. Therefore we have come to lead anxious lives characterized by ontological insecurity. To decry this state of affairs as narcissism or self-deception is insufficient and hardly offers any way out. In relation to art, in particular, the stakes of auto-consumption are complex. As per the cliché, the artist is understood to be an exalted individuality who gets her artistic fuel from self-fertilization, creative auto-combustion, or even self-abuse—creating with her demons, burning with inspiration, and so on. A little sociopathic and monstrous, in fact, there is a reason why we mistrust these people. In the 1990s, the role of the artist was attempted to be translated into a paradigm of individualized entrepreneurship. The then U.K. prime minister Tony Blair likened the worker in the creative industries to the artist: a genetically independent and innovative subject, burning for each project and producing from an inner need—presumably while not caring too much about labor rights and collective identities that might hamper his creativity, which nominally allows for a state of chronic productivity.

With this in mind, let us look into some of the cultural mechanisms that encourage auto-consumption. Not to attempt to counter it dialectically (the zombie reminds us) nor necessarily with a view to undo this pernicious logic but to ask, how can one take back auto-consumption as a kind of *expenditure* that may trump and exceed this particular economy of attention—an overspending of the self?

The visual signifier of auto-consumption is the selfie. A ubiquitous symptom of subjectivity panic, it establishes the pictured self in the consumption loop of visual commodities. There is an aspect of soul death in the selfie. Ultimately, reduced to the selfie, there is not a lot for the body to do anymore. Just think of the less benign versions of selfies and other types of visual documentation of people's intimate lives: revenge porn, for instance, and the documentation and dissemination of violence toward others are also examples of selves being consumed. This is self-consumption: the use and destruction of oneself and other subjects as image. The philosopher Beatriz Preciado makes no bones about it: "Rip away everything from life to the point of death and film the process, record it . . . distribute it live over the Internet, make it permanently accessible in a virtual archive."[25] Our desire and power to mediate the embodied and pictured self have a sinister dimension when the political economy dictates that all that lives get commodified.

The capitalization of creativity has in the past decade or two exerted a major pressure on artistic practice and thinking. Art has become a norm, in a different way than it was under the cultural order of the bourgeoisie. Within the so-called experience economy, art's normative power consists in commodifying a conventional idea of art's mythical otherness with a view to the reproduction of subjectivity and economy. It is the experience economy that gives us the most cynical and concise formulation of functional auto-consumption.

Around the turn of the millennium, management thinkers James H. Gilmore and B. Joseph Pine II launched the concept of the experience economy with their book *The Experience Economy: Work Is Theatre and Every Business a Stage.* Here they describe an economy in which experience is a new source of profit to be obtained through the staging of the memorable. What is being produced is the experience of the audience, and the experience is generated by means of what may be termed "authenticity effects." In the experience economy, it is often art and its markers of authenticity—creativity, innovation, provocation, and the like—that ensure economic status to experience.[26]

Entirely unironically, Gilmore and Pine advise manufacturers to tailor their products to maximize customer experience—thus valve manufacturers could profitably increase the "pumping experience"; furniture manufacturers might correspondingly emphasize the "sitting experience"; and home appliance manufacturers could capitalize on the "washing experience," the "drying experience," and the "cooking experience."[27] The "psychological premise" of being able to "alter consumers' sense of reality" is a theme that is as central as it is ominous.[28]

With their hapless neologism the *experience economy*, Gilmore and Pine's mission is to highlight the profitability of producing simulated situations. Their arguments will not be subverted simply by pointing out this fact: the experience economy is beyond all ideology inasmuch as it is their declared intention to fake it better and more convincingly. In the profitable displacement toward a psychotic phenomenology, it becomes irrelevant to verify the materiality of the experienced object or situation. Memorable authenticity effects are constituted exclusively in a register of subjective experience. My experience of things differs from your experience; hence both are gratuitous, unnecessary, because an individual experience is something that you don't need to have from any material point of view. As an isolated event unto itself, how you experience something is ultimately your pleasure, or your problem. In this sense, the experience economy implies a triple cancellation: it cancels out the experiencing subject, the experienced material object, and the premise and possibility of a shared, collective experience. Again, the experience economy is not about what something is, it is about how it works—*on you,* as you consume yourself.[29]

In other words, one's own subjectivity becomes a product one consumes, by being provided with opportunities to consume one's own time and attention through emotive and cognitive responses to objects and situations. Similarly, when the experience economy is applied to cultural institutions and the presentation of artworks, it revolves around ways of providing the public with the opportunity to reproduce itself as consumers of cultural experiences. It is difficult not to see the consequences of the experience economy as the dismantling of social coherence too. Thus the syllabus for the master's-level experience economy course offered by the University of Aarhus in Denmark explains how consumers within an experience economy function as "hyper-consumers free of earlier social ties, always hunting for emotional intensity," and that students of the course are provided with "the opportunity to adopt enterprising behaviours."[30]

Delightfully, cultural critic Diedrich Diederichsen calls such self-consumption *Eigenblutdoping*, "blood doping." Just as athletes dope themselves with their own blood, cultural consumers augment their self-identity by consuming the products of their own subjectivity. According to Diederichsen, this phenomenon is a "solipsistic and asocial horror," which reduces life to a loop we can move in and out of without actually participating in any processes.[31] Inside the loop, time has been brought to a halt, and the traditional power of the cultural institution is displaced when audiences are invited to play and participate in an ostensible "democratization" of art. Audiences ironically lose the possibility of inscribing their subjectivities on anything besides themselves and are hence potentially robbed of the opportunity to respond to the power of the exhibitionary complex. In the bigger picture, this relates to what Adorno and Horkheimer in a Pavlovian turn of phrase called the culture industry's reduction of people to *Zentren von Verhaltensweisen*—"centers of behavior patterns." We can compare this to the way in which biopolitical government conceives of citizens as patterns of information that manage and control their individual selves in cybernetic feedback loops.[32]

Rip everything from your life, prepare it for consumption, dig into your nervous system and format your living flesh to flows of signs and images . . . Self-consumption is interesting because it arguably has a reach beyond any social reproduction of subjectivity, beyond what we think it is to be somebody as an individual subject. Understood as self-destruction, it reaches well into structures and systems that are entangled with production, technology, life, and symbolic orders, but it also has some lacunae and not-so-obvious depths. As the philosopher Rosi Braidotti reminds us, life can become a habit. It can become a matter of mere continuation, of clinging to one's known existence for the sake of it. The way out may be auto-consumption, the cannibalistic way. In other words, become your own zombie. Destroy and devour yourself in ways that have nothing to do with the death drive.

The zombie returns at this point, then, to stalk a new cultural configuration that is already no longer current. No doubt the experience economy was integrated long ago into our commercialized life environments. But nor is it ever outdated, because it, in its isolated focus on the interiority of individual experience, cancels cultural time measured in decades and centuries. The time of the experience economy is that of an impoverished present. Žižek comments that just like ghosts, zombies return "as collectors of some unpaid symbolic debt." His insight that "the return of the dead signifies that they cannot find their proper place in the text of tradition" is one that we can use for our own ends.

Similarly, the experience commodity haunts art, its traditions and mythologies.[33] The experience economy's ushering in of a mercantile concept of self-consumption calls up an aesthetic subjectivity capable of fashioning itself into required forms, for coexisting with its represented and circulating doubles and versions of itself, and for entering social reproduction in highly mediated ways.

This instrumentalized caricature of an aesthetic subject that consumes itself having experiences proliferates across diverse cultural phenomena, from advertising to social media, and also determines the act of consuming art as purely personal. Since this subject is not to be found in the text of tradition, the marginal and extratraditional figure of the zombie comes to our aid to dramatize and perform its compromised, exhausted forms of self-transformation.

The Death of Death

The zombie is always considered a post-being, a no-longer-human, an impossible subject. But can we also think of it as a pre-being, still not somebody? Can we turn it into a child—that most poignant and delicate embodiment of the monster: the "child-player against whom we can do nothing," as Spinoza put it—or at least allow it to indicate a limit of not-yet-being?[34]

The lack incarnated by zombie is also present at the level of enunciation in the zombie narrative. The zombie, always mute, is never at the center of the plot the way Dracula or Frankenstein is. Hence its presence cannot be explained away as a mechanism for reintegrating social tension through fear. A strange, tragicomic monster, the zombie isn't evil, nor has it been begotten by evil. Instead, it deflects itself in order to show that our imagination cannot stop at the monster. It is irrelevant if you kill it or analyze it away; there will always be ten more rotten arms reaching through the broken windowpane. The zombie pushes a horizon of empty time ahead of it; whether that time will be messianic or apocalyptic is held in abeyance. The zombie represents the degree zero of our capacity to imagine the future. How can we look over its shoulder? What future race comes after the zombie? How do we cannibalize self-cannibalization?

Sooner or later, the zombie exhausts sociological readings of it. There is ultimately no way to rationalize the visceral skepticism that the zombie drags in. A similar mechanism is at work in art: whereas sociology is based on positive knowledge, art is based on the concept of art and on culture's reimagining of that concept. Beyond all of this lie new thinking and imagining. Thus we can witness how it all falls apart in the end: sociology, the zombie as allegory, even the absence of the end that turns out to be one. Left are material traces to be picked up anew.

Notes

1. "The Playboy Interview: Marshall McLuhan," *Playboy*, March 1969, http://web.cs.ucdavis.edu/~rogaway/classes/188/spring07/mcluhan.pdf. I am grateful to Jacob Lillemose for this reference.

2. Sigmund Freud, *The Uncanny*, trans. David McLintock (1899; repr., London: Penguin Books, 2003), 150.

3. Karl Marx and Friedrich Engels, *The Communist Manifesto*, trans. Samuel Moore (1848; repr., London: Penguin Classics, 1967), 78, 94.

4. Ibid.

5. Ibid., 83.

6. Jacques Derrida, *Specters of Marx: The State of the Debt, the Work of Mourning, and the New International*, trans. Peggy Kamuf (1993; repr., New York: Routledge, 2006), 57.

7. This was before the former became a curatorial trope: I am thinking of Mike Kelley's *The Uncanny* (1993; repr., Cologne: Walther König, 2004), Christoph Grunenberg's *Gothic: Transmutations of Horror in Late-Twentieth-Century Art* (Boston: Institute of Contemporary Art, 1997), and Paul Schimmel's *Helter Skelter: LA Art in the 1990s*, ed. Catherine Gudis (Los Angeles: Museum of Contemporary Art, 1992), which had the subtitle *Art of the Living Dead*.

8. David Deitcher, "Social Aesthetics," in *Democracy: A Project by Group Material*, ed. Brian Wallis (New York: DIA Art Foundation, 1990), 37. (Deitcher erroneously states that *Dawn of the Dead* appeared in 1979; the correct year is 1978. I have corrected this in the quotation.)

9. Franco Moretti, "Dialectic of Fear," in *Signs Taken for Wonders: On the Sociology of Literary Forms*, trans. Susan Fischer, David Forgacs, and David Miller (London: Verso, 1983), 84.

10. Steven Shaviro, *The Cinematic Body* (1993; repr., Minneapolis: University of Minnesota Press, 2006), 91.

11. Brian Holmes, "The Affectivist Manifesto: Artistic Critique in the 21st Century," in *Escape the Overcode: Activist Art in the Control Society* (Eindhoven: Van Abbemuseum; Zagreb: What, How, and for Whom, 2009), 14.

12. See Julia Kristeva, *Powers of Horror: An Essay on Abjection*, trans. Leon S. Roudiez (New York: Columbia University Press, 1982).

13. Hal Foster, *The Return of the Real* (Cambridge, Mass.: MIT Press, 1996), 156.

14. Jean Comaroff and John L. Comaroff, "Alien-Nation: Zombies, Immigrants, and Millennial Capitalism," *South Atlantic Quarterly* 101, no. 4 (2002): 779–805. I am grateful to Kodwo Eshun for this reference. The allegorical impulse behind bringing the zombie back to the Marxian concept of alienation derives from the dynamics of the zombie's ruinous (lack of) existence. Thus George Romero's famous trilogy is a sequence of allegorical variation: a critique of racist America (*Night*), a critique of consumerism (*Dawn*), and a critique with feminist overtones (*Day*).

15. See Gilles Deleuze and Félix Guattari, *Anti-Oedipus: Capitalism and Schizophrenia*, trans. Robert Hurley, Mark Seem, and Helen R. Lane (1972; repr., Minneapolis: University of Minnesota Press, 1983).

16. Karl Marx, "Estranged Labour," in *Economic and Philosophical Manuscripts of 1844*, https://www.marxists.org/archive/marx/works/1844/manuscripts/labour.htm.

17. Franco "Bifo" Berardi, *The Soul at Work: From Alienation to Autonomy*, trans. Francesca Cadel and Mecchia Giuseppina (New York: Semiotext(e), 2009), 23.

18. Deleuze and Guattari, *Anti-Oedipus*, 335.

19. Wade Davis, *The Serpent and the Rainbow* (New York: Simon and Schuster, 1985), 80.

20. Ibid., 139.

21. Achille Mbembe, "Necropolitics," *Public Culture* 15, no. 1 (2003): 11–40.

22. Max Brooks, *World War Z: An Oral History of the Zombie War* (New York: Gerald and Duckworth, 2007), 96.

23. In the Spanish translation, the body snatchers are *ultracuerpos*: ultrabodies, as if particularly well-adapted mutations.

24. Michel Foucault, "Nietzsche, Genealogy, History," in *The Foucault Reader*, ed. Paul Rabinow, 76–100 (London: Penguin, 1984).

25. Beatriz Preciado, *Testo Junkie*, trans. Bruce Benderson (New York: Feminist Press, 2013), 346.

26. See also my *Kunst er Norm* (Aarhus: Jutland Art Academy, 2008).

27. James H. Gilmore and B. Joseph Pine II, *The Experience Economy: Work Is Theatre and Every Business a Stage* (Boston: Harvard Business School Press, 1999), 16.

28. Ibid., 175.

29. In English and the Latin languages, the term *experience* is one-dimensional, unlike in German, in which one differentiates between *Erfahrung*, which is the selective, interpretive, and reflexive elaboration of the unpredictable, eventful *Erlebnis*—that which happens unexpectedly to you and enriches you.

30. See the Aarhus University Faculty of Humanities website at http://studieguide.au.dk/kandidat _dk.cfm?fag=1062.

31. Diedrich Diederichsen, *Eigenblutdoping: Selbstverwertung, Künstlerromantik, Partizipation* (Cologne: Kiepenheuer and Witsch, 2008).

32. Theodor W. Adorno and Max Horkheimer, *Dialektik der Aufklärung: Philosophische Fragmente* (1947; repr., Frankfurt am Main, Germany: Fischer, 2008), 93.

33. Slavoj Žižek, *Looking Awry: An Introduction to Jacques Lacan through Popular Culture* (Cambridge, Mass.: MIT Press, 1992), 22–23.

34. Quoted from Gilles Deleuze and Félix Guattari, *Qu'est-ce que la philosophie* (Paris: Minuit, 1991), 70.

Abject Posthumanism
Neoliberalism, Biopolitics, and Zombies

SHERRYL VINT

The posthuman has been a provocative site of theoretical enquiry for at least the last twenty years, establishing connections between science fiction scholarship and wider academic explorations of fragmented, postmodern subjectivity. Key texts have used the figure of the posthuman to prompt us to imagine subjectivity beyond the constraints of liberal humanism and its rapidly outdated ideal of the autonomous self. N. Katherine Hayles's *How We Became Posthuman* reassessed our understanding of subjectivity, consciousness, and embodiment through an interrogation of cybernetics, making a powerful argument that the self was more than information and that in embodiment we might find the key to another kind of being. Similarly, Donna Haraway's "A Cyborg Manifesto" celebrated this figure of hybridity precisely because it refused discourses of purity and origin, opening up a space to think otherwise about our "joint kinship with animals and machines"[1] and suggesting a way out of "the maze of dualisms in which we have explained our bodies and our tools to ourselves."[2] Both of these influential figures of the posthuman promised an expanded horizon for thinking about the human, a new discursive approach rooted in partial and fragmentary identities, multiple standpoints of knowledge, and politics of affinity. Refusing key binaries of the Western philosophical tradition, these potent figures promised much. Yet, as early as 1990, in an interview with Andrew Ross and Constance Penley, Haraway was already questioning the emerging mythology of cyborg figures in popular culture as compared to her vision.[3] The hypermasculine, armed, and relentlessly single-minded cyborgs of the Terminator (1984–2009) franchise, for example, hinted at a politics exactly in opposition to Haraway's deconstructive trickster. Things have changed even further in the twenty-first century. From the more-than-human subject dialectically interrogated and embraced in sf texts such as Octavia Butler's Patternist (1976–84) series or Iain M. Banks's Culture (1987–2010) novels, we have moved into an era in which posthumanity is a generalized condition. New and abject posthumans raise anxieties about massification and material collapse that emblematize our current state of neoliberal crisis and biopolitical governance. This version of the posthuman bears little relation to Haraway's ironic cyborg and instead partakes of the experiences of exclusion and abjection epitomized by Agamben's *homo sacer*, the one who can be killed but not sacrificed because this figure is constituted only by the bare life of existence, not full human being. These abject posthuman figures—most evident in the reconfiguration of zombies from the living-dead to the infected-living—deconstruct the binary of living and death: surviving, but not really alive, they persist in a future without hope, a paradoxical future without a future.

The prevalence of such images in our cultural imagination suggests, as the title of one of Žižek's works proclaims, that we feel we are living in end times. Žižek identifies as the "four riders" of our ongoing apocalypse "ecological crisis, the consequences of the biogenetic revolution, imbalances within the system itself, . . . and the explosive growth of social divisions and exclusions."[4] As he, among others, points out, although it is urgent that we change systems of global capitalism, today we find it "easier to imagine a total catastrophe which ends all life on earth than it is to imagine a real change in capitalist relations."[5] We revel in the imagination of apocalyptic disaster in recent popular culture for this reason. This fascination is so pronounced that a review in *Time* magazine, commenting on the zombie colonization of much popular culture beyond the horror film, declared them "the official monster of the recession."[6]

Zombi(e)s, Labor, Neoliberalism

The relationship between zombies and abjection is well established in the critical tradition, often focused on issues of labor, thereby acknowledging the connection to a pre-Romero mythology of the zombi[7] as someone compelled by Vodou to rise from the grave and work. Although post-Romero zombies are more commonly associated with images of overwhelming consumption, the capitalist dialectic of production and consumption links these states. As David McNally argues in *Monsters of the Market*,[8] such creatures are ways of working through the alienation of capitalist extraction of surplus value: they mirror how humans' living labor is turned into a dead thing, a commodity. The frequent images of dismemberment in monster texts, McNally contends, revisit the traumatic violence of historical moments like the enclosures of land through which peasants were forced into dependence on a wage, now repeated in the predations of neoliberal globalization and reflected in the rise of such mythologies in sub-Saharan Africa. Capitalism is damaging beyond physical suffering, Marx insists: it destroys the spirit or essence of the human, transforming creative energies and full being into interchangeable units of work via its equivalizing logic. The interchangeability of zombies, who appear always as a mass, whose inhumanity is emblematized by this very failure to be distinct individuals, suggests something of their appropriateness as a symbol for disenfranchised labor.

Workers everywhere are now reduced "to the lowest common denominator, to a disposable cost, compelling them to compete with sweatshops,"[9] and this new, more generalized condition of abjection is reflected in texts that at times ask us to sympathize with rather than—or, better, in addition to—fear the zombie. Hints of such a change are present in Romero's shifting mythology, from the implication that reactionary law enforcement is just as happy to execute an out-of-place black man as they are to dispatch ghouls in *Night of the Living Dead* (1968), to what K. Silem Mohammad has diagnosed as "a permanent state of crisis for two competing 'class' structures, the privileged but besieged living and the disenfranchised but ever-more organized Undead"[10] in *Land of the Dead* (2005), to the metafictional blurring of film and reality in *Diary of the Dead* (2007) that ends by asking whether humanity is worth saving given its wanton brutality. In popular culture more widely, the shifting position of the zombie is indicated by films that blend zombie apocalypse with other genres, such as comedy *Shaun of the Dead* (dir. Edgar Wright, 2004), buddy film *Zombieland* (dir. Ruben Fleischer, 2009), or satire *Fido* (dir. Andrew Currie, 2006).

Our obsession with the living-dead speaks also to our *epistēmē* of biopolitics in which the boundary between the living and the dead is precisely what is at issue politically and philosophically. While "the right of sovereignty was the right to take life or let live," the new right established with the modern security state is "the right to make live or to let die."[11] Crucially, there are two aspects to the new exercise of biopower. Not only are certain kinds of lives fostered and shaped through its disciplinary institutions, while others are let expire through neglect or design, but also—and more importantly—this new biopower establishes a logical connection between the making-live and letting-die that institutes a paradoxical logic. The metaphor of the body politic shifts from taking as its referent the body of the sovereign to the aggregate body of the population whose "health" is now the object of good governance. One of the ways of fostering this body is by expelling or excising that which is unhealthy: thus letting die is integrally bound up with making live. As Foucault documents, the shift of sovereign power toward biopower was concomitant with a shift toward membership within a nation-state being understood as a matter of biology or race. Racism allows what is homogenous (the human species) to be conceptualized as divided between the "good," healthy citizens and the "bad," unhealthy specimens, construed as fundamentally different from the human/ citizen. Thus, Foucault argues, the political project of liberation focused on protecting the aggregate population from the excesses of the sovereign state turned into a politics of medical-hygienic conformity and the defense of society from biological dangers. The enemy is no longer "the race that came from elsewhere or that was, of a time, triumphant and dominant" but "a race that is permanently, ceaselessly infiltrating the social body, or which is, rather, constantly being re-created in and by the social fabric."[12]

This context of biopolitics is crucial for understanding why the image of the zombie in many recent films has shifted from the living-dead to the infected-living: zombies emerge more clearly as our possible selves, as abjected and expelled parts of the body politic—just as labor is expendable to global capital and migrant laborers as people are unwanted by many nation-states. The threat of these new zombies is double, to be incorporated literally by being consumed, or to be incorporated by infection. Furthermore, global capitalism has made monsters of us all, reproducing the kind of subjectivity that guides corporate decisions that privilege profit above people, an ironic turn from corporations having the legal status of persons to organic people behaving with the utter self-interest characteristic of corporate personhood. Henry Giroux calls this a zombie politics that "views competition as a form of social combat, celebrates war as an extension of politics and legitimates a ruthless Social Darwinism in which particular individuals and groups are considered simply redundant, disposable."[13] The world of such laborers whose physical bodies but not human subjectivities are required by capital parallels the subjectivity produced by what Achille Mbembe, discussing the nonhuman status of slaves, calls "necropolitics," where the subject is "kept alive but in *a state of injury*, in a phantom-like world of horrors and intense cruelty and profanity."[14]

Giorgio Agamben's biopolitical work on the distinction between *zoē* (the simple fact of living) and *bios* (the proper human life, infused with essence or spirit) is also pertinent, repositioning as it does the human–animal boundary to a caesura *within* the human that reveals how contingent is the category of *bios*. A number of philosophers have been concerned with the ease with which biopolitics thus becomes thanatopolitics, a governance of life inevitably producing massive death in a model that finds its ultimate exemplar in the Nazi regime. Although it is important to preserve a distinction between the thanatopolitical "letting die" of liberal biopolitics and the "making die" of totalitarianism, it is nonetheless valuable to trace their connections as well. Indeed, Timothy Campbell contends that "this distance grows ever smaller under a neoliberal governmentality" that is concerned with a reduction of persons to things, or rather with the attempt "to crush the person and thing, to make them coextensive in a living being."[15]

Campbell goes on to outline the original Greek distinction, which also informs Agamben's work, by which a quality called "charisma" or "grace" was understood to separate the mere living of *zoē* from the fully human existence of *bios*, marking those humans who had sufficiently separated themselves from the animal within. Under neoliberalism, he concludes, "the 'truth' of the market, becomes the final arbiter of who has made sufficient moves toward deanimalization."[16] Zombies, with their historical ties to abject labor, and who combine a human form with signs that it has been robbed of grace—reduced to decomposing flesh—thus epitomize the crisis of subjectivity today. The speed of many of these new infected-living zombies only makes them more dangerous, reflecting the vicissitudes of an unstable, globalized labor market in which we all could quickly and catastrophically slip from the *bios* of being gainfully employed to the *zoē* of economically irrelevant biological life.

Danny Boyle's film *28 Days Later* (2002), which popularized the new zombie paradigm, exemplifies the most negative aspects of our neoliberal order figured as zombie future. It establishes a number of motifs that have become staples of the genre: the protagonist, Jim (Cillian Murphy), wakes from a coma, enabling the representation of the transformation as a single decision shift;[17] the many scenes of him wandering around an abandoned London feed our fascination with images of a world depleted of humans; the rapidity of the change from human to infected, requiring the surviving humans to turn instantly upon their fellows, embodies neoliberalist ethics; and the violence, both the rapid and animal-like movements of the infected and the splatterpunk aesthetic of their dispatch, indulges a dehumanization of all, both infected and human. Although the film ultimately concludes on a hopeful note for rescue and suggests the restoration of the heteronormative family at the end, early scenes work to challenge our faith in restoration rather than transformation as key to a better future. The state of normality before and after the disaster, we are reminded, is "people killing people," and black actors Naomi Harris (who wields a machete) and Marvin Campbell, an infected soldier kept as an experiment, both evoke the image of Haitian rebellion against slavery and the injustices of the "civilized" order before.

Infected-Living, Biopolitics, Contagion

In their critique of the fantasy of restoring "normal" civilization via the abject bodies of slaughtered zombies, recent zombie narratives challenge us to rethink life beyond the anthropocentrism of the liberal subject. In *Remnants of Auschwitz*, Agamben suggests that biopolitics requires a theory that moves beyond the binary of making-die–letting-live or making-live–letting-die, a theorization that is adequate to a situation in which "man's animal functions survive while his organic functions perish completely."[18] Building on his example of someone in a persistent comatose state, Agamben offers the new formulation of "*to make survive*" to capture the "decisive activity of biopower in our time [that] consists in the production not of life or death, but rather of a mutable and virtually infinite survival."[19] Biopower works to separate *within the individual subject* that which is human (*bios*) from that which is merely living (*zoē*), to keep what it can make into a thing and exploit (labor-power) and jettison what is inconvenient, inefficient, and irrelevant (the full human subject). Biopolitics produces a kindred creature to the infected-living zombies. Like capital's fantasy of labor-power without human workers, the infected-living persist, *survive*, as biological bodies without human subjectivity. Foucault also connects the biopolitical divisions of the modern state to economic shifts of neoliberalism, which increasingly turned to managing populations and territories rather than disciplining individuals, requiring new regimes of statistical governance in which things such as scarcity, starvation, and unemployment are no longer problems to be solved but rather rates to be calibrated to ensure each occurs in sufficient quantity to preserve the health of the overall system of capitalist circulation.

Agamben's contention that the concentration camp is the paradigmatic expression of late modernity, and his writings on the figure of the *Muselmann*, are perhaps the myth for this new and more sinister posthuman. The *Muselmann* is not only or "not truly a limit between life and death," he tells us; "rather, he marks the threshold between the human and the inhuman."[20] The *Muselmann* is a particularly horrifying figure because he continues to live after the limit of life, showing "the insufficiency and abstraction of the limit"[21] we have set to the category of the human. What is uniquely horrifying about such figures, Agamben observes, is not that "their life is no longer life," a condition of degradation suffered by all camp inhabitants, but instead that "their death is no longer death."[22] Drained of all affect and denied the possibility of communication, these figures die as human beings before their physical deaths.

Žižek suggests something similar in his discussion of the dispossessed and stateless subjects of contemporary biopolitics, figures similarly stunned into a shuffling semblance of human existence. These victims of natural disasters and global economic collapse are the new living-dead, alive but without place in the life-worlds of neoliberal governance. Such figures cannot rightfully be described using the familiar language of posttraumatic stress disorder, Žižek insists, because trauma has become the normalized rather than the disruptive condition. What is also true, but which Žižek does not explore, is that this more generalized condition is not new but rather is newly extended to many subjects who previously saw themselves as protected from such damage by the discourse of liberal humanism and its state institutions. I call such narratives ones of abject posthumanism, in which humanity becomes split between surviving "real" humans and infected, dangerous posthumans (the zombies; the infected), a literalization of what Foucault has termed the racism of modern biopolitical governance.

Viruses, which are both "natural" and manufactured as a technology of warfare, are an apt image for this abject posthuman, another kind of living-dead–infected-living. They are alive but incapable of reproduction on their own, and so they take over the functions of "healthy" cells, forcing them to reproduce the virus and become more agents of infection. This is precisely the trajectory of the abject posthumans who prey on surviving humans. Yet, as Priscilla Wald points out, the image of contagion does not have only pejorative associations. The word originally was used to describe the rapid circulation of ideas, not disease, and even the virus itself, although it often results in death, is not inherently about killing but rather about *changing*. Intrinsic to the idea of the virus is not only the model of the invading outsider but also the transmission of shared immunity and thus group belonging. Contagion, Wald points out, "dramatizes the dilemma that inspires the most basic of human narratives: the necessity and danger of human contact."[23]

Similarly, Roberto Esposito seeks to think about biopolitics that does not inevitably become thanatopolitics and uses the paradigm of immunity to explore the dialectical relations between self and community that are captured in the body's biological defenses. He characterizes post-9/11 America as a society suffering from an autoimmune disorder, in which the possibility for community is destroyed by a too-vigilant mechanism for detecting and annihilating infection,[24] a dynamic that is also operative in recent zombie narratives. For example, the AMC series *The Walking Dead* (2010–) is an extended meditation on the problems of community and individuality. It partakes equally of zombie and postapocalyptic traditions and is about what kind of human community will be built on the ashes of the preinfection world as much as about the flight from zombie attack.

The show is ambivalent in its depiction of zombies as *zoē* or *bios*: on one hand, in the many and familiar scenes of zombie hordes converging on our protagonists, the zombies are represented simply as monstrous threat and are killed in volume and with violent abandon; on the other, and in contrast to *28 Days Later*, when one of the core group, Amy (Emma Bell), becomes infected in the first season, the group is divided between those who want to dispatch her immediately and those willing to allow her sister, Andrea (Laurie Holden), time to grieve. In her phase of zombie infection, death, and rebirth as monstrous, then, Amy occupies a space in which she is not human and yet also not *fully* Other. In the end, her death is deemed inevitable, and thus this moment of hesitation does not offer a way to think through community and contagion in new ways, but it nonetheless treats the community's autoimmune responses as a difficulty, something questioned as well as naturalized. The series shifts further toward a reactionary us–them binary in the second season, when the hope for reversal, promised by the Centers for Disease Control and Prevention, has been destroyed. Its narrative arc concerns the differences in leadership style between Rick and his second in command, Shane Walsh (Jon Bernthal). Shane quickly adapts to the harsh new realities of the postapocalyptic world, willing to sacrifice human lives as easily as zombie ones if it proves advantageous to those he identifies as *his* community, a narrow group that does not extend to their entire collective. Shane puts himself at risk, but only for those in his self-identified family, whereas Rick strives to be the leader for the entire group and is willing to risk himself to help any people they encounter.

The first half of season 2 is taken up by a long search for a missing child, Sophia (Madison Lintz), whom they finally discover in the final moments of "Pretty Much Dead Already" (November 27, 2011). In the episode's final moments, Rick and his group confront Hershel (Scott Wilson) and his family, the owners of the farm where they are staying, over the infected that Hershel has kept quarantined in the barn rather than killed. Hershel insists upon seeing the zombies as ill rather than monstrous. Rick disagrees but has sufficient investment in the old order to respect Hershel's autonomy. Shane repeatedly insists that the old world is dead and, to survive, they must embrace new, harsher values. This debate over how to interpret the zombies—as within or beyond human community—is abruptly ended when Shane begins shooting, releasing the penned-up zombies and continuing the massacre until the final one—the missing Sophia, now changed—emerges from the barn. Crucially, it is Rick, not Shane, who kills her, representing his reluctant capitulation to the values Shane epitomizes. Sophia's change is an outcome they could easily—yet tellingly did not—predict, undermining the surface narrative's support of Rick's kinder, gentler postapocalyptic regime. *The Walking Dead* shares with Rick a desire for a sense of humanity that can persist beyond the zombie apocalypse—an investment in ideals of community, a condemnation of the autoimmune disorder that will sacrifice all for the sake of the self. Yet the narrative simultaneously endorses Shane's perspective that this dream is not only impossible but also dangerous, a liability in a world understood to have peeled away the veneer of community and revealed the "true" state of nature as a war of all against all. The series tries to balance these two impulses by vilifying Shane (who is killed for his crimes by the end of this season) and by making Rick loath to change: yet change he does, implying that the division of community into full and less-than human subjects is inevitable rather than a result of human political and economic systems.

The abject posthuman in *The Walking Dead*, then, is ultimately less the monstrous zombies than it is the monsters that the human community must become to survive in a world founded on such rapacious values. Shane is representative of the ethos of the neoliberal order, a discourse that acts on the population "to make survive," in Agamben's terms, but one that simultaneously dehumanizes and makes monstrous these survivors. This is true both of the zombies in the series, reduced to endless walking and consuming, and of those humans able to adjust themselves to the new order, who draw a narrow circle of community and demonize all those outside it. This perspective reflects the logic of neoliberalism that fragments human subjects across geographic, ethnic, and class boundaries and its refusal to allow one to recognize that survival is often at a cost for and of others.

In "The Imagination of Disaster," Susan Sontag analyzes the dehumanization in formulaic 1950s disaster films and argues that films such as *Them!* (dir. Gordon Douglas, 1954) and *Invasion of the Body Snatchers* (dir. Don Siegal, 1956) provide their audiences with the "fantasy of living through one's own death and more, the death of cities, the destruction of humanity itself,"[25] seeing in their repeated motifs an effort to come to terms with the violence of contemporary technology and pervasive xenophobia. Such films rely on an unacknowledged similarity between the dehumanized invaders and the logical and impersonal values of the savior-scientists, resulting in narratives that deny rather than enable social critique. Such films, Sontag contends, are an *"inadequate response"* to the problems they narrativize, texts complicit "with the abhorrent" since they neutralize it and "perpetuate clichés."[26] Just as the soulless and hyperrational aliens of 1950s disaster movies reflected limitations of the contemporary political ethos, the recent films of zombie infections, in their depictions of the "necessary" extremes of human violence to counter this threat, similarly demonstrate an unacknowledged homology between their antagonists and their heroes. Texts, such as *The Walking Dead*, that seem to question the exclusion of abject posthumans, only to insist on the necessity of their annihilation, enact a similar bad faith. They maintain that the split between abject and human subjects, between *zoē* and *bios*, is "natural" rather than made by contingent human choice and thereby normalizes and naturalizes the competition of capitalism and its dehumanization.

Contradictions, Profanations, the Promises of Monsters

I want to conclude by asking whether it is possible to think of the abject posthuman in ways other than as the monstrousness of bare life detached from the protections of the subject-citizen. In thinking about the posthuman infected-living zombies, can we recover anything of contagion's roots in shaping shared immunity/community?[27] Life should be "pure relation and therefore absence or implosion of subjects in relation to each other: a relation without subjects,"[28] Esposito contends. It is the logical categories of modernity (identity, causality, noncontradiction) that create a situation in which the impulses of life turn on themselves: such categories "construct barriers, limits, and embankments with respect to that common *munus*."[29] When humans refuse to be what liberal philosophy has constituted as "the human," new possibilities emerge, including new models of the relationship between individual and community. Campbell describes Esposito's biopolitics as a "philosophy of the impersonal,"[30] drawing on the work of Simone Weil and the idea that what is sacred in a person is precisely what disrupts the self-focused individual and prevents the immune response from coming into play. To develop this idea of impersonal *bios*, Campbell returns to Agamben and his idea of profanation. If something becomes sacred by removing it from the realm of ordinary human activity and separating it to the supernatural, then the reverse process, to profane, restores "to common use what sacrifice had separated and divided."[31]

Agamben refers to this reverse action as "a profane contagion"[32] and further contends that capitalism introduces this division with the commodity form that "splits into use-value and exchange-value."[33] Capitalism separates the human spirit from the human body, requiring that humanity does not work to live (that is, produce use-values to reproduce itself) but rather lives to work (that is, produce surplus-value for capital). In order to profane, in Agamben's sense, we must remove objects from this service to capital and return them to service to humanity, via embracing the same actions emptied "of their sense and of any obligatory relationship to an end."[34] Campbell suggests that humor is one way that we might separate our actions from a given or obligatory end and thus restore them to the human realm of profanation. The Argentinean film *Fase 7* (dir. Nicolás Goldbart, 2011) uses humor to redirect the zombie narrative to a new end, reading the world of zombie capital from the point of view of those subjects damaged rather than enriched by neoliberalism. *Fase 7* profanes the zombie narrative.

Fase 7 is a zombie film without any zombies. It begins with our unlikely hero, Coco (Daniel Hendler), who is shopping with his pregnant girlfriend, Pipi (Jazmín Stuart). Although crowds rush through the street in a panic as these two load their groceries and go home, they are oblivious and carry on bickering about quotidian tasks. Later that evening, as they eat dinner, we overhear a television news report talking about the virus having spread to the United States, Canada, Mexico, Spain, and the United Kingdom, concluding that Argentina may now be under threat. When the broadcast shifts to a World Health Organization representative explaining the risk, it simultaneously shifts from Spanish to the representative's English. Most of the film follows Coco and Pipi as their apartment building is quarantined by hazmat-suited agents who speak to them through megaphones and continually defer answering their questions. Rather than fleeing zombie hordes or learning to kill, Pipi and Coco play board games, bicker, make ration lists, and otherwise settle in for a boring apocalypse. We learn of the outbreak only through occasionally overheard bits of dialogue from television broadcasts, and most of this information continues to be in English.

When violence does break out, it begins as an attack on one of the building's residents, Zanutto (Fredrico Luppi), whose persistent cough has turned the others, organized by the paranoid Horacio (Yayo Guridi), against him. Horacio tries to involve Coco in these plots, but the inept, bumbling, and generally well-meaning Coco resists and even tries to warn Zanutto. The war among residents that breaks out is represented as a series of comic escapades, as Zanutto emerges not as a vulnerable old man but rather as a stylized, larger-than-life action hero. The death toll mounts, but the killing is entirely by paranoid residents turning on one another, a parody of the new ethos promoted by zombie narratives. Coco is given a mysterious videotape by Horacio that offers a conspiracy theory about the manufacture of the virus as part of a plot to implement "a new world order that guarantees the status of corporations, the ones responsible." We never see the full video but overhear parts of its narrative, including excerpts from George Bush's New World Order speech of 1991 given after the first U.S. invasion of Iraq. In the dénouement, almost everyone is killed, except Coco and Pipi, who leave the building and head north.

Fase 7 is simultaneously a playful and a serious film. It mocks the easy capitulation to the zero-sum-game ethics of neoliberalism naturalized in many other zombie films and reminds us of the connections between such fictional new world orders and the material one constructed for us by American hegemony and global capital. In leaving the city, Coco and Pipi refuse Bush's New World Order, revealing the emptiness of the supposed "rule of law rather than the law of the jungle,"[35] and seek a different kind of future than the hypocrisies of United Nations interventions that have made the world safe for global corporations. Throughout, Coco has retained his humanity and refused to adopt the new ethos of generalized killing; he remains committed to community rather than individuality, and his escape with pregnant Pipi at the end suggests a possibility for the birth of something new. Pipi and Coco escape with Horacio's paranoid survivalist supplies but with their own plan to live a rural life beyond the pressures and pace of the city. Although this film cannot undo the dominant thanatopolitical theme of zombie narratives, it nonetheless offers a glimpse at how such images might otherwise be deployed: a way of seeing that the end times can also be those of new beginnings.

Notes

1. Donna Haraway, "A Cyborg Manifesto: Science, Technology, and Socialist- Feminism in the Late Twentieth Century," in *Simians, Cyborgs, and Women: The Reinvention of Nature* (New York: Routledge, 1991), 154.

2. Ibid., 181.

3. Donna Haraway, "The Actors Are Cyborg, Nature Is Coyote, and the Geography Is Elsewhere: Postscript to 'Cyborgs at Large,'" in *Technoculture*, ed. Constance Penley and Andrew Ross, 21–26 (Minneapolis: University of Minnesota Press, 1991).

4. Slavoj Žižek, *Living in the End Times*, rev. ed. (London: Verso, 2011), x.

5. Ibid., 334.

6. Lev Grossman, "Zombies Are the New Vampires," *Time*, April 9, 2009, http://www.time.com /time/magazine/article/0,9171,1890384,00.html.

7. Gerry Canavan, "Fighting a War You've Already Lost: Zombies and Zombis in *Firefly/Serenity* and *Dollhouse*," *Science Fiction Film and Television* 4, no. 2 (2011): 173–203. This is an excellent overview of the distinctions and similarities between zombis and zombies and their relevance to capitalist critique.

8. David McNally, *Monsters of the Market: Zombies, Vampires, and Global Capitalism* (Leiden, Netherlands: Brill, 2010).

9. Jean Comaroff and John Comaroff, "Alien-Nation: Zombies, Immigrants, and Millennial Capitalism," *The South Atlantic Quarterly* 101, no. 4 (2002): 784.

10. K. Silem Mohammad, "Zombies Rest, and Motion: Spinoza and the Speed of Undeath," in *Zombies, Vampires, and Philosophy: New Life for the Undead*, ed. Richard Greene and K. Silem Mohammad (Chicago: Open Court, 2006), 94.

11. Michel Foucault, *Society Must Be Defended*, trans. David Macey (New York: Picador, 2003), 241.

12. Ibid., 61.

13. Henry A. Giroux, *Zombie Politics and Culture in the Age of Casino Capitalism* (New York: Peter Lang, 2010), 2.

14. Achille Mbembe, "Necropolitics," trans. Libby Meintjes, *Public Culture* 15, no. 1 (2003): 21.

15. Timothy Campbell, *Improper Life: Technology and Biopolitics from Heidegger to Agamben* (Minneapolis: University of Minnesota Press, 2011), 72.

16. Ibid., 94.

17. I am thinking of the parallels between the insertion of the protagonist and viewer quickly in medias res of the new world of zombie politics, and the strategies of neoliberalism that utilize a rhetoric of urgency and crisis to compel people to accept rather than question rapid changes of policy. See Naomi Klein, *The Shock Doctrine: The Rise of Disaster Capitalism* (New York: Picador, 2007).

18. Giorgio Agamben, *Remnants of Auschwitz: The Witness and the Archive*, trans. Daniel Heller- Roazon (New York: Zone Books, 2002), 155.

19. Ibid.

20. Ibid., 55.

21. Ibid., 70.

22. Ibid.

23. Priscilla Wald, *Contagious: Cultures, Carriers, and the Outbreak Narrative* (Durham, N.C.: Duke University Press, 2007).

24. Roberto Esposito, *Bios: Biopolitics and Philosophy*, trans. Timothy Campbell (Minneapolis: University of Minnesota Press, 2008).

25. Susan Sontag, "The Imagination of Disaster" (1965), in *Science Fiction: Stories and Contexts*, ed. Heather Masri (New York: Bedford, 2009), 1005.

26. Ibid., 1014.

27. Other scholars have found liberating possibility in the figure of the zombie, a subject that refuses individuation and one whose excessive, unchanneled energy may partake of the spirit of the multitude. See Simon Orpana, "Spooks of Biopower: The Uncanny Carnivalesque of Zombie Walks," *Topia* 25 (Spring 2011): 153–76, and Sarah Juliet Lauro and Karen Embry, "A Zombie Manifesto: The Nonhuman Condition in the Era of Advanced Capitalism," *boundary 2* 35, no. 1 (2008): 85–108. Orpana sees in the popular celebration of zombies a model for collectivity premised on notions other than a mutually beneficial contract among otherwise distinct individuals but notes as well that such a "collective constellation . . . only appears as a threatening, monstrous Other to those still trapped within the individualist, bourgeois paradigm" (158). Similarly, Lauro and Embry argue that the zombie's very lack of subjectivity is precisely what makes it a fitting image of the posthuman, "a subject that is not a subject" (96).

28. Esposito, *Bios*, 89.

29. Ibid., 90.

30. Campbell, *Improper Life*, 66.

31. Ibid., 52.

32. Giorgio Agamben, "In Praise of Profanation," in *Profanations*, trans. Jeff Fort (New York: Zone Books, 2007), 74.

33. Ibid., 81.

34. Ibid., 86.

35. This line is a direct quotation from Bush's speech. In the film's final sequence, as the survivors drive out of the apartment's garage, we hear a voice-over of this speech (in Bush's voice) as we view them leaving.

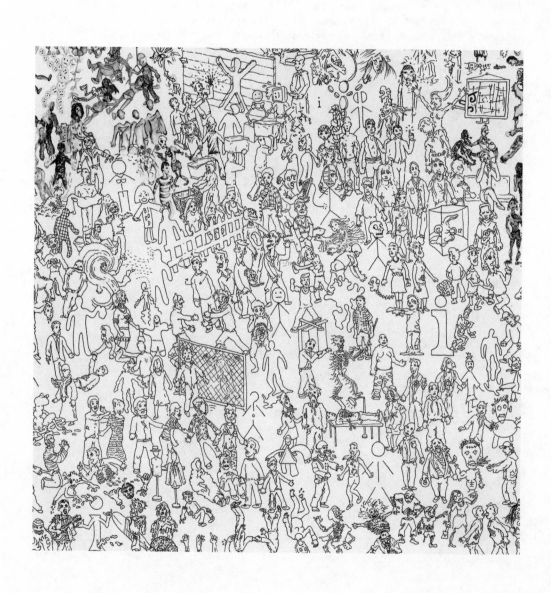

PART III
Zombies and Other(ed) People

Vital Ambivalence

In an opinion piece for the *New York Times* on the subject of recent police violence against people of color, and in particular the case of Sandra Bland, a woman who was found hanged in her jail cell after being arrested on faulty charges, Roxane Gay concluded her article with the following powerful words: "increasingly, as a black woman in America, I do not feel alive. I feel like I am not yet dead." Gay's bold statement reverberates with the language of living death as it has been activated in political theory and calls to mind Giorgio Agamben's *Homo Sacer,* Orlando Patterson's work on *Slavery and Social Death,* Achille Mbembe's description of "Necropolitics," and Judith Butler's recent work on *Precarious Life.* It is beyond the purview of this preface to deconstruct the many subtleties of this statement and its commentary upon the political nature of the crisis in police prejudice against minorities, and the list of names of people of color killed by those in positions of authority in the past months and years is too long and troubling to reproduce here. But I open with Gay's quotation as a figurehead to announce the coming discussion, for her description is a potent reminder of both the contemporary relevance of imagery of living death and of the historical lineage of the zombie—that personification of the inhumane treatment of humans, of lives that are not valued.

The government-sanctioned mistreatment of certain types of bodies, especially that which is critiqued by Gay here—"On the Death of Sandra Bland and *Our Vulnerable Bodies,*"[1] that is, specifically those belonging to African Americans—falls in a direct historical line from those displaced and dehumanized by the transatlantic slave trade, which explicitly privileged certain lives above others and characterized some types of bodies as little more than service and labor machines. Gay's choice of words makes clear that the ongoing crisis in U.S. society (which has garnered recent media attention but is by no means a recent problem) reflects the survival of that racist philosophy that so many would like to pretend was vanquished with the end of the Civil War or the civil rights protests of the last century. Black life has been devalued for centuries: itself zombielike, the ethos that perpetuated the slave trade slogs on, and in cases of police prejudice, for example, we often find people of color treated as Gay asserts, like zombies, as less than living.

As was stated in the introduction, this theme is endemic to the zombie's origins. The zombie myth was, in its first incarnation, an analogy for the slave's ambivalent status as expendable life, as a subhuman commodity. The first zombie films highlighted racial difference, and though such films did not offer an enlightened perspective, they have made for useful criticism of the period's brand of exoticized racism, particularly regarding fears of miscegenation. In large part because of the prevalence of African American protagonists in George Romero's Living Dead films, race has remained a visible component of the evolving zombie narrative. In her broader study of "Capitalist Monsters," Annalee Newitz traces the way films about the undead from the 1980s, 1990s, and 2000s highlight the "anachronistic race relations [that] exist alongside those of the present day" (91), but she writes that the undead are "best understood in the context of anxieties about many kinds of race relations that develop in the wake of colonialism" (90).

Truly, although the zombie's reflection on the treatment of people of African descent is the logical remainder of its folkloric origins, a subject treated in the first section of this volume, others have read zombie narratives for their commentary on orientalism, anti-Semitism, Islamophobia, and the genocide of the native peoples of North America. Still others read zombie narratives for their commentary on different categorizations—like gender and sexuality, bodies that transgress national borders or that defy expectations of what a body or mind should be "able" to do—that have led to the privileging of one type of body or human life over another. As the essays collected in this section of the book demonstrate, zombie narratives make visible the way various types of "vulnerable bodies," to borrow Gay's term, are *othered* by our society: zombie stories highlight racial tensions and the demonization of particular religions, but they also sometimes provide space for these *others*—female, black, Muslim, homosexual, disabled, homeless and displaced, aging and infirm—to fight back. The five essays included in this section of the book offer a glimpse of the way certain types of people who are traditionally devalued by mainstream society find a place of critique (and even, in cases, empowerment) in zombie narratives.

Edward P. Comentale's "Zombie Race" begins with a succinct history of the zombie's transmission in popular culture, from its origins in Afro-Caribbean folklore to American film. Providing some beautiful close readings that highlight the issue of appropriation, particularly through the thematic of voice, this essay captures the undead aesthetic in literary works that directly address the zombie (Zora Neale Hurston's *Tell My Horse*) and well as those that don't (Richard Wright's *Uncle Tom's Children*). The second half of the essay turns to investigate zombie figures in music, from Fela Kuti's "Zombie," to Michael Jackson's "Thriller," to Kanye West's figurations of monstrosity. The zombie's transmission is not limited only to cultural appropriation, however, but also works in a manner similar to "sonic contagion," working on the listener to create a transformative aural experience in "the lively space of death and dissent."

This essay might belong as much in a discussion about zombies and media (for its developed argument on sound, voice, and other devices of recorded music, like repetition, with its disorienting zombic quality) as it does in a selection of essays on "Zombies and Other(ed) People." In fact, though the majority of the primary texts here are the work of artists of African descent, the discussion of race is actually rather oblique, but I think this is one of the essay's strengths: it doesn't hit you over the head but subtly influences the viewer, like a driving backbeat. For example, Comentale draws our attention to a recurring image of a black man holding a white woman as it exists in a zombie movie poster, the frontispiece of Richard Wright's *Native Son*, and a Kanye West album cover, without really ever spelling out what this trope means. Of George Clinton's "Dr. Funkenstein," Comentale writes that he uses "the machines of electronic sound production to restore something like racial vitality." What this essay offers is a vision of the way the aesthetic of the zombie can be a tool for expressing the tension between one's race and one's perception by society, even when that vitality is considered "monstrous" by others.

First published in his edited collection *The Dread of Difference: Gender and the Horror Film* (1996), Barry Keith Grant's essay "Taking Back the *Night of the Living Dead*: George Romero, Feminism, and the Horror Film" is a must-cite for any work engaging substantively with feminism in zombie films. This highly regarded piece specifically treats the character of Barbra in the 1968 film *Night of the Living Dead* and the feminist update that the character receives in the Tom Savini remake of the film in 1990, but there are a couple of things that are too often overlooked about the essay. For example, Grant widens his scope to investigate Romero's female characters more broadly for their success in terms of survival skills, connecting this to the ethos of masculine professionalism patterned in the films of Howard Hawks, a model for Romero. This essay thereby suggests the way that contemporary definitions of success in survivalist video games and other zombie narratives (like *The Walking Dead*) are mired in an outmoded conception of gender and traces the way that Romero's films were subverting the patriarchy well before the 1990 remake of *Night of the Living Dead*. This essay thereby highlights the intertwined mesh of categories like capitalism, gender, morality, and professionalism in survival narratives, providing a foundation on which contemporary scholarship should continue to build.

Readers interested in gender and sexuality will want to investigate the broader work of Shaka McGlotten, particularly his edited collection (with Steve Jones) *Zombies and Sexuality*. But in his study of queer online sociality and Bruce LaBruce's gay zombie film *Otto; or, Up with Dead People* that I include here, McGlotten underscores a significant (and heretofore undertheorized) binary that the zombie straddles: the loneliness/community of the zombie (in the) horde. In opposition to those who would read the nonreproductivity of homosexual sex as antifuture (and thus as zombielike), McGlotten suggests that the "openness" of the figure provides an overlooked site within the mythology for potential empowerment. Other criticism of *Otto* has tended to highlight the film as a narrative about AIDS, which makes McGlotten's pivot here to online sociality all the more relevant in the era of meet-up apps like Grindr and Tinder. Even further, one of my favorite things about this essay is its brief but poignant discussion of zombies and addiction, an area into which I hope to see scholarship expand. McGlotten's assertion that there is vitality in addiction—as he notes, addiction is often discussed in terms of possession—is a striking inversion that deserves more discussion.

Next, in a treatment of zombies and disability, "Dead *and* Disabled: The Crawling Monsters of *The Walking Dead*," Anna Mae Duane looks at the prevalence of disabled bodies in *The Walking Dead* series alongside the aesthetics of the freak show. This piece, which was previously published online and expanded for this volume, marks an important contribution to a field of inquiry within zombie studies that needs to be developed. Particularly striking is Duane's profile of disabled teenager Nick Santonastasso, who uploads videos to the Internet of his "zombie pranks," in which he accosts strangers in public. Santonastasso has no legs and only one arm, and in these forced encounters, he highlights how his natural form resembles various zombies, like the Bicycle Girl zombie from *The Walking Dead*'s pilot episode. This essay raises important questions about the zombie's commentary on disability and challenges the way this prevalent movie monster preserves notions that non-"normal" bodies are "monstrous." Tying the latest iteration of the zombie narrative to contemporary concerns like Ebola outbreaks; depictions of "supercrips" like Helen Keller, who overcome terrific obstacles to normalize; and the spectacle of freakery more broadly, this short essay extends several shoots into areas that might later be afforested by future scholars.

Jon Stratton's selection is a chapter from his book *Uncertain Lives: Culture, Race, and Neoliberalism in Australia* that is devoted to zombie narratives and their characterizations of immigrants, refugees, and asylum seekers. In "Trouble with Zombies: *Muselmänner*, Bare Life, and Displaced Peoples," Stratton expands on his well-known essay "Zombie Trouble: Zombie Texts, Bare Life, and Displaced People," in which he connected Agamben's theoretical work in *Homo Sacer* to contemporary depictions of zombies, reading the fantastical undead as placeholders for those perceived as "threatening" to the state. This expansion of that critical work pays particular attention to the characterization of the Muslim in contemporary Western societies, a topic that is increasingly pressing, especially alongside geopolitical shifts of power in the Middle East, rising anti-immigrant tensions in Europe, and Islamophobia in the United States. Another of its contributions is that it compares the zombie to both the vampire and the werewolf, illustrating the inhumanity of the lycanthrope, which Agamben discussed, as a trait that reappears in the living dead. Connecting texts from *Pride and Prejudice and Zombies* and *Fido* to the concentration camp and its *Muselmänner*, this essay gives an in-depth explanation of what the zombie connotes as a figuration of "bare life" and for whom the zombie stands in contemporary fiction and film about the denigration and displacement of people.

Further Reading

The original zombie "other" was a helpless slave of a Vodou master and, thereby, was implicitly connected to the history of the transatlantic slave trade, furnishing commentary on the legacy of oppression and abuse of persons of African descent under colonial and postcolonial rule. On the period of early cinema and its racial politics, see—in addition to the previously cited "Dead Subjectivity" by Fay—Edna Aizenberg's treatment of *I Walked with a Zombie*, or Lizbeth Paravisini-Gebert's address of "Women Possessed" in early zombie cinema, or Chera Kee's "They Are Not Men . . . They Are Dead Bodies."

Perhaps because of these origins, zombies often remain coded as racially different. The collection edited by Moreman and Rushton on *Race, Oppression, and the Zombie* gives a nice overview of the topic, especially the essays by Ann Kordas on racist enjoyment of early zombie narratives and Barbara Bruce on "the ambivalence of race" in Romero's *Night of the Living Dead*. See also the aforementioned section of Newitz's book, "The Undead: A Haunted Whiteness." In a similar register to Comentale's piece here, Kobena Mercer's discussion of Michael Jackson's *Thriller* in *Welcome to the Jungle* is a classic reading in black cultural studies, while Justin Ponder's essay "Dawn of the Different" provides a novel take on the zombie's hybridity as inherently "mulatto." The video game Resident Evil 5, with its setting in Africa, sparked renewed discussion of race and the zombie. See the aforementioned essay by Richard Brock and Tanner Higgin's address of the topic in his dissertation "Gamic Race" as well as Hanli Geyser's essay "Return to Darkness: Representations of Africa in Resident Evil 5." The essay by Gretchen Bakke, "Dead White Men: An Essay on the Changing Dynamics of Race in U.S. Action Cinema," profiled by Elizabeth McAlister's piece in the first section, may also be of interest for its discussion of white zombies and black vampires.

For investigation of the zombie read as othering *other* races or creeds, see especially Eric Hamako's "Zombie Orientals Ate My Brain!," which details the way zombie narratives are colored by terrorism panic and anti-Muslim fervor. For its brief discussion of *World War Z*'s treatment of the Israel–Palestine conflict, Aalya Ahman's "Gray Is the New Black" bears some relevance, as does Matthew Rovner's article in the *Jewish Daily Forward* on Israel's recent zombie films. More work in this area, connecting the French series *Les Revenants* to antirefugee panic, for instance, is also being done, as by Claire Mouflard in her essay "Zombies and Refugees." For an address of the zombie as symbolic of Native peoples, see Robert Saunders's essay in *Undead in the West* on a 1999 film called *Ravenous*, about a zombielike Native American curse, and, on Cutcha Risling Baldy's blog, "Why I Teach *The Walking Dead* in My Native Studies Class." Those interested in the theme in terms of Mexican American immigration should see the essay by Christopher Gonzalez, "Zombie Nationalism: Robert Rodriguez's *Planet Terror* as Immigration Satire."

Naturally, there is much more to read on the topic of gender and sexuality in horror more broadly, and those unacquainted with the field should start with Clover's *Men, Women, and Chainsaws* and Halberstam's *Skin Shows*. Barry Keith Grant's collection *Dread of Difference*, which has just come out in an exciting new edition, provides a nice introduction to the topic. Those interested in reading more widely on zombies and gender specifically might also enjoy Andrea Ruthven's critique of "Zombie Postfeminism" and Natasha Patterson's "Cannibalizing Gender and Genre," but readings of gender and sexuality are often found together in discussion of zombies, as in the article "A Zombie Apocalypse" by Jessica Murray, on South African zombie narratives as providing space for "alternative constructions of gender and sexuality," and Stephen Harper's essay in *Jump Cut*, "I Could Kiss You, You Bitch," on the "racist, sexist, and homophobic elements" of the Resident Evil films.

On the topic of "Zombies and Sexuality," in addition to the essay reproduced here and the edited collection produced by McGlotten and Steve Jones, see also Jones's many other essays as well as Marc Leverette's "The Funk of Forty Thousand Years" in *Zombie Culture*. Much has been written, as has been previously stated, about Bruce LaBruce's gay zombie films and AIDS, but for a reading of the film's optimism that is more in line with McGlotten's piece reproduced here, see Kathleen Frederickson's short piece

"Up with Dead Privates" and Arnau Roig Mora's "The Necropolitics of the Apocalypse: Queer Zombies in the Cinema of Bruce LaBruce."

In McGlotten and Jones's edited volume *Zombies and Sexuality*, Cathy Hannabach's essay "Queering and Cripping the End of the World" brings together two different types of zombie others. Under the subheading of zombies and disability, we can include comparisons made between the living dead and the elderly. In particular, the zombie has been compared to the Alzheimer's patient and fears of the aging body; see the articles by Susan Behuniak, "The Living Dead? The Construction of People with Alzheimer's Disease as Zombies," and Elizabeth Switaj's "Ageing, Disability, and Zombies." Aside from Duane's offering in this collection, the topic of the zombie as disabled figure remains, as yet, underdeveloped, but Mel Chen's article "Lurching for the Cure" should also be required reading.

Although it is not literally concerned with the "living dead" in the same way that the articles here are, those looking for more discussion of the theory presented by Stratton might see Andrew Norris's article "Giorgio Agamben and the Politics of the Living Dead" for its discussion of biopolitics and political identity as articulated by Agamben and Heidegger. Seth Morton's "Zombie Politics" performs a very nice synopsis of Agamben and explains why he has fallen out of academic favor, going "beyond Agamben" (320) with its attention to contemporary biopolitical thinkers like Martin Hägglund, Eugene Thacker, and Roberto Esposito.

For more on the displaced zombie in a different context than that of the political refugee or the immigrant profiled in Stratton's piece, see George Pfau's essay "Homeless, Feverish, Cannibal" or my own essay "For the Ethical Treatment of Zombies" on the "Miami Zombie," Rudy Eugene, and his attack of homeless man Ronald Poppo. The article by Linnemann, Wall, and Green that is included in the next section, "Zombies in the Street," also addresses this incident and the way different types of bodies are dehumanized by the state and the media.

Note

1. Emphasis added.

CHAPTER 11

Zombie Race

EDWARD P. COMENTALE

It begins with a thump, or rather, a scrape and a thump. *Shhh-thump*. The monster appears first as sound and then as rhythm, or rather, counter-rhythm. Its presence is made known, paradoxically, by its double absence, one physical and the other temporal.

It lags, behind itself, drags itself, before itself, somewhere in back of you, in front of you, over your shoulder—always where it is not. *Shhh-thump*. Its second beat is scarier than the first, not just because it is louder, closer, but because it recalls the first. The monster is always in two—two spaces, two times. It approaches as it recedes. It coheres as it falls apart. Each step revives as it destroys. Each step is the death of death, the death of death, over and over again.

Shhh-thump. Shhh-thump. It returns, not like a ghost, referring back each night to the same secret crime, but like a siren, always again itself, not itself, in a process of becoming itself. The footprint, the bloodstain, the heavy breathing—as Jeffrey Cohen notes, the monster is always also a demonstration, both a sign and the process of its own signification, a sign of its own passing, a sign of its own lumbering movement in time.[1] In its repetition, its representation, the zombie performs the living death of language, of representation, and thus opens up the time and space of terror, of encounter. It is not so much an "other," an essence, or even an expression of such essence but an indication, a dark index, of what is already happening or about to happen.

Shhh-thump. Shhh-thump. Shhh-thump. In time, this foot—always metrical and yet always uneven—becomes a groove. The terror of its empty beat, everywhere and nowhere, implies something like pleasure as well as protest. Agent Mulder had it right; the zombie only wants to dance:

> MULDER: You know, Scully, I was just thinking about Lazarus, Ed Wood, and those tofurkey-eating zombies. How come when people come back from the dead they always want to hurt the living?
>
> SCULLY: Well, that's because people can't really come back from the dead, Mulder. I mean, ghosts and zombies are just projections of our own repressed cannibalistic and sexual fears and desires. They are who we fear that we are at heart—just mindless automatons who can only kill and eat.
>
> MULDER: Party pooper. Well, I got a new theory. I say that when zombies try to eat

people, that's just the first stage. You see, they've just come back from being dead so they're going to do all the things they miss from when they were alive. So, first, they're going to eat, then they're going to drink, then they're going to dance and make love.

SCULLY: Oh, I see. So it's just that we never get to stay with them long enough to see the gentler side of the undead.

MULDER: Exactly.[2]

The best zombie flicks, like the best of funk and hip-hop, work through the rhythms and counter-rhythms of this foregone conclusion: the delay and drag of inevitable assault; convergent and divergent lines of hands-in-the-air flight; the chase too soon, too slow, toward and away from some impossible event. The best moments of these films exist, spasmodically, between two beats, two deaths, as a dark dance out of which emerges something like an alternative art and a possible politics. They present the zombie not as an expression of something else, as a screen for personal trauma or historical crisis, but as a rhythmic field of intensities, and thereby as it raises a different set of demands: disincorporation, decentralization, and dissemination. In a word, the rhythm of the zombie is the rhythm of *diaspora*—the spread, the sporing, of zombie culture as cultural politics.

In talking race and zombies, we begin with the deathliness dispersed everywhere through slavery and colonial power. If the figure of the zombie emerges from the slave trade of Africa and stalks the West bearing traces of this trauma, its threat lies precisely in its forced abandonment of humanist ethics and expression.[3] Take, for instance, Jean-Paul Sartre's famous introduction to Frantz Fanon's *Wretched of the Earth*. Here, in an explicitly Marxist reading, Sartre casts colonization as a violent system of exploitation that results in the production of "monstrosities."[4] The humanist claims of the colonizers, he argues, serve only to justify the inhuman reduction of the colonized, an objectification of the other as slave. For Sartre, though, as for Fanon, this very deathliness, this inexpressive thingliness, becomes the precondition for revolutionary violence:

> Europeans, open this book, look inside it. After taking a short walk in the night you will see strangers gathered around a fire, get closer and listen. They are discussing the fate reserved for your trading posts and for the mercenaries defending them. They might see you, but they will go on talking among themselves without even lowering their voices. Their indifference strikes home: their fathers, creatures living in the shadows, *your* creatures, were dead souls; you afforded them light, you were their sole interlocutor, you did not take the trouble to answer the zombies. The sons ignore you. The fire that warms and enlightens them is not yours. You, standing at a respectful distance, you now feel eclipsed, nocturnal, and numbed. It's your turn now. In the darkness that will dawn into another day, you have turned into the zombie.[5]

In this scenario the very thingliness of the ex-natives grants them both a new objective vision and a steely commitment to necessary violence. In fact, for Sartre, only the violence wielded by the colonized, in its radical indifference and inhumanity, can restore anything like their lost humanity. At the moment of attack, the death of his own death, the victim of colonization—"this walking dead man"—is renewed as a subject, while the colonizer is in turn reduced to an object.[6] We cannot help "seeing in this trial by strength," Sartre writes, "a perfectly inhuman method used by subhumans to claim for themselves a charter for humanity. . . . The colonized are cured of colonial neurosis by driving the colonist out by force. Once their rage explodes, they recover their lost coherence, they experience self-knowledge through reconstruction of themselves."[7] This revolt occurs on the other side of humanism and expression, waged through death as the sheer objectification of colonizer *and* colonized, situating both within a single horizon of monstrous form and force.

And yet there's another story to be told here, or less a story than another kind of negotiation, one that, by emphasizing the undeadness of form itself, looks beyond any specific instance of revolutionary violence and, in its emphasis on displacement and diaspora, bypasses the utterly Western and potentially fatal logic of subject and object. In this we take our cue from Edouard Glissant's later description of the Caribbean as a "dead-end situation," ensnared "in nothingness."[8] For Glissant, the average Martinican is a "happy zombi," simply "passing through his world." His life is governed by "remote control," possessed, mindlessly, by foreign languages, foreign economies, and foreign ideologies.[9] For Glissant, as for all the writers and singers and dancers discussed in this essay, "deadness," the deadness of form as it slips past the expressive sovereignty of self and nation, informs a negotiation that cannot be reduced to binary systems of relation. In Glissant's work, Martinique is less a unified region or culture than the site of manic repetition and radical derision. Caught between the inaccessible motherland of Africa and the impossible dreamland of France, the region knows nothing but empty forms, a constant shuddering into and out of competing ideologies. Here, "double consciousness" appears as endless "diversion," the ceaseless shuffling into and away from foreignness, a kind of empty possession that is also always a form of dispossession, the infection of and by other cultures and discourses. In turn, Glissant's own discourse abandons expressions and clarifications for repetitions and mutations, for densities, distortions, and obscurities. "Banging away incessantly at the main idea," he writes, "will perhaps lead to exposing the space they occupy in us. Repetition of these ideas does not clarify their expression; on the contrary, it perhaps leads to obscurity," and, thus, perhaps, "the recognized inscrutability of the other."[10] Similarly, the zombie, as a figure of colonization and its reversal, seeks nothing of expression or metaphor; rather, in the dark movement of its body, in its voice, and in the rhythms and repetitions of its presence, it exposes a different kind of modernity and a different kind of politics. Simply put, when it comes to the postcolonial zombie, we're dealing less with monster as other than with monster as form of becoming, less with trauma and violence, and even less with expressions of such, than with performances, with issues of voice and vocal possession, of media and mediation—again, disincorporation, decentralization, and dissemination.

This seems to be the strangely threatening subtext of the first sensationalist blast of ethnographic writings that emerged from Haiti during the U.S. Occupation between 1915 and 1934. Take, for example, W. B. Seabrook's 1929 Haitian travelogue *The Magic Island*, the book most often credited with introducing the figure of the zombie to Western audiences.[11] In his chapter on zombies, "Dead Men Working in the Cane Fields,"

Seabrook strains to uphold the representational boundaries between the Western world and its primitive other, but he constantly comes up against the unsettling hybridity that marks Haitian race, class, religion, and science. Here the skeptical ethnographer, seeking to unearth the dark origins of the zombie legend, turns first to a Haitian farmer, Polynice, a man whose doubleness—"half peasant born and bred"—bespeaks the doubleness of the island as a whole.[12] With Polynice as his guide, Seabrook's fantasies of Haitian otherness slowly begin to crumble. At one point he witnesses a woman murmur a prayer to Papa Legba and then cross herself before an image of Christ. He marvels, in turn, at a procession of "little black boys in white lace robes, little black girls in starched white dresses, with shoes and stockings, from a parish school, with coloured ribbons in their kinky hair."[13] As Seabrook notes, this cross-cultural contamination swings both ways, an apparent by-product of colonial history. Western culture and civilization might find itself perverted by the heart of darkness here, but such darkness proves already tainted by Western enlightenment. In what is perhaps his story's most ghastly moment, Seabrook learns that most of the island's zombies are associated with Hasco, an American corporation. "Hasco is perhaps the last name anybody would think of connecting with either sorcery or superstition," he explains. "The word is American-commercial-synthetic, like Nabisco, Delco, Socony. It stands for the Haitian–American Sugar Company—an immense factory plant, dominated by a huge chimney, with clanging machinery, steam whistles, freight cars. It is like a chunk of Hoboken. . . . It is modern big business, and it sounds it, looks it, smells it."[14]

Civilization and primitivism, modernity and myth, technology and ritual—as Seabrook probes deeper and deeper into the Haitian heart of darkness, he slowly realizes that none of his cherished categories seem to apply. While Polynice fears the zombie because it signals the endless indenture of black slavery, Seabrook himself seems most horrified by the way it defies the representational system upon which Western power is based. When he finally comes face-to-face with a set of dead-eyed zombie laborers, "plodding like brutes, like automatons," he is struck by nothing so much as their *opacity*— their simple refusal to express either humanity or its other. The face of one zombie appears not simply pained but "vacant, as if there were nothing behind it. It seemed not only expressionless but incapable of expression. . . . 'Great God,'" Seabrook exclaims aloud, "'maybe this stuff is really true, and if it is true, it is rather awful, for it upsets everything.'" The death in the zombie's face signals the deathliness of all form—the sheer arbitrariness, the unnaturalness of the sign, its apparently senseless circulation in time and space. By "everything," Seabrook explains, he means nothing less than "the natural fixed laws and processes on which all modern human thought and action are based."[15] Ultimately, though, this opacity is as much notable for its effects as for its causes. In his panic, Seabrook turns to science, medicine, and ultimately the rule of law to re-master what has already been enslaved. Seeking a "fixed rule of reason," he turns to Dr. Antoine Villiers, a "scientifically trained mind," who reveals an article within the current Haitian Penal Code that states, "Also shall be qualified as attempted murder the employment which may be made against any person of substances which, without causing actual death, produce a lethargic coma more or less prolonged. If, after the administering of such substances, the person has been buried, the act shall be considered murder no matter what result follows."[16] But the blow has been struck, and a certain uneasiness marks the rest of Seabrook's study, as well as each zombie text that follows in its colonial wake. Despite calling in the law here, Seabrook seems capable of only telling more zombie stories, coming across less like a rational investigator and more like an anxious folklorist—a "sensationalist"—offering his own performance to counter what seems to be the eternal return of the zombie. He finishes his travelogue in bad faith, telling more and more anxious zombie tales that work to extend the very thing he fears the most.

According to Kyle Bishop, for "a Western, white audience," the "real threat and source of terror" in such stories lies not in "political vagaries of a postcolonial nation, the plights of the enslaved native zombies, or even the dangers posed by menacing armies of the walking dead, but rather the risk that the white protagonists—especially the *female* protagonists—might turn into zombies (i.e., slaves) themselves. In other words, the true horror in these movies lies in the prospect of a Westerner becoming dominated, subjugated, symbolically raped, and effectively 'colonized' by pagan representatives."[17] In all such stories, though, the threat of "reverse colonization" occurs at the borders of representation, via sound and rhythm rather than symbol and narrative. The clichéd markers of "primitive" culture—tribal drums, ecstatic dancing, crude totems, "voodoo" dolls—do not merely symbolize the primitiveness of non-Western culture but demonstrate something of the mimetic and decisively repetitive nature of anti-imperial power. In fact, in both high modernist texts such as Joseph Conrad's 1902 novel *Heart of Darkness* and popular schlock like the 1932 film *White Zombie*, the threat of "going primitive" occurs through a series of specifically rhythmic encounters—encounters that are defined as much by copying as by contact and thus inevitably leave power itself up for grabs.[18] Moreover, the threat of "going primitive" could just as easily be experienced as a kind of thrill, an ultimate release from the strictures of Western enlightenment and the pain of being a Western subject. As Barbara Browning observes, the Western account of African diasporic culture "relies on the figure of cultural contagion," but "artists and performers in the diaspora sometimes invert, ironically, the metaphor, such that 'Western influence' is itself shown as a pathogen. Or, more typically, they recuperate the notion of African 'infection' by suggesting that diasporic culture *is* contagious, irresistible—vital, life-giving, and productive."[19] Indeed, if the American consumers of early zombie pop culture seemed themselves possessed by a "voodoo" spell, they were—by virtue of the very repetition of genre—entwined in a similar negotiation of power. In the pulpy short stories and mainstream Hollywood films of the 1930s and 1940s, the threat of cultural contagion is everywhere on display, but the details of plot and image make it nearly impossible to determine the origin or even the direction of colonial power. More often than not, the anxious logic of cultural contagion—in which the colonial world is negatively defined as dirty, diseased, and crudely mimetic—undermined the very ideology it was meant to uphold, a reversal that extended well beyond the colonial scene through the very proliferation of zombie films, stories, and pop songs that defined zombie culture more generally.

Take, for example, Jacques Tourneur's 1943 classic *I Walked with a Zombie*.[20] The film signals its weirdly progressive politics early on, with the suggestion that the corruption of the Caribbean island of Saint Sebastian began with the slave trade. In high gothic

Figure 11.1.
(Dis)Possession 1: Carrefour and
Jessica from the poster for *I Walked
with a Zombie* (dir. Jacques Tourneur,
RKO Radio Pictures, 1943).

mode, it sketches out the dark secrets of the seemingly glamorous Holland clan—the tragic death of the planter-patriarch, the incestuous squabbling between the two half brothers, the mother's obsessive love for her sons. Toying with its audience's expectations, the film takes no small delight in dashing Betsy's naive attraction to the island's exotic beauty against the family's inherent cynicism: "It's easy enough to read the thoughts of a newcomer," Paul Holland grouses. "Everything seems beautiful because you don't understand. Those flying fish—they are not leaping for joy. They're jumping in terror. Bigger fish want to eat them. That luminous water—it takes its gleam from millions of tiny dead bodies. It's the glitter of putrescence. There's no beauty here. It's death and decay." Everywhere, though, this death and decay are brought about by a radical mimesis, the rhythmic appropriation and misappropriation of formal power. Just as the two sons come across as decadent copies of their once great father, Betsy has arrived as a replacement for a now zombified Jessica, who had previously replaced Mrs. Rand, the family's matriarch. In the film's most effective sequence, Betsy, having lost faith in Western medicine, leads Jessica to the ritual *houmfort* (a Vodou temple), where she hopes to gain the advice of the local *bokor* (sorcerer or priest). The two women sneak through the cane past an ominous set of bones, a screech owl, and then a giant naked zombie (Carrefour, played with eerie stiffness by Darby Jones), only to emerge upon what seems the true heart of darkness: a ritual gathering, where they witness first a sword dance, a sultry spirit possession, and then, with a burst of manic drumming, an erotic stomp between two black women who seem to represent Betsy's and Jessica's own primitive doubles. The girls join in the line of worshipers seeking advice from the father of the gods, Damballa, whose voice emerges from a nearby hut. When they get to the door, though, it opens unexpectedly upon Mrs. Rand, the matriarch of the Holland clan, who has been impersonating the father of the gods in order to maintain control over the local population.

Just as the local practitioners of Vodou use little dolls to control their white oppressors, Mrs. Rand crudely mimics the formal properties of Vodou ritual in order to assert her authority. It's a fascinating twist, not simply because it upsets the now familiar plot of "going native" to make room for something like female empowerment but also because it restages the possession of colonial power via the native's own logic of possession. As Mrs. Rand explains, in her own brittle voice,

> When my husband died I felt helpless. They disobeyed me—things went from bad to worse. All my husband's dreams of good health, good sanitation, good morals for these sweet and gentle people seemed to die with him. Then, almost accidentally, I discovered the secret of how to deal with them. There was a girl with a baby—again and again I begged her to boil the drinking water. She never would. Then I told her the god, Shango, would be pleased and kill the evil spirits in the water if she boiled it. She boiled the water from then on. . . . I found it was so simple to let the gods speak through me. Once started, it seemed such an easy way to do good.

Such possession apparently comes with a price. The surreptitious reversal in gender is just part of the story: this switch takes place via the abstraction of sound and voice and thus suggests a more radical decentering of power. Going primitive here figures less as an anarchic release of repressed energy than as a sacrifice to form. Mrs. Rand is just as much possessed by Vodou as she uses Vodou to possess others. The end of the film suggests that in a fit of jealousy, she herself caused Jessica's zombification, in a ritual initiated under the sway of the jungle rhythm. "That night," she explains, "I went to the houmfort. I kept seeing Jessica's face—smiling—smiling because two men hated each other—because she was beautiful enough to take my family in her hands and break it apart. The drums seemed to be beating in my head. The chanting—the lights—everything blurred together. And then I heard a voice, speaking in a sudden silence. My voice. I was possessed. I said that the woman at Fort Holland was evil and that the Houngan [the male Vodou priest] must make her a zombie."

African American writers of the same era adopted similar strategies in their depictions of racial power and authority, and their work—either free of Western colonial anxiety or actively resisting its effects—helps to clarify this power and its possibilities. Everywhere in the literature of the Harlem Renaissance and the writings of Afro-modernity, the very deadness of cultural form as it inflects the possibilities of human voice and human body becomes the precondition of political vitality, putting a radical racial spin on the aesthetic innovations of modernism at large. For example, in her famous 1938 study *Tell My Horse: Voodoo and Life in Haiti and Jamaica*, Zora Neale Hurston turns to the zombie as a "remnant" and a "relic."[21] As "wreckage," Hurston suggests, the zombie figures the wreckage of the region at large, but less as metaphor or expression than as a form of indication, darkly illuminating its social condition and its own historical moment.[22] Hurston characterizes Haiti as a split nation, violently torn between races, classes, and ideologies. Its zombies seem to exist in a sort of a limbo, hopelessly detached from origins, forced to wander between otherwise incompatible worlds. Tapping into a folkloric tradition that extends well back to the colonial trade of nineteenth-century Africa, Hurston first explores the economic motives of zombie production. The centerpiece of her account concerns the "Give Man" process, a dark Vodou ritual in which local mulatto owners trade their own souls to the dark *loa* (spirits or gods) in order to develop a zombie workforce. But Hurston, the writer, seems most interested in zombification as an act of inscription, one in which a human body is taken out of one story and forced to inhabit another. The bokor uses a strange and secret language to speak with the gods and then capture the soul of a man or woman; during the zombification process, money is exchanged for speech, vocal authority, which then commands the body of the zombie to serve other ends. In this, Hurston's zombies appear both excessively mediated and remarkably unmediated, at once named and unnamed, possessed and dispossessed. In fact, Hurston is drawn to the opaque voice of the zombie itself, which she describes as a "broken sound" or "broken noise."[23] As the body of the zombie is disconnected from any organic community, she suggests, so its voice seems broken off from any coherent language. Its homelessness is made manifest in the wreckage of its speech.

At the same time, Hurston's text famously struggles with its own voice. In constructing her ethnography, the writer slips somewhat anxiously between folkish and professional discourses, and she frets everywhere about her own voice as it distorts or violates its objects of study. She specifically worries what it means to speak of and for the figure of the zombie. In one horrific scene, she visits and then photographs what is believed to be a real zombie. A local doctor forcibly uncovers the zombie's head and holds it in position while Hurston snaps away at the "blank face with dead eyes."[24] Here anthropology itself, especially when conjoined with Western technology, figures zombification, the rendering undead of an otherwise vital subject. But it is precisely this deathliness at work in signs and significations that becomes a valid literary strategy and a form of resistance in Hurston's text. Hurston's chapter on zombies is succeeded by an account of vocal possession. Here we learn that the book's title phrase "Tell My Horse" refers to a process in which Guede, the boisterous god of the Haitian lower classes, mounts a person and speaks through his mouth. The phrase refers to the physical shuddering of the human mount, who, once gripped by the god, gives voice to the injustice and unfairness of his or her life, calling out bossmen, politicians, the police, children, and even former lovers. For Hurston, the voice that speaks through the mount is the voice of the ancestral past, connecting the possessed Haitian to a lost homeland, as well as the voice of unconscious desire, giving vent to the repressed energies of the underclass. But it is mostly, she claims, a "blind for self-expression," a way of circumventing censorship and allowing the Haitian peasantry to speak truth to economic and political power without consequences. In this, Guede's voice becomes a voice of derision, of chatter and gossip. Celebrated on the eve of All Saints' Day, Guede is the god of burlesque and mockery, upending authority via citation and exaggeration. His voice does not represent or express power but eats through it. A radically deidealized, decentered voice, a voice without a subject, it exposes both the arbitrary dimensions of all voice and the pleasure of vocal mediation.[25] In fact, for Hurston, the voice of Guede is the voice of death and the voice of death in signs. "Perhaps that is natural," she writes, "for the god of the poor to be akin to the god of the dead, for there is something about poverty that smells of death."[26] In this, Hurston's study ultimately appears less like a scholarly treatise than like a scholarly burlesque, mocking the authority of both folklore and science as it clears space, through ventriloquism, for personal intervention. Her Vodou-inflected version of modernist form entails a campy graveyard deconstruction of power that, in emphasizing voice and vocal performance, inflects African American culture at large.

Richard Wright, on the other hand, was too much of a realist to be interested in zombies, and he could not be further opposed to Hurston in terms of politics and style. Still, in his work, undeadness is thematized as both an affective state and a formal principle, bound up with narrative itself, and thus becomes the basis of a much more direct negotiation of racial politics. Wright announces his undead agenda with the stunning epigraph of his first collection, *Uncle Tom's Children*.[27] "Uncle Tom is dead," claims the new generation of black Americans, thereby asserting their own revolutionary protocol even amid the persistence of racial injustice in the States. Wright's fiction as a whole is notable for its depictions of extreme affective states, but the stories presented here, from first to last, present racial subjectivity as a provocative state of undeadness. Wright's protagonists are all notably subhuman; sometimes mere "blobs"; often shapeless; always defenseless, barren, and bare. In their fear and confusion, they experience intense discombobulation, occult suggestibility, and sheer paralysis, a kind of manic stiffening that destroys all thought and will. In fact, most are literally condemned to death, awaiting some ultimate demise at the hands of their white tormentors. In turn, they play at death, staring blankly, nullifying gesture and expression, hiding in plain sight of the white world, and sometimes literally burying themselves in the ground to elude their white captors. The zombified state of Jim Crow blackness is perhaps most clearly displayed in a story titled "Down by the Riverside." Forced to shoot a white man in order to protect his pregnant wife (who also happens to be already dead), Wright's protagonist feels himself suspended over a black void, detached from his own body, which he then watches as it moves listlessly through a series of scenes until its final execution. Led through a hostile white crowd toward his grave, the protagonist "wanted to look around, but could not turn his head. His body seemed encased in a tight vise, in a narrow black coffin that moved with him as he moved."[28] Still, in each of these stories, living death proves the precondition of a certain clarity and then agency. Specifically, as a form of numbness and indifference, of stiffening and hardness, living death signals the death of a limiting cultural tradition and an emptying of racial ideology. In his zombification, the protagonist of "Down by the Riverside" achieves a state of knowingness beyond the romances of religion, family, and, ultimately, property: "None of it really touched him now," the narrator explains. "He was beyond it all now; it simply passed in front of his eyes like silent, moving shadows, like dim figures in a sick dream."[29] In turn, the protagonist wields his literal death in a final act of defiance, using it to expose the forces of power that shaped his life. Shot from behind in the very act of escape, his body falls into the river; as his corpse reveals the watery currents that pass around it, so his death, in its opacity, points openly to the terror of the Jim Crow South.[30]

More pointedly, Wright's characters are famously caught up in forms over which they have little control; zombies all, they seem driven by larger ideological forces and often discover themselves committing, against their own will, horrendous acts of violence. Similarly, Wright's own fiction seems to slip into and out of undead genres—gothic horror, courtroom drama, the flood tale—as if somehow fated to repeat, if only provisionally, the literary forms of the past. However, it is precisely this dark and often inscrutable play of form and repetition that signals the undeadness of Afro-American modernism as a vital aesthetic mode. In fact, each of the stories in *Uncle Tom's Children* begins with a song, and each replays (samples) that song in ways that transfigure its meaning. One tale, "Long Black Song," presents the subject of African American modernity as, specifically, a phonographic subject. Here a lonely Southern housewife is visited by a phonograph salesman and finds herself instantly drawn in by the mechanically spinning song—an old spiritual—that he plays for her. The rhythm of the song is disruptive, violent even, but also, in its repetition, erotic and seductive; it lures the woman away from her everyday routine and its racially inflected expectations. As sheer sound, spinning abstractly, opaquely, beyond the everyday spectacle of Southern life, it frees the woman to experience her body and thus her identity anew. However, once the woman's husband returns and discovers her affair with the phonograph salesman, the "Long Black Song" of the South becomes sheer repetition, inevitable deathliness. Silas chases his wife out of the house with a whip and then shoots the salesman when the latter returns the next day for his pay. Later a white mob circles the house and, after a few gunshots, tries to burn it down with Silas inside. As the male protagonists replay the past in all its furious violence, the woman fretfully "circles" the scene, like a record needle, listening to the voices that are already "echoes," helpless to intervene in a history that must replay itself once more.[31] If earlier, phonographic sound, in its undead repetition, signaled sensual release and radical otherness, it now—as the silent structure of racial trauma—seems to lock history into its own violent groove. Still, the phonograph has done its work—a break has occurred. At the moment of trauma's repetition in sound, history loses force, and its actors are made aware of its inherent ghostliness, its utter emptiness. Time itself begins to slip, to jump its groove. Afro-modernity as zombie modernity seems poised to move, jerking to a new technoaffective order.

Because, really, the zombie only wants to dance. Tellingly, Browning's model of diasporic contagion is explicitly musical. "Hip Hop," she explains, "is one moment in the history of the dispersion and popularization of black musical idioms, a process of cultural exchange which was concomitant with the first processes of global economic exploitation—that is, colonization. Reggae represents another such moment. Funk. Soul. Mambo. All 'infectious rhythms'—all spread quickly, transnationally, accompanied by equally 'contagious' dances."[32] In the cultural history of the zombie that follows the slave trade from Africa through the West Indies to America and beyond, there are nearly as many dancing zombies as there are laboring zombies. In the earlier literature of Haiti, the dancing zombie stands in as a form of exploited labor, manipulated to perform—in a kind of blank-face blackface—for his or her white masters.[33] Later in the century, on American soil, the dancing zombie comes to reflect the commercial manipulation of teen culture, the lusty hordes whipped up into a rhythmic frenzy by cool beats. It was only in the 1970s, however, that this shambolic figure took a more self-consciously political turn. In the punk movements of England and America, the dancing zombie figures white alienation and dissension. As Dick Hebdige notes, the image of the punk—blank face, tattered clothes, twitchy movements—served to hollow out the social markers of postindustrial capitalism. Stomping around in chains and safety pins, the punk as zombie defied the expressive ethos of the marketplace and exposed the arbitrary nature of its signifying code.[34] At the same time, though, the zombie became a central figure in the struggle for African and African American civil rights in its musical form. In the Afrobeat of Fela Kuti and the funk of the band Parliament, the dancing zombie figures as both victim and threat, his body mangled by technomodernist regimes yet still jerking and twitching to some revolutionary protocol within the music itself. Today, post-*Thriller*, the zombie's identification with popular dancing is strong enough to reverse the order of connotation; dancing now—whether as Lady Gaga, Beyoncé, Kanye West, or Thom Yorke—means to drag the foot, jerk the shoulder, or stumble backward, and in this it maintains its critical implications. Most important, from this perspective, popular culture seems less like a negotiation of competing identities and expressions than the dynamic work of orientation itself, bodies falling in and out of preestablished forms, seeking out rhythms and counter-rhythms, modes of fit and resonation, effectively staging an alternative public sphere within the official one.

Take, for example, Fela Kuti's "Zombie," one of the earliest and most famous songs in the undead canon.[35] Fela's influential Afrobeat fusion is remarkable in itself as an example of postcolonial hybridity. Born in Nigeria to a feminist activist mother and a Protestant minister father, Fela Kuti was sent to the Western world to study medicine and wound up messing with new musical forms—here, jazz and a Ghanaian horn-and-guitar-based genre called "highlife." Later, inspired in America by the Black Panthers, his music took an explicitly political turn, its multiethnic rhythmic complexity revamped to address the injustices of colonial rule. In Nigeria he formed the Kalakuta Republic, a commune cum recording studio (named after his first prison cell), declared his independence from the state, and changed his middle name to Anikulapo, meaning "he who carries death in his pouch." In this revolutionary spirit, in 1977, Fela and his band Afrika '70 released the album *Zombie*, the title track of which contained a scathing critique of the Nigerian military. Backed by a needling funk guitar riff and a shuffling African rhythm section, Fela barks off a series of military commands meant to expose the empty-headedness of the police:

> Zombie no go go, unless you tell am to go (zombie)
> Zombie no go stop, unless you tell am to stop (zombie)
> Zombie no go turn, unless you tell am to turn (zombie)
> Zombie no go think, unless you tell am to think (zombie)

Recalling Hurston's claims regarding the god of the poor, Fela's vocal performance is astounding in its mockery; this is no bland political diatribe but a raucous satire, with Fela sneering and giggling his way through the military routine. In live performances, his backing band responded to the song's shouted military commands with broad goofy dance steps. In this the deathliness of the martial rhythm came up against its own dance hall double, as if, by following mechanization and the rule of law to the letter, the group had been freed, at least momentarily, from its oppression. The song's rhythms are lock-tight but empty, and together they set the song into giddy motion, preparing the way for Fela's cracked sax solo, which both recalls and ridicules something like a national anthem. As Dorian Lynskey writes, "the song's sheer reckless jubilance is jawdropping. Mischievous boys would sing it to taunt nearby soldiers, marching sarcastically with sticks under their arms instead of rifles."[36] Within days of the song's release, in fact, a thousand members of the Nigerian army showed up at Fela's compound, seeking to re-assert their original rhythmic protocol. They burned down the barricades and stormed through the dwelling, beating and raping its inhabitants. Fela's seventy-eight-year-old mother was thrown from a window, sustaining injuries that resulted in her death, while Fela himself was beaten to within an inch of his life. Afterward the pop star went into exile in Ghana, where his thinking about politics and identity retreated into an other-worldly mysticism, but sound and rhythm remained a vital force in his life and his politics. "With my music I create a change," he explained in an interview. "So really I am using music as a weapon. I play music as a weapon."[37]

We might simply note here the undead nature of any cultural code, the necessary repeatability, or iterability, of the sign that makes a mockery of human expression and identity as original or unique. The very abstraction of the sign allows artists such as Hurston and Fela to travesty the law it presumably serves, adopting and adapting its undead forms in order to undermine them from within. But when it comes to dancing zombies, we must also consider the specific uncanniness of the recorded voice, which, when wielded by a bokor-DJ, becomes a strange source of both social order and social chaos. As Mladen Dolar writes, if the human voice serves to mediate body and sign, to reconcile matter to meaning, it also everywhere threatens to expose the incoherence and incompletion of being.[38] On one side, voice teeters on the brink of physicality, meaning-less sound, the zombie's low, dumb growl; on the other, it passes into mere signage, the empty language of the law, the directive still transmitted from the abandoned radio tower.[39] In this doubleness the voice wreaks havoc on the coordinates of both personal and social identity, at once providing an ideal reflection of existence and vexing it. As

Richard Middleton argues, "reflections of the vocal body have a capacity to short-circuit the 'normal' distinctions between inside and outside, self and other—for the moment we enter into the symbolic order, an unbridgeable gap separates forever a human body from 'its' voice. The voice acquires a spectral autonomy, it never quite belongs to the body we see."[40] In stressing the vexed ontological status of such voices, however, we begin to see how they might establish identity and agency on new terms. Recording technology, Middleton argues, exposes the voice as an always already undead voice, as a constant displacement of human nature beyond nature, and thus as the constant mediation of human identity beyond itself. At times, even, this same voice—as undead voice—grants the pleasure of such slippage, the pleasure of losing and finding the nonself beyond the self. The traumatized self is released from its pain, restored not just in the idealization of an immaterial voice but in a vital sound that is not its own, not its own expression. Such, I hope to show, seems to be the pleasure and the politics of zombie pop. Recording technology and the sheer repetition of the refrain works this cut or break, the deathly repetition that precedes restitution, allowing us to indulge in a pleasure that is neither fully natural nor fully artificial. As Middleton writes, "this is what the 'loss' of the body documented in the record form actually reveals—that these bodies . . . *are the only ones we ever had.* It is within this space of sonic invention—a space not so much between two deaths as between two lives—that recorded voice, including even the work of the DJ, can contribute to saving a life."[41]

Enter Dr. Funkenstein, "the disco fiend with the monster sound / the cool ghoul with the bump transplant . . . / preoccupied and dedicated / to the preservation of the motion of the hips."[42] George Clinton's P-Funk mob found its stride in the mid-1970s as a ragtag musical horde at times consisting of more than one hundred musicians. The band emerged out of a troubled political climate (the civil rights struggle and the Detroit riots) and brought together a range of dissonant styles (African rhythms, modern jazz, doo-wop, slave spirituals, rock and roll), but their sound explicitly embraced monstrosity and freakishness as a source of renewal. "All that is good is nasty!" Clinton howled in the early days, like some corrupt revivalist, and from that point on his band—in sound, looks, message—dedicated itself to the funked-up body as a source of personal renewal, communal strength, and political dissent. In 1976, however, Parliament began to develop a more technological approach to the funk revolution. Here, Clinton introduced his alter ego Dr. Funkenstein, a sexy space alien—leader of the "Afronauts"—who had come down to earth to spread his ancient wisdom of "clone funk" and repopulate the future in his image. Part mad scientist, part ghetto pimp, and part bokor, Dr. Funkenstein prescribed a technorhythmic cure for the repressed and alienated bodies of Western modernity, using the machines of electronic sound production to restore something like racial vitality. In concert, Clinton emerged from the P-Funk Mothership in sunglasses, furs, and diamond-studded boots and, with his kinky commands and gestures, set to "body snatchin'"—first his band and stage crew (in tribal robes and face paint) and then the audience itself. For Funkenstein, musical production is also always reproduction. His studio figures as a jungle laboratory, and the recording apparatus is a genetic operator, splicing and spinning the cultural code in order to spit out hot new configurations of being. "The mad scientist's funk is engraved in the groove," Middleton writes, the bodies of the dancers animated by system loops. Etymologically, "groove" and "grave" have linked origins, but there are sexual connotations as well . . . as well as drug overtones—being possessed by grooviness. The record groove spins into the cybernetic apparatus. In its discursive nexus, life and death, subject and object, body and machine, are tightly conjoined.[43]

In turn, Funkenstein's listeners are all happy "clones," "children of production," re-animated from death via the deathliness of form itself. Despite Clinton's preaching about African mysteries and the metaphysics of sex, his followers are animated through purely technological processes—the mechanical production of sonic difference in and as repetition. "Everything is on the one," they chant together, but their essential oneness is founded decisively on their own doubleness, in the rhythmic repetition of the "one" as the "two," in its undead return. Tellingly, the term *funk* refers to a nasty stench, a syncopated rhythm, and the act of fucking, but these three meanings here seem to overlap. At once primitive and futuristic, monstrous and mechanical, sexual and cybernetic, the "children of production" stage their protest in a series of rhythmic gestures that everywhere overturn not just the moral implications of their degradation but the very logic of repetition and originality through which that degradation is enforced.[44]

As Alexander Weheliye argues, in the audiovisual break that defines phonographic culture—the "cut" between sound and source—the black subject is dematerialized and rematerialized in his sounding.[45] His sonic invisibility entails neither expression nor even its negation but becomes the precondition for another kind of presence altogether; the body folded into sound entails a version of selfhood as a series of contingent *opacities* or *intensities*, at once open and defined, immanent and singular.[46] The phonographic subject, Weheliye claims, born out of this sonic disjuncture, bypasses the limited logic of origin and copy, of essence and expression, and becomes instead a series of "potent, yet fragile singularities as modes of becoming-in-the-world."[47] At the same time, phonography transforms history into a series of competing tracks or grooves, varying rhythms that sound with and against one another in a more or less dynamic mix. Such grooves—as they imply both writing (graphism) and an affective mo(o)vement—suggest a mode of temporal change that is multivalent and nonlinear; sonic culture, like zombie culture, entails a proliferation of affectively charged spaces and temporalities, all cross-fading into and out of one another, creating ruptures, displacements, and syncopations within history proper. As Kanye West snarls on a track called "Power," "The system broken, the school's closed, the prison's open / We ain't got nothing to lose motherfucker / we rollin'." Here, backed by tribal chants and a sample from King Crimson, Kanye offers up his music—his intensely rhythmic "shit"—as an alternative politics.[48]

But even in considering rhythm, what emerges at the other end of this process—this *shit*—is undetermined, undecidable. If the politics of expression and liberal humanism are replaced in this art by an opacity that is both more and less than human, at once prehuman and posthuman, and open on all sides to an uncertain history, as—in a word—a form of waste, barren and abject, it also seems easily contained within the logic of monster as other, as abject. What does it mean to embrace such monstrosity, especially as a kind of kinky, rhythmic pleasure? Or, rather, how does one embrace monstrosity without letting it signal little more than lack, absence, or, worse, trash, dereliction, and impoverishment?

We might ask the question in a more pointed way: why did Michael Jackson need to wear monster makeup in order to perform? Or why, in a life mocked by personal abjection and cultural shame, a life reduced to a dancing, shuffling thingliness, bereft of maternal comfort, put on stage by a corrupt father to entertain a hostile crowd, why would a performer choose to redouble his own monstrosity, his own loss and decay, and perform it a second time? By the time Michael Jackson rose to fame, the racial logic of minstrelsy had long been subsumed under the postmodern logic of citation. From the start, Jackson came across as an astounding mimic, borrowing from both black and white sources, male and female, American, British, and Caribbean. But above all else the performer was drawn to the lonely, misunderstood monsters of classic Hollywood cinema and even the schlocky slime creatures of the 1950s B movies. His first solo hit was the title song to *Ben*, a 1972 horror film about the uncanny bond between a lonely boy and a psychically controlled horde of killer rats. In the song, Jackson adopts the perspective of the lonely boy and addresses the leader of the evil rat pack, using the opportunity to express his own feelings of alienation: "Ben, you're always running here and there / You feel you're not wanted anywhere."[49] No doubt Jackson's identification with monsters ran deep. In fact, he often wore monster makeup to the studio to practice his song and dance moves, a habit that ultimately led to the conceptualization of "Thriller," his 1983 hit single, and the groundbreaking video produced in its wake.[50]

Arguably, Jackson's identification with monstrosity inspired his infamous experiments in plastic surgery and skin pigmentation. As David J. Skal suggests, however, the star's experiments figure less as anxious attempts at eternal youth or racial disidentification than as performances of monstrous change and the destabilization of identity:

> Perhaps it wasn't surprising that the star of "Thriller" should be intent on transforming his face into a kind of living skull. From some angles, the bone-white skin, cutaway nose, and tendril-like hair resembled nothing so much as Lon Chaney's Phantom of the Opera.
>
> The comparison is apt, because it underscores Jackson's and Chaney's parallel cultural function: the embodiment of a powerful transformation metaphors [*sic*] for a public basically unsure and fearful about the actual prospects of change in a supposedly classless and mobile society.[51]

In other words, for Jackson, quotation and monstrosity go hand in hand; in performance, more so, they figure a kind of alienation as well as an escape from that alienation. As Peggy Phelan argues, "Jackson's introjection of other performance tropes allowed him to simultaneously exploit and unravel the distinction between source and quotation. . . . The embodied nature of live performance transforms referencing from the textual realm of quotation and allusion to the psychic realm of introjections, one constituted by diffuse and ephemeral systems of notation."[52] Jackson's monstrous system of notation, enacted everywhere on his decaying body and faltering voice, functions at the borderline of presence and absence, agency and abjection, revealing, in its own shambling form, both the thrill and threat of zombie culture at large.

In "Thriller," the originally recorded song, Jackson presents himself as both monster and victim, one perhaps suffering because of his own monstrosity.[53] He seems drawn both toward and away from some horrific event, caught between a traumatic past and an impossible future. But the drama is all vocal and, as such, encapsulates what Phelan describes as Jackson's lifelong struggle "to come into voice, into public consciousness."[54] In other words, in "Thriller," Jackson reveals that the anxious project of selfhood relies upon the voice and the voice's shifting relation to some other. Here, in fact, his demand for a response, for human recognition ("I have something I want to tell you," he chirps in the video, "I'm not like other guys"), exposes the monstrous nature of all voice; its own errant drift toward and away from the other. As Phelan writes, "Jackson's strongest works are performative speech acts, creating the feeling they express—love, hope, grief, anger, resignation."[55] Here, though, the dance of the voice around some unnamed and inherently threatening other ultimately frees it to come into its own.[56] In fact, using all the empty clichés of the horror tradition and the vocal clichés of black soul and funk—clichés that presumably get in the way of anything like personal expression—Jackson manages to convey not just his own uncompromising presence or even his own power but also something like pleasure. Like Elvis before him, another monstrous minstrel, Jackson riffs through a compelling category of vocal identities—pop, soul, funk, blues, and so on. As voice, though, as a shambling vocal form, at once empty and aggressive, his performance turns its own monstrosity into something other than lack or abjection. In its frantic dance around the moment of encounter—"You're out of time," he sings—his voice translates the terror of its situation into something playful; the pain of the past and the threat of the future, in their rhythmic syncopation and tonal modulation, become the disarming thrill of *now*, sheer sonic becoming.

In the famous video that accompanied the release of *Thriller*, Jackson appears as not just one monster but several—werecat, Frankenstein's creature, mummy, and, of course, zombie. His image, like his voice, appears to be caught in a series of campy mediations, a fact brought home by the film-within-a-film narrative that doubles Jackson as monster and then hero, only to reverse it all over again to expose yet another monster within. One by one, each of these transformations is emptied of its threat, as just another copy, so that when the zombies finally emerge from their graves, they embody not so much the pain but the rhythmic possibilities of undeadness. No doubt, with their rotting flesh and distorted movements, Jackson's dancing ghouls are menacing, as is Jackson himself when he turns, glares at his girlfriend with nothing but hate in his sunken eyes, yet the horde seems so thoroughly gripped by their own monstrosity that it shudders them into dance. As with Jackson's voice, these bodies raise a certain demand, but their expressions and gestures are not outwardly aggressive; all of the menace is drawn inward, into the syncopated transitions of their own movements. As Jackson's voice dances in and around the impossible event, so their bodies shuffle in and out of time, stumble into and out of space. They kick one foot out to the side and then—slowly—drag it back in before stomping on the beat. *Shhh-thump*. Hands swing like cat claws to the right and then to the left, before landing again in the middle. *Shhh-shhh-thump*. Shoulders lurch forward, while legs stomp backward. *Thump-shhh-thump-shhh- thump*. In this the rotting *ballet de corpse* performs composition as much as decomposition. Together, the dancers shake off corporeal constraints only to take on new ones, decoding as recoding, and vice versa, until the entire process begins to resemble something like pleasure. Ultimately, they stomp off down the road and, one by one, turn to face the spectator, until Jackson himself whips his head around and the makeup is gone. "'Cause this is Thriller!" he shouts and then immediately launches into a set of signature moves. As Phelan notes, in reference to Jackson's famous moonwalk, Jackson created a future for himself by moving backward, by repeating the steps of the past.[57] Here, though, with "Thriller"—in the midst of death and disfigurement, through the very deathliness and displacement of form—he attains something like the power of *now*. Monstrosity reveals itself not as simple otherness or even abjection but as the syncopated process of becoming, the halting movement of bodies within and against the official regimes of space and time.

To see the zombie as an opacity, as an obscure density of noncalcified substance, shuffling within fields of similar densities, strips the genre of all humanist claims. To see not just the zombie but a human protagonist such as Ben in *Night of the Living Dead* as an opacity, as a cut and a groove, circulating within and against the cuts and grooves of white history at large, transforms the very terms of all politics as cultural politics.[58] At the end of Romero's film, Ben's body—killed, mutilated, and dragged—appears in a series of grainy newspaper photos, apparently reduced over time to a tiny black blob, yet one that still moves, albeit negatively, to the rhythms of power at large. Even as he's killed and killed again, "Ben" continues to raise a demand, a counter-rhythm of form and force. Here, in fact, the rhythm of the body competes with a series of other repeating rhythms—of the survivor, the police force, the press, the cinematic machine, the academic essay machine—exposing the political nature of each. In this the zombie's body appears less as a dancing machine than more generally as a territorializing refrain, an aggregate of forms that in its jerky repetition marks out a space and time of operation—rhythm, in Gilles Deleuze and Félix Guattari's formulation, as a functional assemblage, a series of motifs and counterpoints that works to catalyze bodies in relation to one another and thus as an instance of power. "Meter," the two authors write, "assumes a coded form whose unit of measure may vary, whereas rhythm is the Unequal or Incommensurable, that is always undergoing transcoding. Meter is dogmatic, but rhythm is critical: it ties together critical moments, or ties itself together in passing from one milieu to another."[59] The zombie, then, as rhythmic refrain, moves toward and away from its own death, jammed up and then loose again, at the threshold of existential consistency. The moment of repetition—the second beat, the second footstep, the second revolution—becomes, as it does on the dance floor, both the moment of death and the death of death, a dub-beat death march, at once freezing and freeing up the entire mechanism in relation to the livid field of the whole.

Perhaps, even in this terrifying gap between one death and another, zombie culture as dance culture opens up a radical ethical domain and serves as a vernacular mode of ethical exploration. Here, Benedict de Spinoza provides the best model, for his early modern view of bodies and ethics speaks most clearly to our late modern, posthuman view of hordes and masses. As philosopher of immanence, Spinoza deals only in substances and modes; in his *Ethics,* the human body figures as a mode of extension, a modality, affected by other modalities, by the shapes, sizes, and speeds of all other bodies.[60] "All bodies either move or are at rest," Spinoza writes, as if constructing his own zombology. "Each body moves now more slowly, now more quickly." For Spinoza, such bodies do not vary in substance but in affect, insofar as they are affected by one another, modified in their relations with one another, and sometimes, together, form a composite body or a horde:

> When a number of bodies, whether of the same or of different size, are so constrained by other bodies that they lie upon one another, or if they so move, whether with the same degree or different degree of speed, that they communicate their motions to each other in a certain fixed manner, we shall say that these bodies are united with one another and that they all together compose one body or individual, which is distinguished from the others by this union of bodies.[61]

Importantly, for Spinoza, the virtue of any body is defined as its power to persist in its own form and relation. "Virtue" is nothing other than acting, living, and preserving our being by the guidance of reason, insofar as such being is opposed or augmented by other forces in a single environment. Thus, lurching forward and back, referring to nothing other than its own assemblage, the zombie body collapses self-serving categories of right and wrong and forces us to consider the nature of good and bad encounters, to think beyond the humanist imaginary of the ego and instead consider relations and proportions of corporeal and corporate well-being. Indeed, *zombie* may be merely another name for "virtue" itself, the body's ability to persist in its own being and power. The zombie attack appears as an attack only from within a humanist worldview; it merely exposes power as such, as the rhythmic appropriation of time and space, and, in response, we need to translate our affective terror into adequate reason and ethical inquiry.

In fact, "Thriller" is no less important for the copies it has inspired. Watch, for example, the viral video of the dancing inmates of the Cebu Provincial Detention and Rehabilitation Center, a maximum-security prison in the Philippines.[62] In 2007, more than three hundred inmates, many of whom were imprisoned for murder, performed a truncated version of Jackson's zombie dance from "Thriller." The footage, uploaded onto YouTube, quickly generated millions of hits and inspired copycat performances in prisons across the world. Here, sure, the zombie dance—with its classic foot drag—serves as a way of disrupting, or at least challenging, official order; the prisoner, doing time, facing the end of time, uses his body as a mechanical assemblage to insert himself and his horde back into vital time (or at least the vital time of cultural consumption). By submitting to a dead form, by performing "Thriller" for a second time, the group affects something like the death of death, and, so while facing death's row, they reverse their own sentencing, gaining, at least for a moment, some reprieve. Byron F. Garcia, the Cebu prison chief who planned the prison dance, claims that his decision to use "Thriller" was based on an identification between Jackson and the prisoners: "I saw in the lyrics and video of Thriller much of what jail culture is like. Because of the hideous conditions in jails, prisons are like tombs and inmates are like ghoulish creatures. The only difference is that dancers in the MJ Thriller video come with make-up and costumes. The Dancing Inmates come as themselves. People perceived to be evil." According to Garcia, however, the dance ultimately works beyond the logic of identity and expression to expose and perhaps reset the power relations between prisoners and society: "The message is, governments must stop looking at jails darkly. We have to stop being entertained and thrilled by the sting of sin. We have to look at prisons beyond the cycle of crime and punishment and certainly look inside underlying social, cultural and psychological implications of rehabilitation." But the moment cuts both ways. Subsequently, the dance was revealed as an attempt by the prison chief to keep prisoners in line and quell gang violence between rival cell blocks. According to prison authorities, the dance was staged as an example of "revolutionized penology," and since then it has become a lucrative stage show, performed once a month for paying public audiences, who watch from viewing platforms surrounding the exercise yard. At the jail, visitors can have their pictures taken with the zombie inmates, and they can buy souvenir zombie prison shirts. Here, then, the zombie dance figures as a double act of deterritorialization and reterritorialization, but its ethical force is not at all blunted by its spectacular regimentation. In fact, its mediation is precisely what makes it available as an instance and negotiation of power, one that inspires both terror and critical insight. Certainly, here, as in the best zombie films, the exercise of pop culture and government power becomes as much an issue of machinery and rhythmic assemblages as it is an issue of rights and expression and indicates, even in this commodified form, a violent encounter that is always already under way as well as impending.

Ultimately, then, to see the zombie as rhythmic opacity, as a cut and a groove, circulating within and against the cuts and grooves of Western history at large, means to rethink the terms and implications of diasporic culture—and to rethink diasporic culture, perhaps, as all culture today. Taking the evolution of dub music in Jamaica as his model, scholar Steve Goodman (aka Kode9, a London-based DJ and producer) redefines the "Black Atlantic" as a site of sonic outbreak and contagion.[63] Everywhere along the migrational pathways of Afro-modernity, Goodman argues, the viropolitics of rhythm and frequency confront the corporate viropolitics of consolidation and branding. Sonic parasites ride on the back of the expanding economy, hijacking local populations via the nervous system, possessing individual bodies one at a time and swaying them into rhythmic group motion. Here, Goodman argues, postmodern culture takes one funky step forward. In the hands of the studio engineer, sonic contagion pushes "memetics" beyond memory and cognition, repackaging the meme as an "individuated block of affect," a "synaesthetic pulse pattern," at once affective and machinic, alive and dead. Hence, Ishmael Reed's "Jes Grew" virus—"unprintable" and yet "irresistible," at once virtual and visceral[64]—a fully Spinozist virus, incubated in the studio lab, dispersed through the empty air, replicated across space and time, and thus rhythmically engaged in a tactical redesign of power relations.[65] But more than just a hipper, blacker version of postmodern play, or a politically charged version of remix culture, diasporic virology theorizes itself on the actual dance floor, creating in the body of each dancer an "alternative, diasporic orientation" to the world.[66] This sonic contagion—locally contracted and yet globally displaced, affectively charged and yet technologically abstract—proves nothing if not radically ecological. Eschewing universalism and downplaying humanist fantasies of expression, it demands, like the zombie attack itself, an affective inventory of forces, frequencies, and economies, and then a tactical deployment of rhythmic and vibrational process for mobilization on a global scale.

Zombie culture, as a popular subculture, takes many forms these days—the zombie flash mob, the zombie march, the zombie prison dance. These phenomena work in similar ways, abandoning expression, even the expressive potential of style, in order to crack open, with their own opacity, the official regimes of space and time. I'd like to conclude, then, with an example that suggests just how far the zombie mode can be extended as a convention as it exposes convention itself as an undead form and thus as a mode of survival. In 2009, indie rock icon Bon Iver released a small four-song EP that concludes with an a cappella tune titled "Woods."[67] The song consists of only four lines, a small pastoral song about living in the woods and building a "still" as a means of slowing down time and renewing one's sense of self and purpose. It is constructed out of no more than a series of Auto-Tuned voices, which, in their rhythmic rise and fall,

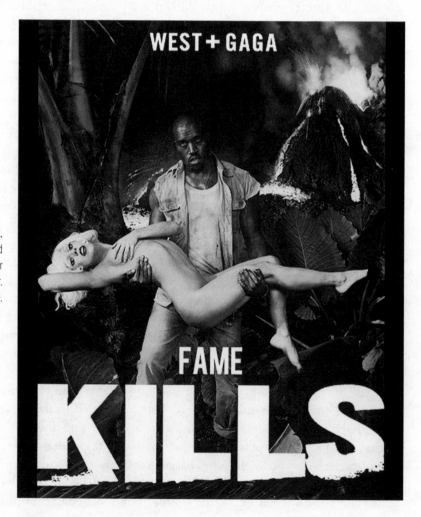

Figure 11.2.
(Dis)Possession 2: Lady Gaga and Kanye West, in a promotional poster for the ill-fated Fame Kills tour. Photograph by David LaChapelle.

do not so much name as create an abstract space of comfort and persistence. The use of Auto-Tune here proves significant, because it allows the artist to emphasize the artificial nature of the voice as it works to reconstruct nature as such. But that's nothing. In 2010, hip-hop star Kanye West picked up Bon Iver's tune and used it as the basis of another song, "Lost in the World," the culminating track on his critically acclaimed album *My Beautiful Dark Twisted Fantasy*.[68] Here, Kanye extends a long tradition in soul and funk by depicting himself and his music in monstrous terms, born of undead forms, remixed and remodeled in order to create a new space of identity and power. His song begins with Bon Iver's white pastoral but slowly reterritorializes it with a tribal beat and then a politically charged rap about the dangers of black life in the city. The jumble of styles and sentiments is held together by both the steady rhythm and Kanye's voice, rising to a fascinating crescendo, singing,

> I'm lost in the world
> I'm down on my mind
> I'm new in the city
> But I'm down for the night.

Here, Kanye layers Bon Iver's "still" with the word "city," so the line becomes "I'm building a city," and then layers "time" with "night," at once extending Bon Iver's pastoral gesture and reclaiming it as an alternative space and time for himself. As Virgil covers Theocritus, as Danny Boyle covers George A. Romero, so Kanye covers Bon Iver, reterritorializing an indie pastoral as a space of hip-hop survivalism. The point is driven home by the introduction of a snippet from Gil Scott-Heron's revolutionary diatribe "Comment #1," which outlines the long history of racial violence and slavery that underpins the American pastoral.[69] The entire undead assemblage culminates with Scott-Heron's black power vocal, intoning,

> Who will survive in America?
> Who will survive in America?
> Who will survive in America?

—a refrain that proves both the power of convention and its sheer provisionality. Thus, as cultural refrain, the zombie dance remains a significant form of construction and critique, a horizon of expectation and exhortation, a lively space of death and dissent.

Notes

1. Jeffrey Jerome Cohen, "Monster Culture (Seven Theses)," in *Monster Theory: Reading Culture*, ed. Jeffrey Jerome Cohen, 3–25 (Minneapolis: University of Minnesota Press, 1996).
2. "Hollywood, A.D.," *The X-Files*, season 7, episode 19, directed by David Duchovny, aired April 30, 2000, Fox Broadcasting.
3. For the history of the zombie figure in its relation to migrant labor and the slave trade within Africa, see Jean Comaroff and John Comaroff, "Alien-Nation: Zombies, Immigrants, and Millennial Capitalism," *South Atlantic Quarterly* 101, no. 4 (2002): 779–805.

4. Jean-Paul Sartre, preface to *The Wretched of the Earth*, by Frantz Fanon, trans. Richard Philcox (New York: Grove Press, 2004).

5. Ibid., xlviii.

6. Ibid., lvii.

7. Ibid., lv.

8. Edouard Glissant, *Caribbean Discourse: Selected Essays*, trans. Michael J. Dash (Charlottesville: University Press of Virginia, 1999).

9. Ibid., 57.

10. Ibid., 4.

11. William Seabrook, *The Magic Island* (New York: Paragon House, 1989).

12. Ibid., 92.

13. Ibid., 97–98.

14. Ibid., 95.

15. Ibid., 101.

16. Ibid., 103.

17. Kyle Bishop, *American Zombie Gothic: The Rise and Fall (and Rise) of the Walking Dead in Popular Culture* (Jefferson, N.C.: McFarland, 2010), 65–66.

18. Here my argument draws on Michael Taussig's astounding observations in *Mimesis and Alterity: A Particular History of the Senses* (New York: Routledge, 1993).

19. Barbara Browning, *Infectious Rhythm: Metaphors of Contagion and the Spread of African Culture* (New York: Routledge, 1998), 6–7.

20. *I Walked with a Zombie*, directed by Jacques Tourneur (RKO Radio Pictures, 1943).

21. Zora Neale Hurston, *Tell My Horse: Voodoo and Life in Haiti and Jamaica* (New York: Harper Perennial Modern Classics, 2009).

22. Ibid., 179.

23. Ibid.

24. Ibid., 195.

25. See excellent commentary in Ed Cameron, "The Voice against the Voice: Vodou, Psychoanalysis, and Zora Neale Hurston," *Women Writers: A Zine*, August 2008, http://www.womenwriters.net/aug08 /cameron.htm; Amy Fass Emery, "The Zombie in/as the Text: Zora Neale Hurston's *Tell My Horse*," *African American Review* 39, no. 3 (2005): 327–36; and Annette Trefzer, "Possessing the Self: Caribbean Identity in Zora Neale Hurston's *Tell My Horse*," *African-American Review* 34, no. 2 (2000): 299–312.

26. Hurston, *Tell My Horse*, 223.

27. Richard Wright, *Uncle Tom's Children* (New York: Harper Perennial, 2008).

28. Ibid., 114.

29. Ibid., 112.

30. Ibid., 123.

31. Ibid., 145–46.

32. Browning, *Infectious Rhythm*, 5–6.

33. See, e.g., G. W. Hutter, "Salt Is Not for Slaves," in *Zombie! Stories of the Walking Dead*, ed. Peter Haining (London: W. H. Allen, 1985), 39–53; Inez Wallace, "I Walked with a Zombie," ibid., 95–102; and Charles Birkin, "Ballet Negre," ibid., 189–208.

34. Dick Hebdige, *Subculture: The Meaning of Style* (New York: Routledge, 1979).

35. Fela Kuti (and Afrika '70), "Zombie," *Zombie* (Celluloid Records, 1977), track 1.

36. Dorian Lynskey, *33 Revolutions per Minute: A History of Protest Songs, from Billie Holiday to Green Day* (New York: HarperCollins, 2011), 240.

37. Quoted ibid., 244.

38. Mladen Dolar, *A Voice and Nothing More* (Cambridge, Mass.: MIT Press, 2006).

39. Ibid., 59, 71.

40. Richard Middleton, "'Last Night a DJ Saved My Life': Avians, Cyborgs, and Siren Bodies in the Era of Phonographic Technology," *Radical Musicology* 1 (2006): para. 11, http://www.radical-musicology .org.uk/2006/Middleton.htm.

41. Ibid., para. 25.

42. Parliament, "Dr. Funkenstein," *The Clones of Dr. Funkenstein* (Casablanca, 1976), side 1, track 3.

43. Middleton, "Last Night a DJ Saved My Life," para. 20.

44. See related commentary in John Corbett, *Extended Play: Sounding Off from John Cage to Dr. Funkenstein* (Durham, N.C.: Duke University Press, 2004), 20ff.

45. Alexander G. Weheliye, *Phonographies: Grooves in Sonic Afro-Modernity* (Durham, N.C.: Duke University Press, 2005).

46. Ibid., 32, 54.

47. Ibid., 68.

48. Kanye West, "Power," *My Beautiful Dark Twisted Fantasy* (Roc-a-Fella/Def Jam, 2010), track 3.

49. Michael Jackson, "Ben" (Motown, 1972), side 1.

50. See Jackson's revealing 1999 interview with MTV, "MTV: The 100 Greatest Music Videos Ever Made," http://www.youtube.com/watch?v=b_VmQzVF-CI.

51. David J. Skal, *The Monster Show: A Cultural History of Horror* (New York: Faber and Faber, 2001), 318–19.

52. Peggy Phelan, "'Just Want to Say': Performance and Literature, Jackson and Poirier," *PMLA* 125, no. 4 (2010): 944.

53. Michael Jackson, "Thriller," *Thriller* (Epic, 1983), side 1, track 4.

54. Phelan, "Just Want to Say," 945.

55. Ibid.

56. See my related work on Elvis and the "vocal drive" in *Sweet Air: Modernism, Regionalism, and American Popular Song* (Urbana-Champaign: University of Illinois Press, 2013), chapter 4.

57. Phelan, "Just Want to Say," 944.

58. *Night of the Living Dead*, directed by George A. Romero (Image Ten, 1968).

59. Gilles Deleuze and Félix Guattari, *A Thousand Plateaus: Capitalism and Schizophrenia*, trans. Brian Massumi (Minneapolis: University of Minnesota Press, 1987), 313.

60. Benedict de Spinoza, *A Spinoza Reader: The Ethics and Other Works*, trans. Edwin Curley (Princeton, N.J.: Princeton University Press, 1994).

61. Ibid., 126–27.

62. "Thriller," as performed by inmates of the Cebu Provincial Detention and Rehabilitation Center, commentary by Byron F. Garcia, July 17, 2007, http://www.youtube.com/watch?v=hMnk71h9M3o.

63. Steve Goodman, *Sonic Warfare: Sound, Affect, and the Ecology of Fear* (Cambridge, Mass.: MIT Press, 2010).

64. Ibid.

65. Ibid., 157.

66. Ibid., 159.

67. Bon Iver, "Woods," *Blood Bank* (Jagjaguwar, 2009), track 4.

68. Kanye West, "Lost in the World," *My Beautiful Dark Twisted Fantasy* (Roc-a- Fella/Def Jam, 2010), track 12.

69. Gil Scott-Heron, "Comment #1," *Small Talk at 125th and Lenox* (Flying Dutchman/RCA, 1970), side 1, track 4.

CHAPTER 12

Taking Back the
Night of the Living Dead
George Romero, Feminism, and the Horror Film

BARRY KEITH GRANT

Near the beginning of George Romero's original *Night of the Living Dead* (1968), Barbra, one of the film's three female characters, sinks into near-catatonic helplessness to become a burden on the other living characters. She remains this way until near the end, when she attempts to help free another woman from the clutches of the zombies, only to be dragged out the window by her now undead brother. In the remake of *Night of the Living Dead* (1990), written by Romero, no longer can it be said that the character of Barbra, as Gregory A. Waller aptly puts it, "would seem to support certain sexist assumptions about female passivity, irrationality, and emotional vulnerability."[1] Indeed, in the remake, Barbara is the only one of seven characters in the farmhouse to survive the night, and she is an active, assertive character, not only within the diegesis but as a narrative agent as well.[2] This revision warrants closer examination, for it is at once simple yet stunning in its implications.

Romero's broad knowledge of the genre in which he has most often worked is signaled in his films by numerous references to other horror movies, both in dialogue and visual style.[3] In the afterword to his novelization of *Martin* (1978), he explicitly writes that his intention was to "re-vamp" the vampire story.[4]

The film's treatment of the vampire makes it clear that, as the pseudo-vampire himself says, "there's no magic"—but there *is* ideology. And clearly, Romero has been particularly concerned about the ideology of gender representation in the horror film, attempting to "revamp" that tradition of the genre as well. Many of his films address this issue, especially the living dead series.

As has often been noted, movies such as Wes Craven's *The Hills Have Eyes* (1977), John Carpenter's *Halloween* (1978), the sequels to both these films, and the seemingly endless Friday the 13th and Nightmare on Elm Street series—all those horror shows Robin Wood describes as "a single interminable chronicle of blood-letting"[5]—owe much to the original *Night of the Living Dead*. The film inaugurated a cycle of zombie movies

Figure 12.1.
The helpless Barbra (Judith O'Dea) is aided by Ben (Duane Jones). *Night of the Living Dead* (dir. George Romero, Walter Reade Organization, 1968).

that eventually turned what Herschell Gordon Lewis, director of *Blood Feast* (1963) and *2000 Maniacs* (1964), once called the "gore film" into the more ominous-sounding "meat movie" or "splatter film." Romero himself is credited with having coined the term *splatter cinema* to describe those films that revel in physical violence and maiming to the extent that such spectacle becomes their sole raison d'être.[6] And it is, of course, no secret that such movies concentrate their violence upon women.

Night of the Living Dead has had astounding commercial success: made for a paltry $14,000, the film has grossed more than $30 million worldwide and become a cult classic.[7] But if it was such a critical and commercial success, the immediate and obvious question is, why should Romero bother to remake it? The cynical view would be that the director is exploiting his own past success, feeding on himself like an ironic variation of his own horrible creatures in a calculated attempt to bolster a sagging career. (None of his films outside the horror genre have been commercially successful.) But as certain auteurs have returned to their fictional worlds and, over time, deepened their characters and themes—Truffaut with Antoine Doinel, Lang with Mabuse, Coppola with Michael Corleone—so here Romero has returned to his original zombie narrative and fashioned a more politically progressive view than in the original, particularly in terms of the gender issues raised by the first *Night*'s influence on the subsequent development of the genre.

It is this unfortunate heritage—his own monstrous offspring, so to speak—that Romero increasingly attempts to confront in his living dead movies. In the living dead trilogy—*Night of the Living Dead*, *Dawn of the Dead* (1978), and *Day of the Dead* (1985)—the zombie becomes as crucial a metaphor of social relations for Romero as the prostitute for Godard.[8] *Night*, which David Pirie calls "probably the only truly modernist reading of the vampire myth," has been read variously as a critique of the Nixonian "silent majority," of American involvement in Vietnam, and of the family under capitalism. *Dawn* self-consciously uses the zombie as a conceit for macho masculinism and conspicuous capitalist consumption, "the whole dead weight of patriarchal consumer capitalism," as Robin Wood puts it. (Romero's own description of the film as "a satirical bite at American consumerism" is equally apt.)[9] *Day* shows the extent to which society has collapsed five years later, concentrating the political connotations of zombiedom on the issue of sexual politics. Men in the film are consistently shown to be as much of a threat to life as the zombies that are forever surrounding the band of human survivors.

Romero wrote the screenplay for the new version of *Night*, which was directed by Tom Savini (makeup chief on *Martin, Dawn, Day,* and *Creepshow* [1982] and leading player in *Knightriders* [1981]—all directed by Romero). The original was certainly a "personal" film: Romero cowrote it based on his original story, and he directed, photographed, and edited it as well. His low-budget horror films that followed the first *Night*—*Jack's Wife* (aka *Hungry Wives/Season of the Witch*) (1973), *The Crazies* (aka *Code Name: Trixie*) (1973), and *Martin*—all approach the genre from a similarly subversive perspective, clearly revealing Romero as an auteur before he was officially so dubbed in *Film Comment* by Dan Yakir in 1979.[10] So even though he did not direct the remake of *Night*, Romero's authorship is evident throughout the film.

Surprisingly—especially given Savini's reputation for physically gruesome special effects—the new *Night* downplays graphic violence. Rather, following the trajectory of the trilogy, it consistently foregrounds the dramatic implications of the first version, concentrating on social tensions embodied in relations between living characters. So, for example, the bickering of the bourgeois couple, Harry and Helen Cooper, is now more pronounced and unambiguously involves physical abuse, and the racial tension raised by the presence of the black hero, Ben, whose racial difference is never mentioned by the other characters, is now more explicit.

But I want to focus here on the rewriting of the character of Barbra. Like her predecessor, the new Barbara initially seems "mousy," as conventionally coded by her tightly buttoned high-neckline blouse, brooch and neckerchief, and inevitable eyeglasses. She, too, is frightened at the beginning of the film by her brother Johnny's scary stories, and it initially seems as if she, like the first Barbra, will quickly fall into a catatonic stupor. But when implored by Ben to maintain her composure, she quickly rallies herself. Confronted with some approaching zombies, she and Ben dispatch them at the same time, Barbara in fact disposing of the larger of the two with a poker. "I'm not panicking," she coolly tells Ben afterward. "You told me to fight, so I'm fighting." In the course of the narrative, she exchanges her traditional female attire for clothing found in the farmhouse resembling military fatigues and combat boots. She emerges as the fittest to survive and is the only one of the group in the farmhouse alive at the end of the film. Interestingly, according to the original script, Barbra was to have survived the 1968 film as well—albeit reduced to catatonic paralysis.[11] In the remake, she not only survives but does so by deducing the correct strategy in response to the zombie attacks: neither to defend the house (Ben) nor to retreat to the cellar (Harry) but to flee, since the zombies can easily be outrun. She acts more effectively, in other words, free of the territoriality associated in the film with masculinism.

This change in the character of Barbra/Barbara should not be surprising, for, although it seems to have gone largely unnoticed, a crucial aspect of Romero's vision almost from the beginning has been his generally positive treatment of women, even a striking empathy with them. Romero's third film, *Jack's Wife*—which he wrote, photographed, edited, and directed—is unambiguously sympathetic toward its female protagonist, a bored housewife experiencing growing dissatisfaction with her patriarchal husband and prescribed lifestyle. Like Fellini's Giulietta, Joan escapes into her imagination, and her fantasies and dreams, to which the viewer is privileged, become indistinguishable from reality. She becomes interested in witchcraft, its appeal for her obviously a fantasy inversion of her real disempowerment. In one of her dreams, Joan imagines her husband, Jack, leading her around with a dog collar and leash, attacking her in her car, and slapping a newspaper on the window in a deliberate reference to the zombie with the brick who attacks Barbra in the opening scene of *Night*.

Indeed, if there is an agent of horror in the film, it is not the witch Joan but her husband, who here and in several other scenes is visually coded as the monster. The film thus demythifies witchcraft as supernatural, its ideological project perfectly summed up by the image of Joan buying her witchcraft paraphernalia in a trendy shop and paying for it with a credit card. Her official induction as a witch near the end of the film shows her again being led about on a leash around her neck—witchcraft, that is to say, is just another oppressive ideology (superstition) that prevents this woman from being herself. Romero explicitly describes the film as "feminist," saying of Joan that "she's got everything she could possibly want, except a life."[12]

The clearheaded, unsentimental resourcefulness of the new Barbara in response to the crucible of the undead follows from the treatment of Fran in *Dawn* and Sarah in *Day* and calls to mind another central aspect of Romero's zombie films: their striking similarity to the adventure films of Howard Hawks and the code of professionalism these films explore. Waller has shown how stories of the undead are about humanity's fitness for survival, although he nowhere links this to the Hawksian theme.[13] Romero himself has explicitly acknowledged the influence of Hawks on his work and of the 1951 Hawks-produced science-fiction horror film *The Thing (from Another World)* (ostensibly directed by Christian Nyby) in particular.[14] The Hawksian influence on Romero is pronounced both in his films' plots—the familiar narrative situation wherein a small group is cut off from society and must accomplish a certain dangerous task—and in their mise-en-scène, particularly in the kind of gesture so crucial to the Hawksian universe. Roger's lighting of Peter's tiparillo in *Dawn*, for example, is clearly indebted to similar gestures in Hawks's work: Clift's lighting of Wayne's cigarettes in *Red River* (1948), for instance, or the similar interplay between Bogart and Bacall in *To Have and Have Not* (1944).

The much-underrated *Knightriders*—which Romero describes as a personal film and, after *Martin*, his own favorite[15]—is an unabashed homage to the Hawksian code of professionalism. *Knightriders* is about a traveling band of performers who go from town to town engaging in jousting tournaments on motorcycles. The troupe adheres to a rigid moral code that determines both their actions and their social position, the feudal chain of being by which they abide serving as a perfect metaphor for the world of Hawksian professionalism, which is defined in large part by knowing one's limits and abilities. King Billy (Ed Harris), the troupe's leader, fights to uphold the code and prevent its corruption by commercialism and egotism. Both temptations are lures to which the unprofessional rebels, led by Sir Morgan (Savini), succumb. Personal grudges and partisan politics rather than the code begin to influence the jousts, and King Billy ultimately keeps the troupe together through his martyrdom, sacrificing himself on the chrome altar of the front grille of an oncoming commercial semi. (This is, of course, corny and melodramatic stuff—the very words Wood uses to describe the comparable work in Hawks's oeuvre, that "completely achieved masterpiece" *Only Angels Have Wings*.)[16]

The world of the living dead films is a brutally Hawksian one, in which the primary task is survival itself. Being able to survive in this world requires a philosophical detachment and existential determination in order to cope with the zombies physically, psychologically, and spiritually. As with, say, the cowboys on the Chisholm Trail in *Red River* or the men in the Arctic in *The Thing*, the characters in the living dead films are cut off from established codes of ethics, forced to survive on an existential precipice even steeper than the mountains surrounding the flyers in *Only Angels Have Wings*. Dr. Grimes's remark on TV in the first *Night* that "the bereaved will have to forgo the dubious comforts that a funeral service can give" explicitly establishes this theme, and the films go on to explore both the failure and inappropriateness of such institutions as family, religion, even traditional humanism, to defeat the legions of the undead. This total collapse is shown most powerfully in the opening sequence of *Dawn*, in which a tenement roomful of dying people sequestered by a priest for the giving of last rites becomes a hellish pit of ghoulish violence, and in *Day*, when Sarah unhesitatingly cuts off her lover's arm after he is bitten by a zombie to prevent the infection from spreading.

In the second version of *Night*, Romero clearly has recast Barbara as the film's one true Hawksian professional. The others in the farmhouse are unable to deal with the zombies in a professional manner because of egotism and sentimentality. Tom admits that he could never have shot the first zombie dispatched by Barbara because he was "Uncle Rege," and soon after, as she kills another, Judy screams hysterically, "You shot

Figure 12.2.
Hawksian professionalism in the apocalypse. *Dawn of the Dead* (dir. George Romero, Walter Reade Organization, 1979). U.K. press kit photograph, copyright 1978 Dawn Associates. Distributed by United Film Distribution Company.

Mr. Magruder." Barbara coolly demonstrates the necessity of so doing (despite the invitation to sentiment in the shot of a granny zombie) by proving to them that these attackers are already dead: as a zombie comes through the door, she calmly shoots it several times in the chest first, allowing it to keep coming at them as vivid empirical proof of her rational assessment of the phenomenon before hitting it between the eyes. Ben accuses Barbara of "losing it," but she emphatically denies this as she blows away another zombie with the shotgun. "Whatever I lost, I lost a long time ago. I'm not planning on losing anything else," she retorts, and then turns the accusation around by telling Ben and Harry that they seem like squabbling children. In the film's dramatic climax, Harry, like Tom and Judy earlier, cannot bring himself to shoot his daughter once she becomes undead, even though he knows he must—it is a job that only the true professional can accomplish, and again it falls to Barbara to perform the unpleasant but necessary task.

Romero's treatment of gender in relation to the philosophy of professionalism seeks to resolve the thorny problem for feminism of assessing the value of the Hawksian worldview. Feminist critics have been divided in their opinion of Hawks. Peter Wollen and Robin Wood (even in his later, more politically conscious criticism) clearly articulate the classic auteurist understanding of the relation between Hawks's comedies and adventure films as a dialectic between the "feminine" and "masculine" principles of human nature. The comedies, according to this orthodox view, privilege the emotional life of female characters who are shown to provide a healthy balance to the professionalism of male characters in the adventures.[17] This is precisely the reason Molly Haskell and other early feminist critics also value Hawks's work. As Naomi Wise puts it, "while the men in Hawks' adventure films are professionally skilled . . . , Hawksian women are professional human beings."[18] Nonetheless, critics as diverse as Claire Johnston and Raymond Durgnat disapprove of these films for the very same reason, finding unacceptable the fact that Hawks's women must constantly prove themselves within a masculine world according to masculine standards. As Johnston notes, the problem with Hawks is that for him, "there is only the male and the non-male: in order to be accepted into the male universe, the woman must *become* a man. . . . She is a traumatic presence which must be negated."[19]

By contrast, Romero is considerably more progressive. *Knightriders* shows that it is unnecessary for women to struggle throughout a narrative to demonstrate their professionalism, for it is a fait accompli, a given: after a victorious joust in the troupe's first performance, Sir Rocky (Cynthia Adler) removes "his" helmet to reveal that the knight is a woman. Furthermore, nowhere is she shown to have a heterosexual attachment ("I know who I am," she declares at one point, in contrast to Jack's wife); she is simply there, one of the group. Romero is also willing to allow homosexuals into his professional group, as when Pippen, the troupe's master of ceremonies, is unintentionally brought out of the closet and no one thinks twice about it, since his sexual preferences are irrelevant to his professional function within the group. And if Hawks can be seen as an apologist for capitalism by equating it with manliness (most clearly in *Red River*),[20] then Romero's films attack capitalism as consistently as they do the ideology of masculinity. The shots of cash registers in the mall in *Dawn* filled with now useless money and of bills blowing in the bank entranceway in the zombie-filled streets of Fort Myers in

Day are clear comments about the irrelevance of capitalism and materialism to the new morality contemplated by the zombie films.

In fact, it is more often the *men* in Romero's horror films who fail to prove themselves professionally. In *The Crazies*, the first person to become insane is a father, who kills his wife and sets fire to the family house. And in *Creepshow*, the comic-book morality tales of monstrous revenge and poetic justice can be read as the unleashed imagination of a boy against his patriarchal and repressive father in the movie's frame story. This depiction of men as insane oppressors is consistent in the zombie movies. In *Dawn*, Roger becomes so taken with the sporting pleasure of killing zombies that he acts recklessly and, as a result, is fatally bitten. The internecine conflict among the living in *Day* is obviously motivated by the threat to phallic control represented by the presence of the professional woman—she is, in Johnston's words, a "traumatic presence," but significantly, Romero refuses to allow her to be "negated." And in the second version of *Night*, as before, Harry and Ben lock horns, so to speak ("playing rooster" is how Judy describes it), in a struggle for masculine dominance and territorial control.

Social order quickly collapses—("It doesn't take long for the world to fall apart, does it?" Ben remarks when the farmhouse telephone goes dead)—because of the inability of Romero's male characters to work together. Threatened with violence and dissolution, masculine power oppressively asserts itself in attempts to impose order through authorial control rather than group cooperation. Waller aptly describes the scene in *Dawn* in which the men arm themselves: "The fetishistic objects flash by: high-powered rifles, derringers, revolvers, western-style handguns and holsters, cartridge belts, shotgun shells, and more . . . , the central icons in the so-called male action genres."[21] Social organization and law revert merely to physical power, like Freud's primal horde. The roving band of bikers in *Dawn* is Romero's most explicit image of this masculine power principle, although this is also clear in the new ending he has provided for *Night*.

The territorial battle in the farmhouse between Harry and Ben is a microcosm of the larger social breakdown, as we see toward the end of the film. Radically unlike the first *Night*, Barbara escapes from the farmhouse and, after wandering in the dark wary of approaching zombies, comes upon the local paramilitary unit scouring the countryside for zombies. In the original film, the group appears the next morning and brutally shoots Ben, who has survived the night alone in the cellar but whom they assume (?) is just another zombie. In the remake, these men are shown at first like zombies: in a sudden, startling close-up, the first man is shown wide-eyed, his arm threateningly stiff around Barbara's neck. "What in the name of Jupiter's balls are you doing out here alone, little lady?" he asks. The next morning she awakes (physically and politically) to this barbarism fully institutionalized: some of the men taunt the zombies in a pen, treating them like animals for sport; other zombies are hung for the spectacle of watching them wriggle before they are shot.

This is the debasement of professionalism, its requisite lack of sentiment souring into callousness. Barbara acts as a *corrective* to the narrowness of "masculine" professionalism rather than, as in Hawks, having to be measured *by* it (in that key Hawksian phrase, to be as "good" as men). The image of a truck selling hot sausages and pork roasted on a spit to hungry participants of the spectacle makes clear the link between zombies and patriarchy, its own monstrousness: like the customers ordering fried chicken in the diner in Hitchcock's *The Birds* (1963), it is an ironic sign of a brutish, insensitive, phallic culture.

Crucially, we see the sudden appearance of the zombie hunters and the society they represent from Barbara's horrified perspective. Indeed, the second *Night* adopts the same strategy of narrative viewpoint as the earlier *Jack's Wife*, in which all but a very few shots are motivated from Joan's physical or psychological perspective. Initially the camera adopts Barbara's physical point of view: thus, when the first zombie attacks her in the car in the opening cemetery scene, we are inside, with her, looking out. But then, more importantly, from the moment when she begins to assert her professionalism, we see from her perceptual, or moral, perspective. As soon as Barbara asserts herself, the film dispenses with shots of her frightened looks at the monsters—that crucial moment in horror films when, as Linda Williams has argued, the aspiring independent woman is punished for attempting to assert her own gaze.[22] So when the now zombified Uncle Rege approaches her from behind, Barbara experiences no horrified discovery; rather, at the last possible moment—and without any indication that she was aware of his presence, so that, perhaps, we are encouraged to expect her to respond with fear and surprise—she wheels about and promptly dispatches him. The viewer is thus prevented from delighting in the voyeuristic spectacle of a frightened and helpless woman.

Yet Barbara *does* look horrified after being "rescued" when, seeing the zombies being hung from a tree and then shot, she says, "We're them and they're us" (a line also heard in both *Dawn* and *Day*). Seen from her point of view, patriarchy is made exceedingly strange, becoming, in fact, repugnant and monstrous. Significantly, the film provides no opportunity to view Barbara undressed before she dons her Rambette costume—as is the case in *Alien* (dir. Ridley Scott, 1979), where it can be argued that the Sigourney Weaver character is recuperated for male pleasure in the concluding shots of her wearing implausibly flimsy space underwear. In refusing to provide the viewer with the dominant male gaze typical of the horror film generally and of the slasher cycle—with its conventional alignment of camera viewpoint and the monster victimizing women—in particular, the second *Night* subverts the form's characteristic sexual politics.[23]

Robin Wood's observation that horror films are progressive to the extent that they

Figure 12.3.
Barbara (Patricia Tallman) emerges as the fittest to survive in the new *Night of the Living Dead* (dir. Tom Savini, Columbia Pictures, 1990).

refuse to depict the monster as simply evil seems clearly borne out by these films,[24] for even as Romero progressively downplays the Otherness of the zombies, he depicts patriarchy as increasingly monstrous. If the zombies are indeed "nothing but pure motorized instinct," as they are described in *Day*, then the automatic relegation of the women to subordinate roles by the men in the trilogy makes them very much "undead." By contrast, the literal living dead are depicted with increasing sympathy in the trilogy. Beginning as an undifferentiated mass of murderous machines in the first *Night*, they become the pathetic victims of the bikers' crude violence in *Dawn*. *Day* features Bub, described by Romero as a "zombie with a soul," who in the end uses a gun to kill the macho army captain with at least partial moral approval by both filmmaker and audience. According to Romero, "you have to be sympathetic with the creatures because they ain't doin' nothin'. They're like sharks: they can't help behaving the way they do."[25]

The second *Night* encapsulates the trilogy's depiction of patriarchy, for at the beginning of the film, the zombies are the monstrous threat, but at the end, it is hysterical masculinity that is truly horrifying. In the conclusion, Barbara returns to the farmhouse the next morning to rescue Ben, followed by some of the men. They let Ben out of the basement to find that, unlike in the original, he has indeed become a zombie, and they shoot him. Barbara, having wandered off alone, discovers Harry, who, wounded but still alive, has crawled into the attic (ironically, given his earlier unyielding commitment to the basement). Perceiving Harry as a horrible patriarch, she shoots him in the head at point-blank range without hesitation. When the men come into the room, she says, "There's another one for the fire," correctly guessing that they will assume Harry also had been a zombie. In the original, Barbara's concluding line belongs to the redneck sheriff instructing his men what to do with Ben's corpse; in the remake, it accompanies a woman's response to patriarchy as defiant as the killing of the salesman in Marleen Gorris's militantly feminist *A Question of Silence* (1982). The newer *Night* endorses Harry's fate no less than that of the macho Captain Rhodes in *Day*, who lives just long enough to see his lower body torn off and dragged away by zombies.

The remake of *Night*, then, attempts to reclaim the horror genre for feminism, for all those female victims in such movies who attempt to resist patriarchal containment. Where, say, R. H. W. Dillard finds the original *Night* to be so effectively frightening because it articulates a fundamental nihilism and negation of human dignity,[26] it is more accurate to say that all four zombie films are so powerful because Romero's undead demand the suspension of normal (bourgeois) values, particularly those of patriarchy. Wood is, I think, exactly right about the apocalyptic yet progressive politics of Romero's zombie films.[27]

My concern here is not simply to validate another male director for classic auteurism but to read these films, instances of a genre notorious for its brutalization of women, against the grain for their possible value for progressive gender politics. Indeed, Romero's work offers a perfect instance of the exploitation film's potential, as noted by such critics as Pam Cook and Barbara Klinger, for incorporating progressive ideas.[28] When the search team at the beginning of *Day* lands in Fort Myers, which has become populated entirely by zombies, it is significant that they are shown in front of an empty, now meaningless cinema—for Romero, as an independent regional filmmaker, has managed to make several progressive and commercially viable features while remaining on the margins of the mainstream. (In this sense, *Knightriders* gains additional significance as an autobiographical work about the attempt of a filmmaker, in the guise of King Billy as the head of his troupe of actors, to maintain integrity and avoid ideological compromise for commercial reasons.) "Have we conjured up creatures and given them mystical properties so as not to admit that they are actually of our own race?" Romero has asked.[29]

The remake of *Night of the Living Dead* shows that Romero has put this question to himself, and even if, ultimately, he falls into the trap of defining women in terms that one could argue are still masculinist, he has nevertheless provided one of the most significant feminist perspectives in the history of the horror film.

Notes

1. Gregory A. Waller, *The Living Dead and the Undead* (Urbana-Champaign: University of Illinois Press, 1986), 283.

2. [Editor's note: In the original, the character is Barbra; in the remake, it is Barbara.]

3. Paul Gagne, *The Zombies That Ate Pittsburgh: The Films of George Romero* (New York: Dodd, Mead, 1987), 11; John McCarty, *Splatter Movies: Breaking the Last Taboo of the Screen* (New York: St. Martin's Press, 1984), 58.

4. George A. Romero and Susanna Sparrow, afterword to *Martin* (New York: Day Books, 1980), 209.

5. Robin Wood, *Hollywood from Vietnam to Reagan* (New York: Columbia University Press, 1986), 195.

6. See McCarty, *Splatter Movies*, 1, 5.

7. *Dawn of the Dead*, released without an MPAA rating because of its predecessor's cult reputation, still managed to become, like *Night*, one of the most commercially successful American independent features ever made.

8. Subsequent to the original publication of this essay, Romero directed a fourth film in the series, *Land of the Dead* (2005).

9. David Pirie, *The Vampire Cinema* (New York: Crescent Books, 1977), 141; Elliott Stein, "The Night of the Living Dead," *Sight and Sound* 39, no. 2 (1970): 105; David Pirie, "New Blood," *Sight and Sound* 40, no. 2 (1971): 73–75; Wood, *Hollywood from Vietnam to Reagan*, 118; Gagne, *Zombies*, 87.

10. Dan Yakir, "Mourning Becomes Romero," *Film Comment* 15, no. 3 (1979): 60–65.

11. John Russo, *The Complete Night of the Living Dead Filmbook* (New York: Harmony Books, 1985), 35; Gagne, *Zombies*, 25.

12. Yakir, "Mourning Becomes Romero," 65; Gagne, *Zombies*, 56.

13. Waller, *The Living and the Undead*, 18.

14. Gagne, *Zombies*, 7, 11.

15. Ibid., 108.

16. Robin Wood, *Howard Hawks* (London: British Film Institute, 1981), 17.

17. See Wood, *Howard Hawks*, esp. chapters 2 and 3, and Peter Wollen, *Signs and Meaning in the Cinema*, rev. ed. (Bloomington: Indiana University Press, 1972), chapter 2.

18. Molly Haskell, "The Cinema of Howard Hawks," *Intellectual Digest* 2, no. 8 (1972): 56–68; Haskell, "Howard Hawks: Masculine Feminine," *Film Comment* 10, no. 2 (1974): 34–39; Haskell, *From Reverence to Rape: The Treatment of Women in the Movies* (Baltimore: Penguin, 1974), 208–13; and Naomi Wise, "The Hawksian Woman," *Take One* 3, no. 3 (1972): 17.

19. Claire Johnston, "Women's Cinema as Counter Cinema," in *Movies and Methods*, ed. Bill Nichols (Berkeley: University of California Press, 1976), 1:213; Raymond Durgnat, "Hawks Isn't Good Enough," *Film Comment* 13, no. 4 (1977): 15–16.

20. Durgnat, "Hawks Isn't Good Enough," 9, 11.

21. Waller, *The Living and the Undead*, 310.

22. Linda Williams, "When the Woman Looks," in *Re-Vision: Essays in Feminist Film Criticism*, ed. Mary Ann Doane, Patricia Mellencamp, and Linda Williams, 83–99 (Frederick, Md.: University Publications of America/American Film Institute, 1984). Reprinted in *The Dread of Difference: Gender and the Horror Film*, 2nd ed., ed. Barry Keith Grant, 17–36 (Austin: University of Texas Press, 2015).

23. See Williams, "When the Woman Looks," and Barbara Creed, "Phallic Panic: Male Hysteria and *Dead Ringers*," *Screen* 31, no. 2 (1990): 125–64.

24. Robin Wood, "An Introduction to the American Horror Film," in *The American Nightmare: Essays on the Horror Film*, ed. Robin Wood and Richard Lippe (Toronto: Festival of Festivals, 1979), 23.

25. Yakir, "Mourning Becomes Romero," 62. In *Land of the Dead*, one zombie kills another out of mercy, to spare him pain, ironically a more humane gesture than is shown by the living characters.

26. R. H. W. Dillard, "*Night of the Living Dead*: 'It's Not Just Like a Wind Passing Through,'" in *Horror Films*, ed. R. H. W. Dillard, 55–82 (New York: Monarch Press, 1976).

27. Robin Wood, "Apocalypse Now: Notes on the Living Dead," in Wood and Lippe, *The American Nightmare*, 91–97. Reprinted in Wood, *Hollywood from Vietnam to Reagan*, 114–21.

28. Pam Cook, "Exploitation Films and Feminism," *Screen* 17, no. 2 (1976): 122–27, and Barbara Klinger, "'Cinema/Ideology/Criticism' Revisited: The Progressive Genre," in *Film Genre Reader IV*, ed. Barry Keith Grant, 93–109 (Austin: University of Texas Press, 2012).

29. Romero and Sparrow, afterword to *Martin*, 210.

Dead and Live Life

Zombies, Queers, and Online Sociality

SHAKA McGLOTTEN

Deep as first love, and wild with all
regret, O, Death in Life, the days that are no more!
—**Alfred, Lord Tennyson**

In ten years of talking to gay men about their online and offline intimacies, no one ever told me, "I feel like a zombie." And it would be unfair to (most of) my informants to call them zombies. But I did hear many stories about death and the numbing or exciting habituation that comes with loneliness, boredom, and addiction—affective modes that blur the lines between dead and (a)live life. Here I use "dead and live life" to index different states of liveness, the different ways we might feel more or less alive. These states include the heightened sense of our own phenomenological encounter with the world that comes in moments of vitality, excitation, and the crises (minor and major) that animate so much of ordinary life.[1] Then, there are the attenuated forms of liveness that appear as affective numbness, flatness, and the narrowed but intense focus of hunger or addiction; or those that manifest as the cast out, abject, animal, refugee, poor, or queer whose "bare" life marks out the limits of life writ large. And finally, there are those sorts of liveness that haunt our labors and aspirations: the banal and brutal repetition that structures working middle-class Western everyday life as much as it defines the figure of the walking dead.

In thinking through the variously sad, funny, and ordinary stories these men have told me, I marvel at the stubborn persistence of desire and wonder if the hungry-yet-dead animatedness of zombies might not offer ways of reading forms of intimate liveliness that fall outside of a live intimate life—that is, those hetero- and homonormative ideologies of the good, coupled life, or what Lauren Berlant has called "dead citizenship."[2] The stories of intimacy that my friends, lovers, and informants told me included experiences of hot sex or expressive creativity (two things that might indicate a lively life), but they were as often about mourning dead friends and worlds, feeling lonely or bored, anxiously awaiting or avoiding STD tests, or worrying about whether the time they spent online meant they were addicted to something, whether sex or the Internet.

In this essay I story instances of dead and live life culled from interviews with gay men about their real and virtual intimacies.[3] I read their narratives alongside Canadian underground filmmaker Bruce LaBruce's 2008 gay zombie film *Otto; or, Up with Dead People*[4] to consider the trafficking between forms of dead and live life in contemporary queer sociality, which, I suggest, is animated by death, reflecting banal and strange configurations of death-in-life. And at the same time, the essay eschews the antifutural, antirelational polemic of Lee Edelman's *No Future*.[5] Edelman's critique of "reproductive futurism," an ideology that depends on and reproduces the figure of the Child as a basis on which political hopefulness and the rhetorics that articulate it depend, is forceful and compelling. I am especially impressed by the ways he locates the power and "dignity" of queerness in the refusal to believe in a redemptive future. My work, however, differs insofar as the theoretical and political orientation he deploys refuses *absolutely*; it negates not only normative models of relationality or politics but any models a priori. In his framing, all politics are routed through reproductive futurism, and thus the ethical demand of queer life and sociality is regarded as merely the negation of politics and the social itself. Like Edelman, I am similarly critical of the equivalence established between futurity and the sentimental and normative notion that "children are the future." I am less convinced, however, that all political futurities necessarily operate in this way. Framed within the context of this essay, then, I understand our collective zombification as still possessing an openness, an expansive and ever-expanding capacity to act in ways that are as creatively animated as they are expected. Thus, even as we continue to hungrily desire (whether bodies or stuff or politics), and labor within the constraints of advanced capitalism, we can nonetheless cultivate enlivening modes of agency, or at least imagine them.

I'm Hungry for You

Like many of the stories told me, Todd Ahlberg's 2003 documentary film *Hooked: Get It On(Line)*[6] begins with an optimistic framing of gay online spaces—"It's awesome," says one of Ahlberg's subjects, speaking of the erotic opportunities available. Ultimately, however, the film uses men's experiences in online spaces to tell a less interesting story about addiction: one that conflates the instantaneity of gay online spaces like Gay.com or ManHunt.net with technological innovation and gay male sexuality more generally. In Ahlberg's framing, these sites are symptomatic of larger problems with gay men's sexual culture like promiscuity and anonymous sex. Glazed eyes, drooling, open-mouthed desire: the film's telos imagines technology and the desires and practices of men who go online as zombied. While Ahlberg's documentary interest in online gay life and addiction resembles my own ethnographic one, I find an ongoing animatedness where he finds only a deadness that cries out for therapeutic interpretation and intervention.

If *Hooked* is a closed text in that men's narratives about technologically mediated sex reproduce stereotypes about gay sexual excess, then Bruce LaBruce's *Otto* is a radically open one that addresses contemporary queer sociality more broadly. The film follows the rebirth of Otto, an amnesiac young gay zombie new to the unlife, who stumbles into a new documentary project by filmmaker Medea Yarn. Yarn is simultaneously completing her "magnum corpus," a political-porno-zombie film about the "Che Guevara of the undead," who fucks a zombie army into undead life to revolt against "living civilization."[7] LaBruce's film and Yarn's film-within-the-film level variously camp, blunt, astute, and sincere critiques of the "deadened living" of modern life. In spite of what her goth comportment and fascination with the undead might suggest, Medea Yarn's polemic is not antilife, but she reads, rather perversely, sites of death-in-life as potentially vital. This approach will be familiar to Marxist, environmental, queer, and antiglobalization activists. Shooting a scene at a garbage dump, a "graveyard of advanced capitalism," Medea gives Otto notes to prepare for the scene, suggesting that, as a zombie, he should imagine the dump as "a lotus land, an idyll of truth and beauty, a symbol for mankind's quest to turn the earth into an industrialized wasteland of casual extermination and genocide." If that's too heady, she condenses the sentiment neatly: "Just think of it as a metaphor for the heartless technocracies that govern the earth and you'll be fine."

Even as Yarn employs Otto's unlife to highlight the creeping "putrescence and decay" of capital, they are also each themselves subject to the critique of deadened living. They are both affectively flat, even boring. Medea Yarn's pedantic self-importance and exploitative entrepreneurism mock and mobilize stereotypes about experimental filmmakers (her name is an anagram of Maya Deren); and Otto sometimes reads as chemically zoned-out goth hipster (Belgian actor Jey Crisfar's good looks and his dusty but unmistakably fashionable clothes likely save Otto from being wholly unsympathetic).

If my reading of *Otto* thus far suggests an ambivalent anticapitalist moralism rather than the openness I note earlier, then the film's layered structure, intellectual precocity, camp sincerity, and ambivalence make matters more complex. The film, and Yarn's film-within-a-film, seriously and playfully offers up different forms of life and death as more or less animate. Taking the characters of Medea Yarn and Otto, for example, it's unclear who is more lively, the amnesiac zombie or the stock avant-gardist. More to the point, LaBruce leaves Otto's undead status deliberately unclear. Viewers are left wondering whether Otto is a zombie or just confusedly acting like one. As LaBruce puts it in an interview with the cultural critic Ernest Hardy,

> I wanted to make a zombie who was a misfit, a sissy and a plague-ridden faggot. I deliberately leave it open to interpretation whether Otto is supposed to be a "real" zombie or merely a screwed-up, homeless, mentally ill kid with an eating disorder, who believes that he's dead. I had been running into a lot of young people who told me they felt kind of like the walking dead already, owing to the alarming, apocalyptic state of the world, or the deadening effects of technology, or whatever. *Otto* is my dead valentine to the youth of today.[8]

Rather than considering them to be merely inanimate, the condition of death-in-life afflicting the "youth of today" suggests a contagious affective atmosphere in which death itself is open, a transmissible and ongoing movement rather than a frozen inertness.[9]

Responding to my request for informants in a Gay.com chat room, EvilAndroids engaged me in an anxious conversation about my research, the motives of the men who frequent online publics, and his own troubled relationship to life online. In his search for connection online, EvilAndroids describes deadness as something he is in the process of becoming through his interactions with other men, a condition he views as a desirable end:

> <EvilAndroids> i think its killing me
> <EvilAndroids> everyone takes a little bit mroe then the last
> <EvilAndroids> and somedays i keep going thinking this is it, and when i am empty
>   there will be nothing left to take and i can be at peace
> <EvilAndroids> like a robot

In *Otto*, Medea Yarn says of the eponymous lead, "He vaguely reminded me of the other boys I had already cast in *Up with Dead People*: lonely, empty, dead inside. In a way he fit the typical porn profile: the lost boy; the damaged boy; the numb, phlegmatic, insensate boy willing to go to any extreme to feel something, to feel anything." If Otto and EvilAndroids share a queer emptiness, they differ in their relation to it. Yarn reads Otto's zombie identity, and/or mental illness, as an index of an extant emptiness (or a present absence); his willingness to participate in her agitprop documentary evidences his desire to interrupt that emptiness. EvilAndroids, by contrast, yearns for a more spacious emptiness that opens after desire is exhausted. Of course, his longing for a robotic peace, one that presumes "there [is] nothing left to take," resembles the blank subjectivity of the zombie:

> <shakaz26> it's killing you—or you're killing yourself—if you do really crazy risky
>   things . . . but then that's just desire
> <EvilAndroids> just the motions
> <EvilAndroids> but it never goes away
> <shakaz26> i know what you mean
> <EvilAndroids> its killing me on the inside

But, as Dominic Pettman and others point out,[10] exhaustion doesn't signal the end of desire, only its affective reconfiguration (into anxiety, depression, or indifference, for example). EvilAndroids acknowledges this persistence—"but it never goes away"—and at the same time reemphasizes an ongoing deadening that is paradoxically an anxiously enlivening, a decomposition without end rather than a flat or full stop.

So Over It

If I were a more quantitatively rather than ontologically preoccupied social scientist, I could tell you exactly how many times I had an online exchange that went like this:

> <shakaz26> hi, how's it going?
> <standinzombieinformant> good, just bored.

Suffice to say I had *a lot* of them start that way, as most online cruisers can attest. Boredom shares with emptiness the sense of lacking something (whether that lack is something we want or not), yet it varies from absence in that it indexes a form of depleted stillness that blocks more lively forms of engagement.[11] "Just bored" simultaneously conveys an indifferent sufficiency, "just enough," while inviting a more exciting interruption: "Will you offer to relieve my boredom?" In a face-to-face interview, EvilAndroids, now JonJon, articulated the ways the anticipating and uncomfortable stillness of feeling bored got him into trouble. He went online looking for authentic connections but, bored and lonely (more on the latter below), settled for the temporary "self-validation" sex offered. He lamented the homogeneity of the men in Austin, Texas, noting that the promise of queerness lay in its capacity to be different, to differ:

> That's another thing about Austin. All the guys are normal, average, straight-acting. . . . I'd rather be with someone who is a piece of work, someone I can hate or fall in love with. I'm ashamed of how we've homogenized, I mean, HOMOgenized. We're so set on being normal. Being gay is like having a license to be out there. . . . People forget in gay culture that it's important to be an individual. Somedays I get bored waiting for someone of that caliber and so I hook up with someone and feel terrible afterwards. I'm still lonely and I still get bored.

For EvilAndroids/JonJon, hooking up is effected through an angry disenchantment with the banality and cultural HOMOgeneity of his environment. His sentiments echo a broader disenchantment with changing forms of sociality, especially virtually mediated ones. That is, if online spaces were once imagined to offer a utopian cyber public sphere to supplement the disappearing zones of public encounter (those inter-class/race/generation forms of contact celebrated by Samuel Delany), this fantasy was quickly interrupted by the accelerated mainstreaming of gay male life, as it was incorporated within the neoliberal political imaginary and subject to the dictates of commodity fetishism.[12] In an interview, Keith Griffith, owner of Cruisingforsex.com and a producer/director of amateur pornographic films, suggested that the disappearance of public sex venues and increasingly rarer "out there" queer life had less to do with limitations imposed by the antigay right than, paradoxically, with the success of the gay and lesbian rights movement itself. In a now well-rehearsed argument, mainstream visibility and acceptance of queer people corresponded to the assimilation of queer culture to the logic of capital, in which alternative sexualities come to represent one among a field of available lifestyle options. This process of normalization suppresses the radical potential of a politics of sexual liberation that emphasizes pleasure and openness over static identity categories (particularly when the stability of those categories in large part derives from the ways they cleave to particular patterns of consumption). As Keith argues,

> It isn't the conservative agenda. It is that we have created another box that we've forced people to go inside of, and that is: you've gotta be gay. You're either straight or you're gay. And that has had a profound impact on the ability of men to have sex. A good friend of mine who now lives in Fresno, California, and moved there specifically

for the good opportunities for sex, says that his first rule of thumb, because he's a traveling nurse, so he can be pretty much anywhere he wants to be, his first rule of thumb is to see if there's a gay community center in the town, and if there is, he *will not* move there! Because it does something to change the dynamics. The men are absolutely convinced that if they have one sexual encounter with another man, they are gay, and of course the gay community will say "you are gay, you're just in denial." Well, maybe sex is much more fluid than that. Maybe we are now as guilty as straight people for forcing people into one more choice, one more box.

Keith's conviction that identity categories limit the fluidity of sex, or his friend's instrumental avoidance of towns with a gay community center, both nostalgically evoke a disappeared golden age of queer sociality that escaped the fetters of identification and critique contemporary gayness as a deadened imitation of an earlier, more capacious, gay (and explicitly not gay) erotic life (even if that life is a utopian fantasy!). In *Otto*, Bruce LaBruce enacts a polyvalent critique against boredom and the boring. As he tells Ernest Hardy, he undertook *Otto* in part as a response to and repudiation of the rise of cruel and shallow torture porn films. LaBruce hoped to excavate earlier and more compelling forms of horror storytelling, imagining *Otto* as a thinking person's existential horror.[13] Furthermore, as I suggest earlier, *Otto* imagines its leads as themselves navigating the razor's edge between boredom and interest. Medea Yarn's cringe-inducing experimental films, in arty black and white, complete with Grecian drapery and self-consciously performative dance/movement, come to mind, as does her pedantic voice-over. Even Otto's existential crisis sometimes comes across as an adolescent identity crisis ("To unlive, or not to unlive?"). Yet LaBruce's (and, perhaps, Yarn's) critique of contemporary queer life is altogether less ambivalent; the new gay is boring, already zombied and getting deader. Early on, a clip from Yarn's film features a recently converted gay zombie couple drinking tea and reading the paper, uttering the occasional, if affectionate, snarl and groan in a parodic condemnation of a banal couplified gay life. And, as the film later reveals through idyllic romantic flashbacks with another young man, his ex-boyfriend Rudolf, Otto's own couplification couldn't save him from his melancholic existential crisis (and might have made it worse). Finally, in a pivotal scene, Otto is picked up outside a Berlin bar called Flesh, which, in layered irony, is hosting a zombie night. Gay men swishily mime Otto's own shambling and are likewise drawn to the bar by a not wholly articulate hunger. Otto and the queens he sees outside the bar are in their own way "window shopping." When Otto is picked up outside the bar, it's because, as Kathleen Frederickson observes, "the public proffered inside the bar is unpromisingly dead."[14]

The lack of animation, or desaturation,[15] of contemporary queer sociality is something that Peter, a young journalist, and his friends hoped to interrupt in their "lulz"[16]-hunting "stakeouts." In these stakeouts, Peter and his friends would playfully, if also a bit cruelly, respond affirmatively, but with false information, to ads on Craigslist or requests for private chats on Gay.com:

> We called them stakeouts. It started out innocent. We were drunk and we were upset about old, ugly people, that they thought they could private us—

—lookin?

—want some head?

—sup?

We went to the Ford model site and copied an "ugly"-looking model and we invited someone and hid behind a dumpster and between a laundry mat. And we enjoyed watching as people came by and knocked on doors and didn't get answers.

Our group was mixed—straights and gays and there was only so much hair waxing and fingernail painting we could do. We had to keep people entertained!

Responding to a horrified and, likely, judgmental expression on my face, Peter elaborated,

Let me tell you the rationale. We'd never private someone—they'd private us. Like, there was a guy down the hall. We didn't like him, so we staked him out and sent five suitors at specific times. We never got tired of it—never. One time we hooked up a couple who thought they were meeting other people.

These stakeouts, like *Otto*'s critique of cloneish gay male life, highlight the stubborn zombie dumbness of desire. In the stakeouts, ordinary men, or "old, ugly" ones, persisted in improbably believing that young models were authentically interested in them and demonstrated a pathetic willingness to shamble after these imaginary ideal types. The stakeouts provided a respite from boredom for Peter and his friends, and they cruelly promised a more intimate relief for the men they tricked, some of whom likely sought an interruption of their atomized apartness, the desperate loneliness that makes one gullible, and that is one of the imagined origins of boredom.[17] They capitalized on the desperate hunger of the one, the loneliest number.

One Is the Loneliest Number

Zombies possess an impersonal sociality.[18] That is, they are frequently imagined together as a mass, a crowd, or a swarm, yet they remain alone even among others. Noting the shared predilection for grouping among both zombies and humans, Jen Webb and Sam Byrnand point out in their essay "Some Kind of Virus" that "zombies aren't social isolates—they seem to prefer to live in groups, within built environments; like us, they actively colonize spaces for themselves; like us—at least in the West—they seek to spread well beyond their local region, and to dominate people and places."[19] Indeed, in related and distinct ways, *Otto* and antinormative theory and activism alike despair of the apparently contagious banalization of queer life. Although similar in its viral patterns of consumption and expansion, zombie togetherness is distinct from human belonging. Their sociality differs in that they do not possess the reflective self-awareness or empathetic identification we take as the hallmarks of meaningful intimate connection with ourselves and others. This, along with their boundary-crossing reanimatedness, is part of what makes them inhuman. As one of the performers in the performance mashup *Nonfiction Zombie* puts it, "these creatures are nothing but pure, motorized instinct."[20] Even when stumbling alongside other zombies, zombies are imagined as singular members of crowds or mobs, absent of consciousness and affinal or communitarian ties. Their solitude is assured even when they clump together in their hungry search of living flesh. In this way, zombies epitomize the unnatural or terrorized solitude that attends loneliness.[21]

In his essay "Lonely," Michael Cobb works to imagine a queer theory "after sex." He attaches sexlessness to singleness to suggest that loneliness can elaborate analyses of non-majority intimacy and sexuality beyond the couple form. Moreover, reading Hannah Arendt's *On the Origins of Totalitarianism*, he looks to the ways "the world wants people to feel desperate, lonely, and ready for toxic forms of sociality."[22] To feel lonely is to be "too much of a one";[23] it is to feel "deserted, abandoned,"[24] and a sharp hunger for connection, even if that connection isn't especially healthy. Following Arendt, Cobb points to the ways that the demand to be together capitalizes on the forms of loneliness induced, counterintuitively, through the overabundant proximate "pressing up" that comes with modern life and governance. In other words, we don't have the space to be alone in productive ways and so become susceptible to the terror of loneliness, to which totalitarian logics proffer the love plot and/or sex as relief.[25]

Otto passively resists the demand to be together, to be intimate with himself or others. He disinterestedly investigates his past after discovering clues to his identity in his wallet. He's alone even when he's with others, whether the gay clones at "Flesh" (they don't speak), the skinhead trick he fucks/eats (does he really want the punk, or is he just hungry?), and the gay undead in Medea Yarn's film (he evinces no interest in participating in this revolutionary undead sex public). His soft refusal is not wholly a rejection of intimacy or (un)life, however. After all, he chooses not to self-immolate as his double does in Medea Yarn's documentary, and his relationship with her ends amicably enough. Following his necro/homophobic bashing, Otto permits Fritz, the star of Yarn's *Up with Dead People*, to take care of him, even if he insists on taking off his own shirt; they share a tender love scene. Nonetheless, at the film's conclusion, Otto heads north, alone, if speculatively optimistic about finding more of his kind.

Unlike Otto's detachment, however, EvilAndroids's online sociality was pierced by the sort of claustrophobic loneliness Cobb describes. When, for example, EvilAndroids said that his online life was killing him, he described an affective frame of desperate longing: "But somedays a person just needs to not feel alone," "I'm still lonely," "It never goes away."

Another participant I interviewed, named Redy, a black artist and activist, noted the still-palpable impact of his inability to connect online in a largely white southern university town. His earlier online experiences in a predominantly black city were, by contrast, nearly utopian:

And at first it was just kinda like, wow, I can be in my own world and home and have this whole other portal in which to live. And I wasn't out at the time and it was probably just too intense for me to actually ever, to, uh, really understand how imaginative that world was. Here I was sitting in my household not out with my family and bein' able to withdraw into this whole new world of tops and bottoms and leatherdaddies and hookups and white guys comin' to my house and picking me up from my home and older black guys and guys my age. It was just this whole other imaginative world. And then with a click of a button I could be just back inside my house, or not even the click of a button, just turning my head around, or a sound from inside the house could take me back to the world that I was in. So I mean it was really like fucking like some serious time travel that was going on. And I really found fun in it too.

His early experiences online represented opportunities to playfully engage a range of intimate and erotic possibilities. But a handful of years later, Redy felt the menacing pressure of loneliness, created through the fear that racial difference created a barrier to proximity: "There were so many people who were not into me! Not like [now in] New York, where I can get dick everyday. It really fucked with my psyche for a long time." This loneliness is tied, as Peter suggested to me, to the inability to connect: "We're social beings. No one likes to be alone. . . . Something does happen when you don't have a connection to the world. Especially if you're gay. You're that gay guy who is alone and this is a way to connect." For my informants, loneliness felt like a creeping deadness in their online and offline lives; feeling dead is to be blocked from those palliative forms of "connection to the world," however infected they may be by normative ideologies or neoliberal political economies.

I wonder, though, if my informants (and the rest of us) might not find ways to recuperate the "impersonal intimacy"[26] of Otto and other zombies. In the psychoanalytic approach of Leo Bersani and Adam Phillips, impersonal intimacy describes an ethics that embraces one's own narcissism, but one divested of ego, as well as the other's difference as obdurate rather than as a source for identification. In the context of LaBruce's film, then, I look to Otto's ability to indifferently choose the course of his unlife. Otto presents a powerful fantasy/model of an agency that is as empowered as it is automatized. Indeed, this is perhaps an underexplored approach of zombie theory; rather than operate only as fearful metaphors for racialized difference, infection, consumerism, or the failures of sovereign power, zombies might also offer compelling sites for identification. After all, Otto's abdication of coercive loneliness and traditional forms of relating means he gets to enact a freedom from the responsibilities and obligations that are the ordinary stuff of life and, perhaps, forms of attachment that are a viscous drag on living life in more novel ways.

Addiction Is Desire on Zombie Mode

Loneliness, like boredom, invites changes that, as much as they are attempts to soften the blows of life or enliven some felt deadness, can lurch into excesses that dampen the freedom to choose. Addiction is one such excess, an "epidemic of the will"[27] that compels a destructive liveliness that is distinct from the compulsions toward liveness produced by the many automatisms of life, like perspiration or breathing. In my ten years talking to gay men, addiction repeatedly emerged as a way to make sense of online sociality. Indeed, many of my informants mirrored the sentiments of the men in Ahlberg's *Hooked*. EvilAndroids understood hooking up online as tied to problems of self-esteem, both in himself and others:

<EvilAndroids> maybe they just need to be validated so badly
<EvilAndroids> they;d compromise integrity
<EvilAndroids> and thats the release
<EvilAndroids> being free from all inhibition
<EvilAndroids> like a drug

In an in-person interview, he made this relationship between sex and drugs even more explicit, saying, "Like heroin, you need that validation. Sex is a form of self-validation. That's the addiction—to that validation that self-doubt creates." John, a graphic designer who worked from home, was likewise explicit about online sociality and addiction:[28]

> I found a lot of this stuff really addictive. I'd work on a project for a couple of hours and then I'd get bored and so I'd look for a distraction. Since I do my [design] work on a computer, it was easy to log in to Gay.com or look for porn. Before I knew it, I'd be downloading a dozen porn movies from some site or I'd be chatting in Gay.com, even arranging for a hookup. I always thought it'd be nice to just have the program up and running and if someone interesting wanted to chat with me, great, then I'd chat for a bit and get back to work, but I always ended up giving this distraction my full attention. . . . And I did start thinking, you know, maybe this is a problem, because I can't seem to work at the computer and stay focused on what I need to do. I had a friend who was a sex addict, but he was into public sex stuff; he didn't even have a computer. He got in trouble for it even, with citations and what not, but I don't think he was ever arrested. Anyway, he started going to these sex addicts meetings that are structured like AA [Alcoholics Anonymous] and that seemed to work for him. I borrowed this book from him about sex and love addiction and that gave me some perspective. You know, I really saw myself in it. But I was resistant to going to any kind of meetings. I mean that would be admitting I had a real problem, and I didn't think it was that bad yet. But it was interesting to think of this thing that had started out being a kind of distraction as being connected to other stuff. . . . Like, maybe I was online or looking for distraction because I was really looking for something else, something deeper, like sex, I guess, but also stuff like attention, affection . . . or love.

Ahlberg and his subjects, like EvilAndroids and John, understand the compulsion toward forms of online sociality, toward hooking up and other forms of pleasure, as belonging to the dominant discourse of addiction, that is, as a problem of the healthy self or will. Within this framework, they have failed to construct or exert their own moral agency. Rather than choosing life, the addicted self chooses a supplementary form of death-in-life that offers, but can never deliver on, a transcendent alter-life. Reading William Burroughs and others, Ann Weinstone notes the ways immortality is something addiction promises and suggests that addiction is willingly traded for transcendence: "The addict is not addicted to junk but to junk as a way of life."[29]

It's hard to escape the gravity well of addiction narratives, narratives that convert at least potentially agentive persons into juridical, epidemiological, or therapeutic objects, regarding them as zombies that need to be quarantined, helped, or put down. Not everyone, however, was as attached to addiction's explanatory force. Daniel, aka TXPops, a retired lawyer and activist, for example, who went into the Gay.com chat rooms every morning and evening "to be in a gay social space," didn't interpret this habit as an addiction, though he could have:

> You're addicted or you're not. You can get addicted to table sugar. I became a diabetic and I had to get over that [table sugar addiction]. I'm not one of those people who gets too worked up about whether I need to be using my time more productively. If there is some sort of addiction [to chat rooms/online sex], I don't have that one. But I am a big one for letting people self-define. If they think they're addicted, well then . . .

Like Daniel, I want my informants to be able to self-define; I don't want to suggest that my informants, or anyone attached to addiction as a means of narrating or moving through the world, suffer from false consciousness. Nevertheless, there are key ways in which addiction, or desire on zombie mode, is vital rather than merely dead. Less desire run amok than desire unfettered, addiction is what happens when the pursuit of an object, a person, a fetish, a feeling—pleasure, but not only pleasure—takes on a life of its own. This is why, in a range of everyday/therapeutic contexts, people talk about addiction as a thing that has taken possession of them rather than as a set of choices they're engaged in making: addiction is a live animal hungering for more. It appears as an anxious relationship to habits as well as a repetition that grooves the promise of an individuated sovereign self, gesturing toward a not wholly coherent beyond, in which, pace Freud, one has mastered pleasure (or life and death). Again, *Otto*, though it doesn't address addiction per se, can be illustrative here. In the persistent hunger (for sex, flesh, or revolutionary politics) of dead and living gay zombies, desire operates alongside *and* independently of reflective self-awareness. Zombies model not only forms of impersonal sociality, as I suggest earlier, but impersonal personhood as well. This is not the melodramatic self-shattering of Leo Bersani's "Is a Rectum a Grave" or Lee Edelman's elegant, arch-bitch antifutural death drive but something altogether less overmuch; a flatter, more passive, limp-wristed or indifferent, *yet still vital*, affirmation of an easygoing "whatever." Sometimes it's just better to be on autopilot. Otto (Auto?) manages his existential crisis impersonally and indifferently;[30] he navigates his rebirth into the unlife, learns about his past life, makes art, and decides to leave Berlin mostly by going with the flow. What I call his "soft refusals" represent another way of conceiving zombie desire not only as a deadening drive toward repetition compulsion or explosive *jouissance* but as a desubjectivized way of being "in the flow" of desire. Hunger, then, appears less as a failure of the sovereign self than as an intransigent repetition that refuses a before (the healthy self or the couple form) and after (recovery or kids) in favor of something beyond the established teloi of life and death.

Conclusion: No Dead Matter

In a range of work, cultural geographers Nigel Thrift and Ben Anderson elaborate social scientific and philosophical conceptions of matter and materiality to include the affective, performative, and other constitutive but physically immaterial stuff of space, time, and life/liveliness.[31] The emphasis on the openness of matter has been an especially productive consequence of this work. That is, no matter is considered dead. Zombies, to take an obvious example, are alive not just because they have been reanimated but because their decomposing bodies participate in ecologies of energy transfer and because their contagiousness imputes an immanent continuity. Their hunger performs the obstinate movement of desire's passing. Desire induces changes, and it returns. This hunger transcends the constraints of life as we know it, or sparks at its edges.

This approach to the openness of matter has inspired many of my ethnographic and theoretical engagements (and evasions) in this essay. On one hand, I have looked to the ways boredom, loneliness, and the compulsion to repeat appear to dampen or block access to an expressive, creative, or free life, to a life that flows rather than one that groans and jerks about. On the other hand, drawing on the rich material available in Bruce LaBruce's *Otto*, I have gestured toward an excess, a liveliness that is still vital in spite of or even because of its impersonal, indifferent, and automated drives. I have tried to affirm my informants' experiences with loneliness, boredom, and addiction as powerful adhesions to (digital) queer sociality as neither wholly vital nor deadened but as simultaneously constrained and animate. So that, finally, zombie personhood, rather than representing the fearful antithesis of human self-awareness, emerges instead as a model for ontologies neither self-possessed nor self-coherent, thereby pressing against the constraints of what we imagine to be an enlivened life. Zombies refract queerness as dead and live life; we're here and queer, but we might not be going anywhere; we're contagious and, hopefully, spreading; our productive differences are as caught up in the circuits of capitalist production and exchange as they are immanent and sometimes realized interruptions. Put differently, and a bit cynically, we may be gay zombies condemned to hunger after the cock and ass of the deadened living or to accede to the demands of a consumerist economy of desire more broadly, but that doesn't mean we aren't also alive and capable of choosing a more livable unlife. Here, we can again follow Otto, who asks, not rhetorically, "how do you kill yourself if you're already dead?" Otto decides to head north, where he hopes to discover "a whole new way of death." But barring a northern holiday with Otto and other movie monsters, we remain tasked with creatively reanimating dead life in ways that will open us to a yet more vital life, even one that hungers and lurches about.

Notes

My thanks to Thomas Farringer-Logan, Bill Baskin, and the editors of *Generation Zombie*, in which this essay first appeared, for generous readings and critiques. I am deeply grateful for the assistance of my colleague Sarah Van Gundy, who helped with researching and developing many of the key ideas in this essay through an earlier collaboration and repeated viewings of LaBruce's film.

1. On "crisis ordinariness," see Lauren Berlant's essay "Intuitionists: History and the Affective Event," *American Literary History* 20, no. 4 (2008): 845–60, and Kathleen Stewart, *Ordinary Affects* (Durham, N.C.: Duke University Press, 2007).

2. Lauren Berlant, "Live Sex Acts," in *The Queen of America Goes to Washington City: Essays on Sex and Citizenship*, 155–81 (Durham, N.C.: Duke University Press, 1997).

3. See Shaka McGlotten, "Virtual Intimacies," in *Queers Online: Media Technology and Sexuality*, ed. Kate O'Riordan and David Phillips, 122–37 (New York: Peter Lang, 2007).

4. Bruce LaBruce, dir., *Otto; or, Up with Dead People* (Strand Releasing, 2008), DVD. LaBruce's film isn't the first to tackle the subject of gay zombies. There's also *La Cage Aux Zombies* (1995), *Creatures from the Pink Lagoon* (2006), and the now unavailable *At Twilight Comes the Flesh-eaters* (1998). The latter film retells Romero's *Night of the Living Dead* as gay porn and, like *Otto*, features a film-within-a-film. See Darren Elliott for a longer list, "Consuming Masculinity and Community in Bruce LaBruce's *Otto; or, Up with Dead People* and *L.A. Zombie*," in *Zombie Sexuality: Essays on Desire and the Living Dead*, ed. Shaka McGlotten and Steve Jones, 140–58 (Jefferson, N.C.: McFarland Press, 2014).

5. Lee Edelman, *No Future: Queer Theory and the Death Drive* (Durham, N.C.: Duke University Press, 2004). This critique of Edelman's significant contribution owes a good deal to José Esteban Muñoz, *Cruising Utopia: The Then and There of Queer Futurity* (New York: New York University Press, 2009). See also Sarah Juliet Lauro and Karen Embry, "The Zombie Manifesto: The Nonhuman Condition in the Era of Advanced Capitalism," *boundary 2* 35, no. 1 (2008): 85–108. Like Edelman, Lauro and Embry either cynically or playfully (or both) resist the hopefulness of reproductive futurism. "The Zombie Manifesto," in its articulation of and argument for the zombie as antisubject, symptomatizes the ways zombies trouble distinctions between subject and object; indeed, by troubling both the groundedness of being and returning to haunt the living, zombies are, as Lauro and Embry put it, useful "ontic/hauntic" critical objects. Their manifesto also symptomatizes an ironic intellectual tendency to propose a nihilistic negative dialectic, here in the form of the zombii/zombie as swarm, as the only remedy for infected (by histories of power relations, or bad power) liberal humanism. For Lauro and Embry, the zombie allegorizes (among other things) humanity and its antithesis, a systemwide, but not to be celebrated, disruption. In this way, they distinguish their own intellectual project from that of other notable posthuman theorists, Gilles Deleuze and Félix Guattari; unlike them, Lauro and Embry are interested only in *unbecomings* and the ways the zombie offers us a way out of the trouble humanism and, ultimately, global capitalism have gotten us into. Rather than use the zombie to ask what it means to be human or to consume, or to be dead or alive, or to be agentive or automated, "The Zombie Manifesto" asks us to accept that the end of power relations as we know them won't come through the conscious actions of the multitude (pace Hardt and Negri) but from the consciousnessless hunger of the unthinking zombii swarm. And if I am sympathetic to their provocation regarding an impersonal or passive revolutionary politics, I'm less certain about where this provocation leads. In their view, the end times brought about by the zombapocalypse certainly won't be liberating, because, after all, as zombii, we won't be equipped with the rational subjectivities to discern freedom or anything else.

6. Todd Ahlberg, dir., *Hooked: Get It (On)Line* (Eclectic DVD, 2003), DVD.

7. Dialogue and press kit available at http://www.ottothezombie.de/press.html.

8. Ernest Hardy, "Zombie Deep Throat," http://ernesthardy.blogspot.com/2010/01/zombie-deep-throat.html.

9. See Ben Anderson, "Affective Atmospheres," *Emotion, Space, and Society* 2, no. 2 (2009): 77–81. See also Teresa Brennan, *The Transmission of Affect* (Ithaca, N.Y.: Cornell University Press, 2004).

10. Dominic Pettman, *After the Orgy: Toward a Politics of Exhaustion* (Albany: State University of New York Press, 2002). See also the Feel Tank Manifesto's articulation of "political depression" at http://www.chicago-red.org/feeltank/.

11. See Ben Anderson, "Time-Stilled Space Slowed: How Boredom Matters," *Geoforum* 35, no. 6 (2004): 739–54.

12. See Samuel Delany, *Times Square Red, Times Square Blue* (New York: New York University Press, 1999); Urvashi Vaid, *Virtual Equality: The Mainstreaming of Gay and Lesbian Liberation* (New York: Anchor Books, 1995); Michael Warner, *The Trouble with Normal: Sex, Politics, and the Ethics of Queer Life* (New York: Free Press, 1999); Lisa Duggan, *The Twilight of Equality? Neoliberalism, Cultural Politics, and the Attack on Democracy* (Boston: Beacon Press, 2003).

13. Hardy, "Zombie Deep Throat."

14. Kathleen Frederickson, "Up with Dead Privates," http://mediacommons.futureofthebook.org/imr/2010/05/07/dead-privates. As Darren Elliott notes, in *Otto*, LaBruce advances his ongoing critique of gay male subcultures, especially their articulation or conflation of eroticism and fascism. Elliott, "Consuming Masculinity and Community."

15. Anderson, "Time-Stilled."

16. "Lulz" is a variation of the Internet slang LOL, or "laugh out loud." "Lulz" is more frequently used in the context of pranks and is commonly found on the message boards of the website 4chan and employed by "trolls," hackerish and adolescent pranksters for whom "'lulz' means the joy of disrupting another's emotional equilibrium." See Mattthias Schwartz, "The Trolls among Us," *New York Times Magazine*, August 3, 2008, http://www.nytimes.com/2008/08/03/magazine/03trolls-t.html?_r=2&ref=technology.

17. Ben Anderson critically reads these four ways of conceiving boredom in relation to a disenchantment with the modern world as secularization, calculable individualism, the changing nature of leisure, and standardized/standardizing time-space. Anderson, "Time-Stilled," 741.

18. I borrow this subheading, and many key ideas, as my subsequent discussion evidences, from Michael Cobb, "Lonely," *South Atlantic Quarterly* 106 (Summer 2007): 445–57.

19. Jen Webb and Sam Byrnand, "Some Kind of Virus: The Zombie as Body and as Trope," *Body and Society* 14, no. 2 (2008): 84.

20. Tracy Stephenson Shaffer, "Scripting and Staging a Theoretical Mashup: *Nonfiction Zombie* in a Dance Club," *Liminalities* 6, no. 1 (2010), http://liminalities.net/6-1/zombie.html.

21. Some recent zombie texts offer counterevidence to the account I give here. That is, zombies are increasingly imagined as entangled in rather than only apart from human society and sociality. To take only a few examples, the conclusion of the zom-rom-com *Shaun of the Dead* (dir. Edgar Wright, 2004) finds Shaun's dim-witted but brave best friend Ed, now a zombie, still playing video games, albeit chained in the shed. In *Fido* (dir. Andrew Currie, 2006), zombies are the mostly benign servants in an alternate 1950s America. And in *28 Weeks Later* (dir. Juan Carlos Fresnadillo, 2007), a zombified father's desire to be near his children morphs into a rage-fueled incestuous desire to infect them.

22. Cobb, "Lonely," 447.

23. Ibid., 448.

24. Ibid., 447.

25. Ibid., 448–49.

26. Leo Bersani and Adam Phillips, *Intimacies* (Chicago: University of Chicago Press, 2008).

27. Eve Sedgwick, "Epidemics of the Will," in *Tendencies*, 129–40 (London: Routledge, 1994).

28. McGlotten, "Virtual Intimacies," 131–32.

29. Ann Weinstone, "Welcome to the Pharmacy: Addiction, Transcendence, and Virtual Reality," *Diacritics* 27 (Autumn 1997): 81.

30. I am tempted to call Otto "detached," but that would suggest a more active rejection or working through of forms of attachment that I'm not convinced he ever possessed. Attachments are intense, while indifference shrugs.

31. Anderson, "Time-Stilled"; Anderson, "Affective Atmospheres"; Ben Anderson and John Wylie, "On Geography and Materiality," *Environment and Planning A* 41, no. 2 (2009): 318–35; Nigel Thrift, *Non-Representational Theory: Space/Politics/Affect* (New York: Routledge, 2008).

Dead *and* Disabled

The Crawling Monsters of *The Walking Dead*

ANNA MAE DUANE

In Katherine Dunn's 1989 novel *Geek Love*, two freak show performers debate the merits of reading horror stories. "Don't you get scared reading those at night?" Oly asks her older brother Arty. Arty, and indeed all the siblings in the freak show family in this novel, has a body that elicits awe, or fear, or hatred at first sight. They have learned from an early age that Americans like to divide the world into what's normal and good and then place everything else in an all-purpose bin called "other." And they know all too well which side of the equation they live on. Arty is particularly used to the horrified, fascinated stares his extraordinary body evokes—all four of his limbs are quite a bit shorter than average, and every one of them tapers off into a flipper. So Arty reads the horror novel, not as entertainment, but as an instruction manual to get ahead in the world. "These [stories] are written by norms to scare norms," Arty tells his sister.

> And do you know what the monsters and demon spirits are? Us, that's what. You and me. We are the things that come to the norms in nightmares. The thing that lurks in the bell tower and bites out the throats of the choirboys—that's you, Oly. And the thing in the closet that makes the babies scream in the dark before it sucks their last breath—that's me. And the rustling in the brush and the strange piping cries that chill the spine on a deserted road at twilight—that's the twins singing practice scales while they look for berries.[1]

Instead of lamenting the fearful stories his body conjures, Arty delights in the power others' reactions can give him. As he sees it, those who fear him—the "norms" who see his body as an emblem of weakness, decay, or monstrosity—are trapped in their own stories. For Arty, it's the person inhabiting the "monster's" body who has the advantage: he can leverage an outsider's power over the horror-struck audience. Arty's gleeful immersion in the narratives that seek to contain the horror imposed upon him can be read as a primer in the double-consciousness of disability, a state in which the person with disability becomes responsible for managing the often oppressive narratives of others while somehow holding on to a sense of self outside these often dehumanizing stories.

As Rosemarie Garland-Thomson has written, the weight of stereotype often skews social encounters between people with disabilities and the able-bodied, or normates. Such interactions are "usually strained because the nondisabled person may feel fear, fascination, repulsion or merely surprise, none of which is expressible according to social protocol."[2] Often, Thomson relates, it falls to the person with disability to manage the anxiety such encounters provoke in others. "To be granted fully human status by normates, disabled people must use charm, intimidation, ardor, deference, humor or entertainment to relieve nondisabled people of their discomfort."[3] People with disabilities must distance themselves from the bogeymen their bodies evoke, even as they acknowledge that their interlocutor can see little else.

Nick Santonastasso, like Arty in *Geek Love*, is not interested in managing the anxieties of the able-bodied. Rather, this real-life teenager from New Jersey has gathered considerable Internet fame by wholeheartedly inhabiting the monster that his body evokes. An avid fan of AMC's popular series *The Walking Dead*, Santonastasso sets up pranks that transport the relentless, decaying zombies off of the television screen and into the spaces of everyday suburban life.[4] He stages zombie attacks at everyday locales like parking garages and supermarkets, all the while filming his victims' frightened reactions at the horror crawling toward them. Santonastasso is able to evoke the zombie's onslaught so effectively because his body fits the profile of many of the monsters who appear on *The Walking Dead*. To be specific, he has one limb instead of the typical four.

As this anthology testifies, there's no shortage of theories to explain our current obsession with zombies. A rich body of literature examines the zombie as a product of racial and colonial histories and as a metaphor for the continued legacies of those histories.[5] There are compelling analyses that read the shuffling hordes of the undead as symbols of our mindless, voracious consumerism. Parades of shambling zombie capitalists were a regular feature in Occupy protests on both sides of the Atlantic.[6] Santonastasso's savvy performances demonstrate that there is one zombie attribute that requires no metaphorical reading. No matter how divergent the origin stories might be, zombies are both the product and emblem of illness and disability. Zombies' bodies are, quite literally, falling apart. As such, they reflect the terrifying lack of control that comes with bodies that won't do as they're told.

The very first episode of *The Walking Dead* series depicts Rick Grimes as a weak, disoriented protagonist who wakes up in a hospital gown to find a world destroyed by an infection that defies all human ingenuity. Once he makes it to the outside, the stakes of maintaining able-bodiedness are rendered in stark terms. For in the bleak world of *The Walking Dead*, physical weakness is a death sentence. Any departure from full health is just a quick downhill progression to the world of zombies. A difficult pregnancy, a pronounced limp, extreme youth, or old age are all a one-way ticket to shambling, mindless zombification.

Activists in disability rights organizations such as Not Dead Yet contend that American culture's fear of imperfection often manifests in the assumption that it is better to be dead than disabled.[7] *The Walking Dead* removes the middle ground between the two choices. If you're disabled, you will soon be dead, and the dead function with all sorts of disability. It's striking how often the "Walkers" are incapable of walking at all. One of

Figure 14.1.
Still from *The Walking Dead* (dir.
Frank Darabont), pilot episode of the
AMC Studios series, 2010.

the first zombies Rick kills is missing her legs (Figure 14.1). In a later season, we watch the villainous Governor narrowly escape a building filled with zombified nursing home patients whose disabilities prevent them from being effective predators.

If, as disability theorists have long argued, ableist assumptions treat disability as a problem that requires one either to cure or kill it, the zombie narrative distills this binary logic into a moral imperative.[8] Zombies, after all, allow for no middle ground. In *The Walking Dead*, the possibility of accommodating the monsters is always a disastrous idea. Early in the series, a good-hearted farmer named Herschel tries to keep his former wife and neighbors contained in a barn on his property. Several other characters, including the heroic Michonne and the villainous Governor, try unsuccessfully to create a space for their infected loved ones to inhabit, only to fail miserably. The stark choices demanded by zombie narratives clarify the anxiety of having to engage with the uncertainty disability evokes. *The Walking Dead*, like other zombie narratives, repeatedly assures us that it's foolish to imagine any sort of continuum between physical health and repulsive decay. You are on one side of the equation or the other. Thus the terror of our own treacherous, unpredictable embodiment becomes transferred to monstrous bodies we must eradicate to be safe.

While *The Walking Dead* is perhaps the most popular version of a story conflating disability with the horror of the zombie, it is far from the only story in circulation. As Mel Y. Chen contends, all zombies inevitably queer and crip comforting stories about how bodies are "supposed" to work. They are too hungry and too damaged to properly assuage their terrible needs. "That zombies' voracious appetites cannot be satisfied," Chen writes, "is only confirmed by disarrayed and clearly nonoperational organs."[9] In other words, what zombies desperately want—food, and the energy it supplies to a healthy body—is precisely what their dysfunctional bodies disqualify them from having.

Even in venues we might imagine far from the realm of the horror story, we see zombies linked to disability, particularly a disability resistant to cure. For instance, zombies quickly found their way into the language describing the fearful spread of illness occasioned by the 2014 Ebola outbreak. In a trend that combined the racialized colonial origins of zombies with the disability their unwieldy bodies conjure, sources from Twitter memes to local newspaper accounts to edicts from the Chinese government

When Bae gets Ebola but you still love her

Figure 14.2.
A meme often retweeted at the height of the Ebola scare in October 2014. Origin unknown.

rendered Ebola the stuff of horror movies. A Twitter meme linking *The Walking Dead* to the Ebola crisis humorously reinforced the connection that many were taking quite seriously.

In October 2014, a local Liberian paper recounted that "two Ebola patients who died of the virus in separate communities in Nimba County have reportedly resurrected in the county. The victims, both females, believed to be in their 60s and 40s respectively, died of the Ebola virus recently in Hope Village Community and the Catholic Community in Ganta, Nimba."[10] With a flourish worthy of the best zombie novels, the journalist sets up this strange event as an origin story. "Since the Ebola outbreak in Nimba County," the story recounts, "this is the first incident of dead victims resurrecting." Apparently, Patient Zero in the forthcoming zombie apocalypse had been identified.

This incredible story was picked up, retweeted, and covered in several publications, including the *International Business Times*.[11] Even before the Liberian paper's account, the narrative linking Ebola patients to zombies had international purchase. In August 2014, a public service announcement on China's official news agency, Xinhua, assured citizens that Ebola was not a "zombie disease." Yet even as officials sought to dismiss fears of zombies, they offered wholly unsubstantiated descriptions of Ebola symptoms that reiterated a connection between the disease and the undead. "An Ebola sufferer may lose consciousness or faint, making him or her appear dead," Xinhua explained. "But a few hours or even days later the patient may suddenly come to and enter an extremely violent state, tearing at and biting anything that moves, including people and animals."[12] Even as Chinese officials, African journalists, and American tweeters turned to zombie fiction to explain terrifying realities, writers of zombie literature had researched the real-life potential of the Ebola virus to add weight to the terror their fictional stories might evoke. The Feed and First Days trilogies are just two examples of texts tracing a zombie outbreak to the Ebola/Marburg family of viruses.[13]

The connection between disability and (un)death is so common that it can be found in narratives normally considered the polar opposite of horror stories. Even inspirational tales of disability can evoke the terrors of the zombie, in which voracious, uncontrollable bodies wield power over a mind seemingly gone dark. Helen Keller might be the last person to come to mind when thinking of zombies, yet some of the most iconic visual language used to depict her resonates with the aesthetics of many zombie films. The first film version of William Gibson's *The Miracle Worker* (1962) predates George Romero's *Night of the Living Dead* (1968), but the film's depiction of Helen Keller's disability visually anticipates the lurching, desperate hunger Romero would come to invest in his representation of the walking dead. One of the most famous scenes in both film versions of *The Miracle Worker* takes place at the dinner table, where a dramatic clash occurs as Helen's voracious, ungainly appetites shock her teacher, Ann Sullivan, who watches Helen wreak havoc upon what would have otherwise been a civilized family meal. The scene ends with Sullivan's physically beating the writhing, wordless Keller into submission.

Figure 14.3.
Still from *The Miracle Worker* (dir. Arthur Penn, United Artists, 1962). Copyright 1962 United Artists. All rights reserved.

Helen Keller's first autobiography doesn't include the film's scene of violence set off by her unseemly feeding habits. There are, however, numerous references that cast her early years of disability as an experience of walking death. She speaks of the time before the arrival of Anne Sullivan as a time of dark isolation and credits Sullivan with "restoring her to her human heritage."[14] Of course, Keller—thanks to the "miracle" she attributes to her teacher—ultimately crosses over to desirable territory in the kill or cure battle. She is able to move from the uncivilized desires of an incommunicative creature into a refined, educated, charming young woman, or as she puts it, she moves from "darkness into light, from isolation to friendship, companionship, knowledge, love."[15] Once her mind is again connected to the world of the able-bodied, she goes on to achieve feats (attendance at Radcliffe and friendships with Alexander Graham Bell and Thomas Edison, to name just a few) well beyond the reach of most able-bodied women of her time.[16]

Helen Keller's inspirational journey from darkness to light, from a living death to a well-lived life, might seem far from the terrors depicted in *The Walking Dead*, but her sunny optimism illuminates the logic that renders the Walkers so frightening. A zombie—the manifestation of disease and disability run amok—is the doppelgänger of the inspirational supercrip that Keller represents so powerfully. The supercrip, as defined in disability studies scholarship, is a person with disabilities who cheerfully, bravely, resolutely, overcomes the obstacles posed by his body and thus represents the possibility of triumph over the perils of embodiment.[17] If the monstrously uncontrollable body scares us, the story of the supercrip offers a soothing balm. These are the disabled people who thrill us as they run marathons, climb mountains, and break records. Their stories reassure us that no matter what physical difficulties might arise, we can still bend the body to our will. We—our minds, our desires—are still in charge. Helen Keller can "overcome" her blindness and deafness and become an international star. Thus, readers extrapolate, we can all invest in a logic of mind over matter.

While advances in medicine have improved the lives of many, an absolute investment in the medical model of disability gilds the supercrip's heroic tales of overcoming with an air of manic overcompensation.[18] If, as the medical model argues, successfully engaging with disability means isolating a problem that must be fixed rather than accommodating a sometimes painful reality, the stakes around the supercrip are high indeed. Their extraordinary bodies show no sign of weakness or discomfort as they achieve remarkable things—their disability is completely overcome by force of will. As we seek to deny what embodiment and mortality will inevitably ask of all of us, the story of the supercrip assures us that we are in ultimate control of our bodies, not the other way around. The supercrip is, in other words, the antizombie.

Indeed, the only possible respite from the relentless need to kill the shuffling, crawling creatures populating *The Walking Dead* comes from a medical solution that would rightfully restore the body to its role as instrument rather than prime mover. The few hopeful arcs in the five-season story line have revolved around the hope of a cure. The group of survivors first makes its way to the Centers for Disease Control and Prevention in Atlanta, only to be horribly disappointed by the government agency's lack of a remedy for zombie plague. The protagonists later spend several episodes heading toward

Washington, D.C., because of a rumor that the government had produced an antidote to the virus. Again, the show takes pains to place the defeat of medical knowledge at the center of the horror.

So Nick Santonastasso's decision to place his body in the dichotomous play of kill-or-cure that rules *The Walking Dead* is not without risk. By gleefully inhabiting the creatures that—as the television show incessantly reminds us—must be eliminated because they cannot be fixed, Santonastasso evokes a long history of conflating disabled bodies with monstrous ones. By rendering his extraordinary body as a monstrous one in his pranks, Nick evokes, for at least some viewers, the painful memories of the freak show. As YouTube videos show him crawling across the floors of supermarkets and car garages, the similarities between his antics and the most frightening scene in Tod Browning's cult classic film *Freaks* (1932) are striking. In that film's horrific climax, disabled circus workers—who had been portrayed sympathetically up until that moment—morph into monsters, crawling through the mud to mutilate and murder able-bodied characters who had dared to cross them. The scene is so iconic that Pixar's *Toy Story* (dir. John Lasseter, 1995) even pays homage to it in the scene where the broken, disabled toys act out a monstrously vengeful drama. In these stories, among others, we find Helen Keller's progress reversed. The monster isn't tamed by curative able-bodiedness. Instead, the formerly friendly disabled characters devolve into murderous freaks. We are taught, in these horror stories, as in the zombie tale, that there is no accommodation—if the disabled characters cannot be cured, then they pose a deadly threat.

The vacillation between fear and fascination that Tod Browning's *Freaks* exploits was indeed central to the affective structure of the American freak show itself. The history of these shows does little to support the idea—shared by the fictional Arty and the real-life Nick—that people with disabilities can play the monster while escaping the monster's fate. Throughout the late nineteenth and early twentieth centuries, freak show managers and audiences exploited people like Julia Pastrana, a hirsute woman whose husband/manager exploited her before and after death.[19] Her husband gave her dead body—and that of her stillborn child—a second commercial life, or perhaps more accurately a prolonged state of undeath. He embalmed both mother and child and put them on display for the edification and entertainment of onlookers.

Nick Santonastasso, unlike Julia Pastrana, wields control over his representation, determining when the story stops and starts. Santonastasso would likely balk at a comparison with Helen Keller, but his zombie pranks do share Keller's entrepreneurial talent for inserting a disabled body into a story line that resonates strongly with able-bodied audiences. His YouTube videos have gathered thousands of hits, and his fame won him a trip to Japan to play one of his pranks on a cast member of *The Walking Dead*. Even as his videos offer frightening vignettes depicting an uncontrollable disabled figure, Santonastasso's curation and distribution of these tableaus also evoke the story of the supercrip. It's not every teenage boy, after all, who scores international trips to mingle with some of the most famous people in the world.

It's precisely the tension between "good" and "bad" stories about disability that makes Nick Santonastasso's pranks so smart, and so powerful. Santonastasso's initiative and skill evoke the admiration normally reserved for the supercrip, even as he plays a zombie, a role crafted out of fear of bodily havoc associated with illness and disability. In so doing, he demonstrates that the angelic and demonic portrayals of disability—the hero that rules the body and the zombie who destroys it—are two sides of the same coin. In a culture that so often looks to the bodies of disabled people to reaffirm our need to feel in control of uncontrollable forces, Nick makes the "norms" watch themselves. Rather than petitioning for his humanity by putting the able-bodied at ease, he insists upon it by exposing their anxieties. The freak show often exploited people with disabilities who were subject to the fearful, fascinated stares of others. Nick Santonastasso, with the aid of a camera and the Internet, has turned the gaze back on the audience—on the "norm" who reveals her fear and can do little but grin sheepishly at how silly it is to be afraid of monsters. In these stories, we side with the encroaching zombie, laughing nervously at the misguided fantasy that we can ever keep what he brings at bay.[20]

Notes

1. Katherine Dunn, *Geek Love: A Novel* (New York: Vintage, 2011), 46.
2. Rosemarie Garland-Thomson, *Extraordinary Bodies: Disability in American Literature and Culture* (New York: Columbia University Press, 1997), 12.
3. Ibid., 13.
4. For coverage of Santonastasso's zombie stunts, see http://uproxx.com/tv/2013/12/one-armed-zombie and http://gawker.com/walking-dead-recruits-one-limbed-teen-for-terrifying-zo-1503534374.
5. Christopher M. Moreman and Cory James Rushton, eds., *Race, Oppression, and the Zombie: Essays on Cross-Cultural Appropriations of the Caribbean Tradition* (New York: McFarland, 2011).
6. Stephen Harper, "Zombies, Malls, and the Consumerism Debate: George Romero's *Dawn of the Dead*," *Americana: The Journal of American Popular Culture* 1, no. 2 (2002): 2000; Tavia Nyong'o, "The Scene of Occupation," *The Drama Review* 56, no. 4 (2012): 136–49.
7. http://www.notdeadyet.org/.
8. For a particularly astute reading of this dynamic, see Rosemarie Garland-Thomson, "The Cultural Logic of Euthanasia: 'Sad Fancyings' in Herman Melville's 'Bartleby,'" *American Literature* 76, no. 4 (2004): 777–806.
9. Mel Y. Chen, "Lurching for the Cure? On Zombies and the Reproduction of Disability," *GLQ—A Journal of Lesbian and Gay Studies* 21, no. 1 (2015): 25.
10. "Dead Ebola Zombies Resurrect?," *New Dawn*, September 24, 2014, http://www.thenewdawnliberia.com/general/3212-dead-ebola-patients-resurrect.
11. Mangala Dilip, "Ebola Zombies? Liberian Newspaper Claims Victims Are Rising from the Dead," *International Business Times*, October 2, 2014, http://www.ibtimes.co.in/ebola-zombies-liberian-newspaper-claims-victims-are-rising-dead-610439.
12. http://qz.com/249592/chinese-official-media-assures-citizens-that-ebola-doesnt-create-zombies/.
13. Mira Grant, *Feed* (New York: Orbit, 2010); Rhiannon Frater, *First Days* (New York: Tom Doherty Associates, 2011).
14. Helen Keller, Annie Sullivan, and John Albert Macy, *The Story of My Life; with Her Letters (1887–1901) and a Supplementary Account of Her Education* (New York: Doubleday, 1921), 26.
15. Ibid.
16. Ibid.
17. Carla Filomena Silva and P. David Howe, "The (In)validity of Supercrip Representation of Paralympian Athletes," *Journal of Sport and Social Issues* 36, no. 2 (2012): 174–94; Rosemarie Garland-Thomson, "Seeing the Disabled: Visual Rhetorics of Disability in Popular Photography," in *The New Disability History: American Perspectives*, ed. Paul K. Longmore and Lauri Umansky, 335–74 (New York: New York University Press, 2001).
18. For more on the medical model, see Sara Goering, "Beyond the Medical Model? Disability, Formal Justice, and the Exception for the 'Profoundly Impaired,'" *Kennedy Institute of Ethics Journal* 12, no. 4

(2002): 373–88; Simon Brisenden, "Independent Living and the Medical Model of Disability," in *The Disability Reader: Social Science Perspectives* (1998): 20–27; Longmore and Umansky, *New Disability History*.

19. J. Sokolov, "Julia Pastrana and Her Child," *Lancet* 1 (1862): 467–69; Rosemarie Garland-Thomson, "Narratives of Deviance and Delight: Staring at Julia Pastrana, 'The Extraordinary Lady,'" in *Beyond the Binary: Reconstructing Cultural Identity in a Multicultural Experience*, ed. Timothy Powell, 81–106 (New Brunswick, N.J.: Rutgers University Press, 1999).

20. My reading of how performance can interfere with the logic asserting "better dead than disabled" is greatly influenced by Carrie Sandahl's work, particularly "Queering the Crip or Cripping the Queer? Intersections of Queer and Crip Identities in Solo Autobiographical Performance," *GLQ— A Journal of Lesbian and Gay Studies* 9, no. 1–2 (2003): 25–56.

Trouble with Zombies

Muselmänner, Bare Life, and Displaced People

JON STRATTON

This chapter is about the relationship between zombies and displaced people, most obviously refugees, asylum seekers, and illegal immigrants. It is founded on a realization that the underlying characteristics of zombies are similar to those attributed to displaced people—people, predominantly from non-Western states, striving for entry into Western states. The chapter begins from the recognition that during the 2000s, there has been a tremendous increase in the number of films released featuring zombies. At the same time, zombies have started appearing in other media. A video game series called Resident Evil, which includes biologically mutated flesh-eating undead, founded a genre now called "survival horror." Released originally for Sony PlayStation in 1996, by September 30, 2004, the various forms of the game had sold more than twenty-five million units.[1] In 2002, the series spawned a film also called *Resident Evil* (dir. Paul Anderson). The film became the fourteenth highest grossing R-rated film in the United States that year and the fiftieth highest grossing film globally.[2] There are now multiple sequels. In 2009, Quirk Books released *Pride and Prejudice and Zombies,* a mash-up in which author Seth Grahame-Smith introduced zombies into Jane Austen's 1813 romance novel. The book became an instant success. In April it had reached the third spot on the *New York Times* best-seller list, and by the end of the year, it had sold more than seven hundred thousand copies.[3] Such was the success of the revisioned novel that Quirk Books was inspired to commission a prequel, Steve Hockensmith and Patrick Arrasmith's *Pride and Prejudice and Zombies: Dawn of the Dreadfuls.*

At the same time, since the 1990s, there has been an increasing anxiety in Western countries over the numbers of displaced people attempting to gain entry across their borders. The reasons for this are many, but not my main concern here. Certainly there has been an overall increase in refugee numbers. One set of figures released by the United Nations High Commissioner for Refugees tells us that, whereas in 1960, 1,656,669 people were classified as refugees, in 2006, this number had climbed to 9,877,703.[4] However, most of these refugees are situated in countries outside the developed West. Similarly, between 1980 and 2000, there has been a significant increase in asylum seeker applications in Europe, from around 150,000 to around 450,000, with a spike up to 700,000 in the early 1990s, and in Australia and New Zealand from virtually nothing in the mid-1980s to around 5,000 a year. In North America, the figure increased significantly in the mid-1990s to nearly 200,000 and then declined to around 50,000 by 2000.[5] Anxieties over border protection in all countries but, perhaps, especially in the West were heightened in the wake of the 2001 attacks on the World Trade Center in New York. The link between these anxieties and concerns over displaced people attempting to gain entry to Western countries was made, for example, in Alfonso Cuarón's *Children of Men*, released in 2006 and set in 2027.

I will be arguing that, in many of the recent zombie films, the zombie threat can be read in terms of the fears of many members of Western countries about being overwhelmed by displaced people. What might be the justification for this connection between zombies and displaced people? The recent renaissance in zombie films lifts off from the revision of zombies in Western popular culture that is traced to George A. Romero's now classic 1968 film *Night of the Living Dead*. This film began what is now colloquially called the zombie apocalypse trope, in which entire communities, whole countries, and even the world are subject to destruction by increasing numbers of zombies that appear from nowhere, often originating as a consequence of radiation from outer space, if any rationale for their existence is proffered. In these films the zombie presence is qualitatively different from the earlier zombie trope, derived from claims about the existence of zombies in Haiti, in which witches or evil scientists turned individuals into zombies as a means of controlling them. Nevertheless, the foundational idea of the zombie as a dead person resurrected to a state that remains nearer death than life is a constant.

What audiences find most frightening in the zombie idea is not the resurrection from death but the state of living death that is the fate of the zombie. Indeed, in some films that are identified as a part of the zombie genre, such as *28 Days Later* (dir. Danny Boyle, 2002), the person doesn't even die before turning into what is now being described as a zombie. In this case, if the key to the identification of a zombie is the interstitial state of being between life and death, then, I will argue, the zombie takes on the characteristic of what Giorgio Agamben calls "bare life." Bare life is difficult to define because it has two aspects. The first is, for want of a better word, social. Setting up his discussion of the relationship between bare life and aesthetics, Anthony Downey writes that

> lives lived on the margins of social, political, cultural, economic and geographical borders are lives half lived. Denied access to legal, economic and political redress, these lives exist in a limbo-like state that is largely preoccupied with acquiring and sustaining the essentials of life. The refugee, the political prisoner, the disappeared, the victim of torture, the dispossessed—all have been excluded, to different degrees, from the fraternity of the social sphere, appeal to the safety net of the nation-state and recourse to international law. They have been outlawed, so to speak, placed beyond recourse to law and yet still in a precarious relationship to law itself.[6]

Members of all these groups, including displaced people, can be thought of as experiencing bare life in its modern form.

Bare life also describes the existential state of a person placed in this circumstance. Following Agamben, I will argue that the typifying existential state is that to which many Jews were reduced in the concentration and death camps of Nazi Germany; a person in this condition was called in many camps a *Muselmann*. This state, often described as a living death, closely resembles that of the zombie. The difference being that zombies, living after death, are portrayed as fundamentally threatening to the living, while the *Muselmänner* lived only until their transformation into the dead was complete. The point here is twofold. First, that, excluded from the rights and privileges of the modern state, those displaced people are positioned legally as bare life. Second, in this legal limbo, these people can be treated in a way that enables them to become associated with a condition mythically exemplified in the zombie. The consequence is that not only can the zombie texts of films and other media be read as reproducing this connection, drawing on present-day anxieties to increase the terror produced by these texts, but displaced people are characterized using the same terminology that describes the threat that zombies generate in zombie apocalypse texts.

The Popularity of Zombies

Through the first decade of the twentieth-first century, there was a very significant increase in the cultural presence of zombies. In January 2006, Steven Wells, in an article in the *Guardian*, wrote that "there were zombies everywhere in 2005."[7] That same year, in March, Warren St. John, in the *New York Times*, commented that "in films, books and video games, the undead are once again on the march, elbowing past werewolves, vampires, swamp things and mummies to become the post-millennial ghoul of the moment."[8] What St. John's remark signals is something quite important: that it is not just that there has been an increase in visibility of zombies as a consequence of their appearance in an increased number of texts but that this increase outstrips other conventional horror characters such as werewolves and vampires. Agamben has discussed the werewolf, and I shall return to this creature later.

Here, it is worth noting that vampires have also recently enjoyed a renaissance in popularity. At the end of *Our Vampires, Ourselves*, Nina Auerbach writes that "the reversibility of vampirism in 1980s movies . . . suggests that at the end of the twentieth century, vampirism is wearing down and vampires need a long restorative sleep."[9] That sleep did not last long. In the late 1990s, Angel and Spike appeared in *Buffy the Vampire Slayer*, helping to start the shift to more humanized vampires that could be love objects. Since then, vampires have appeared in the four Twilight books by Stephenie Meyer, the first of which was published in 2005, and the immensely popular film, *Twilight*, made from the books, was released in 2008, with a sequel, *The Twilight Saga: New Moon*, being released the following year. In 2008, *Twilight* was the seventh highest grossing film in the United States.[10] Among other recent texts, vampires also feature in a number of television series. *Moonlight* ran for one season in late 2007 and early 2008. The protagonist was a private investigator who was also a vampire. His love interest was a mortal woman who was a reporter. The show achieved a cult following and was very successful with adults in the eighteen to forty-nine range. Originally broadcast on CBS in the United States, signaling its particular popularity with women, it was rerun on the CW television channel, which its president of entertainment has said is aimed at women in the eighteen to thirty-four demographic.[11] *The Vampire Diaries*, in which a mortal woman becomes romantically entangled with vampires, began in September 2009 on CW. It rapidly won its time slot for a female viewing audience aged up to thirty-four. In these texts, vampires, which, to put it quickly, used to suggest, among other things, forbidden sexual desire, now, in a more liberated time, constitute the love interest.[12] Vampires are also a key character component of HBO cable television network's *True Blood* series, which is based on Charlaine Harris's Southern Vampire Mysteries first published in 2001. In these texts, vampires are either the source of forbidden romance or integrated problematically into everyday society, or both. Vampires, then, have lost their traditional fear factor and are positioned more as a strange Other who have different cultural ways and are sometimes still a threat but one generally manageable. In other words, coming out of an American society dealing with major changes in its racial profile, these vampire texts suggest a racial reading, one in which the dominant society is struggling to come to terms with a rapidly changing racial order. As we shall see, zombies can also be read racially, but this reading interprets them as a racial threat to Western civilization.

There is nothing benign about zombies. In short, as Simon Pegg, the writer of, and actor in, *Shaun of the Dead*, a British zombie film released in 2004, remarks, "as monsters from the id, zombies win out over vampires and werewolves when it comes to the title of Most Potent Metaphorical Monster."[13] It needs to be noted that Pegg has an ahistorical view of these monsters. He writes that

> where their pointy-toothed cousins are all about sex and bestial savagery, the zombie trumps all by personifying our deepest fear: death. Zombies are our destiny writ large. Slow and steady in their approach, weak, clumsy, often absurd, the zombie relentlessly closes in, unstoppable, intractable.[14]

As I have argued, the sex and bestial savagery of vampires have now been tamed into a disturbing and disruptive cultural difference, fear transformed into a romantic frisson, within a cultural pluralist multiculturalism. And the fear of zombies is now not so much about death as it is about those excluded from Western societies who seem to be threatening civilization as we, in the West, know it.

Zombies, then, have become the most important mythic monster at the present time. Peter Dendle, in an astute discussion of the zombie phenomenon, "The Zombie as Barometer of Cultural Anxiety," published in 2007, writes about "the resurgence of zombie movie popularity in the early 2000s."[15] For him, this "has been linked with the events of September 11, 2001."[16] Making a different, but still generalizing, claim to Pegg's, Dendle goes on to argue that

> apocalypticism has always been ingrained into the archetypal psyche of any society defining itself—as all human endeavours must—in the context of history and time. The possibility of wide-scale destruction and devastation which 9-11 brought once again into the communal consciousness found a ready narrative expression in the

zombie apocalypses which over thirty years had honed images of desperation subsistence and amoral survivalism to a fine edge.[17]

Following Dendle, Kyle Bishop makes a similar point: "Although the conventions of the zombie genre remain largely unchanged, the movies' relevance has become all the more clear—a post-9/11 audience cannot help but perceive the characteristics of zombie cinema through the filter of terrorist threats and apocalyptic reality."[18] As we shall see, there is certainly a link between zombies and a terrorist threat that is claimed to be of Islamic origin. And, it can be argued, as both Dendle and Bishop have done, that 9/11 had a considerable impact on the American national imaginary and that this is expressed in the way that Americans make, and read, zombie films.

However, films made outside the United States, and even a recent American zombie film such as Romero's *Land of the Dead*, released in 2005, evidence a quite different anxiety. To understand this, we need to begin with a discussion of what constitutes a zombie. Dendle argues that

> the essence of the "zombie" at the most abstract level is supplanted, stolen, or effaced consciousness; it casts allegorically the appropriation of one person's will by another. It is no coincidence that the creature flourished in the twentieth century, a century whose broad intellectual trends were preoccupied with alienation.[19]

Dendle is here extrapolating from a history that refers back to the zombie as a characteristic of Haitian Vodou. In doing so, he elides the recognition that the zombies of the zombie apocalypse films after Romero's *Night of the Living Dead* are often not created by someone. They do not have will, but they are not in somebody's control. Indeed, this is one of things that makes them so frightening; their existence is entirely alien. We shall see that this is one way that the zombie as terrorist threat functions. That is, while in the American, and indeed Western, imaginary, terrorists are thought to be controlled by some evil master, usually personified as Osama bin Laden, they are also thought to be a mindless threat coming from outside the West, from outside any Western country.

Dendle traces the American popular cultural interest in zombies to the American occupation of Haiti between 1915 and 1934. He writes that

> ghosts and revenants are known world-wide, but few are so consistently associated with economy and labour as the shambling corpse of Haitian vodun, brought back from the dead to toil in the fields and factories by miserly land-owners or by spiteful *houngan* or *bokor* priests. . . . The zombie, a soulless hulk mindlessly working at the bidding of another, thus records a residual communal memory of slavery: of living a life without dignity and meaning, of going through the motions.[20]

Dendle links the rise of American interest in zombies to the Great Depression and the crisis of labor. It is an important point. In post–*Night of the Living Dead* zombie apocalypse films, the link between the zombie and slavery, and by extension the worker in a capitalist economy, has been repressed. As we shall see, in the films where the zombies can be read as displaced people, this connection is reappearing.

Joan Dayan, an anthropologist, has provided this description of the zombie: "Born out of the experience of slavery and the sea passage from Africa to the New World, the zombi tells the story of colonization: the reduction of human into thing for the ends of capital. For the Haitian no fate is to be more feared."[21] Dayan goes on to explain that, in the present day,

> in a contemporary Caribbean of development American style, the zombi phenomenon obviously goes beyond the machinations of the local boco. As Depestre puts it, "This fantastic process of reification and assimilation means the total loss of my identity, the psychological annihilation of my being, my zombification." And Laënnec Hurbon explains how the zombi stories produce and capitalize on an internalization of slavery and passivity, making the victims of an oppressive social system the cause: "The phantasm of the zombie . . . does nothing but attest to the fulfillment of a system that moves the victim to internalize his condition."[22]

Dayan's purpose is to explain how, in the present Haitian context, the zombie functions as an explanation for the destruction of Haitian culture by American colonialism disguised as development. The mindless zombie, laboring for another, becomes a way of understanding the impact of American capital on Haiti and the Caribbean more generally.

Jean Comaroff and John Comaroff make a similar point about the rise in zombie stories in South Africa. They write that

> there can be no denying the latter-day preoccupation with zombies in rural South Africa. Their existence, far from being the subject of elusive tales from the backwoods, of fantastic fables from the *veld*, is widely taken for granted. As a simple matter of fact. In recent times, respectable local newspapers have carried banner headlines like "Zombie Back from the Dead" illustrating their stories with conventional, high-realist photographs.[23]

The Comaroffs argue that the zombie narrative is a useful way for people who do not understand the complexities of international, neoliberal capitalism to account for how some people seemingly get rich very quickly without doing any visible work: they create zombies who work for them and do not have to be paid. Looking over the history of zombies in Africa, the Comaroffs write that "zombies themselves seem to be born, at least in the first instance, of colonial encounters, of the precipitous engagement of local worlds with imperial economies that seek to exert control over the essential means of producing value, means like land and labor, space and time."[24] In other words, at a conceptual level, zombies are a local response of the colonized to the impact of colonial capitalism, a way of understanding how those capitalist practices produce wealth for some and immiseration for others.

From *Pride and Prejudice* to *Pride and Prejudice and Zombies*

At this point we can return to the Caribbean. Two years before Romero's *Night of the Living Dead* revisioned the zombie trope, Jean Rhys published a book in England which is now written about as a key postcolonial novel. *Wide Sargasso Sea* is a kind of answer text, what Bill Ashcroft, Gareth Griffiths, and Helen Tiffin describe as a text that writes back to the book that inspired it, illuminating the colonizing assumptions that underpin the earlier novel.[25] In this case that novel is Charlotte Brontë's *Jane Eyre*. Published in 1847, thirty-four years after *Pride and Prejudice*, to which we shall shortly turn, *Jane Eyre* tells the story of a young woman's rise from a straitened childhood eventually to marry Edward Rochester, the owner of Thornfield Hall. What Jane does not know until the day she is supposed to marry Rochester is that he is already married. He keeps his first wife, whom he regards as mad, locked in the attic under the ministrations of Grace Poole. This wife is Bertha Mason, the Creole woman from Jamaica whose dowry of thirty thousand pounds is the source of Rochester's wealth. Unable to marry, Jane refuses to cohabit with Rochester and leaves. Later, Bertha escapes her prison and sets fire to the Hall, committing suicide by jumping from the roof. Rochester loses his sight and his left hand in trying to save her. Finally, though, Jane and Rochester are able to marry.

What Rhys divined was that behind this romance lay the story of an abused first wife, married for her colonial wealth and then discarded. *Wide Sargasso Sea* tells Bertha's story. In this novel, we find that Bertha was originally named Antoinette and that it is Rochester who renames her. Rhys's narrative highlights the power imbalance between the Caribbean colonies and Britain while also showing how, at the time of the novel, much of the wealth on which Britain's gentry depended came from these colonies, in which slavery had only been abolished in 1834 and where many remained slaves for a further six years. In a discussion of the novel, Thomas Loe has argued that the zombie is "an extremely potent central image associated with Antoinette."[26] One of its purposes would seem to be to give an exotic quality to the Caribbean as compared with the mundane realism of Rochester's England. However, the zombie motif does other work. Loe argues that Antoinette's mother is made into a zombie, that Antoinette tries to zombify Rochester in the hope of keeping his love, and that, most important of all for my purpose here, Rochester attempts to turn Antoinette into a zombie. For Loe, "the figure of the zombie provides Rhys with an astonishingly appropriate metaphor for dramatizing her vision of the powerless and displaced woman against [what Judith Gardiner calls] the 'unified ideology' of 'capitalism, colonialism, and patriarchal domination.'"[27] Rochester tries to transform Antoinette as he moves her to England, attempting to remake her as a woman of the gentry, even going so far as to change her name from the French-influenced Antoinette to the solidly English Bertha. He does not succeed. Instead, Antoinette becomes "mad," a victim of a failed zombification, displaced from her Jamaican home to an England she neither likes nor understands, caught between two cultures.

On a blog called *BoingBoing*, in response to a review of *Pride and Prejudice and Zombies*, nanuq comments, "Any classic book could be improved with a few zombies around. Charles Dickens seems a natural for that (Zombie versions of *A Tale of Two*

Cities or *Oliver Twist* practically write themselves). *Jane Eyre* and *Wuthering Heights* would be great too (Catherine coming back as a zombie! Mr Rochester keeping his zombie wife locked in the attic!).["28] nanuq does not realize that Rochester's wife has already been made into a zombie by Rochester, a consequence of Rochester's wanting to live off the wealth acquired by Antoinette's family's colonial Jamaican plantation. What is unknown in *Jane Eyre*, and remains obscure in *Wide Sargasso Sea*, is whether Bertha/Antoinette has a black ancestor. The implication, though, is that she has. Nevertheless, in metaphor, Antoinette's journey to England, her displacement, reveals the slave past in terms of a zombie present.

We can now turn to *Pride and Prejudice and Zombies*. Austen's *Pride and Prejudice* remains her most popular book. It is a romance that is also a comedy of manners about the early-nineteenth-century English landed gentry, and its setting is restricted to England. Stimulated by the work of Edward Said, there has been some debate over Austen's awareness of the slavery in the colonial Caribbean, the plantations of which provided some of the wealth which made the life of the English gentry possible. In 1772, Lord Mansfield's judgment in the case of a recaptured runaway slave owned by a man from Boston visiting England, known after the slave's name as the *Somersett* case, established the basis for ending slavery in England. However, as I have already mentioned, slavery in the British colonies continued until the Emancipation Act came into force in 1834. Austen published *Pride and Prejudice* in 1813 and *Mansfield Park* in 1814.

In *Mansfield Park*, the wealth that sustains Sir Thomas Bertram and his family at the home that bears the name of the man who ended slavery in England derives from Sir Thomas's plantation in Antigua. There are problems on the plantation that require Sir Thomas's presence. Commenting on the narrative, Said remarks, "Whatever was wrong there—and the internal evidence garnered by Warren Roberts suggests that economic depression, slavery, and competition with France were at issue—Sir Thomas was able to fix thereby maintaining his control over his colonial domain."[29] I do not want to enter the debate whether Austen approved of slavery—though it seems to me that the evidence points to her disapproval of it.[30] Said explains that "the Bertrams could not have been possible without the slave trade, sugar, and the colonial planter class; as a social type Sir Thomas would have been familiar to eighteenth- and early nineteenth-century readers who knew the powerful influence of this class through politics, plays, . . . and many other public activities (large houses, famous parties and social rituals, well-known commercial enterprises, celebrated marriages)."[31] Robin Blackburn, in his history of British colonial slavery, argues that the wealth derived from New World slavery formed the necessary basis for the Industrial Revolution.[32]

Austen's indication of the presence of slavery in the colonies, and its importance, occurs in the novel following *Pride and Prejudice*. As Suvendrini Perera remarks, "this growing visibility of the navy in *Mansfield Park* supplements the increasing presence of empire at the edges of Austen's texts; progressively, her '3 or 4 Families in a Country Village' . . . come to encompass and incorporate more extensive portions of the globe."[33] Only a decade earlier, in 1804, the slaves of Haiti had completed a successful rebellion

against the French, and as Perera suggests, "the terrifying possibility of a Haiti-style rebellion in the English slave colonies had instantly become a national obsession."[34]

What, then, are we to make of the zombies that increasingly threaten the social
life of the gentry in *Pride and Prejudice and Zombies*? As is usual in zombie apocalypse
texts, we are not told whence they came. In this text, Elizabeth Bennett and her sisters
are trained in martial arts so that they can act as vigilantes, killing zombies. They have
visited China, where they learned kung fu from Shaolin monks. What we do know
is that zombies have been roaming the English countryside for a generation or more.
We know that London has been walled and that the army moves from area to area of
England trying to keep the zombies under control. We know also that zombies are
comparable to "savages" because Mr. Darcy remarks to Sir William Lucas that "every
savage can dance. Why, I imagine that even zombies could do it with some degree of
success."[35] Zombies, then, have some similarity with the black slaves, who were thought
of as savages, who work the colonial Caribbean plantations that supply the wealth that
supports the lifestyle of the gentry.

Zombies do not appear to infest anywhere but England—or possibly Britain. With
the connection between slavery and zombies that we have already established, we can
now understand the zombie threat as a return of the repressed. Whether we read the
text literally in terms of a slave revolt that has spread to England or metaphorically as
an expression of the vengeance of the enslaved Africans on which the gentry's wealth
was built, what we have is a movement of the displaced from the Caribbean colonies
to England. It is a zombie apocalypse set back in the early nineteenth century that can
be read as making clear the connections between English wealth and colonial slavery,
which, in this early novel at least, Austen had elided.

Zombies, Bare Life, and Muslims

Bringing this zombie apocalypse back to the present, we can turn again to Comaroff
and Comaroff. They write that

> the fear of being reduced to ghost labor, of being abducted to feed the fortunes of a
> depraved stranger, occurs alongside another kind of specter: a growing mass, a shad-
> owy alien-nation, of immigrant black workers from elsewhere on the continent. Like
> zombies, they are nightmare citizens, their rootlessness threatening to siphon off the
> remaining, rapidly diminishing prosperity of the indigenous population.[36]

The Comaroffs are describing how poor, black South Africans experience the displaced
people arriving in South Africa through its porous land border. One of the established
themes of zombie apocalypse films is the siege—the scene where the humans seek sanctuary somewhere and find themselves surrounded and besieged by increasing numbers
of zombies striving to get in.

At this point, we shall turn to Romero's first film, the film that transformed the
zombie genre, *Night of the Living Dead*. The film offers little more than the siege theme.
Seven people find themselves trapped in a house and attempt to protect themselves from

zombie attack as gradually each, except one, is killed by the zombies, or in the case of the young daughter, becomes a zombie, eating her father and killing her mother. What, ultimately, was so shocking about this film was its nihilism. The man who survives the zombie attack is himself killed in the mistaken belief that he is a zombie. The first thing to know about this low-budget, black-and-white film is that Romero never envisaged it as a zombie film. He thought of the creatures as ghouls. As he has said, "I never called them zombies, I called them 'flesheaters' or 'ghouls'—back then, zombies were those boys in the Caribbean who were doing wetwork for Lugosi—I never thought of them as zombies."[37] Ghouls are demons that entered Western popular culture from the Arab world in the nineteenth century. They are supposed to haunt graveyards and feed on the flesh of corpses. Indeed, Romero's original title for the film was *Night of the Flesh Eaters*. The title was changed by someone at the Walter Reade Organization, the film's distributors, because of objections by the connections of a film called *The Flesh Eaters*, released in 1964. Here, it is necessary to realize how the change of name, which was not Romero's doing, contributed to the change in the type of creature that audiences thought was being depicted. When the film was released, these were still understood to be ghouls. Roger Ebert, for example, in a review published in *Reader's Digest* in January 1969, in which he discussed his shock at the horrifying nature of the film, wrote about the creatures as ghouls.[38]

It is unclear when the creatures became zombies, but probably around the end of the 1970s. When Romero's sequel, *Dawn of the Dead*, was released in the United States in 1978, he was still thinking of the creatures as ghouls. When the film was released in Italy, it was called *Zombi*, and Lucio Fulci's notorious *Zombi 2* was given that title as if it was somehow related to the Romero film. In the United States, when it was released in 1980, Fulci's film was titled *Zombie*. At the same time, *Variety*, in a negative review of *Dawn of the Dead* published in January 1979 that rivaled the paper's earlier review of *Night of the Living Dead*, described the creatures as "carnivorous corpses." In many European countries, such as Italy, Greece, West Germany, and France, the film carried a title associating it with zombies. What seems to have justified the changed perception of Romero's creatures is that they were resurrected corpses.

The shift from ghouls to zombies brought a different set of connotations into play. Romero's father was a Cuban migrant. His mother was from Lithuania. Romero tells this story about his father, who always denied he was Cuban and claimed his family was from Spain: "I grew up in New York with a Spanish dad right in the days of West Side Story, where you know the Puerto Rican gangs and shit? My dad telling me Puerto Ricans are shit. I have a Latino dad who's telling me that Puerto Ricans are shit (laughs). I mean this is a very confusing situation."[39] Commenting on this autobiography, Cindy Casares writes, "Perhaps this confusion is what led Romero to express his angst through monsters."[40] Seemingly glossing Romero, she goes on: "He got the idea for a low-budget horror film with an apocalyptic theme about the invasion of a new kind of monster—a monster that was tearing the world as we knew it apart because the audience didn't know who was one and who wasn't."[41] Could these monsters be migrants transforming America's racial structure? Eric Hamako notes that "George Romero has raised—and critiqued—the idea of Latino immigration and zombies-as-Latinos, in at least two of his films."[42] Of course, the audience could tell who was a monster and who was not. However, the white men hunting down the zombies in *Night of the Living Dead* seem unable to. The man who is mistaken for a zombie and shot dead is African American. Reading this as a statement about American race relations can distract from reading the zombies as nonwhite migrants. These invading monsters were even more threatening than a black American who had taken charge and successfully defended the besieged house; these were mindless, living dead.

To understand what is going on here, we need to think about Giorgio Agamben's idea of bare life. Bare life is key to understanding the functioning of the modern state. Indeed, the presence of bare life within the state is foundational to its form. Agamben begins by distinguishing two complementary ways of thinking about life as they are used by Aristotle. These are *zoē* and *bios*. *Zoē* is a term that unites species-being and embodiment. *Bios* can be translated as "form of life." It can be used to think about how *zoē* is lived. Agamben writes that "in the classical world . . . simple natural life is excluded from the *polis* in the strict sense and remains confined—as merely reproductive life—to the sphere of the *oikos*, 'home.'"[43] "Simple natural life" is a translation of *zoē*. This is not bare life. Bare life is the constituting feature of political life. As Agamben describes it, *"no simple natural life, but life exposed to death (bare life or sacred life) is the originary political element."*[44] Sacred life is a reference to a particular Roman legal idea. Agamben uses it as a way of defining not only bare life but also sovereignty: *"The sovereign sphere is the sphere in which it is permitted to kill without committing homicide and without celebrating a sacrifice, and sacred life—that is, life that may be killed but not sacrificed—is the life that has been captured in this sphere."*[45] Bare life is a description of life in a political context.

If *zoē* is simple natural life, bare life is what gives meaning to sovereignty. However, this life is revealed in its exclusion from premodern political life: "The sovereign and *homo sacer* are joined in the figure of an action that, excepting itself from both human and divine law, from both *nomos* and *physis*, nevertheless delimits what is, in a certain sense, the first properly political space of the West distinct from both the religious and the profane sphere, from both the natural order and the regular judicial order."[46] *Homo sacer*, and its equivalents in other premodern political orders, is the person who does not have the protection of the sovereign. It is not the state that has the right to kill this person reduced to bare life but anybody. This person exists on the borderline of the *polis*, both included and excluded—their inclusion making their exclusion possible. Death marks the limit of sovereignty.

Agamben goes on to make another point that will be important later in my argument: "Contrary to our modern habit of representing the political realm in terms of citizens' rights, free will, and social contracts, from the point of view of sovereignty *only bare life is authentically political*."[47] Here, Agamben is extending the idea of bare life into the practice of the modern state. But more of this shortly.

Agamben illustrates his point that bare life exists on the margin of the premodern state with a discussion of the werewolf. He explains: "Germanic and Anglo-Saxon sources underline the bandit's liminal status by defining him as a wolf-man."[48] The bandit was the medieval equivalent of *homo sacer*. Agamben continues:

What had to remain in the collective unconscious as a monstrous hybrid of human and animal, divided between the forest and the city—the werewolf—is, therefore, in its origin the figure of the man who has been banned from the city. That such a man is defined as a wolf . . . is decisive here. The life of the bandit, like that of the sacred man, is not a piece of animal nature without any relation to the city. It is, rather, a threshold of indistinction and of passage between animal and man, *physis* and *nomos*, exclusion and inclusion: the life of the bandit is the life of *loup garou*, the werewolf, who is precisely *neither man nor beast*, and who dwells paradoxically within both while belonging to neither.[49]

Agamben is implicitly reworking Claude Lévi-Strauss's idea that myths ultimately mediate between nature and culture. Here, the werewolf was a way that members of premodern political orders could understand the relationship between existence in a political order and the natural world, that is, the place of bare life. We should also note, and it is something to which we shall return, that being excluded from the *polis* diminishes a person's humanity. They exist between human and animal. The werewolf, like the bandit, is essentially predatory, threatening the existence of the *polis* while living off of it. It both requires the *polis* but threatens its destruction. In the modern world, the position of bare life changed fundamentally. In doing so, the power of the werewolf myth dissipated. What I want to suggest is that, equating with the werewolf in the premodern world, the zombie has become the emblematic figure for bare life in the modern world.

Agamben argues that "the entry of *zoē* into the sphere of the *polis*—the politicization of bare life as such—constitutes the decisive event of modernity and signals a radical transformation of the political-philosophical categories of classical thought."[50] As we have seen, *zoē* is not bare life, but its presence within the arena of the political transforms it into bare life. Elsewhere, in *Remnants of Auschwitz*, and referring to Michel Foucault's work, Agamben provides a more extensive insight into this crucial political shift:

In its traditional form, which is that of territorial sovereignty, power defines itself essentially as the right over life and death; it concerns life only indirectly, as the abstention of the right to kill. This is why Foucault characterizes sovereignty through the formula *to make die and to let live*. When, starting with the seventeenth century and the birth of the science of police, care for the life and health of subjects began to occupy an increasing place in the mechanisms and calculations of states, sovereign power is progressively transformed into what Foucault calls "biopower."[51]

At this point, bare life, which previously existed on the margin of political orders, now begins its move to becoming the basis of political practice; to rephrase Agamben, "in modernity life is more and more clearly placed at the center of State politics (which now becomes in Foucault's term, biopolitics), . . . in our age all citizens can be said, in a specific but extremely real sense, to appear virtually as *homines sacri*."[52] Agamben does not mean that anybody is allowed to kill the citizen of such a state. Rather, the lives of everybody within the state are governed by the power of the sovereign; everybody exists not as potentially bare life but as bare life with a reprieve.

The consequence is itself horrifying: "It is almost as if, starting from a certain point, every decisive political event were double-sided: the spaces, the liberties and the rights won by individuals in their conflicts with central powers always simultaneously prepared a tacit but increasing inscription of individuals' lives within the state order, thus offering a new and more dreadful foundation for the very sovereign power from which they wanted to liberate themselves."[53] Bare life has become increasingly cloaked with the panoply of citizenship and rights, but this is simply a disguise for what is really at stake in modern politics, bare life itself.

We now need to make a brief detour. Gil Anidjar has written a history of the development of the discursive construction of Muslims in the modern West. His interest is in how the Muslim world has come to be understood in the political terms of despotism and total subjection. He explains that it was Montesquieu, following Jean Bodin, who first introduced the idea of despotism as a political form. Anidjar details this:

> The invention of despotism . . . involves the translation of a domestic term into a political one—the *despotes* was the head of the household, *not* a political figure. Yet this inventive gesture was structurally linked to another no less potent, if perhaps less visible invention: the "apathy" and the "faithful resignation" of the despot's subjects. What emerged at this momentous historical point in the writings of Montesquieu and others was also the invention of absolute subjection, its rapid and unceasing translation, . . . religion and politics as the conflictual union of incomparables.[54]

Anidjar quotes from Montesquieu's *De l'esprit des lois,* published late in his life in 1748: "'The flood tide of Mahommedans brought despotism with it,' and despotic government 'is most agreeable' to the Mahommedan religion."[55] Glossing Montesquieu, Anidjar writes that "such subjection, like blind fatalism, excludes reason and excludes one from reason."[56] Anidjar notes that Montesquieu describes despotism, and its associated absolute subjection, as an absurdity. We might think it not so much an absurdity as a fantastic description of the dark side of the modern politics that Agamben outlines. Despotism and mindless submission represent the possibility of modern politics once bare life has been made its foundation. Montesquieu, and later thinkers from Kant to Hegel and onward, image this awful phantasm as the political life of the Orientalized Other, the Muslims.

Anidjar takes one more step. His interest is in how a certain type in the concentration and death camps of Nazi Germany came to be called *Muselmänner,* Jews who become identified as Muslims. The immediate question is why these victims of the camps were named Muslims. In an insightful and complex discussion that does not concern us here, Anidjar suggests that, "as figures of absolute subjection, the Muslims can no doubt represent a degree zero of power, the sheer absence of a political displaced by a (negative) theology."[57] The Jews in the camps who had lost their ability to think, lost their will, appeared like the fantastic absurdity of Muslims under a despotic religiopolitical regime.

Muselmänner and Zombies

We now need to consider these Muslims, *Muselmänner*. The *locus classicus* for the *Muselmann* is Primo Levi's account in his first book, called in its original Italian *Se questo è un uomo* and published in England as *If This Is a Man* and in the United States as *Survival in Auschwitz*:

> To sink is the easiest of matters; it is enough to carry out all the orders one receives, to eat only the ration, to observe the discipline of the work and the camp. Experience showed that only exceptionally could one survive more than three months in this way. All the mussulmans who finished in the gas chambers have the same story, or more exactly, have no story; they followed the slope down to the bottom, like streams that run down to the sea. On their entry into the camp, through basic incapacity, or by misfortune, or through some banal accident, they are overcome before they can adapt themselves; they are beaten by time, they do not begin to learn German, to disentangle the infernal knot of laws and prohibitions until their body is already in decay, and nothing can save them from selections or from death by exhaustion. Their life is short but their number is endless; they, the Muselmänner, the drowned, form the backbone of the camp, an anonymous mass, continually renewed and always identical, of non-men who march and labor in silence, the divine spark dead within them, already too empty to really suffer. One hesitates to call them living: one hesitates to call their death death, in the face of which they have no fear, as they are too tired to understand.[58]

We can add to this description from an account published by Agamben in *Remnants of Auschwitz*:

> The other inmates avoided *Muselmänner*. There could be no common subject of conversation between them, since *Muselmänner* only fantasized and spoke about food. . . . I can still see them returning back from work in lines of five. The first line of five would march according to the rhythm of the orchestra, but the next line would already be incapable of keeping up with them. The five behind them would lean against each other; and in the last lines the four strongest would carry the weakest one by his arms and legs, since he was dying.[59]

These descriptions of *Muselmänner* make them appear remarkably similar to the creatures invented by Romero, the ones that, by the end of the 1970s, were beginning to be called zombies. I do not want to suggest that Romero had read Levi. Rather, Romero was tapping in to an anxiety about those excluded from the protection of the modern state, those reduced to bare life.

Like Romero's creatures, *Muselmänner* have no will; they stagger along; they are interested in only one thing, food; and they do not speak—the zombie attribute is a groan. Here we can think about Elaine Scarry's comment on the experience of severe pain: "Physical pain does not simply resist language but actively destroys it, bringing about an immediate reversion to a state anterior to language, to the sounds and cries a human being makes before language is learnt."[60] The zombie is a creature without language, which Western thought has considered a founding characteristic of human society. The zombie groan can be read as the expression of the pain of bare life, of the living dead.

It is instructive that, when the title of Romero's film was changed, the new title included the words "living dead." Since then, this has become the characteristic description of zombies. It is also a term often used to describe the *Muselmänner*. Aldo Carpi may have been the first person actually to have applied the term "living dead" to the *Muselmänner* in his *Diario di Gusen*, the diary he kept of his time in that concentration camp, first published in 1971. In the translation given in *Remnants of Auschwitz*, "I remember that while we were going down the stairs leading to the baths, they had us accompanied by a group of *Muselmänner*, as we later called them—mummy-men, the living dead."[61] In the title of Romero's film, "living dead" is an inspired shorthand for Levi's: "One hesitates to call them living: one hesitates to call their death death." The translation, *Survival in Auschwitz*, had been published in the United States in 1961. However, JoAnn Cannon tells us that "it seems hardly to have been noticed when it first appeared" but that Holocaust literature "began to be read as a sub-genre in the mid-sixties."[62] It is possible that someone in the Walter Reade Organization made the connection. But perhaps not. By the late 1960s, there was a growing awareness of what was beginning to be termed the Holocaust in the United States. The scene toward the end of *Night of the Living Dead* where we watch on television as the sheriff and his men hunt down and destroy zombies, and kill the African American survivor, can be read in the context of the stories of the Nazi *Einsatzgruppen*, the SS death squads whose role was to search out and murder Jews, gypsies, and others who were unwanted in the conquered territories. However, the scene also has a general resonance with those reduced to bare life, including displaced people, people denied the protection of the state.

We must not forget the literal meaning of the *Muselmannn*, that is, the Muslim. I have discussed the background to the use of the term in the camps, the association of Muslims with total, mindless submission. This link also works the other way around. In the post-9/11 American fear of Islamic terrorists, Muslims can get figured as zombies. Referencing the historical association of Muslims with submission, and with the *Muselmannn*, on the Web, buttub wonders about the increase in zombie films in the 2000s, telling us that "the theory that most interests me, and that strikes me as likely most responsible for zombie mania, is that our culture's zombie fascination stems from widespread fear of Muslim terrorists."[63] Hamako makes the same point:

> [The] Orientalist characterization of Muslims is not different . . . from the characterization of modern zombies. The modern zombie expresses Orientalist fears of Violent "Islamic" (and perhaps soon, "Confucian") opposition to modernity and secularism.[64]

Where Dendle and Bishop focus on the apocalypse aspect of the zombie apocalypse motif, buttub and Hamako identify the continuity with the discursive construction of the Muslim. The emphasis on apocalypse does not account for why the apocalyptic vehicle should be zombies. The Orientalist connection of zombies with Muslims does. The zombie apocalypse, then, becomes a meaningful way to represent the so-called Islamic terrorist threat to the United States.

Awful as the *Muselmänner* state is, it is by no means unique. Alexander Esquemelin was a Dutchman who was indentured with the French West Indies Company and shipped to Tortuga, an island off the coast of Haiti, in the seventeenth century. He wrote a book called *Bucaniers of America*:

> Esquemelin deplores the condition of the many men kidnapped in Europe as "servants" and sold as slaves. These bonded men, he asserts, are used worse than African slaves; for their masters, with only three years to get their money's worth, often extracted that value at the price of the worker's life. Pressed beyond the limits of human endurance, they literally take leave of their senses: "These miserable kidnap'd people, are frequently subject to a certain disease, which in those parts, is called *Coma*; being a total privation of the senses. And this distemper is judged to proceed from their hard usage." Experienced as a coma in the days when Haiti was called Hispaniola, this state of death-in-life induced by the [quoting Joan Dayan] "reduction of human into thing for the ends of capital" is now called zombification. The zombie, like the comatose indentured servant, is a being whose identity and will are slaughtered in service to the exactions of unfree labor.[65]

We find here a more direct connection between the condition of the *Muselmannn* removed from the protection of the state and, as bare life, reduced to the barest condition of the experience of life, and the classical ideas of zombies.

Agamben reinforces the *Muselmann*'s threshold state. He writes, "That one cannot truly speak of 'living beings' is confirmed by all witnesses. Améry and Bettelheim define them as 'walking corpses.'"[66] Agamben provides this reading:

> It is . . . possible to understand the decisive function of the camps in the system of Nazi biopolitics. They are not merely the places of death and extermination; they are also, and above all, the site of the production of the *Muselmannn*, the final biopolitical substance to be isolated in the biological continuum. Beyond the *Muselmannn* lies only the gas chamber.[67]

We can now understand what is so terrifying about the zombie. It is not that the zombie reminds us of our own forthcoming demise but that the zombie is the mythic expression of bare life in the modern world. The zombie apocalypse is the fantastic representation of the modern state being overwhelmed by the bare life that underpins its existence—the bare life that is lived by those people excluded from the privileges of citizenship and rights. This includes those displaced people who, for many reasons, seek entry to Western states. In the neoliberal world, where inclusion has been supplanted by exclusion, or, in Agamben's terms, where the state of exception is becoming the norm, those attempting to gain entry to the state are part of a continuity with those within the state—all are treated as bare life to a greater or lesser extent; all have the possibility of being reduced to the condition of *Muselmänner*.

Zombies and the Displaced

Given what I have already said about Romero and *Night of the Living Dead*, it is not surprising to find that, in his fourth zombie film, *Land of the Dead*, released in 2005, the parallel between the zombie siege of Pittsburgh and the fear over illegal entry to the United States across the Mexican border is easily made:

> To ensure the status quo, Dennis Hopper's Kaufman, the self-appointed leader of Pittsburgh, constructs the world's most extreme border security—blown up and barricaded bridges make the rivers impassible, and electric fences and armed guards protect the area from any intrusion; in an extreme example of xenophobia, soldiers shoot any invaders on sight. These forms of immigration control have become even more jarringly familiar with recent debates about erecting a fence between the United States and Mexico and the redeployment of National Guard troops to guard the United States' southern border during George W. Bush's presidency.[68]

Here, the zombies can with facility be read as illegal migrants threatening traditional American society. With this reading, the zombie acquires again its earlier reference—a worker who either already is, or is able to be worked into, a state of coma. Indeed, the worker with no protection can become a slave.

In zombie films made outside the United States, this reading is more available. In *Shaun of the Dead*, with the sudden transformation of people into zombies, Shaun and his white friends make for their local pub, the Winchester, as the most defensible place he can think of. In British films, the pub is historically the place of community, as it is, for example, in *Passport to Pimlico* (dir. Henry Cornelius, 1949). By extension, in *Shaun of the Dead*, the pub is a synecdoche for a white England under siege from a range of illegal immigrants, asylum seekers, and so forth, all trying to breach the pub's defenses. Finally, the British army comes to the rescue of Shaun and his friends, killing off the besieging zombies.

Pegg, in his *Guardian* article from which I have already quoted, comments on his dislike of Charlie Booker's use of "fast" zombies, that is, zombies that walk and run, in his television series *Dead Set*.[69] In what I presume is supposed to be read as a jokey riposte, Booker responds, "Simon: your outright rejection of running zombies leaves you exposed, in a very real and damning sense, as a terrible racist."[70] If zombies stand for those displaced people attempting to enter Britain, then they are, indeed, mostly nonwhite. The immiseration of the displaced people at the border is expressed in the bare life that is represented in the zombies. The racialized difference of those people is metaphorized in the zombies' difference from humans.

With this in mind, we should not be surprised that, in a voice-over at the end of *Shaun of the Dead* that tells us what happens after the zombie threat has been quelled, we are told that the few remaining zombies are used as game show participants and domestics. Domestic work is characteristic labor for illegal immigrants across the West. *Shaun of the Dead* can be read analogically where *Children of Men* presents a literal image of Britain falling to the pressure of displaced people entering the country.

In *Fido* (dir. Andrew Currie, 2006), a Canadian zombie film, zombies are fitted with a specially invented collar that renders them harmless to humans.[71] They can then be used for menial work, and any household that does not have at least one zombie domestic is considered to be socially embarrassing. *Fido* goes even further in the development of the zombie–displaced people connection. Set in a 1950s America after the Zombie Wars, towns are fenced off from the Wild Zone where the zombies without collars still prowl, attempting to enter the areas where humans live. In an information film that we see at the beginning, made by ZomCom, the company that makes the zombie collars, we are told in rhetoric that echoes the anxieties about border security that stretches from illegal immigrants to terrorists that the advent of the zombies meant that "we were forced to defend our homeland . . . mankind pitted against legions of the undead." ZomCom also "built security systems like the perimeter fence that encloses our towns in a wall of protective steel." The film's title comes from the name Timmy, the Robinsons' young son, gives the zombie his mother acquires for their home. It is, of course, a name that is typically given to a dog, though nobody in the film acknowledges this. When Timmy plays baseball with Fido, he acts toward him in the way that black servants were historically treated, telling him to get the ball: "Go fetch it, boy." These zombies are racially different and, indeed, not human. In these films, but especially in *Fido*, the zombie as bare life is linked with the zombie as unenfranchised worker.

An Australian low-budget film called *Undead* is perhaps one of the stranger recent additions to the zombie genre.[72] Made over a number of years by the Spierig brothers, Michael and Peter, it was released in 2003. It includes both zombies and an alien visitation from space. A small town in Queensland is the focus of a zombie outbreak caused by something raining down from outer space. Marion is a survivalist who has been affected by this development before, when fish he was catching turned into zombies. He is convinced that the aliens are a part of the zombie threat. When asked by Sallyanne, "Have you ever seen anything like this before?" he answers, "I have. It's an invasion. The end of life as we know it." The police are shown to be incompetent and unable to understand what to do in the new circumstances. Marion takes charge of protecting the small group of people who have escaped being transformed into zombies. He is a characteristic figure in recent Australian film. Similar to Mick Taylor, the kangaroo shooter and serial killer in *Wolf Creek* (dir. Greg McLean, 2005),[73] and the unnamed kangaroo shooter in *Lucky Miles* (dir. Michael James Rowland, 2007),[74] who both appear to be patrolling Australia's border, Marion attempts to protect the village from what he thinks are the depredations of the aliens. By the film's end, it turns out that the aliens are actually trying to stop the zombie plague and return everybody to being human. Thinking they have succeeded, they leave. Unfortunately, one of the townsfolk, who has been bitten by a zombie, escapes and infects the rest of Australia. This time the aliens do not return.

This somewhat confusing combination of zombie apocalypse and sci-fi film can make sense in the context of the ramping up of the Australian population's anxieties about asylum seekers by the government of John Howard in the early 2000s. In 2001, the government refused entry to shipwrecked asylum seekers picked up by the MV *Tampa*, started the so-called Pacific Solution where asylum seekers were sent to detention camps in other countries in the Pacific region, and changed Australia's migration zone to exclude the Australian islands around the north of the country. Also in 2001, shortly before a federal election, the government promoted the idea that asylum seekers on a boat had thrown their children overboard. The consequence of these and other acts by the government were that the general population became increasingly concerned about the threat posed by asylum seekers and voted the government back into power.

With this history, we are now better able to read *Undead*. Here, again, the zombie threat is a translation of the fear generated by, in this Australian case, specifically asylum seekers attempting to find a home in Australia. Only here, it seems, nothing can stop them, certainly not the police or even the local survivalist, except aliens. We now need to think about these aliens. They emit light, they wear what look like cassocks with cowls, and, as they cure people of zombification, those people are taken into the clouds until the aliens have eradicated the zombie scourge. The Christian connotations are spelled out by Rene, near the end of the film, when she is trying to convince Marion that he has been wrong about the intentions of the aliens. She says, "Aliens are the saviors. It's not us." It seems that "we" are simply not powerful enough to save Australia from the zombies. At one point in the film, when Rene is shooting down zombies in the town's general store, she has the Australian flag behind her. We need God, or some Christian force allied to God, to save us. When that is no longer available, Australia is overrun.

Rhetoric

Fido can make such a clear analogy between displaced people and zombies because the same rhetoric is used for each. Zombies provide a monster for our time because they express our anxieties over the relationship between bare life and the modern state. The displaced people attempting to enter the countries of the West are, from the point of view of the members of those countries, bare life. They have no protection from any state. This underlying similitude enables the same metaphors to be used for both zombies and displaced people. Where zombies appear as a remorseless threat laying siege to wherever humans manage to collect to defend themselves, displaced people are constructed in the same way, as a threat at the border of the state. In an article on the way Austrian newspapers write about asylum seekers, Elisabeth El Refaie describes how "Kurdish refugees are quite regularly represented as an 'army' on the point of 'invading' Europe, and their arrival is often referred to as an *Ansturm* [onslaught] or *Invasion* [invasion]."[75] She quotes from a newspaper article that writes of "new hordes of applicants for asylum."[76] While an onslaught or invasion might conjure up an image of an organized, rational army, "horde" implies a disorganized, irrational mass. El Refaie explains that "in other articles, the 'war' metaphor is also evoked by verbs, which describe the refugees as 'forcing their way' [*drängen*] over the border into Europe, of 'invading' [*eindringen*] Germany, and of 'storming' [*stürmen*] Fortress Europe."[77] All these metaphors suggest that Europe is under siege from a mindless throng.

In describing the language used in Australia, Sharon Pickering lists some of the terms she found in the *Brisbane Courier Mail* and the *Sydney Morning Herald* between 1997 and 1999 to describe the threat posed by asylum seekers: "we are soon to be 'awash,' 'swamped,' 'weathering the influx,' of 'waves,' 'latest waves,' 'more waves,' 'tides,' 'floods,' 'migratory flood,' 'mass exodus' of 'aliens,' 'queue jumpers,' 'illegal immigrants.'"[78] Terms like "wave" and "flood" use the water reference to conjure up some overwhelming and amorphous force. They are dehumanizing expressions that identify the asylum seekers as a mass rather than as individuals. These people are "aliens," constructed, as Pickering points out, in a system of binary logic "which routinely renders one normal and the other strange/other."[79] Thinking of the zombie as bare life, this is the binary Other of the humanizing effect of membership of the *polis*.

As in zombie films, Pickering shows that it is the human members of the Australian state who are the ones under siege, their civilized existence always at threat from the zombified bare life attempting to enter the protected space. Pickering writes that

> in the case of asylum seekers, the boundaries [between "us" and "them"] are easily identified by the discrete nation state—not only fixed national and geographic boundaries in the case of Australia but also those of race. In "record arrest," "swoop," "incident," "criminal gangs" and "illegal run," criminal justice discourse becomes interwoven with that of war: "incursion," "sustained assault on Australian shores," "gathering to our north," "massing in Indonesia," all to invade the "land of hope."[80]

Here again, this "war" that Australia is fighting is actually a siege in which the country is being defended against the invasion of a racial Other that is disorganized, massified, and relentless. These people may not be *Muselmänner*, though many of them are Muslims, but they are bare life in that they do not have the protection of any state. They appear, like apocalyptic zombies, as a faceless, unthinking mass of less-than-human people that accumulates at the border, threatening to overwhelm the state's defenses by their sheer pressure and destroy the human beings and the social order inside.

These examples are drawn from work studying the rhetoric used for asylum seekers in Austria and Australia. The same terms are used across the West. Displaced people, that is, those officially classified as illegal immigrants, asylum seekers, refugees, and the like, are bare life striving to enter states where they will be given protection. Those states experience them as an unregulated threat to life within the border. As Aihwa Ong writes, "in camps of the disenfranchised or displaced, bare life becomes the ground for political claims, if not for citizenship, then for the right to survive."[81] At the same time, in the modern state, bare life is the basis for the treatment even of citizens of the state. The zombie is the mythic expression of bare life striving to enter the state, but at the same time, the zombie is the condition that awaits all of us from whom the state withdraws protection. The zombies besieging the places of sanctuary in zombie apocalypse films can be read as displaced people seeking recognition from the countries of the West. As *Pride and Prejudice and Zombies* makes clear, they bear the histories of the enslaved whose labor enabled the quality of life at the heart of the colonial empires and that provided the wealth for the Industrial Revolution. But the zombies are also an image of what we, members of the modern state, might become. In the modern state, bare life founds the political order. In the neoliberal version of that state, where rights are dependent on what people within the border of the state can offer to the economic well-being of the state, the degree to which one is reprieved from bare life depends on one's economic worth. In this way, within the state, labor returns as an inverse measure of zombification, while, without the protection of the state, bare life equates with the most menial and unprotected forms of labor—exemplified in the zombie as domestic.

In most zombie films, it is the population near to hand, often from outside the neighborhood, who are turned into zombies and become the threat to the remaining citizens. While, as I have argued, these zombies can be read as threatening, racially Othered, displaced people, they can also be read as the citizens of the state whom that state no longer finds economically useful. In many recent zombie films, one of the more shocking elements is how ordinary the zombies look. They often have little in the way of physical transformation. Any member of the neoliberal state might find herself turned into a zombie. In *Shaun of the Dead,* Shaun mistakes his local, neighborhood zombies for the same people whom he had often seen blearily trudging off to work early in the morning. This sense of how easy it is for the members of the neoliberal state to become zombies is also an aspect of the horror engendered in recent zombie texts. In the American television series *The Walking Dead,* which began in 2010, Rick Grimes, a deputy sheriff, wakes up from a coma to find that almost everybody in the United States has become a zombie. Neoliberal America has itself imploded in a zombie apocalypse.

Bare life, as I have explained, has a dual meaning. In the first place, it refers to the lack of legal protection by the state. Without that protection, the person reduced to bare life can become transformed into the second understanding of bare life: the liminal condition of death in life, coma. Indeed, such a person can become one of the living dead. This is the existential condition represented in the zombie. The equation of the zombie and the displaced person occurs through the construction of bare life in both aspects of the term. The new fascination with zombie apocalypse films can be understood in relation to (but of course is not limited to) the increasing anxiety of members of Western states founded in the threat that these states feel is posed by displaced people. Both manifestations of bare life are described using the same discursive terms. The fear of what is perceived to be an external threat from the racialized zombie Other helps those who live in Western states to repress the awareness of how easily their own existence can become reduced to bare life.

Notes

1. Capcom, "Capcom's Million-Selling Series, Resident Evil, Expanding to the Nintendo GameCube and Sony PlayStaion2!," 2010, http://www.capcom.co.jp/ir/english/news/html/e041101.html.
2. Box Office Mojo, "Resident Evil," 2013, http://www.boxofficemojo.com/.
3. Stephanie Merritt, "Pride and Prejudice and Zombies by Jane Austen and Seth Grahame-Smith," *The Guardian,* December 23, 2009, http://www.guardian.co.uk/.
4. UNHCR, "Refugee Population by Origin 1960–2008," http://www.unhcr.org/.
5. UNHCR, "The State of the World's Refugees 2000: Fifty Years of Humanitarian Action," 2000, http://www.unhcr.org/.
6. Anthony Downey, "Zones of Indistinction: Giorgio Agamben's 'Bare Life' and the Politics of Aesthetics," *Journal of Popular Film and Television* 223, no. 2 (2009): 109.

7. As cited in Kyle Bishop, "Dead Man Still Walking: Explaining the Zombie Renaissance," *Journal of Popular Film and Television* 37, no. 1 (2009): 19.

8. Ibid.

9. Nina Auerbach, *Our Vampires, Ourselves* (Chicago: University of Chicago Press, 1995), 192.

10. Box Office Mojo, "Twilight," 2016, http://boxofficemojo.com/.

11. CW Television Network, "Overview," *New York Daily News,* November 10, 2010, http://www.nydailynews.com/.

12. David Punter and Glennis Byron write that "early vampires are not only aristocrats, but also seducers, and from the start the vampire has been associated with sexuality." Punter and Byron, *The Gothic* (Malden, Mass.: Blackwell, 2004), 269.

13. Simon Pegg, "The Dead and the Quick," *The Guardian,* November 4, 2008, http://www.guardian.co.uk/.

14. Ibid.

15. Peter Dendle, "The Zombie as Barometer of Cultural Anxiety," in *Monsters and the Monstrous: Myths and Metaphors of Enduring Evil,* ed. Niall Scott (New York: Rodopi, 2007), 54.

16. Ibid.

17. Ibid.

18. Bishop, "Dead Man Still Walking," 24.

19. Dendle, "Zombie as Barometer," 47–48.

20. Ibid., 47.

21. Joan Dayan, "Vodoun, or the Voice of the Gods," in *Sacred Possessions: Vodon, Santeria, Obeah, and the Caribbean,* ed. Margarite Fernández Olmos and Lizabeth Paravisini-Gebert (New Brunswick, N.J.: Rutgers University Press, 1997), 33.

22. Ibid.

23. Jean Comaroff and John Comaroff, "Alien-Nation: Zombies, Immigrants, and Millennial Capitalism," *South Atlantic Quarterly* 101, no. 4 (2002): 786–87.

24. Ibid., 795.

25. Bill Ashcroft, Gareth Griffiths, and Helen Tiffin, *The Empire Writes Back: Theory and Practice in Postcolonial Literatures* (London: Routledge, 1989), 190.

26. Thomas Loe, "Patterns of the Zombie in Jean Rhys's *Wide Sargasso Sea,*" *Journal of Postcolonial Writing* 31, no. 1 (1991): 35.

27. Ibid., 41.

28. nanuq, "Pride and Prejudice and Zombies: Adding Much-Needed Zombies to the Austen Classic," *BoingBoing* (blog), November 12, 2009, http://m.boingboing.net/.

29. Edward Said, *Culture and Imperialism* (London: Chatto and Windus, 1993), 87.

30. See, e.g., Susan Fraiman, "Jane Austen and Edward Said: Gender, Culture, and Imperialism," *Critical Inquiry* 21, no. 4 (1995): 805–21.

31. Said, *Culture and Imperialism,* 94.

32. Robin Blackburn, *The Making of New World Slavery: From the Baroque to the Modern, 1492–1800* (London: Verso, 1997).

33. Suvendrini Perera, *Reaches of Empire: The English Novel from Edgeworth to Dickens* (New York: Columbia University Press, 1991), 47.

34. Ibid., 20.

35. Jane Austen and Seth Grahame-Smith, *Pride and Prejudice and Zombies* (Philadelphia: Quirk Books, 2009), 22.

36. Comaroff and Comaroff, "Alien-Nation," 789.

37. James Rocchi, "Interview: 'Diary of the Dead' Director George A. Romero," moviefone, February 16, 2008. http://www.cinematical.com/.

38. Roger Ebert, "Night of the Living Dead," 2004, http://www.rogerebert.com/.

39. Romero in interview with Lee Kerr as cited in Cindy Casares, "The Cuban American Who Created Zombies as We Know Them," November 1, 2009, http://guanabee.com/.

40. Ibid.

41. Ibid.

42. Eric Hamako, "Response to 'Dawn of the Dead (1978): Zombies and Human Nature,'" October 2, 2009, http://mediacommons.futureofthebook.org/.

43. Giorgio Agamben, *Homo Sacer: Sovereign Power and Bare Life* (Stanford, Calif.: Stanford University Press, 1998), 2.

44. Ibid., 88, emphasis original.

45. Ibid., 83, emphasis original.

46. Ibid, 84.

47. Ibid., 106, emphasis original.

48. Ibid., 105.

49. Ibid., emphasis original.

50. Ibid., 4.

51. Giorgio Agamben, *Remnants of Auschwitz: The Witness and the Archive* (New York: Zone Books, 1999), 82.

52. Agamben, *Homo Sacer*, 111.

53. Ibid., 121.

54. Gil Anidjar, *The Jew, the Arab: A History of the Enemy* (Stanford, Calif.: Stanford University Press, 2003), 125.

55. Ibid., 126.

56. Ibid., 127.

57. Ibid., 145.

58. Primo Levi, *Survival in Auschwitz: The Nazi Assault on Humanity*, trans. Stuart Woolf (New York: Touchstone, 1996), 83.

59. Goscinki, as cited in Agamben, *Remnants of Auschwitz*, 169–70.

60. Elaine Scarry, *The Body in Pain: The Making and Unmaking of the World* (New York: Oxford University Press, 1985), 4.

61. Agamben, *Remnants of Auschwitz*, 41.

62. JoAnn Cannon, "Canon-Formation and Reception in Contemporary Italy: The Case of Primo Levi," *Italica* 69, no. 1 (1992): 33.

63. buttub, "Notes on Zombies," *Ghost Island* (blog), July 16, 2009, http://ghostisland.wordpress.com/.

64. Hamako, "Response to 'Dawn of the Dead.'"

65. Erin Mackie, *Rakes, Highwaymen, and Pirates: The Making of the Modern Gentleman in the Eighteenth Century* (Baltimore: Johns Hopkins University Press, 2009), 135.

66. Agamben, *Remnants of Auschwitz*, 64.

67. Ibid., 85.

68. Bishop, "Dead Man Still Walking," 24.

69. I have no room to discuss *Dead Set* here, but, in short, it is a classic zombie apocalypse siege film but this time on the set of a reality television show. The zombies, who are easily read as the show's audience, lay siege, and the series ends with them killing and eating the show's cast. Once again, though, the zombie siege can also be read as an expression of British anxiety about the threat of displaced people pressing on Britain's border.

70. Charlie Booker, "Is Obama Really President or Am I Just Watching a Fantasy? It's Almost Too Good to Be True," *The Guardian*, November 10, 2008, http://www.guardian.co.uk/.

71. For reviews of *Fido*, see, e.g., Steve Biodrwoski, "*Fido*: A Boy and His Zombie," *Cinefantastique Online*, 2007, http://cinefantastiqueonline.com/. Also see http://thehorrorgeek.com/ and http://www.cinerina.com/.

72. It is not the first Australian zombie film; that would seem to be *Zombie Brigade*, released in 1986. In this film the zombies are Vietnam War veterans risen from the dead to take revenge on the attempt by Japanese developers to build a theme park on the site of the war memorial. The anxieties here would seem to connect with long-standing Australian fears of Asian invasion.

73. On the kangaroo shooter in *Wolf Creek*, see Jon Stratton, "Dying to Come to Australia: Asylum Seekers, Tourists, and Death," in *Our Patch: Enacting Australian Sovereignty Post-2001*, ed. Suvendrini Perera, 167–96 (Perth, Australia: Network Books, 2007).

74. On *Lucky Miles*, see Jon Stratton, "'Welcome to Paradise': Asylum Seekers, Nostalgia, and *Lucky Miles*," *Continuum: Journal of Media and Cultural Studies* 23, no. 5 (2009): 629–45.

75. Elisabeth El Refaie, "Metaphors We Discriminate By: Naturalized Themes in Austrian Newspaper Articles about Asylum Seekers," *Journal of Sociolinguistics* 5, no. 3 (2001): 364.

76. Ibid.

77. Ibid., 364–65.

78. Sharon Pickering, "Common Sense and Original Deviancy: News Discourses and Asylum Seekers in Australia," *Journal of Refugee Studies* 14, no. 2 (2001): 172.

79. Ibid.

80. Ibid.

81. Aihwa Ong, "Mutations in Citizenship," *Theory, Culture, and Society* 23, no. 2–3 (2006): 501.

PART IV
Zombies in the Street

In Memoriam: The Toronto Zombie Walk (2003–2015)

On August 29, 2015, the Royal Theatre in Toronto, Canada, hosted a funeral. It was not, as so many memorials purport to be, a celebration of life but, unapologetically, of death—and it recognized not the death of a person but of a movement. It eulogized the annual zombie walk that Thea Faulds, or Thea Munster (as she prefers to be called), had been organizing in Toronto for more than a decade. An annual event that became a phenomenon, the zombie walk was a macabre movement that swept the North American continent (and, indeed, the world) with a strange pox in which people broke out in tattered clothes and fake blood and appeared in public dressed as the living dead.

Although the *Guinness Book of World Records*'s superlative for largest number of zombies in attendance is currently held by Minneapolis, for an event in October 2014 that certified 15,458 zombies, there was more to the movement than just record breaking for hometown bragging rights. Mass numbers of people in cities as diverse as Pittsburgh, Detroit, Seattle, London, Stockholm, Mexico City, and Brisbane were willing to put time and effort into playing dead—most often, as with Toronto's annual walk, for no stated reason whatsoever. More than any statistics on the number of zombie films or books or comics or video games produced, or the number of zombie preparedness bumper stickers sold, it was the spectacle of thousands (and, in some cases, tens of thousands) of people turning up in city streets and town squares dressed as ambulant corpses that served as incontrovertible proof that there was something profound about the imagery of living death speaking to people at that historical moment, now ended, of the first decade of the new millennium.

The zombie's occupation of public space has long been a central feature of its narrative in cinema, an element that Fred Botting's essay in this section engages and that Jeff May addresses directly in his excellent piece "Zombie Geographies and the Undead City." A geographer, May highlights zombie films' usefulness for his discipline as "expressions of a bodies-cities theory" (285) and illustrates the zombie narrative's reconceptualization of city space. Reading together the zombie's binary living-deadness and the dichotomy of public and private, May's article attempts to read "the role that spatial and bodily otherness plays in the constitution of bodies and cities" (285). (As such, this article should appear on a list of suggested reading concerned not only with the zombie and space but with the zombie's inherent otherness.) Of particular importance is May's description of the zombie's creation of what he terms "blank space":

> Blank space reflects the spatial inbetweenness and otherness that exists when a zombie outbreak disrupts pre-zombie codifications. . . . If the city's main operating functions are drastically altered, as occurs in a zombie outbreak, then the soft spaces of the city are writ clean, reduced to blank space and made potentially *new*. (290)

This is precisely what Thea Munster's zombie walk reveled in: a willful interruption and redirection of the ordered mechanics of city space.

I've written about both the Toronto Zombie Walk and the broader zombie walk phenomenon in more detail elsewhere. In my essay in *Better Off Dead*, "Playing Dead," I read the zombie walks as in line with the pedestrian street acts of the Situationist Internationale and connected such happenings to the art events of Jillian Mcdonald. However, I hazarded a guess that the significance of zombie mobs and zombie walks amounted to "voided signifiers" with "the shape and form of insurrection" and that, like a zombie, these were "just contour, devoid of sense" (220). In sum, my assessment of the zombie walk was that it served as an intermediary between play and protest, and I had wondered what would become of the inchoate demonstration of the zombie mob in an era when demands for social or political change were being more explicitly articulated—a theory I later tested by mapping the declining popularity of zombie events alongside a flurry of activity of student protests in 2009 in an article called "Sois Mort et Tais Toi: Zombie Mobs and Student Protests"; it yielded few concrete conclusions other than the suggestion that the zombie could just as easily be incorporated into protest as eclipsed by it.

In short, my own attempts at understanding the zombie walk movement produced more questions than answers. To me, the act of playing dead seemed like an unintelligible wail issuing deep from within society's collective unconscious. But there was rarely a stated translation. What did it mean that people were doing *this* "for fun"? Was this a sign of collective grief, and if so, what was the subject of that lament? This section turns to the work of other scholars who have pondered the zombie's occupation of public space (in narrative and in real life) for answers to these questions and more: the essays herein connect the zombie's transversals of space and appearances in public to literary predecessors and to historical antecedents; they investigate zombie performances as both protest and play; they push further at our understanding of how space is constituted and delimited and characterized as either public or private and the role that time plays in such performances; and they foretell, in the description of mounting social discontent regarding income inequality and police brutality, a reason why the zombie walk may now be disappearing.

From within a book collection called *London Gothic*, Botting's chapter, "Zombie London: Unexceptionalities of the New World Order," investigates both Danny Boyle's 2002 film *28 Days Later*—which depicts an abandoned, postapocalyptic London—and the sequel to this film, *28 Weeks Later* (dir. Juan Carlos Fresnadillo, 2007), which moves a group of protagonists from a rural farmhouse to the "new London," a walled city regimented and surveilled by armed forces. Botting reads the movement of characters through space, from urban to rural and from rural to the new, posturban compound, in contrast to the gothic and romantic trajectory and in line with the dream of bio-politics in the new world order. This article argues that we see in the 28 series of films a new type of zombie brought forth, one that Botting dubs "zoombies" for their in-creased speed and which he reads alongside theories of the posthuman and postmodern (Thacker, Virilio, Deleuze, Hayles, Jameson) as "the speedy, hyperactivated nonsubjects of a media-saturated postindustrial high-performance economy." Drawing explicitly from Hardt and Negri's theories of *Empire,* Botting underlines the way that, in this pair of films, "global financial capital and the militarization of social control" inform each other so that a state of perpetual war and the strictly controlled space of the city constitute each other.

Botting's article provides a foundational study of several key concepts visible in the public performance of zombie walks. The regimented space of the city, for example, is one of the mechanisms of the everyday that the zombie walk seeks to disrupt with its arrest of traffic flows and its spectacle of surprising bodies in the public square. This is addressed more directly in the piece I have chosen as representative of this facet of zombie scholarship.

Simon Orpana's "Spooks of Biopower: The Uncanny Carnivalesque of Zombie Walks" profiles the Toronto Zombie Walk alongside a detailed reading of Mikhail Bakhtin's musings on the uses of the grotesque within traditional carnival (from *Rabelais and His World*). In total, this piece sketches out the ways that zombie walk events nego-tiate the spatial and temporal restriction of the late capitalist subject as they play with notions of collectivity and social subversion in a manner similar to carnival. Yet, Orpana argues that the modern zombie walk, as he wrote in the original article's abstract, "*con-trasts* with the older versions of carnival in its morbid *suspension* of life and death"[1]—that "the zombie subject is excluded from the processes of rebirth and regeneration," which are an integral part of carnival's theatrical operation, a response to and reflection of the modern power formations critiqued by Foucault, Deleuze, Agamben, and Hardt and Negri. Most innovatively, perhaps, this essay discusses the "inoculation" provided by laughter in zombie events (as in carnival), but I am still left wondering whether the critique of biopower engendered by zombie walks goes far enough in the face of gross social injustice.

Furthering this line of questioning, in a special issue of *The Drama Review* devoted to "Precarity and Performance," Tavia Nyong'o elucidates the zombie's uptake into protest, profiling the presence of zombies at Occupy London and Occupy Wall Street. In "The Scene of Occupation," Nyong'o relates this use of the zombie to "the everyday weight of reproducing social life under capital"; "moving 'laterally,' as Lauren Berlant puts it, we *feel* zombified." Nyong'o reminds his readers that such events call on us to consider the politics of *time* as much as *space*. The theoretical heft of the essay comes from its in-depth discussion of "the *precarious time* of occupation," which Nyong'o relates to Antonio Negri's writings on *kairòs* and to broader discussions of rupture, temporality, refuge, and the multitude in a materialist discussion of history and struggle. Nyong'o acknowledges that there is performative potential in the zombie, an attempt at dezombification; however, the essay also illustrates the layered complexity in such rehearsals, as of Michael Jackson's *Thriller,* examining in particular the choreographed, and coerced, rendition of Jackson's zombie dance by inmates at the Cebu Provincial Detention and Rehabilitation Center in the Philippines, which Comentale referenced in his chapter in the previous section. Nyong'o emphasizes here that the video of this performance went viral, alluding to the complicated understandings of private and public space in the digital age that are likewise dramatized in Occupy events.

Finally, we turn to the piece by Travis Linnemann, Tyler Wall, and Edward Green for its harrowing representation of a different type of zombie in the street, one that is not performative but pejorative: a denigration of human life as less than living. In "The Walking Dead and Killing State: Zombification and the Normalization of Police Violence," the authors describe this form of real-life zombification as a "politicocultural production" of those whose lives are deemed not to matter. Profiling, for example, the Miami Zombie incident that occurred on May 26, 2012, the authors read this event's salacious media coverage, "a powerful example of the cultural production of a spectral sort of monstrosity," as they introduced the work in its previous publication.[2] The authors situate this maneuver as part of the "larger ideological frame that normalizes state violence and conceals the fundamental inequalities of late capitalism." The relevance of this essay in the contemporary moment, in the wake of recent attention to police violence against black bodies and investigation of the media's use of terms like "thug," should be obvious, but the piece makes many other points about the types of bare life that are deemed expendable humanity—for example, I'm grateful for the piece's discussion of drug use and police violence.

This essay might have been placed just as easily alongside those grouped under "Zombies and Other(ed) People" for its illustration of lives that don't (appear to) matter; and its inclusion here signals to the inseparability of the issues discussed in this volume, especially colonialism, capitalism, and the privileging of certain lives above others. We might weave together many threads from these four very different essays on "Zombies in the Street": looking specifically at time versus space, the uses and abuses of media, bare life and "barer life" (as Botting writes), and even laughter—the discussion of humor in Orpana's essay might be productively contrasted with its treatment in Linnemann, Wall, and Green's piece. I've curated this section as I have because I want to map a kind of narrative progression in the rise and decline of the Toronto Zombie Walk—a topic adumbrated by this section's discussion of the movement's history, the zombie's transversal of public space in cinema, and the limits of zombie performance elsewhere—and link this to the overt social expressions of discontent and political action that we've witnessed lately.

Inaugurated in 2003 as the first of its kind, if the Toronto Zombie Walk hung up its latex flesh wounds and its milky contact lenses in 2015, does this signify that we are done grieving now? Or merely that the zombie's indecipherable moan is no longer a fitting container for our angst? Were there people dressed as the living dead at Ferguson?

I'm not certain, but I doubt it, because the "zombification" in question had already happened (in just the way that Linnemann, Wall, and Green's essay describes), and the task at hand now is to break the witch doctor's spell.

Further Reading

As I've mentioned, I have authored two pieces on the subject of zombie walks, "Playing Dead: Zombies Invade Performance Art . . . and Your Neighborhood" and "Sois Mort et Tais Toi: Zombie Mobs and Student Protest." Those interested in the walks as performance art should investigate the work of artist Jillian Mcdonald, who staged a live zombie event at Toronto's Nuit Blanche art festival in 2008. They seem to have also inspired Bernadette Corporation's work titled "Be Corpse." On the latter, see the article in *Afterall: A Journal of Art, Context, and Enquiry.*

As in my own work, Sasha Cocarla draws a comparison between the walks and the Situationist Internationale in her essay "Reclaiming Public Spaces through Performance of the Zombie Walk." In the same issue of *The Drama Review* from which Nyong'o's piece comes, see also Rebecca Schneider's excellent essay "It Seems as If . . . I Am Dead: Zombie Capitalism and Theatrical Labor," in which she reads the Occupy Wall Street zombies as "reflection machines, flexible theatres of the crowd, aimed to catch the visages of those who worship corporate wealth" (153).

Those interested in the topic as performance should see especially Emma Austin's "Zombie Culture: Dissent, Celebration, and the Carnivalesque in Social Spaces," Attia Sattar's "Zombie Performance," and Jennifer Rutherford's treatment of the subject in her short book. Austin's essay, for example, draws the zombie walk together with the space of the cemetery, celebrations of Día de Muertos, and the zombie narrative's occupation of space in cinema, providing useful musing even on the privilege inherent in zombie performances. Sattar's article is an investigation of the phenomenon of playing zombie, as in zombie walks, zombie runs, and zombie tag. The author's perspective here shifts from one of "collective behavior and sociohistorical movements" to look instead at the singular zombie performance.

Other essays on the topic to consider besides those previously mentioned include Phillip Mahoney's "Mass Psychology and the Analysis of the Zombie: From Suggestion to Contagion," Simone do Vale's "Trash Mob," John Morehead's "Zombie Walks, Zombie Jesus, and the Eschatology of Postmodern Flesh," and Andrew Tripp's "Zombie Marches and the Limits of Apocalyptic Space." Bryce Peake and Michele White look specifically at performance of gender and racial identity in zombie walks. See Bryce Peake's "He Is Dead, and He Is Continuing to Die: A Feminist Psycho-semiotic Reflection on Men's Embodiment of Metaphor in a Toronto Zombie Walk" and Michele White's "Killing Whiteness: The Critical Positioning of Zombie Walk Brides in Internet Settings."

Those interested specifically in the dichotomy of the urban and the rural in zombie narratives should see, in addition to May's previously referenced article, Dan Hassler-Forrest's "Zombie Spaces." Somewhat tangentially related, Christine Heckman's essay in Dawn Keetley's collection on *The Walking Dead* treats the place of the automobile in

American identity and in this popular zombie narrative. See "Roadside 'Vigil' for the Dead: Cannibalism, Fossil Fuels, and the American Dream."

Finally, for a further analysis of the cinematic zombie's relationship to the grotesque and carnivalesque, see Linda Badley, "Zombie Splatter Comedy from *Dawn* to *Shaun*."

Notes

1. Simon Orpana, "Spooks of Biopower: The Uncanny Carnivalesque of Zombie Walks," *Topia: Canadian Journal of Cultural Studies* 25 (Spring 2011): 153, emphasis added.

2. Travis Linnemann, Tyler Wall, and Edward Green, "The Walking Dead and Killing State: Zombification and the Normalization of Police Violence," in *Theoretical Criminology* 18, no. 4 (2014).

CHAPTER 16

Zombie London
Unexceptionalities of the New World Order

FRED BOTTING

Not Anything to Show More Fair

A patient awakes, naked, in an empty hospital twenty-eight days after a deadly virus has been released from a medical test facility. The city outside is also deserted. An old newspaper headline in close-up tells of the city's evacuation. He wanders, a solitary figure amid familiar London sights: the Houses of Parliament and Whitehall; Horseguards, Horseguards Parade, and the Guards Memorial; Pall Mall and the Mall; Mansion House, the City, and Piccadilly, with its statue of Eros; St Paul's and the London Eye. The journey offers a tour of historical and heritage locations, places of tourism and entertainment, centers of government and commercial power, and sites of regal and martial tradition. The opening scenes of *28 Days Later* (dir. Danny Boyle, 2002) replay fictional (literary-cinematic) apocalyptic scenarios of modern urban devastation. Daniel Defoe, Mary Shelley, Richard Jeffries, laid out a pattern of modern urban apocalypse subsequently developed in genre fictions and further elaborated on film. *The Last Man on Earth* (dir. Ubaldo Ragona, 1964), with its "vampires" (that move like zombies), is set in an evacuated modern Rome. The same story (Richard Matheson's *I Am Legend*) becomes *The Omega Man* (dir. Boris Sagal, 1971), with a lonely survivor bunkered in a Los Angeles house and harassed by radioactive mutants, and, ultimately, *I Am Legend* (dir. Francis Lawrence, 2007), where New York hosts a fast-moving swarm of zombie-vamps. The films *28 Days Later* and *28 Weeks Later* (dir. Juan Carlos Fresnadillo, 2007) acknowledge their trash zombie horror apocalyptic forebears: *Night of the Living Dead* (dir. George Romero, 1968), with its besieged farmhouse; *Dawn of the Dead* (1978), with its consumerism; *Day of the Dead* (1985), with its military presence; *Land of the Dead* (2005), with its corporate tower. The virus theme, too, comes from the TV series *Survivors* (BBC, 1975–77) and *Resident Evil*'s (dir. Paul Anderson, 2002) genetic experimentation and fast-moving zombie-mutants. The reflexive awareness of *28 Days Later*'s citations of its zombie horror apocalypse precursors are given a wider frame of reference in its very striking and recognizably unfamiliar opening scenes. Prominent among the shots of London is a sequence in which the wandering survivor crosses a rubbish-strewn Westminster Bridge. The camera pans across the river to Big Ben and the Houses of Parliament warmly illuminated against a gentle sky as the city sun sets. More than a provision of a distinctive location scene for a global cinema audience, crossing the bridge in an empty city recalls Wordsworth's sonnet "Upon Westminster Bridge," in which London is majestic and beautiful in the morning sun, sublimely touching the romantic (urban) wanderer's soul with its stillness, its absence of crowds, smoke, and noise. At this moment the city becomes admissible to nature rather than at odds with its rhythms. As a singular "mighty heart" lying still, the urban body is unusually peaceful and unified, thereby containable in a single imaginative vision.[1] The mighty heart, however, suggests another London, a sleeping giant ready to awake and beat faster. The other city is more apparent in Wordsworth's poetry. In *The Prelude,* London is reduced to the chaos of Bartholomew Fair, a "city within a City" that exceeds and threatens romantic visionary unity as a messy multiplicity of disorganized sights, sounds, sensations, not properly humane or natural, a "parliament of monsters."[2] Overwhelming individual consciousness with an excess of spectacle, the city is seen as a place of subjective and physical otherness in which sense and self-assurance lose themselves to the pressures of other egos: "the sublime renewal of our consciousness and desire for self-presence" both "frees us" and returns us to a "world of circumstances beyond our control."[3] The price, it seems, paid by romantic consciousness to overcome the sublime threat of the monstrous urban spectacle is utter devastation, a destruction and evacuation of all other bodies, signs, and symbols pressing upon and competing with a singular poetic vision. It is an apocalyptic tendency played out in various romantic guises, Byron's "Darkness" notably. For Percy Shelley, in "Peter Bell III," "hell is a city like London," a "crepuscular demi-world" of commerce and politics in which ruination forms the prelude for nature to reclaim urban space.[4] For Mary Shelley in *The Last Man,* the scale of devastation is global and destructive: a worldwide plague—a monstrous force of nature—wipes out humanity and its centers of civilization (London, Paris, Rome) until "everything was desert."[5]

The opening of *28 Days Later* prepares the film's romantic trajectory, skipping over the more prevalent features of the darkly modern city as charted by Edgar Allan Poe, Charles Baudelaire, and Walter Benjamin. Poe's story "The Man of the Crowd" provides one of the key aesthetic figures of modernity and outlines another London, frightening, dark, and ruined and associated with crime and debauchery: the other side of prosperous Victorian modernity. Poe's crowd is multiple, but its effects draw out a sense of a danger and contagion, a place of poverty and crime in which the city itself "becomes almost a drunken mob."[6] Unlike Paris, it engenders a "paranoid wandering subject" whose experience is one of terror: "the outer environment has returned like a wave, threatening to engulf him, and instead of consuming, he is consumed in a neatly twisted version of cannibalism."[7] Benjamin, working through Baudelaire and Poe, charts urban experience in a context in which subjectivity, vision, and visual culture move to the rhythms of industrial and urban organization; the crowd's heterogeneous singularity repeats the relation of worker and mechanical labor. Shock—both shattering tradition and breaking into everyday experience—becomes the dominant mode of work, life, and leisure.[8] Technology, Benjamin notes, "has subjected the human sensorium to a new kind of training";[9] it decenters romantic humanity and aesthetics, based on the "aura" of artistic experience.

The legacy of modernity's technological shocks, in particular of its mass visual media, is laid out in the precredit sequence of *28 Days Later.* Providing the backstory to the release of infection, it begins in a research laboratory with its experimental subject watching an array of screens depicting scenes of urban violence from around the world, visual images of rage correlated to the production or cure of the virus. Media, it seems, mime or (re)produce urban violence. Television news, indeed, has been analyzed as both creating and curing shocks.[10] It suggests a process of production and evacuation of sensation that subjects all viewers (all experimental animals) to the shocks and stimulation of multiple screened events. A cycle of exciting and deadening spectatorial responses is manifested, on the screens within the screen and in the camerawork and the editing, as soon as the RAGE virus is released. The slow, suspenseful close-ups and pans across a darkened lab are quickly replaced by closed-circuit TV shots of balaclava-wearing activists breaking in. As the animals are freed, so, too, is the highly contagious virus; slow, blurry motion, rapid and jerky camera movements, sudden close-ups of bloodshot eyes and bloody vomit, angry chimps battering their own cages and violently attacking their rescuers. These scenes present a media form that has accelerated modernity's modes of mechanical reproduction, producing sensation and stimulation to enraged excess, movements too rapid for consciousness to process or screen off. The cinematic tradition in which the film locates itself, however, is very much bound up with modernity. Zombies, despite their colonial origins, are figures of industrial production and mechanical reproduction.[11] Fritz Lang's *Metropolis* (1927) provides a stark and gothicized vision of urban life and labor in its shots of the city, of the slow-moving and homogeneous mass of workers marched to and from their dark, subterranean habitations, reduced to a state of automation, "depersonalized, faceless, dressed identically."[12] The "gothic modernism" of *Metropolis* stresses the darkness of factory labor and urban society and links it to monstrous and oppressive technological innovations (the scientist Rotwang and the robot double Maria) that turn workers into a mass of "dehumanized mechanical actions."[13] From the emergence of film, zombies connote the mass of modernity as subjects of both production and reproduction: before the camera, the moving images of a shambling, shocked, and submissive workforce present repetitive industrial dehumanization; before the screen, the desensitized and shocked mass of workers turned spectators are shocked again. The pattern continues: 1950s B movie monsters and alien invaders are "zombie-like" figures of Fordist and bureaucratic society, manifestations of the "depersonalising conditions of modern urban life."[14]

The allusions of *28 Days Later* acknowledge and transform the cinematic history of zombification and urban modernity. From the start, and the evacuation of the city, the film plots a romantic arc to the Lake District. The emptying of London and of the institutions of urban modernity (government, banking, family) serves as the basis for imagining the reconstitution of human, even humane, social relations based on assured individuality in the context of an imaginary family unity and a post-Blairite masculinity.[15] In the city, distinctions between a private, domesticated realm and the pressures of urban public spaces remain difficult to sustain, the latter endlessly and insistently encroaching upon the other.[16] The modern city is double, a duplicity, both legible and illegible, and textual and more than readable, like the modern romantic apocalypse, calling for and confounding the limits of representation.[17] It exists on several intersecting planes simultaneously, ordered vertically in maps, towers, lines, and grids and reshaped incessantly by cultural, subjective, and aesthetic movements—horizontal, plural—of inhabitants, pedestrians, wanderers, migrants. Lived space, traversed horizontally, metaphorically, textually, re-creates the city, drawing out its "disquieting familiarity," its deportations, relations, interdependences, creating an "urban fabric," a dense network, like the multiple weaves of Barthes's text.[18]

Though rewritten, the film's ending, with its imaginary family and idyllic rural retreat, appears to remain within a persistently romantic cultural fantasy.[19] However, it and structures of modernity—public–private, home–abroad, country–city—are adjusted. Just as domestic and urban space and individual and crowd were placed in tension from the start, one interpenetrated, if not overwhelmed, by the other, the fantastic distinction between city and country (urban hell vs. rural idyll) appears less secure. The vision of the city as a "dystopian nightmare" is part of a "long-cultivated habit" of those with power and privilege able to move as far as possible from the city: "the upshot has been not only to create endless suburbanization, so-called 'edge-cities,' and sprawling megalopolis, but also to make every village and every rural retreat in the advanced capitalist world part of a complex web of urbanization that denies any categorization of populations into 'urban' and 'rural.'"[20] City and village are relocated in wider global political-economic networks. These appear clearly in *28 Weeks Later*, where the fantasies of apocalyptic evacuation, familial reconstitution, and rural ideal are unpacked in a reversal of *28 Days Later*'s romantic trajectory. The film *28 Weeks Later* begins in a farmhouse. A husband and wife prepare dinner, talking of their absent children. She looks at a photograph, an archaic reminder of the family that used to live there. A still image of a frozen, dead past, anachronistic in the rapidly moving currents of infected times. The refuge is soon invaded, and this remainder of family life is forcibly broken up, a rent exacerbated by the husband's act of cowardice, leaving his wife to a fate worse than death. His flight returns him to a London no longer recognizable in modern terms but subjected to the forces and protocols of a new global order. In this context, the family is no longer viable; not only has the husband betrayed his wife but he lies to his children about her "death." Paternal figures, it seems, in the tradition of horror films (*Amityville*; *The Shining*), are not to be relied on.[21] The family itself, like old photographs, seems to be redundant, no longer a bulwark against the pressures of social change and global shifts;[22] or a locus of resistance;[23] or little points of cohesion, "social solidarities," in an unstable and highly charged urban context.[24]

Speed

"Rapidity is always a sign of precocious death for the fast species."[25] Speed reconfigures bodies and urban environments; it registers a movement beyond life. The "infected," too, take the idea of zombies beyond their modern parameters, notably due to their distinctively rapid movement. The world of *28 Weeks Later* retains only traces of modernity, like the still images of family life; these "zombie categories" hint at the persistence of lost ideals and institutions in times that have superseded them.[26] Modernity's (zombie) subjects have changed—and more than in the way they move. Not really undead, multiple genre references notwithstanding, these "zombies"—as a sequence of captions early in *28 Weeks Later* indicates—can starve after five weeks. They are as much figures of global anxieties about migrations of bodies, capital, and infection (HIV, SARS, influenza epidemics). In terms of their medium, their movement suggests a speedier, saturated, and sensational environment of stimuli, one in which shocks and countershocks are relayed globally and daily in a more intense fashion. Mutants in the strict zombie tradition, no longer figures of mass modernity and mechanical cinematic reproduction, their mutation, nonetheless, is calibrated to the shifts of a postindustrial, mediatized global sphere. In a review of the TV zombie series *Dead Set*, Simon Pegg (director/star/writer of *Shaun of the Dead*) complains at the failure of that series to adhere to a "key detail": "ZOMBIES DON'T RUN!" Acknowledging the absurdity of debating "the rules of a reality that doesn't exist," he offers a convincing case for the slow, relentless, and inevitable potency of zombies: they manifest "our deepest fear," "our destiny writ large"—death. For him, rapid movement reduces their power to "a quick thrill at the expense of a more profound sense of dread." Hence *28 Days Later* is "misconstrued by the media as a zombie flick," Boyle and Garland drawing on *Day of the Triffids* as much as Matheson and Romero to develop "a new strain of survival horror." Pegg, however, acknowledges the context for the change and criticizes Zack Snyder's "pointless" remake of *Dawn of the Dead*: the "upgraded zombie 2.0" appears "at the behest of some cigar-chomping, focus-group happy movie exec desperate to satisfy the MTV generation's demand for quicker everything—quicker food, quicker downloads, quicker dead people."[27] "Quicker everything"—the injunction to go faster dominates all activities; the demand for speed in media, information, consumption, accelerates away from the modernity that produced zombies lumbering to the pace set by the manufacturing industry. Zombies, slow, relentless, and modern, are replaced by "zoombies," fast-moving figures of a fast-food culture and fast-camera cinema.

Speeding up not only heightens the repetitions and shocks of industrial, urban modernity; it marks an acceleration beyond its rhythms, disturbing its borders, frames, and categorizations. Paul Virilio, one of the cultural critics developing Benjamin's insights in a contemporary context, traces the effects of new optical and military technologies on urban spaces and bodies, identifying an acceleration beyond, an eclipse of, modern logic and structures. Speed changes the relationships between subjects, objects, screens, and their environments; retrains senses, bodies, selves; inaugurates new and shifting alignments between physical space and media, a development of the historical interaction between war and vision in which urban space passes from fortress city to open, planned commercial flows regulated by military planning (Hausmann's Paris) and on to cities that are as much virtual as they are physical, "overexposed" cities shaped by media, signs, image, and spectacle, encountered, not by crossing a gated threshold, but through an "electronic audience system."[28] Pressed by new media laws of real time and instantaneous communication, conforming to the "terrorist aesthetic of optical impact," monitor screens transform the viewer "into an agent or potential victim, as in war."[29] The subject that emerges, shocked beyond the quality and characteristics of its modern human forebear, is barely a subject at all, given that a shocked subject already teeters on the brink of oxymoronism;[30] numbed, automatic, zombielike, it is a victim of sense and sensation and also a hypermodern organism stimulated, hyperactivated, and reactive, an effect of an incessant "bombardment" of images and signs. With speeds being set by computer and relayed instantly on monitor screens, mind and body become equally penetrable and more rapidly hardened so that the process of blocking and protection demands a countervailing pressure toward increased excitement: "superstimulants are the logical extension of metropolitan sedentariness."[31] Science is able "to attack," Virilio suggests, "what is alive, 'natural,' vitality finally being eliminated in the quasi-messsianic coming of the wholly hyperactivated man."[32] Accelerated beyond nature, the movement exceeds life and death, to the point that bodies, in entertainments, thrill rides, say, are not even alive until excited to the maximum. To the point of crashing, or death.[33] The bombardments of media and telecommunications are aligned with new economic formations in which imperatives of "hyperproductivity" lead to new work-related illnesses for mind and body—stress and repetitive strain injury, for example—winding them up beyond natural tolerance thresholds, numbed and enervated in a hyperdialectic of shock.[34] On a wider scale, the "structural unemployment" caused by technological and economic innovation transforms the working mass of industrial society into redundancy, castoffs individuated by postindustrial practices, reduced to the "passivity of individuals made useless" yet remaining a "social menace." Romero's zombies—Pittsburgh's fading industrial environment in the background—appear in this form: without work, aspiration, useless, they are the meat thrown out by corporate postindustrial change.[35]

In contrast, and opposed, to the neolumpenproletariat cast off by postindustrial practices, "hyperactivated man," the revved-up, flexible, fragmented, plural bodies defined by multiple gazes and microsystems of control, complies with contemporary corporate imperatives: "in the context of the flexibility demanded by contemporary capitalism, there has been a great compression of time and space, and the body comes to be seen as a chaotic, hyperflexible site, ridden with contradictions and warfare."[36] Early in *28 Weeks Later* (following the retreat from country to city), a very specific site is shown from a range of angles; high aerial shots from aircraft and buildings dominate the mise-en-scène. All are mediated, showing that the movie camera is no longer alone: telescopic rifle sights, surveillance helicopters, security cameras, CCTV, command center monitors, and optical scanners. The impression of this city, other than its familiar views, is of a space entirely captured by visual technologies (and the accompanying buzz of audio telecommunications), real-time surveillance, and control fully wired into military command.

Docklands–Baghdad

The central location of *28 Weeks Later* situates London within a new alignment of gothic local and global forces. The location is distinct from the previous film, and its allusion to an older romantic and modern tradition of gothic London, not so historical, nor dark, nor criminal, nor the touristic landmarks of a heritage past (despite shots of Tower Bridge), nor the shadowy spaces of labyrinthine alleys nor netherworlds (a brief journey through the tunnels of the Underground aside). A new London is framed in a sequence of aerial establishing shots, transformed, rebuilt, and relocated in the economic and political upheavals of the 1980s. Shots of Docklands, Canary Wharf, and the Millennium Dome offer recognizable architectural emblems of Thatcherite economic and social transformation and Blairite "Cool Britannia." Views of shiny corporate towers and plazas, city airport lounges, metro stations, and walkways are light, shiny, open, and open, too, to very evident controlling gazes; these sites seemingly anathema to an older gothic darkness. Canary Wharf stands as the "most public and visual expression of 1980s aggressive monetarism," a "city within a City populated by a migrant army of executive, managerial and office staff serving the productive signifiers of postmodernity—microelectronics, telecommunications and international capital."[37] Docklands draws out the tensions transforming urban space: "the urban wasteland has been repositioned within the circuits of international finance capital and recoded as a site of consumption and pursuit of leisure."[38]

The very literal de- and reterritorialization of urban space occurs as an effect of the more abstract deterritorializations associated with a global shift in flows of capital. As Fredric Jameson argues, finance capital evinces capitalism's general ability to feed on and exploit economic crises and turn away from older—and failing—economic and industrial practices and processes. It pursues a destructive, almost cannibalistic logic as its moves from the first stage of capitalization associated with the realism and secularization of the Enlightenment. Moving away from industrial competition and national division, capital's abstraction, through an imperialistic stage, leaves behind the materiality of production to find profits in financial transactions themselves: capital becomes "free-floating," separated "from the concrete context of its productive geography."[39] Its dematerialization is akin to the virtual and informational Fights associated with posthumanism.[40] As materiality and the globe are superseded, new ghosts appear to redefine financial exchanges: "specters of value . . . vying against each other in a vast, worldwide, disembodied phantasmagoria."[41] Ghostly, capital moves out of reach of what once might have been called a real world. The "Thatcherite dream of remaking Britain through private development and corporate finance under the combined ideologies of enterprise, regeneration and heritage" has a darker dimension, "the nightmare of deregulated planning and massive redevelopment" evinced in the tearing down of nineteenth-century living spaces and social infrastructures and discarding of less visible—or rich—urban populations and their histories.[42] For Roger Luckhurst, diverse gothic and occult Londons tell different stories and engage different histories and politics. On one hand, ghosts are part of a process that seeks "to revivify the pasts continually swept away in the ceaseless churning of London development and redevelopment," revenants of other lost histories, figures holding on to, or warding off, the forgetting of pressed and enforced change.[43] In the face of progress, however, gothic fragments operate "as the emblems of resistance to the tyranny of planned space."[44] The "deliberate evisceration of London's democratic public sphere" is paralleled by the evacuation, reconstruction, and repopulation of Docklands, a transformation that is given gothic form in Iain Sinclair's *Downriver*, which "transposes the tyranny of one era onto another," the London Docklands Development Corporation (LDDC) refracted through the eighteenth-century gothic.[45] Gothic, in this instance, provides a language to register political concerns, a figure of tyranny that arises as one of the "symptoms of stalled representative government." The spectrality of capital comes to the fore as a shadowy and powerful tyrant operating outside law, regulation, or restraint.

Losing Control

In employing Docklands as the point of entry for London's (and Britain's) repopulation after viral infection has apparently subsided, *28 Weeks Later* signals its geopolitical importance, not so much as a national capital city, but in its role as a commercial zone of deregulated financial flows, a nodal point in the network of international finance capitalism. As a "security zone," and renamed as "District 1," the Isle of Dogs is an enclave protected by barbed-wire fences, snipers, and cameras. All flows of bodies are directed, surveyed, managed. The connection between finance capital and military control was already implied in the development of Docklands. The Big Bang and Canary Wharf disclose a military subtext insofar as neoliberal economic theory and digital technology adapt netrocentric military strategy. Furnished with hi-tech telecommunications equipment, with open trading floors, the post–Big Bang financial business takes the form of a "command center" directing operations "at a distance," working through digital networks in a militarized model of the control society.[46] What *28 Weeks Later* offers are starker and more direct images of the link between global financial capital and the militarization of social control; its attention to surveillance technologies and telecommunications, all operated by military personnel, is emphasized further by the shots from the point of view of snipers on top of buildings. Camera is equated with rifle as numerous shots track crowd movements below, individuals in their apartments, all seen through telescopic sights strategically placed high on the buildings above. Space is controlled and observed, a city newly closed off and closed in, like Jameson's Bonaventura hotel or the special zones,[47] the "closed-off" areas of corporate plazas, shopping malls, freeways, gated communities, and out-of-town business "campuses."[48]

For Virilio, war and the city constitute each other, from a period of walled fortifications through to a nuclear era in which the city—as polis—met its end in a sprawl beyond central urban boundaries.[49] The "third era," that of the "postindustrial metacity," appears in a different relationship: the "progressive militarization of science and the economy of nations" aims at "total peace" counterpoised with a "state of siege" no longer centered on the metropolis but threatening the entire world.[50] National security cedes to "global security" in the post–Cold War period, the call for total peace calibrated against "a global and total civil war" in which cities are rife with internal conflicts and antagonisms, a "Lebanonization" of urban zones.[51] Docklands, separate from the old financial City of London, closed off to the masses, but remaining electronically open to world finance, is itself a place of migration, a fortress and a kind of ghetto, a militarized, defended zone built in the wasteland of modern urban decay. The supposed borderlessness of its successor throws up a diversity of new barriers and divisions, boundaries that remain proximate, penetrable, and in flux even as they try to close themselves off. Where the city begins and ends, in virtual, physical, and psychological terms, given global openness and increasing internal division, remains a question for Virilio: in a situation of "generalized desertion," a sense of generalized anxiety arises, an uncertainty as to where the city gates are, of how to live without borders.[52]

Globalization "involves new movements and new instabilities, from 'transmigration' of capital and people to new urban forms that are 'fragile' in being centered on an economy of high productivity, advanced technologies and intensified exchanges"; it is "multiscalar," occupying places and nonplaces and denationalizing state institutions.[53] Boundaries become unclear, identities shift. Even the increased power of corporate formations remains subject to "whole networks of urbanization that move to rapid shifts and flows of manufacturing capital" and create a dispersed global proletariat.[54] As the frontiers of the city blur to form internal boundaries and virtual nonspaces, so distinctions between global and local interpenetrate and transform each other in a fluid and dynamic relation.[55] While global forces and media (capital, advertising) are absorbed into the local,[56] a new interior is hollowed out, "a global delocalization, which affects the very nature not merely of 'natural,' but of 'social' identity, throwing into question not so much the nation-state, but the city, the geopolitics of nature."[57] The turning inside out of global and local relations is evident in another of the major features of globalization: the migration of populations.[58] Globalization is not a homogenizing force, as Appadurai notes, but a "cannibalizing" one in which sameness and difference, East and West, begin to consume each other in a "cultural flux."[59] A splitting of traditional expectations and identifications occurs. Appadurai discusses the sense of "rage" and "betrayal" that arises in translocal ethnic contexts as a result of misunderstandings and the disclosure that one's neighbors are not necessarily identified with the same communal, ethnic, or political values:

> a perceived violation of the sense of knowing who the Other was and of rage about who they really turn out to be. This sense of treachery, of betrayal, and thus of violated trust, rage, and hatred has everything to do with a world in which large-scale identities forcibly enter the local imagination and become the dominant voice-over in the traffic of ordinary life.[60]

Rage defines one of the cultural responses to shifting urban constitutions. It is also an identifiable social effect of shifting economic priorities: "the only available response on the part of those left marginalized is urban rage."[61]

RAGE

The virus released from the laboratory showing images of urban violence is called "RAGE." The global context in which *28 Weeks Later* locates itself takes issues further; occupied and under reconstruction, Britain, it seems, is no different from any country in the world, no more privileged or secure than, say, Iraq or Afghanistan. Its returning population is being "repatriated" under the protection of an external force; they are housed in a "Green zone," like in Baghdad, and under constant surveillance.[62] Turning an erstwhile global financial center into a refugee camp stages a striking reversal that forcibly underlines the ease with which national fortune can be transformed in the precarious flux of global change. Third and first world, like rich and poor in cities, are never too far apart. In globalization, the city undergoes reversals of assumptions in which the third world reappears in the first, in the shape of migrants, unemployment, and homeless figures.[63] As Virilio argues, "our post-industrial world is already the spitting image of the old colonial world," while Hardt and Negri note that the "Third World does not really disappear in the process of unification of the World market but enters into the First, establishes itself at the heart as ghetto, shantytown, favela."[64]

While, visually and verbally, U.S. forces are the main occupiers, early captions announce that a "U.S.-led NATO force" is in control. Legitimated by transpolitical sanction and identifying the context as post- or hypermodern, the occupation is enforced by international authority. Other visual and verbal markers underline this difference; public announcements declare that "the U.S. army is responsible for your safety," warning civilians not to leave the "security zone." Traveling shots from the Docklands railway show soldiers in biological protection suits disposing of bodies in biohazard bags. Security—the lives of the returning population—is the main stake of this militarily supervised repatriation. Soldiers do not wage war but act as police to protect lives by maintaining security against civil disorder (the return of the infected) and disease (viral contagion); snipers train their sights on people within the perimeter, looking down on crowds moving in plazas below or on individuals relaxing in their quarters. Their task is one of management and control, a task supported by advanced technological systems. New arrivals are processed by medical teams; eye scans in close-up indicate that control operates in genetic as well as corporeal terms: the boy's eyes are shown to be of different colors, a hereditary trait that he, significantly, shares with his mother. The new order is biopolitical rather than political: "biopolitics is the nexus of biology, code, and war, in which the distinction between disease and disorder is made indistinct." It spreads a highly flexible and extensive net over all aspects of life, materializing the shift identified by Foucault from disciplinary mechanisms to biopolitics.[65]

Biopolitics has become one of the cornerstones of the new world order. For Hardt and Negri, this order takes the form of a new "Empire" and functions with an intensely biopolitical version of life. Rather than employing disciplinary modes, rules, and norms sustained in diffuse discursive formations and aimed at individuals—their bodies, resistances, subjectivities—it involves protocols of command and control whose network appears even more democratic, diffuse, and immanent, intensifying and generalizing discipline "through machines that directly organize brains . . . and bodies . . . toward a state of autonomous alienation from the sense of life and desire for creativity" into a biopolitics targeting the "whole social body comprised by power's machine" as it penetrates "the ganglia of the social structure," now a "single body."[66] This body's nervous system, as much as its behavior and organs, is placed under "a network of powers and counterpowers structured in a boundless and inclusive architecture" that accelerates beyond "a liberal notion of the public, the place outside where we act in the presence of others," to a space "universalized"—and transformed—by a gaze "monitored by safety cameras and sublimated or de-actualized in the virtual spaces of the spectacle."[67] Thus, biopower "simply *produces* the obedient subjects it needs," a combination of postmodern warfare and post-Fordist production "based on both mobility and flexibility; it integrates intelligence, information, and immaterial labour."[68] Empire is monstrous in its totality, vampiric in its operations, feeding off the multitude that is a new monster of life, creativity, and nomadic affinities.[69] The multitude is a singular and multiple entity (distinct from notions of the masses, the mob, the crowd, the populace), a mode of "life in common" that provides the basis for Empire's sovereignty and power, as well as hinting at the possibility of an affirmative excess.[70] Multitude is found in relations among the poor and in the resistance and mobility of migrancy; with the destitute, the excluded, the repressed, and the exploited lies the potential to transform relations of power in a more creative and affirmative manner. Biotechnical transformations based on the energy of the multitude suggest an outside or limit to an Empire that is conceived as boundless, immanent, and total. Yet Empire, while constituting multitude, also feeds off its life and creativity, a life and creativity not its own but which it consumes and on which it depends. Divisions, antitheses, and ambivalences remain, despite the claims to the totalizing homoheterogeneity of Empire's immanent and global network. On one hand, Empire denotes a global condition beyond the borders, frameworks, and categories of modernity, but without outside, the possibility of differentiation and delineation becomes difficult. With all exceptions, even multitude itself, included as part of its operations, Empire works through a state of permanent crisis, an "omni-crisis."[71] In this state of omni-crisis, war is transformed into a permanent and civil condition. Generalized as a constant call to vigilance and action, war is a permanent activity: the "war on" (drugs, terror, poverty) is a matter for everyone. As a result, the enemy is no longer a specific nation or threat but "banalized (reduced to an object of continued police repression) and absolutized (as the Enemy, an absolute threat to the ethical order)."[72] Like the RAGE virus, the threat is everywhere and nowhere, to everyone and no one—outside the secure zone, or among the population within, disease and disorder form abstract and routine threats to the management of life.

Fuck the Chain of Command

Requiring constant policing at every level, the virus sustains the operations of biopolitical control and further enhances the stakes as an uncertain object of fear and anxiety. As the film develops, it is shown to be both inside and beyond networks of command and control, a point of excess to the totalizing reach of Empire. As a form of the "Enemy," its effects are double: it crosses and restores intangible or impossible boundaries, fueling Empire's boundlessness (its invisibility legitimating any security measures whatsoever), and in the process, it implies a limit to the enveloping expanse of Empire and the inclusivity and immanence of power's ability to absorb and feed off any resistance at all. Furthermore, this banal and absolute threat, this particular and general Enemy, serves well as a means of introducing "new segmentations" within network control; it offers an empty figure for projection, recoil, fear, thus enabling the redrawing of new boundaries. "Fear of violence, poverty and unemployment," note Hardt and Negri, "is in the end the primary and immediate force that creates these new segmentations."[73] The ambivalence extends to the relation between Empire and multitude, the latter the necessary living and creative force constituted by and feeding the former. As a site of fear and new segmentations, however, it also retains something in excess—of life, perhaps, disclosing a negativity lying within and outside Empire at the same time. Negativity, as Ernesto Laclau observes, remains a serious theoretical problem in the general affirmations of *Empire*.[74] Life's excess discloses Empire to be double also: its "corruption" is evident in the manner its command "is directed toward the destruction of the singularity of the multitude through its coercive unification and/or cruel segmentation."[75] Divide and rule and/or unify and rule. Either way, unifying or segmenting, Empire consumes the living creativity of the multitude, the negativity of fear and the destructiveness of power part of its consumptive armory. In part, excess precisely serves in the "function of exception" through which Empire takes and maintains control of the ever-fluid situations of heterogeneous, chaotic global milieus.[76]

For Virilio, the move beyond nation to a transpolitical and militarized state in which "peace" and "security" are elevated over "defense" means that the "enemy" disappears, "making way for the indeterminacy of constantly redefined threats" to life and ways of life: the citizen, now "a danger to the *constitution of internal pacification*," becomes "a subject who is a 'living-dead' [*mort-vivant*], no longer akin to the Spartan Helot or the Roman slave, but a kind of 'zombie' inhabiting the limits of a devalued public life."[77] Placing everyone under the absolute injunction of peace, however, means that all are also potential threats. In this state of transpolitical life, death becomes a vanishing horizon, incorporated (undeath) and evanescent. The new (non)subject of this form of life is unliving and undead and, significantly in Virilio's account, a zombie situated at the borders of this regime—its enemy and threat, and its internal horizon of control. Civil peace remains—imminently—in danger of losing itself. Zombies—zoombies, rather—thus manifest the (internal) excess that biopolitics produces and needs; ambivalent, uncivil, unliving, undead, destructive figures of fear situated along the crossing of the categories out of which the new world order emerges and on which it legitimates itself. The specter of negativity disturbs the affirmations of Empire and Multitude alike and returns in zombie fears and zombie consumption, destruction and death. Rapid, violent, corporeally excessive, destructive—the embodiment of disorder and disease, zombies manifest a "necrology" of the body politic and disclose the limitations of sovereignty in the new world order. Distinct from the redundant, slow, unproductive dejecta of modern industrial organization, zoombies are the speedy, hyperactivated nonsubjects of a media-saturated, postindustrial, high-performance economy, the other face of Empire's multitude, wired up (like chimpanzee and patient in *28 Days Later*) to screens, machines, drips, and monitors. While they might look like the "People" of modern democracy—and their negatives, the masses or violent urban mob—they are not mechanized automatons but the singular body of the multitude hooked up to the digital networks of hypermodernity, its power flowing "through machines that directly organize brains" and producing "a state of autonomous alienation from any sense of life or desire for creativity."[78] The multitudes retain a positive, affirmative political potential. In contrast, zombies are alienated from life and creativity to the extent that they destroy and are eliminated by forces of Empire. Neither do they hold out any promise of manifesting the "singular power of a *new city*."[79]

The setting of *28 Weeks Later* and its elaboration of a zombie plague point toward excess. Not only is "life" policed, managed, secured, and manipulated by a technological, military, and medical network; it is also, in the form of the RAGE virus itself (a living organism and agent of violent death), the point at which control exerts its most extreme and dramatic pressure. Responding to the army doctor's concern about the virus returning, the local commander asserts that it will be subjected to "code red": it will be "killed." At the limits of pacification lies extermination. When the virus does return, spreading rapidly through the civilian population of District 1, security measures prove useless and panic ensues. At first, security forces are urged to "watch out for friendlies" and "only target infected," but the hysterical crowd makes it difficult to distinguish enraged infected from panicking civilians, all unruly bodies demanding pacification. The command is given to "shoot everything," targeting all at ground level with the explicit instruction of making "no exceptions." As snipers shoot indiscriminately into the zombie–human melee, power's last-ditch attempt to secure itself fails: "we've lost control." Its last resort is more extreme still: the order is given for the aerial firebombing of District 1, pacification and purification at once. "No exceptions" evinces the absolutization of Empire's enemy and the way that death and destruction mark the limit and outside of its power; it belies the securing of life on the basis of an always-imminent threat: not any life, not individual life, but life in general, the life of Empire's population, must be protected, the life of abstracted and abstractable biotechnological power, that is, life under control. When life goes too far—as virus; as rage; as exuberant, unruly excess (the condition also of creativity)—then an unbearable negativity comes to the fore. Though "completely incapable of submitting to command," zombies do not express any desire to create life anew, only to perpetuate death/undeath. Hence they come into closer proximity with, replicating even, the operations of Empire itself, consuming, feeding off, destroying, life and creativity. Empire is the "ou-topia," the nowhere (and everywhere), the "nonplace" where global production occurs, a nonplace that "has a brain, heart, torso and limbs, globally."[80] Empire's nonplace is positioned against the multitude and "defined here in the final instance as the 'non-place' of life, or, in other words, as the absolute capacity for destruction. Empire is the ultimate form of biopower as it is the absolute inversion of the power of life."[81] Just as Empire is the nonplace of life, so, too, the zombie, reconfiguring its body in hideous terms, assumes the shape of the "ou-body," the "no-body," its impossible embodiment and excess—its life-death. Zombies offer themselves as the barely inverted image of Empire; the virus that creates them comes to figure as the mirror of global capitalism's capacity to mutate, undermine, and destroy its precedents. With each crisis, capital mutates, spreading its reach, penetrating further and more devastatingly: "the system is better seen as a kind of virus—its development is something like an epidemic (better still, a rash of epidemics, an epidemic of epidemics)."[82] As virus, capitalism is a kind of life, less and more than life, a barer life that escapes the controls that produce it.

In biopolitical discourse, the establishment of the new world order's legitimacy requires a sovereignty predicated on exceptionality, on life stripped down to its most basic level and located in a "zone of indistinction" that allows for "the circulation of 'life' as an exception." "At once excluding bare life from and capturing it within the political order, the state of exception actually constituted, in its very separateness, the hidden foundation on which the political system rested." When borders blur, Agamben argues, bare life "frees itself in the city" as "place for both the organization of State power and emancipation from it."[83] For Thacker, zombies serve as an image of bare life's exceptionality. He cites the figure of the leper, from the twelfth century, as an example of "living death" and goes on to assert, with reference to movie monsters, their continuity with "the living dead, the mass of living corpses that are *only bodies. that are only bare life.*"[84] While the equation of zombie and bare life works, it only does so up to a point, the point where exceptionality is eclipsed by unexceptionality, by "no exceptions." In *28 Weeks Later,* zombies pose and exceed bare life and exceptionality (to have no exceptions is to equate everything and, at the same time, to make exceptionality general, a norm to be removed); bare life becomes absorbed, like zombies/civilians, onto and into the reflexive plane of Empire's operations and exposes a barer life beyond it. For Hardt and Negri, "there is nothing, no 'naked life,' no external standpoint, that can be posed outside the field permeated by money; nothing escapes money."[85] Only, perhaps, the specter of zombie capital, ruinously toxic, or the total collapse of the banking system, which, in *28 Days Later*'s apocalyptic scenario, is depicted as Jim bends down near a cash machine to pick up piles of notes, just more litter blowing through the street. The exception that produces sovereignty and is to be exterminated is no exception at all when absorbed into the abstracted circulation of money and capital's own living death.

"No exceptions": the phrase is uttered—again under "code red" in *28 Weeks Later*— once before the command to start shooting indiscriminately. The military doctor argues with a soldier that the children, the boy especially, should remain in her care. The boy, with his mother's genetic makeup, may be immune to the virus (and also have the capacity to be a carrier). Hence he has immense value (and danger) in the search for a cure. His value is as an exception, but it is measured by the doctor, and it appears in medically humane terms, not, like the soldier, through biopolitical protocols: "no exception" dictates the need for pacification—in the interests of life and population—over the need to cure, in the same interests. Life, again, finds itself divided within the imperatives of Empire. As a life that has the potential to save many lives, his existence legitimates her disobedience in refusing military authority, an act of negativity performed in the interests of a higher value that, ultimately, leads her to sacrifice her own life, bodily and material being given up for a human ideal. She is not alone. The friendly and jokey sniper Sergeant Doyle also responds negatively to the "no exceptions" command; he leaves his post and descends to ground level to help the remaining humans flee District 1. His disobedience and refusal of authority are performed with a defiantly negative series of statements: "it's all fucked"; "fuck the code red"; "fuck the chain of command." His act of insubordination positions him outside Empire's chain of command and against its zombie mirror; its negativity, moreover, is associated with a sense of human compassion and commonality. Refusing Empire's coupling of life and undeath, Doyle takes responsibility for the survival of doctor and children; they escape District 1 with the help of a helicopter pilot and flee into the deserted city—pursued by escaping zombies. Doyle's negativity implies that some humanity is still alive as the film reaches its climax; it enables him to discover a cause and meaning to his own life (and death), locating value outside the parameters of biopolitical control in a reassertion of human values. Between the excess of control manifested by the U.S. Army (and dramatized in its explosive violence) and the excess of the zombies rampaging through streets and parks, another excess emerges from the act of negativity, one that seems to permit human survival, almost sentimentally, in its focus on the lives of two young siblings. The film, however, refuses a return to human and humane values. All acts of negativity seeming to constitute a basis for or belief in something sacred are shown to be well intentioned (like the protestors freeing animal torture victims—and the virus—in the first film) but at best misguided and futile.

The negativity that ends the film (and prepares the way for *28 Months Later*) is not a prelude to a (dialectical) restoration of human values. Though the children survive, flown by a reluctant pilot across the Channel, the boy (having been infected by his father) is now a carrier of RAGE. Humane acts, acts of compassion and kindness, are just preludes to disaster, spreading rather than containing the virus. The last two scenes underline the devastating effect of such misidentification: a crashed helicopter is filled only with the crackling of defunct communication signals; a dark Eiffel Tower announces the next urban location to be infected with silhouettes of rampaging zombies appearing against the evening skyline. Barer life spreads fast and violently. Only RAGE persists, not life or death: "It's all fucked."

Notes

1. William Wordsworth, "Composed on Westminster Bridge," in *The Poetical Works* (London: Oxford University Press, 1920), 269.

2. Neil Hertz, "The Notion of Blockage in the Literature of the Sublime," in *Psychoanalysis and the Question of the Text*, ed. Geoffrey Hartman (Baltimore: Johns Hopkins University Press, 1978), 78–80.

3. Frances Ferguson, "The Nuclear Sublime," *Diacritics* 14 (1984): 7.

4. Julian Wolfreys, *Writing London* (Basingstoke, U.K.: Macmillan, 1988), 77–79.

5. Mary Shelley, *The Last Man* (Oxford: Oxford University Press, 1994), 242.

6. Ben Highmore, *Cityscapes* (Basingstoke, U.K.: Macmillan, 2005), 30.

7. Alexandra Warwick, "Lost Cities: London's Apocalypse," in *Spectral Readings*, ed. Glennis Byron and David Punter (Basingstoke, U.K.: Macmillan, 1999), 82.

8. Walter Benjamin, *Illuminations*, trans. Harry Zohn (London: Fontana, 1973), 178, 17.

9. Ibid., 176.

10. Mary Ann Doane, "Information, Crisis, Catastrophe," in *Logics of Television: Essays in Cultural Criticism*, ed. Patricia Mellencamp, 222–39 (London: BFI and Indiana University Press, 1990), and Patricia Mellencamp, "TV Time and Catastrophe, or Beyond the Pleasure Principle of Television," ibid., 240–66.

11. Tony Williams, "*White Zombie*: Haitian Horror," *Jump Cut* 28 (1983): 18–20.

12. John Tulloch, "Mimesis or Marginality? Collective Belief and German Expressionism," in *Conflict and Control in the Cinema*, ed. John Tulloch (Melbourne: Macmillan, 1977), 41.

13. Tom Gunning, *The Films of Fritz Lang* (London: BFI, 2000), 55.

14. Susan Sontag, "The Imagination of Disaster," in *Film Theory and Criticism*, ed. Gerald Mast and Marshall Cohen (New York: Oxford University Press, 1974), 435.

15. Linnie Blake, *The Wounds of Nations* (Manchester, U.K.: Manchester University Press, 2008).

16. Maria Kaika, *City of Flows* (London: Routledge, 2005).

17. See Wolfreys, *Writing London*; Warwick, "Lost Cities"; Michel de Certeau, *The Practice of Everyday Life*, trans. Steven F. Rendall (Berkeley: University of California Press, 1984); Steven Goldsmith, *Unbuilding Jerusalem: Apocalypse and Romantic Representation* (Ithaca, N.Y.: Cornell University Press, 1993).

18. De Certeau, *Everyday Life*, 96, 103.

19. G. Christopher Williams, "Birthing an Undead Family," *Gothic Studies* 9, no. 2 (2007): 3–44.

20. David Harvey, *Justice, Nature, and the Geography of Difference* (Oxford: Blackwell, 1996), 404.

21. Tony Williams, "Trying to Survive on the Darker Side: 1980s Family Horror," in *The Dread of Difference*, ed. Barry Keith Grant, 164–80 (Austin: University of Texas Press, 1996).

22. Arjun Appadurai, *Modernity at Large* (Minneapolis: University of Minnesota Press, 1996), 44.

23. Paul Virilio, *Lost Dimension*, trans. Daniel Moshenberg (New York: Semiotext(e), 1991), 63.

24. Harvey, *Justice*, 425.

25. Paul Virilio, *The Art of the Motor*, trans. Julie Rose (Minneapolis: University of Minnesota Press, 1995), 87.

26. Ulrich Beck and Elisabeth Beck-Gernstein, *Individualization* (London: Sage, 2002).

27. Simon Pegg, "The Dead and the Quick," *The Guardian*, November 4, 2008, http://www.guardian.co.uk/media/2008/nov/04/television-simon-pegg-dead-set/.

28. Virilio, *Lost Dimension*, 1.

29. Virilio, *Art of the Motor*, 73.

30. Hal Foster, *The Return of the Real* (Cambridge, Mass.: MIT Press, 1996), 131.

31. Virilio, *Art of the Motor*, 102.

32. Ibid., 120.

33. SHaH, "How It Feels," in *Crash Cultures*, ed. Jane Arthurs and Iain Grant, 23–34 (Bristol, U.K.: Intellect, 2003).

34. Virilio, *Art of the Motor*, 134.

35. Steve Beard, "No Particular Place to Go," *Sight and Sound*, April 1993, 30–31, and Steven Shaviro, "Capitalist Monsters," *Historical Materialism* 10, no. 4 (2002): 281–90.

36. Appadurai, *Modernity at Large*, 44.

37. Jon Bird, "Dystopia on the Thames," in *Mapping the Futures*, ed. Jon Bird (London: Routledge, 1993), 123, 126.

38. Ibid., 125.

39. Fredric Jameson, "Culture and Finance Capital," in *The Jameson Reader*, ed. Michael Hardt and Kathi Weeks (Oxford: Blackwell, 2000), 259.

40. N. Katherine Hayles, *How We Became Posthuman* (Chicago: University of Chicago Press, 1999).

41. Jameson, "Culture and Finance Capital," 273.

42. Bird, "Dystopia on the Thames," 135; Andy Coupland, "Docklands: Dream or Disaster," in *The Crisis of London*, ed. Andy Thornley (London: Routledge, 1992), 161.

43. Roger Luckhurst, "Occult London," in *London: From Punk to Blair*, ed. Joe Kerr and Andrew Gibson (London: Reaktion, 2003), 335.

44. Roger Luckhurst, "The Contemporary London Gothic and the Limits of the Spectral Turn," *Textual Practice* 16, no. 3 (2002): 532.

45. Ibid., 539; Luckhurst, "Occult London," 340.

46. Charlie Gere, "Armagideon Time," in Kerr and Gibson, *London: From Punk to Blair*, 120.

47. Fredric Jameson, *Postmodernism, or, The Logic of Late Capitalism* (London: Verso, 1991).

48. Michael Hardt and Antonio Negri, *Empire* (Cambridge, Mass.: Harvard University Press, 2000), 188.

49. Paul Virilio, *Desert Screen*, trans. Michael Degener (London: Continuum, 2002), 5.

50. Ibid., 11–13.

51. Ibid., 34.

52. Virilio, *Lost Dimension*, 29.

53. Saskia Sassen, "Globalization and the Formation of Claims," in *Giving Ground*, ed. Joan Copjec and Michael Sorkin (London: Verso, 1999), 102, and Sassen, "The Repositioning of Citizenship," in *Reading Hardt and Negri*, ed. Paul A. Passavant and Jodi Dean (London: Routledge, 2004), 176.

54. Harvey, *Justice*, 222–23.

55. Virilio, *Lost Dimension*, 9.

56. Appadurai, *Modernity at Large*, 42.

57. Paul Virilio, *The Information Bomb*, trans. Chris Turner (London: Verso, 2000), 10.

58. Harvey, *Justice*, 415.

59. Appadurai, *Modernity*, 43–44.

60. Ibid., 43–44.

61. Harvey, *Justice*, 404.

62. Joshua Clover, "All That Is Solid Melts into War," *Film Quarterly* 61, no. 1 (2008): 6.

63. Michel Serres, *Angels: A Modern Myth*, trans. F. Cowper (Paris: Flammarion, 1993), and Slavoj Žižek, *Tarrying with the Negative* (Durham, N.C.: Duke University Press, 1993).

64. Virilio, *Information Bomb*, 55; Hardt and Negri, *Empire*, 253–54.

65. Michel Foucault, *The History of Sexuality: Vol. I. An Introduction*, trans. Robert Hurley (Harmondsworth, U.K.: Penguin, 1981), 136–37, and Foucault, *Society Must Be Defended*, trans. David Macey (London: Penguin, 2003), 249.

66. Hardt and Negri, *Empire*, 23–24.

67. Ibid., 166, 188–89.

68. Ibid., 53.

69. Ibid., 62.

70. Michael Hardt and Antonio Negri, *Multitude* (London: Penguin, 2006), xv.

71. Hardt and Negri, *Empire*, 189.

72. Hardt and Negri, *Multitude*, 13.

73. Hardt and Negri, *Empire*, 335.

74. Ernesto Laclau, "Can Immanence Explain Social Struggles?," in Passavant and Dean, *Reading Hardt and Negri*, 21–23.

75. Hardt and Negri, *Empire*, 391.

76. Ibid., 16.

77. Paul Virilio, *Negative Horizon*, trans. Michael Degener (London: Continuum, 2008), 160–61.

78. Hardt and Negri, *Empire*, 25.

79. Ibid., 395.

80. Ibid., 190.

81. Ibid., 345.

82. Jameson, "Culture and Finance Capital," 258.

83. Giorgio Agamben, *Homo Sacer* (Stanford, Calif.: Stanford University Press, 1998), 9.

84. Eugene Thacker, "*Nomos, Nosos,* and *Bios,*" *Culture Machine* 7 (2005), http://www.culturemachine.net/index.php/cm/article/viewArticle/25/32.

85. Hardt and Negri, *Empire*, 31.

Spooks of Biopower
The Uncanny Carnivalesque of Zombie Walks

SIMON ORPANA

The viral zombie of contemporary horror fiction seems to have entered popular imagination in 1968 with George A. Romero's film *Night of the Living Dead*.[1] In that low-budget, black-and-white horror film, recently dead humans become reanimated and wander about in search of live victims. Though prone to damage and decomposition, the zombies can only be killed by trauma to the brain, and the bite of a zombie will turn living victims into zombies themselves. Variations on this formula have informed what has become a thriving culture industry, spawning numerous films, television shows, comic books, and video games that depict grim futures in which the bulk of humanity has been turned into zombies. The simplicity of the zombie trope makes it a useful vehicle for political allegory and cultural critique; however, the flexibility and diversity of the genre make uncovering the latent psychosocial trauma that lends horrific energy to these films a difficult task. Romero's first three zombie films suggest specific anxieties over technology, racism, consumerism, and the military, alongside a general sense that an undead collectivity threatens human society and individuality.[2] The calamitous breakdowns of social order depicted in zombie apocalypse narratives offer a critical perspective on the various horrors implicit in everyday social life.

It is with this aspect of the genre in mind that I examine a recent manifestation of zombie culture: the zombie walk. In celebration of the zombie mythos, zombie walk participants make themselves up like the undead and shamble through the city, disrupting pedestrian and auto traffic but causing no lasting damage to actual property or people. The first recorded zombie walk occurred in Toronto in October 2003. The walk was organized by Thea Faulds (who goes by the moniker Thea Munster) and involved only her and six friends.[3] True to form, the zombie walk spread, and more than three thousand people participated in the 2008 Toronto Zombie Walk. The 2008 walk was also organized by Faulds and conducted under permit with the cooperation of the municipal police force.[4] Zombie walks rapidly became a global phenomenon, with nearly fifty cities hosting walks to celebrate World Zombie Day on October 26, 2008.[5] Toronto's 2009 zombie walk involved more than a thousand participants, and the same year saw zombie walks take place in cities such as Glasgow, Prague, and Helsinki.[6] From humble beginnings, these decomposing denizens of popular subculture have limped, lunged, and gnawed their way to the status of a mass movement.

As a popular celebration of zombie mythology, the zombie walk contains strong echoes of Mikhail Bakhtin's characterization of the carnivalesque. Bakhtin argues that the feasts, spectacles, and particular language of the medieval carnival festivities were the expressions of a folk culture that celebrated the biological grounds of social cohesion. The carnival creates a kind of second life set apart from the rigid hierarchies of feudal social systems.[7] Bakhtin's understandings of grotesque realism, physical degradation, and folk laughter—as inoculation against the "cosmic terror"[8] of hegemonic social control—are particularly relevant for characterizing zombie walks as modern manifestations of the carnivalesque. In a mode comparable to Bakhtin's carnivalesque, the zombie walk provides a temporary and imaginary dissolution of modern power structures. The walks create a spectacular performance that cathartically addresses social anxieties regarding contagion, exclusion, and the increasing incursion of the modern state into the bodily, collective life of its citizens. I will argue that a major difference between the zombie carnival and the Bakhtinian carnivalesque is the manner in which the zombie subject is excluded from the processes of rebirth and regeneration traditionally associated with carnival culture. This exclusion can be seen as a response to the modern power formations that Michel Foucault calls "biopower" and that Michael Hardt and Antonio Negri, following Gilles Deleuze, call the "society of control."[9] In light of the biopolitical turn in modern politics, the zombie walk offers an uncanny return of the repressed formation of carnival; the zombie walk's celebration of collectivity takes on a ghoulish appearance in response to the encroachment of modern power structures into regions of life and culture that have historically provided temporary refuge from systems of control.

Zombie Carnival and Grotesque Realism

Though separated from the historical milieu in which carnival culture flourished by at least four hundred years, the zombie walk nevertheless incorporates many elements reminiscent of Bakhtin's characterization. In keeping with the nature of countercultures in general, impersonating the undead gives zombie walk participants second, secret identities and can simply be seen as a refinement and extension of North American Halloween festivities. However, in contrast to the free-form costume invention and individualistic, mercantile character of Halloween, the particularities of the zombie narrative allow for the creation of a mass identity similar to the biologic collectivity expressed in Bakhtin's carnival. Though each zombie walk participant takes pride in his particular interpretation of the zombie trope—a Victorian umbrella lodged in the head, for instance, or a zombie mother holding her half-devoured child—the social differentiation and individuation reflected in the zombie walk population are underscored by the presentation of a collectivity affected by the zombie virus en masse. We are offered a modern memento mori reminiscent of the medieval danse macabre: a public spectacle illustrating the idea that indiscriminate death (or unlife) is the master of us all.

In celebrating the social body over the discrete individual, Bakhtin named grotesque realism the dominant mode characterizing the carnivalesque treatment of the body.[10]

Owing to its focus on the common biological materialism of the human subject over unique individual traits, grotesque realism is of particular relevance to the zombie walk and its re-creation of the human form. Bakhtin notes,

> The grotesque ignores the impenetrable surface that closes the limits of the body as a separate and completed phenomenon. The grotesque image displays not only the outward but also the inward features of the body: blood, bowels, heart and other organs. The outward and inward features are often merged into one.[11]

It is just these inward features that the collectivizing zombie virus makes visible, upsetting categories of inside–outside in its exposure of muscle, bone, and organs and disrupting the post-Enlightenment ideal of the discrete individual from whom "all attributes of the unfinished world are carefully removed."[12] The figure of the zombie signifies the breakdown or eclipse—the literal decomposition—of this discrete, polished, individuated modern subject. In enacting the zombie walk, participants enter into an imagined subjectivity, the transformative essence of which sees the individual and the whole topography of social differentiation subsumed under a macabre form of collective representation. But to understand the negative, undead manifestation of carnival in zombie culture, we need to place zombie walks within a historical framework that charts the suppression of the carnivalesque form of collectivity and its possibility of reemergence.

Allon White provides a historical sketch of carnival's modern trajectory, characterizing its repression and decline as "the gradual, relentless attack on 'the grotesque body' of carnival by emergent bourgeois hegemony from the Renaissance onward."[13] White describes how

> bourgeois society from the seventeenth century through to the late nineteenth century systematically suppressed the material body of festivity once common to the entire society for a large part of every year. Carnival became confined to certain sites on the edge of town or on the litoral and was then largely dislodged altogether, no longer able to control the whole urban milieu during its reign. More important perhaps, carnival was marginalized in time as well as spatially. The whole carnival calendar, which had structured the European year, reluctantly gave way to the working week, under the pressure of capitalist industrial work regimes.[14]

Alienated from the collective social and grotesque body, the bourgeois individual subjectivizes and interiorizes carnival's focus on such transpersonal material elements as food, fluids, and filth. These elements are experienced in the register of "private terror, isolation and insanity rather than a robust, communal celebration."[15] White links the bourgeois regime of cleanliness and the "repudiation of reveling in mess" to the nineteenth-century emergence of hysteria as a psychological disorder in which "terrors associated with the lower bodily stratum are converted into symptoms of the top half of the body."[16] White's analysis also provides a convincing rationale for the emergence of hysteria as a disorder diagnosed predominantly among Victorian women; excluded from the mostly masculine realm of "peripheral 'bohemias'" that provided carnival's nineteenth-century substitutes (such as burlesque shows and circuses), women developed hysterical symptoms because they had no designated social spaces in which to give expression to carnivalesque impulses.[17] As a return-of-the-repressed formation of carnival, hysteria is thus revealed as a historically and socially conditioned behavior: a symptom of the class and gender suppression of popular carnival culture rather than a malady rooted in a universalized view of human nature and gender difference.

Reading the zombie apocalypse narrative in light of White's thesis about hysteria as a displaced *phobic representation* of the corporeal pleasures of carnival helps illuminate a particularity of zombie mythology that runs through the entire genre.[18] The focus on human brains—as zombies' sought-after nourishment and as the only part of the zombie body that can be effectively harmed—might serve as a marker for the cultural moment when the "lower bodily strata" celebrated in carnival reassert themselves over and against the sense of cleanliness and decorum inherent in bourgeois values and high-cultural production.[19] This reading would couple the rise in popularity of zombie films to the emergence of postmodern modes of analyzing popular culture in the late 1970s and early 1980s. These new modes of analysis moved beyond the elitist, largely production-oriented critiques of the earlier twentieth century (such as those of the Frankfurt school or the British culturalists) to suggest recuperative reading practices that recognize popular culture as an arena of conflicting interests, desires, and political potentials. Most useful for the present purpose is Fredric Jameson's assertion of a utopian and critical element within popular culture and his categorization of class as the latent, determinative content of narrative production.[20] If the class suppression of a popular culture grounded in the corporeal celebration of the collective social body informs the latent, political content of zombie walk celebrations, then these events can be read as real-life social enactments of some of the ideological critiques posited by zombie cinema.

Jameson provides the insight that ideology is "necessarily Utopian" even as it serves the negative function of justifying and disguising class domination.[21] Ideology incites our desires for collectivity and inclusion while simultaneously masking the extent to which these goals are foreclosed by sociohistorical circumstance. Thus in Jameson's reading of the film *Jaws* (dir. Steven Spielberg, 1975), the polysemousness of the shark as a symbol for various threats to American society—communist conspiracy, consumerism—is what allows the film to function ideologically by displacing historically conditioned social anxieties onto a monstrous natural figure. The shark can then be effectively dispatched, deflecting attention from the actual causes of social anxiety to which it referred.[22] Jameson also highlights the utopian elements of *Jaws* by analyzing the key protagonists as allegorical types who represent small business and individual private enterprise (Quint), law and order (Hooper), and "the new technocracy of multinational corporations" (Brody).[23] A union of multinational capital and state security supersedes the old social order of postwar liberal democracy symbolized by the sacrificed character of Quint. This plot resolution thus legitimizes the postmodern social order. By displacing the actual social anxieties registered by the film onto the shark, the film's opportunities for social critique are recaptured by the dominant discourse of multinational, neoliberal capitalism. When Quint's death cements Hooper and Brody's alliance, *Jaws* offers the utopian fantasy of a reconstituted collectivity "in which the viewer rejoices without understanding that he or she is excluded from it."[24]

A more recent example of the utopian-ideological mechanism can be found in Jason Reitman's *Up in the Air* (2009). Addressing anxiety over the precariousness of employment in the United States following the 2008 economic crisis, the film focuses fears over job loss on George Clooney's character Ryan Bingham, a hatchet man for a human resources consultancy who, jetting across America, delivers job termination notices to employees of various companies. But rather than address the government and corporate malfeasance that precipitated these austerity measures, the film depicts a silver lining in the impending cloudscape by asking us to celebrate the value of local support networks such as friends and family and the opportunity to pursue one's dreams that is supposedly afforded by the loss of a steady, nine-to-five schedule. Through its subtle, carnivalesque inversions of power hierarchies and identity (Bingham is repeatedly humbled; the dignity of family and ordinary folk is asserted; everyone, Bingham included, is threatened with displacement), the film produces a utopian feeling of "we're all in this together" that obfuscates the actual class dimensions of the economic crisis.

The dystopian yet carnivalesque vision of most zombie films provides an exceptionally good mechanism for revealing and even reversing the process of critique and reification through which much popular culture works to maintain political hegemony. In many zombie films, the dissolution of the social fabric due to the zombie crisis allows for class, gender, and racial antagonisms to be highlighted. The utopian promise of a reconstituted collectivity is often thwarted—not by the zombies but by the continued momentum of already existing prejudices and antagonisms on the part of the human protagonists. The zombies provide the horizon of a collective constellation that can only appear as a threatening, monstrous Other to those still trapped within the individualist, bourgeois paradigm. As Robert Stam points out, "carnivalesque art is uninterested in psychological verisimilitude or conventional audience identification with rounded personalities." Rather, the figures of carnival "are those of the Menippea, walking demonstrations of man's 'non-coincidence with himself,' ambulatory oxymorons given to sudden and improbably ethical turnabouts."[25] The zombie film is situated precisely at the border between bourgeois individualism and the clownish, decentered, and intractable noncoincidence of self supplied by carnival's grotesqueries. For this reason, the zombie trope offers a particularly useful engine of social critique, while also opening a new site of potential colonization for a postmodern, reconstituted, and transnational capitalism.

To provide just one example of carnivalesque social critique (and possible capitalist recuperation) in zombie cinema, I would revisit a seminal moment in Dan O'Bannon's *Return of the Living Dead* (1985). Echoing the simultaneously comic and demonic portrait of excessive consumption in Joe Dante's *Gremlins* (1984), the promotional poster for *Return of the Living Dead* features a cartoon of three punks-turned-zombies spray painting headstones in a graveyard beneath the tagline "They're back from the grave and ready to party!" Both movies draw on punk subculture: the chief gremlin, Stripe, sports a proud mohawk hairdo, and the red-haired punk rocker, Trash (played by Linnea Quigley), returns from the dead to lead the zombie horde as a kind of queen. With its emphasis on piercing, self-mutilation, and the metaphorical inversion of social hierarchy through the skewed appropriation of mainstream codes and symbols, the punk movement itself indicates a return of the repressed formation of carnival.[26] The linking of punk with the excesses of commodity consumption and youth culture in *Gremlins* and *Night of the Living Dead* might be seen as both a critique of the punk movement's difficulty in escaping the very commodity culture it rejects *and* a form of ideological incorporation on the part of a threatened mainstream.

The pertinent moment of O'Bannon's film occurs when three of the still-human protagonists manage to secure the remaining upper torso and head of a (once?) female zombie to a morgue gurney. In a scene that mixes the clinical mood of a medical theater with the haunted air of Victorian séance, the humans interrogate the half-zombie in an effort to understand the monster's motivations. As the undertaker, Ernie (Don Calfa), leans his ear toward the craned neck of the bound ghoul, we learn that zombies feast on human brains in an effort to annul the pain of being dead. But the depiction of the zombie who supplies this information on behalf of her kind as female gendered and missing the lower half of her body speaks to White's hypotheses that women have borne the brunt of the suppression of carnival culture and that hysterical symptoms can be mapped back onto a contradiction between the upper and lower regions of the body. As an expression of the film's political unconscious, the half-zombie's bisection graphically suggests that the pain of being dead can be read as code for pain over the social death of the lower body under the bourgeois suppression of carnival collectivity. The cure— eating brains—becomes symptomatic of this circumstance in a strikingly literal way, by targeting the cerebral organ necessary for the individual subject's self-repression.

In a scene almost immediately following the one just described, Quigley's punk character, Trash, rises from the dead as a kind of zombie sex symbol. We might read the close sequencing of the abject Victorian half-corpse with the sexualized and fetishized risen body of Trash as signaling the cultural resurrection of the libidinal impulses of carnival, but in an ambiguous manner that questions the cooptation of carnivalesque energies within postmodern capitalism. The shift in Western economies from the production of material goods to a greater emphasis on consumption allows and even necessitates transcending the older, ascetic paradigms expressed by Max Weber's iron cage metaphor.[27] This transcendence gives rise to an ideological milieu in which "it is possible to market and to sell the contemporary capitalist city as a well-nigh Bakhtinian carnival of heterogeneities, of differences, libidinal excitement and a hyperindividuality that effectively decentres the old individual subject by way of an individual hyperconsumption."[28] In light of these new market possibilities, I would risk overallegorizing by pointing out that *Return of the Living Dead*'s resurrected Trash zombie takes a homeless man pushing a shopping cart overstuffed with personal articles as her first victim, her newly undead body somehow unscathed by the horde of zombies who precipitated her transformation.

The viral nature of the zombie trope (viral in the mythos established by zombie films and in the growing popularity of the walks themselves) lends zombie walks an expansive, egalitarian energy characteristic of the carnival banquet for which "there is no separation between spectator and participant."[29] Because of the viral nature of the epidemic, every nonzombie is also a potential zombie, and the filmic zombie's ravenous hunger for living flesh or brains turns the zombie walk spectacle into a kind of mass banquet that carries an implicit, metaphorical threat of incorporation to the urban population with whom the parade comes in contact. Shambling through the city, a zombie mob collects new participants as it goes, while the infective nature of the trope turns casual observers and passersby into potential victims of the horde. This transformation extends to the physical infrastructure of the city as well: the zombie walk leaves a trail of fake stage blood, gooey brains (made from gelatin), and rubber body parts in its wake, incorporating the city streets into the grotesque realist aesthetic.

These elements of filth, fluids, and degradation are essential to the functioning of Bakhtin's grotesque realism; it is through them that power hierarchies are overturned, the high is brought low, and the low is both degraded and renewed through contact with the fecund, terrestrial processes of death and rebirth.[30] A vision that understands life and

death as two aspects of a single, greater process that envelops the entire human and natural world finds metaphoric expression in the grotesque body, a body that Bakhtin stresses
is always "in the act of becoming."[31] In contrast, the undead body of zombie mythology
stands starkly outside of the processes of death, change, and renewal. Zombification is a
death in suspension—an indefinite prolongation of the process of decay. It is this factor
that generates part of the sense of horror surrounding zombies as creatures who, like
vampires, are forever excluded from the transformative cycles of death and regeneration, which perpetuate life. Unlike the cosmic process of organic becoming celebrated
in traditional carnival, the zombie body is *frozen* in a state of degradation: no longer
truly living, yet unable to die by natural processes. The carnivalesque feast or banquet
of traditional folk culture, which Bakhtin describes as the transformation of death into
life, gets inverted into a feast on the living by the undead in zombie mythology, in an
act of incorporation that transforms the living victims into zombies. Through the insatiable hunger of the individual zombies, the collective zombie body grows ever larger,
thus providing a pathological expression of the traditional grotesque body that Bakhtin
characterizes as "never finished, never completed."[32] In transcending the limits of both
biological and bourgeois individualism, the zombie mob becomes a hyperbolic figure
for the collective body of the people, at once "grandiose, exaggerated, immeasurable."[33]
It is the expansive, epidemic, and depersonalizing nature of the zombie virus that am-
plifies the horrific aspects of the genre (a horror rooted in the primal fear of being
consumed alive) and points toward the particular social formation that zombie culture
reacts *against* in its carnivalesque inversion of power structures.

Figure 17.2.
The crowd at the Toronto Zombie Walk
in Trinity Bellwoods Park. Photograph
courtesy Lara Willis.

Zombies and Biopower

We might see popular zombie mythology and the zombie walk in particular as modern illustrations of Bakhtin's grotesque realism, but with this major difference: while the zombie walk's collective, grotesque body acts like that of the traditional carnival, disrupting and offering cathartic release from the hierarchies of social differentiation, the zombie carnivalesque celebrates the *morbid suspension* of the regenerative, redemptive aspects of corporeal degradation celebrated in the traditional carnival forms. Though it does construct an alternative system of distinction based on the creativity and elaborateness of the participants' costumes, the zombie walk challenges the bourgeois social order's emphasis on the individual agent through caricature and the hyperbolic degeneration of forms. In place of the autonomous individual, the zombie horde constitutes a pathological, collective social body; but in contrast to traditional carnival cultures, organic life is not reaffirmed or reconstituted on some more fundamental level—and we must now investigate why it is so.

Running through Bakhtin's thoughts regarding carnival is the idea of folk humor or humor of the people.[34] Bakhtin describes this cosmic laughter not as "an individual reaction to some isolated 'comic' event" but as a "laughter of the people," "universal in scope" and "directed at all and everyone, including the carnival's participants."[35] In the celebration of common bodily functions, the physical degradations of slapstick and genital humor, and the distortions and magnifications of hyperbole and excess, laughter is the force that reunites alienated humanity with its common roots in the cycles of life and death. Through humor, carnival helps inoculate participants from a sense of cosmic calamity—impending doom from dimly perceived natural or supernatural quarters that haunts our ancestral memory and is exploited by hegemonic authority in its attempt to cow the populace into submission.[36] Bakhtin writes that medieval festive laughter, as an expression of the social and resistant consciousness of the people, "presents an element of victory, not only over supernatural awe, over the sacred, over death; it also means the defeat of power, of earthly kings, of the earthly upper classes, of all that oppresses and restricts."[37] Zombie culture also exhibits dark humor that laughs in the face of overwhelming power, but the terror and oppression that zombie culture addresses are fundamentally different than the problems familiar to medieval humanity.

The territory Bakhtin maps in his study of carnival or folk culture incorporates the medieval period of European development up to and including the fifteenth century and extends "to all languages, all literatures, and the entire system of gesticulation." It is modern Western culture of the last four hundred years that Bakhtin presents as an exception to this folk culture. In comparison to premodernity's "boundless ocean" of "grotesque bodily imagery," the post-Enlightenment European focus on the individual body, belles lettres, and polite conversation is "a tiny island."[38] This tiny island, populated by discrete and self-directed individuals, has grown to incorporate much of the modernized world, while producing a backlash "return of the repressed" in the form of new focuses on corporality and mass collectivity.

In *Discipline and Punish*, Michel Foucault describes the society of *monarchical control*, characteristic of the Middle Ages and the Renaissance, in which power was exercised directly on the body of subjects in more or less public displays by representatives of a centralized monarch. This monarchical formation gave way to a society of *disciplinary power* toward the end of the eighteenth century. Administered indirectly through institutional structures run by trained specialists, disciplinary power is imposed in private as much as possible, leaving an impression of society's will on the interior soul rather than on the external body of the individual who is punished. Foucault shows how the dramatic metamorphosis of the spectacular public executions of the eighteenth century into the orderly, administrative prisons of the nineteenth illustrates this shift; disciplinary measures become hidden away, and their aims become less the punishing of physical bodies and more the correcting and rehabilitation of one's subjective consciousness.[39] Bakhtin seems to prefigure the shift in disciplinary structures when he describes how the sixteenth century saw the overthrow of older, bodily oriented carnival vulgarity in favor of more strict and formalized norms of language, decorum, and individuality. Bakhtin writes how in the modern model,

> all attributes of the unfinished world are carefully removed, as well as all the signs of inner life. The verbal norms of official and literary language, determined by the canon, prohibit all that is linked with fecundation, pregnancy, childbirth. There is a sharp line of division between familiar speech and "correct" language.[40]

The change from explicit to implicit power structure described by Foucault is mirrored (actually prefigured) by a shift in language about, and cultural attitudes toward, the body. If we map the shift away from the folk culture of dissent described by Bakhtin onto the changes in the formulations of power charted by Foucault, we can see how carnivalesque laughter in the face of terror and the celebration of the physical is replaced by the decorum, interiority, and individualism of the disciplinary society that saw its fulfillment in the Victorian and contemporary periods. We might go further and suggest that the interior trajectory of the emergent disciplinary model (and the attendant technologies that made it possible, such as print culture and panoptic surveillance) is what actually *allows* hegemonic power to exert new pressures on the social collective, pressures that change the form of power's antithetical but also compensatory shadow-self, the culture of carnival. By interiorizing the narrative of social tension and catharsis that was physically enacted in the institution of carnival, disciplinary society molded the compensatory mechanisms supplied by folk culture into new forms that have the popular films and celebrity iconography of the modern mass culture industry at their terminus. Between the "passive" mass audience, whose hypothetical existence is a presupposition of the modern culture industry, and the active participants of traditional carnival culture, intermediary stages of development can be charted. These intermediary sites included the popularity of pub events and music halls, where audiences could sing along with performers, and more bawdy forms of entertainment, such as the burlesque and freak shows, where the Victorian subject could hide away from the society of surveillance to surreptitiously enjoy the last vestiges of carnival culture. Such entertainments flourished in the blind spots of the panoptic eye, providing zones for the regulated

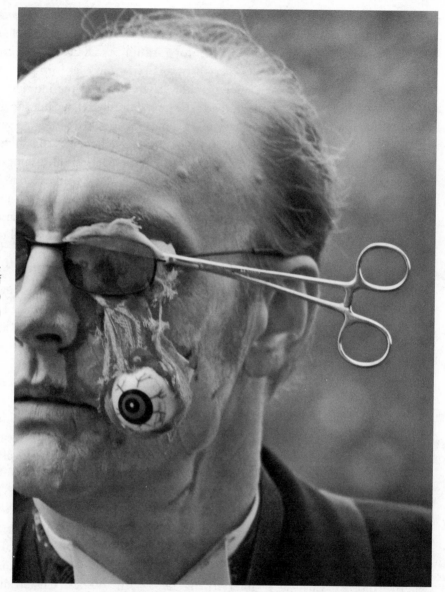

dispersal or containment of oppositional energies. For systems of control to implant themselves in the very roots of human subjectivity, further refinements of the social machinery were required.[41]

Cosmic Terror and Biopolitical Production

Hardt and Negri add a third mutation of power to Foucault's developmental model, for which they borrow Deleuze's epithet, the *society of control*.[42] This last model character-izes our current late-capitalistic society and is framed in conjunction with Foucault's conception of biopower as the complete internalization of social regulation, which leads to a state where "the whole social body is comprised by power's machine."[43] Hardt and Negri's society of control actually incorporates the biologic collective celebrated in Bakhtin's carnivalesque, bringing us full circle to a new configuration of the grotesque body:

> this [power] relationship is open, qualitative, and affective. Society, subsumed within a power that reaches down to the ganglia of the social structure and its processes of development, *reacts like a single body*. Power is thus expressed as a control that extends throughout the depths of the consciousness and bodies of the population—and at the same time across the entirety of social relations.[44]

Biopower as the functional model of the society of control is concerned with the "production and reproduction of life itself."[45] Like the carnivalesque, biopower's domain is that of birth and death, of the individual in her biological aspect as a member of the social body. The biological physicality of common human nature—which, according to Bakhtin, was the medieval site of a collective escape from hierarchical power structures of church and monarch—is subsumed by the dominant model of power used for the control, regulation, and maintenance of the populace in contemporary society.

Under the auspices of the society of control, carnival has few places left to go.[46] In modernized societies, the traditional carnivalesque domains of death, regeneration, and the corporeal foundations of life have been absorbed in toto by hegemonic forces that have subsumed "not only the economic or only the cultural dimension of society but rather the social *bios* itself."[47] Karl Marx describes the shift from the formal to real subsumption of labor under capitalism; this shift extends, in Hardt and Negri's theory, to the social, cultural, and personal realms. The subjectively experienced fabric of human nature itself reconstitutes individuals into a biologically based collectivity that is the very antithesis of the carnival celebration described by Bakhtin.[48] It is as a reaction *against* this

Figure 17.4.
The crowd in character at the Toronto Zombie Walk. Photograph courtesy Lara Willis.

subsumption of human nature and subjectivity by modern societies of control that the popularity and particular character of the carnivalesque zombie walk can be properly understood.

The zombie virus enacts a suspension of those very realms over which biopower attempts to exert its dominance. The zombie reproduces through consumption, not procreation, perpetuating a state of being removed from the provinces of birth and death, depletion and regeneration, illness and well-being—which biopower annexes as its primary areas of concern. Personal subjectivity and affective relations, further realms infiltrated by the power networks of the society of control, are likewise effaced or compromised by the zombie virus. Many zombie movies depict the unsettling process through which a friend or loved one loses his social and affective capacities as the virus gradually takes effect. The zombie's loss of higher human functioning in terms of language use, reasoning, response to affect, facial expressions, and other social cues signifies a devolution from full human sociality into a vegetative persistence of the biological organism. This reduction of the human element to its minimal "bare life" constitutes the zombie as a cultural expression of the *homo sacer* figure theorized by Giorgio Agamben.[49] Zombies are beings that exist outside of all organized systems of protection but that also provide the hidden template and justification for societal power structures, such as increased security measures, racial and patriarchal violence, and class division. The cultural prominence currently enjoyed by the zombie might thus register a popular apprehension of what Agamben argues is the concealed final term *and* foundational unit of biopolitical society.[50] However, the primary characteristic distinguishing zombies from the powerlessness of the victim position described in Agamben's theories is that zombies bite back.

We can see that by challenging the newly subsumed regions over which modern power structures exert their dominance, what might be called the inverted biopolitical aesthetic of the zombie walk is actually in keeping with the spirit of carnival as articulated by Bakhtin. With its undead, grotesque bodies, zombie carnivalesque makes visible the internal ruptures, traumas, and anguishes of being socially, collectively "dead," which normally remain hidden from view in our everyday relationships and experience. This new visibility challenges what Jacques Rancière calls the "distribution of the sensible" that conditions the way social space, value, and subjectivities are experienced.[51] As Ben Highmore points out, what Rancière calls political subjectification "doesn't consolidate an identity already in existence: it is a moment of fundamental disidentification."[52] For Rancière, political art acts in a disruptive manner to "reconfigure the map of the sensible by interfering with the functionality of gestures and rhythms adapted to the natural cycles of production, reproduction and submission."[53] While the medieval carnival supplied a form of resistant, artistic spectacle that asserted corporeal excess over and against the hierarchies of the feudal order, modern zombie carnival disrupts and suspends the natural, productive cycles that biopolitical capitalism has annexed into its control strategies. If political art employs fictional constructs that "introduce lines of fracture and disincorporation into imaginary, collective bodies," then it is the biologically grounded collectivity of modern biopower that the zombie virus dissolves.[54] In doing so, zombie carnival reconstitutes a new solidarity whose primary content celebrates the negation of the preexisting order. In our modern world, the network technologies of control have been refined to such an extent that only the macabre suspension of both individuated consciousness and social *bios*, playfully enacted in the zombie walk and ironically represented in zombie cinema, can reassert the carnivalesque celebration of physicality and reconfigure alienated humanity into a liberated collectivity.

Subaltern Laughter of the People

Having noted the differences in power articulation between medieval and modern society, we are now in a better position to understand how the overarching Bakhtinian theme of laughter as inoculation against a sense of cosmic terror plays itself out in the performance of the zombie trope. For Bakhtin, this terror was "an obscure memory of cosmic perturbations in the distant past and the dim terror of future catastrophes" and "the fear of the immeasurable, the infinitely powerful . . . the starry sky, the gigantic material masses of the mountains, the sea, cosmic upheavals, elemental catastrophes." These overpowering displays of sublime, natural power are used "by all religious systems to oppress man and his consciousness."[55] I might add that the Judeo-Christian tradition, though often interpreted as supporting the idea of natural calamity (whether it be earthquake, flood, or an epidemic like HIV) as the expression of divine disfavor, also includes a strong critique of this tendency—in, for instance, the Book of Job and the redemptive message of the New Testament. Following a certain eucharistic logic, Bakhtin argues that the banquet or feast aspect of carnival was a way of overcoming terror of the external cosmos through metaphorical ingestion. In the feast, the material elements of earth, water, air, and fire are reincorporated into one's own materiality; fear of the macrocosmic world is vanquished through a homeopathic incorporation of the microcosmic. Laughter is a crucial part of this process when the material world is hyperbolized through humor about urine and excrement and cosmic calamity is "degraded, humanized, and transformed into grotesque monsters" through its equation with primal bodily functions.[56]

The tactic of employing grotesque realism to challenge the use of fear in the coercion of political subjects finds expression in zombie culture as well. Just as zombies disrupt biopower by suspending the biological and neurological systems on which it is predicated, so too does zombie culture appropriate the trope of cosmic terror, employing cosmological elements of sublime nature *against* the ideological structures that support biopower. In regard to the combination of disciplinary technologies (aimed at individuals) and regulatory mechanisms (aimed at populations) that Foucault saw as characteristic of the modern expression of biopower, the zombie as individual and mass unit constitutes a nightmare image *par excellence*.[57] Not only is the individual undead zombie wholly beyond the realm of biopower's sovereignty over procreation but the lack of nerve receptivity and the limited self-consciousness of zombies also make them poor candidates for disciplinary models of social control. However, it is in their collective

Figure 17.5.
Toronto Zombie Walk
participant Adam Invader.
Photograph courtesy
Lara Willis.

aspect as epidemic virus that zombies pose the greatest threat to the regulatory structures of biopower.

Whereas Western religion interprets death as a transfer of the soul from earthly to heavenly power, Foucault notes how death becomes "the moment when the individual escapes all power, falls back on himself and retreats, so to speak, into his own privacy" under the modern, largely secular regime of biopower.[58] The zombie's uncanny living dead status allows space for imagining what is impossible in Foucault's formulation: the individuals "infected" are removed from the realm of biopower's influence *without* the attendant privatization of death and instead remain part of a collective mass with its own rudimentary sense of agency. This agency takes the form of a voracious hunger, the product of which is not a rebirth and return of the subject to the realm of life—as in the medieval carnival's banquet of excess; it is, rather, the removal of ever more subjects from the field over which biopower holds sway. The resulting calamitous breakdown of the social order is the challenge to biopower chronicled in countless zombie films and theatrically enacted in the zombie walk.

The zombie epidemic thus provides a nightmare image that concretizes the usually diffuse anxieties of the society of control under biopower. Foucault notes that death under biopower is "no longer something that suddenly swoop[s] down on life—as in epidemic," but is "now something permanent, something that slips into life, perpetually gnaws at it, diminishes it and weakens it."[59] As a permanent, cloying presence around which the remainder of humanity must reorganize its social structure, the slow but persistent zombies of Romero's classic films illustrate the collective unease generated by the gnawing, hidden presence of death within biopolitical society. While generally lethargic and easily avoidable as *individual* menaces, the zombies get the better of the human population through sheer number and a process of attrition; people typically succumb to these shambling predators when weakened by psychological stress, physical injury, or momentary carelessness. The zombie thus becomes a trope for all of the antagonistic but self-generated elements threatening what Ulrich Beck has described as the "second modernity" of a society whose prime concern has shifted: from the transformation of nature into profitable forms to managing the risks associated with the very success of this process.[60] Linking risk theory and biopolitics is the notion that a great number of modern societal challenges relate to the problems produced by the activity of populations rather than individuals. As an expression of a collectivized *homo sacer*, the excess population excluded from the social and political order can be neither sacrificed nor killed but is rather left to die; zombie deaths are a social nonevent that legitimizes the social order, and zombies emerge as a limit marker for contemporary biopolitical risk society. Existing beyond the pale of social protection *and* coercion, the monstrous image of the zombie provides the excluded ground around which society configures itself and also becomes the repository of unintegrated and ostracized meaning, identity, and possibility.

In the grotesque and cosmic laughter celebrated by carnival, "the people play with terror and laugh at it," thereby appropriating the mythologies used by the ruling classes to keep them in check and employing these same hegemonic devices to challenge dominant power hierarchies.[61] In the medieval period, this mythology emphasized the terrors of hell in the afterlife; in our modern period, to cite the tagline of Romero's *Dawn of the Dead* (1978), "When there's no more room in hell, the dead will walk the earth." The zombie walk performs a mythos in which the predominant concern is not fear of judgment after death but anxiety over a more mundane and existentially unintelligible death that haunts the social imagination in the form of overcrowded urban living conditions, viral epidemics, random accidents, terrorism, and environmental catastrophe. Threats such as these are the peripheral but ever-present specters that lurk at the borders of modern risk society. While fear of these biopolitical bogeymen's ability to undermine our sense of security is manipulated by dominant power in service of hegemonic ends, this same fear is simultaneously undermined through the dark humor of the carnivalesque zombie walk spectacle.[62]

Zombie Walks and Heterotopia

In a definition that echoes the carnivalesque confusion of categories and inversion of hierarchies, Foucault describes heterotopia as a space that is simultaneously a "mythical and real contestation of the space in which we live," a zone in which diverse social relations are at once "represented, challenged and overturned."[63] While Foucault's category is more expansive than carnival proper because he makes the anthropological claim that all cultures likely include heterotopias, carnival might be considered one example of the kind of heterogeneous space that he envisions. The breaching of productive workaday time with "time viewed as celebration" and the rendering of a sense of unreality to the allegedly "real" space of social relations are two facets of heterotopias shared by carnival.[64] The confusing of the categories of life and death in the zombie walk makes a heterotopic challenge to the visible order that has interesting historicospatial nuances when viewed in light of Foucault's concept. Foucault provides a telling example of heterotopia with the cemetery, charting the history of its relocation in the nineteenth century from the heart of the city to the suburbs, where it became "the 'other city' wherein each family possesses its gloomy dwelling."[65] Foucault's explanation of the reasons for this displacement echoes White's account of the removal of carnivalesque entertainments from the city center to the outskirts:[66] an individualizing emphasis on death, not as transcendence but as the final act of a private history; fear of contamination by the sickness and filth believed to be attendant upon death; and the present-oriented and hedonistic nature of a modern society in which "the inactivity of old age [and death itself] constitutes not only a crisis but a deviation."[67] If nursing homes can be read as examples of the "heterotopias of deviance" that Foucault sees replacing the older "heterotopias of crisis," then graveyards as the spatial enclosure for the ultimate form of human inactivity provide an even more paradoxically problematic *and* inclusive challenge to predominant modern norms.[68] In light of the historical displacement of death by bourgeois society, the zombie walk again appears as a return of the repressed, with participants disguised as the tenants of suburban cemeteries migrating back to the heart of the city, transforming the downtown streets through which they pass into a momentary, heterotopic destabilization of geographic and necromantic categories.

The challenges to dominant social order posed by the zombie walk are not merely metaphorical but extend to the disruption of everyday life posed by thousands of zombie actors shambling through the city. Systemic stress to urban infrastructure has become a tangible threat in recent years as these events have grown in popularity. As far as the Toronto Zombie Walk is concerned, collaboration between Faulds and municipal authorities allowed the event to continue for many years, with an estimated six thousand people showing up for the eighth annual walk on October 23, 2010. While the zombie walks started as a planned but more or less renegade appropriation of the city, their growing popularity impelled Faulds to negotiate with the city, securing permits for the use of the municipal parks in which the zombies congregate at the beginning and end of the route. The year 2010 was also the first in which Faulds and her team of volunteers asked participants to fill out registration forms, with the aim of establishing a mailing list to better promote fund-raising events. In terms of the demographics of zombie walk participants, Faulds highlights the diversity of people who come out for the event. By

Figure 17.6.
Toronto Zombie Walk
participants. Photograph
courtesy Lara Willis.

no means limited to the subculture interested in campy horror movies, zombie walks are currently seen by many as a fun family event, and Faulds is surprised by the number of e-mails she receives from mothers asking about zombie-related books, products, and events that they can share with their kids. Interestingly, the demographic information gathered at the 2010 Toronto walk indicates that upward of 70 percent of participants actually came from outside of the downtown Toronto area, adding a new dimension to the metaphor of suburban infiltration suggested by the graveyard example.[69]

Zombie walks might thus be seen as part of the increased interest suburban residents have taken in the downtown core of cities—a reinvigoration of city centers influenced by the recent linking of economics to cultural growth and the so-called creative economy. This turn to the culture of cities is also evidenced in cultural festivals such as Toronto's annual Nuit Blanche and the monthly Art Crawls organized by the gallery and business owners on Hamilton, Ontario's, burgeoning James Street North. As Foucault suggests, heterotopias may well be crucial to the healthy functioning of social formations as cathartically liberating zones of regeneration and transformation.[70] The renewed popularity of street and art festivals helps recast the downtown cores of our cities into just such spaces of exploration, excitement, and discovery. At the same time, many heterotopias might be more properly described as a form of bourgeois or alienated carnival, a strategy for containing, taming, sanitizing, and turning a profit from the unruly energies of deviant, grotesque bodies. To this end, questions need be raised about the ultimate beneficiaries of these zones of libidinal investment and category confusion. For instance, even art festivals that are not sponsored by corporate or business interests can work to legitimate forms of cultural capital that further the interests of the propertied classes while masquerading as a populist celebration of common culture. As a grassroots and largely spontaneous, viral form of cultural celebration, zombie walks embody the dialogical and heterogeneous nature of carnival as depicted by Bakhtin. A celebration of the people and of a popular culture that has emerged from the underground, zombie walks maintain a critical tension between the visible and invisible currents that structure social life, holding up an uncanny mirror to our fragmented, individualized modern culture and giving expression to a sense of collective human energy that the conduits of biopolitical capitalism struggle to dissect and capture in ever-subtler ways.

Conclusion: Zombies Walking the City

We can see how the same tropes of carnival—grotesque realism, degradation, the feast, laughter at cosmic terror—operate in the zombie walk but appear in uncanny garb due to the modern incursion of the apparatus of power into regions to which humanity once repaired as a source of regeneration and respite from the oppressive aspects of societal configuration. I suggest that at least part of the popular appeal of zombie culture is due to the opportunity it allows for the creation of a collectivity that is conceptually outside the hegemonic field of late-capitalistic societies of control. The appropriation of apocalyptic mythology enacted in zombie culture also engages modern systems of power in a carnivalesque manner that may add unconsciously to zombie culture's draw as a disguised oppositional stance. Whether carnival-type inversions of social structure offer a truly oppositional political position or simply a cathartic release that actually helps to maintain political hegemony is an open question. What zombie narratives and their performance in the zombie walks do provide is a conceptual space from which to perceive and perhaps evaluate the social totality in a manner that is not accessible through the private, individualized engagement with social space encouraged by modern capitalist society. While the heterotopic space that zombie walks construct might offer a harmless release of oppositional energies, it might also lead to the production of new structures of value and feeling that could manifest in unexpected and politically regenerative ways.

In organizing the Toronto Zombie Walk, Faulds has thus far refused most corporate sponsorship, despite the mounting costs of procuring permits and city personnel and the increased time commitment associated with organizing the event. At the 2009 Toronto walk, Capcom, the maker of a popular zombie video game series, supplied a free zombie makeup station for walk participants; aside from this contribution, however, Faulds herself raised most of the money needed to cover permits and other municipal fees through fund-raisers and T-shirt sales. This situation is in contrast to the 2008 World Zombie Day festivities, for which the local Pittsburgh television program organizing the event offered four different levels of corporate sponsorship.[71] Toronto was *not* one of the forty-eight cities that officially joined in the 2008 World Zombie Day festivities (though London, Ontario, was), and the Toronto walk appears to be remaining true to its grass roots. Issues of incorporation aside, the carnivalesque aspects of the zombie walk illustrate the manner in which a second life that once took place through celebrations of human collectivity over a large part of the calendar year has been relegated to relatively marginal and temporally limited foci of resistance to the dominant culture. More heartening is the apparently irrepressible drive for a spontaneous, celebratory human community that continues to express itself in the most unexpected of constellations, even when the manner of expression involves an enactment of the overwhelming desire to gnaw off a neighbor's arm.

Notes

1. Zombie movies before George Romero's *Night of the Living Dead* (1968) most often featured variations of the Vodou zombie in which victims appear hypnotized or brought back to life by a single, evil master who gains control over them. See, e.g., *White Zombie* (dir. Victor Halperin, 1934) and *Teenage Zombies* (dir. Jerry Warren, 1960). The viral zombie genre started by Romero reduces the zombified human to an undead state akin to the "bare life" described by Giorgio Agamben in *Homo Sacer: Sovereign Power and Bare Life*, trans. Daniel Heller-Roazen (Palo Alto, Calif.: Stanford University Press, 1998). At the same time, the viral zombie registers anxieties over collectivity that link them to atomic monster movies such as *Them!* (dir. Gordon Douglas, 1954) and science fiction films like *Invasion of the Body Snatchers* (dir. Philip Kaufman, 1978).

2. Romero's subsequent zombie films, such as *Land of the Dead* (2005), *Diary of the Dead* (2007), and *Survival of the Dead* (2009), address such themes as class division, mass media, and mourning.

3. Thea Faulds mentions the 2003 Toronto Zombie Walk in Valerie Hauch, "Lurching on a Street Near You—the Undead," *The Star*, October 22, 2010, https://www.thestar.com/news/gta/2010/10/22/lurching_on_a_street_near_you_the_undead.html. Jackson Griffith describes that on August 19, 2001, in Sacramento, California, organizers of the annual Trash Film Orgy horror film festival hosted a "zombie parade" as a promotional event leading up to one of their film screenings. Griffith, "Friends, Seen and Unseen," *News Review*, July 25, 2002, http://www.newsreview.com/sacramento/content?oid=12731. While this event predates the inaugural 2003 Toronto Zombie Walk, the latter event was (and remains) an open and nonpromotional event. One participant of the 2003 Toronto walk went on to organize Vancouver's first zombie walk in 2004, creating an event that drew about one hundred people. The next year, the zombie walk spread to San Francisco and other cities. Thea Faulds, in discussion with the author, March 12, 2011. In an e-mail message to the author on April 20, 2011, Faulds, commenting on her reasons for starting the zombie walks, wrote, "Well, I like to shake things up. . . . I also didn't seem to know anyone who liked to dress up as the dead—at that time. So I decided to seek the undead through flyering and making an event."

4. Roger Cullman, "Toronto Zombie Walk 2008 Post Mortem," *blogTO* (blog), October 20, 2008, http://www.blogto.com/city/2008/10/toronto_zombie_walk_2008_postmortem.

5. "World Zombie Day 2010," http://www.theitsaliveshow.com/zombiefest2008/wzd.htm.

6. Roger Cullman, "Toronto Zombie Walk 2009," *blogTO* (blog), October 26, 2009, http://www.blogto.com/city/2009/10/toronto_zombie_walk_2009/.

7. Mikhail Bakhtin, *Rabelais and His World*, trans. Helene Iswolsky (Indianapolis: Indiana University Press, 1984), 8, 10.

8. Ibid., 335.

9. Gilles Deleuze, "Postscript on the Societies of Control," *October* 59 (Winter 1992): 3–7; Michel Foucault, *Society Must Be Defended: Lectures at the Collège de France, 1975–76*, ed. Mauro Bertani and Alessandro Fontana, trans. David Macey (New York: Picador, 1997), 263–93; Michael Hardt and Antonio Negri, *Empire* (Cambridge, Mass.: Harvard University Press, 2000), 41.

10. Bakhtin, *Rabelais and His World*, 18–19.

11. Ibid., 318.

12. Ibid., 320.

13. Allon White, "Hysteria and the End of Carnival: Festivity and Bourgeois Neurosis," *Semiotica* 54 (1985): 100.

14. Ibid., 104.

15. Ibid., 103.

16. Ibid., 105, 107.

17. Ibid., 108.

18. Ibid., 105.

19. The brain-eating zombie seems to have entered the genre with Dan O'Bannon's film *Return of the Living Dead* (1985), though many zombie films, including Romero's, do not highlight this aspect of zombie behavior.

20. Fredric Jameson, *The Political Unconscious: Narrative as Socially Symbolic Act* (Ithaca, N.Y.: Cornell University Press, 1981); Jameson, "Reification and Utopia in Mass Culture," *Social Text* 1 (1979): 130–48.

21. Jameson, *The Political Unconscious*, 286.

22. Jameson, "Reification and Utopia," 141–43.

23. Ibid., 143–44.

24. Ibid., 144.

25. Robert Stam, *Subversive Pleasures: Bakhtin, Cultural Criticism, and Film* (Baltimore: Johns Hopkins University Press, 1989), 109.

26. Dick Hebdige, *Hiding in the Light: On Images and Things* (New York: Routledge, 1998), 35.

27. Max Weber, *The Protestant Work Ethic and the Spirit of Capitalism* (New York: Dover, 2003), 181–82.

28. Fredric Jameson, *The Cultural Turn: Selected Writings on Postmodernism 1983–1998* (New York: Verso, 2009), 72.

29. Bakhtin, *Rabelais and His World*, 265.

30. Ibid., 19–21.

31. Ibid., 317.

32. Ibid.

33. Ibid., 19.

34. Ibid., 4.

35. Ibid., 11.

36. Ibid., 335.

37. Ibid., 92.

38. Ibid., 319.

39. Michel Foucault, *Discipline and Punish*, trans. Alan Sheridan (New York: Vintage, 1990).

40. Bakhtin, *Rabelais and His World*, 320.

41. Foucault argues that the modern production of sexuality acts as a form of social control that is centered on "the body that produces and consumes" rather than simply restricting desire. Michel Foucault, *The History of Sexuality: Vol. 1. An Introduction*, trans. Robert Hurley (London: Penguin Books, 1990), 107. Slavoj Žižek's observation that "the direct injunction [to] 'Enjoy!' is a much more effective way to hinder the subject's access to enjoyment than the explicit Prohibition which sustains the space for its transgression" also points to the internalization of productive and permissive control mechanisms by the individual psyche. Žižek, "The Big Other Doesn't Exist," *European Journal of Psychoanalysis* 5 (Spring/Fall 1997): section 3, para. 10, http://www.psychomedia.it/jep/number5/zizek.htm.

42. Deleuze, "Postscript on the Societies of Control"; Hardt and Negri, *Empire*, 41.

43. Hardt and Negri, *Empire*, 24.

44. Ibid., emphasis added.

45. Ibid., 24.

46. The Internet is one possible refuge for carnivalesque social formations, with sites like Second Life and other multiplayer video games providing obvious examples.

47. Hardt and Negri, *Empire*, 25.

48. Hardt and Negri's characterization of the society of control in *Empire* is in keeping with Bakhtin's distinction between dialogic and monologic discourse. Dialogic discourse is the open-ended, intertextual and necessarily relational interaction between a multiplicity of voices, in contrast to monologic discourse, which attempts to deny this multivocal process and establish itself as authoritative. In Hardt and Negri's vision, empire represents itself as a fixed, eternal order, outside of history yet unbounded by space. Hardt and Negri, *Empire*, 14. It thus exhibits similarities to the monologic tendencies of authoritarian regimes.

49. Agamben, *Homo Sacer*.

50. Ibid., 83; Giorgio Agamben, *Survival in Auschwitz: The Witness and the Archive* (New York: Zone Books, 2008), 156.

51. Jacques Rancière, *The Politics of Aesthetics: The Distribution of the Sensible*, trans. Gabriel Rockhill (New York: Continuum, 2004), 12–13, 85.

52. Ben Highmore, *Ordinary Lives: Studies in the Everyday* (New York: Routledge, 2011), 48.

53. Rancière, *Politics of Aesthetics*, 39.

54. Ibid.

55. Bakhtin, *Rabelais and His World*, 335.

56. Ibid., 336.

57. Foucault, *Discipline and Punish*, 250.

58. Ibid., 248.

59. Ibid., 244.

60. Ulrich Beck, *Risk Society: Towards a New Modernity*, trans. Mark Ritter (London: Sage, 1992).

61. Bakhtin, *Rabelais and His World*, 91.

62. This is not to say that every zombie movie exhibits subversive humor. For instance, David Slade's *30 Days of Night* (2007), Zack Snyder's remake of Romero's classic *Dawn of the Dead* (2004), and Breck Eisner's recent remake of Romero's early film *The Crazies* (2010) provide few opportunities for laughter. Even Romero's original films are characterized more by ironic social commentary than by outright humor. Films such as Andrew Currie's *Fido* (2006) and Bruce McDonald's *Pontypool* (2008) typify the sense of subaltern laughter I see as present in the zombie walks.

63. Michel Foucault, "Of Other Spaces: Utopias and Heterotopias," in *Architecture Culture 1943–1968*, ed. Joan Ockman and Edward Eigen (New York: Rizzoli, 1993), 422.

64. Ibid., 424–25.

65. Ibid., 424.

66. White, "Hysteria and the End of Carnival," 104.

67. Foucault, "Of Other Spaces," 423.

68. Ibid., 423. Foucault distinguishes between the older "heterotopias of crisis," which the modern world is replacing with "heterotopias of deviance." Ibid., 422–23. The former are characterized as aiding the individual to navigate a transition in her life course (such as adolescence or marriage), whereas the latter function to regulate "individuals whose behaviour differs from the current average or standard" (423).

69. Thea Faulds, discussion with the author, March 12, 2011.

70. Foucault, "Of Other Spaces," 426.

71. The Pittsburgh event was staged as an attempt to get the Monroeville Mall (the setting of Romero's original *Dawn of the Dead* film) into the *Guinness Book of World Records*. For the different levels of sponsorship available, see the website of The It's Alive! 2008 Zombie Fest, "Zombie Fest Sponsor Information," http://theitsaliveshow.com/zombiefest2008/sponsors.htm.

The Scene of Occupation

TAVIA NYONG'O

I was going to prison then, and—in so far as in those places the re-education to virtue is reached through idleness—I asked myself: what is there more idle than to still occupy myself with a little materialism?

—**Antonio Negri,** *Time for Revolution*

On a gray Sunday in late October, I go in search of Occupy London. I locate St. Paul's Cathedral on a map (having never noted its existence on any prior visit to London) and take the Tube, wondering as I go what reasoning or happenstance had led activists to choose a center of state religion as a staging ground for their confrontation with the forces of capital.[1] A short walk and I am approaching the cathedral from the side; I wander through the encampment of tents, run my hands along a wire fence covered in protest signs—the snarky, stinging anonymous murmuring of the multitude—before arriving at the church's august west front, with the two towers, wide steps, and fountain. Although Christopher Wren's baroque architecture was designed to lift the eyes heavenward in pious contemplation of eternity, the hum of life in and around the tented encampment of the occupation instead drew the eyes, ears, and shoulders down. One stooped to enter a kitchen, info tent, or place of discussion or simply squatted outside to watch the circulation of tourists, occupiers, and passersby, and to watch oneself being watched.

The Thursday prior to my visit, a prominent cleric in the Diocese of London had resigned (and another would days later) over plans to evict the occupiers, by force if necessary, from cathedral grounds. I listen, half-comprehendingly, as an English friend explains the local and national politics of this controversy, which was on the cover of the tabloids that week and was enmeshed in the complex legal, ecclesial, and political web linking the contemporary metropolitan city known as London, the City of London (its financial center and counterpart to Wall Street), and the Diocese of London, of which St. Paul's is the cathedral. I began to intimate, if not fully comprehend, why occupying these particular church grounds might resonate within the context of a protest against the looting and pillaging of the world economy by finance capital, protected, in the case of the City of London, by privileges accorded to it as a private corporation established by royal edict in 1694, beyond the reach of democratic accountability. Knowing even a little of this background, I felt more able to speculate as to how the looming threat of eviction and violence might hang over that particular Sabbath, the day before All Hallow's Eve.

In front of the cathedral steps, a young woman of color is teaching a dance as Michael Jackson's "Thriller" blasts intermittently from the loudspeakers (which Occupy London, unlike Occupy Wall Street, possesses). Behind her, a group rehearses dance moves that bear a family resemblance to the famous zombie dance choreographed by Jackson and Michael Peters for the 1983 music video *Thriller*, directed by John Landis. Many of the dancers wear Guy Fawkes masks, an icon associated with Anonymous (the group of activist hackers). Anonymous appears to have initiated this dance rehearsal; at least one of its members is handing out masks to newly recruited dancers. Going into mock ethnographic mode, I accentuate my American accent and ask him in the most oblivious-sounding tone I can muster who the mask depicts. He snorts and replies that it is an effigy of the only man who ever entered Parliament with honest intentions. The following day, these and other participants will dress up as corporate zombies and descend on the Bank of England, in a Halloween action fronted by banners reading "Dancing on the Grave of Capitalism" and "This Has Just Begun."

The church location lends the London occupation a different *Stimmung* than that which I had felt during my visits to Occupy Wall Street (which held its own zombie walk earlier in October).[2] Whether by decision or happenstance, encamping under the shadow of a cathedral placed the London occupation within a "vortex" of sacred resonances.[3] In New York, occupiers chose a privately owned plaza known as Zuccotti Park from 2006—until occupiers reclaimed its prior name of Liberty Plaza Park in 2011—that is required by law to remain open to the public. Liberty/Zuccotti Park is the kind of privatized public space that developers concede in exchange for zoning exemptions from the city, typically to permit developers to build higher than zoning laws permit (colonizing shared sky as well as land). They are fig leaves draped over the naked takeover of the city by its finance, insurance, and real estate industries in the wake of the city's near-bankruptcy in the 1970s.[4] The park is unusual only in its freestanding status

Figure 18.1.
Rehearsing the zombie dance at Occupy London to Michael Jackson's "Thriller," October 30, 2011. Photograph by Tavia Nyong'o.

Figure 18.2.
Rehearsing the zombie
dance at Occupy London,
October 30, 2011. Photograph
by Tavia Nyong'o.

(it occupies an entire city block) and the requirement for twenty-four-hour access, re-interpreted in the wake of the November 15, 2011, eviction of occupiers to exclude sleeping. The decision to take a stand there—in a sliver of "public" land carved out from rapaciously expanding privatized space—contrasts with the symbolism of occupying hallowed ground, land set apart neither for commerce nor for public recreation but for the transport of communicants into the presence of the divine. Where the former acted on a nexus of the political–commercial power governing urban space, the latter did the same for a political–commercial–religious nexus, unearthing a connective grid of economic, ecclesial, and state power that lay deep in the history of the city.

To the wandering tourist, in other words, Occupy London could initially appear to be an act of religious refuge. This impression, while not fully accurate, is telling in that it brings forward one significant aspect of occupying: the manner in which it seeks to strike at a common root that unites what we typically accept as the divided realms of the sacred and secular. This common root was Foucault's great theme in his lectures on governmentality.[5] As his recent commentator Giorgio Agamben has argued, the term Foucault selected to describe the instruments of governmentality—*dispositif* in French, translated as "apparatus" in English—may descend from early Christian theological strategies for accounting for the administration of things by a unitary and sovereign divinity, an administration covertly but continuously linked to the contemporary sovereignty of "the economy" over politics and society:

> The Latin term *dispositio*, from which the French term *dispositif*, or apparatus, derives, comes therefore to take on the complex semantic sphere of the theological *oikonomia*. The "dispositifs" about which Foucault speaks are somehow linked to this theological legacy. . . . The term "apparatus" designates that in which, and through which, one realizes a pure activity of governance devoid of any foundation in being.[6]

If early Christian theology found in the concept of "apparatus" an account of the ontological separation of God from the administration of his creation, then, Agamben argues, this division remains at the base of our contemporary concept of "economy." Economy, in other words, is a fundamentally theological term that has been subsequently secularized without losing its subjectifying power, based in the "pure activity of governance." Today we may have exchanged the sovereignty of God for the sovereignty of the market. But, according to Agamben, this shift has not abolished but only intensified the separation between being and the subject of governmentality produced by the apparatus. It has resulted in a proliferation of apparatuses to the point where we are perpetually being subjectified and desubjectified by a capitalism that continuously profanes the sacred even as it sets up its own sacred cows (like the Wall Street Bull). This violent oscillation leaves the subject in a "spectral" or "larval" state, Agamben argues, in language suggestive of an encounter with the haunted, protean figure of the zombie.[7]

For Agamben, we are now engaged in an "everyday hand-to-hand struggle with apparatuses."[8] Occupation clearly counts as an intensification of such everyday hand-to-hand struggles with governmentality, and it throws into relief three aspects, time, space, and the act of naming, which all seem primed for performance analysis. Performance analysis helps unpack the concept of "everyday struggle," revealing the immanent tension between everydayness and struggle, between stasis and movement, between "resistance" and "potentiality."[9] For such a performance analysis of the time, place, and act of naming, two additional theorists from the autonomist tradition assume importance: Antonio Negri and Paolo Virno. Known as theorists of the multitude, they are also theorists of the time and place of the virtuosic performance of occupation.

To extend and radicalize Agamben's concept of the everyday hand-to-hand struggle against apparatuses, I propose to use Negri's writings on *kairòs*, collected in the book *Time for Revolution*,[10] in order to theorize what I would call the *precarious time* of occupation. What does it mean to occupy time precariously? Clearly it is connected to occupying space by and for the commonweal. But even if occupying the commons profanes the religious–secular divide that captures and captivates us in the economy, such a profanation cannot return us to a prior time before industrial capitalism or neoliberalism.[11] And after all, as Marx and Engels noted in *The Communist Manifesto*, it is under capitalism that "all that is holy is profaned."[12] This capitalist profanation presents occupation with a paradoxical political task; "the profanation of the unprofanable," Agamben concludes, "is the political task of the coming generation."[13] Such a paradoxical task, Negri's analysis of time shows, involves a precarious emancipation of temporality from the binds of eternity.

What might it mean to profane the unprofanable through the emancipation of time? Is this the familiar injunction of the generation of 1968: to live without dead time? Or is it, perhaps, a different engagement with the pervasive profanation of the life world by capitalist apparatuses—apparatuses enjoining us to preoccupy ourselves constantly, to aspire to a commercial simulacrum of "life without dead time"? Is it perhaps necessary to learn how to live *with* dead time? To live in *undead time*, the zombie time of austerity and financial chaos?

Precarious times for precarious life, no doubt.[14] But an ethics of human dignity and mutual recognition are but a part of the complex of power-knowledge that occupation diagrams. Pitching a tent at St. Paul's undoubtedly drew upon the symbolism of the church as *refuge*, casting the occupiers not only as protestors against capitalist greed but as vulnerable lives seeking protection from dreaded or predatory forces. When I was there, a banner left the question hanging in the air: "What would Jesus do?" We might point here to the precedent, in recent years, of asylum seekers protesting the unjust immigration laws of Fortress Europe—squatting, occupying, and hunger-striking in churches in cities such as Barcelona (2001), Dublin (2006), and Zurich (2008). We

Figure 18.3.
Occupy London encampment at St. Paul's Cathedral, October 30, 2011. Photograph by Tavia Nyong'o.

might profitably employ this association to connect occupation to Paolo Virno's dialectic of dread and refuge in the contemporary multitude. This dialectic is itself doubled, between "two forms of protection" and "two forms of risk": "In the presence of real disaster, there are concrete remedies," Virno writes. "Absolute danger, instead, requires protection from . . . the world itself. . . . The permanent mutability of the forms of life, and the training needed for confronting the unchecked uncertainty of life, lead us to a direct and continuous relation with the world as such, with the imprecise context of our existence."[15] If squatting a church to prevent deportation sits on one side of this doubled dialectic, as a concrete remedy to real disaster, Occupy London is a response to its obverse, to *absolute* (or generalized) danger, and the forms of anguish and dread into which such danger propels us. Such absolute danger is not necessarily *greater*: in perhaps the majority of cases, the *concrete* danger to the lives of those seeking concrete asylum is much more immediate than the *absolute* danger to occupiers, even when it is visibilized in the form of the direct force of police brutality. Absolute danger, rather, involves a strategic and ensemblic giving over of oneself to risk, an infinite abandon to the imprecise context of being human, not as the bearer of rights or dignities but as the nexus for a nondeterministic range of capacities and debilities.[16]

Occupying the absolute danger of being human brought Occupy London into a range of quotidian conflicts with the ordinary functions of St. Paul's as a vortex of ecclesial, political, and commercial power. But this contest over access to space and the rights to the city was woven into the fabric of another contest: that between *chronos*, the mundane, clock time of the everyday, and *kairòs*, the intensified, suspended time that Negri sees as key to revolution. The scene in October—with an impending Feast of All Saints—disclosed something of that tension between *chronos* and *kairòs*. Halloween is a secular, at times even irreligious festivity. In New York, a popular Halloween supply store, Ricky's, had decided to make "zombies" the theme of 2011, and the zeitgeist was apparently cross-Atlantic. The zombie is a complex icon for Halloween, for capitalism, and for the protest of capitalism. As David McNally usefully argues, zombies are potent symbols because they work simultaneously as agents and victims of rapacious capitalism. They capture—in their corporeal intensities, appetites, movements, and undeadness— the otherwise naturalized "risks to bodily integrity that inhere in a society in which individual survival requires selling out life-energies to people on the market."[17] Zombie flesh is thus itself a nexus—hence its decay, its bleeding, its stumbling, and its viral bite—for competing temporalities of *chronos* and *kairòs*. The video *Thriller* remains an Ur-text for a global pop culture of the zombie, even as Michael Jackson's status as *the* icon of crossover black pop indirectly evokes the Afro-Caribbean roots of zombie lore.[18] To adopt the guise of the zombie and go stumbling through the streets is a breaching of "the here and now of a stultifying straight time," as José Esteban Muñoz terms it, a hand-to-hand combat with the subjectifying power of the "soul" that the Church traditionally shepherded and for which neoliberal governmentality now takes responsibility.[19] That such a combat could ground itself at a place devoted to the management of the passage from secular to sacred time speaks to an at least tacit recognition of the rigorous demands of a contemporary revolutionary profanation of the unprofanable.

Kairòs as Precarious Time

"Eternity is in love with the productions of time," wrote William Blake, antinomian poet of radical British romanticism.[20] In the current context, we can understand his proverb as pointing to the affinity between the desiring-production of *kairòs*—intensive, revolutionary, occupied time—and the eternity for which the Church takes responsibility through its yearly cycle of feast days and fast days, its providential administration of a worldly economy of souls for which no rigid distinction is maintained between secular and sacred governmentality (particularly not in the neoliberal era of "faith-based initiatives" and "the big society"). Certainly there are many of the cloth in love with the revolutionary desires of occupation (however much that love finds expression primarily in acts of resignation). The Church itself has, entombed within its most formal rituals, a messianic time that holds open an elsewhere to the economy over which it ordinarily presides. So, how do we make sense of this affinity between two modes of time that are in such agonistic contention? How can we think about the productive performance of *commoning* within *kairòs*?

Here, Negri's speculations, in *Time for Revolution*, are helpful for placing the affinity of eternity and *kairòs* within a materialist conception of history and struggle. Negri wrote the essay "Kairòs, Alma Venus, Multitudo" on the way to prison, the Epicurean materialist Lucretius's *On the Nature of Things* in hand ("my book during this period").[21] In this duration of imprisonment, he occupied himself with a little materialism, to paraphrase my epigram. His essay is concerned with the ability, the need, to name the event that throws us out of ordinary chronology and into the intensiveness of desiring-production. The three terms in its title draw an arc between the revolutionary time of *kairòs*, "Alma Venus" (his figure for Lucretius's love of "the swerve" at the heart of things), and the contemporary multitude, whose capacity to decide against the apparatuses of governmentality is Negri's preoccupation. The first stage of this tripartite analysis appears to have the most to do with both performance and precarity (understanding that all three levels are interlocking and interdependent). *Kairòs* is caught up with time, turning, and embodiment, insofar as "a thing called into existence in the act of naming . . . *takes on corporeal characteristics, for the body is the predicate of any subject that lives in time*, i.e., of something that exists in the moment in which it names."[22]

Kairòs, Negri insists, is different time. Not *different from* eternity but, following Deleuze, *difference in itself.*[23] The love or affinity of eternity for the productions of time is a love for this difference, for the cycle of efforts and defeats of the desiring, commoning production that we call revolution. Negri comments:

> In the classical conception of time, kairòs is the instant, that is to say, the quality of time of the instant, the moment of rupture and opening of temporality. It is the present, but a singular and open present. Singular in the decision it expresses with regard to the void it opens upon.[24]

It is possible to point to such a rupture, such an opening of temporality, inaugurated by the fall 2011 occupations in cities across the United States, the United Kingdom, and beyond. It was a rupture that self-consciously inherited a sequence of prior openings, beginning most obviously with the revolutionary sequence of the Arab Spring. But the question of the revolutionary nature of this time of *kairòs* is often wrongly conflated with the immediate question asked by journalists: what will be the final effect or consequence of the occupations? Such questions prematurely yoke *kairòs* to *telos*, to destiny, and remain inattentive to the lived immediacy of the present moment and the void it opens out onto. It is in the face of this void that great anguish is experienced, great innovations are accomplished, and—in a performative enactment of the swerve at the heart of both phenomena—the zombie walk breaks out.

There is something of the mundane about the zombie. Crushed by the everyday weight of reproducing social life under capital, moving "laterally," as Laurent Berlant puts it, we *feel* zombified.[25] And yet, to *perform* the zombie is to experiment with the pleasures of terror, shock, and surprise. It is, paradoxically, a form of *dezombification*, particularly when it gets you out into the streets dancing. The zombie march enacts the sudden swerve of matter as it falls through the void.[26] The march is part of, but nonidentical to, occupation. It seems worth considering as an aesthetic mode that could expand upon more economistic understandings of precarity (such as increasingly familiar theories of the precariat), but without falling back on the models of "precarious life" associated with moral philosophy.[27] The zombie dances, swerves, and stumbles along a staggered line that Negri and others associated with autonomist Marxism have sought to identify with the political. Insofar as the autonomist tradition has sought to read Marxism *politically*, and not as either ethics or economics, it serves a particularly useful role in interpreting the aesthetic politics of dezombification.

Again, the particular politics we are addressing here are the politics of time, and it is important to think these politics alongside the more expected (when it comes to the Occupy movement) politics of space. Negri associates *kairòs* with a series of images we can think of as images of precarious time: "being on the brink," "being on a razor's edge," and "the instant in which 'the archer looses the arrow.'"[28] *Kairòs*, we could say, possesses its distinctive *affect*, one that we need to attend to and describe in all its variety and complexity (where journalistic coverage has always remained fixated on considering its *effects*). This affective account of *kairòs* as precarious time does not restrict itself to felt emotions but rather takes up the idea of affect as *extensible* in time and space, of affect as possessing a *movement* vocabulary and a set of principles for the *navigation* of a terrain. The politicized zombie supplies one image of this extension of affective dread, moving beyond the scene of occupation and into the pedestrian crush of the corporate city.

Occupy London certainly felt "on the brink" that weekend before All Hallow's Eve (as Halloween is traditionally known in the Church's cycle of yearly feasts). At that evening's General Assembly (the governing body of the occupation), a fervent struggle broke out, with denunciations and counterdenunciations, over a statement that had been released to the press, and attributed to Occupy London, demanding some specific revisions to the City of London's legal charter. As in New York, the contention centered on whether and how to issue demands and thus participate in party politics, the inefficacy of which the occupations had, at least in part, meant initially to highlight. That it was the

Figure 18.4.
Halloween zombie march,
London, October 31, 2011.
Photograph by Tavia Nyong'o.

City of London Corporation that ultimately brought suit over the occupiers (leading to their forcible eviction, in February 2012, from the "public highways" they were adjudged to have obstructed) would only underscore the diagram of ecclesial, capitalist, and political power that the occupation had already activated by October. At All Hallow's Eve, however, repercussions from that summer's urban rebellions, themselves following upon the infamous kettling of schoolchildren earlier in November 2010, were foremost on everyone's mind. This context made a potential face-off with the Metropolitan Police that much more anxiety provoking. The encampment had been there only days it seemed, and its time was already running out. Would the occupation fold up its tents before it had a chance to live up to its historical mission? Would it let the threat of violence force it into a premature reformism? The archer had loosed the arrow, and Occupy London felt like it was on the brink.

Rather than conclude this story, I want to dwell in this particular stage of the occupation and ask what we can possibly ask of it regarding revolutionary innovation, if we do not ask after its ultimate result. At least to me, two possible alternative questions suggest themselves: how does revolutionary innovation emerge out of *kairòs*? And what does it mean to say that eternity is in love with the productions of time? For Negri, a materialist answer must incorporate "the dimension of temporality as the ontological fabric of materialism."[29] That is to say, a materialist conception of time is one in which eternity becomes the name for that prior accumulation of time that launches, so to speak, the arrow of *kairòs* into the void of the to-come.[30] Negri writes,

> Eternity is the time that comes "before." It is indeed the power of accumulated life, of an irreversible and indestructible temporality; it is the common name of the being that is. Every *kairòs* is installed in this eternity.
>
> What we are saying—i.e., that *kairòs* is installed in the eternal, that is in the time that comes "before"—does not push *kairòs* into the past, but rather it renders the eternal present to the present of *kairòs*. The "here" of *kairòs* is not detached from the

"here" of the eternal; there is no order by which its temporal distance can be measured; neither is it possible to think a sort of contemporaneity of *kairòs* and of the eternal: for the eternal is a consisting in the place of *kairòs*, a simultaneous consisting.[31]

Revolutionary time, in Negri's exposition of it here, does not occupy a separate space of *telos* or destiny within history, as if the to-come were either predetermined or else a monotonous repetition of the present. He even rejects the notion of positing any temporal distance between *kairòs* and eternity. *Kairòs* is *installed* within eternity, or in our new parlance, it *occupies* it. For Negri, in each moment is installed its own arrowing arc of revolutionary affect, much as Walter Benjamin argued, at the conclusion of his own account of historical materialism, that "every second was the small gateway of time through which the Messiah might enter."[32]

How to Live with Dead Time

How do we know when an event filled with *kairòs* is upon us? How do we name it? As Lauren Berlant has argued, one thing that can be so unsettling about an event is the arresting realization—amid the ordinary ongoingness of everyday occurrence—that *something* is happening at all.[33] It is the event itself, much more than the presence or absence of our expectations for it, that can prove so jarring, spurring its retroactive codification into *genre*. Berlant notes,

> In these narrative histories of the present, a shift between knowing and uncertain intuitionisms enables us to think about being in history as a densely corporeal, experientially felt thing whose demands on survival skills map not the whole world in one moment but a way to think about the history of sensualized epistemologies in the atmosphere of a particular moment now (aesthetically) suspended in time.[34]

It is in this sense of a sensual epistemology of a particular moment suspended in time that I return to an analysis of the zombie. I again wish to avoid nominating the zombie as *typical* of occupation, or even of the contemporary precarious condition. Rather, thinking Berlant's account of eventilization together with Negri's account of *kairòs*, I want to explore the *particular* figuration of zombification as a mode of delaying the becoming-object of the event, of holding open the swerve or, in the zombie's case, the *shamble*, of matter moving into the void.[35]

Marx's political writings point to one aspect of this phenomenon: the frequent recourse to figures and genres draped in historical familiarity at the very moment of rapid and accelerating revolution. Here the zombie inherits the Atlantic cycle of speculation and "accumulation through dispossession" that Ian Baucom anatomizes in *Spectres of the Atlantic*.[36] The zombie effigies dead, congealed labor. In Marx's *Eighteenth Brumaire*, such theatricality served a reactionary, cloaking function, but we can also note its ambiguity.[37] Consider the cloaking of the zombie march on the Bank of London in the globally recognizable sounds and dance moves of Michael Jackson's "Thriller." The infectious and enduring rhythm of his iconic hit became the subject of a viral video in 2007, when coerced performances of the dance by inmates of the Cebu Provincial Detention and Rehabilitation Center (CPDRC) in the Philippines were uploaded to the Internet. In J. Lorenzo Perillo's lucid analysis of these performances, the CPDRC video intersected with a strategy of containment, as the Internet viewer looked on via the panoptic position of a camera stationed high above the courtyard in which the orange-jumpsuited men—and one *bakla* transgender performer—danced.[38] I myself was part of a group that screened the video as part of an impromptu tribute to Jackson in the wake of his death in 2009, enthusiastically participating in the infectious joy his dance and music brought, until sharply, and correctly, upbraided by a colleague who pointed out the video's enactment of carceral power and imperial enjoyment. This episode brings forward the ambivalence I now see to be key to any approach to current uses of the zombie (or, for that matter, reclamations of the name "occupation," which is equally weighted with the history of ongoing settler and apartheid regimes). It seems to be that rather than the innocent or newborn subject, rather than the ecstatically joyous figure that might have sought "to live without dead time," the zombie performs the body as an accumulation strategy: an accumulation of genre, of history, of gesture, and of race. The zombie dance is a survival skill for living with dead time.

Shaka McGlotten's work on zombification and queer (a)sociality is especially productive for developing this insight into contemporary zombie aesthetics. Demurring before straightforward celebrations of the zombie as the latest avatar of the posthuman, McGlotten nonetheless wants to construe our "collective zombification as still possessing an openness."[39] Particularly useful are the possibilities he detects for new materialist conceptions of the zombie in what he describes as the new "emphasis on the openness of matter":

> That is, no matter is considered dead. Zombies, to take an obvious example, are alive not just because they have been reanimated, but because their decomposing

Figure 18.5.
Dancing on the Grave of Capitalism protest, London, October 31, 2011. From Divi58, "Dancing-on-grave. mp4," YouTube, November 1, 2011, http://www.youtube.com /watch?v=FbQ4cuGOqWk. Screen grab courtesy of Tavia Nyong'o.

Figure 18.6.
Dancing on the Grave of Capitalism protest, London, October 31, 2011. From Divi58, "Dancing-on-grave.mp4," YouTube, November 1, 2011, http://www.youtube.com /watch?v=FbQ4cuGOqWk. Screen grab courtesy of Tavia Nyong'o.

bodies participate in ecologies of energy transfer, and because their contagiousness imputes an immanent continuity. Their hunger performs the obstinate movement of desire's passing. Desire induces changes, and it returns. This hunger transcends the constraints of life as we know it, or sparks at its edges.[40]

The particular, atypical shamble of the zombie—its asocial sociality, its decomposing ecology—choreographs a relation to the tense, dreadful time of precarity. In a literal way, becoming-zombie is a release from boredom and anxiety, as interviews with occupiers attest.[41] But release of energy should be seen as a *transfer* of energy, as itself evincing, if it is not too paradoxical to speak of this: a *surplus of time*. The scene of occupation, as William Scott has found in his historical research into workers' occupations of factories, and also in his own service as an Occupy Wall Street librarian, produced a surplus, an elongation and intensification of time.[42] Within *kairòs*, Scott notes, hours felt like days, and days felt like months. Time became elongated or *stretched* out, as striated (clock time) became smooth (haptic, felt time).[43] *Time takes longer.* The zombie, shambling across the perimeter of occupation in roving hunger, transfers this time, makes it contagious.

Another way to put this is to address the blackness of the zombie, attached equally to laboring and racialized histories of the "many-headed hydra."[44] Rebecca Schneider has pointed to the theatricality of Marx's historical materialism, both in the *Eighteenth Brumaire* and in the dramaturgical possibilities inherent in the theoretical figure of "dead labor."[45] I am very much drawn to this idea, as I am to Fred Moten's powerful reinterpretation of Marx's trope of the "commodity that speaks," which Moten reads both with and against the Marxian grain to proffer a conception of black performance as a scene of resistance by the object.[46] That the zombie dance is black performance seems overdetermined, given its burlesqued roots in cinematic fantasies of Haitian Vodou. Disavowing—as Jackson did—the zombie as a generalized figure of the "occult," one associated with a white, juvenile, male fan base for B movies, only redoubles the musical ironies of a black artist "crossing over" into the black-derived musical landscape of rock via a figure encrypted with such an accumulation of African meanings. Such musical and choreographic virtuosity steps around the many potential dead ends his character confronts in his attempts to escape the horrors of the occult, the many jump cuts the video makes between layers of a reality that turns out to be a movie, within a television show, within a dream. As an allegory of racial capitalism, and of lateral agency within it, *Thriller* could not work better. It seems at least for this reason that it, rather than the B movies it ostensibly cites, provides the Ur-text for contemporary zombie marches such as the one that was organized at Occupy London.

To think the zombie not as a generic figure of B movie cliché, then, nor even the zombie as it has enjoyed a popular and critical resurgence in the 2000s (most recently on TV in *The Walking Dead*), is to think the zombie through Jackson's body as an accumulation strategy for politicized, anarchic dances. Compared side by side, the dance being rehearsed at Occupy London and the one performed in the *Thriller* video resemble each other only in idea. Jackson and his dancers have a virtuosic speed and "infectious rhythm" that the occupiers do not attempt.[47] Instead, in their amateurish, simplified gestures that afford room for joining and leaving, for error and improvisation, they enact both the affective tonality of the zombie, characterized by slowness and shambles, and the depressive contagion of the zombie bite, enlivening the socially deadened matter it comes into contact with. Whether that matter is other pedestrians, traffic, police, or buildings, they all become surfaces the zombie shambles into and across. There is an arrested "adolescence" at play in the adoption of zombie marches as a political tactic: it is a throwing of the dead affect of aggrieved and aggressive youth into the face of an overdeveloped, ravenous economy that feeds on the bodies, desires, and aspirations of the young. Would crowds of youthful wizards and vampires, or werewolves and demons, have done the trick? Or is there too much of either the agentially evil or the simply bestial to permit such figures to do the same cultural work of representing the bad sentiments of precarity?

Let me answer that with one last narrative from the month before my visit to London. In October, I had been initially reluctant to take my own first trip down to New York's financial district. I was, in a former life, a Wall Street zombie. Technically, I never worked on Wall Street. But, for a difficult year in my early twenties, I did don a suit at the crack of dawn and schlep down to one bank or another in the financial district (or, occasionally, to one of its outposts in Long Island City, Queens, or Stamford, Connecticut, where I worked the graveyard shift). Citibank, Chase Manhattan, American Express, Swiss Bank. I was a permatemp in a series of postmodern secretarial pools, the highest paid work my liberal arts degree could secure me even in the middle of the 1990s dot-com boom. But when dressed up as "computer skills," typing documents for a series of soulless financial corporations was a fairly high-paying job. In fact, it was the best I could do.

When, about a decade later, I returned to New York City a newly minted assistant professor, my annual salary, when converted to an hourly rate, barely exceeded what Wall Street had paid me, if, indeed, it did exceed it. That simple conversion, however, belied the transformation from insecure hourly waged work to a stable salaried career. What chilled my spirit back in those early days, what filled me with dread and drove me from the workforce into the impoverished ranks of humanities graduate education, was the zombified state I felt myself enter into each morning, a state that persisted all day and lingered long into the night. Like the marchers in the zombie march on Wall Street and the Bank of England, I felt that doing precarious labor for high capital was slowly draining my lifeblood, taking away my dream of being young and alive in New York and slowly transforming it into a gray nightmare. Ever since escaping the corporate hellhole, I had been reluctant ever to voluntarily reenter lower Manhattan. So I was surprised, when I began taking trips in October to witness and participate in Occupy Wall Street, at the number of tourists milling around the financial district, snapping pictures of the Exchange, happily threading their way amid the crush of police, brokers, street vendors, and occupiers. Considering the Stock Exchange and the geography of lower Manhattan from the point of view of a postmodern *flâneur* was an arresting thought. Were these shutterbugs appalled, or excited, to hear that the zombies were coming?

"Make a hole and let the zombies through!" was the refrain as the zombies broke out of Zuccotti Park and shambled toward the Stock Exchange. I immediately understood their impulse to take their bad sentiments and externalize them into "corporate zombie makeovers," effigying the accumulated power and rapacious hunger of dead labor over live labor while, at the same time, identifying with the swarming movements, roving tactics, and monstrous affect of the zombies. Zombie marches, I was somewhat surprised to learn, are a phenomenon of only this past decade.[48] They are officially designated as a form of "cosplay" (costumed play) and, along with everything else it seems, now have their own websites, conventions, documentaries: the whole apparatus of contemporary subculture. Their rise is attributed, reasonably enough, to the resurgence of the zombie film as a Hollywood genre in the 2000s. But it hardly strains credulity to understand the phenomenon against the backdrop of awful carnage of the post-9/11 world, in particular, the War in Iraq conducted by former U.S. president Bush and former British prime minister Blair. Occupations in London, Boston, and New York have adopted the zombie walk as a recognizable performance genre of our times, drawing on B movies, music videos, and zombie kitsch as a commodified cultural unconscious, an accumulation of dead and congealed labor that is reanimated through the theatricality of makeup and make-believe. Occupying the zombie march is a hand-to-hand combat with the everyday apparatuses of entertainment and distraction, not a pious refusal of popular culture but a politicized immersion in its commodified affect for the purposes of its possible rerouting; not a recusal from the desires that result in a "larval" or "spectral" subject but an ensemblic desiring-production of precarious time.

And what about the name of "occupation"? What can the precarious time of *kairòs*, as performed through the zombie, tell us about that name? Others have mentioned the numerous pitfalls associated with that name. But here, too, Negri's discussion of *kairòs* comes to our assistance. Occupation, we might argue along the lines of Negri's analysis, is not a concept in the strict sense, not a transhistorical category, but a name, immanent to the event that it names. And "the truth of a name," he asserts, "cannot be given by anything other than its insistence in *kairòs*." Occupation "does not ask language for its truth, because it has already asked it of *kairòs*. But in language it finds a place to 'inhabit.'"[49] I have sought in this essay to find a place in the language of performance for such an occupation.

Notes

1. I subsequently learned that St. Paul's was a recourse after an attempt to occupy the London Stock Exchange was thwarted. "Protestors 'to Continue Stock Exchange Demo,'" *The Independent*, October 16, 2011, http://.independent.co.uk/news/uk/home-news/protesters-to-continue-stock-exchange-demo-2371469.html.

2. Tavia Nyong'o, "I Was a Wall Street Zombie," *Social Text* (blog), October 6, 2011, https://socialtextjournal.org/i_was_a_wall_street_zombie/.

3. Joseph Roach, *Cities of the Dead: Circum-Atlantic Performance* (New York: Columbia University Press, 1996).

4. Begun in the late 1960s, the privately owned public park that is today known as Zuccotti Park (it was so named in 2006) was only completed in 1980, when the lease of the last remaining holdout on the block ran out. See David Dunlap, "Holding Out at Zuccotti Park Is a 44-Year-Old Tradition," *City Room* (blog), October 11, 2011, http://cityroom.blogs.nytimes.com/2011/10/19/holding-out-at-zuccotti-park-is-a-44-year-old-tradition/. The story of the destruction of the economic base of the city by predatory capitalists (including John Zuccotti) is told in Robert Fitch, *The Assassination of New York* (New York: Verso, 1993).

5. Michel Foucault, *Security, Territory, Population: Lectures at the Collège de France, 1977–78*, ed. Michel Senellart, trans. Graham Burchell (New York: Palgrave Macmillan, 2007).

6. Giorgio Agamben, *What Is an Apparatus? and Other Essays*, trans. David Kishik and Stefan Pedatella (Stanford, Calif.: Stanford University Press, 2009), 11.

7. Ibid., 21.

8. Ibid., 15.

9. Gilles Deleuze, *Foucault*, trans. Seán Hand (London: Continuum, 2006), 74.

10. Antonio Negri, *Time for Revolution* (London: Continuum, 2003).

11. Although the day I visited Occupy London, I *did* take part in a spirited debate over the legacy and future prospects of the Luddite rebellion against industrial tools.

12. Karl Marx and Friedrich Engels, *Manifesto of the Communist Party* (1848), http://www.marxists.org/archive/marx/works/1848/communist-manifesto/.

13. Giorgio Agamben, *Profanations*, trans. Jeff Fort (New York: Zone Books, 2007), 92.

14. Judith Butler, *Precarious Life: The Powers of Mourning and Violence* (New York: Verso, 2004).

15. Negri, *Time for Revolution*, 32–33.

16. Jasbir Puar, "Ecologies of Sex, Sensation, and Slow Death," *Social Text* (blog), November 22, 2010, https://socialtextjournal.org/periscope_article/ecologies_of_sex_sensation_and_slow_death/.

17. David McNally, *Monsters of the Market: Zombies, Vampires, and Global Capitalism* (Boston: Brill, 2011), 3.

18. A devout Jehovah's Witness, Jackson himself denied that his video indicated any personal belief in what he called "the occult."

19. José Esteban Muñoz, *Cruising Utopia: The Then and There of Queer Futurity* (New York: New York University Press, 2009), 155.

20. William Blake, *The Complete Prose and Poetry*, ed. David V. Erdman (New York: Random House, 1988), 37.

21. Negri, *Time for Revolution*, 139.

22. Ibid., 150, emphasis added.

23. Gilles Deleuze, *Difference and Repetition*, trans. Paul Patton (New York: Continuum, 2010), 36–89.

24. Negri, *Time for Revolution*, 152.

25. Lauren Berlant, *Cruel Optimism* (Durham, N.C.: Duke University Press, 2011).

26. "Unless inclined to swerve," Lucretius writes, "all things would fall right through the deep abyss like drops of rain." Lucretius, *The Nature of Things*, trans. A. E. Stallings (New York: Penguin, 2007), 42.

27. Butler, *Precarious Life*.

28. Negri, *Time for Revolution*, 152.

29. Ibid., 157.

30. Negri distinguishes between the "to-come" pointed to by *kairòs* and the "future" of chronological, homogenous time. This distinction is necessary because, for instance, finance capitalism has already colonized the future of chronological, homogenous time, occupying it with its apparatuses of insurance,

futures markets, risk assessments, four-year plans, mortgage-backed securities, and so on. Punk rock prophetically declared, in the early stages of the neoliberal era, that there was "no future," aligning itself with the alternative time of the to-come. My use of Negri's argument here clearly dovetails with José Muñoz's reading of Ernst Bloch's concept of the "not yet." Muñoz, *Cruising Utopia*, 3.

31. Negri, *Time for Revolution*, 165.

32. Walter Benjamin, *Walter Benjamin: Selected Writings, 1938–1940*, vol. 4, ed. Howard Eiland and Michael William Jennings (Cambridge, Mass.: Harvard University Press, 2003), 97.

33. Lauren Berlant, *Cruel Optimism* (Durham, N.C.: Duke University Press, 2011).

34. Ibid., 64.

35. On the distinction between the typical and the particular, see Ian Baucom, *Specters of the Atlantic: Finance Capital, Slavery, and the Philosophy of History* (Durham, N.C.: Duke University Press, 2005), 39–46.

36. Ibid.

37. Karl Marx, "The Eighteenth Brumaire of Louis Bonaparte," 1852, in *Later Political Writings*, ed. Terrell Carver, 31–127 (Cambridge: Cambridge University Press, 1996).

38. Lorenzo J. Perillo, "'If I Was Not in Prison, I Would Not Be Famous': Discipline, Choreography, and Mimicry in the Philippines," *Theatre Journal* 63, no. 4 (2011): 607–21.

39. Shaka McGlotten, "Dead and Live Life: Zombies, Queers, and Online Sociality," in *Generation Zombie: Essays on the Living Dead in Modern Culture*, ed. Stephanie Boluk and Wylie Lenz, 182–93 (Jefferson, N.C.: McFarland Press, 2011).

40. Ibid., 190.

41. See "Wall Street Zombie March," *New York Daily News* Channel, October 4, 2011, http://www.youtube.com/watch?v=RMsgN2WF0-M.

42. William Scott, *Troublemakers: Power, Representation, and the Fiction of the Mass Worker* (New Brunswick, N.J.: Rutgers University Press, 2012); Scott, "Winning the Crisis," paper presented at the Department of Social and Cultural Analysis, New York University, March 21, 2012.

43. Gilles Deleuze and Félix Guattari, *A Thousand Plateaus: Capitalism and Schizophrenia* (Minneapolis: University of Minnesota Press, 1987).

44. Peter Linebaugh, *The Many-Headed Hydra: Sailors, Slaves, Commoners, and the Hidden History of the Revolutionary Atlantic* (Boston: Beacon Press, 2000).

45. Rebecca Schneider, *Performing Remains: Art and War in Times of Theatrical Reenactment* (New York: Routledge, 2011); Schneider, "It Seems as If . . . I Am Dead: Zombie Capitalism and Theatrical Labor," *TDR* 56, no. 4 (2012): 150–62.

46. Fred Moten, *In the Break: The Aesthetics of the Black Radical Tradition* (Minneapolis: University of Minnesota Press, 2003).

47. Barbara Browning, *Infectious Rhythm: Metaphors of Contagion and the Spread of African Culture* (New York: Routledge, 1998).

48. Simone do Vale, "Trash Mob: Zombie Walks and the Positivity of Monsters in Western Popular Culture," in *The Domination of Fear*, ed. Mikko Canini, 191–202 (Amsterdam: Rodopi, 2010).

49. Negri, *Time for Revolution*, 155.

CHAPTER 19

The Walking Dead and Killing State

Zombification and the Normalization of Police Violence

TRAVIS LINNEMANN, TYLER WALL, and EDWARD GREEN

Yet the demons are not only the strangers that have come among us, but the people who have become strangers.

—Jock Young, *The Exclusive Society*

On the afternoon of May 26, 2012, police shot thirty-one-year-old Rudy Eugene dead as he "ate the face" of a homeless man on a deserted Miami causeway. Because of the bizarre gruesomeness of the attack, some in the news media immediately took to calling Eugene, a black man of Haitian descent, the "Miami Zombie" and "Causeway Cannibal."[1] Five days later, a New Jersey man mutilated himself with a knife and "threw his skin and intestines" at police.[2] That same day, in Maryland, a man confessed to eating the heart and brain of his murdered roommate. Later, another report emerged from China, leading some to declare that a terrifying pandemic—a "zombie apocalypse"—had begun.[3]

These events, however they actually happened, were a boon for an ever opportunistic and decadent news media. On one hand, what "leads" could "bleed" more than reports of flesh-eating maniacs who hurled their entrails at police? Yet, on the other, "zombies" summon the mysteries of life and death and thus fears far more profound than lurid tabloid sensationalism. Given this, it should be of little surprise that the media had a hand in actually raising the dead, and yet it is quite troubling that it forecast a zombie apocalypse with such little sense of parody. That the end did not come at the rotting hands of an undead horde perhaps reveals the whole affair as yet another instance of media-fueled panic. Certainly descriptions of monstrous "zombified" others seem to fit the social reflex to look on in horror rather than confront the proliferating insecurities of late-modern life. Still, as entwined as spectacle and spectator are, much of what the public consumes in this regard settles into a background of white noise made up of a collection of tired scapegoats and populations superfluous to the neoliberal social order. The "Miami Zombie" and attendant "zombie apocalypse," however, seem to have briefly escaped the murmuring background of mediated spectacle to animate a particular sort of violent monstrosity in the social imaginary. Here we witness the mediatized transformation of a mother's religious son to—something unrecognizable[4]—the "Miami Zombie":

> crouched over Ronald Poppo's limp body, naked and growling, chewing off chunks of the man's face. It took several bullets fired by a stunned police officer to stop him. At 31, the son who had carried a Bible, quoted scripture and worn a 4-inch cross on a chain around his neck had become *something unrecognizable* known across the nation as the Miami zombie.[5]

We must recognize reports of "zombies" and "cannibals" not only as salacious, thoughtless reporting but also as part of a larger ideological frame that normalizes state violence and conceals the fundamental inequalities of late capitalism. As such, our reading of the case helps detail the process of *zombification*—the politico-cultural production of those who, in the words of Sharon Patricia Holland, "never achieve, in the eyes of others, the status of the living"—what we call the *walking dead*.[6] In this reading, zombification is a long-standing practice of white supremacy and the walking dead, its product. As bell hooks writes,

> reduced to the machinery of bodily physical labor, black people learned to appear before whites as though they were zombies, cultivating the habit of casting the gaze downward so as not to appear uppity. To look directly was an assertion of subjectivity, equality. Safety resided in the pretense of invisibility.[7]

Some might also suggest that the walking dead as we conceive them here bear close resemblance to *homo sacer* or "bare life."[8] That is, while (un)dead, these zombified others exist outside the juridical order and protections of the state.[9] However, in what follows, we argue that the walking dead do not simply "exist" outside the benevolence of the state and social conventions but are active constituents in the fabrication and maintenance of police and state power.[10] Which is to say, the reproduction of police and state power occurs through "legitimate" violence most often exercised against those dispossessed and "socially dead" others like Rudy Eugene.

While there has been much written about the zombie in popular culture, we should be clear that our aim here is not necessarily to expand or critique this literature. Rather, we treat the spectacle of the "zombie apocalypse" seriously in order to explore the ways in which ideological production reaffirms disparate social relations. Violent street crimes, even those hidden within the so-called zombie apocalypse, are a convenient and durable symbol that stirs middle-class social anxieties that are in many ways analogous to those brought on by the rising inequalities and precarity of late capitalism.[11] Quite often, however, the media present and the public discusses violent crime ahistorically, as if it results simply from the pathology of the individual and bears no relation to broader structural inequalities. Cases such as this one are important, then, because the ensuing media coverage often proposes and reinforces uncomplicated explanations for seemingly inexplicable behaviors. These shorthand schema, what we could call the "quasi-criminological," help circulate and reinforce individual, rational, and moral explanations for violent crimes, thereby impeding any sustained critique of existing social arrangements. As we will argue here, while the media and authorities failed to provide a suitable explanation for Rudy Eugene's violent outburst, they did effectively depoliticize and normalize his death at the hands of police. It is our aim, then—by way of engaging the politics of zombification—to draw attention to and contest the ways in which the logics of security, state violence, and punitive disposability are imagined and schematized as livable parts of late capitalism. To accomplish this, we begin with a critical reading of the news media's coverage of the case to detail currents of insecurity sewn into the cultural production of zombification. We then situate zombification within a broader system of violence to detail the ways in which cultural production helps reaffirm race and class domination and the existing social order.

State Killing, Ideological Production, Zombification

Police violence is often difficult to recognize as anything but legitimate and necessary because it is a category of understanding produced and guaranteed by the state. For example, a common rationalization for "police-perpetrated homicides" is that the victim was an immediate threat to the life of another.[12] And though several U.S. courts[13] have ruled that police actually bear no such responsibility, the supposed "duty to protect" is routinely invoked to make police killings appear legitimate, necessary, and within the boundaries of legally permitted force. Some suggest that police public relations departments foreground and sometimes fabricate "immediate danger" and "duty to protect" narratives in order to justify or obfuscate state killings.[14] Likewise, reports elaborating an officer's biography and connections to the community bolster "duty to protect" logics, while accounts that a "suspect was shot" without reporting who did the shooting or that euphemize killings as "deadly force" are linguistic diversions that remove the actions of police and the act of state killing altogether. Most crucial for our purposes here, tales of the "evil," "strange," and "monstrous" among us exaggerate the perceived dangerousness of police work and encourage the public to evaluate police killings in stark "him or me" terms. Together, these discursive ruses fashion what Slavoj Žižek calls a "fetishistic disavowal" in which the public glosses over the causes and consequences of police and state violence so that it may continue acting "as if it doesn't know."[15] This was certainly the case with Rudy Eugene, as his street-level execution failed to generate any sustained criticism of police violence or police power more generally.

Despite the brutality of his attack, we must recall that Eugene was unarmed, in fact, naked, when killed in a hail of bullets fired by officers apparently so panicked that his victim, Ronald Poppo, received two gunshot wounds of his own. Here we can take the phrase "naked before the state" quite literally, as the hasty decision to shoot to kill marked Rudy Eugene the embodiment of bare life. Yet, with some two thousand[16] people killed by U.S. police in a so-called justified and justifiable manner in recent years, this case, however spectacular, exemplifies a routinized sort of state violence that too often passes into the white noise of the everyday—unquestioned and unchallenged.

We therefore treat Eugene's case as an instance of state killing—a death of a person at the hands of state agents. From this vantage, zombification is not merely escapism or entertaining fantasy but an ideological production that disowns very real, human, material circumstances and consequences. As such, we do not intend to argue the killing's legality but rather confront the fetishistic disavowal of subjective violence and everyday state killing. Eugene's case and the contemporary interest in zombies more generally are analytically useful as they demonstrate how obscene, sometimes laughable propositions excuse and normalize brutal violence. For instance, following the mass shooting at Newtown, Connecticut, zombies appeared in deliberations among members of the U.S. Senate Judiciary Committee over questions of gun control. Perhaps a crude attempt to bring levity to volatile debates, Senator Patrick Leahy quipped, "Maybe if zombies attacked, you might need a semiautomatic assault weapon for self-defense," but short of that, he would be happy with his ".45 caliber at home."[17] This sort of ironic distancing—making light of the brutality of slaughtered children through the absurdity of a "zombie apocalypse"—props up and reproduces long-standing systems of ideological thinking. Žižek writes,

> Ideology is not constituted by abstract propositions in themselves, rather, ideology is itself this very texture of the lifeworld which "schematizes" the propositions, rendering them "livable." Take military ideology for instance: it becomes "livable" only against the background of the obscene unwritten rules and rituals (marching chants, fragging, sexual innuendo . . .) in which it is embedded. Which is why, if there is an ideological experience at its purest, at its zero-level, then it occurs the moment we adopt an attitude of ironic distance, *laughing at the follies in which we are ready to believe*—it is at this moment of liberating laughter, when we look down on the absurdity of our faith, that we become pure subjects of ideology.[18]

Through the lens of the obscene and absurd, we see all the talk of apocalypse—and the zombification of Rudy Eugene—as a once laughable proposition, rendered somehow more livable. That some were more willing to entertain zombified fantasies than they were to question and challenge circumstances that left Eugene dead and Poppo disfigured reveals the force and effect of such thinking. What zombification schematizes and renders livable, then, is a particular sort of enemy, an unrecognizable, killable other, seen as the fodder for police and state violence. As Matthew Shepherd, author of the zombie-themed graphic novel *Dead Eyes Open*, put it, zombies provide a very simple dynamic—us versus them:

> The thing about zombies is they are, in some ways, the perfect tool to establish a really simple dynamic. If you want to tell a story about "us versus them" they are not like us and they must be destroyed. Zombies are really at base, the simplest way to do it. So,

Zombies become some of the last bastion of an easy way to find an enemy, fight and kill, and feel really good about fighting and killing.[19]

If the popularity of the genre lies in its ability to allow the public to fantasize about killing a monstrous "them," as Shepherd suggests, we must seriously question whether this logic encourages a similar sort of violence in the real and the everyday. Thus our focus here is not only on what was rendered livable in the rush to report on and view the "zombie apocalypse" but also what promises to settle into the background of the everyday as the "Miami Zombie" recedes from memory.

"The Unraveling of Rudy Eugene"

Beyond the absurdity of a zombie apocalypse, the coverage of Eugene's case is important because of the simplified explanations given for his violent attack on Ronald Poppo.[20] Like quasi-criminological theories sewn into scripts of television crime dramas and Hollywood films, these explanations, what Nicole Rafter and Michelle Brown call popular criminology, also grow from speculation strewn across the pages of newsprint and the offhand comments and best guesses of "expert" commentators.[21] Focusing our analysis on the quasi-criminological, we reviewed the balance of the new media's coverage of the case and identified three different yet entwined explanations for Eugene's attack on Poppo.[22] Underlying Eugene's mediatized zombification is a risk-crazed focus on his "abnormal normality," the transformative power of illicit drugs, and the supernatural gothic. While unique in its own right, each of the quasi-criminological explanations that we document is structured by the unknown and thus characteristic of the insecurities of contemporary social life. As Leonidas Cheliotis[23] has recently argued, the punishment and imprisonment of "violent street criminals" provides a means of catharsis for the stubborn middle-class anxieties of life under late capitalism. We argue that Eugene's street-level execution enables a similar sort of catharsis, the violence of which is obscured by his mediatized zombification. To that end, the following traces the unconscious expressions and justifications for state killings entwined with the zombification of Rudy Eugene.

The "Zombie" Next Door

In the wake of Anders Breivik's assault on a Norwegian youth camp that left seventy-seven people dead, an acquaintance of the killer offered a familiar, now almost obligatory observation: "It was very, very strange.[24] *He just seemed like a normal, nice guy.*"[25] Like Breivik and countless others who emerged from the crowd only after some terrible act, much of the "Miami Zombie" coverage described Eugene as a "fairly ordinary guy" before his crimes made him "infamous." From the *Miami Herald*: "Before Rudy Eugene became infamous, he was a fairly ordinary guy—he liked sports, fast cars and action movies. But even those closest to him say Eugene was introspective and private."[26] Even family and friends, it appears, were left struggling with Rudy's apparent transformation from everyman to monster, leaving many not only grasping for an explanation but also battling for his humanity. A friend pleaded,

> I am shocked by the situation. I don't know what to say about it, how to interpret it, how to express it. The only thing I know for sure is Rudy was something other than this monster people talk about.[27]

As pop psychologist Martha Stout[28] argues in her widely discussed book *The Sociopath Next Door*, a frightening proportion—one in twenty-five people—of remorseless, predatory "sociopaths" circulate in the banalities of the everyday. The vision of social life sketched by Stout—one teeming with sadistic corporate managers and killers "possessed of blood lust" who murder on a whim—provides a familiar and somehow comforting conceptual frame for the public to understand Eugene's brutal and seemingly unprovoked attack on Poppo. Rather than confronting the myriad social and psychological forces that could produce such violence, Stout's theory suggests that many among us are simply hidden monsters waiting to act out terribly. Here the most awful crimes, indeed all tragedies, reduce to simple chance, and no matter the preparation, when your number is up—your number is up.[29] Yet, as familiar and oddly comforting as the "sociopath next door" trope may be, we see something else at work here. By highlighting an utterly normal complexion exploded by terrifying violence, cases like Eugene's reveal the power and pervasiveness of the cultural logics of insecurity and security. By falling back to Eugene's normality, media accounts such as these support a vision of criminality closely aligned with contemporary visions of the lone-wolf gunman or terrorist, that is, an all-pervading threat that is nearly impossible to predict, locate, or prevent. Anonymous, loosely affiliated, or lone-wolf actors pose a daunting task for the security state and are at the center of increasingly invasive antiterror measures. For instance, the aptly named "lone-wolf provision" of the U.S. Foreign Intelligence Surveillance Act allows law enforcement to monitor those thought to be preparing for a terrorist act, even if they have no proven connection to terrorist organizations.[30] Following this logic, critics argue, all are suspect and potential lone-wolf actors. The implications of this risk-crazed thinking are frightening. Indeed, if Eugene, described by those who knew him as "normal" and "nice," could act out so violently and unpredictably, then every stranger on the street could be a "zombie" waiting to rise from a grave of anonymity. Assuming violent monstrosity hidden behind a facade of banality also draws interesting connections to the "abnormally normal" conception of serial killers.[31] As a psychiatrist testified during the trial of "the quiet man in apartment 213," Jeffrey Dahmer, "dress him in a suit and he looks like 10 other men."[32]

As with lone wolves and serial killers, the cultural logics of pervasive danger and unknowable monstrosity are clearly represented by the zombie. Launched by the Centers for Disease Control and Prevention (CDC) months before the zombie apocalypse exploded onto the scene, a public service advertisement campaign engaged zombies as the ideal figure of unpredictability, risk, and danger (Figure 19.1). From a CDC press release:

The rise of zombies in pop culture has given credence to the idea that a zombie apocalypse could happen. In such a scenario zombies would take over entire countries,
roaming city streets eating anything living that got in their way. The proliferation of
this idea has led many people to wonder "How do I prepare for a zombie apocalypse?"

Here zombies stand in for more knowable and thinkable dangers of environmental
disaster and nonstate terrorism. As a CDC official reasoned, "if you are generally well
equipped to deal with a zombie apocalypse you will be prepared for a hurricane, pandemic, earthquake, or terrorist attack."[33]
Again proving the zombie's cultural import, followers of CDC's Twitter feed jumped
from around twelve thousand to 1.2 million followers just one day after the campaign's
launch.[34] While it may provide the CDC a hip, up-to-date take on disaster preparedness,
success of the program also presupposes that some do not consider prospects of a zombie apocalypse pure fantasy. As one "zombiephile" interviewed in the days following

Eugene's case urged, "zombies, they might happen. Vampires, werewolves, they ain't going to happen. There is a lot more suspension of disbelief. *But zombies could happen.*"[35] In fact, in the midst of Eugene's case, so widespread were fears of zombie attacks that the CDC released an official statement denying knowledge of any condition that would reanimate the dead or present zombielike symptoms in the living.[36]

This sort of necrophobic anxiety extends beyond the CDC's tongue-in-cheek attempts at responsibilization. For instance, Halo Corporation, a private security firm with several U.S. government contracts, recently held what it described as a "groundbreaking, multijurisdictional, counter-terrorism summit" to train the "entire range of national security stakeholders."[37] The centerpiece of the three-day event was a "drill" organized around an imagined zombie apocalypse. Defending the drill as a "very real exercise, not some type of big costume party," Brad Barker, president of Halo Corp, argued that "everything that will be simulated at this event has already happened, it just hasn't happened all at once on the same night."[38] Regardless of the veracity of Barker's assertion, for him zombies are the perfect planning tool, a lone-wolf danger that is somewhere out there yet completely unknowable and unpredictable. So, as both Barker and the CDC jokingly suggest, if "prepared for the zombie apocalypse you will be prepared for anything," we warn that an insidious violence—*if you can kill a zombie, you can kill anyone*—underpins the current fascination with zombies and the zombification of Rudy Eugene.

The Drugged and Walking Dead

It should come as no surprise that running through all of the reports on zombies and cannibals were threads of a rather mundane drug panic.[39] In this case, law enforcement and news media focused on a nascent family of synthetic stimulants known colloquially as "bath salts." An article written by celebrity physician Dr. Oz for a late May 2011 edition of *Time* magazine was just one of many media reports in circulation at the time to warn of the drug. Despite a clear lack of evidence, the article, "Bath Salts: Evil Lurking in Your Corner Store," described it as a "supercharged instrument of suffering" and a "pharmacological hell," linking it to a host of health problems, violent behavior, and suicide.[40] Law enforcement was in concert with tabloid media, distributing safety bulletins nationwide warning officers of the violent unpredictability of bath salts users. One bulletin, published by the Ohio Strategic Analysis and Information [fusion] Center, reported twenty-seven cases where officers "used force" on "hostile, violent, unpredictable, out of control, paranoid and reckless" subjects "high on bath salts." Given reports of users "having unusual superhuman strength" and being able to "shoot off the ground" like a "flash of light," we can make better sense of how events in Miami unfolded as they did later that year.[41] On May 23, just three days before the "Miami Zombie" made headlines around the world, Rick Scott, governor of Florida, signed a law[42] criminalizing bath salts and synthetic cannabis. Amid the anguish over bath salts, apparently only a passing mention was needed to link Rudy Eugene to the drug and the rash of "zombified" behaviors that followed. In an interview with ABC News just three days after Eugene's killing, Armando Aguilar, president of the Miami Fraternal Order of Police, flippantly remarked,

> The [bath salts] cases are similar minus a man eating another. People taking off their clothes. People suddenly have super human strength. They become violent and they are burning up for [*sic*] the inside. Their organs are reaching a level that most would die. By the time police approach them they are a *walking dead person*.[43]

The link between Eugene and bath salts apparently played well with the public as it originated here and was reproduced as fact by the national media. We should not take Aguilar's speculative diagnosis as coincidence, however. According to journalist Frank Owen, the drug was a convenient dodge to defuse the volatility of a black man's killing at the hands of a Hispanic police officer. Frank Owen suggests,

> Nobody could say this wasn't a good shooting. Aguilar thought. Ramirez had a clean record, and this was the first time he had used his weapon in his four years with the department. Still, the fact remained that a Hispanic officer had shot an unarmed black man in a city with a long history of racially charged police killings. Aguilar was well aware of the ongoing Department of Justice investigation into the Miami Police Department: Hispanic cops had fatally shot seven African American civilians in the span of eight months. The shootings raised tensions in a city already known as a racial tinderbox.[44]

If Owen is correct, Miami police quite literally fabricated the "bath salts" connection and hence the zombification of Rudy Eugene to obfuscate and diffuse an instance of state killing. Even without such motivations, this sort of drug-driven expurgation has been in use by news media and authorities for quite some time. In fact, many of the initial reports invoked the history of past drug panics describing bath salts as the "new LSD."[45] Today, law enforcement and the security industry, represented here again by Barker and Halo Corporation, circulate similar myths about the transformative power of illicit drugs. Barker argues,

> No one knows what the zombies will do in our scenario, but quite frankly no one knows what a terrorist will do. If a law enforcement officer sees a zombie and says, "Freeze, get your hands in the air!" What's the zombie going to do? He's going to moan at you. If someone on PCP or some other psychotic drug is told that, the truth is he's not going to react to you.[46]

Here the cultural logics of security arrange familiar dangers (terrorists and drug users) under the edifice of the zombie—a mimetic, universal, *killable* enemy. Following Eugene's case, more "cannibal attacks" in the "zombie drugs plague" dotted mediascapes worldwide. One such incident involved a man who allegedly growled "I'm going to eat you" at officers attempting to rein him in. According to reports,

> a drifter high on drugs was put in a Hannibal Lecter–style mask after threatening to eat two police officers in a new cannibal attack in the United States. Brandon de Leon is believed to have taken "bath salts" just like Rudy Eugene who ate 75% of

homeless man Ronald Poppo's face in Miami and only stopped when police shot and killed him.[47]

The "new" drug said to transform "drifters" into "Hannibal Lecter" fashions a narrative where big-budget Hollywood movies bleed into the routine—where everyday life becomes the stuff of nightmares. Troubling the lines between fantasy and reality, the "Miami Zombie" maps the liminal spaces where the "street scripts the screen and the screen scripts the street."[48]

Despite panicked screams of cannibalism, in the end, medical examiners found no flesh in Eugene's digestive system. Some weeks later, toxicologists also dismissed the bath salts connection, finding only trace amounts of marijuana in Eugene's tissue. These facts have failed to dispel the link between bath salts and violent behavior, further underscoring the power and resilience of myth in the punitive imagination. When confronted with Eugene's toxicology reports, Aguilar remained incredulous, insisting,

> I still believe there was something else in Rudy Eugene's system other than marijuana that the medical examiner didn't detect. There was definitely something there, something we just can't test for yet, maybe a new form of bath salts or maybe even a completely new compound that we don't know about.[49]

Aguilar's stubborn refusal to admit there wasn't "something else" in Eugene's system illustrates how useful, in fact, crucial, drugs are in the justification of police violence. Following the videotaped beating of Rodney King, for instance, an LAPD spokesperson speculated that King "may have been dusted" (on PCP), as if King's intoxication would somehow excuse his brutalization.[50]

Aguilar's allusions to "something else" bear something more sinister, however. Like King, Eugene's case shows that the imaging of drug use is a possession of sorts—a gateway into the supernatural. As some have recently described, methamphetamine users circulate in the insecure and punitive imagination as "meth zombies" and "shadow people"—supernatural monstrosities indeed.[51] More recently, the District of Columbia Department of Public Health launched a public service advertisement campaign warning of the dangers of "fake weed" (Figure 19.2). Taking a cue from the CDC, the campaign exploits the current zombie craze, situating its grotesque aesthetic at the center of

Figure 19.2. District of Columbia Department of Health "Fake Weed" public service advertisement.

a familiar fear-appeal drug control campaign. As these and many other examples attest, zombification is an increasingly visible and popular analytic for subjective degradation, monstrosity, and social disposability.

Zombification and the Powers of Horror

Unable to arrive at a suitable explanation, and perhaps spurred on by Eugene's Haitian ancestry, many, even those closest to him, pondered supernatural explanations for his attack. His girlfriend explains:

> What happened to Rudy had to be supernatural, something humans cannot explain, something that leaves us with a lot of questions. I just wish he would come to me in a dream and answer all the questions. I wish he would tell me what happened that day.[52]

Somewhere in the dreamland of Eugene's abnormal normality, the mystery of his motivations and the blood and gore of his attack are boundaries of the gothic. Here we glimpse crime's symbolic core—its horrific energies and affects—in this case "demons" that "came out" of Rudy Eugene on a deserted Miami causeway. As another of Eugene's bewildered friends speculated, "drugs can open the gateway to the demons inside of you. Whatever he took open[ed] that gateway and a demon came out. Whatever he was fighting, it came out. I believe in spiritual battles. *I believe in demons.*"[53]

Characterized by darkness, grisly rotting flesh, and ravenous cannibalism, zombies are perhaps the ultimate gothic monsters.[54] Rising from almost every corner of social life—from uniformed police to schoolchildren—the shambling herds of rotting bodies imagined by contemporary zombie films are a demographic cross section and thus a faceless homogeny. Indeed, as author of the book *Zombiemania* notes, zombies "are the closest type of monster to us. They are us and we are them."[55] In this way, zombies are endlessly mimetic—everyone and no one at all, everywhere and nowhere—a ghostly, spectral monstrosity. As such, zombification perhaps broadens, transcends, or encloses criminalizations built on racial stereotypes and the ambiguities of intersectionality.[56] Yet, as a cause of Eugene's violent outburst, however, the gothic is no explanation at all but something beyond human sight and understanding.

Still, it is not only the unknown and supernatural but bloody gruesomeness and subjective violence of the attack that conjures the gothic. As one shocked onlooker described, "he was like a zombie. It was intense. He was tearing the other man to pieces with his mouth. There was blood everywhere. It was really horrific."[57] Highlighting the cultural fascination with ripped flesh and splayed bodies—what some describe as "wound culture"—cases such as this reveal or perhaps fashion a "pathological public sphere" where private fantasy and sociality coalesce around the spectacle of blood and gore.[58] As he had done previously with unfounded speculation about bath salts, Aguilar animated the spectacle of the "Miami Zombie" with vivid descriptions of Poppo's wounds: "His mouth, his nose and his ears were ripped off. . . . In my 30 years as a cop, I've never seen anything like this."[59] Here the violence of the attack and gruesomeness of the wounds underpin a collective trauma that justifies Eugene's street-level execution.

In that, when confronted with a possessed, ravenous zombie "tearing another man to pieces," the assumption is that police have no choice other than to shoot and kill. Yet it is this uncritical assumption that renders Eugene killable, obscures the act of killing, and shields individual officers and police power from public scrutiny.

Moving away from Eugene's biography and the mystery of his motivations, reports focused on the gore of Poppo's wounds and resilient character further animate the collective affective dimensions of the crime and embolden the cultural logics of killability. For instance:

> The homeless drifter whose face was largely eaten by the "Miami Zombie" was once a brainy 1964 graduate of New York's prestigious Stuyvesant High School. It was a long road from being one of the city's smartest and most driven kids to lounging under a Florida bridge Saturday, when a maniac attacked him at random in one of the most gruesome crimes on record.[60]

Like Eugene, a young man with a hardscrabble past and uncertain future, Ronald Poppo was unrecognized by a public that passed him on the street and unrecognizable to a family who wondered whether he was even alive. It was not until the media and certain sectors of the public figuratively hoisted him on their shoulders as the resilient survivor of a horrific crime that he became anything more than a member of the walking dead in his own right. Giving a human—however mangled—face to Eugene's monstrosity, Poppo represented a particular understanding of grievable and resilient victims of violent crime.

Underpinning the anxious concern for Poppo's recovery is what Mark Neocleous calls a "training in resilience" that hardens the public to the spectacle of violent crime.[61] That is, viewing the spectacle through Poppo's eyes as victim, we are encouraged to ignore his very real suffering and focus only on his ability to survive the attack. For a profligate news media, Poppo is simply a victim-commodity. For the state, Poppo is a grievable victim who justifies and disavows the unremitting violence of police power. The irony is that the state—city governments and local police—has reinvigorated its techniques of banishment to ensure the dispossessed remain invisible.[62] Yet, as survivor of the "Miami Zombie," Ronald Poppo is no longer a faceless member of the walking dead but a symbol of the public's collective fears and of its desires to triumph over and destroy the underserving and "evil."

The cathartic affects of violence, trauma, and symbolic victimization perhaps come better into view when considering how the voyeuristic public treats the suffering of offenders' families and friends. After four different churches turned her away, Rudy's mother, Ruth Charles, was forced to hold his funeral in the chapel of a local funeral home. Still struggling for his humanity, she publicly pleaded, "Everybody says that he was a zombie, but I know he's not a zombie; he's my son."[63] No obituary mourned Rudy Eugene; the circumstances of his life were left to fade into the spectacle of a bizarre crime, along with his identity as son and brother. This is important, as public mourning is a way to recognize the life lost but also the suffering of those who remain.[64] By denying Eugene the status of the living, the public also failed to recognize the fundamental human dignity and moral equality of his family.[65] It is this sort of dehumanizing and ironic distancing at work in ideological production that transforms the pain of others into absurd spectacles such as a zombie apocalypse. From the *Miami Herald*:

> You'd think a face-eating naked man shot dead along the postcard blue landscape of the MacArthur Causeway would be bad for tourism, but not in our steamy Magic City. We've developed crocodile skin when it comes to police news, no matter how dehumanizing, and now we embrace our wackiness. History and our fine-tuned reputation as a storyteller's paradise have taught us that how 31-year-old Rudy Eugene met his maker—shot by police after he bit off most of a man's face right next to the Miami Herald building, the scene creating a hellish traffic jam—is the kind of news that draws tourists and filmmakers like mosquitoes to standing water.[66]

Here Eugene's encounter with Poppo, "no matter how dehumanizing," is just another bit of "police news" filling the twenty-four-hour news cycle. And with an armored "crocodile skin" sort of indifference and the liberating laughter Žižek describes, the public is encouraged to dismiss the whole affair—Poppo's disfigurement, Eugene's execution, the suffering of friends and family, and the horror of spectators—as "the kind of [wacky] news" that might inspire a film or at least lure tourists. And with that, Rudy Eugene's humanity dissolved into the gothic horrors of an unrecognizable, killable monster—the "Miami Zombie."

The Walking Dead and Killing State

While exactly what led Rudy Eugene to act out so violently is unclear and may remain a mystery, critical reflection on the quasi-criminological underpinnings of the case details the ways in which zombification works to normalize state violence and a sort of "guilt-free" killability. As Trevor Fencott, maker of the zombie-themed Land of the Dead video game, suggests, "zombies are an absolutely no guilt snack. You can put them down and because they're already dead, you need not feel guilty about them."[67] While this comment is necessarily useful, it is important to be clear that we do not conceive the walking dead simply as metaphor but rather as the literal embodiment of those dispossessed and socially dead others born of late capitalism.

As worldwide financial collapse looms, the once contented American middle class, long ensconced in the securities of stable employment, health care, and homeownership, is increasingly aware of its own precariousness and perhaps even more aware of a growing rank boiling beneath them.[68] Fencott again offers,

> We live in a world where you consume fast food and you're irradiated with cell phone waves and you're really under assault all the time. I think in many ways we feel like zombies. . . . Rather than a demonic force that possessed someone and they're hanging out in the graveyard. They're not in the graveyard anymore. The graveyard is a very religious thing. Zombies are now in your shopping mall.[69]

Though once animated by premodern fears of god and nature, as insatiable consumers wandering shopping malls, zombies remind all that they too may one day confront or join the walking dead and other threatening, flawed consumers cut adrift by late-capitalist precarity.[70] The entwinements of zombification and widespread social (in)security are further evidenced by a groundswell of "doomsday" survivalists and "zombie preppers." One such prepper and member of an "Anti-Zombie Militia" interviewed for the Discovery Channel's *Zombie Apocalypse* had this to say about a government bio-research facility set to relocate to his town:

> I live about five minutes away from where the proposed facility is. There is a high possibility of having some kind of zombie outbreak with a bio-lab that's being moved in here. We formed together to be a preparation group. We are a group of individuals with different skills, some of us, ex-military, police officers, people trained in firefighting, paramedics. Home is supposed to be where you feel safe at. *I no longer feel safe, knowing that something like this is coming at me.*[71]

This sort of necrophobic apocalypticism buoys a vibrant market for all manner of zombified weapons and gear. One such offering is Zombie Max Ammunition, which, according to its manufacturer, "is for the Zombie apocalypse" and for "use on Zombies only."[72] From ammunition to "zombie-proof" cars and condominiums, threats of zombification, however absurd, are a boon for capital.[73] This collage of spectacular violence and commodified security, what Žižek might call the obscene underside of American popular culture—the collective unconscious, the real of our desires—permits the punitive and voyeuristic public to fantasize about destroying what it fears. Through this lens, the killing of Rudy Eugene, a young man of Haitian ancestry from inner-city Miami, can quite literally be read as the street-level execution of a young, black, inner-city, drug-using "monster."

Masked by the absurd, obscene, and spectacular, zombification enables further violent scapegoating of those dispossessed, nonwhite, and working-poor subjects historically brutalized by police power. In fact, recalling Owen's accusation that the "bath salts" link was engineered to diffuse the volatility of yet another black man killed by Miami police, we might argue that zombification depoliticized Eugene, rendering him effectively raceless.[74] This is where zombification appears particularly dangerous, as the underlying themes—unknowable and inescapable danger, drug-fueled transformation, and gothic monstrosity—offer no explanatory power but do reinforce a variety of fears, misguided assumptions, and superstitions. Clearly the zombie represents a particularly monstrous and racialized other. To zombify is to conceal the violence and dehumanization of the existing racial order. Yet we also suggest that zombification is a cultural imaginary that may perhaps expand the logics of killability beyond skin color and other racial signifiers. That is, while clearly invoking disparate racial logics, the zombie's mimesis also schematizes a broader understanding of killability to include all those socially excluded and dispossessed others on the business end of police and state violence. Indeed, as Gerry Canavan suggests, the figure of the zombie represents both the racially abject, invisible, labor of the third world and the unproductive labor and flawed consumption of the first.[75]

If authorities and news media offered explanations for crimes such as this, linked directly to the history of racialized violence and broad structural inequities, then the public spectacle of violent acts could necessarily foment rejection of existing socioeconomic arrangements. As this case details, however, zombification effectively depoliticizes the act of killing and obscures the ways in which violence secures bourgeois social order. As the Halo security training and, to a lesser degree, the CDC preparedness campaign show, the depoliticization of zombification is not confined to cases like Eugene's. Consider, for instance, the article "Firearms Training for When the 'Zombies' Attack." Written by a police firearms instructor, the article outlines several scenarios meant to help police hone "key skills [they] might use in a real gunfight" by bringing "Hollywood to the range" in the form of an imagined zombie attack. Recommending targets depicting zombies attacking "innocent people," the author suggests that his "good-old-fashioned zombie shoot" will encourage officers to "have fun" and "use [their] imaginations." Here, quite clearly, we see the imaginative production of "criminals" as the killable walking dead. And though he is clear to remind officers that it is "unlikely they would have to shoot real zombies any time soon," the instructor nevertheless conceals the horrific act of shooting and killing other human beings within the tone-deaf humor and banal absurdity of a "zombie attack."[76] If we continue to view the figure of the zombie as fantasy and amusing gimmick, as this author does, then it is likely to remain as such. However, if we resist adopting an attitude of indifference and ironic distance and take more seriously the words and actions of police and the state, then we may perhaps better reckon zombification as the "very texture of the life world" that renders livable, in fact, celebrates, state killing.[77]

Radical critique of ideology allows us to see that Eugene's killing, though hidden within the absurd spectacle of zombification, is no different than other police killings, even those openly challenged by an outraged public. For instance, consider the 1999 killing of Amadou Diallo, an unarmed Guinean immigrant who died in front of his Bronx apartment building in a forty-one-shot barrage launched by NYPD officers, and the 2006 killing of Sean Bell, who died in a hail of fifty rounds fired by NYPD officers, who, like those in the Diallo killing, were cleared of any wrongdoing. The obscene overkill of ninety-one rounds spent to ostensibly "protect" the public from two unarmed black men seems more reminiscent of a Hollywood horror film than the material realities of crime control in the contemporary United States. Yet we should be clear that these and countless other killings do not represent some unfortunate circumstances or the indiscriminate violence of a few "bad apples." Rather, Diallo, Bell, Eugene—all police-perpetrated homicides—expose the violent fantasies animating police power.[78] That is, we should not dismiss police violence solely as the misdeeds of a few officers, nor should we assume that the spectacle of the "Miami Zombie" reflects *only* the unconscious desires of a voyeuristic public. Rather, we must see the actions of police and public as entwined and inseparable from the unconscious desires of criminal justice and the state itself.

It is the "institutional unconscious" that for Žižek "designates the obscene disavowed underside that, precisely as disavowed, sustains the public institution."[79] Put differently, the act of killing—zombie or unarmed immigrant—allows policing as a symbolic institution to reaffirm and sustain itself. First, exercising its monopoly on legitimate violence, policing demonstrates its ability to "protect" and "secure" the public by annihilating violence and danger in effigy. It is here that even the most brutal *and* banal violence is disavowed, depoliticized and normalized in the name of security. Even in cases where evidence is too damning to deny, prosecuting and punishing the offenders helps policing seem reflexive and faithful to its ethos of "protect and serve." Through the eternal demand for security and its superficial reforms, the violence of police power endures. For these reasons, we can say that police killings are no last resort of a "thin blue line," nor are they an unfortunate outcome of human error or weakness. Rather, we must

Figure 19.3.
Advertisement for zombie firearms training target. VisiColor Zombie Targets by Champion.

see police killings as elemental to police power and a fundamental practice of the *killing state*. As the cruel announcement "dead man walking!" traditionally bellowed by prison guards escorting condemned prisoners to their deaths reveals, the walking dead is a category of material existence fashioned by state power, in which physical death is a mere formality. In the death house, on city streets and terrains of distant battlefields, the state—the final arbiter of life and death—generates its sovereign power through its killable subjects. The violence administered by its police and prisons is not "volatile and contradictory," then, but rather the routine death-dealing practices of the U.S. killing state as it (re)produces sovereign power by securing insecurity.[80]

For some reason, Rudy Eugene tore Ronald Poppo's body and life apart. As brutal as the attack was, it does not excuse the spectacle that ensued. In the crime's aftermath, there was little discussion of use-of-force policies or "less-than-lethal" technologies and virtually no reflection on the fact that police killed a naked, unarmed man. Rather, media, police, and public wrote it off as another of the innumerable dangers of modern life, offering instead contemptible "explanations" of drug-induced and supernatural zombification. And whether it was met with panic or laughter, the "apocalypse" was a boon for capital as "real" zombies riled the insecure imaginary.

"Spectacle is a form of camouflage. It does not conceal anything; it simply renders it *unrecognizable*."[81] As such, zombification is simply the latest veneer to adorn timeless fears and animus, as George Romero, forerunner of the contemporary zombie genre, seems to suggest: "[Zombies] could be anything. They could be an avalanche, they could be a hurricane. It's a disaster out there. The stories are about how people fail to respond in the proper way."[82] Yet hidden by the "failure to respond properly" is the sadomasochist marriage of the state and its subjects. While the sadistic execution of a "violent street criminal" may provide a modicum of relief from the terrors of life under late capitalism, for the uncritical public, this catharsis comes at the price of having to disavow the contradictions and inequalities of the present social order. As Franco Moretti writes,

> fascinated by the horror of the monster, the public accepts the vices of its destroyer without a murmur, just as it accepts his literary depiction, the jaded and repetitive typology which regains its strength and its virginity on contact with the unknown. The monster, then, serves to displace the antagonisms and horrors evidenced within society to outside society itself.[83]

Awash in the horror of the present, the public masochistically accepts the many failings of the state and its police. It may be that all who are locked into such a relationship are zombified. Mindlessly devouring the material *and* ideological, *homo consumens* are the ideal subjects of late capitalism.[84] And those state agents who kill without question or conscience are beasts of burden—(un)dead labor in the service of a wicked master.[85] Police power will always be in the service of the social order that authorizes it. To reject police violence and state killing is also to reject existing social arrangements. For us, this rejection, however monumental, begins with the critique of ideology. Yet we are not necessarily hopeful that the public will awaken from its own zombification and better recognize the pain and suffering of life under late capitalism, because after all, zombies do not suffer—they are already dead.

Notes

1. Nadege Green and Audra Burch, "The Unraveling of Rudy Eugene, aka the Causeway Face Attacker," *Miami Herald,* July 14, 2012, http://www.miamiherald.com/news/special-reports/causeway-attack/article1941239.html.

2. Marlene Naanes, "Police: Hackensack Man Stabbed Himself and Threw Intestines at Officers," May 29, 2012, http://www.northjersey.com/news/Hackensack_man_stabs_self_throws_intenstines_at_police.html.

3. Robert Gutsche Jr., "Zombies, Drugs, and Florida Weirdness: 'Imaginative Power' and Resonance in Coverage of Miami's 'Causeway Cannibal,'" *Journalism Studies* 14, no. 4 (2013): 555–67.

4. We use "unrecognizable" here to denote a particular form of monstrosity, as does Jacques Derrida, *The Beast and the Sovereign* (Chicago: University of Chicago Press, 2010). We also recognize that this draws interesting links to the politics of misrecognition.

5. Green and Burch, "Unraveling of Rudy Eugene," emphasis added.

6. Sharon Patricia Holland, *Raising the Dead: Readings of Death and (Black) Subjectivity* (Durham, N.C.: Duke University Press, 2000).

7. bell hooks, *Black Looks: Race and Representation* (Boston: South End Press, 1992), 168.

8. Giorgio Agamben, *Homo Sacer: Sovereign Power and Bare Life* (Stanford, Calif.: Stanford University Press, 1998).

9. Jon Stratton, "Zombie Trouble: Zombie Texts, Bare Life, and Displaced People," *European Journal of Cultural Studies* 14, no. 3 (2011): 265–81.

10. Mark Neocleous, *The Fabrication of Social Order: A Critical Theory of Police Power* (London: Pluto Press, 2000).

11. Leonidas Cheliotis, "Neoliberal Capitalism and Middle-Class Punitiveness: Bringing Erich Fromm's 'Materialistic Psychoanalysis' to Penology," *Punishment and Society* 15, no. 3 (2013): 247–73.

12. Paul Hirschfield and Daniella Simon, "Legitimating Police Violence: Newspaper Narratives of Deadly Force," *Theoretical Criminology* 14, no. 2 (2012): 155–82.

13. See Warren v. District of Columbia, 444 A.2d. 1, DC Ct of Ap. (1981); Castle Rock v. Gonzales, 545 U.S. 748 (2005); Balistreri v. Pacifica Police Department, August 23, 1988; DeShaney v. Winnebago County, February 22, 1989.

14. Rob Mawby, *Policing Images: Policing, Communication, and Legitimacy* (London: Willan, 2003).

15. Slavoj Žižek, *Violence: Six Sideways Reflections* (New York: Picador, 2008), 58.

16. Uniform Crime Reports, "Crime in the US 2011," Expanded Homicide Data Table 14. http://www.fbi.gov/about-us/cjis/ucr/crime-in-the-u.s/2011/crime-in-the-u.s.-2011/tables/expanded-homicide-data-table-14.

17. Alisa Chang, "Talk of Zombies Aside, Gun Bills Face Political Reality," NPR, March 16, 2013, http://www.npr.org/2013/03/16/174461553/talk-of-zombies-aside-gun-bills-face-political-reality.

18. Slavoj Žižek, *Living in the End Times* (London: Verso, 2011), 3, emphasis added.

19. Donna Davies, *Zombie Mania* [documentary] (Canada: Starz, 2008).

20. The title of this section is from an article published by the *Miami Herald,* July 14, 2012.

21. Nicole Rafter and Michelle Brown, *Criminology Goes to the Movies* (New York: New York University Press, 2011).

22. To gather data for our case, we performed a number of LexisNexis Academic searches with several combinations of key words: "Rudy Eugene," "Miami Zombie," and "Miami Cannibal." After eliminating articles that did not pertain to Eugene, we identified 134 articles published between May 25, 2012, and March 22, 2013. Using a grounded approach, we read each thoroughly, concentrating on the various explanations offered for Eugene's attack on Poppo.

23. Cheliotis, "Neoliberal Capitalism," 252.

24. Twenty (14.9 percent) of the articles countered discussions of Eugene's violence with descriptions of his "normality."

25. Antoinette Kelly, "Norwegian Mass Killer Seemed Like 'Normal Guy' Says Irish Friend," August 5, 2011, http://www.irishcentral.com/news/norwegian-mass-killer-seemed-like-normal-guy-says-irish-friend-126828123-237404371.html.

26. Green and Burch, "Unraveling of Rudy Eugene."

27. Ibid.

28. Martha Stout, *The Sociopath Next Door* (New York: Broadway, 2006).

29. Steve Hall and Simon Winlow may perhaps refer to this as a Luhmannesque social system, fashioned of luck and bad luck, cunning and stupidity, losers and winners.

30. Raymond Spaaij, "The Enigma of Lone Wolf Terrorism: An Assessment," *Studies in Conflict and Terrorism* 33, no. 9 (2010): 854–70.

31. Mark Seltzer, *Serial Killers: Death and Life in America's Wound Culture* (New York: Routledge, 1998).

32. Ibid., 10.

33. Centers for Disease Control and Prevention, "Zombie Preparedness," https://www.cdc.gov/phpr/zombies.htm.

34. Melissa Bell, "Zombie Apocalypse a Coup for CDC Emergency Team," *Washington Post*, May 20, 2011, http://www.washingtonpost.com/blogs/blogpost/post/zombie-apocalypse-a-coup-for-the-cdc-emergency-team/2011/05/20/AFPj3l7G_blog.html.

35. John Williams, "Undying Affection; They're in Video Games, TV Shows, Fun Runs, Amusement Parks—We Can't Seem to Escape Our Love for Zombies," *Baltimore Sun Sunrise*, June 12, 2012, 1C.

36. Irving DeJohn, "No Living Dead: CDC Clears the Air over Threat of 'Zombie Apocalypse,'" *New York Daily News*, June 2, 2012, 14.

37. Julie Watson, "'Zombie Apocalypse' Training Drill Organized by Halo Corp. for Military, Police Set for Oct. 31 in San Diego," Associated Press, October 27, 2012.

38. Ibid.

39. Ninety (67.9 percent) of the articles made some mention of illicit drug use as quasi-criminological explanation for Eugene's attack on Poppo.

40. Mahmet Oz, "Bath Salts: Evil Lurking in Your Corner Store," *Time*, May 29, 2011, http://content.time.com/time/magazine/article/0,9171,2065249,00.html.

41. SAIC, "Awareness: Officer Safety and Bath Salts," May 29, 2012, http://info.publicintelligence.net/OHSP-BathSalts.pdf.

42. http://www.myfloridalegal.com/pages.nsf/Main/E8A7D22B0760FDEF85257A45004C799A.

43. Seni Tienabeso, "Face-Eating Attack Possibly Prompted by 'Bath Salts,' Authorities Suspect," ABC News, May 29, 2012, http://abcnews.go.com/US/face-eating-attack-possibly-linked-bath-salts-miami/story?id=16451452.

44. Frank Owen, "The Miami Zombie," *Playboy*, December 29, 2012, http://www.playboy.com/playground/view/the-miami-zombie.

45. Kristen Gwynne, "The Dumb and Dangerous Anti-drug Propaganda in the Miami Zombie Story," Alternet, May 31, 2012, http://www.alternet.org/story/155671/the_dumb_and_dangerous_anti-drug_propaganda_in_the_miami_zombie_story.

46. Watson, "'Zombie Apocalypse' Training Drill."

47. Melissa Thompson, "Dawn of the Zombie Drugs Plague; Panic Spreads after Two More Cannibal Attacks," *Daily Mirror*, June 8, 2012.

48. Keith Hayward and Jock Young, "Cultural Criminology: Some Notes on the Script," *Theoretical Criminology* 8, no. 3 (2004): 259.

49. Owen, "Miami Zombie."

50. Houston Baker, "Scene . . . Not Heard," in *Reading Rodney King: Reading Urban Uprising*, ed. R. Gooding-Williams (London: Routledge, 1993), 42.

51. T. Linnemann and T. Wall, "'This Is Your Face on Meth': The Punitive Spectacle of 'White Trash' in the Rural War on Drugs," *Theoretical Criminology* 17, no. 3 (2013): 315–34.

52. Green and Burch, "Unraveling of Rudy Eugene."

53. Ibid.

54. Mark Neocleous, "Gothic Fascism," *Journal for Cultural Research* 9, no. 2 (2005): 133–49.

55. Williams, "Undying Affection."

56. Jennifer Nash, "Re-thinking Intersectionality," *Feminist Review* 89, no. 1 (2008): 1–15.

57. Thompson, "Dawn of the Zombie Drugs Plague."

58. Seltzer, *Serial Killers.*

59. Kevin Gray, "Drug LSD May Be behind Miami Face-Eating Attack, Police Say," *Chicago Tribune*, May 30, 2012, http://articles.chicagotribune.com/2012-05-30/business/sns-rt-us-usa-miami-attackbre84t16d -20120530_1_armando-aguilar-bath-salts-top-police-officer.

60. Helen Kennedy, "Victim of 'Miami Zombie' Attack Graduated from Manhattan's Stuyvesant High School," *New York Daily News*, May 30, 2012, http://www.nydailynews.com/news/crime/victim -miami-zombie-attack-graduated-manhattan-stuyvesant-high-school-article-1.1086770.

61. Mark Neocleous, "'Don't Be Scared, Be Prepared': Trauma–Anxiety–Resilience," *Alternatives: Global, Local, Political* 37, no. 3 (2012): 188–98.

62. Katherine Beckett and Stephen Herbert, *Banished: The New Social Control in Urban America* (New York: Oxford University Press, 2009).

63. Nadege Green, "He's Not a Zombie; He's My Son," *Sydney Morning Herald*, May 31, 2012, http:// www.smh.com.au/world/hes-not-a-zombie-hes-my-son-20120531-1zkj8.html.

64. Judith Butler, *Precarious Life: The Powers of Mourning and Violence* (London: Verso, 2006).

65. Majid Yar, "Critical Criminology, Critical Theory and Social Harm," in *New Directions in Criminological Theory*, ed. Steve Hall and Simon Winlow (Abingdon, U.K.: Routledge, 2012), 59.

66. Fabiola Santiago, "Face-Eating Story Just One More Weird Miami Tale," *Miami Herald*, May 29, 2012, http://www.miamiherald.com/2012/05/29/2822961/face-eating-story-just-one-more.html.

67. Davies, *Zombie Mania.*

68. By no coincidence, in the still settling rubble of the 2008 crash, analysts described several major financial institutions as "zombie banks," lumbering along in a "dead but dominant" state (see Jaime Peck, "Zombie Neoliberalism and the Ambidextrous State," *Theoretical Criminology* 14, no. 1 [2010]: 104–10), unable to perform basic functions, while "threatening everything else" (see Chris Harman, *Zombie Capitalism: Global Crisis and the Relevance of Marx* [Chicago: Haymarket Books, 2010], 12).

69. Davies, *Zombie Mania.*

70. Steve Hall, Simon Winlow, and Craig Ancrum, *Criminal Identities and Consumer Culture: Crime, Exclusion, and the New Culture of Narcissism* (Cullompton, U.K.: Willan, 2012).

71. Discovery, *Zombie Apocalypse* [documentary] (United States: Discovery Channel, 2012).

72. "Zombie Max Ammunition," http://www.hornady.com/ammunition/zombiemax/.

73. Some estimates place the entire genre at a $5 billion a year industry. Jon Ogg, "Zombies Worth over $5 Billion to Economy: The Walking Undead Reflect Our Anxieties over Scary Times," NBC News, October 31, 2011, http://www.nbcnews.com/id/45079546/ns/business-stocks_and_economy/t/zombies -worth-over-billion-economy/#.UUczi4U1aEU.

74. Owen, "Miami Zombie."

75. Gerry Canavan, "'We Are the Walking Dead': Race, Time, and Survival in Zombie Narrative," *Extrapolation* 51, no. 3 (2010): 450.

76. Bill Campbell, "Firearms Training for When the 'Zombies' Attack," September 15, 2011, http://www.policeone.com/police-products/firearms/articles/4275398-Fire-arms-training-for-when-the -Zombies-attack/.

77. Žižek, *Living in the End Times*, 3.

78. Steve Martinot and Jared Sexton, "The Avant-Garde of White Supremacy," *Social Identities* 9, no. 2 (2003): 169–81.

79. Žižek, *Violence*, 168.

80. Mark Neocleous, *Critique of Security* (Montreal: McGill-Queen's University Press, 2008).

81. Martinot and Sexton, "Avant-Garde of White Supremacy," 174, emphasis added.

82. Daniela DiGuido, "Zombie Apocalypse in Pop Culture: Miami 'Zombie' Bath Salts Attack Is No Laughing Matter," June 6, 2012, http://www.policymic.com/articles/9281/zombie-apocalypse-in -pop-culture-miami-zombie-bath-salts-attack-is-no-laughing-matter&op=.

83. Franco Moretti, "The Dialectic of Fear," *New Left Review* 136 (1982): 68.

84. Cheliotis, "Neoliberal Capitalism," 255.

85. Jean Comaroff and John Comaroff, "Alien-Nation: Zombies, Immigrants, and Millennial Capitalism," *South Atlantic Quarterly* 101, no. 4 (2002): 779–805.

PART V
New Life for the Undead

Some Kind of #Bite

There's something missing. But then, the zombie is a creature that is *always* missing something: today the zombie is understood as a fleshly, material entity devoid of sense, as in the virally afflicted, or, risen from the dead, as lacking some internal essence that makes us human. In an older sense of the word, however, *zombi* had two meanings:[1] it signified either a body without a soul, the archetypical zombie; *or* as a soul without a body, an immaterial being, a disembodied ghost forced to wander; or (as in the earliest text in which the word appears, 1697's *Le Zombi Du Gran Perou*) as a maleficent spirit. The how and the why of the zombie's solidification as a tangible rather than ethereal specter is beyond the purview of this study (though I discuss it somewhat in *The Transatlantic Zombie*), but I'd like to suggest here that the immaterial zombie is making a comeback in the most likely of places: on the Internet.

In one form, computer scientists have been talking of zombie PCs and zombie networks, used to infect or hack systems, for a decade, but there are other examples of virtual zombies all around us. Investigations of how the virtual world of the Internet has changed our relationship to our own lived bodies is a central issue in posthumanist theory taken up by Anne Balsamo, Scott Bukatman, N. Katherine Hayles, Brian Massumi, and many others, as the technology that surrounds us today makes Marshall McLuhan's musings on media seem ever more prophetic. I always think of a line from the first season of *House of Cards*: before the reporter Zoe Barnes sends a damning tweet, she tells the villainous protagonist and ambitious congressman Francis Underwood, "Remember, these days, when you're talking to one person, you're talking to a thousand." It's perhaps, then, not at all surprising that a material monster like the zombie has an expansive, unbounded, immaterial incarnation online. I'd like to draw a distinction between the digital zombie, as it appears in video games and online computer games, which come with visual and sonic approximations of zombie wars and the destruction of bodies—though obviously they are part of any conversation on zombies in media—and the virtual zombie, which is further abstracted. Let me provide an illustration of what I mean by the latter.

The virtual zombie is evidenced in Pete Rorabaugh and Jesse Stommel's online experiment Twitter vs. Zombies, a game they curated in November 2012 in which participants used a series of hashtags (like #bite, #dodge, #safezone, #weapon) to play an online version of Humans vs. Zombies, a tag game popular on college campuses. In their online article about the experience, "Twitter vs. Zombies: New Media Literacy and the Virtual Flash Mob," they explain that the point was to create "an epic zombified experiment in Twitter literacy, gamification, collaboration and emergent learning."[2] Their article explains the initial rules of the game: an original patient zero infects victims with the hashtag #bite, after which those infected attempt to #bite others and those playing (as was designated by the hashtag #TvsZ for Twitter vs. Zombies) attempted to #dodge bites or protect others by means of a #swipe. The rules of the game, as is stated on the Google Docs "Rule Manifest," were emergent, and this document was updated as the game was played. Rorabaugh and Stommel's article chronicles the way that the game evolved as the players contributed new aspects to the gameplay, such as the inclusion of a "twitpic" (an uploaded picture) of a household object—I saw one of knitting needles, another of a kitchen knife—with the hashtag #weapon to signify that they would use this as an instrument to defeat or hold off the zombie's attack. Safe zones were also improvised, virtual spaces in which humans could shelter themselves and others, and one could buy an hour of invincibility by contributing a substantive blog post reflecting on any aspect of the game.

For Rorabaugh and Stommel, the point was to engineer a collaborative space, a MOOC in which, through playing, novices could learn about Twitter and even experienced Twitter users could learn how to use it with other online platforms like Storify. They write,

> We wanted Twitter vs. Zombies to create a flexible system for learning how to use a specific social network and to study how the users of that system would adapt it for their own creative purposes. As the game advanced from the use of simple actions (#bite, #dodge, and #swipe) to more involved activities like blogging and photo-sharing (#safezone and #weapon), players within the game constructed a collaborative narrative of the simulated apocalypse. Each new rule, built "on the fly" as the game progressed, tried to engage increasingly complex skills. Over the course of the game, players new to Twitter learned to tweet with a hashtag, insert a link into a tweet, build lists, follow other users, publish media to WordPress and YouTube, watch individual feeds, use Twitter as a collaborative tool, direct message, and archive content in Storify. They wrote to save their lives, they negotiated, and they reflected on their learning about a tool from both within the tool and outside it.

What Rorabaugh and Stommel engineered, in short, was a virtual space for learning and for play, in which the communicability of the zombie infection emulated the speed and form of contemporary online communication. (Stommel's other writings on the topic are also valuable on this subject; see especially "'Pity Poor Flesh': Terrible Bodies in the Films of Carpenter, Cronenberg, and Romero.")

Rorabaugh and Stommel's essay is a valuable resource for those interested in the zombie's cyber (un)life, but I haven't sought to include it here because there is really no substitute for the online version, which provides hyperlinks to a variety of example tweets from the game, pictures and videos created by players, the Google Docs scoreboard and rules manifest, the official game site, the Storify narrative, crowdsourced reflections on the game, and pertinent articles. As such, their work calls to our attention what scholarship increasingly looks like in the digital age, where so much intellectual labor takes shape first in the form of online blogs. It is apt that, instead of being ensconced among the pages of this book, this piece be located elsewhere, in virtual space, so that it can stand for the thing that is here but isn't here, the immaterial aspect of the zombie, an ever elusive but exceedingly important aspect of the mythos that is suggested in the zombie's appearances in digital and virtual media. In this, the final section of the book, we attend to some "new" approaches to the undead.

First in this section, Eugene Thacker's "Nekros: or, The Poetics of Biopolitics" will take us back to the beginning. This essay considers Plato, Aristotle, Homer, Dante, medieval demonology and Thomas Aquinas, Hobbes, Kant, and Burke—not merely for figurations of living death in these works but to extrapolate from these classic texts a definition of what constitutes life—a strange thing in that Life itself is not living but an "inhuman" flow, a vital circulation of affect. Reading together the body politic (as in Hobbes's *Leviathan*) and biopolitics (as in Foucault), Thacker's essay draws little connection to the zombie until the final section: Thacker concludes that the zombie reveals how "biopolitics always implicates an ontology of life that it nevertheless is always attempting to supersede." This essay has relevance not only for new approaches to biopolitics but also for new vitalism and affect studies, but for me its most fertile moments come out of its discussion of sympathy and empathy as *contagious*. In particular, this essay helps me think through the "viral" sharing of images and videos of recent tragedies from the terror attack in Nice, France, on Bastille Day 2016 to the homicides (often perpetrated by police) of young men of color that are caught on tape and livestreamed on Facebook. How the mediation of affect flow contributes to new "problems of multiplicities," as Thacker calls it—especially in an era in which solidarity is often pronounced with the somewhat colonizing gesture of claiming "Je Suis Paris" or "I am Orlando"—seems to me to be conjured by work like this essay.

Jeffrey Jerome Cohen's poetic meditation "Grey" from the book *Prismatic Ecologies* is "A Zombie Ecology," a treatment of the recent fascination with zombies and its implications for movements in ecology and trends in ecotheory. This essay considers what our obsession with the zombie reveals about the turn away from anthropocentrism in so many fields within the "new materialism," including object-oriented ontology (OOO). As an alternative, Cohen puts forth ZOO (zombie-oriented ontology), which reminds us of the body's object status. Cohen sees undeadness as signifying more than just terminality; he sees it as offering a reminder of our own various states of being: it is the perfect monster to represent the enchantment of objects under global capitalism, or the sense of "embodiment as a drag against the internet-induced fantasy of incorporeality," but embodiment is also itself a kind of "drag"—a fantasy of wholeness, singularity of being. A grey ecology, in contrast, promotes "lived ethics (the anthropomorphic) as well as the coinhabitance and alien thriving of the nonhuman (the disanthropocentric)." In this offering, Cohen deftly cross-pollinates the political concern for human others with an interest in nonhuman beings by, for instance, placing weight upon the important issue of "environmental justice," the notion that ecological catastrophe affects certain groupings of people, such as the impoverished, more than others. Drawing together two poles that have often been considered diametrically opposed, this essay illustrates that an interest in different ontologies need not come at the expense of the living.

Drawing upon and departing from Donna Haraway's classic text "A Cyborg Manifesto," Karen Embry and I illustrated that, at its most basic level, the living dead zombie represents a defiance of the binary categories imposed by Enlightenment reason, many of which, like the self–other distinction, undergird capitalism. In our article "A Zombie Manifesto: The Nonhuman Condition in the Era of Advanced Capitalism," we argued that the zombie bears the marks of the dawn of modernity in its basic irresolvability, as it resists classification as either living or dead, inanimate or animate, subject or object, human or animal. My feeling about the essay was that its major contributions lay in its address of the figure's colonial history, which emphasizes that because of its historic association with Haiti, the zombie always carries with it the wraith of rebellion and the age of revolutions. I am also proud of the article's discussion of the zombie as a negative dialectic, drawing on Horkheimer and Adorno. In this piece, I see the germ of the idea that carried through my dissertation and first book: that the zombie is an embodiment of an irresolvable dialecticality that always holds in tension slavery and slave revolt. The larger point of the article, to my mind at the time that Karen and I wrote it, was to illustrate a fundamental incompatibility between capitalism and posthumanism and to argue, tongue in cheek, that the zombie offers a more accurate glimpse of a truly postcapitalist, posthuman future. I think some have misunderstood us as actually locating a liberatory potential within the nonsubjecthood of the zombie; the takeaway, as I see it today, is only a restatement of Marx: that *self* is the enemy of economic justice and that we have to find a way of moving beyond it in order to make change. If the zombie points the way forward, it is not in the deadened nonsubjectivity of Romero's brand of living dead but in the swarm species, hive-mind variety seen in *World War Z* (dir. Marc Forster, 2013).

Gerry Canavan's article "'We *Are* the Walking Dead': Race, Time, and Survival in Zombie Narrative" begins in dialogue with Steven Shaviro's important essay "Capitalist Monsters" and with "A Zombie Manifesto." Despite all of the associations with the zombie as capitalist consumer, Canavan stresses here that the zombie is always Other people and warns that embracing the potential of the zombie as posthuman risks dismissing too quickly its political implications as a societal mirror. Most importantly, the author sees as inherent to all zombies the colonial gaze described by John Rieder. The idea that the zombie refuses not to be *always* about slavery, in some capacity, provides a useful spin that returns us to the figure's origins at the same time as we investigate how the metaphor takes on new resonances today. Canavan reads the zombie narrative's depiction of the colonial gaze and its emphasis on the racial panic that structure colonialism and capitalism. In an important (re)turn to the human, Canavan reads the aftermaths of Hurricane Katrina and the earthquake in Haiti through the lens of the zombie narrative to remind us (as have others in this volume) that the real acts of zombification exist when we dehumanize our fellows. I wanted to end with this essay because this theoretical maneuver remains especially important in the wake of media attention to police brutality against minorities, as the grip of Islamophobia dehumanizes waves of refugees seeking asylum, and as anti-immigrant rhetoric is ratcheted up to new heights in political discourse.

Further Reading

In this section, we see the zombie used as a kind of prism through which new trends in philosophy are refracted to make visible the reality of our lived experience or to reveal the significances of the mythology in new contexts. Even as I'm writing this, there are probably scholars putting the zombie to uses that I cannot even imagine, and there are many others who defy my taxonomy and are difficult to fit neatly into one nice slot, such as Aaron Jaffe's oblique and performative take on Wallace Stevens: "13 Ways of Looking at a Zombie."

In this final section of suggested reading, I'll point to a few essays that correspond roughly to the trends singled out in the part's selection: including discussion of zombies in new media; new approaches to biopower and affect studies; treatment of zombies as posthuman; and new ways of thinking about capitalism and its effect on the world, including ecological consciousness.

First, there are many different ways of approaching the zombie and media—for example, the concept of "Zombie Media" is articulated by media theorists (see Garnet Hertz and Jussi Parikka) as a reinvigoration of so-called dead media, contra planned obsolescence and the wastefulness of consumer culture. Most often, however, one finds attention to the zombie film's treatment of media, as in the essay in the first section by Jeffrey Weinstock. This trend continues to evolve as technology evolves; see, for example, Dawn Keetley's "Zombie Evolution: Stephen King's *Cell*, George Romero's *Diary of the Dead*, and the Future of the Human," in which she writes of "zombies [as] media images" in a kind of posthuman figuration. See also, on this front, Mark Deuze's essay "Living as a Zombie in Media Is the Only Way to Survive," in the special issue of the *Journal of the Fantastic in the Arts* devoted to the topic "After/Lives: What's Next for Humanity?" Many other essays in that collection may also interest the reader exploring the undead as posthuman, as might some of the framing remarks of the introduction or afterword to Deborah Christie's and my *Better Off Dead: The Evolution of the Zombie as Posthuman*. Those just beginning to explore the field should look at Peter Dendle's discussion of "Zombie Movies and the 'Millennial Generation'" for its discussion of the zombie's relationship to technology. For concrete engagement with some of the foundational posthumanist concepts, see Patricia MacCormack's essay "Zombie without Organs: Gender, Flesh, and Fissure," Martin Rogers's "Hybridity and Post-human Anxiety in *28 Days Later*," or K. Silem Mohammad's discussion of Spinoza, Deleuze, and zombies as representing "a counter-human ethology" (98) in "Zombies, Rest, and Motion."

As for attention to zombies and digital media, the bulk of the work to date is (unsurprisingly) on video games. In addition to those previously mentioned in regard to Resident Evil 5's problematic depiction of Africa, see in particular Tanya Krzywinska's

"Zombies in Gamespace" and Diane Carr's "Textual Analysis, Digital Games, Zombies." Ewan Kirkland's "Horror Videogames and the Uncanny" is broader in scope but still relevant, and Richard J. Hand's "Proliferating Horrors: Survival Horror and the Resident Evil Franchise" ends with a beautiful comparison between the labyrinthine structure of video games and Walter Benjamin's *Arcades Project*.[3] Regarding the zombie and cyberspace, see again McGlotten's essay included here and Brendan Riley's discussion of "The E-Dead." A recent collection edited by Laura Hubner devoted to *The Zombie Renaissance* has a subheading for the category "Zombie Fans and Digital Cultures." Amanda Firestone profiles the app Zombies, Run! in the book collection *The Last Midnight*, and artist Winnie Soon has described her work "Hello Zombies" as a response to Internet spam. As the zombie's virtual incarnations multiply, more work in this area will doubtlessly follow.

There's nothing similar to Thacker's piece other than his own works. His short piece "Nomos, Nosos, and Bios" also has a brief discussion of zombies, but much of his work's focus on the apocalyptic is related; see, for example, *After Life* and *In the Dust of this Planet*, from his Horror and Philosophy series published by Zero Books. To pick just one strand in Thacker's piece here and trace its vibration in zombie scholarship, I would single out Fred Botting's "Affect-less: Zombie-Horror-Shock" for its discussion of affect in recent zombie films, with emphasis on media and new media. Using *28 Days Later* as a set piece, this essay explores "Zombie-Horror-Shock" and its wider implications for our mediatized culture.

Obviously, there are many trends in zombie scholarship that I'm neglecting. One is attention to the zombie's renaissance as a response to 9/11: a causal argument of which I've never been convinced because of the global scope of the zombie obsession but one often read through British director Danny Boyle's 2002 film. Better is a piece like Anna Froula's "Prolepsis and the 'War on Terror': Zombie Pathology and the Culture of Fear in *28 Days Later*," especially for its useful application of Adam Lowenstein's "allegorical moment." Nonetheless, those interested in the effect of terrorism on the genre might see Nick Muntean and Matthew Thomas Payne's "Attack of the Livid Dead: Recalibrating Terror in the Post–September 11 Zombie Film" or Christopher Zealand's article on "The National Strategy for Zombie Containment: Myth Meets Activism in Post 9/11 America," to name but a few. The most interesting work in this area seems to be that which raises the issue of affect in an age of permanent war. To that point, see Nick Muntean's articulation of the "trauma zombie" in *Better Off Dead* and Frances Auld's reading of posttraumatic stress disorder in the show *In The Flesh*.

In a similar vein to Cohen's essay here, see also Greg Pollock's "Undead Is the New Green: Zombies and Political Ecology" in *Zombies Are Us: Essays on the Humanity of the Walking Dead*, which uses a framework taken from Bruno Latour to look at the complicated nature of environmental politics. My essay on "The Eco-Zombie" in *Generation Zombie* may also be useful: it looks at ecophobia in the zombie film, highlighting a few instances in which zombies are depicted as the henchmen of Mother Nature, avenging criminal treatment of the environment.

Pushing further our thinking on the reach of capitalism, the final section of Michael Newbury's article "Fast Zombie/Slow Zombie" is titled "Zombie Ecology." This important article attends to the relatedness of capitalism and the current crises of the ecosphere: in the main, the argument treats the depiction of food in zombie films but also the rhetoric of apocalypse in food writing. Those interested in food in zombie films should also see Stephen Watt's delightful reading of two scenes in *Zombieland* in his piece "Zombie Psychology": that Tallahassee (Woody Harrelson) quests for a Hostess Twinkie but abhors the coconut-flavored Sno-ball is juxtaposed with Columbus (Jesse Eisenberg), who experiences shock when an attractive neighbor transforms into a zombie before his eyes. The essay probes the line between desire and disgust and the way the contemporary zombie narrative explores this territory. See again Attia Sattar's piece in the same volume. Sattar provides a glimpse into the way the zombie food economy is tied to insecurities about mass food production.

Finally, those who enjoy Canavan's piece here will certainly want to read his excellent study "Fighting a War You've Already Lost," in which he draws on the work of Roberto Esposito, Achille Mbembe, and others to investigate the zombie in examples from science fiction and cyberpunk as a figure of biopower's inherent contradictions.

Notes

1. Hans-W. Ackermann and Jeanine Gauthier, "The Ways and Nature of the Zombi," *Journal of American Folklore* 104, no. 414 (1991): 467.

2. Pete Rorabaugh and Jesse Stommel, "Twitter vs. Zombies: New Media Literacy and the Virtual Flash Mob," http://jessestommel.com/twitter-vs-zombies-new-media-literacy-the-virtual-flash-mob/.

3. Walter Benjamin, *The Arcades Project*, trans. Howard Eiland (Cambridge, Mass.: Harvard University Press, 2002).

20 Nekros; or, The Poetics of Biopolitics

EUGENE THACKER

Biopolitics

A question: what is the "bio" of biopolitics? Contemporary theories of biopolitics often emphasize medicine and public health, political economy and governmentality, or the philosophical and rhetorical dimensions. But if biopolitics is, in Michel Foucault's terms, that point at which "power takes hold of life," the moment in which "biological existence was reflected in political existence," then it follows that any theory of biopolitics will also have to interrogate the morphologies of the concept of "life" just as much as the mutations in power.[1]

It is remarkable how the concept of "life itself" has remained a horizon for much biopolitical thinking.[2] There is, for instance, the naive position, in which one presumes something called "life" that preexists or exists outside of politics, which is then co-opted into specific power relations (e.g., political economy, public health, statistics and demographics). The problem with this approach is that it forces one to accept a concept of life that is either excessively vague (life as experience) or reductive (life as a molecule, life as data). The presumption of a preexistent life also puts one in the dubious position of arguing for a protectionism regarding life, effectively making the removal of politics from life the goal of the critique. While we may disregard this position as naive, it is important to note how it surreptitiously haunts contemporary critiques of medicine and health care, from "big pharma" to the ongoing debates over public health security and bioterrorism.

The opposite of this is the cynical position, in which one assumes that there is no extrapolitical, essential concept of "life itself" that is then co-opted by politics or recuperated in power relations. Life is always already political, not only at the literal level of medicine but also in the way subjects are interpolated at the level of social, economic, and political life. Life is a concept that is constructed not only within scientific discourse but equally within political discourse—even when that discourse articulates an "outside" called natural law, human rights, or bare life. More sophisticated as a form of critique, the problem with the cynical approach is that it can end up leveraging critique on behalf of an empty concept. Since there is no preexistent life that is co-opted by power, either one is left dispensing with the concept altogether—a difficult task, since

Figure 20.1.
L'inferno, Gustave Doré, 1857.
Courtesy of Karl Hahn,
Wikimedia Commons.

the concept of life remains politically operative in a variety of contexts—or one argues for a renewed concept of life that has yet to be envisioned—in effect producing a concept of preexistent life similar to the one in the naive position.

The Problem with Multiplicities

Perhaps what life is, or how it is defined, is less important than the question of whether something called "life" comes under question at all in biopolitical theories—and one that is also not simply an empty yet functional shell. Foucault's Collège de France lectures offer several ways of addressing this dilemma. In Foucault's 1978 course, biopolitics is often characterized in terms of multiplicity—but the particular multiplicity of the collective, aggregate life that is the population. Foucault mentions three examples of epidemics as correlated to particular forms of power. In the Middle Ages, leprosy is aligned with sovereignty, and its ritual dividing practices and exclusion. The example of plague during the sixteenth and seventeenth centuries is, for Foucault, aligned with disciplinary power and its practices of inclusion and ordering. Finally, Foucault mentions smallpox and vaccination as an example of a third type of power, the apparatus of security, which "pulls back" and carefully observes the outcome of an event so as to selectively intervene. It is from this third type of epidemic that Foucault isolates a power that stitches together medicine, politics, and a concept of "population"—that is, an awareness of a novel object of power that is defined at once by its multiplicity, its temporal dynamics, and its statistical fluctuations. What emerges, Foucault argues, is a form of power that operates at the level of highly specified perturbations, one that intervenes at the level of the flux and flow, the manifold circulations, that is the population itself. "Circulation understood in the general sense as displacement, as exchange, as contact, as form of dispersion, and as form of distribution—the problem presented is: how can things be ordered such that this circulates or does not circulate?"[3]

Biopolitics is unique in Foucault's analysis because it expresses power as a problem of managing circulations and flows—something like *biopolitical flow*. It makes use of informatic methods, including statistics, demographics, and public health records, to insert a global knowledge into the probability of local events; it identifies and reacts to potential threats based on a whole political economy of the regulation of state forces; and, instead of a dichotomy between the permitted and forbidden, it calculates averages and norms upon which discrete and targeted interventions can be carried out. In a striking turn of phrase, Foucault suggests that, in this correlation between a distributed power and a distributed life, the central issue becomes "the problem of multiplicities" (*le problème des multiplicités*).[4] In this sense, biopolitics "is addressed to a multiplicity of people, not to the extent that they are nothing more than their individual bodies, but to the extent that they form, on the contrary, a global mass that is affected by overall processes characteristic of birth, death, production, illness, and so on."[5]

If we follow Foucault's leads here, then the "bio" of biopolitics has to be understood as a concern over the governance of "life itself," and this notion of life itself is principally characterized by what Foucault describes as the processes of circulation, flux, and flow. The problem of multiplicities is therefore also a problem concerning the government of the living, the governance, even, of "life itself." This is, to be sure, life understood as *zoē* and *bios*, as biological life and the qualified life of the human being, but it must also be understood in terms of what Aristotle called *psukhē*—a principle of life, a vital principle, the Life of the living.[6] While human agency both individual and collective is implicated in this notion of life as *psukhē*, it is also a nonhuman, unhuman form of life—one that nevertheless courses through us and through which we live. Thus the primary challenge to biopolitical modes of power is this: how to acknowledge the fundamentally unhuman quality of life as circulation, flux, and flow, while also providing the conditions for its being governed and managed. Biopolitics in this sense becomes the governance of vital forces, and biopolitics confronts what is essentially a question of scale—how to modulate phenomena that are at once "above" and "below" the scale of the human being.

Dead Tropes, Resurrected Bodies

In biopolitics, the conjunction of life and power raises the specter of the body politic, a figure of political philosophy that is at once anachronistic and yet continually resurrected. Foucault, for example, talks about both the "anatomo-politics of the human body" and the "biopolitics of the population." In his Collège de France lectures, Foucault points out that biopolitics conceives of a body that departs from the anatomical and mechanistic body politic of Hobbes's *Leviathan*. While this is true, the logic of the body politic continues to inform the concept of biopolitics, especially considering the centrality of a concept of "life" for both concepts. What is needed, then, is a way of thinking biopolitics in relation to its figural dimension—not just a biopolitics but a *poetics of biopolitics*.

The figure of the body politic resolves a number of conceptual problems: it not only posits a form of political organization nested in the truth of the body's anatomy but also implies a further analogy between the life of the natural–biological body and the life of the collective body, be that configured in terms of the political–theological community, the organismic nation-state, or, more recently, the global informatics of the multitude. Consider the primary question that occupies every discussion of the body politic—its building up or its construction. We know the conditions for the need of a body politic—the state of brutish nature, the war of all against all, "man is a wolf to man," and so forth. Once this irrevocable and universal mistrust of the human is established, how exactly does the body politic come to be? Quite simply, piece by piece, part by part, limb by limb. *Leviathan* gives us what is perhaps the clearest example of this building-up process, one in which

> the *sovereignty* is an artificial *soul*, as giving life and motion to the whole body; the *magistrates* and other *officers* of judicature and execution, artificial *joints*; *reward* and *punishment* . . . are the *nerves*, that do the same in the body natural . . . *counselors*, by whom all things needful for it to know are suggested unto it, are the *memory*; *equity* and *laws*, an artificial *reason* and *will*; *concord*, *health*; *sedition*, *sickness*; and *civil war*, *death*.[7]

Figure 20.2.
Still from *Zombi 2* (dir. Lucio Fulci, Variety Film, 1979).

Leviathan is, of course, picking up on a long tradition of analogizing the body politic and the body natural. Plato offers what is perhaps the earliest coherent example in the West. In the opening discussion of *Republic*, Socrates suggests that the question of justice in the individual should be sought by analogizing to the question of justice in the *polis*, the latter simply an individual "writ large." What results is a view of the *polis* as an integrated, tripartite order based on a tripartite anatomy of the human body: the philosopher-king (the head, or reasoning part), the auxiliaries or soldiers (the torso, or passional part), and the peasant class (the groin, or productive/reproductive part). Today, this building up of the body politic has become a mainstay of dystopian science fiction. In the graphic novel *V for Vendetta*, the government establishes its oppressive unity through a pervasive, high-technology surveillance system which is the "eyes," the "ears," and the "hands" of the body politic.

The Gothic Body Politic

The body politic is built up, but it can also break down. The building up also leads to a problem, however, for if the body politic can be constructed, then is it not also vulnerable to the inverse processes of destruction, dissolution, and decay? This is a major preoccupation in the literature of the gothic, which dwells on the processes of decay and degeneration, paradoxical processes that are at once generative and yet destructive. Consider the following passage:

> I am filthy. Lice gnaw me. Swine, when they look at me, vomit. The scabs and sores of leprosy have scaled my skin, which is coated with yellowish pus. I know not river water nor the clouds' dew. From my nape, as from a dungheap, sprouts an enormous toadstool with unbelliferous peduncles. Seated on a shapeless chunk of furniture, I have not moved a limb for four centuries. My feet have taken root in the soil forming a sort of perennial vegetation—not yet quite plant-life though no longer flesh—as far as my belly, and filled with vile parasites. My heart, however, is still beating. But how could it beat if the decay and effluvia of my carcass (I dare not say body) did not abundantly feed it? In my left armpit a family of toads has taken up residence, and whenever one of them moves it tickles me. Take care lest one escape and come scratching with its mouth at the interior of your ear: it could next penetrate into your brain. In my right armpit there is a chameleon which endlessly chases the toads so as not to die of hunger: everyone has to live. But when one side completely foils the tricks of the other, they like nothing better than to make themselves at home and suck the dainty grease that covers my sides: I am used to it. A spiteful viper has devoured my prick and taken its place.

Relentlessly perverting the classical body politic inherited from Hobbes, the text continues its anatomical litany, moving down into the nether regions of the body:

> Two small hedgehogs, that grow no more, have flung to a dog—which did not decline them—the contents of my testicles; inside the scrupulously scrubbed scrotal sac they

lodged. My anus has been blocked by a crab. Encouraged by my inertia, it guards the entrance with its pincers and causes me considerable pain! Two jellyfish crossed the seas, at once enticed by a hope which did not prove mistaken. They closely inspected the two plump portions which comprise the human rump and, fastening on to these convex contours, so squashed them by constant pressure that the two lumps of flesh disappeared while the two monsters which issued from the kingdom of viscosity remained, alike in colour, form, and ferocity. Speak not of my spinal column, since it is a sword.[8]

This is from *Les Chants de Maldoror,* the enigmatic nineteenth-century text by Isidore Ducasse, Comte de Lautréamont. What we are given here is something like a gothic body politic, one that is still built up but that is ridden with natural decay and monstrous hypergrowth. This body politic is not simply sick, lacking some essential component or nutrient that would make it healthy again. Instead, it seems to exist in this state of growth-decay as its natural state. In the gothic body politic, the body politic has not simply died, but there is also no "getting better." It remains a sovereign body, seated on a calcified throne—in fact, violently fixed there through the sword-backbone (perhaps the same sword depicted in the frontispiece to *Leviathan*). What Lautréamont gives us is not an anatomical body politic but a necrological one, a body whose natural state is this contradictory hyperdecay, at once generation and dissolution.

The gothic body politic therefore opens onto the inverse of the building-up process—the process of decay and dissolution. Not surprisingly, this is also a major motif of the body politic concept. But it is rarely foregrounded in the same way as the "heroic" building-up process. Often it is expressed in the somewhat furtive, later chapters dedicated to the "diseases" of the body politic. Here the figure of the body politic takes hold in a way that is, from Plato onward, strikingly modern. Hobbes, for instance, is forced to acknowledge that if "concord" is analogous to "health," then "sedition" would have to correlate to "sickness," and "civil war" to the death of the body politic itself. The body politic is not only built up; it is also governed by a logic of antiproduction, a breaking down. Hobbes gives us such an image in *Leviathan*: "Though nothing can be immortall, which mortals make; yet, if men had the use of reason they pretend to, their Common-wealths might be secured, at least, from perishing by internall diseases."[9] The problem, for Hobbes, is when the body politic is dissolved, "not by externall violence, but intestine disorder"—is the cause of such disease to be located within the anatomy of the body politic itself, and if so, are such pathologies of the body politic in fact innate or internal to it? Hobbes ambivalently affirms this, noting that "amongst the *Infirmities* therefore of a Common-wealth, I will reckon in the first place, those that arise from an Imperfect Institution, and resemble the diseases of a naturall body, which proceed from a Defectuous Procreation."[10]

Here Hobbes is aware of a central dilemma in the figure of the body politic. Insofar as the body politic is predicated on an analogy to the human body, it is also vulnerable to the contingencies and pathologies of the natural body. Plato also demonstrates an acute awareness of this dilemma. Early on in *Republic*, Socrates follows up his analogy of the body natural and the body politic with a medical qualifier: "there is an exact analogy between these states of mind [justice in the individual] and bodily health and sickness."[11] As Socrates notes, "health is produced by establishing a natural relation of control and subordination among the constituents of the body, disease by establishing an unnatural relation."[12] The implications of this are laid out in detail near the end of *Republic*: "Just as a sickly body needs only a slight push from outside to become ill, and sometimes even without any external influence becomes divided by factions within itself, so too doesn't a city that is in the same kind of condition as that body, on a small pretext . . . fall sick and do battle with itself, and sometimes even without any external influence become divided by faction?"[13]

Despite their historically different points of reference (Hippocratic medicine and Greek democracy for Plato, mechanism and the English Civil War for Hobbes), the commonality between them is this way in which the construction of the analogy has brought with it a dilemma concerning the pathologies of the body politic. And this leads both thinkers to assert what is perhaps the central lesson of the figure of the body politic—that the greatest threat to the body politic comes from within. This in itself—more than the literal, anatomical analogies—ties the figure of the body politic to biopolitics. If the latter, in Foucault's treatment, deals with the governing of "life itself" in terms of circulation, flux, and flow, then biopolitics can be understood as the management of the circulations that constitute the body politic—not an opening up or a shutting down of the body politic's boundaries but a calculated pull-back and targeted perturbation within this flux and flow, within this "problem of multiplicities."

Poetics and Pathos

The body politic—whether it is built up or breaking down—is always an issue of form, figure, and the figurative, always an issue of a poetics specific to a politics.

Aristotle gives us what remains a basic premise of poetics—the relation between poetics and *pathos*, or affect. As is well known, Aristotle's case study is tragedy, for it is in the weighty and serious matters of Greek tragedy that one finds the intimate coupling between *poiesis* and *pathos*. Tragedy delivers in dramatic form some statement about, for instance, fate and determinism, and this has the effect of a release, expunging, or purification in the audience members. This effect thus turns into an affect, something that flows and that circulates among those present at the play. This then encircles the effect of this affect as something "common," as something collectively experienced. The combination of these three elements—circulation/flow of affect, the feeling of purification, and its collective aspect—is famously dubbed "catharsis" by Aristotle.[14]

The term *catharsis* has connotations that draw together a notion of healing that is inseparable from a ritual or social function. Catharsis is "purgation" or "purification," both terms that denote a ritualistic process by which a body or bodies are made clean and free of any elements that would threaten the coherence, not only of the individuated body natural, but of the body politic as well. The *pathos* of catharsis is thus a process of separating out, of expunging, of rendering homogenous, of forcibly articulating an interior and an exterior. But it is also important to note that, in *Poetics,* it is not only the feeling of release or purification that defines catharsis but the fact that it circulates. Catharsis is less an emotion and more an affect—it proceeds by a sort of logic of miasmatic contagion or swarming, passing from stage to amphitheater, from actor to audience, and between one audience member and another.

If catharsis is the indissociability of poetics and *pathos*, then what kinds of *pathos* are produced? There is, for example, the pathos of sympathy and empathy in moral philosophy. If, generally speaking, sympathy is "feeling-with," then empathy is "feeling-in." The latter is often taken as a more extreme version of the former (which is why, in science fiction, "empaths" are often used to detect what an alien creature is feeling). While Immanuel Kant argues for an axiomatic approach to ethical relations based on sympathy as an innate character of human beings, Burke argues for a passage from sympathy to empathy as the basis for ethical relations. Burke's famous example is itself rather gothic—the witnessing of a public execution and the pathos it produces in the observers. One passes from a more distanced feeling-with (acknowledging the fear that must accompany the executed) to a more dangerous feeling-in (the hypothetical that the executed could also be me), and then—ideally—to a final *pathos*, a kind of feeling-together, in which I recognize my common humanity with others present at the execution. Thus *pathos* is not just feeling or emotion but the circulation of such feelings or emotions. Putting *pathos* into circulation implies that the tonality of such feelings or emotions is experienced as a passing, as a circulation, and as a connecting.

Death governs the circulation of pathos in Burke's example. But it is not a scene of total extinction, for something persists or resists afterward—that is, *pathos* persists and becomes something like *antipathos*, or antipathy ("feeling-against"). Something still circulates and flows, some affect swarms throughout a given collective site that becomes the basis for the commonality of pathos. Burke no doubt chooses this scene for its dramatic effect—it literally has a stage, an audience, and a tragic event. This is similarly highlighted by Antonin Artaud's essay "The Theater and the Plague." For Artaud, interested precisely in this theater of swarming affect, the pathos that circulates and flows is not simply a quantized emotion felt by receptacle-like individuals; rather, *pathos* is at once a form of life—identified with breath—and also a form of contagion. The same affective principle that is life giving is also life destroying, not through negation but rather through an excess that is part and parcel of that life principle. Breath is life, but

Figure 20.3.
Still from *Zombi 2* (dir. Lucio Fulci, Variety Film, 1979).

a form of life that endlessly circulates, that in fact cannot circulate. For Artaud, *pathos* is also pathological, in the sense that it is a form of life defined by its propensity for circulation and flow.

Pathological Life

The duplicity of *pathos*—donation and negation, feeling-with and feeling-against, crossing over and dividing—is directly tied to an ontology of life that is defined in terms of *pathos*. Poetics is, for Aristotle, indelibly connected to life: "tragedy is not an imitation of persons, but of actions and of life."[15] But at the same time, this life-affirming aspect of catharsis often functions through its inverse, and objects that would normally be repulsive, such as a corpse, become objects of understanding: "We take delight in viewing the most accurate possible images of objects which in themselves cause distress when we see them (e.g. the shapes of the lowest species of animal, and corpses)."[16]

In the *De anima*, Aristotle notes that any attempt to think about life must encounter the problem of *pathos*, or affections. Aristotle's initial move here is to distinguish an inquiry concerning "life itself" from an inquiry concerning living beings. The real challenge, for Aristotle, is to seek "the first principle of living things" rather than any analysis of living things, viewed individually or as a species. It is this principle that Aristotle refers to as *psukhē*, traditionally translated as "soul" but better translated as "life principle."[17] A basic distinction is made, then, between an essence or principle of life—*psukhē*—and the myriad of specific living things, such as plants, animals, and people. We might, then, suggest that Aristotle here posits a difference between "Life" as an ontological foundation and "the living," or the various specific instantiations of Life.

Yet, at the beginning of the treatise, this search for a principle of life immediately opens onto a number of problems. For one, Aristotle notes that the distinction between a principle of life and living things raises the question of their relation. Is *psukhē*, the principle of life, "in" each living thing entirely, or is it distributed or shared among particular living things? What, then, is the relation between Life and the living, between *psukhē*-as-principle and *psukhē*-as-manifestation?

The crux of this apparent confusion may not lie in the inexactness of Aristotle's prose but rather in the way in which *relation* itself is conceptualized. In book I, Aristotle's initial response is to suggest that *psukhē* is quasi-autonomous with respect to living things. While there can be affections peculiar to *psukhē* itself, there can also be other types of affections that are specific to living beings—but then this also means that those affections specific to living things are indirectly specific to *psukhē* in itself. And this is where the language of *pathos* becomes important. As Aristotle notes, the "affections of the soul also present a difficulty. It is unclear whether all these are shared also with the ensouled thing or whether some one of them is peculiar to the soul itself."[18] On one hand, *pathos* is central in that it connects *psukhē* in itself to the various instances of *psukhē*—*pathos* connects Life to the living, and vice versa.

Aristotle's comments on *pathos* are noteworthy, for the relation between *psukhē* as Life and as the living seems to hinge on the meanings that relation itself—*pathos*—has in this nexus between Life and the living. Here *pathos* is less like emotion and more like a relation, "what a thing undergoes." A body—be it plant, animal, or human—undergoes or is capable of undergoing any number of affections. Thus, affection (*pathos*) is itself the relation between Life and the living.

But now the question is, if *pathos* is in some way constitutive of the very relation between Life and the living—that is, if *pathos* actually conditions *psukhē*—then why would *pathos* need to be purged or expunged? If *pathos* conditions life generally, then the purification of *pathos* would seem to amount to a deconditioning of life, to a negation of life, the *antipathos*. The central political question that the example of Greek tragedy poses is "what does *pathos* purge?" If one of the functions of *pathos* in this case is to cleanse, purify, and rearticulate the body politic, then what are the criteria that define what is to be purged, expelled, and healed? The answer—posed, for example, by Aeschylus's *Oresteia*—would seem to be that it is not only a person or a person's wrongful deeds that are deserving of purgation; rather, it is a whole class of persons, of actions, of *life-forms*, that constitute that which must be purged. Again, "tragedy is not an imitation of persons, but of actions and of life." It is not so much persons or actions that must be purged as a chain of events, temporalities, and bodies—forms of life that are marked as threatening to the coherence of the body politic. In such instances, *pathos* becomes *pathological*, not just by its propensity to circulate and flow but by the way it raises the political problem of managing such circulation and flow. This class of life-that-is-marked-for-purgation is that which we can call *pathological life*.

If *pathos* designates not just emotions of suffering and pity but circulations of affects, then what would a "pathology" be in this context? From the modern epidemiological standpoint, what is pathological is a virulent microbe, abetted by the technologies of transportation, global trade, and the passage of peoples and animals across borders. One of the central affects of epidemics, plague, and pestilence is their pervasiveness, their seeming to at once be tied to stigmatized "others" but at the same time capable of connecting the most unlikely conjunctions of bodies, economies, and territories. But these ways of thinking give us an image of *pathos* that is, like the pathological life of disease, at once *everywhere*—in the air, all around us, pervading the very space of the body itself—and yet which must "emerge" from *somewhere*—even if this "somewhere" lies in the nebulous gray zones of an Orientalized "East" or a biopoliticized and racialized "other."[19]

But an epidemic is not just the passing of a "thing" like a message along a channel. What circulates are also affects, affects that are also relations of bodies. In fact, epidemics illustrate, in a highly ambivalent manner, the way that bodies are affects, and vice versa. So, if pathological life is not simply the biological life of the virulent microbe, and if it is not simply the representation of the patient's suffering, then what is the relationship between *pathos*-as-circulation and the view of the body politic as constituted by circulation, flux, and flow?

I Am Legion

Interestingly, the characteristics of pathological life are central to early modern demonology, which identifies a *pathos* unique to the politico-theological interests in the body politic. We can suggest, then, that there is a hidden genealogy to this Foucauldian biopolitics of flux, flow, and circulation. Not surprisingly, the descriptions of demonic possession during the early modern era often overlap with descriptions of epidemic disease. There are, of course, a number of precedents for this analogy in early Christianity. The most well known of these is the scene in Mark 5 (also repeated in Luke 8–9) in which Jesus, passing through a village with his followers, performs an exorcism on an old man possessed by demons. Jesus asks the demon's name, and a multitude of voices ring out, "I am Legion, for we are many." The demons are then cast out of the old man's body and into a herd of swine, which are then driven off a cliff. Word of Jesus's healing powers spreads throughout the village, and, in fear, the villagers ask Jesus to leave. The entire scene is depicted in quasi-medical terms, the exorcism as a "healing" or "curing."

In the "I Am Legion" fable, we see *pathos* stratified in the three ways we've mentioned. The demons are explicitly identified—and identify themselves—as a multiplicity, not only by the multitude of voices that ring out but by the multitude of quasi-material demonic bodies that inhabit the single body of the old man. There is also the animality of *pathos* in the herd of swine, which themselves swarm in a kind of "dance of death" frenzy. Here *pathos* is implicitly linked to the many animal instances of swarming in insects, flocking in birds or bats, or schooling in fish. Finally, *pathos* is also expressed in a linguistic dissemination of word of mouth. The exorcism incites both reverence and fear in the villagers, and word spreads to such an extent that Jesus's reputation precedes him to the next village.

Scenes such as this provided Scholastic demonology with a set of references against which individual cases of demonic possession could be verified, judged, and incorporated into Church doctrine. The result was not only a new set of juridical procedures but a new discourse and way of thinking about the supernatural in terms of the unhuman. This culminates in the early modern debates over the ontological status of demonic possession—works such as Jean Bodin's *De la Démonomanie des sorciers*, Johann Weyer's *De praestigiis daemonium*, and Reginald Scot's *Discoverie of Witchcraft* shape this debate. Each text makes claims about the role that medicine plays in either dispelling demonic possession or distinguishing it from other nonsupernatural causes (e.g., epilepsy, melancholia, trickery). They draw out the boundaries of the demonic, which become formalized in the great "handbooks" on demonology, such as the *Malleus Maleficarum*. In this way, the attempt to control epidemic disease, like attempts to control cases of demonic possession and their potential heresies, is, in modern terms, a "problem of multiplicities," or, to be more precise, the political challenges posed by epidemics and demonic possession point to a key relationship, that between sovereignty and multiplicity.

Spiritual Biopolitics

Though medieval thinkers from Anselm to Peter Lombard had commented on Satan and the Fall, it is Thomas Aquinas's treatise *De malo (On Evil)* that serves as the blueprint for Scholastic demonology. Aquinas's treatise places the demon within an ontological framework of Aristotelian naturalism, examining not just the biblical Satan but the demon itself as a kind of life-form—as a perturbation within the "flow of life," the *spiritus*. Aquinas considers demons to be intermediary beings like angels, lacking the absolute omnipotence of God but also lacking the limits of mortality of human beings. The theological and ontological status of spiritual creatures was, in effect, an act of boundary management between the natural and supernatural.

It is in the final eight questions of the *De malo,* in which Aquinas addresses the impact of demons in the human world, where the question of *spiritus* is raised. While Aquinas acknowledges the existence of demons as such, his dismissal of demonic powers is strangely modern—demonic signs, possession, and necromancy are all given Aristotelian-naturalistic explanations. This is the case when Aquinas discusses the impact demons can have on life processes such as generation and decay and, in particular, on the lives of human beings. Aquinas explains demonic possession as a misapplication of demonic intellect outside of its appropriate domain (this alone distinguishes demons from angels). The demonic is the aberrant intellect that then results in the aberrant form of life that is the possessed subject.

The technique by which the demon does this is through a perturbation of *spiritus,* a term Aquinas uses in its theological sense of "life-spirit," "breath," or "flow of life." Borrowing from Aristotelian hylomorphism, Aquinas suggests that demonic possession operates neither in the purely supernatural realm, nor purely in the mind of the possessed, but in the intermediary flux that connects them:

> Therefore, what happens in the case of those asleep regarding the apparitions of dreams from the local movement of vapors and fluids (spirituum et humorum) can happen by the like local movement achieved by devils, sometimes in those asleep, and sometimes in those awake. And in the case of those awake, devils can sometimes indeed move internal vapors and fluids (spiritus et humores) even to the point that the use of reason is completely fettered, as is evidently the case with the possessed.[20]

Spiritus is precisely that which mediates the natural and supernatural, earthly and divine—as well as managing the distinction and separation between them. The result, according to Aquinas, can be as simple as erratic behavior or as opaque as necromancy and the raising of the dead. Aquinas makes a key point here, however—the demon does not possess the power to create life, though it may have the impression of animating and reanimating. This is because, for Aquinas, the demon itself is not living; it does not have animation in the Aristotelian sense of living, natural beings. And yet it can have the effect of animating. The demon, then, seems to be that which can animate but which itself is not animated—that which perturbs and disturbs the flow of life but which is not itself living.

While Aquinas grants little in the way of real effectiveness to demons, this question of animation and vitalization remains an important part of Scholastic demonology. As Maaike van der Lugt notes in a recent study, the question of demonic generation is not just a question of whether angels or demons have bodies but whether they partake in the vital processes that having bodies affords. This includes generation and decay but also digestion, putrefaction, respiration, even communication. In her readings of Scholastic thinkers, van der Lugt focuses on the idea of "demonic generation," or the capacity of the demon to take on human or animal life qualities:

In the theological discourse, the concept of the possessed body presupposes and is opposed to the notion of life and the human person. The Scholastics had refined and made more precise this distinction between the possessed body and the living body in a series of questions concerning the activities of angels and demons at the moment of their appearance. . . . Were they capable of feeling, of moving, of speaking, or eating, or, finally, of generating life? Could they, according to the expression of Saint Thomas, exercise the opera vitae?[21]

The demon manifests in its generative capacity through its "vital works" or "vital signs," what Aquinas and other Scholastics referred to as *opera vitae*. But the *opera vitae* presumed a more basic action, which was the occupation of the body and, by extension, the occupation of vital or life forces, resulting in the possessed or "assumed" body, the *corpora assumpta*. The *corpora assumpta*, or the endowing of (human) life to the nonliving (demon), produced a strange disunity within the body, manifested in the vital signs or *opera vitae* of the demon.

Not only was Scholastic demonology—and the Church laws that elicited it— concerned with the identification and verification of the demonic, and not only was it important to be able to distinguish divine possessions from demonic ones, but there was also a concern with the "spiritual biopolitics" of life forces or principles of animation, a biopolitics of *spiritus*. As Alain Boureau notes, "divine rapture was the mirror image of diabolical possession, which itself was held in the obscurity of extracted confessions, denials, or medical loopholes. The analogous nature of possessions, either divine or diabolical, was the result of a similarity in the modes of action of the *spiritus*, of the divine spirit, either angelic or demonic."[22]

There is a further twist to this biopolitics of the demon. In Scholastic demonology, demonic possession involves not just the life of the demon itself as a supernatural creature but the vitalization of the demon by the body of the possessed. In this sense, demonic possession is not an appropriation of body or life but rather the taking on of life processes. It is the "ensouling," in Aristotelian terms (*empsukhē*), of that which is not living, the vitalization of the nonliving. This is an important distinction. Demons often possess nonliving things as well as living bodies. This is what Boureau refers to as

Figure 20.4.
Still from *Zombi 2* (dir. Lucio Fulci, Variety Film, 1979).

the "epidemiological" demon, the demon that enters the host unawares, either through food, via objects, or even as borne on the wind. The demon—that which is not animated but which animates—is also that which animates the inanimate—objects, mists, clouds, even the bodies of the dead. Demons can thus often take on an "elemental" quality. In such cases, the demonic becomes almost purely abstract, nearly identical to multiplicity itself.

Medical Demonology, Theology of Plague

At stake in the development of Scholastic demonology is the extent to which a form of power is produced that at once establishes and governs a supernatural—or, we might say, unhuman—field of circulations and flows. At stake, in other words, is the governance of the unhuman itself, the biopolitics of life-beyond-life—perhaps, even, a supernatural biopolitics.

In cases such as these, medicine and theology are brought together in ambivalent ways. There is, first, what we might call "medical demonology," or the ways in which medicine and medical knowledge came into relation with religious doctrine on, for instance, necromancy or the existence of demons. As early modern scholars have noted, medicine does not simply debunk or secularize demonology—quite the opposite. If anything, medicine comes to complete demonology, or at least serve as an arbitrator in disputed cases of demonic possession. The debate between Bodin, Weyer, and Scot is instructive. Bodin, an important early theorizer of sovereignty, argues for the reality of demonic possession—a threat to the religious order is also a threat to the secular order, and sovereignty undermined in the divine is also an undermining of sovereignty in the earthly. Bodin writes his treatise as an explicit retort to Weyer, who, as a physician, tentatively argues for a more medicalized and secular view of demonic possession. But even Weyer's text is filled with uncertainties; medicine's role is not simply to debunk all cases of demonic possession but to distinguish authentic cases from inauthentic ones (which may be symptoms of melancholy, epilepsy, or hysteria). If Weyer allows for the real existence of demons, then Scot goes the distance and argues for a general dismissal of the reality of demonic possession—again, medicine serves as the fulcrum of his argument, explaining the supernatural by recourse to the natural.

While that explanation varies, from the theological to the medical, and while the response varies, from persecution to diagnosis, what remains constant in medical demonology is the concern over the governance of the circulation and flow of *pathos*. If medical demonology pits medicine against a theological event, then we can also think about the inverse—the case in which theology is pitted against a natural-medical event. We can call this the "theology of plague," and it involves, quite simply, religious explanations of epidemic disease. Not surprisingly, the "angry God" motif is a recurrent one, both in the classical context—Thucydides reports it as a popular explanation of the plague of Athens—and in the Christian context—for instance, in the many accounts of the Black Death. But more than the angry God or references to the Book of Revelation, these narratives of epidemic disease often contain a number of insights into the politics of plague and pestilence. Chroniclers of the Black Death often note how epidemic disease brings with it a disruption of social hierarchy and political order, often necessitating forms of intervention, from enforced quarantines to the shutting up of houses to the mass graves and legal interdiction on public gatherings, festivals, plays, and funerals.[23]

All of these cases take place in an early modern or even premodern context. At the same time, they overlap significantly with contemporary concerns over global pandemics and biodefense. What if biopolitics is not simply immunological but also demonological? Demonology, in this case, would have to be understood less as the all-too-human drama of temptation and sin and more in terms of the governance of circulation, flux, and flow. It would also revolve around a phenomenon that is radically unhuman (the *antipathos*) or that serves as that which does not fit within the human framework. And it would also involve a form of life or vitalism that is often expressed as a contradiction (generative decay, the bestial and divine, communicable communication). In short, if biopolitics is demonological and not just immunological, this is because it raises the problem of the management of ambivalently vitalistic flux and flow—that is, the politics of unhuman life.

Poetics of Biopolitics

The classical term *nekros* encapsulates many of the dichotomies of the biopolitics concept. In its traditional sense, *nekros* names the corpse, the body that is no longer living. When, for example, Odysseus holds funeral rites for his deceased companions, it is the *nekros* that is cremated. But when Odysseus makes his way to the underworld, what he encounters is not simply the dead body or the corpse but "the ghosts of the dead" (*nekuōn kataethneōtōn*).[24] Here *nekros* names "the dead" as a form of life, one that resists any reliable distinction between the living being and the corpse. And this second type of *nekros* is also a collective, politicized form of life (*ethnea nekrōn*, the "nations of the dead").

Nowhere is this more effectively demonstrated than in Dante's *Inferno*, where we see stratifications of the living dead that are at once the product of divine punishment and, as such, are meticulously managed as massing or aggregate bodies. In the sixth circle, where Dante and his guide Virgil come up to the giant, fortress-like gates of the infernal City of Dis, guarded by hordes of demons, Virgil must enlist divine intervention in order to pass through the gates. Once Dante and Virgil enter, what they see is a city in ruins, an uneven landscape of burning, open graves:

> And we our feet directed tow'rds the city,
> After those holy words all confident.
> Within we entered without any contest;
> And I, who inclination had to see
> What the condition such a fortress holds,
> Soon as I was within, cast round mine eye,
> And see on every hand an ample plain,
> Full of distress and torment terrible.[25]

In this landscape, at once *terra*, *fortezza*, and *campagna*, Dante and Virgil come across another type of terrain—a landscape of open graves:

> The sepulchres make all the place uneven;
> So likewise did they there on every side,
> Saving that there the manner was more bitter;
> For flames between the sepulchres were scattered,
> By which they so intensely heated were,
> That iron more so asks not any art.
> All of their coverings uplifted were,
> And from them issued forth such dire laments,
> Sooth seemed they of the wretched and tormented.[26]

This harrowing vision of a field of burning graves blurs the boundary between corpse, grave, and the terrain itself. The scene prompts Dante to ask Virgil, "My Master, what are all those people / Who, having sepulture within those tombs, / Make themselves audible by doleful sighs?" His response: "Here are the Heresiarchs, / With their disciples of all sects, and much / More than thou thinkest laden are the tombs."[27]

In Dante's version of the dead walking the earth, the living dead are explicitly ordered within the City of Dis; indeed, the living dead are the "citizens" of this city. Furthermore, as Virgil notes, the living dead are politicized: they are the heretics, those who have spoken against the theologico-political order and, importantly, who have done so from within that order. In this way, Dante links the heretics to the other circles of lower Hell, including the "sowers of discord" (who are meticulously, anatomically dismembered) and the "falsifiers" (who are ridden with plague and leprosy).

Nowhere else in *Inferno* are we presented with such explicit analogies to the classical body politic. The City of Dis is, of course, very far from the idealized *polis* in Plato's *Republic* or the *civitas Dei* described by Augustine. The City of Dis is not even a living, human city. Instead, what we have is a necropolis, a dead city populated by living graves, by the dead walking the earth. The City of Dis is, in this guise, an inverted *polis*, an inverted body politic.

Again we have the ambiguous vitalism of the "shades," as well as their massing and aggregate forms. But here the living dead are not simply an instance of judgment or divine retribution; in fact, they are the opposite, that which is produced through sovereign power. This sovereign power not only punishes (in the famous *contrapasso*) but, more importantly, orders the multiplicity of bodies according to their transgressions or threats. In *Inferno*, the living dead are not only a threat to political order; the living dead are also organized and regulated by sovereign power. Sovereign power determines the living dead through an intervention into the natural workings of things, thereby managing the boundary between the natural and the supernatural. It does this not only to preserve the existing theological-political order but also to identify a threat that originates from within the body politic.

Within this mortified body politic, we witness two forms of power—a sovereign power that judges and punishes, but also a regulatory power that manages the flows and

Figure 20.5.
L'inferno, Gustave Doré, 1857.
Courtesy of Wikimedia
Commons.

circulations of multiple bodies, their body parts and bodily fluids. In this way, Dante's underworld is utterly contemporary, for it suggests to us that the body politic concept is always confronted with this twofold challenge—the necessity of establishing a sovereign power in conjunction with the necessity of regulating and managing multiplicities.

Living, Dead

This is a remarkably persistent motif, one finds in the contemporary lowbrow example of the living dead. The peculiar subgenre of the zombie film has, for many years, provided us with different cultural expressions of Dante's living dead. The American and Italian traditions are the most prominent examples in this regard. While early Hollywood thrillers such as *White Zombie* (dir. Victor Halperin, 1932) or *Revolt of the Zombies* (dir. Victor Halperin, 1936) placed Western doctors and heroes within the context of Vodou and colonialism, American zombie films after George Romero's landmark *Night of the Living Dead* (1968) place the living dead within a decidedly postindustrial, American context, self-reflexively stressing the "silent majority" and the uses of political satire.

By contrast, the Italian tradition of zombie films displays parts of both the early and later American traditions. Though many well-known directors have dabbled in the genre, it is Lucio Fulci who has explored (some would say exploited) the motif of the living dead in the most detail. Not only do Fulci's zombie films pick up on the idea of the colonial encounter as a medical encounter but medical power is always linked to the supernatural—perhaps we can even say sovereign—power to raise the dead. Critics of Fulci dismiss his work, noting that Fulci basically made one film, over and over. Admittedly, it is hard to deny such dismissals, for Fulci's films, such as the cult classic *Zombie* (1979; released in Italy as *Zombi 2*), *The Beyond* (1981), and the strangely uneventful *City of the Living Dead* (1980) repeatedly present an archetypal scene, one that visually encapsulates each of the films—that of the dead walking the earth.[28]

There is, to be sure, a political romanticism to these modern variants of the living dead; eventually, the multitude prevails through sheer persistence, and all symbols of hierarchy eventually fall. But more than this, what is instructive is the way such films demonstrate the problem of biopolitics as the governance of circulation, flux, and flow. These scenes of the dead walking the earth often signify moments of retribution, the living dead—themselves the product of a medical-sovereign power—taking vengeance upon their creators. Similar scenes are found in Romero's zombie films *Dawn of the Dead* (1978), *Day of the Dead* (1985), and, more recently, *Land of the Dead* (2005); all contain key, climactic scenes of the living dead as a contagious mass moving through the fences, barricades, and bunkers that human groups construct to manage them. The spaces through which the living dead move—houses, suburbs, malls, city streets, military bases, and corporate towers—all become porous spaces to the miasmatic logic of the living dead. They occupy the borderland not only between the living and the dead but between the One and the Many, sovereignty and multiplicity. Their massing and their aggregation are a matter not only of number but also of circulation and movement (albeit a maddeningly slow, persistent movement . . .). The movement of such massing and aggregate forms is that of contagion and circulation, a passing-through, a passing-between, even, in an eschatological sense, a passing-beyond.

In these archetypal scenes of the dead walking the earth, the living dead are driven by an ambiguous vitalism. Occupying the grey zone between the living and the dead, the zombie is "animated" in an Aristotelian sense; put another way, the living dead are living precisely because they are a construed threat. But, at the same time, they are the not-living because they are excluded from the body politic and the fortifications of security and political order—especially when they always reside within such spaces.

From this perspective, what begins to become apparent is that biopolitics always implicates an ontology of life that it nevertheless is always attempting to supersede. That ontology is at once medical and theological, medical demonology and the theology of plague. Something that decomposes and that is living; perhaps this conjunction between *psukhē* and *pathos*, between life and circulation/flux/flow, is the central dilemma for biopolitics today—the intelligibility of the "bio" of biopolitics.

Coda: The Incorruptibles

Theologians often talk about the incorruptibility of the corpses of saints, corpses touched by divine intervention and miraculously impervious to the temporal processes of decay. The corpses of mystics such as John of the Cross and Teresa of Avila are counted among the Incorruptibles of the Catholic Church. By contrast, I would like to be absolutely corruptible—nothing of my body would remain, not even the clothes I'm wearing or the notebook in which I'm writing. Finally all words and memories would evaporate, leaving not even an echo or resonance. It's a political fantasy—but no less fantastical than the Incorruptibles.

Notes

This text is derived from a talk given at Amherst College in 2009. Some of this material is found in modified form in my book *In the Dust of This Planet—Horror of Philosophy*, vol. 1 (Winchester, U.K.: Zero Books, 2011).

1. Michel Foucault, *The History of Sexuality, Vol. I* (New York: Vintage, 1990), 142.

2. An important exception is the work of Roberto Esposito, whose trilogy *Bíos, Immunitas,* and *Communitas* examines the philosophical underpinnings of biopolitics as a concept.

3. Michel Foucault, *Sécurité, Territoire, Population—Cours Au Collège de France, 1977–1978* (Paris: Gallimard/Seuil, 2004), 16.

4. Ibid., 12.

5. Michel Foucault, *Il Faut Défendre la Société—Cours Au Collège de France, 1976* (Paris: Gallimard/Seuil, 1997), 216.

6. This idea is further explored in my book *After Life* (Chicago: University of Chicago Press, 2010), 1–24.

7. Thomas Hobbes, introduction to *Leviathan: With Selected Variants from the Latin Edition of 1668*, ed. Edwin Curley (Indianapolis: Hackett, 1994).

8. Comte de Lautréamont, *Maldoror and the Complete Works of the Comte de Lautréamont,* trans. Alexis Lykiard (Cambridge: Exact Change, 1994), 142–43.

9. Hobbes, *Leviathan,* part II, chapter 29 ("Of those things that Weaken, or tend to the Dissolution of a Common-wealth").

10. Ibid.

11. Plato, *Republic,* trans. Desmond Lee (New York: Penguin, 2003), IV, 444c, 153.

12. Ibid., IV, 444d, 154.

13. Plato, *The Republic of Plato,* trans. Alan Bloom (New York: Basic Books, 1991), VIII, 556e, 235.

14. Aristotle, *Poetics,* trans. Malcolm Heath (New York: Penguin, 1996), 1449a24–28. Aristotle's famous definition is as follows: "Tragedy is an imitation of an action that is admirable, complete, and possesses magnitude; in language made pleasurable, each of its species separated in different parts; performed by actors, not through narration; effecting through pity and fear the purification *(katharsis)* of such emotions."

15. Ibid., 1450a15.

16. Ibid., 1448b10–14.

17. Aristotle, *On the Soul/Parva Naturalia/On Breath,* trans. W. S. Hett, Loeb Classical Library (1936; repr., Cambridge, Mass.: Harvard University Press, 2000). Aristotle reiterates several times: "Let us then,

taking up the starting point of our inquiry, say that the ensouled is distinguished from the unsouled by its being alive" (II.1.413a).

18. Ibid., I.1.403a.

19. See, e.g., Sheldon Watts, *Epidemics and History: Disease, Power, and Imperialism* (New Haven, Conn.: Yale University Press, 1999).

20. Thomas Aquinas, *On Evil,* trans. Richard Regan (Oxford: Oxford University Press, 2003), q.III, art.iv.

21. Maaike van der Lugt, *Le Ver, le demon, et la vierge: Les théories médiévales génération extraordinaire* (Paris: Belles Lettres, 2004), 238.

22. Alain Boureau, *Satan the Heretic: The Birth of Demonology in the Medieval West,* trans. Teresa Lavender Fagan (Chicago: University of Chicago Press, 2006), 174.

23. Literary accounts, from Giovanni Boccaccio's *Decameron* to Daniel Defoe's *Journal of the Plague Year* to Mary Shelley's *The Last Man,* Richard Matheson's *I Am Legend,* and Octavia Butler's *Clay's Ark,* all take up these basic motifs—the disruptive event, the lack of adequate explanation, the political shutting down, and the ensuing threat of social chaos.

24. Homer, *The Odyssey,* trans. Robert Fagles (New York: Penguin, 1996), XI.39.

25. Dante Alighieri, *Inferno,* trans. Henry Wadsworth Longfellow (Cambridge: Houghton, Mifflin, 1886), Canto IX, ll. 104–11.

26. Ibid., ll. 115–23.

27. Ibid., ll. 124–29.

28. The final scene in *Zombi 2* depicts the living dead slowly descending on New York City (they are crossing Brooklyn Bridge—apparently zombies come from Brooklyn . . .).

CHAPTER 21

Grey
A Zombie Ecology

JEFFREY JEROME COHEN

Grey is the fate of color at twilight. As the sun's radiance dwindles, objects receive less light to scatter and absorb. They yield to the world a diminishing energy, so that the vibrancy of orange, indigo, and red dulls to dusky hues. A grey ecology might therefore seem a moribund realm, an expanse of slow loss, wanness, and withdrawal, a graveyard space of mourning. Perhaps with such muted steps, the apocalypse arrives, not with a bang but with a dimming. Or maybe ashen grey is all that remains after the fires of the world's end have extinguished themselves, when nothing remains unburned.

Yet this affective disposition in which greying signals depletion and lifelessness reveals only the stubborn embedding of our anthropocentricity: as if the earth greys to mourn with us, to lament the absence of our tread. *Entre chien et loup,* twilit grey is materialized uncertainty. The shade marks a moment of mesopic vision, when the colors constituting the small portion of the spectrum humanly apprehensible recede, but they do not take the world's vitality with them. The grey hour is liminal, a turning point at which owls, mosquitoes, monsters, and the wind thrive, when stone cools for a while and persists in its epochal process of becoming dust, when animals and elements continue indifferent to our proclivity to think that an evening's color drain is a metaphor for human impermanence, a cosmic acknowledgment of our little fits of melancholy. Grey includes exhaustion, even obliteration, but also reminds that death is a burgeoning of life by other means. Grey is unimpressed by fantasies of disaster and finality. We are too enamored of the red and blue of catastrophe—of a world destroyed in flame and flood—and of the etiolation that follows. We like to imagine our own end and assume at our demise the world likewise terminates (fade to black) or that planet Gaia returns to the balance it possessed before apes became profligate humans (fade to deepest green). The apocalyptic imagination has difficulty discerning the vibrancy of grey. The gloaming is a place of life, but not necessarily in those sublime forms we expect life to assume. Despite our indolent habit of aligning dusk and evening with the declining and the still, neither is terminal. Grey mornings inevitably arrive, with roiling fogs and air restlessly astir.

A sensual grey ecology is inhuman, but that does not render it misanthropic, disembodied, or wholly foreign. *Inhuman* signifies "not human," of course, and therefore

includes a world of forces, objects, and nonhuman beings. But *in-human* also indicates
the alien within (any human body is an ecosystem filled with strange organisms; any
human collective is an ecosystem filled with strange objects) and requires as well a consideration of the violently inhumane.[1] Grey, polychrome hue of the in-between and the
uncertain, a miscellaneous zone, is not easily circumscribed. Like a cloud bank, a grey
ecology teems with varying densities of matter and shifting velocities: stormy thicknesses
as well as serenely heterogeneous clumps (*cloud*, after all, comes from the same word
as *clot* and *clod*), composites, and microclimates. Grey rolls, thins, inspissates, comes on
little cat feet. It is an open aesthetic.

If an ecology is an *oikos*, a dwelling or a home, it must also include the one who
writes about grey materiality while sitting at a laptop on a particularly fine morning just
at the border of Washington, D.C., listening to traffic and birdsong through an open
door. I know that nature is not outside with the melodies of trucks and finches but
resides also within this house (a structure built of trees, after all: birds are not the only
architects of arboreal habitations), a home shared with a spiny-tailed lizard named Spike
and a basil plant and dust mites and a ridiculous number of small rocks I have brought
indoors. This porous and fragile dwelling is built on both life and death, and not just
because its foundational soil is a seething expanse of decay and renewal, a necropolis of
vitality. This field become a little yard was probably at some point worked by enslaved
people. Not far from here is the church attended by those transported into hard lives
they did not choose, the ruins of the segregated school built for their descendants, the
remains of a burial ground. When this small brick house was erected quickly in 1940,
one of many hundreds for an influx of wartime workers, the neighborhood's covenant
declared what skin color and what religion would bar potential owners from possession.
As I was reminded by a neighbor when we moved here, Jews like us were not allowed.

A grey ecology will not forget this difficult past, limned by exclusions and brutality. A community comes into being through boundary. Forces, beings, and things left
outside dwell in an unsettled, "inexcluded" space. This liminal expanse marks the habita-
tion of unfinished business. The story it conveys includes histories of injustice, trauma,
violence. Grey is the realm of the monster, what appears at the perilous limit between
what we know and what we do not wish to apprehend, what we are and what we must
not be, what we fear and what we desire.[2] Like the monster, a grey ecology will often
take anthropomorphic form. Our perceptions of the world are irremediably shaped by
our humanity, and although we can attempt to discern what it is like to be a thing, "one
can never entirely escape the recession into one's own centrism."[3] Grey is an expanse for
what might be called disanthropocentrism: a sweep in which an environmental justice
may flourish, with its attention to lived human existence, as well as the vibrant matter,
dark ecologies, and object orientations that are so much a part of the new materialism.
In grey—a process more than a color—can be discerned the inhumanity through which
dominating notions of the human come into being hegemonies that emerge through the
sorting of who and what gets to dwell in the house and own a proper life, who and what
will be excluded. Grey reveals the inhuman as a thriving of life in other forms, a vitality
even in decay that demonstrates how the nonhuman is already inside, cohabitating and
continuing. Grey is the human in the microbe and the stone as well as the virus and the

rock in the human. It propels us beyond our own finitude, opens us to alien scales of both being (the micro and the macro) and time (the effervescent, barely glimpsed; the geologic, in which life proceeds at a billion-year pace).[4] A grey ecology is an expanse of monsters, but that is not in the end such a dark place to dwell.

Grey is the tint our flesh acquires as cells deprived of nutrients become energy for other creatures, for whom our demise is a flourishing. At this mortal boundary, grey is undead—that strangely evocative word, the negative of a noun that is already a kind of ultimate negative. *Undead* names the zone of restless and perplexing activity from which monsters arrive, a sensual as well as epistemic threshold at which the familiar loses certainty. *Undead* marks a kind of contact zone between the human and the nonhuman, in which the human reveals the monster always already enfolded in whatever dispersed amalgamation we are.

A green ecology judges a culture by its regard for nature, where "nature" is typically regarded as an external entity, culture's other. A grey ecology refuses such separations and believes that the haunting of monsters reveals communal values, shared aspirations, and lived ethics (the anthropomorphic) as well as the coinhabitance and alien thriving of the nonhuman (the disanthropocentric). Changes in a people's dominant monster manifest restless processes of transformation. The undead with the most enduring history of haunting are no doubt ghosts: sublime, frighteningly aesthetic creatures with cerebral narratives and noble pedigrees, tracing their descent from Virgil, Shakespeare, Henry James, Karl Marx, Jacques Lacan, and Jacques Derrida. The specters haunting Europe and its former colonies have a deep history and long postcolonial reach. Yet these intangible spirits have yielded over the last decade to a relentlessly corporeal zombie onslaught. The discarnate enigma of *The Turn of the Screw* seems anemic compared with the harrowing eyewitness accounts of apocalypse in Max Brooks's *World War Z* (2006), modeled on an oral history of World War II.[5] Our monsters are no longer ethereal and philosophical specters but shambling, putrefying corpses. Existential riddles, ghosts, and the vampires that followed them sought to challenge our minds. Now the undead just want to eat our brains. What is at stake in this material turn, this movement from cognition to consumption, from subjectivity to grey matter, from ectoplasm to ashen flesh, the human as yet another object in an object-filled world? Whereas a ghost is a "soul without a body," the zombie (according to Zora Neale Hurston in her seminal account of folklore in Haiti) is a body deprived of soul.[6] A corpse unearthed from the cemetery, the zombie is reanimated without possession of its personhood and forced into interminable labor on a Caribbean plantation. Zombies are therefore intimates of colonial history and the burgeoning of capitalism. Hurston published her research in 1938, and although zombies enjoyed a brief vogue in contemporary film, they did not so thoroughly saturate pop culture until the last decade or so. Their Haitian origin has mainly been forgotten, as the animated dead have migrated from film into novels, video games, and advertisements. With tiresome repetition, the future now promises a zombie apocalypse, an end to all hope of righting an unjust world. Our inevitable fate is to become zombies ourselves or to perish within their insatiable stomachs.

Because they possess a subjectivity that makes them seem like us, a ghost or a vampire is a monster to which a connection is easily felt. Not so the zombie. Despite its human form, these undead are far less anthropocentric. Their barrier to desire is evident in the love poems in the recent collection *Aim for the Head: An Anthology of Zombie Poetry*, replete with ironic lines like "gazing deep into your glazed eyes / you make me feel so vaguely alive,"[7] in variations like "I love you for your brains"—tongue-in-cheek effusions that replace soul with mere body are the best intimacies that zombie verses muster. Grey ecology, it seems, is a space of foundering attachment, of withdrawal rather than collaborative composition. Yet to write poetry about zombies, to dress as them during "zombie runs," and to imagine at such great literary lengths their depredations enacts a kind of desire, indicating their monstrous pull. Ugly, gauche, and anything but ethereal, zombies possess a shadowy but undeniable magnetism. Like vampires, they are embodied monsters; unlike their debonair cousins, zombies are nothing but their bodies. Whereas many familiar monsters are singular and alluring characters, zombies are a collective, a herd, a swarm. They do not own individualizing stories. They do not have personalities. They eat. They kill. They shamble. They suffer and they cause suffering. They are dirty, stinking, and poorly dressed. They are indifferent to their own decay. They bring about the end times. They are the perfect monster for a human world more enamored of objects than subjects, in which corporations are people and people are things.

The notion of an impending zombie apocalypse is so widespread that a best-selling handbook instructs readers on the supplies, shelter, and proper selfish behaviors necessary to survive the event. More than a million copies have been sold of Max Brooks's *Zombie Survival Guide: Complete Protection from the Living Dead*.[8] Its ardor for a doomsday when the ear is so catastrophically unbalanced that humans forfeit their dominion is a translation into a monstrous register of the vibrant genre of ecocatastrophe, what James Lovelock calls *The Revenge of Gaia*.[9] Inspired perhaps by the success of Brooks's book as well as the triumph in the United States of a secular apocalyptic imagination (the intoxication of imagining all things coming to their catastrophic end), the Centers for Disease Control and Prevention (CDC) in Atlanta recently published the graphic novel *Preparedness 101: Zombie Pandemic*. The book is described as "a fun new way of teaching about emergency preparedness."[10] The CDC also offered a tongue-in-cheek Web page devoted to the management of virally induced zombie plagues, where the following announcement appeared:

> If zombies did start roaming the streets, CDC would conduct an investigation much like any other disease outbreak. CDC would provide technical assistance to cities, states, or international partners dealing with a zombie infestation. . . . CDC and other federal agencies would send medical teams and first responders to help those in affected areas.[11]

Viewers of the AMC series *The Walking Dead* as well as readers of the graphic novels on which the show is loosely based know that the CDC will not live up to any of these promises. In season 1, episode 6, the Atlanta headquarters of the CDC is self-incinerated after its last remaining scientist fails to identify any means of combating the agent reanimating the brain stems of the dead. To the survivors seeking its refuge, the CDC promises knowledge and safe harbor. The institution delivers neither. Stealing a topos from Richard Matheson's vampiric zombie novel *I Am Legend* (1954), the lone scientist who mans the abandoned headquarters has been traumatized by the death and subsequent reanimation of his wife. His experiments have demonstrated that whatever agent causes corpses to become ravenous zombies has already infected the living. To be human means to inhabit the zombie's juvenile form. The scientist can see no escape from the future's bleakness, despite his frantic efforts to restore the past. He blasts the CDC to fiery pieces, perishing in the explosion. The scene is typical of the zombie's doom-laden domain, an out-of-kilter ecology that systematically robs family, neighborhood, city, and nation of protective power. Grey, the ashen shade that colors Atlanta after the blast vaporizing the CDC, is the color that moves the earth toward its ecological destiny as *The World without Us.*[12]

Like the meteors, plagues, floods, alien invaders, and personified earth that also populate the apocalyptic imagination, the advent of the zombie heralds the termination of human hegemony. The sleepers of *The Walking Dead* and *28 Days Later* awaken to a reconfigured world, a history that is literally posthuman. They are tasked with navigating a landscape of catastrophe but do so without much hope. They suffer so that their audience will not have to. Such narratives are not alarmist but instead are excellent at inculcating passivity. The world we know may well be coming to its horrible and human-caused close. It is perversely reassuring to be told that there is not much we can do about this ruinous advent besides spectate and carry on.

Because the word *zombie* migrated from Africa to Haiti to the United States and thence to Europe, zombies are transnational and epochal, but that does not mean they are not historicizable. George Romero's ghouls in *Night of the Living Dead*, for example, offered "an allegorical condemnation of the atrocities of Vietnam, violent racism, and the opposition to the civil rights movement."[13] Like all monsters, zombies are metaphors for what disquiets their generative times. But while it is clear that images of the violence in Vietnam resonated with the early viewers of Romero's film, few who watch today will associate that war with the movie's profaned bodies. Yet *Night of the Living Dead* remains powerful decades later. No single interpretation can capture a monstrous totality, no matter how persuasive that analysis might be. Monsters are more than the contexts that attended their births. They move through spaces even more potent than their own bodies. A monster is best understood as an extension of and collaboration with the unsettled ecology in which it dwells.

Zombies seem wholly natural. They are "just" dead human bodies, after all. Yet their haunting is the product of prosthetics, special effects, and digital enhancement, rendering them among the most industrially mediated of monsters. Multiple technologies have aided the exponential growth of the zombie population. Anyone with a smartphone, friends, and inexpensive makeup can create a zombie video for YouTube. Zombies are the perfect fodder for munitions-centric action films and video games (and sometimes, as with the Resident Evil series, it is impossible to tell the two apart). While social media can enable us to be more connected, more affiliated, more humane, the callous culture of the Internet can also trigger a profound affective disconnect. Zombies are its perfect monster. They are human beings against whom the most horrendous violence may be ethically perpetrated. They are to be shot through the head, and such execution is never a war crime. Offering the possibility of a murder that does not count, the zombie is the perfect monster for guilt-free slaughter. They are also relentless. Video games require enemies that turn us into zombies, pounding away at the FIRE button without cessation and without remorse. Maybe that is why games used to be marketed as enjoyable but now they simply announce themselves as addictive.[14]

Our dreams used to be bucolic, pastoral, green. Now we fantasize the past in violent shades of crimson. The Gaia hypothesis in its many guises offers either an agrarian or georgic reverie of primeval subsistence. We do not imagine the past in such pacific frames anymore. Now prehistory is a space for eating meat, running, and having our genes inalterably set to propel us toward destructive choices (evolutionary biology in its pop forms is the best thing ever to happen for white male privilege, because what used to be horrendous can now be naturalized as a response hardwired through environmental conditioning). Zombies are proliferating at the same time as our reigning fad diet is the Paleolithic, extolling the consumption of raw foods.[15] Meat loving and contemptuous of grains, the Paleo Diet renounces agricultural humanity for a fantasy of primitive hunter-gatherers who devoured what they killed or snatched with their own hands, a primal masculine ecology. Everyone was supposedly healthier when they resembled Bear Grylls, despite the fact that most hunter-gatherers probably lived very short lives that terminated in the stomachs of predators. Like the "Born to Run" movement, which insists that human bodies were designed on the savanna to run long distances without shoes, this diet is propelled by a fantasy that the past was a better space and that the current imperfections of our bodies were in distant history its flawless adaptations. The Paleo Diet, like the Zombie Diet, imagines that it is best to consume without adding culture to food (do not process what you devour) and that what we eat should arrive through no intermediary (nature offers bounty enough). We might even be tempted to label both diets *green*: what could be more natural, more ecofriendly, than a locavore culinary regime that leaves so small an environmental footprint? In the end, however, zombie diets are actually the more sustainable, since humans are the most-neglected meat in a flesh-loving culture. Zombies know that deer, horses, and humans all make good eating, and they were early practitioners of snout-to-tail dining. A grey ecology has very little waste—or rather, what would be waste is revealed as intimate to life in other forms.

Environmental justice is a mode of analysis that urges close attention to the populations paying the highest price for the comfortable modes of living enjoyed by elites. In Stacy Alaimo's words, "environmental justice insists upon the material interconnections between specific bodies and specific places, especially the peoples and areas that have been literally dumped upon."[16] These are the poor and the underserved: those who live downstream from toxic chemical spills, those whose drinking water has been poisoned, those who economic necessity compels to mine toxic substances without proper protective gear. Racism is as environmental as it is social.[17] The undead as another category of "unthought" share much with such victims, most of whom suffer in their bodies for ecological devastation. The state of undeath is frequently triggered by environmental hazards: radiation, toxic chemical spills, viruses. Racism is intimately entwined within monsterization, and so it is perhaps not surprising to discover that the zombie offers a racialized body. Never individualized, zombies present the single human collective about whom we can without hesitation speak in terms of determinative mental traits, communal bodily designators, and stereotyped characteristics. Zombies offer a permissible groupthinking of the other, the slough where we find ourselves besmirched by modes of thinking we claim to have surpassed. We feel no shame in declaring the discolored bodies of the undead repulsive. Zombies eat disgusting food. They possess no coherent language; it all sounds like grunts and moans. They desire everything we possess. They are a danger from without that is already within. We need to erect walls, secure borders, build fortresses, and amass guns against their surging tide. Applied to any other group, such homogenizing reduction and obsession with physicality, communal menace, and fantastic consumption should be intolerable. But the zombie is a body from which the person has departed, so we can talk about it without worry over bigotry.

The word *zombie* came into English by way of Haiti, where it arrived from Africa along with that island's population of enslaved peoples.[18] The folkloric zombie is a reduction of person to body: an utterly dehumanized laborer, compelled relentlessly to toil, brutally subjugated even in death. Old tropes gain new life in the contemporary zombie's body. Regardless of its skin color, we speak of the undead in terms inherited from racialist discourse. This undeath of some fairly ugly rhetoric suggests that, despite the fervent assertions of some political commentators, the United States is nowhere near postracial. As *The Walking Dead* TV series made clear in an episode titled "Vatos" (season 1, episode 4), featuring a Latino gang whose bluster hides the fact that they are caring for the elderly in an abandoned nursing home, life after the zombie apocalypse does not mark a radical break for everyone. Guillermo, the leader of the group and the nursing home's former custodian, declares that things did not really change all that much once the zombies appeared. Survival has always been difficult.

Derrida obliquely predicted the zombie advent (where zombies convey real human suffering) when he composed a ghostly book, *Specters of Marx*, critiquing the triumphalism that attended the fall of the Berlin Wall. Before we start celebrating the end of history or ideology, Derrida wrote, we should recall that

> never have violence, inequality, exclusion, famine, and thus economic oppression affected as many human beings in the history of the earth and of humanity. . . . Instead of celebrating the "end of ideologies" and the end of the great emancipatory discourses, let us never neglect this obvious macroscopic fact, made up of innumerable singular sites of suffering: no degree of progress allows one to ignore that never before, in absolute figures, have so many men, women and children been subjugated, starved or exterminated on the earth.[19]

These words have become only more true since Derrida penned them in 1993. Our exultant self-satisfaction at communism's end—our very love of things coming to ends—blinds us to abiding, proliferating human suffering. From specter to zombie: is it any wonder that an ardor for the end of history has been swept along by an apocalypse that involves "violence, inequality, exclusion, famine . . . innumerable singular sites of suffering"? The zombie figures the return of the injustices we quietly practice against people we prefer to keep dim in a twilight that marks a willed blindness.

In its limbo of body enduring beyond death, the zombie offers a vision of an afterlife that we have decided is otherwise impossible. Imagine there's no heaven, no hell below us, and we get the endless nightfall of the zombie apocalypse, a place indifferent to good and evil, a hereafter without gods. Yet the walking dead are also very much of this world. We are haunted by zombies because we experience embodiment as a drag against the Internet-induced fantasy of incorporeality. Perhaps we no longer dream of ghosts because we have become them. We disidentify with zombies by slaughtering them en masse, allowing us to sustain our desire for an electronic realm where we are freed from fleshly restraint. Battling zombies is a wild liberation—or at least a powerful vehicle for our fantasy that we can escape our own embodiedness and become high-speed avatars, quick souls divorced from slow flesh, from our own worldedness.[20] Paradoxically, however, a bond of desire continues to entwine us with the zombie we murder. During a television interview to promote *Land of the Dead* (2005), George Romero asserted that should zombies actually appear, he would offer himself to be bitten so that he could live forever. As Sarah Juliet Lauro and Karen Embry observe in "A Zombie Manifesto," "the irony is that while the statement prompts us to ask what kind of life that would be, it reveals that our fascination with the zombie is, in part, a celebration of its immortality and a recognition of ourselves as enslaved to our bodies."[21] And lovers of the world we inhabit as well. We will stay here forever, even if the price is undeath.

Zombies are a kind of ultimate enemy, because they are so utterly inhuman, yet we the living always turn out to be worse than the zombies we fight. We form our collectives to do battle with these monsters, and then we turn on each other and display a zombielike aggression against what should be community. In *Night of the Living Dead*, the "hero" Ben participates in but survives the violence practiced within the besieged farmhouse. Emerging from the place the next day, he is shot by the police. *The Walking Dead* series seethes with brutality perpetrated by the living against each other, offering a sustained meditation on racism and class enmity. Its cast of traumatized men also exposes as a lie the idea that zombies have no feelings. Men in the narrative have trouble articulating needs, desires, and emotions; when they do, disaster ensues. The zombies, meanwhile, are not emotionally dead; they are unremittingly expressive—of anger, of insatiable hunger, of trauma. They are raw. The zombies embody what the men feel.

To return to the "Vatos" episode of *The Walking Dead* and its ecology askew, though sometimes too saccharine, the narrative of the Latino gang brilliantly juxtaposed a fortress-like industrial building where the elderly had been placed to spend their last days with the transformed streets of Atlanta, an urban space made strange because traversed by nonnormative bodies. The zombies crowding the city blocks offer the corporeal forms communities typically render invisible, now released from their warehousing in assisted living centers, group homes, mental hospitals, and hospices to fill spaces once purged of all signs of nonablebodiedness. We live in a disability-fearing, youth-loving, death-phobic culture. When the elderly and the disabled are institutionalized to dwell secluded from public view, when cognitive and physical disability are conflated first with mere corporeality and then with the moribund, when we associate the end of life with the smell of disinfectant and the scrubbed walls of a hospital, when bodies simply vanish after the person inside perishes, quietly carted away by people paid a trifling wage to ensure that we do not have to stand in the presence of a corpse, to stand in the presence of our own mortality, then the zombie offers a chance to behold our bodily future. What lies ahead for most of us is disability and for all of us death. The zombie is the perishable carnality that we hide from ourselves, the declaration of our own thingly existence.

Yet the zombie's decay is not an indication of its deadness. The zombie is our window to the visceral world to which we have always belonged and into which we are absorbed as food for growth. It is a world we close off from ourselves yet yearn to see. We know that we are something more and something less than human, yet we hide that knowledge from ourselves. Surrounded by injunctions to conceal, costume, and enjoy, we outsource the corpse to morticians, health care personnel, hospice workers, and custodians. The zombie vividly exhibits the indifference of our materiality to the supposed superiority or control or beauty of the subjectivity that is supposed to reside within, grey life in death. Decomposition is the flourishing of bacteria, the autonomy of the world, an unyielding demonstration of the inhuman agency that resides in the pieces and substances that we totalize for a while into a body we call ours. Decay is a process of transformation. It seems final, fatal, and terminal, but this activity is future directed, creative, and uninterested in our mourning.

Such inhuman indifference finds a parallel in our propensity to regard others in ways patently inhumane, a withdrawal of ethical relation. As I compose this chapter, the news has been full of stories of cannibalism labeled, tongue in cheek, as signs of the advent of the zombie apocalypse. High on drugs, a man in Miami was shot by the police while chewing the face from a homeless victim. The event illustrates some profound human failures: of a social safety net that should ensure a world where indigent people do not have to sleep under bridges, of a health care system in crisis. To say that a mentally ill substance abuser and a person without a home should be omens of a zombie apocalypse is to guard ourselves from knowledge we possess but prefer to dismiss: that we are a class-riven society, that ablebodiedness is impossible to maintain, that we are in the end too selfish to care adequately for the elderly, the impoverished, the disabled. There are no monsters visible at such horrific encounters, at such foundering of our sympathy, only us.

Humans ought never to be reduced to the bare life of an object. Yet our inclination to imagine that things have no agency, vitality, or autonomy also deserves interrogation. Thingly existence is very different from existence reduced to inert thingness. What if the world is not passive? What if objects are livelier than we suppose? In the zombie's ongoing putrefaction, in its inability to remain still long, in its status as animated body indifferent to human subjectivity is evident what has been called an object-oriented ontology (OOO). Graham Harman defines this thing-centric mode of philosophical analysis as one in which "individual entities of various different scales . . . are the ultimate stuff of the cosmos," and "these entities are never exhausted by any of their relations or even by their sum of all possible relations."[22] OOO is a nonanthropocentric philosophy in which things possess agency, autonomy, and ultimate mystery. The walking dead offer what might be called a ZOO, a zombie-oriented ontology—or, even better, a ZOE (zombie-oriented ecology), which makes evident the objectal status of the body as a heterogeneous concatenation of parts, working in harmonious relation, or exerting their own will, or entropically vanishing, or willfully relating to other forces, other things. The zombie becomes organs without a body, an assemblage of autonomous zones without a necessary totality. The zombie is the inhuman reality of the body, our composition by volitional objects that sometimes work together and sometimes do not, as well as the dependence of this composing process on an agentic, active nonhuman world. We do not like to behold our own viscerality, our own material composition, and the zombie is therefore repugnant. Obscure, worldly, challenging, and embodied, the zombie's grey is also strangely beautiful.

Like dragons and giants, the walking dead are transcultural monsters, haunting nearly every geography and history. Our hope and our fear that death is not the end of life amount to the same thing, yielding gods who rise from the dead to redeem us as well as humans who rise from the dead to feed on us. Yet the world is seldom so small as this anthropocentric feeding-and-believing cycle would posit. A vigorous tradition of animated corpses unfolds (for example) in medieval Icelandic texts, where the sagas speak of a revenant called the *draugr* or *aptrgangr* who, once interred, will not remain still. In *Grettir's Saga,* a work of the fourteenth century, we learn of Glam, a pagan from Sweden hired by a farmer to tend sheep on a haunted mountainside.[23] Glam refuses participation within the farmhouse community and will not attend Christmas services or even fast before the holy day.[24] He is murdered by an unseen monster during a snowstorm, and his employer finds it impossible to bring the corpse to Christian burial. Once interred in a cairn—beneath a heft of stones that cannot hold him down—Glam begins haunting the farm, riding atop its roof at night and descending to smash to pieces the bones of any animal or human foolish enough to slumber nearby. The young warrior Grettir offers to rid the farm of this *aptrgangr,* this "again-walker." In life Glam had been "extremely large . . . a strange appearance, with wide-open blue eyes and wolf-grey hair," and in death "large and horribly deformed, with strange oversized features," an intimacy of the pre- and postmortem.[25] Grettir wrestles with this monster furiously, destroying parts of the house and then tumbling through the door:

> Glam, now off balance, came crashing out of the house with Grettir on top of him. Outside it was bright in the moonlight, with gaps here and there in the cloud cover. On and off, the moon shone through. Just as Glam fell the clouds moved, revealing the moon. Glam stared up at the light, and Grettir later said that this sight was the only one that ever scared him.[26]

At this moment when Grettir himself seems undead ("he lay between life and death"), Glam curses his foe, declaring that he will never reach more than half his strength, that he will forever fear the dark. Grettir recovers, decapitates Glam, and places the head against the buttocks, ensuring the monster will not return. Glam's prediction will, however, hold true. Grettir forever fears darkness and isolation. His death will unfold as a result.

Glam is clearly the walking dead, but not exactly a zombie in the contemporary sense. He murders, but not for food. After death, his personhood endures within his body. Yet the episode well illustrates something lurking within but often hidden by modern zombie narratives: the twilight environmental aesthetic of the undead. Zombies are creatures who have no need of shelter. They do not build. They exist in an uncultured state. Perhaps they incarnate our fantasies of nature as an exterior and inimical force, our ecophobia.[27] They are also in the end too separate from their worlds, too solitarily human. Zombies never break anthropomorphism. Humans living and undead continue to inhabit a shared and limited ambit. Even if they sometimes devour animals, zombies generally eat only live human beings, not each other, never plants. Their limited diet is evidence enough of how circumscribed their monstrosity remains. Creatures of relation, found only in herds, their insistent human connection also constitutes a silent sociality, one that disallows the invention of wider modes of worldly inhabitance. Unlike some of the lonely bodies described by object-oriented philosophy—dim, rogue, and dark objects, things that recede infinitely from relation, objects that cannot ever directly touch—zombies are unremittingly gregarious.[28] They do not thrive in solitude but seek others with whom to compose their vagrant herd. A zombie is a body in insistent relation, but only with other human bodies.

Zombies could learn much from their forebears. Frankenstein's Creature, who apprehends the language of the earth through the groaning of glaciers in the Alps, who is spotted most often in resplendent, icy spaces, knows as undead Glam does that a continuity binds body and world. Glam could have taught our modern monsters the potency of lunar radiance, of dwelling at margins, of trackless snow. The love of icescapes shared by Frankenstein's Creature and Glam, expanses where the movement of the earth is constant, suggests that their undeath is perhaps the same as the animation of what was never supposed to have held life. They are undead as the world is undead—which is to say, that the world is differently alive. Monster, human, and world are *transcorporal.* I take that term from Alaimo, who coins it to designate the "entangled territories of material and discursive, natural and cultural, biological and textual,"[29] where "concern and wonder converge" in a material ethics that involves "the emergent, ultimately unmappable landscapes of interacting biological, climatic, economic, and political forces," where "human corporeality" intermeshes with the "more-than-human."[30]

And so Glam's power is not fully exerted until he is outdoors, in those wild spaces where during his life as a shepherd he dwelled. His curse is delivered only when clouds cease to obscure the moon, when the cold night is bathed in a radiance that makes Glam's eyes glisten. A being of lunar luminescence, broken stones, and blizzards, Glam in his undeath is that against which we build our houses, the excluded as well as the inhuman. The *aptrgangr,* the again-walker, is a monster whose life in death makes us realize the precariousness of our own dwellings, of our lives: the weakness of our doors and roofs, the penetrative power of the moon, storms, and night. This inhuman ecology is a part of our zombie-oriented ontology, one in which we realize it is not simply the human body that is an assemblage of discordant, agential, and envitalized objects but the earth itself. "Undead" means "differently alive." The very ground we walk on, our future tomb, is alive in its supposed inertness, forever on the move, a foundation as well as our ruin, the undead material from which we construct our worlds. No wonder our zombies revive through the agency of inhuman but fully mundane agents like radiation and viruses.

A *kakosmos* of flowing crimson and grey body parts autonomously alive, the zombie aesthetic is disturbing, and thereby fruitful to think with.[31] Yet, in the end, I wish we could have our zombies without desiring so ardently an apocalypse to accompany them. Apocalypse is a failure of the imagination, a giving up on the future instead of a commitment to the difficult work of composing a better present. Those who dream of the purgation of our problems rather than delivering themselves to the labor of repair choose an easier path. No wonder the zombies devour them. To be undead might mean something more than to inhabit a terminal world, a vastness reduced to the grey of an earthbound despair. Zombies without apocalypse might offer a future in which we recognize the suffering, the possibilities, the potency, and the dignity of humans and nonhumans alike: grey as the color of unexpected life.

Notes

A substantially different version of this chapter appears in *Journal for the Fantastic in the Arts*. I thank the journal for permission to reprint some of that material here. I would like to thank the audiences in Orlando and Edinburgh who gave me valuable feedback on this chapter; China Miéville and Kanlillea Aghtan for their critical responses; and Karl Steel, Lara Farina, Alan Montroso, Richard Morrison, and Michael O'Rourke for their suggestions for revision.

1. I quietly argue throughout this chapter that a grey ecology is consonant with scholarly work being conducted under the rubrics "object-oriented ontology" and "the new materialism" and cannot exclude a consideration of ethics, especially in the form of environmental justice. Profoundly helpful in framing this investigation have been Stacy Alaimo, *Bodily Natures: Science, Environment, and the Material Self* (Bloomington: Indiana University Press, 2010), and Jane Bennett, *Vibrant Matter: A Political Ecology of Things* (Durham, N.C.: Duke University Press, 2010).

2. For some of my early work on monsters, see "Monster Culture (Seven Theses)," in *Monster Theory: Reading Culture*, ed. Jeffrey Jerome Cohen, 3–25 (Minneapolis: University of Minnesota Press, 1996). For a vivid exploration of the confluence of monster theory and ecocriticism, see Simon C. Estok, *Ecocriticism and Shakespeare: Reading Ecophobia* (New York: Palgrave Macmillan, 2011), 67–83.

3. Ian Bogost, *Alien Phenomenology: or, What It's Like to Be a Thing* (Minneapolis: University of Minnesota Press, 2012), 80. On the unavoidability of anthropocentrism, see also page 64. Bogost's work, like that of Graham Harman, Timothy Morton, Levi Bryant, and the other writers associated with object-oriented philosophy, is often carelessly accused of possessing no evident ethics or politics. Yet thickening human understanding of the inhuman world and interrogating relations to it is an ethical practice (and in the case of Morton and Bryant, one conducted within an explicitly ethical mode). See esp. Timothy Morton, *The Ecological Thought* (Cambridge, Mass.: Harvard University Press, 2010), and Levi Bryant, *The Democracy of Objects* (Ann Arbor, Mich.: Open Humanities Press, 2011). I am attempting in this essay a humane account of a subject ethically, ontologically, and phenomenologically messy, as Jane Bennett accomplishes through her refusal to pathologize hoarding in her essay "Powers of the Hoard: Further Notes on Material Agency," in *Animal, Vegetable, Mineral: Ethics and Objects*, ed. Jeffrey Jerome Cohen, 237–69 (Washington, D.C.: Oliphaunt Books, 2012).

4. In writing these lines, I am thinking both of Quentin Meillassoux, *After Finitude: An Essay on the Necessity of Contingency* (London: Continuum, 2008), especially his disruptive notion of the arche-fossil, and, conversely, Paul Virilio, *Grey Ecology*, trans. Drew Burk (New York: Atropos, 2009), about the scale and the power of finitude as well as the necessity of rethinking progress narratives.

5. Max Brooks, *World War Z: An Oral History of the Zombie War* (New York: Random House, 2006).

6. "The stereotypical zombie is essentially the opposite of such a 'ghost': it is a soulless body, rather than a disembodied soul." Quoted in Peter Dendle, "Zombie Movies and the 'Millennial Generation,'" in *Better Off Dead: The Evolution of the Zombie as Posthuman*, ed. Deborah Christie and Sarah Juliet Lauro (New York: Fordham University Press, 2011), 177. For the zombie as body without soul, see Zora Neale Hurston, *Tell My Horse: Voodoo and Life in Haiti and Jamaica* (New York: Harper and Row, 1938), 179.

7. Sean O'Neil, "Visceral Love," in *Aim for the Head: An Anthology of Zombie Poetry*, ed. Rob "Ratpack Slim" Sturma (Long Beach, Calif.: Write Bloody, 2011), 46.

8. Max Brooks, *The Zombie Survival Guide: Complete Protection from the Living Dead* (New York: Three Rivers Press, 2003).

9. James Lovelock, *The Revenge of Gaia: Why the Earth Is Fighting Back—and How We Can Still Save Humanity* (New York: Basic Books, 2006).

10. https://www.cdc.gov/phpr/zombies_novella.htm.

11. https://www.fema.gov/blog/2011-05-19/cdc-preparedness-101-zombie-apocalypse.

12. *The World without Us* is the title of a best-selling book by Alan Weisman (New York: St. Martin's Press, 2007) that imagines life on the planet should its human population vanish: a delirium of buildings falling apart, forests eagerly expanding, subways aflood with cleansing water, farms that had been sustained by chemical interventions reverting to wilds, human traces reduced to the lines in the geological strata and some lingering synthetic molecules. For a rich exploration of what the "spectral and speculative" *world without us* might offer as a negative concept for thinking about the world itself, on the other hand, see Eugene Thacker's *In the Dust of This Planet* (Winchester, U.K.: Zero Books, 2011), esp. 4–5.

13. Kyle William Bishop, *American Zombie Gothic: The Rise and Fall (and Rise) of the Walking Dead in Popular Culture* (Jefferson, N.C.: McFarland, 2010), 14.

14. Karl Steel made that point to me via Twitter, and it seems exactly right.

15. See the multimedia spectacle of a website at http://thepaleodiet.com/.

16. Alaimo, *Bodily Natures*, 28.

17. Ibid.

18. For the Haitian context of the zombie, see Franck Degoul, "'We Are the Mirror of Your Fears': Haitian Identity and Zombification," trans. Elisabeth M. Lore, in Christie and Lauro, *Better Off Dead*, 24–38.

19. Jacques Derrida, *Specters of Marx: The State of the Debt, the Work of Mourning, and the New International*, trans. Peggy Kamuf (New York: Routledge, 2004), 85.

20. Peter Dendle maps the "relationship between history's least energetic monster and history's most energetic generation" in "Zombie Movies and the 'Millennial Generation,'" 181.

21. Sarah Juliet Lauro and Karen Embry, "A Zombie Manifesto: The Nonhuman Condition in the Era of Advanced Capitalism," *boundary 2* 35, no. 1 (2008): 88.

22. "Brief SR/OOO Tutorial," *Object-Oriented Philosophy* (blog), July 23, 2010, http://doctorzamalek2.wordpress.com/20 to/07/23/brief.srooo-tutorial/. A fuller discussion of OOO may be found in the second half of Harman's recent book *Prince of Networks: Bruno Latour and Metaphysics* (Melbourne: re.press, 2009) and in Harman, *Towards Speculative Realism: Essays and Lectures* (Winchester, U.K.: Zero Books, 2010) as well as in the collection edited by Levi Bryant, Nick Srnicek, and Graham Harman *The Speculative Turn: Continental Materialism and Realism* (Melbourne: re.press, 2011).

23. *Grettis saga Asmundarsonat*, ed. Guoni Jonsson (Reykjavik: islenzk fornrit 7, 1936); trans. Jesse Byock (Oxford: Oxford University Press, 2009). References by chapter number. For a good introduction to undead figures in Norse sagas, see William Sayers, "The Alien and Alienated as Unquiet Dead in the Sagas of the Icelanders," in Cohen, *Monster Theory*, 242–63.

24. "I liked the customs better when men were called heathens," Glam declares, "and I want my food without tricks." *Grettis saga Asmundarsotrar*, 32.

25. Ibid., 32, 35.

26. Ibid., 35.

27. *Ecophobia* is David Sobel's coinage in *Beyond Ecophobia: Reclaiming the Heart in Nature Education* (Great Barrington, Mass.: Orion Society, 1996).

28. This taxonomy of bodies according to their luminescence and relation making (a list also includes "bright") is taken from Levi Bryant, who uses it throughout his work. For an especially lucid explication, see

his blog post "A Brief Observation on Relation, Language, and Logic," *Larval Subjects* (blog), April 22, 2012, http://larvalsubjects.wordpress.com/2012/04/22/a-brief-observation-on-relation-language-and-logic/.

29. Alaimo, *Bodily Natures*, 3.

30. Ibid., 2.

31. *Kakosmos* is Bruno Latour's wonderfully messy term in *Politics of Nature: How to Bring the Sciences into Democracy* (Cambridge, Mass.: Harvard University Press, 2004).

CHAPTER 22

A Zombie Manifesto
The Nonhuman Condition in the Era of Advanced Capitalism

SARAH JULIET LAURO and KAREN EMBRY

The zombie has been one of the most prevalent monsters in films of the second half of the twentieth century, and as many have noted, it has experienced a further resurgence (or should we say *resurrection*) in British and American film in the last five years.[1] Zombies are found everywhere, from video games and comic books[2] to the science textbook. The zombie has become a scientific concept by which we define cognitive processes and states of being, subverted animation, and dormant consciousness. In neuroscience, there are "zombie agents";[3] in computer science, there are "zombie functions."[4] We even find "zombie dogs," "zombie corporations," and "zombie raves" in the news.[5] The ubiquity of the metaphor suggests the zombie's continued cultural currency, and we will investigate why this specter has captured the American imagination for more than a century. We want to take a deeper look at the zombie in order to suggest its usefulness as an ontic–hauntic[6] object that speaks to some of the most puzzling elements of our sociohistorical moment, wherein many are trying to ascertain what lies in store for humanity after global capitalism—if anything.

Our fundamental assertion is that there is an irreconcilable tension between global capitalism and the theoretical school of posthumanism. This is an essay full of zombies—the historical, folkloric zombie of Haitian origin, which reveals much about the subject position and its relationship to a master–slave dialectic; the living-dead zombie of contemporary film, who seems increasingly to be lurching off the screen and into our real world (as a metaphor, this zombie reveals much about the way we code inferior subjects as unworthy of life); and finally, we are putting forth a zombie that does not yet exist: a thought experiment that exposes the limits of posthuman theory and shows that we can get posthuman only at the death of the subject. Unlike Donna Haraway's "Cyborg Manifesto," we do not propose that the position of the zombie is a liberating one—indeed, in its history, and in its metaphors, the zombie is most often a slave. However, our intention is to illustrate that the zombie's irreconcilable body (both living and dead) raises the insufficiency of the dialectical model (subject–object) and suggests, with its own negative dialectic, that the only way to truly get posthuman is to become antisubject.

We propose that reading the zombie as an ontic–hauntic object reveals much about the crisis of human embodiment, the way power works, and the history of man's subjugation and oppression of its "Others." Herein, we trace the zombie from its Haitian origins to its most recent incarnations in popular culture. Given the fact that there are multiple valences in play, it seems best to designate the distinction typographically: there is the Haitian *zombi*, a body raised from the dead to labor in the fields, but with a deep association of having played a role in the Haitian Revolution (thus simultaneously resonant with the categories of slave and slave rebellion),[7] and there is also the *zombie*, the American importation of the monster, which, in its cinematic incarnation, has morphed into a convenient bogeyman representing various social concerns. The *zombie* can also be a metaphoric state claimed for oneself or imposed on someone else. This zombie has been made to stand for capitalist drone (*Dawn of the Dead*)[8] and Communist sympathizer (*Invasion of the Body Snatchers*)[9] and, increasingly, viral contamination (*28 Days Later*). In its passage from *zombi* to *zombie*, this figuration that was at first just a somnambulistic slave singly raised from the dead became evil, contagious, and plural. Our manifesto proclaims the future possibility of the *zombii*, a consciousless being that is a swarm organism and the only imaginable specter that could really be posthuman.

Zombi(i)/es, an Introduction

A recent piece of humorous literature, Max Brooks's *The Zombie Survival Guide: Complete Protection from the Living Dead*, is written as an instruction manual for defeating an onslaught of zombie attacks. The book also may come close to revealing what it is about the zombie that captivates the human imagination: "Conventional warfare is useless against these creatures, as is conventional thought. The science of ending life, developed and perfected since the beginning of our existence, cannot protect us from an enemy that has no 'life' to end."[10] Its immortality is a defining attribute of the zombie that both terrifies and tantalizes. As Brooks notes, in an age when weapons of mass destruction can wipe out whole cities at will, the formidable foe is one who cannot be destroyed by being deprived of "life." Or, as a recent commercial advertising the B movie *Return of the Living Dead: Necropolis* boasts, "you cannot kill what is already dead."[11]

During the summer of 2005, much media hype surrounded the release of *Land of the Dead*, George Romero's fourth installment of his zombie series. In a television interview promoting this latest movie, Romero was asked what he would do if zombies were to take over the planet. He responded that he would go right out and get bitten: "That way I could live forever," he said. The irony is that while the statement prompts us to ask what kind of *life* that would be, it reveals that our fascination with the zombie is, in part, a celebration of its immortality and a recognition of ourselves as enslaved to our bodies.

Why does the zombie terrify, and what explains the enduring currency of the zombie threat? Is it merely that the zombie mocks our mortality, and if so, is the fear it inspires different from that of other immortal monsters, like the vampire? One psychoanalytic interpretation purports that we are most acutely aware of ourselves as subjects when we feel afraid—specifically, when we feel threatened by a force external to our bodies.[12] Quite simply, fear heightens our awareness of ourselves as individuals because our individuality is endangered in life-threatening situations. Nowhere is this drama more acutely embodied than in the model of the zombie attack: for the zombie is an antisubject, and the zombie horde is a swarm where no trace of the individual remains.[13] Therefore, unlike the vampire, the zombie poses a twofold terror: there is the primary fear of being devoured by a zombie, a threat posed mainly to the physical body, and the secondary fear that one will, in losing one's consciousness, become a part of the monstrous horde. Both of these fears reflect recognition of one's own mortality and ultimately reveal the primal fear of losing the "self"; however, in the figure of the zombie, the body and the mind are separated antinomies. The zombie is different from other monsters because the body is resurrected and retained: only consciousness is permanently lost. Like the vampire and the werewolf, the zombie threatens with its material form. Whereas the vampire and even the intangible ghost retain their mental faculties, and the werewolf may become irrational, bestial only part of the time, only the zombie has completely lost its mind, becoming a blank—animate, but wholly devoid of consciousness.[14]

The terror that comes from an identification of oneself with the zombie is, therefore, primarily a fear of the loss of consciousness. As unconscious but animate flesh, the zombie emphasizes that humanity is defined by its cognizance. The lumbering, decaying specter of the zombie also affirms the inherent disability of human embodiment—our mortality. Thus, in some sense, we are all already zombies (but not yet zombiis), for they represent the inanimate end to which each of us is destined.[15] Yet the zombie is intriguing not only for the future it foretells but also for what it says about humanity's experience of lived frailty and the history of civilization, which grapples with mortality in its structure as well as in its stories. Humanity defines itself by its individual consciousness and its personal agency: to be a body without a mind is to be subhuman, animal; to be a human without agency is to be a prisoner, a slave. The zombi(i)/e is both of these, and the zombi(i)/e (fore)tells our past, present, and future.

In its origins and in its folkloric incarnations, the zombi is quite literally a slave, raised by Vodou priests to labor in the fields, but the zombie metaphor also reveals to us our own enslavement to our finite and fragile bodies. As Plato wrote, "the body is the tomb of the soul." Just as the slave's own body becomes his prison, the zombie illustrates humanity's inherent imprisonment, if by counterpoint. The zombie shows us what we are: irrevocably bound to our bodies and already married to the grave. But the zombie also shows us what we are not: man, as we know him, as a cognizant, living creature, does not outlive the death of his body. As such, the zombie metaphor (like its mythological parent, the Haitian *zombi*) is not purely a slave but is also slave rebellion. While the human is incarcerated in mortal flesh, the zombie presents a grotesque image that resists this confinement—animating his body even beyond death. At the same time that the zombie emphasizes human embodiment, he also defies the very limits that he sets. What underlies this symbolic duality, however, is that the zombie, neither mortal nor conscious, is a boundary figure. Its threat to stable subject and object positions, through the simultaneous occupation of a body that is both living and dead, creates a dilemma for power relations and risks destroying social dynamics that have remained—although widely questioned, critiqued, and debated—largely unchallenged in the current economic superstructure.

We attempt to read the zombie as a more effective imagining of posthumanism than the cyborg because of its indebtedness to narratives of historical power and oppression, and we stress the zombie's relevance as a theoretical model that, like the cyborg, crashes borders. Simultaneously living and dead, subject and object, slave and slave rebellion, the zombie presents a posthuman specter informed by the (negative) dialectic of power relations rather than gender. In this essay, we outline the various conversations with which we might put the zombie in dialogue: with Marxist and postcolonial discourse, with psychoanalysis and history, and most promisingly, with philosophy and posthumanist theory.

Borrowing the title and the spirit of Haraway's "Cyborg Manifesto," one of the inaugurating texts of "posthuman theory," we argue here that the zombie can be made to speak only as a somewhat ironic discursive model. The zombie is anticatharsis. Thus, "a zombie manifesto" is one that cannot call for positive change; it calls only for the destruction of the reigning model.[16] Though our essay is at times tongue in cheek and aware of the absurdity of its own suggestions (rather like the zombie film genre itself, which often celebrates itself as "schlock" and "camp"), we are never mocking Haraway's pivotal and enduring piece. We are greatly indebted to the "Cyborg Manifesto," and this is our homage. However, this essay is not a utopic fantasy in which man is liberated from the subject–object conundrum, nor is it a riotous celebration of the apocalypse that would ensue if humanity were able to get free of the subject–object bind. Mostly, it is an ironic imagining of what some of the philosophical concepts that have such currency in critical theory, such as "posthumanism," "negative dialectics," and the "rupture," which is awaited as the second coming of poststructuralism, might look like if incarnated in material form, our zombii.

That said, we do feel that the zombii solves several problems that the cyborg model failed to adequately address: specifically, we read the zombie with and against humanist philosophy and psychoanalysis, but we also discuss the historical significance of the zombie as boundary marker and read it in the context of a Marxist theory of power dynamics, colonialism, and industry. In outlining these various discourses that have defined humanity, we ultimately suggest what a true "posthuman" would look like.

As a figure defined by its liminality, the zombii illustrates our doubts about humanity in an era in which the human condition may be experiencing a crisis of conscience as well as a crisis of consciousness. We will present the zombii as a model of posthuman consciousness (one that is postcyborg) in dispute with the capitalist era's *homo-laborans* as well as a body that speaks to the psyche's fears of dissolution; the zombii is both an effective model for imagining the condition of posthumanity and, quite literally, a post(mortem) human. Above all else, the zombii's "negative dialectic"[17] reshapes the way we think about the boundary between subject–object, resonating especially with the roles of master–slave that so profoundly inform our own sense of human embodiment. We will investigate the significance of the zombi(i)/e across various cultural planes, interrogating the origins of this monstrous figure and proposing some examples of what we ironically posit as *"real-life"* zombies. But first we must turn to the theoretical questions that lead us to the figure of the zombie in order to show how our historical and economic moment summons this apparition as our most apt metaphor.

The Zombie's Brain

Filmmakers and critics have noted the resonance of the zombie with the factory worker's mechanistic performance, the brain-dead, ideology-fed servant of industry, and the ever-yawning mouth of the nation-state. The individual under capitalism is often characterized as a zombie.[18] But as Max Horkheimer and Theodor Adorno write, our zombie individuality is one that relies on the *illusion* of self: under such a system, "nothing is left of him but that eternally same *I think* that must accompany all ideas. Subject and object are both rendered ineffectual."[19] What Horkheimer and Adorno and others illustrate is that the illusory separation of subject and object, the *fata morgana* of individualism, keeps happy the camp of zombies—the slaves to capitalism who are merely deluded into thinking that they are free. Horkheimer and Adorno claim that subject and object are rendered ineffectual categories under capitalism, as the commodity fetish animates objects and reification objectifies the worker. But identifying this conflation is not enough—in the figure of zombie, subject and object are obliterated. This figure, simultaneously slave and slave rebellion, is a more appropriate reflection of our capitalist moment, and even if it holds less promise than a cyborg future, its prophesy of the posthuman is more likely to come to fruition. The zombie, we feel, is a more pessimistic but nonetheless more appropriate stand-in for our current moment, and specifically for America in a global economy, where we feed off the products of the rest of the planet and, alienated from our own humanity, stumble forward, groping for immortality even as we decompose. For Marx, the efficiency of large-scale industry relies on the division of labor that is accomplished "by converting the worker into a living appendage of the machine."[20] Thus, reified as a part of the process of production, the subject has already bled into the object: we are already dwelling in the zombie's interzone.

The history of thought concerning power relations and our servitude to global capitalism has pointed to the humanist constructions of "mind," "self," and the sanctity of "the individual" as the bars of our imprisonment. In *Dialectic of Enlightenment*, Horkheimer and Adorno show that subjectivity remains but a fiction that allows for ideological control.[21] They write, "Subjectivity has volatized itself into the logic of supposedly optional rules, to gain more absolute control. Positivism, which finally did not shrink from laying hands on the idlest fancy of all, thought itself, eliminated the last intervening agency between individual action and the social norm."[22] For thought to break out of the grasp of ideology, which ultimately serves the economic system, it must be devoid of all positivist claims. When it comes to metaphysics, Adorno's model of negative dialectics is preferred, "since reason itself has become merely an aid to the all-encompassing economic apparatus."[23]

For us, the zombii is an enactment of negative dialectics. The living dead, which cannot be divided into parts constitutive of the categories it bridges, raises the insufficiency of the dialectical model. The kind of dialectic the zombii incarnates is not one that strives for resolution; indeed, it cannot, for as we've said, the zombie, by its very definition, is anticatharsis, antiresolution: it proposes no third term reconciling the subject–object split, the lacuna between life and death. The zombie is opposition held irrevocably in tension. We are interested in reading the zombii as a "determinate negation" of the individual in the postindustrial, post-Holocaust era, for the zombie is not merely the negation of the subject: it takes the subject and nonsubject and makes these terms obsolete because it is inherently both at once. The zombii's lack of consciousness does not make it pure object but rather opens up the possibility of a negation of the subject–object divide. It is not, like the cyborg, a hybrid, nor is it like Gilles Deleuze and Félix Guattari's schizophrenic, a multiplicity; rather, the zombii is a paradox that disrupts the entire system.[24]

As we've suggested, our model of the zombii is motivated by our search for a new mode in which to discuss the posthuman subject. A subject that is truly posthumanist would be a subject that is not a subject. Haraway's "Cyborg Manifesto" sought to resolve the antagonism between subject and object binary by reimagining the chasm between the two through the hybrid. In the end, however, the text seems to propose that the subject itself can dissolve the boundary between subject and object through a process of inclusion. Critics have exposed the limitations of this figuration of the cyborg as posthuman. N. Katherine Hayles complicated the model of the cyborg with her argument that the posthuman had lost its body but kept its identification with the Enlightenment position of the liberal humanist subject.[25] Thus the cyborg does not really undo the subject position as much as it just cloaks it in high-tech window dressing. As Hayles and others suggest, to truly move *post* human, we have to shirk not the body but the Enlightenment subject position. In contrast, the zombii does not reconcile subject and object but, rather, as walking antithesis, holds them as irrevocably separate; in the figure of the zombii, the subject position is nullified, not reinvigorated.

We contend that the only way to accurately model a *post* human state is the "neither/nor" of the zombii, which rejects both subject and object categories and is irreducible, anticathartic, antiresolution, and working in the mode of negative dialectics. We put forth the zombii as an analogy to humanity as it exists today and (simultaneously) as a foreboding of a "monstrous future."[26] We avoid making the zombii a "metaphor" for posthumanism, for a metaphor implies equivalence; the analogy connotes only unspecified ratio, and thus, just as the "zombii" manifesto is one that cannot advocate a new model, the zombii analogy functions negatively to suggest only the form, not the substance, of the figural relationship between humanity and its antitheses.[27]

The cyborg seemed to undo the tensions of the opposing slash, which organized life into binary categories (male–female, master–slave, subject–object) and suggested that the model of the hybrid evinced the dissolution of difference. The zombie metaphor itself goes beyond the hybrid by virtue of its inseparability into distinct terms. It is itself an incarnation of presence–absence, yet it complicates the subject–object position because it is the *livingdead*. What we learned from the cyborg is that it is not enough to negate the model "either/or" by claiming "both/and." The zombii doesn't merely do this—in functioning as analogy, it replaces any preposition that could articulate the relation of zombii to human; there is no term joining subject and object. The body of the zombii is itself this indeterminable boundary.

In most contemporary cinematic versions, to kill a zombie, one must destroy its brain. To successfully undo the position of the liberal humanist subject, which has been tainted by an inhumane history shaped by power relations that were perhaps suggested by the opposition of subject and object, one must forfeit the already illusory sense of the individual. In the preface to *Dialectic of Enlightenment*, Horkheimer and Adorno write, "The individual is entirely nullified in face of the economic powers. These powers are taking society's domination over nature to unimagined heights. While individuals as such are vanishing before the apparatus they serve, they are provided for by that apparatus and better than ever before."[28] If, as Horkheimer and Adorno suggest, the individual is a fiction conjured by the economic structure to ensure greater domination, then for us, the only answer to this bind comes in the form of the zombii—a literalization of what has already happened: the death of the individual that continues to lumber forward. The zombii thus suggests how we might truly move posthuman: the individual must be destroyed. With this rupture, we would undo the repressive forces of capitalist servitude. But at what cost? The zombii's dystopic promise is that it can only assure the destruction of a corrupt system without imagining a replacement—for the zombii can offer no resolution.

The Zombie's Body

The zombie is historically tied to, and has been read alongside, the expansion of global capitalism.[29] The zombie is a colonial import: it infiltrated the American cultural imagination in the early twentieth century, at the time of the U.S. Occupation of Haiti. We cannot take up the figure of the zombie without acknowledging its appropriation from Haitian folklore. In *Culture and Imperialism*, Edward Said warns that what may appear "to be detached and apolitical cultural disciplines" actually often depend "upon a quite sordid history of imperialist ideology and colonialist practice."[30] Indeed, though the Haitian zombi has been "cannibalized" by Western film and horror mythology, and though the zombie can therefore be read as a racist denigration of a "savage" people, there is also so much said by the power implicit in this monster's history; the zombie narrative is, in some ways, a reprisal of the Haitian Revolution and a story of slave rebellion. The slaves of Saint-Domingue literally threw off the yoke of colonial servitude, but the country has had an unhappy national history, plagued by foreign occupation, civil unrest, and disease. Similarly, the zombi/e seems to embody this kind of disappointment: it only symbolically defies mortality, and woefully at that—even the zombie's survival of death is anticelebratory, for it remains trapped in a corpse body.

We might read the revision of the zombie qua capitalist as yet another imperialist act—one that dispels the dark fury of the slave and, in turning the iconography inside out, makes the zombie's insatiable hunger figure the white consumer instead, effectively swallowing the slave body as the icon is reappropriated. On some level, this narrativizing recuperates the insurmountable power of the zombie so that it allegorizes the imperial, the colonial, the capitalist structure, rather than the lowly black body.

Our arrival at a historical moment in which the zombie, above other metaphors, reflects the state of the human/posthuman moment must be traced back to the colonial roots of the figure. In Haitian folklore, from which all zombies are derived, the word *zombie* meant not just "a body without a soul" but also "a soul without a body."[31] Therefore the issue of boundaries was never limiting for this mythological figure.[32] However, in contemporary incarnations, the zombie has a fluid body that transgresses its borders by infecting those it bites; the Haitian zombi could only be created by a non-zombi. Thus, in its articulation of Western fears of the infectious spirit of rebellion, this trend manifests within the cinematic zombie in a metaphor of ubiquitous contagion.

In Daniel Cohen's excavation of Haitian folklore rituals, he notes that the embodied zombi is first understood as a soulless, animate corpse and reminds us, "The zombie is not inherently evil, like a vampire; it is merely a servant."[33] Cohen notes that zombis were believed to be created, raised from the dead, by a *hungan,* a witch doctor, so that they could work in the fields at night.[34] That the zombie myth is deeply connected with slavery is obvious, though critics have proffered different readings of the significance of the monster's origins. One anthropologist, Francis Huxley, claims that the zombi is an expression of the population's endurance of slavery.[35] Cohen writes, "Others have speculated that the zombie is sort of a slave's nightmare. For the slave the only hope of release was death and the possible promise of a blissful afterlife. But if a dead slave's body was reanimated for labor as a zombie, then the slave existence would continue even after death, a particularly horrible thought."[36] The roots of the zombie can be traced back to the Haitian Revolution, when reports of the rebelling slaves depicted them as nearly supernatural: "fanatic and insensate hordes of blacks rose as a single body to overwhelm the more 'rational' white troops."[37] The conflict began in "1791, two years after the French Revolution, [when] the colony was shaken and then utterly destroyed by the only successful slave revolt in history."[38] The war lasted twelve years, and the native population defeated the most powerful armies of Europe. The insurgents' battle cry was said to be "We have no mother, no child; What is death?"[39] The slave could not lay claim to family relations because all persons involved were the possessions of their masters; likewise, the zombie has no kin and has lost ownership even of itself.

The zombie is currently understood as simultaneously powerless and powerful, slave and slave rebellion; this is central to our understanding of it as a boundary figure. The dual potential of the zombi to represent both slave and slave rebellion is key to its capture of the Western imagination. In acknowledging its appropriation—and potential *mis*appropriation for ideological purposes—we must not disconnect the zombie from its past. However, if the contemporary zombie body is an indeterminable boundary, no site is perhaps more emblematic of that omnipresent permeability, and insatiable hunger, than the zombie's mouth. For it is always at the mouth that the zombie feeds, and it is where the physical boundary between zombie and not-zombie is effaced, through its bite.

As a nonconscious, consuming machine, the cinematic zombie terrifies because it is a reflection of modern-day commercial society, propelled only by its need to perpetually consume. In this fairly common interpretation of the zombie as capitalist icon, the monstrous figure of global capitalism is fed on the labors of the impoverished, "third world" labor force. The zombie has thus transitioned from a representation of the laboring, enslaved colonial body to a dual image of capitalist enslavement: the zombie now represents the new slave, the capitalist worker, but also the consumer, trapped within the ideological construct that assures the survival of the system. This ravenous somnambulist, blindly stumbling toward its next meal, is a machine that performs but two functions: it consumes and it makes more consumers. Despite the Haitian zombi's roots as imperial slave, the Hollywood zombie of today does not produce anything except more zombies.

Aside from this difference in production, we must pause to consider more deeply the difference between the zombie and the slave. In *The Human Condition*, Hannah Arendt identifies the ancient justification of slavery as an attempt to shift the burden of human necessity; she states that men "could win their freedom only through the domination of those whom they subjected to necessity by force."[40] Both zombie and slave are subject to pure necessity, but the slave is performing someone else's labor, more like a machine, while the zombie labors for no one and produces only more zombies. The zombie's reproductive drive, in the service of zombie "society" (if it can be classified as such), is either an unconscious urge or a mere side effect of its own hunger, for it is through its bite that the zombie reproduces itself. Therefore the zombie cannot even really be said to have two separate functions—consumption and reproduction—for the zombie reproduces as it consumes. Thus the urge of self-preservation is united with the propagation of the species: the urge of the individual body is the same as the will of the collective. Incidentally, this mirrors what Adorno defines as the "rational" impulse that ensures the success of capitalism: the desires of the individual and the state merge.

The figure of the infectious, consuming zombie illustrates humanity's attempt to transfer its burden onto others—as well as our fears of increasingly publicized diseases. In its frenzied state of pure consumption, the zombie seeks to infect those who do not yet share in the oppression of their state: the zombie does not attack other zombies.[41] It seeks to transfer its burden, but the result is only a multiplication of its condition: no zombie body is relieved of its condition by passing it on. Therefore the zombie once again deters the possibility of catharsis. The boundary between man and slave that allows one to shift the burden of necessity onto the other—whether in ancient Greek society or in the global capitalist superstructure of today—is threatened by the zombie: no appetite is sated; all become slaves.

This danger is evident in the figure of the cinematic zombie and its infection of public space. The zombie body is often seen in the public sphere: town squares, cemeteries, schools, streets, and even in malls—providing overt social critique. The fear that the public realm is being invaded by pure necessity, or pure consumption, is expressed through the drama of the inhuman, ever-consuming zombie. For Arendt, the capitalist system's "waste economy" results in the ills of "mass culture," wherein "things must be almost as quickly devoured and discarded as they have appeared in the world."[42] Therefore we see that the insatiable zombie of contemporary cinema incarnates this kind of social critique and forebodes capitalism's monstrous future.[43]

The zombie's collapsed subject–object status recalls, as no other monstrous or posthuman figure can, that this distinctive feature describes both the automaton and the slave. Though the zombie is incapable of thought, it is a two-headed monster. Zombies, like all things that are feared, are the products of the culture that shapes them and bear within their myths the imprint of existing social conditions. Marxist theory resonates with many aspects of this ominous figure (on the most obvious level, the zombie resembles both brain-eating consumer and zombified worker in one), but it can also be read as a fulcrum joining psychoanalytic and materialist approaches.

The zombie speaks to humanity's anxiety about its isolation within the individual body, and our mortality is burlesqued by the zombie's grotesque defiance of the human's finite existence, thus calling into question which is more terrifying: our ultimate separation from our fellow humans or the dystopic fantasy of a swarm organism. What we see in examining the historical trajectory of the zombie's evolution is that our fears, the mediating impulses that translate our psychological makeup, are narratives informed by the material conditions of society. If the zombie articulates anxiety about the division of body and mind/soul, through history this narrative takes on various trappings of political and social crises. The zombie is not purely an expression of the pressing social concerns of the historical moment in which it appears (be it colonization, slavery, or capitalist servitude); rather, it is given structure by these historical events and at bottom represents a crisis as old as the mind itself, concerning the mortality of the flesh. In order to see how the zombie obliterates the fascistic structure of the subject–object split, we have to understand the broader way in which the zombie reconfigures power dynamics—not just between those who make other humans into objects but also between the agentic, conscious subject and the body as object.

Real Live Zombies

The vulnerability of the flesh and the instinctual fear of its decay, as well as the dissolution of consciousness—all things that happen as we approach death—are suggested in the monstrous hyperbolic of the zombie as living corpse. The corpse represents the inherent and inseparable thing-character of human existence, that inanimate state to which we must return.[44] The corpse itself has the ability to terrify by implication, but the animate corpse, a walking contradiction, may frighten most deeply because it represents not only our future but our present. Our bodies are something that we may fear and reject but from which we cannot part. The zombie as bodily specter thus refutes the resistance to embodiment of which many posthumanist models are accused.[45] Like most monsters, the zombie illuminates our own discomfort with various kinds of bodies, but above all, it illustrates the ever-present and real threat of the human body. We are all, in some sense, walking corpses, because this is inevitably the state to which we must return. In imagining that humans are burdened with their own deaths, we can come to see one of the various ways that the zombie terrifies: not as an apocalyptic vision but as a representation of the lived human condition.

We have tried to describe the zombie as it exists in historical and philosophic inquiry and to propose how it can be read in dialogue with Marxist theory. Here we want to put forth a few examples of "real-life zombies" (pardon the paradoxes) in order to illustrate that the indeterminability of the zombie as boundary figure extends to its undecidability as metaphoric or literal, fantastic or real, for this vein of inquiry opens up a discussion of the various power dynamics that are put into play when we take up the zombii as an ontic object.

In her investigation of the "waste body" of the corpse, Julia Kristeva refers to the puerperal fever epidemic that was caused by the introduction of bacteria from decaying bodies into the open wombs of delivering women: "Puerperal fever is the result of the female genitalia being contaminated by a corpse; here then is a fever where what bears life passes over to the side of the dead body. [A] distracting moment when opposites (life/death, feminine/masculine) join."[46] In this example, we see the first of the real-life zombies that we want to posit. This is also an interesting moment where the Western doctor lines up with the Haitian *hungan* as zombi(e) makers. The woman afflicted with puerperal fever was a zombie, a combination of dead and living flesh, if only at the molecular level.[47] Many critics are concerned with illustrating how monsters betray a distrust and discomfort with certain kinds of bodies. The female body has often been characterized as the border between life and death.[48] In the example of the woman with puerperal fever, therefore, this distrust of the female body's ability to regenerate itself, zombie-style, is metaphorized as the reproductive woman becomes a living corpse.

Most critics note that the concept of monstrosity is deeply associated with disabled bodies.[49] The same should, of course, be said of zombies. The mentally ill historically have been portrayed as having a consciousness that is morally suspect or a total lack of subjectivity. As Giorgio Agamben notes, "incurable idiots"[50] were on the Nazis' list of those who occupy the indeterminate state wherein they could be supposed to have neither the will to live nor the desire to die; this is used as justification for their extermination.[51] As a monster without consciousness and without speech, the zombie recalls the mentally ill or the language impaired, such as those with aphasia. Even the lumbering gait of the cinematic zombie, which probably is meant to reflect rigor mortis and advanced decay, looks like a muscular disorder.

In *Madness and Civilization*, Michel Foucault notes many of the treatments that were used to cure mental illness in the eighteenth and nineteenth centuries. Among the rituals associated with attempts to purify the body was the bizarre notion that the corruption of the mind could be prevented if the living body was embalmed like a corpse.[52] In this way, treatment of the mentally ill made them into symbolic zombies long before failed shock treatment and botched lobotomies would, by causing severe brain damage, make them more literally resemble the animated corpses incapable of demonstrating agency or expression that we see in film.

The embalmed madmen are real-life zombies: like the women with puerperal fever, who were contaminated with the bacteria that infest corpses, these were real bodies that straddled the civic and social border that determines the difference between the living and the dead. Just as the cyborg is a body implemented with or affected by technology, these real-life zombies also, on a microlevel, contain within their forms the attributes of the corpse. In the example of the embalmed madmen, we see how the social death of the mentally ill, deemed inferior, is translated into a literal transgression of these vital boundaries, as the living are construed as already dead and treated accordingly. There is yet a third "real *live* zombie" that we want to put forth, one that is a contemporary

406 SARAH JULIET LAURO and KAREN EMBRY

example and that we might claim as both a cyborg and a zombie, thus bearing fruitful discussion of the overlap between these two categories: Terri Schiavo.[53]

Several court cases and a media frenzy were sparked by the petition that Michael Schiavo made to have his wife's feeding tube removed; it was deemed "artificial life support" by one of the ruling judges and brought this woman's story to national attention. What most interests us here, however, is the aspect of the debate that surrounded Schiavo's indeterminability as living or dead. Her parents, who opposed their son-in-law's desire to remove Terri's feeding tube, released video of Schiavo blinking and appearing to smile. The issue of whether the outward appearance of cognition reflects an internal awareness of one's circumstances directed the argument. This alludes to the larger discussion that rages in cognitive neuroscience, concerning the various "zombie" agents that compose what we call consciousness.[54] In order for Michael Schiavo to establish that his wife was truly in a persistently vegetative state, he would have to establish not only that she was unable to communicate but that she was unaware of her surroundings.

This kind of court case pronounces cognizance the determining factor of what constitutes life. If consciousness is found to be illusory, the person in question is decided not to be a "person" at all. The Schiavo debate became the location for a battle between the jurisdiction of the state and the sovereignty of the individual human subject. Therefore Terri Schiavo's case illustrates a limit set on human existence wherein those without social power, or those deemed to have inferior consciousness (like the mentally ill), are considered legally dead.[55] Indeed, it seems an eerie coincidence worthy of mention that *schiavo* means "slave" in Italian, given the origins and continued characterization of the zombie as a slave.

We offer these real-life zombies in direct contrast to Haraway's cyborgs.[56] For Haraway's examples of real cyborgs—a seamstress at her sewing machine and a quadriplegic in her wheelchair—becoming cyborg is not purely a material experience but involves a discursive transformation: we become cyborgs when we decide to be cyborgs. Haraway thus requires a moment of cognition, a moment of consciousness, that always insists upon subjectivity. The zombie may entail a material collision of living and dead tissues, as with the women with puerperal fever, or it may merely be a symbolic or figurative construction, as we might say of the Schiavo "zombie," a comparison that was certainly bandied about in online blogs. Regardless, in the zombii's purest form as an ontic–hauntic object, transformation must be created outside the body, proclaimed by others. The zombii cannot see itself as such, much less claim a zombie identity for itself.

The End?

We have looked at many different ways in which the zombie can be conceptualized: we see the zombie as *animal laborans,* the reified laborer of capitalist production, and the zombie as threatening body, the zombie as brain-dead, the zombie as brain eater, the zombie blindly following its own primal urges; the zombie that is pure necessity, the zombie that is antiproductive, the zombie that is female, the zombie that is avid consumer; we have looked at the zombie as cyborg, the zombie as postcyborg, the zombie as posthuman, the zombie as slave and as slave rebellion. We have mentioned the zombies of folklore and of cinema, as figurative, as symbolic, as literal, as analogy.

Some might be tempted to say that there is, within these various instantiations, something like a "bad" zombie (which has been reduced to an object by the capitalist system, which works as a slave for others, which loses itself in the machine) and something like a "good" zombie (which resists being a tool of capitalism, which is destructive rather than productive, which resists the rational, which becomes the anti-individual, antisubject). Yet judgment always exists outside of the zombie, as a part of the rational ordering of the world: the "goodness" or "badness" of the zombie only exists within thinking "consciousness." If the potential of the posthuman subject exists in its collectivity (and in its multiplicity and its hybridity), then the posthuman zombii is that which forfeits consciousness as we know it—embracing a singular, swarm experience. What the zombii reveals, therefore, is that the inauguration of the posthuman can only be the end of capitalism. This is not a utopic vision, nor is it a call to arms. We are merely noting that capitalism and posthumanism are more linked than has been previously articulated: one has to die so that the other can begin. The zombii "knows" (of course, the zombii *knows* nothing) that the posthuman is endgame: it is a becoming that is the end of becomings. This is why the zombii must remain antiresolution, anticatharsis, and cannot speak.

Capitalism depends on our sense of ourselves as having individual consciousnesses to prohibit the development of a revolutionary collective and to bolster the attitude that drives it: every man for himself. Appositely, posthumanity can only really be attained when we pull the trigger on the ego. To kill the zombie, you must destroy the brain, and to move posthuman, to lay humanism and its legacy of power and oppression in the grave, we have to undo our primary systems of differentiation: subject–object, me–you. In fact, these terms cannot be separated—like the deathlife of the zombie, the capitalist superstructure and the posthuman fantasy have been yoked together in a monstrous body; the existence of one state prohibits the presence of the other. It is important to note that the ego has not always been implicated in capitalism's imperialist, colonial history. Indeed, the slave defied Empire by claiming his individuality, by transgressing the line from object to subject. However, to challenge global capitalism, which has achieved such a stranglehold on the subject position that there is no outside of ideology, the answer may be to throw off the illusory chains of an "identity" based on the division of subject and object. If the subject survives the apocalypse, so will capitalism. As we see in one recent zombie film, Danny Boyle's 2002 film *28 Days Later*, the Haitian Revolution is rehearsed with the effect that the individual is spared.

While *28 Days Later* has been identified as a zombie flick, this claim may seem to require some justification. The "monsters" in this picture are not the resurrected dead, though they are people who have lost their rational senses. One of the pivotal scenes occurs near the end of the film. The protagonists have encountered a group of soldiers who prove to be more monstrous than the zombies. The humans are holding them against their will and are about to rape the two women of the group. The soldiers have kept one zombie, a black man, chained up in the courtyard for observation. Here we see zombie "subjectivity" on display, for *it* remains the subject of scientific observation and the powerless subject of dominant force; still the Queen's subject, the medical subject, and subjected to violence, this zombie has ceased to be an agentic subject and now belongs to the object world. Until, that is, *his* rebellion. With the iron and chains around his neck, this figure cannot help but recall the slave and the origins of the Haitian zombie. When Jim, the protagonist, sets the zombie free to attack the soldiers, we see a replay of the slave rebellion in Haiti, as European soldiers are pitted against the unruly native. Selena, a beautiful black woman and the film's love interest, even wields a machete, obviously alluding to the triangle trade. If our future involves this kind of zombie, the zombie rebelling against its servitude, it suggests the possibility that we can combat the forces that determine our subject status, but this would be a humanist rather than a posthuman future. In the film, the zombie body is sacrificed to save the last humans, and at the end of the film, we get the sense, as a military plane flies overhead, that everything—humanity, government, and most likely capitalism—has survived the attack.[57]

Thus we are left with yet another tantalizing paradox, and without the promise of a completely satisfying ending. When the slave took up arms, he was rejecting his status as object and claiming the position of the subject; thus, to overcome imperialism, the individual had to assert himself as having agency. Here, in an era when global capitalism forecloses all attempts to withdraw from the system, the only option is to shut down the system, and the individual with it. So, to reformulate Franco Moretti's question, will the end be monstrous, or will it be liberating? This is an unanswerable question, but regardless, it is a question that can only be posed in the future tense. When we become zombiis, when we lose our subjectivity and the ability to rationalize, there will be no difference between the two. Therefore, when we truly become posthuman, we won't even *know* it.

Notes

We wish to thank the following persons for their invaluable input and support: Marc Blanchard, Colin Milburn, Caleb Smith, Michael Ziser, Joshua Clover, Tiffany Gilmore, Maura Grady, Courtney Hopf, Shannon Riley, and Jack Martin.

1. Films such as *Shaun of the Dead*, directed by Edgar Wright (Big Talk Productions, 2004); *28 Days Later*, directed by Danny Boyle (British Film Council, 2002); *Dawn of the Dead, 2004 Remake*, directed by Zack Snyder (Strike Entertainment, 2004); *Land of the Dead*, directed by George A. Romero (Atmosphere Entertainment, 2005); and the Resident Evil series, directed by Paul W. S. Anderson (Constantin Film Produktion, 2002) and Alexander Witt (Constantin, 2004). See Peter Dendle's book *The Zombie Movie Encyclopedia* (Jefferson, N.C.: McFarland, 2001), Jay Slater's *Eaten Alive! Italian Cannibal and Zombie Movies* (London: Plexus, 2002), and Stephen Thrower's *Beyond Terror: The Films of Lucio Fulci* (Guildford, U.K.: FAB Press, 1999).

2. E.g., *Bogus Dead, Zombie Commandos from Hell, Carnopolis, Containment*, and *Biohazard*. See All Things Zombie, http://www.allthingszombie.com/comics_reviews.php.

3. Longtime collaborators Christof Koch and Francis Crick (of DNA helix fame) think that "'zombie agents'—that is, routine behaviors that we perform constantly without even thinking—are so much a central facet of human consciousness that they deserve serious scientific attention." "Zombie Behaviors Are Part of Everyday Life, According to Neurobiologists," Caltech Media Relations, February 11, 2004, http://pr.caltech.edu/media/Press_Releases/PR12491.html.

4. Zombie functions or zombie processes in computer science refer to multiple functions: "1. Term used to describe a process that is doing nothing but utilizing system resources. 2. A computer that has been maliciously set up to do work of another program or users. A zombie computer is often a com-

puter or server that has been compromised to help a malicious user perform a Denial Of Service attack (DoS) or DDoS attack. 3. When referring to chat or IRC, a zombie or ghost refers to a user who has lost connection but their user is still logged into the chat server." http://www.computerhope.com/jargon/z/zombie.htm.

5. After scientists at the University of Pittsburgh's Safar Center for Resuscitation Research "announced that they have found a way to revive dogs three hours after clinical death," articles referred to the experiment as involving "zombie dogs." *Pittsburgh Tribune- Review*, June 29, 2005. A recent edition of the *New York Times* Sunday business section ran an article declaring the existence of "biotech zombies," corporations that should be financially extinct yet continue to survive. *New York Times*, February 11, 2007. A shooting occurred at what was termed a "zombie rave" in Seattle. *Seattle Times*, March 25, 2006.

6. In part, we are claiming that there is such a thing as a materially real zombie; an ontic object, for our interest, is not just the zombie as an epistemic thing. However, we are also, following Derrida, taking up the paradoxical nature of the zombie as neither being nor nonbeing; but, of course, the zombie is more substantial than the ghost. The zombie resides somewhere between the ontic and the hauntic. See Jacques Derrida, *Specters of Marx: The State of the Debt, the Work of Mourning, and the New International*, trans. Peggy Kamuf (New York: Routledge, 1994).

7. Vodou rituals were commonly used to communicate and motivate antiwhite sentiment leading up to the Haitian Revolution. See Thomas O. Ott, *The Haitian Revolution, 1789–1804* (Knoxville: University of Tennessee Press, 1973), 47. In many accounts, there is some suggestion that the hordes that rose up to throw off the yoke of oppression had, through Vodou practices, rendered themselves insensible to pain.

8. *Dawn of the Dead*, directed by George A. Romero (Laurel Group, 1978) and *2004 Remake*.

9. *Invasion of the Body Snatchers*, directed by Philip Kaufman (Solofilm, 1978).

10. Max Brooks, *A Zombie Survival Guide: Complete Protection from the Living Dead* (New York: Three Rivers Press/Random House, 2003), xiii.

11. *Return of the Living Dead: Necropolis*, directed by Ellory Elkayem (Denholm Trading Inc., 2005).

12. Max Horkheimer and Theodor W. Adorno write, "The mere idea of the 'outside' is the real source of fear," connecting this primal emotion to self-preservation and the economy's hold on the individual. Horkheimer and Adorno, *Dialectic of Enlightenment: Philosophical Fragments* (Stanford, Calif.: Stanford University Press, 2002), 11. For another interesting discussion of fear, see Julia Kristeva's chapter "Suffering and Horror," in *Powers of Horror: An Essay on Abjection*, trans. Leon S. Roudiez (New York: Columbia University Press, 1982), 140–56, in which fear is described as crucial to subject formation.

13. Though the vampire may, in some legends, travel in packs, it seems always very definitely to retain its individuality. The exception might be the 1964 film *Last Man on Earth*, directed by Ubaldo Ragona (Associated Producers Inc., 1964), which spawned the 1971 sequel *The Omega Man*, directed by Boris Sagal (Warner Bros., 1971), based on Richard Matheson's 1954 novel *I Am Legend* (New York: Fawcett, 1954). (A remake of the same title was slated for release in December 2007.) Though the epidemic overrunning the planet causes "vampirism," the narrative can be understood as belonging to the genre of the zombie plague film: the creatures are nonconscious, and a bacterial outbreak has caused the pandemic.

14. Our ghost stories, in which the body is lost but consciousness remains, usually focus on the individual being threatened or terrorized by a ghost; we do not often see throngs of ghosts infecting others so that they too will become ghosts. The reason for this may be its inability to inspire fear: to live forever and still get to be yourself—would that really be so terrible?

15. Many film critics have offered this kind of psychoanalytic reading of the zombie. See, e.g., Jamie Russell's discussion of the zombie and Kristeva in his *Book of the Dead* (Godalming, U.K.: FAB Press, 2005), 136. Here we present this distinction: the zombie is a metaphoric comparison that can be casually adopted for such discussions; the zombii is always the truly consciousless posthuman.

16. Jamie Russell notes that this is the dominant mode of the "progressive fantasy" of the zombie film: "the old order is overturned without *anything* being offered in its place." Russell, *Book of the Dead*, 83.

17. Theodor W. Adorno "developed the idea of a dialectic of non-identity from a certain distance; Adorno gave this idea the name 'negative dialectics.'" Rolf Tiedemann, editor's afterword to *Metaphysics: Concepts and Problems*, by Theodor W. Adorno (Cambridge: Polity Press, 2000), 191.

18. This trope is so common that even an episode of the children's show *SpongeBob SquarePants* overtly draws this connection, when a character thought to be a zombie takes his rightful place behind

a cash register. See "Once Bitten," *SpongeBob SquarePants,* written by Casey Alexander, Chris Mitchell, and Steven Banks, season 4, episode 73b, September 29, 2006.

19. Horkheimer and Adorno, *Dialectic of Enlightenment,* 26.

20. Karl Marx, *Capital, Volume 1,* 1867, trans. Ben Fowkes (London: Penguin Classics, 1990), 614.

21. "In the bourgeois economy the social work of each individual is mediated by the principle of the self; for some this labor is supposed to yield increased capital, for others the strength for extra work. But the more this process of self-preservation is based on the bourgeois division of labor, the more it enforces the self-alienation of individuals, who must mold themselves to the technical apparatus body and soul." Horkheimer and Adorno, *Dialectic of Enlightenment,* 23.

22. Ibid.

23. Ibid.

24. Gilles Deleuze and Félix Guattari offer their concept of "schizoanalysis" in place of psychoanalysis. See their *Anti-Oedipus: Capitalism and Schizophrenia* (Minneapolis: University of Minnesota Press, 1983). Their schizophrenic "General Freud" is replaced by "the unconscious as an acentered system, in other words, as a machinic network of finite automata (a rhizome)." Deleuze and Guattari, *A Thousand Plateaus: Capitalism and Schizophrenia,* trans. Brian Massumi (Minneapolis: University of Minnesota Press, 1987), 18. Deleuze and Guattari discuss the zombie, vampire, and werewolf; however, they are interested in these figures and their narratives as "becomings." Ibid., 249. Though we are interested in examining the zombie epidemic and its relation to bacterial transformation (something that deeply interests Deleuze and Guattari), we primarily identify the zombie as an "unbecoming."

25. N. Katherine Hayles, *How We Became Posthuman: Virtual Bodies in Cybernetics, Literature, and Informatics* (Chicago: University of Chicago Press, 1999), 287.

26. As Franco Moretti would say, "the monster expresses the anxiety that the future will be monstrous." See Moretti, "Dialectic of Fear," in *Signs Taken for Wonders: Essays in the Sociology of Literary Forms* (London: Verso, 1988), 84.

27. However, the zombie is obviously a metaphor and an allegory in several other regards, especially in the filmmaker's vision; in contemporary cinema, for example, we could say that the zombie is an allegory of contagious disease.

28. Horkheimer and Adorno, *Dialectic of Enlightenment,* xvii.

29. The association of zombies with the capitalist automaton is long standing, but for a recent discussion of how other cinematic monsters "embody the violent contradictions of capitalism," see Annalee Newitz, *Pretend We're Dead: Capitalist Monsters in American Pop Culture* (Durham, N.C.: Duke University Press, 2006). For a discussion of images of the undead in Marx, see Robert Latham, *Consuming Youth: Vampires, Cyborgs, and the Culture of Consumption* (Chicago: University of Chicago Press, 2002).

30. Edward W. Said, *Culture and Imperialism* (New York: First Vintage Edition/Knopf, 1994), 41.

31. David Cohen, *Voodoo, Devils, and the Invisible World* (New York: Dodd, Mead, 1972), 59. Spellings of the word differ in the literature: we have seen "zombi" and "zombie" used to refer to the product of Haitian Vodou. Here we keep to Alfred Métraux's spelling, "zombi," from *Voodoo in Haiti,* trans. Hugo Charteris (London: Deutsch, 1972), in order to make visually apparent the distinction between the Haitian zombi and the cinematic, ontological zombie, except where another spelling has been used in a quotation.

32. The origin of the word *zombie* is debatable. Some speculate it comes from the French *ombres* (shadows); most believe it has African origins and that the Bonda word *zumbi* came to Haiti via Portuguese slave traders. See Wade Davis, *Passage of Darkness: The Ethnobiology of the Haitian Zombie* (Chapel Hill: University of North Carolina Press, 1988), 18.

33. Cohen, *Voodoo, Devils, and the Invisible World,* 60. How the zombie became evil is also of great interest; why the zombie became conflated with that other "savage" stereotype, the cannibal, is, we think, only too obvious.

34. It was Wade Davis who suggested that the reality behind this folk belief might have been indebted to the use of tetrodotoxin, a neurotoxin derived from the poisonous puffer fish, but his work is now considered controversial. See Davis, *The Serpent and the Rainbow* (New York: Simon and Schuster, 1985), 117.

35. Cohen, *Voodoo, Devils, and the Invisible World,* 60.

36. Ibid.

37. Davis, *Passage of Darkness*, 20.

38. Ibid., 18.

39. Ibid., 20.

40. Hannah Arendt, *The Human Condition*, 2nd ed. (Chicago: University of Chicago Press, 1998), 84.

41. Our conflation of the singular and plural pronouns here is intentional, for the zombie is neither single nor plural.

42. Arendt, *Human Condition*, 134.

43. A comparison of the 1978 *Dawn of the Dead* with the 2004 remake exemplifies the significance of the zombie's ability to adapt in order to take on current societal fears. Many similarities remain in the remake, particularly the setting in a shopping mall, but one striking difference is the speed with which the zombies move. The 2004 zombies are notably faster than those of 1978. This trend may parallel the rate at which the capitalist necessity of consumption drives us forward, toward "devouring" and "discarding," as Arendt warned.

44. In *Powers of Horror*, Kristeva writes of the "waste body, the corpse body," that blurs the line between the "inanimate and the inorganic" (109).

45. The posthumanist vision, which exhibits a willingness to disappear into the machine, or to dissolve into cyberspace, is refuted by critics like N. Katherine Hayles, Anne Balsamo, and Deleuze and Guattari, who characterize the overthrow of the material world as either a "nightmare" vision or a flat impossibility rather than as an empowering fantasy.

46. Kristeva, *Powers of Horror*, 159–60. See also Adrienne Rich's detailed account of the epidemic in *Of Woman Born: Motherhood as Experience and Institution* (New York: W. W. Norton, 1976).

47. One such zombie, a real-life woman who was destroyed by puerperal fever, was Mary Wollstonecraft. It is not without significance that her daughter, Mary Shelley, went on to produce a literary zombie, Frankenstein's monster: a man who was a composite of living and dead tissues.

48. Kristeva writes of the "desirable and terrifying, nourishing and murderous, fascinating and abject inside of the maternal body" in *Powers of Horror*, 54. Even the healthy maternal body is made a symbol of this border between life and death; elsewhere, we might argue that the zombie is primarily a female monster.

49. See Lennard J. Davis, *The Disability Studies Reader* (New York: Routledge, 1997); Bram Dijkstra, *Idols of Perversity: Fantasies of Feminine Evil in Fin-de-siècle Culture* (New York: Oxford University Press, 1986); and Erin O'Connor, *Raw Material: Producing Pathology in Victorian Culture* (Durham, N.C.: Duke University Press, 2000).

50. Giorgio Agamben's discussion of "incurable idiots" stems from his analysis of the Nazi document *Authorization for the Annihilation of Life Unworthy of Being Lived* (1920)—the "first appearance on the European juridical scene" of the concept of "life that does not deserve to be lived"—in *Homo Sacer: Sovereign Power and Bare Life*, trans. Daniel Heller-Roazen (Stanford, Calif.: Stanford University Press, 1998), 137.

51. Ibid., 138.

52. Herbs typically used to preserve the dead, like myrrh and aloe, were administered to the patients. Thus the living body was ritually embalmed to prevent the decay of the mind, as the dead are preserved after death, including treatment with bitters, vinegar, and soap, as well as bloodlettings and the cauterization of open sores. See Michel Foucault, *Madness and Civilization* (New York: Vintage Books/Random House, 1988), 163.

53. The undecidability of the coma patient is a long-standing debate, with legal precedents well documented. Giorgio Agamben sites the case of Karen Ann Quinlan, an American girl whose deep coma became a well-known story in the 1980s; he claims her as an example of "pure *zoē*," or pure "life." But rather than seeing this pure, merely biological life as an essential form of the living, Agamben identifies Quinlan as "death in motion" and tells us that "life and death are now merely biopolitical concepts." Agamben, *Homo Sacer*, 186.

54. John R. Searle, in his review of Christof Koch's *The Quest for Consciousness*, states, "Philosophers have invented the idea of a 'zombie' to describe something that behaves exactly as if it were conscious but is not. . . . Many of the mental processes going on inside a conscious subject, according to Koch, are entirely nonconscious." "Consciousness: What We Still Don't Know," *New York Review of Books*, January 13, 2005, 7.

55. Terri Schiavo was determined to be in a purely vegetative state by a Florida court on March 18, 2005, and her feeding tube was subsequently removed. She died on March 31, 2005.

56. Some might claim Schiavo as a cyborg simply because her body was dependent upon machines to sustain her life, but both the zombie and the cyborg are often figured as having suspect consciousness; the automaton and the animate corpse may be the kissing cousins of the fantasy world.

57. Editor's note: At the time of this article's writing, the production of a sequel had been announced, thus seemingly confirming our interpretation of the film's ending. That sequel, *28 Weeks Later*, directed by Juan Carlos Fresnadillo, was released in 2007, though it did not feature any of the characters of the original film.

CHAPTER 23

"We *Are* the Walking Dead"
Race, Time, and Survival in Zombie Narrative

GERRY CANAVAN

The only modern myth is the myth of zombies—mortified schizos, good for work, brought back to reason.
—**Deleuze and Guattari**, *Anti-Oedipus*

Well, there's no problem. If you have a gun, shoot 'em in the head. That's a sure way to kill 'em. If you don't, get yourself a club or a torch. Beat 'em or burn 'em. They go up pretty easy.
—**Sheriff McClelland**, *Night of the Living Dead*

Once banished to the gross-out fringe of straight-to-video horror, all but dead, zombies have come back. Beginning early in the Bush era—even before 9/11, with the filming of *28 Days Later* in London in summer 2001—and continuing unabatedly through the present, the figure of the zombie now lurks at the very center of global mass culture. Alongside the *28 Days Later* franchise, we might name myriad George Romero sequels, remakes, and pastiches; other films like *House of the Dead, Quarantine, I Am Legend*, and *Planet Terror*; zombie video game franchises like Resident Evil, Left 4 Dead, and Dead Rising; best-selling prose works like *World War Z* and *Pride, Prejudice, and Zombies*, both now adapted as films; even, I'd argue, a novel like Cormac McCarthy's critically acclaimed, Pulitzer Prize–winning *The Road*, with its unforgiving landscape of starving inhuman cannibals and universal abjection; zombie-themed crossover events in superhero comics like *Marvel Zombies* and DC's *Blackest Night*; independent comics offerings like Image Comics's hit *The Walking Dead* and Warren Ellis's *Blackgas*; for the first time in television history, zombie-themed series like *Dead Set* in Britain (a reality TV parody) and a version of *The Walking Dead* now greenlit to series on AMC in the United States; so-called zomedies, zombie comedies, like *Fido, Shaun of the Dead*, and *Zombieland*— I might go on.

Playing off Marx's well-known description of capital as vampire in *Capital, Volume 1*,[1] Steven Shaviro suggests in a 2002 special issue of *Historical Materialism* on "Marxism and Fantasy" that our preoccupation with the zombie originates out of the zombie's relationship with contemporary global capitalism:

In contrast to the inhumanity of vampire-capital, zombies present the "human face" of capitalist monstrosity. This is precisely because they are the dregs of humanity: the zombie is all that remains of "human nature," or even simply of a human scale, in the immense and unimaginably complex network economy. Where vampiric surplus-appropriation is unthinkable, because it exceeds our powers of representation, the zombie is conversely what *must be thought*: the shape that representation unavoidably takes now that "information" has displaced "man" as the measure of all things.[2]

When our computers are compromised by hackers or viruses, they become zombie computers, and when our financial institutions fail, it is because they are zombie banks. Remorselessly consuming everything in their path, zombies leave nothing in their wake besides endless copies of themselves, making the zombie the perfect metaphor not only for how capitalism transforms its subjects but also for its relentless and devastating virologic march across the globe. The anti-ecological "proliferation of zombie bodies," Shaviro notes, inevitably culminates in "extermination and extinction"[3]—a final nightmare of exhausted consumption that in our era of endangered species, overfarmed oceans, and Peak Everything does not seem so far off.

But where Shaviro sees the zombie as already identical to the proletarianized subject of late capitalism, I want in this essay to focus on the ways this identification seems troubled and necessarily incomplete. The audience for zombie narrative, after all, never imagines *itself* to be zombified; zombies are always other people, which is to say they are Other people, which is to say they are people who are not quite people at all. A critique like Shaviro's—or, for that matter, like the one advanced by Sarah Juliet Lauro and Karen Embry, who claim the zombie in their "Zombie Manifesto" as the posthuman successor to Donna Haraway's famous cyborg[4]—must first think carefully about the problems of subject position and identification that arise when speaking about the "universal residue"[5] called the zombie. The zombie's mutilation is not one that we easily imagine for "ourselves," however that "we" is ultimately constituted; the zombie is rather the toxic infection that must *always* be kept at arm's length.[6] Because zombies mark the demarcation between life (that is worth living) and unlife (that needs killing), the evocation of the zombie conjures not solidarity but racial panic. To complicate Deleuze and Guattari's proclamation in *A Thousand Plateaus*, then, the myth of the zombie is *both* a war myth *and* a work myth;[7] one of the ways the State apparatus builds the sorts of "pre-accomplished" subjects it needs is precisely through the construction of a racial binary in which the (white) citizen-subject is opposed against nonwhite life, bare life, *zombie* life—that anti-life that is always inimically and hopelessly Other, that must always be kept quarantined, if not actively eradicated and destroyed.

My approach suggests that the major imaginative interest of the zombie lies not as a stand-in for the subject positions of global capitalism but rather in the zombie apocalypse's interrogation of the "future" of late capitalist hegemony, and its concordant state racism, through fantastic depiction of its breakdown and collapse. This essay reasserts, that is to say, the biopolitical origins of the zombie imaginary and therefore insists that before we can ever hope to "become zombies," we first must come to terms with the historical and ongoing colonial violence of which the zombie has always ever been only the thinnest sublimation.

Thinking Zombies: Robert Kirkman's *The Walking Dead*

It seems instructive at the outset to recall briefly Vivian Sobchack's approach to sf in *Screening Space: The American Science Fiction Film*. In contradistinction to the Suvinian approach to sf prose, for Sobchack, the important genre distinction to be maintained is not sf versus fantasy but *sf versus horror,* a divide she finds to be hopelessly muddled by a blurred and indistinct "no-man's land" between the two populated by hybrid films (in our case, zombie cinema) that arguably belong to both modes.[8]

"The horror film," Sobchack says, "is primarily concerned with the individual in conflict with society or with some extension of himself, the sf film with society and its institutions in conflict with each other or with some alien other."[9] It is for this reason that we find a key distinction between horror and sf to be the question of scale; we expect horror to take place in a small and isolated setting (perhaps, as in *Night of the Living Dead,* as small as a single farmhouse), while sf expands to fill large cities and nations, even the entire globe. We might think, for instance, of England after the Rage outbreak in *28 Days Later* or how, in the recent *Marvel Zombies* and DC *Blackest Night* story lines in superhero comics, the zombie outbreak swells to fill the entire cosmos, even the entire multiverse.[10]

If we accept Sobchack's genre definition, we find that the zombie subgenre starts out in horror in its earliest film formulations but winds up in sf in its later ones; while "horror" entries in this *hugely* prolific subgenre certainly remain, the most popular and influential mode of zombie narrative (especially during the Bush-era "zombie revival" period on which I focus) has been the "zombie apocalypse": the large-scale zombie pandemic that leads to the rapid total breakdown of technological modernity and transnational capitalism on a global scale. To put this another way, for Sobchack, the local scale of the horror film is concerned with "moral chaos"—the disruption of the natural order—while the broader scale of sf film lends itself to "social chaos."[11] Unlike horror's Monster, sf's Creature is unparticularized and uninteriorized; it does not hate, nor seek revenge, and it does not even "want" to hurt us. It just does.[12] The sf Creature is an eruption that is only disruption—and it is for this reason that the sf film is so often preoccupied with the *reaction* of society to catastrophe (on one hand) and to a dispassionate, spectacular aesthetics of destruction (on the other). In the end, Sobchack's division between horror and sf comes down to the difference between terror and wonder.[13] If in the horror film we feel "fear," in the sf film we feel "interest." In the horror film we find we want to close our eyes and look away, and the excitement is in forcing ourselves to watch; but in the sf film the narrative pleasure comes precisely in anticipating, and then seeing, what will happen next.

And so, having discovered the zombie right at the intersection of these two modes— the zombie is both local and global, personal *and* depersonalized, symptom of moral chaos *and* cause of widespread social breakdown, gross-out consumer of flesh *and* spectacular

destroyer of our intricately constructed social and technological fortifications—
I want to read the zombie's relationship to contemporary capitalism in the context of
the postcolonial approach to sf John Rieder advocates in his 2008 book *Colonialism
and the Emergence of Science Fiction*. In that vein I will be focusing primarily on Robert
Kirkman's seventy-three-issue comic book series *The Walking Dead* (which began in 2003
and is still ongoing).[14] Kirkman's is a zombie narrative that has been, to coin a phrase,
dehorrored by the diminished immediacy of the comics form, which makes the anticipa-
tory "interest" native to sf all the more evident in his work.

The *Walking Dead* is described by its creator in the introduction to the first trade
paperback in terms that Sobchack would recognize immediately as essentially science
fictional:

> To me the best zombie movies aren't the splatter feasts of gore and violence with goofy
> characters and tongue in cheek antics. Good zombie movies show us how messed up
> we are, they make us question our station in society . . . and our society's station in
> the world.[15]

Here Kirkman describes his objective in *The Walking Dead* as an extension of the work of
George Romero—always the most cerebral and even, in his own way, the most *subdued*
creator of classic twentieth-century zombie cinema, granting his characters long periods
of quiet safety between the catastrophic zombie attacks that typically bookend his films.
Kirkman writes that he hopes to employ the hyperbolic temporal continuity native to
the comic form to create the feel of a Romero film that never ends.[16] In such a story the
fear of "moral chaos" of the early outbreak will necessarily give way to "interest" in the
way society changes in the wake of the zombie disaster—and so it's no surprise that
Kirkman uses the same "waking up from a coma" trope as *28 Days Later* to "skip" the
initial outbreak and get immediately to the postapocalyptic breakdown world.

In his introduction to the first trade paperback, Kirkman tells us *The Walking Dead* is
"not a horror book" but a book about "watching Rick survive."[17] For more than seventy
issues, readers have followed Rick Grimes (before the zombie apocalypse a police officer
and therefore functioning as a synecdoche for the prezombie social order) through a
dizzying disintegration as he has been scarred both physically and mentally in the face
of the ongoing zombie onslaught. Over the year or so of narrative time that has been
depicted in the series, Rick has lost his place in society, his home, his best friend, one of
his hands, his wife and infant daughter, and finally his grip on sanity; by turns paranoid
and murderous, Rick has proven himself willing to do anything, to anyone, in the name
of survival for himself and his surviving prepubescent son, Carl.

In *The Walking Dead*, Rick Grimes and his band of largely expendable survivors—
none of whom are safe—explore the ruins of our own late-imperial America. The story
focus in the earliest issues of the series is on reaching city centers, where (we are told)
the government has ordered all citizens in an effort to better protect them. It used to be
that (white) people *fled* the city for the suburbs "for safety," out of fear of rising crime
rates; here that logic is reversed, and they must go back. But the government's plan is a

Figure 23.1.
Image from Robert Kirkman, *The Walking Dead*. *Top*, issue 1. *Bottom*, issue 52. Image Comics Inc., Berkeley, California. Copyright Robert Kirkman. Reprinted with permission.

disaster, as concentrating survivors in one place only makes it easier for zombieism to spread, and Rick barely makes it back out of Atlanta alive. By chance he meets up with his wife and family, who never made it to Atlanta at all—only to discover that his fellow police officer and best friend Shane has snapped under the pressure of leading the group and ultimately needs to be killed to protect the others (by Carl, no less, in the climactic scene of issue 6 that ends the first trade paperback).[18]

A brief stint at a rural farmhouse turns bad when it is discovered that the owner of the farmhouse has been locking local zombies in his barn in anticipation of a "cure" that, we can be certain, will never be forthcoming. Another inevitable massacre ensues. Finally Rick and his group are able to find a modicum of safety in an abandoned jail. Here the inversion typical to zombie narrative between a privileged "us" and a precarious "them" is made complete: Grimes, a white police officer, will make his desperate home inside a jail, while dangerous and hostile Others array themselves against him outside the walls. In this reversal of the logic of the prison–industrial complex, the book settles for a long time into this new status quo as (in the proud tradition of Romero's zombie films) the survivors work to build fortifications and protect themselves—as a new imagined community under Rick's leadership—against all that is outside.

The Colonial Gaze

So allow me to return again, in this moment of relative quiet for Rick and his tribe, to theory. Where Darko Suvin privileges "cognitive estrangement" as sf's essential feature—the de- and refamiliarizing power of alternative worlds—and where Fredric Jameson privileges the radical retemporalization of our disordered present into the settled historical past of some possible future,[19] Rieder focuses our attention on what he calls sf's "colonial gaze":

> We can call this cognitive framework establishing the different positions of the one who looks and the one who is looked at the structure of the "colonial gaze," borrowing and adapting Laura Mulvey's influential analysis of the cinematic gaze in "Visual Pleasure and Narrative Cinema." The colonial gaze distributes knowledge and power to the subject who looks, while denying or minimizing access to power for its object, the one looked at.[20]

Zombie narrative, I argue, should be understood as operating under precisely this sort of colonial gaze. Zombies—lacking interior, lacking mind—cannot look; they are, for this reason, completely realized colonial objects. Zombies cannot be recognized, accommodated, or negotiated with; once identified, they must immediately be killed.

To shift briefly into a biopolitical register, this is a hyperreal metaphorization of the racial logic that enforces modernity's distinction between that mode of "civilized" living native to the political subject and *zoē*, bare life.[21] For our purposes—concerned as we are about zombie narrative and its vision of "infection" run apocalyptically amok—it seems useful to take a moment here to quote Michel Foucault at length on biopolitics, because in the moment he introduces the concept of biopower, it is to disease, to epidemiology, that he turns to explain its logic:

> This biopolitics is not concerned with fertility alone. It also deals with the problem of morbidity, but not simply, as had previously been the case, at the level of the famous epidemics, the threat of which had haunted political powers ever since the Middle Ages (these famous epidemics were temporary disasters that caused multiple deaths, times when everyone seemed to be in danger of imminent death). At the end of the eighteenth century, it was not epidemics that were the issue, but something else—what might broadly be called endemics, or in other words, the form, nature, extension, duration, and intensity of the illness prevalent in a population. These were illnesses that were difficult to eradicate and that were not regarded as epidemics that caused more frequent deaths, but as permanent factors which—and that is how they were dealt with—sapped the population's strength, shortened the working week, wasted energy, and cost money, both because they led to a fall in production and because treating them was expensive. In a word, illness as phenomenon affecting a population. *Death was no longer something that suddenly swooped down on life—as in an epidemic. Death was now something permanent, something that slips into life, perpetually gnaws at it, diminishes it and weakens it.*[22]

When Foucault writes of death as a sort of all-pervasive, "gnawing" pollutive force against which society imagines it must array itself through careful, rationalized management, he is speaking our language: the language of the zombie. State racism, for Foucault, follows the logic of any zombie film:

> In the biopower system, in other words, killing or the imperative to kill is acceptable only if it results not in a victory over political adversaries, but in the elimination of the biological threat to and the improvement of the species or race. . . . In a normalizing society, race or racism is the precondition that makes killing acceptable.[23]

The biopolitical state—inverting the sovereign power to make dead or let live in its power to make live or let die[24]—*needs* to create this sort of racial imaginary in order to retain its power to kill. Under biopower, those who are imagined to threaten the population as a whole become not merely a danger but a kind of *anti-life* that must be sequestered from (white) life at any cost. Any contact with a zombie, after all, might lead to infection, just as the racial Other must be disciplined and quarantined to prevent "intermingling."

In *Colonialism and the Emergence of Science Fiction*, Rieder demonstrates at length that this colonial discourse of superior and inferior races—the colonial gaze, Foucault's life and anti-life—is a highly unstable positionality that is under constant threat of polar inversion, an instance of the Hegelian master–slave dialectic whose fundamental precariousness is enacted and reenacted throughout the history of science fiction. In an alternate history, or in future days, the colonizer knows he could well be the colonized. In this way, sf engages the violence at the heart of European imperialist expansion by replicating it, over and over, in metaphorical forms both for and against the colonizing subject and the imagined racial hierarchy on which her self-identity depends.

Therefore the exemplary sf novel becomes for Rieder, not Thomas More's *Utopia* or H. G. Wells's *The Time Machine*, but Wells's inverted vision of an imperialized England in flames, *War of the Worlds*, which in its provocative first chapter explicitly equates the Martian colonization of Earth with the British extermination of the native population of Tasmania. Wells's Martians are not generic alien others; they are *colonizers*—they occupy the precise futurological relationship toward Britain that Britain claims to occupy toward its imperial holdings:

> Nor was it generally understood that since Mars is older than our earth, with scarcely a quarter of the superficial area and remoter from the sun, it necessarily follows that it is not only more distant from time's beginning but nearer its end. . . . And we men, the creatures who inhabit this earth, must be to them at least as alien and lowly as are the monkeys and lemurs to us.[25]

Almost a hundred years afterward, in *Time and the Other*, Johannes Fabian would describe this retemporalization as a strategy for what Foucault calls *state racism*:

It is not difficult to transpose from physics to politics one of the most ancient rules which states that it is impossible for two bodies to occupy the same space at the same time. When in the course of colonial expansion a Western body politic came to occupy, literally, the space of an autochthonous body, several alternatives were conceived to deal with that violation of the rule. The simplest one, if we think of North America and Australia, was of course to move or remove the other body. Another one is to pretend that space is being divided and allocated to separate bodies. South Africa's rulers cling to that solution. Most often the preferred strategy has been simply to manipulate the other variable—Time. With the help of various devices of sequencing and distancing, one assigns to the conquered populations a different time.[26]

Wells goes on: "And before we judge [the Martians] too harshly we must remember what ruthless and utter destruction our own species has wrought, not only upon animals, such as the vanished bison and the dodo, but upon its inferior races. The Tasmanians, in spite of their human likeness, were entirely swept out of existence in a war of extermination waged by European immigrants, in the space of fifty years. Are we such apostles of mercy," Wells pointedly asked, "as to complain if the Martians warred in the same spirit?"[27]

The logic of the *War of the Worlds* narrative is one in which the "future" (Mars/Europe/United States) is understood to be invading its own evolutionary "past" (Earth/Tasmania/the Global South) to secure its continued existence. And this was precisely the racist logic employed by the colonial imaginary to justify colonial and imperial violence: whiteness is understood to be humanity's "most advanced" form, and other races are ideologically coded as (at best) primitive or (at worst) dangerously obsolete, subject to disruption, displacement, and even extermination in the name of the European arc of history. What happens in the *War of the Worlds* template, then, is nothing less than European civilization getting a taste of its own medicine—the exterminative logic of the colonial sphere comes back home to the metropole.

The zombie narrative, I argue, is best understood in these terms as a slightly transformed refiguration of *War of the Worlds*. Zombie apocalypses, like imperialistic narratives of alien invasion, repackage the violence of colonial race war in a form that is ideologically safer. Zombie films depict total, unrestrained violence against absolute Others whose very existence is seen as anathema to our own, Others who are in essence living death. In our time, when this sort of unrestrained racial violence is officially suspect but nonetheless *unofficially* still a foundation for the basic operation of technological civilization, zombie narratives serve as the motivating license for confrontation with these sorts of genocidal technologies and power fantasies.

Where zombies might be said to significantly complicate the temporality of *War of the Worlds*-style total violence is through their embodiment of multiple temporalities at once. Rather than invading from the future, as Wells's aliens did, zombies might be said to invade from the *past*: erupting from the graves of our decomposing loved ones to establish their apocalyptic ecology of universal death. But this turns out, dialectically,

Figure 23.2.
Image from Robert Kirkman,
The Walking Dead, issue 24. Image Comics
Inc., Berkeley, California. Copyright Robert
Kirkman. Reprinted with permission.

to be our only possible future all along; the zombie's remorseless, infective hunger is a barely sublimated figuration of the entropic lurch of time and the inevitable degeneration of our own bodies toward death, a horror that technological and social progress may delay but cannot hope to avert.

Both past and future, then, zombies turn out in this way to be coextensive with the present—they are the corpses of our friends and coworkers lurching aimlessly through the sterile environments we all once shared. The rotting zombie corpse inevitably suggests the psychological horror Julia Kristeva called "abjection," the disturbing of the boundary between object and subject.[28] As Rick Grimes exclaims in horror near the end of one trade paperback, it is *we,* not they, who are "the walking dead." In the end,

Figure 23.3.
Image from Robert Kirkman,
The Walking Dead, issue 24.
Image Comics Inc., Berkeley,
California. Copyright Robert
Kirkman. Reprinted with
permission.

no matter what we do or how we live, we too must die and come back and be just like them. Zombies are our only possible future, our already actual present; zombies inherit the earth.

Zombies and Empire

If Empire, especially in the age of never-ending War on Terror, is essentially an attempt to regulate History, to make the present extend forever in both space and time, then zombie narrative is its dark reflection; as zombies flatten time, they obliterate the present alongside the past and the future, only against "us," not for "us." In Agambenian terms, zombies activate the "state of exception," the suspension of all juridical restraint or moral norm in the face of a perceived existential threat:

> modern totalitarianism can be defined as the establishment, by means of the state of exception, of a legal civil war that allows for the physical elimination not only of political adversaries but of entire categories of citizens who for some reason cannot be integrated into the political system. Since [the Third Reich], the voluntary creation of a permanent state of emergency (though perhaps not declared in the technical sense) has become one of the essential practices of contemporary states, including so-called democratic ones.[29]

Faced with the unstoppable progression of what has been called a "global civil war," the state of exception tends increasingly to appear as the dominant paradigm of government in contemporary politics.[30]

Here again we find the zombies allegorizing the racial forms of exclusion and exter-mination that already surround us. Zombie narratives are ultimately about the motiva-tion for and unleashing of total violence; what separates "us" from "them" in zombie narrative is always only the type of violence used. *They* attack *us* (like "animals," "sav-ages," or "cannibals") with their arms and mouths; we attack them back with horses, tanks, and guns.

In *The Walking Dead*—as in any zombie narrative—the tools and technologies of empire are continually borrowed for the purpose of priming precisely this sort of vio-lent colonialist fantasy. Swords and guns, tanks and trucks, repeated references to the brutal physical and sexual violence of slavery and to the cowboy or "frontier" imaginary (especially through the ubiquitous riding of horses and Carl's cowboy outfit and man-nerisms), are all employed in a bizarre postmodern pastiche of the history of U.S. impe-rialism, as different moments of its empire collide into a single simultaneous instant in the face of an essentially inimical and totally implacable racialized threat. There are few moments in the series that suggest this pastiche as well as the splash panel at the end of issue 12, when Rick and his group discover the abandoned jail in which they will make their home through the bulk of the series. The jail is drawn so as to visually double as a frontier fort (and, for that matter, a modern military base); these locations collapse into a single spatial imaginary, with only the polarity of "inside" and "outside" reversed.

Later issues have made the relationship between Rick's story and declinist anxieties about the breakdown of American empire even more explicit: following the final breach of the jail's walls—at the hands, not of zombies, but of their fellow countrymen operat-ing under the orders of a brutally corrupt and impossibly decadent leader known only as the Governor—Rick and Carl eventually fall in with a group claiming to be carrying a cure that they are bringing to Washington, D.C., under the auspices of the U.S. mili-tary. While this (of course) turns out to be a lie, their journey to D.C. does find them a new home to replace the jail, that *other* walled-in space for whiteness characteristic of late American empire: the gated community. In issue 73, the most recent issue as of my writing, they've just moved in, and are looking to take over.

We should see here how the solidarity created among survivors in zombie narrative is always much more unstable than in the typical alien invasion story. Countrymen do not band together in the zombie crisis, and the nation does not have its finest hour; instead, allegiances fragment into familial bands and patriarchal tribes, then fragment further from there. We can see this breakdown everywhere in *The Walking Dead*: Shane, Rick's best friend, must be killed not only because he has become dangerous but because he covets Rick's wife. Later, Carl secretly murders another young boy who is behav-ing sociopathically on the grounds that he too is a threat to the group; we are led to believe this was the "right thing" to do, "because it needed to be done and no one else would."[31] The four prisoners (two of whom are African American) who have been safely inhabiting a sealed-off wing of the jail during the zombie apocalypse must be displaced in order to make room for Rick's group to move in: one of the white prisoners turns out to be a serial killer of young women and is eventually hung, and as soon as the two black prisoners acquire guns, a shootout ensues, in which one is killed and the other is run off—which in the context of these other examples suggests the age-old trope that

Figure 23.4.
Image from Robert
Kirkman, *The Walking
Dead*, issue 12. Image
Comics Inc., Berkeley,
California. Copyright
Robert Kirkman.
Reprinted with
permission.

women cannot be safe around unknown men, particularly black men. The Governor, as already mentioned, finally destroys the jail's usefulness as a fortification in his doomed efforts to seize it for his own people, killing Rick's wife and daughter in the process; the Governor had already proven himself to be utterly reprehensible through both his repeated rapes of a black female protagonist he keeps in chains and a sexualized relationship with a zombified young girl he claims was once his daughter. And in their flight from the ruined jail, after the Governor is dead, Rick's band encounters the Hunters, humans who have embraced zombie-style cannibalism in order to sate their hunger; the Hunters began with eating their own children.

Something important emerges out of these examples. Whatever else might be said about *The Walking Dead*, or about zombie narrative in general, its uncritical relationship to a particular prefeminist narrative about the need to "protect" women and children cannot be glossed over. "Proper" control over wombs, and anxiety that they will somehow be captured, polluted, or compromised, is a kind of Ur-myth for the apocalyptic genre in general and the zombie subgenre in particular; speaking broadly, the function of women in most apocalyptic narratives is to code the ending as "happy" or "sad" based on their continued availability to bear the male protagonist's children when the story is over. This theme is so common in the zombie subgenre as to constitute one of its most ubiquitous and most central ethical clichés: the question of whether or not one should decide to "bring a child into" a zombie-ridden world at all—and, as is common in many such apocalyptic stories (as in, for instance, Cormac McCarthy's 2009 novel *The Road*), the death of Rick's wife and daughter, the moment the circuit of reproductive futurity is cut, is the moment that basically all hope is lost in *The Walking Dead*.[32]

Robin Wood makes the relationship between cannibalism and the breakdown of the patriarchal family central to his analysis of zombie horror, which in our context suggests precisely the sort of multivalent retemporalization at work in zombie narrative: "It is no accident," he writes, "that the four most intense horror films of the 70s at exploitation level . . . all centered on cannibalism, and on the specific notion of present and future (the younger generation) being devoured by the past."[33] Likewise, Alys Eve Weinbaum and Amy Kaplan, among others, have shown how this sort of anxiety over reproductive futurity is essential to the cultural imagination of race, nation, and empire, which are always defined by the question of who is allowed to reproduce, and with whom.[34]

Zombie Ethics

So while in zombie narrative the "enemy" who is killed is always *first* the zombie—who is unthinking and unfeeling and can be killed without regret—as the story proceeds, the violence inevitably spreads to other, still-alive humans as well. Anyone outside the white patriarchal community, anyone who is not already one of "us," is a potential threat to the future who must be interrogated intensely, if not kept out altogether. Even those inside the community have to be surveilled at all times for signs of treachery, weakness, or growing "infection."[35] This is the second way in which the zombie infects us, besides the obvious; they infect us with their vulnerability—their killability makes us "killable" too. One's position in the state of exception is, after all, never secure; the class of dangerous anticitizens, bound for the camps, tends only to grow. In this way, zombie narratives make the latent necropolitical dimensions bound up in both "survival" and modern citizenship explicit; they expose, in the raw, what Achille Mbembe showed in "Necropolitics," that to survive is also to kill:

> the survivor is the one who, having stood in the path of death, knowing of many deaths and standing in the midst of the fallen, is still alive. Or, more precisely, the survivor is the one who has taken on a whole pack of enemies and managed not only to escape alive, but to kill his or her attackers. This is why, to a large extent, the lowest form of survival is killing. Canetti points out that in the logic of survival, "each man is the enemy of every other." Even more radically, in the logic of survival one's horror at the sight of death turns into satisfaction that it is someone else who is dead. It is the death of the other, his or her physical presence as a corpse, that makes the survivor feel unique. And each enemy killed makes the survivor feel more secure.[36]

In this way the zombie narrative always becomes, in the end, a kind of ethical minefield, in which other humans "must" be fought, betrayed, abandoned, and destroyed so that the protagonists, our heroes, might survive. And even the pulse of that "might" is very weak: so much of the pleasure of zombie narrative in both cinema and other forms originates in the audience's knowledge that the heroes' preparations and fortifications will *never* be sufficient, that no matter what happens in the end, the zombies will break through and kill nearly everyone because *this is what zombies do.* In a sense, the zombies are always the real protagonists of the zombie narrative; no matter how long they have been gone from the action, we are always awaiting their eventual, inevitable return. The *telos* of the fortress, like the *telos* of empire, is always, in the end, to fall.

Writing in 1974 of potential negative consequences from U.S. foreign aid, Garrett Hardin called the sort of ethical calculus at work in these zombie narratives "lifeboat ethics," celebrating pitiless self-interest as a necessary and rational Malthusian pragmatism.[37] I call his "case against helping the poor" *zombie ethics.* And while we might be tempted to return already to Shaviro and the sort of zombic universal class consciousness he suggests, we must first follow this ethical trajectory all the way to its end and explore the pernicious ways in which zombie ethics inevitably "infects" our actually existing, *pre*-apocalyptic politics. The "disposability" of the zombie in zombie narrative has a still-ongoing history that simply cannot be ignored. The racial myth of inimical Otherness the zombie narrative replicates, and the forced choices it foists on us, is not just some deceased artifact of the "bad past"; it is alive and well, or if you like, undead, and continues to have real-world consequences.

Fueled by hyperbolic media reporting during the Hurricane Katrina disaster, doctors and nurses at Memorial Medical Center in New Orleans came to believe they were in a zombie story—that no help would ever reach them in time and that outside the walls of their hospital there roamed monsters. The *New York Times Magazine* described the scene this way:

> Thiele didn't know [Dr. Anna] Pou by name, but she looked to him like the physician in charge on the second floor. He told me that Pou told him that the Category 3 patients were not going to be moved. He said he thought they appeared close to death and would not have survived an evacuation. He was terrified, he said, of what would happen to them if they were left behind. He expected that the people firing guns into the chaos of New Orleans—"the animals," he called them—would storm the hospital, looking for drugs after everyone else was gone. "I figured, What would they do, these crazy black people who think they've been oppressed for all these years by white people? I mean if they're capable of shooting at somebody, why are they not capable of raping them or, or, you know, dismembering them? What's to prevent them from doing things like that?"
>
> The laws of man had broken down, Thiele concluded, and only the laws of God applied.[38]

Having heard the news reports proclaiming widespread chaos and mindless violence outside—many if not nearly all of which turned out to be poorly sourced and untrue—and operating in "survival" mode, in a self-declared state of exception, staff at Memorial Medical began refusing treatment to select patients and, in the end, are alleged to have deliberately euthanized as many as twenty-four people.[39]

Just across town, during the same disaster, the mostly white suburb Gretna, Louisiana, used its police force to blockade the bridge that led from New Orleans into the town:

> Paul Ribaul, 37, a New Orleans TV-station engineer from Gretna, said New Orleans and the suburbs have a complicated relationship.
>
> "We say we're from New Orleans, but we're a suburb," he said. "The reason we don't live there is we don't like the crime, the politics."
>
> Ribaul was among Gretna residents who praised the decision to close the bridge. "It makes you feel safe to live in a city like that," he said. . . .
>
> [Mayor Ronnie] Harris said Thursday that closing the bridge was a tough decision but that he felt it was right.
>
> "We didn't even have enough food here to feed our own residents," Harris said. "We took care of our folks. It's something we had to do."[40]

At still another bridge in New Orleans, Danziger Bridge, two African American families searching for food, water, and help were gunned down by seven heavily armed, out-of-uniform police officers for reasons that remain unclear.[41] The state of Louisiana's charges against the officers were eventually dismissed due to prosecutorial misconduct, though local investigation into departmental obstruction of justice is still ongoing.[42] On July 14, 2010, four of the officers involved in the Danziger Bridge incident were federally indicted for deprivation of rights under color of law and use of a weapon during the commission of a crime, charges that could carry the death penalty if they are convicted; that prosecution is ongoing.

When Haiti—of course, the ancestral home of the *zombi*, where this hybridized postcolonial figure first emerged as the nightmarish figuration of a slavery that would continue even after death—was struck by its devastating earthquake in January 2010, the same stories were told: rumors of widespread rapes and murders reported breathlessly by the media as inevitable and obvious fact, baseless (and, in context, often nonsensical) accusations of "looting" hurled at poverty-stricken people of color just trying to survive in the face of an incomprehensible disaster. In her *Precarious Life: The Powers of Mourning and Violence,* Judith Butler writes persuasively of the way the inevitability of grief in human life might be employed as a ground for a Levinasian ethics of mutual vulnerability and shared precariousness, if not for the way ideology persistently codes certain lives as "mournable" and others not. Thinking both of the war in Iraq and the occupation of Palestine, she writes,

> Is a Muslim life as valuable as legibly First World lives? Are the Palestinians yet accorded the status of "human" in US policy and press coverage? Will those hundreds of thousands of lives lost in the last decades of strife ever receive the equivalent to the paragraph-long obituaries in the *New York Times* that seek to humanize—often through nationalist and familial framing devices—those Americans who have been violently killed? Is our capacity to mourn in global dimensions foreclosed precisely by the failure to conceive of Muslim and Arab lives *as lives*?[43]

In postearthquake Haiti, as in post-Katrina New Orleans, as in Iraq and Palestine, we find the moral demand made by shared precariousness once again short-circuited in favor of a prophylactic Othering. Suffering Haitians were quickly recoded as bare life—zombie life—and thereby rendered *unworthy* of proper aid and protection. Haitians couldn't be trusted, we were told, even to accept our help.

An interview at Campus Progress with Dr. Kathleen Tierney of the Natural Hazard Center at the University of Colorado at Boulder memorably called this phenomenon the "looting lie."[44] Misled by this racist imaginary, the international aid response—coordinated, to widespread criticism, by that imperial agency par excellence, the U.S. military—focused on security over support, landing thousands of troops on the island while diverting international aid flights and before allowing a single food drop from the air. Fear of the poor, journalist Linda Polman argued in the *Guardian*, hurt rescue efforts: "CNN won't stop telling aid workers and the outside world about pillaging (the incidence of which for the first four frustrating days at least did not compare with what happened after Hurricane Katrina) and about how dangerous it would be to distribute food, because of the likelihood of 'stampedes.'"[45] In Ben Ehrenreich's report on Haitian rescue efforts at Slate.com, we find this report of the initial days of the disaster:

> "Command and control" turned out to be the key words. The U.S. military did what the U.S. military does. Like a slow-witted, fearful giant, it built a wall around itself, commandeering the Port-au-Prince airport and constructing a mini–Green Zone. As thousands of tons of desperately needed food, water, and medical supplies piled up behind the airport fences—and thousands of corpses piled up outside them—Defense Secretary Robert Gates ruled out the possibility of using American aircraft to airdrop supplies: "An airdrop is simply going to lead to riots," he said. The military's first priority was to build a "structure for distribution" and "to provide security." (Four days and many deaths later, the United States began airdropping aid.)[46]

This is what we do, whenever zombies strike: we build fortifications, we hoard supplies, we "circle the wagons" and point our guns outward. And we do this even, and most tragically, when the zombies don't exist, when outside the walls there are only other people just like us.

Zombie Gaze, Zombie Embrace

Late in the jail period of *The Walking Dead*, there is a brief panel sequence of Carl and his friend, Sophie, staring out through the gates at the zombies outside. We see first the zombies on the chain-link fence, particularly their dark, uncomprehending eyes, their grasping hands, their gaping mouths. The second panel pulls back, cameralike, to see Carl and Sophie from behind, holding hands, looking outward; the white American cowboy man-child and his prospective love interest—who become our last hope for the resuscitation of reproductive futurity—stare at the starving masses behind the fence. On the next page, they talk about what they see. Carl asks if she is still scared of the zombies, and she says no: "Mostly I just feel sorry for them. . . . Because they look so sad. Don't they look sad to you?"

The suggestion here is of a shift from terror of the Other to pity for the Other—which is progress, I suppose, of a type. But this sort of sympathy merely recapitulates the colonial gaze by recoding it into a new, less objectionable form. We, the privileged, still do the looking; they, our objects, are still looked *at*. The *really* radical move for poor Sophie, of course, would be not to feel pity but to throw open the gates: to erase the subject–object division altogether and abandon the zombie gaze. The really radical move, that is, would be to refuse the demarcation between life and anti-life altogether, as Sophie's mother Carol does in a later issue when she deliberately turns herself over to

Figure 23.5.
Image from Robert Kirkman,
The Walking Dead, issue 21. Image
Comics Inc., Berkeley, California.
Copyright Robert Kirkman. Reprinted
with permission.

the zombies to be consumed and turned. "Oh good," she says as the zombie tears into her throat in a perverse lover's embrace, "you *do* like me."[47]

Within the fictional space of the zombie narrative, of course, a move like Carol's makes no sense: this is suicide! But despite the protestations of biopolitical state racism, despite the endless blaring declarations of national emergencies and states of exception, *we* don't live inside a zombie narrative; we live in the real world, a zombieless world, where the only zombies to be found are the ones we ourselves have made out of the excluded, the forgotten, the cast out, and the walled off. To become a zombie would be to obliterate the line dividing "us" from "them" by allowing ourselves to be fully and finally devoured by alterity. To become a zombie is in this way to risk becoming "disposable" ourselves; to do it would mean forsaking the zombie gaze in favor of the zombie embrace. This is why universalism—in either its humanist or zombic guise—should never be named as something easy to achieve, much less something we have already accomplished. It is rather always a struggle of self-decentering and self-deprivileging, of self-renunciation—something easier to say than do, but at the same time the necessary precondition for a final end to our collective zombie nightmare, the nightmare called history itself.

Notes

1. Karl Marx, *Capital, Volume 1*, trans. Ben Fowkes (New York: Penguin Books, 1990), chapter 10.

2. Steven Shaviro, "Capitalist Monsters," *Historical Materialism* 10, no. 4 (2002): 288.

3. Ibid., 286.

4. See Sarah Juliet Lauro and Karen Embry, "A Zombie Manifesto: The Nonhuman Condition in the Era of Advanced Capitalism," *boundary 2* 35, no. 1 (2008): 85–108.

5. Shaviro, "Capitalist Monsters," 288.

6. As Shaviro himself notes near the end of his essay, even as the zombie slips back and forth "between First World and Third," it remains sloughed off always on other bodies, which he suggests is an apt metaphorization of the invisibility of productive labor. Ibid., 288–89. This is especially important in the context of the origins of the *zombi* in colonial Haiti, which, as Lauro and Embry show in "A Zombie Manifesto," was a figure both of the resisting slave *and* of a nightmare of slavery that continues even after death (97–98); the zombie of contemporary mass culture, Shaviro says, instead alternates between figuring invisible/immaterial labor in the third world and antiproductive consumption in the first—both of which are focalized in other people, not ourselves.

7. Gilles Deleuze and Félix Guattari, *A Thousand Plateaus*, trans. Brian Massumi (Minneapolis: University of Minnesota Press, 1987), 425. The full quotation from Deleuze and Guattari reads, "Above all, the State apparatus makes the mutilation, and even death, come first. It needs them preaccomplished, for people to be born that way, crippled and zombielike. The myth of the zombie, of the living dead, is a work myth and not a war myth. Mutilation is a consequence of war, but it is a necessary condition, a presupposition of the State apparatus and the organization of work" (425).

8. Vivian Sobchack, *Screening Space: The American Science Fiction Film* (New Brunswick, N.J.: Rutgers University Press, 2001), 26–27. The best articulation of the Suvinian paradigm can be found in Darko Suvin's *Metamorphoses of Science Fiction*, ed. Gerry Canavan (1979; repr., London: Ralahine Press, 2016).

9. Ibid., 30.

10. See Geoff Johns (writer), *Blackest Night*, no. 0–8 (New York: DC Comics, 2009–2010), and Robert Kirkman (writer), *Marvel Zombies* (New York: Marvel Comics, 2008).

11. Sobchack, *Screening Space*, 30.

12. Ibid., 37.

13. Ibid., 38.

14. [Editor's note: At the time of this article's publication, this was accurate. Today, there are close to

170 issues, and the television show that was developed based on the graphic novel series is in its eighth season.]

15. Robert Kirkman, *The Walking Dead: Vol. 1. Days Gone Bye* (Berkeley, Calif.: Image Comics, 2008), i., collects the first six issues of *The Walking Dead* ongoing comic (Berkeley, Calif.: Image Comics, 2003–).

16. Ibid., ii–iv.

17. Ibid., iii.

18. Dale Knickerbocker has brought to my attention that Atlanta is a particularly interesting city for Rick to journey toward, given the apocalyptic devastation of Sherman's March and the boundless suburban sprawl of the city's recent history. He also suggests Shane as a reference to George Stevens's 1953 Western *Shane*, which the character echoes in both plot and theme; the difference here is that the child is not Shane's mourner but his executioner.

19. Fredric Jameson, *Archaeologies of the Future: The Desire Called Utopia and Other Science Fictions* (New York: Verso, 2007).

20. John Rieder, *Colonialism and the Emergence of Science Fiction* (Middletown, Conn.: Wesleyan University Press, 2008), 7. The cited Laura Mulvey essay is "Visual Pleasure and Narrative Cinema," *Screen* 16, no. 3 (1975): 6–18.

21. These terms are defined on the first page of Giorgio Agamben's *Homo Sacer* as follows: "*zoē*, which expressed the simple fact of living common to all living beings (animal, men, or gods), and *bios*, which indicated the form of living proper to an individual or group." Agamben, *Homo Sacer* (Stanford, Calif.: Stanford University Press, 1995), 1. This is to say that *zoē* is bare (as in mere) life, whereas *bios* is citizenship, political life. Much of Agamben's work focuses on the biopolitical consequences resulting from the exclusion of certain types of bodies from *bios*.

22. Michel Foucault, *Society Must Be Defended: Lectures at the Collège de France, 1975–1976*, trans. David Macey (New York: Picador, 1997), 243–44, emphasis added.

23. Ibid., 256.

24. Ibid., 241.

25. H. G. Wells, *War of the Worlds* (New York: Bantam Books, 1988), 4.

26. Johannes Fabian, *Time and the Other: How Anthropology Makes Its Object* (New York: Columbia University Press, 1983), 29–30.

27. Wells, *War of the Worlds*, 4–5.

28. Julia Kristeva, *Powers of Horror: An Essay on Abjection* (New York: Columbia University Press, 1982).

29. Giorgio Agamben, *State of Exception* (Chicago: University of Chicago Press, 2005), 2.

30. Ibid.

31. *The Walking Dead*, no. 67.

32. We might likewise think of the infamous "zombie baby" moment near the end of the 2004 remake of *Dawn of the Dead*.

33. Robin Wood, "The American Nightmare: Horror in the 70s," in *Hollywood from Vietnam to Reagan . . . and Beyond* (New York: Columbia University Press, 2003), 82.

34. See Alys Eve Weinbaum, *Wayward Reproductions: Genealogies of Race and Nation in Transatlantic Modern Thought* (Durham, N.C.: Duke University Press, 2004), and Amy Kaplan, *The Anarchy of Empire in the Making of U.S. Culture* (Cambridge, Mass.: Harvard University Press, 2005).

35. Priscilla Wald explores zombiism as a science-fictional figure for real-world disease in her book-length study of such "epidemiological horrors," *Contagious: Cultures, Carriers, and the Outbreak Narrative* (Durham, N.C.: Duke University Press, 2008), particularly the way such stories typically employ narratives like the "Patient Zero" origin myth so commonly found in popular accounts of public health crises like SARS and HIV/AIDS.

36. Achille Mbembe, "Necropolitics," *Public Culture* 15, no. 1 (2003): 36.

37. Garrett Hardin, "Lifeboat Ethics: The Case against Helping the Poor," Garrett Hardin Society, June 10, 2003, http://www.garretthardinsociety.org/articles/art_lifeboat_ethics_case_against_helping_poor.html.

38. Sheri Fink, "Strained by Katrina, a Hospital Faced Deadly Choices," *New York Times*, August 1, 2009, http://www.nytimes.com/2009/08/30/magazine/30doctors.html.

39. It should be noted that a grand jury chose not to indict Dr. Pou or two other nurses for the charges brought against them; these charges have now been expunged and the state of Louisiana has agreed to

pay Pou's legal fees. See "Gov. Jindal Signs Bill to Reimburse Anna Pou," Associated Press, July 1, 2009, http://www.abc26.com/news/local/wgno-news-pou070109-story,0,4892289.story.

40. Nicholas Riccardi, "After Blocking the Bridge, Gretna Circles the Wagons: Long Wary of Next-Door New Orleans, the Town Stands by Its Decision to Bar the City's Evacuees," *Los Angeles Times*, September 16, 2005, http://articles.latimes.com/2005/sep/16/nation/na-gretna16.

41. John Burnett, "What Happened on New Orleans' Danziger Bridge?," *All Things Considered*, September 13, 2006, http://www.npr.org/templates/story/story.php?storyId=6063982.

42. Michael Kunzelman, "Cops Could Face Death in Post-Katrina Shootings," Associated Press, July 14, 2010. Since the original publication of this article, the officers involved were convicted of multiple charges related to the case; that conviction was subsequently vacated due to prosecutorial misconduct, with a new trial in 2016 resulting in the officers pleading guilty in exchange for reduced sentencing. See Ken Daley and Emily Lane, "Danziger Bridge Officers Sentenced: 7 to 12 Years for Shooters, Cop in Cover-up Gets 3," *Times-Picayune*, April 20, 2016, http://www.nola.com/crime/index.ssf/2016/04/danziger_bridge_officers_sente.html.

43. Judith Butler, *Precarious Life: The Power of Mourning and Violence* (New York: Verso, 2004), 12.

44. Cord Jefferson, "The Looting Lie," Generation Progress, January 15, 2010, http://genprogress.org/voices/2010/01/16/12964/the-looting-lie/.

45. Linda Polman, "Fear of the Poor Is Hampering Haiti Rescue," *Times of London*, January 18, 2010, http://www.timesonline.co.uk/tol/comment/columnists/guest_contributors/article6991697.ece. It should perhaps be noted that "stampede" is precisely what the zombies do in issues 59–60 of *The Walking Dead*; unthinking, operating on automatic instinct in search of food, they network together into a fierce "herd" and very nearly run our heroes down.

46. Ben Ehrenreich, "Why Did We Focus on Securing Haiti Rather Than Helping Haitians?," *Slate*, January 21, 2010, http://www.slate.com/id/2242078/.

47. *The Walking Dead*, no. 42.

Acknowledgments

This is a many-voiced volume, but beyond the names listed in the table of contents, there are others whose contributions can be heard among these pages. For example, for my part, I would like to acknowledge not only my coauthor of the "Zombie Manifesto," Karen Embry, who indulged me in what must have seemed at the time like a crazy idea, but equally our late professor and mentor Marc Blanchard, who made us write a seminar paper together for his critical theory course as an experiment in transcending intellectual individuality. That was the beginning of our "Zombie Manifesto," of my interest in collaborative scholarship, and of my study of the zombie as an important philosophical figure. Marc's voice carries through the pages of our essay, but also, necessarily, his influence can be felt in the structure of this book as a whole.

There is no one living whose editorial judgment I trust more than Doug Armato's. More than an editor, he is a kind of mentor, and I'm grateful for both his praise and his pushes to do better. I hope that this book is the beginning of a beautiful friendship. His wonderful colleagues at the University of Minnesota Press, especially Erin Warholm-Wohlenhaus but also Gabriel Levin, Mike Stoffel, Rachel Moeller, and Kenneth Wee, have been essential in the endeavor of assembling this volume. I would also like to acknowledge Michel Vrana, who provided the cover design, and copy editor Holly Monteith.

I'm especially grateful to George Pfau for the contribution of his artwork and his thoughtful pairing of his images to the book's parts. George's work is continually an inspiration for my scholarship.

I'd be remiss if I didn't also acknowledge the gang of "zombie scholars" on Twitter (some of whom are students of the monster, others teachers, and all fans) who share their thoughts, reflections, and newly published work and draw attention to their favorite films. This book is for them, but also, in a sense, by them.

Finally, my sweet and long-suffering husband, Joshua Waggoner, is—by virtue of his steadfast support—coeditor and coauthor of everything I do.

All of these voices (and many others, too) can be heard amid the throng.

Further Reading

Ackermann, Hans-W., and Jeanine Gauthier. "The Ways and Nature of the Zombi." *The Journal of American Folklore* 104, no. 414 (1991): 466–94.

Agamben, Giorgio. *Homo Sacer: Sovereign Power and Bare Life*. Stanford, Calif.: Stanford University Press, 1998.

Ahman, Aalya. "Gray Is the New Black: Race, Class, and Zombies." In *Generation Zombie: Essays on the Living Dead in American Culture*, edited by Stephanie Boluk and Wylie Lenz. Jefferson, N.C.: McFarland, 2011.

Aizenberg, Edna. "*I Walked with a Zombie*: The Pleasures and Perils of Postcolonial Hybridity." *World Literature Today* 73, no. 3 (1999): 461–66.

Anderson, Eric, and Taylor Hagood. *Undead Souths: The Gothic and Beyond in Southern Literature and Culture*. Baton Rouge: Louisiana State University Press, 2015.

Auld, Frances. "In the Flesh: The Politics of Apocalyptic Memory." In *The Last Midnight: Essays on Apocalyptic Narratives in Millennial Media*, edited by Leisa Clark, Amanda Firestone, and Mary Pfarr. Jefferson, N.C.: McFarland, 2016.

Austen, Jane, and Seth Grahame-Smith. *Pride and Prejudice and Zombies*. Philadelphia: Quirk Books, 2009.

Austin, Emma. "Zombie Culture: Dissent, Celebration, and the Carnivalesque in Social Spaces." In *The Zombie Renaissance in Popular Culture*, edited by Laura Hubner, Marcus Leaning, and Paul Manning. New York: Palgrave Macmillan, 2015.

Badley, Linda. "Zombie Splatter Comedy from *Dawn* to *Shaun*: Cannibal Carnivalesque." In *Zombie Culture: Autopsies of the Living Dead*, edited by Shawn McIntosh and Marc Leverette. Lanham, Md.: Scarecrow Press, 2008.

Bakhtin, Mikhail. *Rabelais and His World*. Translated by Hélène Iswolsky. Bloomington: Indiana University Press, 1984.

Bakke, Gretchen. "Dead White Men: An Essay on the Changing Dynamics of Race in U.S. Action Cinema." *Anthropological Quarterly* 83, no. 2 (2010): 401–28.

Balaji, Murali, ed. *Thinking Dead: What the Zombie Apocalypse Means*. Lanham, Md.: Lexington Books, 2013.

Baldy, Cutcha Risling. "Why I Teach *The Walking Dead* in My Native Studies Class." *Nerds of Color* (blog), April 24, 2014. http://thenerdsofcolor.org/2014/04/24/why-i-teach-the -walking-dead-in-my-native-studies-classes/.

Balsamo, Anne. "The Virtual Body in Cyberspace." In *The Cybercultures Reader*, edited by Barbara Kennedy and David Bell. New York: Routledge, 2000.

Behuniak, Susan M. "The Living Dead? The Construction of People with Alzheimer's Disease as Zombies." *Ageing and Society* 31, no. 1 (2011): 70–92.

Beisecker, Dave. "Nothing but Meat? Philosophical Zombies and Their Cinematic Counterparts." In *Race, Oppression, and the Zombie: Essays on the Cross-Cultural Appropriations of the Caribbean Tradition*, edited by Christopher M. Moreman and Cory James Rushton. Jefferson, N.C.: McFarland, 2011.

Bernadette Corporation. "Be Corpse." *Afterall: A Journal of Art, Context, and Enquiry* 14 (Autumn 2006): 56–61.

Bishop, Kyle William. *American Zombie Gothic: The Rise and Fall (and Rise) of the Walking Dead in Popular Culture.* Jefferson, N.C.: McFarland, 2010.

———. "Dead Man Still Walking: Explaining the Zombie Renaissance." *Journal of Popular Film and Television* 37, no. 1 (2009): 16–25.

———. "The Idle Proletariat: *Dawn of the Dead*, Consumer Ideology, and the Loss of Productive Labor." *The Journal of Popular Culture* 43, no. 2 (2010): 234–48.

———. "The Sub-Subaltern Monster: Imperialist Hegemony and the Cinematic Voodoo Zombie." *The Journal of American Culture* 31, no. 2 (2008): 141–52.

Bishop, Kyle, and Sarah Juliet Lauro, eds. "After Lives: What's Next for Humanity?" Special issue, *Journal of the Fantastic in the Arts* 25, no. 2–3 (2015).

Bishop, Kyle, and Angela Tenga, eds. *The Written Dead: The Zombie as a Literary Phenomenon.* Jefferson, N.C.: McFarland, forthcoming.

Boehm, Chris. "Apocalyptic Utopia: The Zombie and the (r)Evolution of Subjectivity." In *We're All Infected: Essays on AMC's "The Walking Dead" and the Fate of the Human*, edited by Dawn Keetley. Jefferson, N.C.: McFarland, 2014.

Boelderl, Arthur, and Daniela Mayr. "The Undead and the Living Dead: Images of Vampires and Zombies in Popular Culture." *The Journal of Psychohistory* 23, no. 1 (1995): 51–65.

Bohman, Erik. "Zombie Media." In *The Year's Work at the Zombie Research Center*, edited by Edward Comentale and Aaron Jaffe. Bloomington: Indiana University Press, 2014.

Boluk, Stephanie, and Wylie Lenz, eds. *Generation Zombie: Essays on the Living Dead in American Culture.* Jefferson, N.C.: McFarland, 2011.

———. "Infection, Media, and Capitalism: From Early Modern Plagues to Postmodern Zombies." *Journal for Early Modern Cultural Studies* 10, no. 2 (2010): 126–47.

Boon, Kevin. "The Zombie as Other: Mortality and the Monstrous in the Post-Nuclear Age." In *Better Off Dead: The Evolution of the Zombie as Posthuman*, edited by Deborah Christie and Sarah Juliet Lauro. New York: Fordham University Press.

Botting, Fred. "Affect-less: Zombie-Horror-Shock." *English Language Notes* 48, no. 1 (2010): 177–90.

———. "Zombie Death Drive: Between Gothic and Science Fiction." In *Gothic Science*

Fiction 1980–2010, edited by Sara Wasson and Emily Alder. Liverpool, U.K.: Liverpool University Press, 2011.

———. "Zombie London: Unexceptionalities of the New World Order." In *London Gothic: Place, Space, and the Gothic Imagination*, edited by Lawrence Phillips and Anne Witchard. London: Continuum, 2010.

Braun, Michele. "It's So Hard to Get Good Help These Days: Zombies as a Culturally Stabilizing Force in *Fido* (2006)." In *Race, Oppression, and the Zombie: Essays on the Cross-Cultural Appropriations of the Caribbean Tradition*, edited by Christopher M. Moreman and Cory James Rushton. Jefferson, N.C.: McFarland, 2011.

Brock, Richard. "Of Zombies, AIDS, and 'Africa': Non-Western Disease and the 'Raciocultural' Imagination." *Reconstruction: Studies in Contemporary Culture* 12, no. 4 (2013). http://reconstruction.eserver.org/Issues/124/Brock.shtml.

Brooks, Max. *World War Z: An Oral History of the Zombie War.* New York: Three Rivers Press, 2006.

———. *The Zombie Survival Guide: Complete Protection from the Living Dead.* New York: Three Rivers Press, 2003.

Bruce, Barbara. "Guess Who's Going to Be Dinner: Sidney Poitier, Black Militancy, and the Ambivalence of Race in Romero's *Night of the Living Dead*." In *Race, Oppression, and the Zombie: Essays on the Cross-Cultural Appropriations of the Caribbean Tradition*, edited by Christopher M. Moreman and Cory James Rushton. Jefferson, N.C.: McFarland, 2011.

Bukatman, Scott. *Terminal Identity: The Virtual Subject in Postmodern Science Fiction.* Durham, N.C.: Duke University Press, 1993.

Butler, Judith. *Precarious Life: The Powers of Mourning and Violence.* London: Verso, 2004.

Cameron, Allan. "Zombie Media: Transmission, Reproduction, and the Digital Dead." *Cinema Journal* 52, no. 1 (2012): 66–89.

Canavan, Gerry. "Fighting a War You've Already Lost: Zombies and Zombis in Firefly/Serenity and Dollhouse." *Science Fiction Film and Television* 4, no. 2 (2011): 173–203.

———. "'We Are the Walking Dead': Race, Time, and Survival in Zombie Narrative." *Extrapolation* 1, no. 3 (2010): 431–53.

Carr, Diane. "Textual Analysis, Digital Games, Zombies." Paper presented at the DiGRA Conference, London, 2009.

Carroll, Jordan S. "The Aesthetics of Risk in *Dawn of the Dead* and *28 Days Later.*" *Journal of the Fantastic in the Arts* 23, no. 1 (2012): 40–59.

Carroll, Noël. *The Philosophy of Horror: or, Paradoxes of the Heart.* New York: Routledge, 2003.

Castronovo, Russ. *Necrocitizenship: Death, Eroticism, and the Public Sphere in the Nineteenth-Century United States.* Durham, N.C.: Duke University Press, 2001.

Chalmers, David. "Zombies on the Web." http://consc.net/zombies.html.

Chen, Mel Y. "Lurching for the Cure? On Zombies and the Reproduction of Disability." *GLQ, A Journal of Lesbian and Gay Studies* 21, no. 1 (2015): 24–31.

Christiansen, Steen Ledet. "Speaking the Undead: Uncanny Aurality in Pontypool." *Cinephile* 6, no. 2 (2010): 4–8.

Christie, Deborah, and Sarah Juliet Lauro, eds. *Better Off Dead: The Evolution of the Zombie as Posthuman*. New York: Fordham University Press, 2011.

Clark, Simon. "The Undead Martyr: Sex, Death, and Revolution in George Romero's Zombie Films." In *The Undead and Philosophy*, edited by Richard Greene and K. Silem Mohammad. Chicago: Open Court, 2006.

Clover, Carol J. *Men, Women, and Chain Saws: Gender in the Modern Horror Film*. 1994. Reprint, Princeton, N.J.: Princeton University Press, 2015.

Clover, Joshua. "Swans and Zombies: Neoliberalism's Permanent Contradiction." *The Nation*, April 25, 2011.

Cocarla, Sasha. "A Love Worth Un-undying For: Neoliberalism and Queered Sexuality in Warm Bodies." In *Zombies and Sexuality: Essays on Desire and the Living Dead*, edited by Shaka McGlotten and Steve Jones. Jefferson, N.C.: McFarland, 2014.

———. "Reclaiming Public Spaces through Performance of the Zombie Walk." In *Braaaiiinnnsss! From Academics to Zombies*, edited by Robert Smith. Ottawa: University of Ottawa Press, 2011.

Cohen, Jeffrey Jerome, ed. *Monster Theory: Reading Culture*. Minneapolis: University of Minnesota Press, 1996.

———. *Prismatic Ecology: Ecotheory beyond Green*. Minneapolis: University of Minnesota Press, 2014.

Comaroff, Jean, and John Comaroff. "Alien-Nation: Zombies, Immigrants, and Millennial Capitalism." *The South Atlantic Quarterly* 101, no. 4 (2002): 779–805.

Comentale, Edward P. "Zombie Race." In *The Year's Work at the Zombie Research Center*, edited by Edward Comentale and Aaron Jaffe. Bloomington: Indiana University Press, 2014.

Comentale, Edward P., and Aaron Jaffe, eds. *The Year's Work at the Zombie Research Center*. Bloomington: Indiana University Press, 2014.

Cooke, Jennifer. *Legacies of Plague in Literature, Theory, and Film*. New York: Palgrave Macmillan, 2009.

Davis, Wade. "The Ethnobiology of the Haitian Zombi." *Journal of Ethnopharmacology* 9 (1983): 85–104.

———. *Passage of Darkness: Ethnobiology of the Haitian Zombie*. Chapel Hill: University of North Carolina Press, 1989.

———. *The Serpent and the Rainbow*. New York: Warner Books, 1985.

Dayan, Joan. "The Call of the Gods, the Making of History." In *Kafou: Haiti, Art, and Vodou*, edited by Alex Farquharson and Leah Gordon. Nottingham, U.K.: Nottingham Contemporary, 2012.

———. *Haiti, History, and the Gods*. Berkeley: University of California Press, 1998.

de Blessebois, Pierre-Corneille. *Le Zombi du Gran Perou*. Rouen, France, 1697.

Degoul, Franck. "Dos a la Vie, Dos a la Mort: Une exploration ethnographique des figures de la servitude dans l'imaginaire haïtien de la zombification." PhD diss., Bibliothèque et Archives Canada, 2007.

———. "We Are the Mirror of Your Fears: Haitian Identity and Zombification." In *Better Off Dead: The Evolution of the Zombie as Posthuman*, edited by Deborah Christie and Sarah Juliet Lauro. New York: Fordham University Press, 2011.

Deleuze, Gilles. *Difference and Repetition.* Translated by Paul Patton. New York: Columbia University Press, 1994.

Deleuze, Gilles, and Félix Guattari. *Anti-Oedipus: Capitalism and Schizophrenia.* Minneapolis: University of Minnesota Press, 2003.

Dendle, Peter. "The Zombie as Barometer of Cultural Anxiety." In *Monsters and the Monstrous: Myths and Metaphors of Enduring Evil,* edited by Niall Scott. New York: Rodopi, 2007.

———. *The Zombie Movie Encyclopedia.* Jefferson, N.C.: McFarland, 2001.

———. *The Zombie Movie Encyclopedia.* Vol. 2, *2000–2010.* Jefferson, N.C.: McFarland, 2012.

———. "Zombie Movies and the 'Millennial Generation.'" In *Better Off Dead: The Evolution of the Zombie as Posthuman,* edited by Deborah Christie and Sarah Juliet Lauro. New York: Fordham University Press, 2011.

Deren, Maya. *Divine Horsemen: The Living Gods of Haiti.* 1953. Reprint, New Paltz, N.Y.: McPherson, 1983.

Desjardins, Lisa, and Richard Emerson. *Zombie Economics: A Guide to Personal Finance.* New York: Avery, 2011.

Desmangles, Leslie. *The Faces of the Gods: Voodoo and Roman Catholicism in Haiti.* Chapel Hill: University of North Carolina Press, 1992.

Deuze, Mark. "Living as a Zombie in Media Is the Only Way to Survive." *Journal of the Fantastic in the Arts* 25, no. 2–3 (2015): 307–23.

Dillard, Richard, and Henry Wilde. "*Night of the Living Dead*: It's Not Like Just a Wind That's Passing Through." In *American Horrors: Essays on the Modern American Horror Film,* edited by Gregory Waller. Chicago: University of Illinois Press, 1987.

Do Vale, Simone. "Trash Mob: Zombie Walks and the Positivity of Monsters in Western Popular Culture." *At the Interface/Probing the Boundaries* 70 (2010): 191–202.

Drake, Michael. "Zombinations: Reading the Undead as Debt and Guilt in the National Imaginary." In *Monster Culture in the 21st century,* edited by Marina Levina and Diem-my T. Bui. New York: Bloomsbury, 2013.

Drezner, Daniel. *Theories of International Politics and Zombies.* Princeton, N.J.: Princeton University Press, 2011.

Duane, Anna Mae. "Dead *and* Disabled: The Crawling Monsters of the Walking Dead." *Not Even Past* (blog), February 4, 2014. http://annamaeduane.com/2014/02/04/the-crawling-dead-disability-and-the-zombies-revenge/.

———. "Ebola, Zombies, and Our Viral Past." *Avidly,* October 14, 2014. http://avidly.lareviewofbooks.org/2014/10/14/ebola-zombies-and-our-viral-past/.

Duncan, Glen. "A Plague of Urban Undead in Lower Manhattan." *New York Times,* October 28, 2011.

Eburne, Jonathan. "Zombie Arts and Letters." In *The Year's Work at the Zombie Research Center,* edited by Edward Comentale and Aaron Jaffe. Bloomington: Indiana University Press, 2014.

Ellis, Markman. *The History of Gothic Fiction.* Edinburgh: Edinburgh University Press, 2005.

Fanon, Frantz. *Black Skin, White Masks.* New York: Grove Press, 1967.

———. *The Wretched of the Earth.* New York: Grove Press, 1963.

Fay, Jennifer. "Dead Subjectivity: White Zombie, Black Baghdad." *New Centennial Review* 8, no. 1 (2008): 81–101.

Firestone, Amanda. "Running for My Life: Convergence Culture, Transmedia Storytelling, and Community Building in the Smartphone Application Zombies, Run!" In *The Last Midnight: Essays on Apocalyptic Narratives in Millennial Media,* edited by Leisa Clark, Amanda Firestone, and Mary Pfarr. Jefferson, N.C.: McFarland, 2016.

Frederickson, Kathleen. "Up with Dead Privates." *In Media Res,* October 17, 2010.

Froula, Anna. "Prolepsis and the 'War on Terror': Zombie Pathology and the Culture of Fear in *28 Days Later.*" In *Reframing 9/11: Film, Popular Culture, and the "War on Terror,"* edited by Jeff Birkenstein, Anna Froula, and Karen Randell. New York: Bloomsbury, 2010.

Gay, Roxane. "On the Death of Sandra Bland and Our Vulnerable Bodies." *New York Times,* July 24, 2015.

Geyser, Hanli. "Return to Darkness: Representations of Africa in Resident Evil 5." In *Thinking Dead: What the Zombie Apocalypse Means,* edited by Murali Balaji. Lanham, Md.: Lexington Books, 2013.

Giroux, Henry. *Zombie Politics and Culture in the Age of Casino Capitalism.* New York: Peter Lang, 2011.

Glover, Kaiama. "Exploiting the Undead: The Usefulness of the Zombie in Haitian Literature." *Journal of Haitian Studies* 11, no. 2 (2005): 105–21.

———. *Haiti Unbound: A Spiralist Challenge to the Postcolonial Canon.* Vol. 15. Liverpool, U.K.: Liverpool University Press, 2010.

———. "New Narratives of Haiti; or, How to Empathize with a Zombie." *Small Axe* 16, no. 3 (2012): 199–207.

Gonzalez, Christopher. "Zombie Nationalism: Robert Rodriguez's *Planet Terror* as Immigration Satire." In *Undead in the West: Vampires, Zombies, Mummies, and Ghosts on the Cinematic Frontier,* edited by Cynthia Miller and Bowdoin Van Riper. Lanham, Md.: Scarecrow Press, 2012.

Grant, Barry Keith, ed. *The Dread of Difference: Gender and the Horror Film.* 1996. Reprint, Austin: University of Texas Press, 2015.

———. "Taking Back the *Night of the Living Dead*: George Romero, Feminism, and the Horror Film." In *The Dread of Difference: Gender and the Horror Film,* edited by Barry Keith Grant. Austin: University of Texas Press, 2015.

Greene, Richard, and K. Silem Mohammad, eds. *The Undead and Philosophy: Chicken Soup for the Soulless.* Chicago: Open Court, 2006.

Gunn, Joshua, and Shaun Treat. "Zombie Trouble: A Propaedeutic on Ideological Subjectification and the Unconscious." *Quarterly Journal of Speech* 91, no. 2 (2005): 144–74.

Hakola, Outi. "Colliding Modalities and Receding Frontier in George Romero's *Land of the Dead.*" In *Undead in the West: Vampires, Zombies, Mummies, and Ghosts on the Cinematic Frontier,* edited by Cynthia Miller and Bowdoin Van Riper. Lanham, Md.: Scarecrow Press, 2012.

Halberstam, Judith. *Skin Shows: Gothic Horror and the Technology of Monsters.* Durham, N.C.: Duke University Press, 1995.

Hamako, Eric. "Zombie Orientals Ate My Brain! Orientalism in Contemporary Zombie Stories." In *Race, Oppression, and the Zombie: Essays on the Cross-Cultural Appropriations of the Caribbean Tradition*, edited by Christopher M. Moreman and Cory James Rushton. Jefferson, N.C.: McFarland, 2011.

Hand, Richard J. "Proliferating Horrors: Survival Horror and the Resident Evil Franchise." In *Horror Film: Creating and Marketing Fear*, edited by Steffen Hantke. Jackson: University Press of Mississippi, 2004.

Hannabach, Cathy. "Queering and Cripping the End of the World: Disability, Sexuality, and Race in *The Walking Dead*." In *Zombies and Sexuality: Essays on Desire and the Living Dead*, edited by Shaka McGlotten and Steve Jones. Jefferson, N.C.: McFarland, 2014.

Haraway, Donna J. *Simians, Cyborgs, and Women: The Reinvention of Nature*. New York: Routledge, 2013.

Hardt, Michael, and Antonio Negri. *Empire*. Cambridge, Mass.: Harvard University Press, 2009.

Harman, Chris. *Zombie Capitalism: Global Crisis and the Relevance of Marx*. Chicago: Haymarket, 2009.

Harper, Stephen. "I Could Kiss You, You Bitch: Race, Gender, and Sexuality in Resident Evil and Resident Evil 2: Apocalypse." *Jump Cut: A Review of Contemporary Media* 47 (2007). https://www.ejumpcut.org/archive/jc49.2007/HarperResEvil/.

———. "*Night of the Living Dead*: Reappraising an Undead Classic." *Bright Lights Film Journal* 50 (2005). http://brightlightsfilm.com/night-living-dead-reappraising-undead-classic/#.WOQ5gWTyvBI.

———. "Zombies, Malls, and the Consumerism Debate: George Romero's *Dawn of the Dead*." *Americana: The Journal of American Popular Culture* 1, no. 2 (2002). http://www.americanpopularculture.com/journal/articles/fall_2002/harper.htm.

Hassler-Forrest, Dan. "Zombie Spaces." In *The Year's Work at the Zombie Research Center*, edited by Edward Comentale and Aaron Jaffe. Bloomington: Indiana University Press, 2014.

Hauser, Larry. "Revenge of the Zombies." https://philpapers.org/rec/HAUROT.

———. "Zombies, *Blade Runner*, and the Mind–Body Problem." In *The Undead and Philosophy*, edited by Richard Greene and K. Silem Mohammad. Chicago: Open Court, 2006.

Hayles, Katherine N. *How We Became Posthuman: Virtual Bodies in Cybernetics, Literature, and Informatics*. Chicago: University of Chicago Press, 1999.

Hearn, Lafcadio. *Two Years in the French West Indies*. New York: Harpers, 1890.

Heckman, Christine. "Roadside 'Vigil' for the Dead: Cannibalism, Fossil Fuels, and the American Dream." In *We're All Infected: Essays on AMC's "The Walking Dead" and the Fate of the Human*, edited by Dawn Keetley. Jefferson, N.C.: McFarland, 2014.

Hendershot, Cynthia. *I Was a Cold War Monster: Horror Films, Eroticism, and the Cold War Imagination*. Bowling Green, Ohio: Popular Press, 2001.

Herskovitz, Melville Jean. *Dahomey, an Ancient West African Kingdom*. Vol. 2. Evanston, Ill.: Northwestern University Press, 1967.

———. *Life in a Haitian Valley*. 1937. Reprint, New York: Octagon Books, 1964.

Hertz, Garnet, and Jussi Parikka. "Zombie Media: Circuit Bending Media Archaeology into an Art Method." *Leonardo* 45, no. 5 (2012): 424–30.

Higgin, Tanner. "Gamic Race: Logics of Difference in Videogame Culture." PhD diss., University of California, Irvine, 2012.

Horkheimer, Max, and Theodor Adorno. *Dialectic of Enlightenment: Philosophical Fragments.* Stanford, Calif.: Stanford University Press, 2002.

Hubner, Laura, Marcus Leaning, and Paul Manning. *The Zombie Renaissance in Popular Culture.* New York: Palgrave Macmillan, 2014.

Hurston, Zora Neale. *Tell My Horse.* Philadelphia: J. B. Lippincott, 1938.

Ingles, David. "Putting the Undead to Work: Wade Davis, Haitian Vodou, and the Social Uses of the Zombie." In *Race, Oppression, and the Zombie: Essays on the Cross-Cultural Appropriations of the Caribbean Tradition,* edited by Christopher M. Moreman and Cory James Rushton. Jefferson, N.C.: McFarland, 2011.

Jaffe, Aaron. "13 Ways of Looking at a Zombie." *American Book Review* 33, no. 6 (2012): 9–10.

Jones, Steve. "Gender Monstrosity: Deadgirl and the Sexual Politics of Zombie-Rape." *Feminist Media Studies* 13, no. 3 (2013): 525–39.

———. "Pretty Dead: Sociosexuality, Rationality, and the Transition into Zom-Being." In *Zombies and Sexuality: Essays on Desire and the Living Dead,* edited by Shaka McGlotten and Steve Jones. Jefferson, N.C.: McFarland, 2014.

———. "XXXombies: Economies of Desire and Disgust." In *Thinking Dead: What the Zombie Apocalypse Means,* edited by Murali Balaji. Lanham, Md.: Lexington Books, 2013.

Kay, Glenn, and Stuart Gordon. *Zombie Movies: The Ultimate Guide.* Chicago: Chicago Review Press, 2008.

Kee, Chera. "'They Are Not Men . . . They Are Dead Bodies': From Cannibal to Zombie and Back Again." In *Better Off Dead: The Evolution of the Zombie as Posthuman,* edited by Deborah Christie and Sarah Juliet Lauro. New York: Fordham University Press, 2011.

Keetley, Dawn, ed. *We're All Infected: Essays on AMC's "The Walking Dead" and the Fate of the Human.* Jefferson, N.C.: McFarland, 2014.

———. "Zombie Evolution: Stephen King's *Cell,* George Romero's *Diary of the Dead,* and the Future of the Human." *Americana: The Journal of American Popular Culture, 1900 to Present* 11, no. 2 (2012). http://www.americanpopularculture.com/journal/articles/fall_2012/keetley.htm.

Kenemore, Scott. *The Zen of Zombie: Better Living through the Undead.* New York: Skyhorse, 2007.

Kirk, Robert. *Zombies and Consciousness.* Oxford: Oxford University Press, 2007.

———. "Zombies vs. Materialists." *Proceedings of the Aristotelian Society* 48 (1974): 135–52.

Kirkland, Ewan. "Horror Videogames and the Uncanny." In *Breaking New Ground: Innovation in Games, Play, Practice, and Theory: Proceedings of the 2009 Digital Games Research Association Conference.* N.p.: DiGRA, 2009.

———. "Resident Evil's Typewriter." *Games and Culture* 4, no. 2 (2009): 115–26.

Kirkman, Robert, et al. *The Walking Dead*. Berkeley, Calif.: Image Comics, 2003 to present.

Koch, Christof. "On the Zombie Within." *Nature* 411 (2001): 893.

———. *The Quest for Consciousness: A Neurobiological Approach*. Englewood, Colo.: Roberts, 2004.

Kordas, Ann. "New South, New Immigrants, New Women, New Zombies: The Historical Development of the Zombie in American Popular Culture." In *Race, Oppression, and the Zombie: Essays on the Cross-Cultural Appropriations of the Caribbean Tradition*, edited by Christopher M. Moreman and Cory James Rushton. Jefferson, N.C.: McFarland, 2011.

Kristeva, Julia. *Powers of Horror: An Essay on Abjection*. New York: Columbia University Press, 1982.

Krzywinska, Tanya. "Zombies in Gamespace: Form, Context, and Meaning in Zombie-Based Video Games." In *Zombie Culture: Autopsies of the Living Dead*, edited by Shawn McIntosh and Marc Leverette. Lanham, Md.: Scarecrow Press, 2008.

Laguerre, Michel S. *Voodoo and Politics in Haiti*. New York: St. Martin's Press, 1989.

Langley, Travis, and John Russo. *The Walking Dead: Psychology*. New York: Sterling, 2015.

Laroche, Maximilien. "The Myth of the Zombi." In *Exile and Tradition: Studies in African and Caribbean Literature*, edited by Roland Smith. New York: Africana, 1976.

Larsen, Lars Bang. "Zombies of Immaterial Labor: The Modern Monster and the Death of Death." *E-Flux* 14 (2010). http://www.e-flux.com/journal/15/61295/zombies-of -immaterial-labor-the-modern-monster-and-the-death-of-death/.

Latham, Rob. *Consuming Youth: Vampires, Cyborgs, and the Culture of Consumption*. Chicago: University of Chicago Press, 2002.

Lauro, Sarah J. "Blurred Lines and Human Objects: The Zombie Art of George Pfau." In *Graphic Treatment*, edited by Lorenzo Servitje and Sherryl Vint. University Park: Penn State University Press, 2016.

———. "The Eco-Zombie: Environmental Critique in Zombie Films." In *Generation Zombie: Essays on the Living Dead in American Culture*, edited by Stephanie Boluk and Wylie Lenz. Jefferson, N.C.: McFarland, 2011.

———. "For the Ethical Treatment of Zombies." *Incognitum Hactenus* 3 (2012). https:// incognitumhactenus.wordpress.com/volume3/.

———. "Playing Dead: Zombies Invade Performance Art . . . and Your Neighborhood." In *Better Off Dead: The Evolution of the Zombie as Posthuman*, edited by Deborah Christie and Sarah Juliet Lauro. New York: Fordham University Press, 2011.

———. "Sois Mort et Tais Toi: Zombie Mobs and Student Protest." In *Zombies in the Academy: Living Death in Higher Education*, edited by Andrew Whelan, Ruth Walker, and Christopher Moore. Bristol, U.K.: Intellect, 2013.

———. *The Transatlantic Zombie: Slavery, Rebellion, and Living Death*. New Brunswick, N.J.: Rutgers University Press, 2015.

Lauro, Sarah Juliet, and Karen Embry. "A Zombie Manifesto: The Nonhuman Condition in the Era of Advanced Capitalism." *Boundary 2* 35, no. 1 (2008): 85–108.

Leverette, Marc. "The Funk of Forty Thousand Years; or, How the (Un)Dead Get Their

Groove On." In *Zombie Culture: Autopsies of the Living Dead*, edited by Shawn McIntosh and Marc Leverette. Lanham, Md.: Scarecrow Press, 2008.

Levina, Marina. "Cultural Narratives of Blood." In *Monster Culture in the 21st Century: A Reader*, edited by Marina Levina and Diem-My T. Bui. New York: Bloomsbury, 2013.

Lewis, Tyson. "Ztopia: Lessons in Post-vital Politics in George Romero's Zombie Films." In *Generation Zombie: Essays on the Living Dead in American Culture*, edited by Stephanie Boluk and Wylie Lenz. Jefferson, N.C.: McFarland, 2011.

Linnemann, Travis, Tyler Wall, and Edward Green. "The Walking Dead and Killing State: Zombification and the Normalization of Police Violence." *Theoretical Criminology* 18, no. 4 (2014): 506–27.

Loudermilk, A. "Eating 'Dawn' in the Dark: Zombie Desire and Commodified Identity in George A. Romero's 'Dawn of the Dead.'" *Journal of Consumer Culture* 3, no. 1 (2003): 83–108.

Lowder, James. *Triumph of "The Walking Dead": Robert Kirkman's Zombie Epic on Page and Screen*. Dallas, Tex.: SmartPop, 2011.

Lowenstein, Adam. "Living Dead: Fearful Attractions of Film." *Representations* 110, no. 1 (2010): 105–28.

———. *Shocking Representation: Historical Trauma, National Cinema, and the Modern Horror Film*. New York: Columbia University Press, 2005.

Lucas, Rafaël. "The Aesthetics of Degradation in Haitian Literature." *Research in African Literatures* 35, no. 2 (2004): 54–74.

MacCormack, Patricia. "Zombies without Organs: Gender, Flesh, and Fissure." In *Zombie Culture: Autopsies of the Living Dead*, edited by Shawn McIntosh and Marc Leverette. Lanham, Md.: Scarecrow Press, 2008.

MacGaffrey, Wyatt. *Religion and Society in Central Africa: The BaKongo of Lower Zaire*. Chicago: University of Chicago Press, 1986.

Mahoney, Phillip. "Mass Psychology and the Analysis of the Zombie: From Suggestion to Contagion." In *Generation Zombie: Essays on the Living Dead in American Culture*, edited by Stephanie Boluk and Wylie Lenz. Jefferson, N.C.: McFarland, 2011.

Mantz, Jeffrey W. "On the Frontlines of the Zombie War in the Congo: Digital Technology, the Trade in Conflict Minerals, and Zombification." In *Monster Culture in the 21st Century: A Reader*, edited by Marina Levina and Diem-My T. Bui. New York: Bloomsbury, 2013.

Massumi, Brian. *Parables for the Virtual: Movement, Affect, Sensation*. Durham, N.C.: Duke University Press, 2002.

May, Jeff. "Zombie Geographies and the Undead City." *Social and Cultural Geography* 11, no. 3 (2010): 285–98.

May, Rebecca, ed. *Zombology: A Zombie Anthology*. N.p.: Library of the Living Dead Press, 2009.

Mbembe, Achille. "Necropolitics." *Public Culture* 15, no. 1 (2003): 11–40.

———. "On the Postcolony." In *Post-colonial Studies Reader*, 2nd ed., edited by Bill Ashcroft, Gareth Griffiths, and Helen Tiffin. London: Routledge, 2006.

McAlister, Elizabeth. *Rara! Vodou, Power, and Performance in Haiti and Its Diaspora*. Berkeley: University of California Press, 2002.

———. "Slaves, Cannibals, and Infected Hyper-Whites: The Race and Religion of Zombies." *Anthropological Quarterly* 85, no. 2 (2012): 457–86.

———. "A Sorcerer's Bottle: The Art of Magic in Haiti." In *Sacred Arts of Haitian Vodou*, edited by Donald Cosentino. Los Angeles, Calif.: UCLA Fowler Museum of Cultural History, 1995.

Mcdonald, Jillian. *Horror Makeup.* Exhibition notes. Brooklyn, N.Y., 2006.

———. "Zombie Portraits." 2007. http://jillianmcdonald.net/projects/zombie_lenticular .html.

McFarland, James. "Philosophy of the Living Dead: At the Origin of the Zombie Image." *Cultural Critique* 90 (2015): 22–63.

McGlotten, Shaka. "Dead and Live Life: Zombies, Queers, and Online Sociality." In *Generation Zombie: Essays on the Living Dead in American Culture*, edited by Stephanie Boluk and Wylie Lenz. Jefferson, N.C.: McFarland, 2011.

McGlotten, Shaka, and Steve Jones. *Zombies and Sexuality: Essays on Desire and the Living Dead.* Jefferson, N.C.: McFarland, 2014.

McIntosh, Shawn, and Marc Leverette, eds. *Zombie Culture: Autopsies of the Living Dead.* Lanham, Md.: Scarecrow Press, 2008.

McLuhan, Marshall. *Understanding Media: The Extensions of Man.* Cambridge, Mass.: MIT Press, 1994.

McNally, David. *Monsters of the Market: Zombies, Vampires, and Global Capitalism.* Chicago: Haymarket, 2011.

Mecum, Ryan. *Zombie Haiku.* Cincinnati, Ohio: How Books, 2008.

Mercer, Kobena. *Welcome to the Jungle: New Positions in Black Cultural Studies.* New York: Routledge, 2013.

Métraux, Alfred. *Haiti: Black Peasants and Their Religion.* Translated by Peter Lengyl. London: George G. Haarap, 1960.

———. *Le Vaudou Haïtien.* Paris: Gallimard, 1958.

———. *Voodoo in Haiti.* Translated by Hugo Charteris. New York: Oxford University Press, 1959.

Michel, Claudine, and Patrick Bellegarde-Smith, eds. *Invisible Powers: Vodou in Haitian Life and Culture.* New York: Palgrave Macmillan, 2006.

Miller, Cynthia J., and A. Bowdoin Van Riper, eds. *Undead in the West: Vampires, Zombies, Mummies, and Ghosts on the Cinematic Frontier.* Lanham, Md.: Scarecrow Press, 2012.

———, eds. *Undead in the West II: They Just Keep Coming.* Lanham, Md.: Scarecrow Press, 2013.

Mogk, Matt, and Max Brooks. *Everything You Ever Wanted to Know about Zombies.* New York: Gallery Books, 2011.

Mohammad, K. Silem. "Zombies, Rest, and Motion." In *The Undead and Philosophy*, edited by Richard Greene and K. Silem Mohammad. Chicago: Open Court, 2006.

Mora, Arnau Roig. "The Necropolitics of the Apocalypse: Queer Zombies in the Cinema of Bruce LaBruce." In *Thinking Dead: What the Zombie Apocalypse Means*, edited by Murali Balaji. Lanham, Md.: Lexington Books, 2013.

Morehead, John. "Zombie Walks, Zombie Jesus, and the Eschatology of Postmodern

Flesh." In *The Undead and Theology,* edited by Kim Paffenroth and John Morehead. Eugene, Oreg.: Pickwick, 2012.

Moreman, Christopher M. "Dharma of the Living Dead: A Meditation on the Meaning of the Hollywood Zombie." *Studies in Religion/Sciences Religieuses* 39, no. 2 (2010): 263–81.

Moreman, Christopher M., and Cory James Rushton, eds. *Race, Oppression, and the Zombie: Essays on the Cross-Cultural Appropriations of the Caribbean Tradition.* Jefferson, N.C.: McFarland, 2011.

———, eds. *Zombies Are Us: Essays on the Humanity of the Walking Dead.* Jefferson, N.C.: McFarland, 2011.

Moretti, Franco. *Signs Taken for Wonders: On the Sociology of Literary Forms.* London: Verso, 1983.

Morton, Seth. "Zombie Politics." In *The Year's Work at the Zombie Research Center,* edited by Edward Comentale and Aaron Jaffe. Bloomington: Indiana University Press, 2014.

Mouflard, Claire. "Zombies and Refugees: Variations on the 'Post-human' and the 'Non-human' in Robin Campillo's *Les Revenants* (2004) and Fabrice Gobert's *Les Revenants* (2012–2015)." *Humanities* 5 (2016): 1–11.

Muntean, Nick. "Nuclear Death and Radical Hope in *Dawn of the Dead* and *On the Beach.*" In *Better Off Dead: The Evolution of the Zombie as Posthuman,* edited by Deborah Christie and Sarah Juliet Lauro. New York: Fordham University Press, 2011.

Muntean, Nick, and Matthew Thomas Payne. "Attack of the Livid Dead: Recalibrating Terror in the Post–September 11 Zombie Film." In *The War on Terror and American Popular Culture: September 11 and Beyond,* edited by Andrew Schopp and Matthew Hill. Madison, N.J.: Fairleigh Dickinson University Press, 2009.

Munz, Philip, Ioan Hudea, Joe Imad, and Robert J. Smith. "When Zombies Attack! Mathematical Modelling of an Outbreak of Zombie Infection." *Infectious Disease Modelling Research Progress* 4 (2009): 133–50.

Murray, Jessica. "A Zombie Apocalypse: Opening Representational Spaces for Alternative Constructions of Gender and Sexuality." *Journal of Literary Studies* 29, no. 4 (2013): 1–19.

Nealon, Jeffrey. "Afterword: Zombie Archive." In *The Year's Work at the Zombie Research Center,* edited by Edward Comentale and Aaron Jaffe. Bloomington: Indiana University Press, 2014.

Nelms, Taylor C. "The Zombie Bank and the Magic of Finance: or, How to Write a History of Crisis." *Journal of Cultural Economy* 5, no. 2 (2012): 231–46.

Newbury, Michael. "Fast Zombie/Slow Zombie: Food Writing, Horror Movies, and Agribusiness Apocalypse." *American Literary History* 24, no. 1 (2012): 87–114.

Newitz, Annalee. "This Interactive Painting Can Explain Why We Are Still Obsessed with Zombies." March 5, 2013. http://www.io9.com/.

———. *Pretend We're Dead: Capitalist Monsters in American Pop Culture.* Durham, N.C.: Duke University Press, 2006.

Niehaus, Isak. "Witches and Zombies of the South African Lowveld: Discourse, Accusations, and Subjective Reality." *Journal of the Royal Anthropological Institute* 11, no. 2 (2005): 191–210.

Norris, Andrew. "Giorgio Agamben and the Politics of the Living Dead." *Diacritics* 30, no. 4 (2000): 38–58.

Nuckols, Ben. "Humans vs. Zombies: New Sport Sweeping College Campuses." *The Herald* (Sierra Vista, Ariz.), December 9, 2008. http://www.svherald.com/articles /2008/12/10/sports/features/doc493f5267c6f98956874247.txt.

Nyong'o, Tavia. "The Scene of Occupation." *The Drama Review* 56, no. 4 (2012): 136–49.

Orpana, Simon. "Spooks of Biopower: The Uncanny Carnivalesque of Zombie Walks." *TOPIA: Canadian Journal of Cultural Studies* 25 (2011): 153–76.

Paffenroth, Kim. "Apocalyptic Images and Prophetic Function in Zombie Films." In *The Undead and Theology,* edited by Kim Paffenroth and John Morehead. Eugene, Oreg.: Pickwick, 2012.

———. *Gospel of the Living Dead: George Romero's Visions of Hell on Earth.* Waco, Tex.: Baylor University Press, 2006.

Paffenroth, Kim, and John Morehead, eds. *The Undead and Theology.* Eugene, Oreg.: Pickwick, 2012.

Pagano, David. "The Space of Apocalypse in Zombie Cinema." In *Zombie Culture: Autopsies of the Living Dead,* edited by Shawn McIntosh and Marc Leverette. Lanham, Md.: Scarecrow Press, 2008.

Paik, Peter. "Zombies and Other Strangers." *University of Minnesota Press* (blog), January 26, 2011. http://www.uminnpressblog.com/2011/01/zombies-and-other-strangers -thoughts-on.html.

Paravisini-Gebert, Lizabeth. "Women Possessed: Eroticism and Exoticism in the Representation of Woman as Zombie." In *Sacred Possessions: Vodou, Santeria, Obeah, and the Caribbean,* edited by Margarite Fernandez Olmos and Lizabeth Paravisini-Gebert. New Brunswick, N.J.: Rutgers University Press, 1997.

Patterson, Natasha. "Cannibalizing Gender and Genre: A Feminist Re-vision of George Romero's Zombie Films." In *Zombie Culture: Autopsies of the Living Dead,* edited by Shawn McIntosh and Marc Leverette. Lanham, Md.: Scarecrow Press, 2008.

Patterson, Orlando. *Slavery and Social Death: A Comparative Study.* Cambridge, Mass.: Harvard University Press, 1982.

Peake, Bryce. "He Is Dead, and He Is Continuing to Die: A Feminist Psycho-semiotic Reflection on Men's Embodiment of Metaphor in a Toronto Zombie Walk." *Journal of Contemporary Anthropology* 1, no. 1 (2010): 49–71.

Peck, Jamie. "Zombie Neoliberalism and the Ambidextrous State." *Theoretical Criminology* 14, no. 1 (2010): 104–10.

Pfau, George. "Feverish Homeless Cannibal." In *Zombies in the Academy: Living Death in Higher Education,* edited by Andrew Whelan, Ruth Walker, and Christopher Moore. Bristol, U.K.: Intellect, 2013.

Pifer, Lynn. "Slacker Bites Back: *Shaun of the Dead* Finds New Life for Deadbeats." In *Better Off Dead: The Evolution of the Zombie as Posthuman,* edited by Deborah Christie and Sarah Juliet Lauro. New York: Fordham University Press, 2011.

Pokornowski, Steven. "Insecure Lives: Zombies, Global Health, and the Totalitarianism of Generalization." *Literature and Medicine* 31, no. 2 (2013): 216–34.

Pollock, Greg. "Undead Is the New Green: Zombies and Political Ecology." In *Zombies Are Us: Essays on the Humanity of the Walking Dead*, edited by Christopher M. Moreman and Cory James Rushton. Jefferson, N.C.: McFarland, 2011.

Ponder, Justin. "Dawn of the Different: The Mulatto Zombie in Zack Snyder's *Dawn of the Dead*." *Journal of Popular Culture* 45, no. 3 (2012): 551–71.

Proffitt, Jennifer M., and Rich Templin. "'Fight the Dead, Fear the Living': Zombie Apocalypse, Libertarian Paradise?" In *Thinking Dead: What the Zombie Apocalypse Means*, edited by Murali Balaji. Lanham, Md.: Lexington Books, 2013.

Pulliam, June. "Our Zombies, Ourselves: Exiting the Foucauldian Universe in George A. Romero's *Land of the Dead*." *Journal of the Fantastic in the Arts* 20, no. 1 (2009): 42–55.

Quiggan, John. *Zombie Economics: How Dead Ideas Still Walk among Us*. Princeton, N.J.: Princeton University Press, 2010.

Rhodes, Gary D. *White Zombie: Anatomy of a Horror Film*. Jefferson, N.C.: McFarland, 2001.

Rigaud, Milo. *Secrets of Voodoo*. 1953. Translated by Robert B. Cross. San Francisco, Calif.: City Lights Books, 1985.

Riley, Brendan. "The E-Dead: Zombies in the Digital Age." In *Generation Zombie: Essays on the Living Dead in American Culture*, edited by Stephanie Boluk and Wylie Lenz. Jefferson, N.C.: McFarland, 2011.

Robichaud, Christopher. *The Walking Dead and Philosophy*. Hoboken, N.J.: John Wiley, 2012.

Rogers, Martin. "Hybridity and Post-human Anxiety in *28 Days Later*." In *Zombie Culture: Autopsies of the Living Dead*, edited by Shawn McIntosh and Marc Leverette. Lanham, Md.: Scarecrow Press, 2008.

Rorabaugh, Pete, and Jesse Stommel. "Twitter vs. Zombies: New Media Literacy and the Virtual Flash Mob." July 21, 2003. http://JesseStommel.com/.

Rovner, Matthew. "What's Behind Israel's Zombie Outbreak?" *Jewish Daily Forward*, October 17, 2013. http://forward.com/schmooze/185456/whats-behind-israels-zombie-outbreak/.

Russell, Jaime. *Book of the Dead: A Complete Guide to Zombie Cinema*. Surrey, U.K.: FAB Press, 2006.

Rutherford, Jennifer. *Zombies*. New York: Routledge, 2013.

Ruthven, Andrea. "Zombie Postfeminism." In *The Year's Work at the Zombie Research Center*, edited by Edward Comentale and Aaron Jaffe. Bloomington: Indiana University Press, 2014.

Sattar, Attia. "Zombie Performance." In *The Year's Work at the Zombie Research Center*, edited by Edward Comentale and Aaron Jaffe. Bloomington: Indiana University Press, 2014.

Saunders, Robert. "Hungry Lands: Conquest, Cannibalism, and the Wendingo Spirit." In *Undead in the West: Vampires, Zombies, Mummies, and Ghosts on the Cinematic Frontier*, edited by Cynthia Miller and Bowdoin Van Riper. Lanham, Md.: Scarecrow Press, 2012.

Schneider, Rebecca. "It Seems as If . . . I Am Dead: Zombie Capitalism and Theatrical Labor." *The Drama Review* 56, no. 4 (2012): 150–62.

Scott, Niall, ed. *Monsters and the Monstrous: Myths and Metaphors of Enduring Evil.* New York: Rodopi, 2007.

Seabrook, William. *The Magic Island.* New York: Harcourt, Brace, 1929.

Shaviro, Steven. "Capitalist Monsters." *Historical Materialism* 10, no. 4 (2002): 281–90.

———. *The Cinematic Body.* Theory Out of Bounds 2. Minneapolis: University of Minnesota Press, 1993.

Sheller, Mimi. *Consuming the Caribbean: From Arawaks to Zombies.* London: Routledge, 2003.

Shelley, Mary. *Frankenstein, or the Modern Prometheus.* 1818. Reprint, New York: Dover, 1994.

Sigurdson, Ola. "Slavoj Žižek, the Death Drive, and Zombies: A Theological Account." *Modern Theology* 29, no. 3 (2013): 361–80.

Slater, Jay. *Eaten Alive! Italian Cannibal and Zombie Movies.* London: Plexus, 2002.

Smith, Neil. "Comment: Neo-liberalism: Dominant but Dead." *Focaal* 51 (2008): 155–57.

Soon, Winnie. "Zombification: The Living Dead in Spam." http://www.aprja.net/?p=2471.

Sorensen, Leif. "Against the Post-apocalyptic: Narrative Closure in Colson Whitehead's *Zone One." Contemporary Literature* 55, no. 3 (2014): 559–92.

Stanford Encyclopedia of Philosophy. "Zombies." http://plato.stanford.edu/entries/zombies/.

Stommel, Jesse. "'Pity Poor Flesh': Terrible Bodies in the Films of Carpenter, Cronenberg, and Romero." *Bright Lights Film Journal,* May 1, 2007. http://brightlightsfilm.com/pity-poor-flesh-terrible-bodies-films-carpenter-cronenberg-romero/#.WOROmGTyvBI.

———. "Toward a Zombie Pedagogy." In *Zombies in the Academy: Living Death in Higher Education,* edited by Andrew Whelan, Ruth Walker, and Christopher Moore. Bristol, U.K.: Intellect, 2013.

Stratton, Jon. *Uncertain Lives: Culture, Race, and Neoliberalism in Australia.* Cambridge: Cambridge Scholars, 2011.

———. "Zombie Trouble: Zombie Texts, Bare Life, and Displaced People." *European Journal of Cultural Studies* 14, no. 3 (2011): 265–81.

Sutherland, Meghan. "Rigor/Mortis: The Industrial Life of Style in American Zombie Cinema." *Framework: The Journal of Cinema and Media* 48, no. 1 (2007): 64–78.

Swanson, Carl Joseph. "'The Only Metaphor Left': Colson Whitehead's *Zone One* and Zombie Narrative Form." *Genre* 47, no. 3 (2014): 379–405.

Swanson, Lucy. "Blankness, Alienation, and the Zombie in Recent Francophone Fiction." *International Journal of Francophone Studies* 17, no. 2 (2014): 177–97.

———. "Zombie Nation? The Horde, Social Uprisings, and National Narratives." *Cincinnati Romance Review* 34 (Fall 2012): 13–33.

Switaj, Elizabeth. "Ageing, Disability, and Zombies: The Happy Zombie Sunrise Home." *Femspec* 14, no. 2 (2014): 34–58.

Tait, R. Colin. "(Zombie) Revolution at the Gates: The Dead, the 'Multitude,' and George A Romero." *Cinephile* 3, no. 1 (2007): 61–70.

Teitelbaum, Michael, and Jon Apple. *The Very Hungry Zombie: A Parody.* New York: Skyhorse, 2012.

Thacker, Eugene. *After Life*. Chicago: University of Chicago Press, 2010.

———. *In the Dust of This Planet: Horror of Philosophy*. Vol. 1. Winchester, U.K.: Zero Books, 2011.

———. "Nekros: or, The Poetics of Biopolitics." *Incogitum Hactenus* 3 (2012). http://incognitumhactenus.com/volume3/.

———. "Nomos, Nosos, and Bios." *Culture Machine* 7 (2004). https://www.culturemachine.net/index.php/cm/article/view/25/32.

Tripp, Andrew. "Zombie Marches and the Limits of Apocalyptic Space." *Nomos Journal*, August 7, 2012. http://nomosjournal.org/2012/08/zombie-marches-and-the-limits-of-apocalyptic-space/.

Verstynen, Timothy, and Bradley Voytek. *Do Zombies Dream of Undead Sheep?* Princeton, N.J.: Princeton University Press, 2014.

Vint, Sherryl. "Abject Posthumanism: Neoliberalism, Biopolitics, and Zombies." In *Monster Culture in the 21st Century: A Reader*, edited by Marina Levina and Diem-My T. Bui. New York: Bloomsbury, 2013.

Vossen, Emma. "Laid to Rest: Romance, End of the World Sexuality, and Apocalyptic Anticipation in Robert Kirkman's *The Walking Dead*." In *Zombies and Sexuality: Essays on Desire and the Living Dead*, edited by Shaka McGlotten and Steve Jones. Jefferson, N.C.: McFarland, 2014.

Wald, Priscilla. *Contagious: Cultures, Carriers, and the Outbreak Narrative*. Durham, N.C.: Duke University Press, 2007.

Walker, Matthew. "When There's No More Room in Hell, the Dead Will Shop the Earth: Romero and Aristotle on Zombies, Happiness, and Consumption." In *The Undead and Philosophy*, edited by Richard Greene and K. Silem Mohammad. Chicago: Open Court, 2006.

Waller, Gregory, ed. *American Horrors: Essays on the Modern American Horror Film*. Chicago: University of Illinois Press, 1987.

———. *The Living and the Undead: From Stoker's "Dracula" to Romero's "Dawn of the Dead."* Chicago: University of Illinois Press, 1986.

Warner, Marina. *Fantastic Metamorphoses, Other Worlds*. Oxford: Oxford University Press, 2004.

Watt, Stephen. "Zombie Psychology." In *The Year's Work at the Zombie Research Center*, edited by Edward Comentale and Aaron Jaffe. Bloomington: Indiana University Press, 2014.

Webb, Jen, and Sam Byrnand. "Some Kind of Virus: The Zombie as Body and as Trope." *Body and Society* 14, no. 2 (2008): 83–98.

Weinstock, Jeffrey. "Zombie TV." *Post Identity* 2, no. 2 (1999). https://quod.lib.umich.edu/p/postid/pid9999.0002.201/--zombie-tv?rgn=main;view=fulltext.

Weise, Matthew. "How the Zombie Changed Videogames." In *Zombies Are Us: Essays on the Humanity of the Walking Dead*, edited by Christopher Moreman and Cory James Rushton. Jefferson, N.C.: McFarland, 2011.

Wetmore, Kevin J., Jr. *Back from the Dead: Remakes of the Romero Zombie Films as Markers of Their Times*. Jefferson, N.C.: McFarland, 2011.

Whelan, Andrew, Ruth Walker, and Christopher Moore, eds. *Zombies in the Academy: Living Death in Higher Education.* Bristol, U.K.: Intellect, 2013.

White, Michele. "Killing Whiteness: The Critical Positioning of Zombie Walk Brides in Internet Settings." In *Monster Culture in the 21st Century: A Reader,* edited by Marina Levina and Diem-My T. Bui. New York: Bloomsbury, 2013.

Whitehead, Colson. *Zone One.* New York: Doubleday, 2011.

Williams, Evan Calder. *Combined and Uneven Apocalypse.* Winchester, U.K.: Zero Books, 2011.

Williams, Tony. "White Zombie: Haitian Horror." *Jump Cut* 28 (1983): 18–20.

Wood, Robin. "Apocalypse Now: Notes on the Living Dead." In *American Nightmare: Essays on the Horror Film,* edited by Andrew Britton and Robin Wood. Toronto: Festival of Festivals, 1979.

———. *Hollywood from Vietnam to Reagan—and Beyond.* New York: Columbia University Press, 2003.

Yuen, Wayne. *The Walking Dead and Philosophy.* Chicago: Open Court, 2012.

Zani, Steven, and Kevin Meaux. "Lucio Fulci and the Decaying Definition of Zombie Narratives." In *Better Off Dead: The Evolution of the Zombie as Posthuman,* edited by Deborah Christie and Sarah Juliet Lauro. New York: Fordham University Press, 2011.

Zealand, Christopher. "The National Strategy for Zombie Containment: Myth Meets Activism in Post 9/11 America." In *Generation Zombie: Essays on the Living Dead in American Culture,* edited by Stephanie Boluk and Wylie Lenz. Jefferson, N.C.: McFarland, 2011.

Žižek, Slavoj. *Looking Awry: An Introduction to Jacques Lacan through Popular Culture.* Cambridge, Mass.: MIT Press, 1992.

Previous Publications

Chapter 1 was first published as Steven Shaviro, "Contagious Allegories: George Romero," in *The Cinematic Body*, 83–104. Minneapolis: University of Minnesota Press, 1993.

Chapter 2 was first published as Jeffrey Weinstock, "Zombie TV," *Post Identity* 2, no. 2 (1999), http://hdl.handle.net/2027/spo.pid9999.0002.201. Reprinted with permission.

Chapter 3 was first published as Priscilla Wald, "Viral Cultures: Microbes and Politics in the Cold War," in *Contagious: Cultures, Carriers, and the Outbreak Narrative*, 157–61 and 183–212. Durham, N.C.: Duke University Press, 2007. Copyright 2007 Duke University Press. All rights reserved. Reprinted by permission of Duke University Press. http://www.dukeupress.edu/.

Chapter 4 was first published as Elizabeth McAlister, "Slaves, Cannibals, and Infected Hyper-Whites: The Race and Religion of Zombies," *Anthropological Quarterly* 85 (2012): 457–86.

Chapter 5 was first published as Ola Sigurdson, "Slavoj Žižek, the Death Drive, and Zombies: A Theological Account," *Modern Theology* 29, no. 3 (2013): 361–80. Reprinted with permission of John Wiley and Sons.

Chapter 6 was first published as Jen Webb and Sam Byrnand, "Some Kind of Virus: The Zombie as Body and as Trope," *Body and Society* 14 (2008): 83–98. Reprinted with permission.

Chapter 7 was first published as David McNally, "Ugly Beauty: Monstrous Dreams of Utopia," in *Monsters of the Market: Zombies, Vampires, and Global Capitalism*, 253–69. Leiden, The Netherlands: Koninklijke Brill NV, 2011.

Chapter 8 was first published as Jean Comaroff and John Comaroff, "Alien-Nation: Zombies, Immigrants, and Millennial Capitalism," *South Atlantic Quarterly* 101, no. 4 (2002): 779–805, doi:10.1215/00382876-101-4-779.

Chapter 9 was first published as Lars Bang Larsen, "Zombies of Immaterial Labor: The Modern Monster and the Death of Death," *e-flux Journal* 15 (2010), http://www.e-flux.com/journal/15/61295/zombies-of-immaterial-labor-the-modern-monster-and-the-death-of-death/.

Chapter 10 was first published as Sherryl Vint, "Abject Posthumanism: Neoliberalism,

Biopolitics, and Zombies," in *Monster Culture in the Twenty-first Century*, ed. Marina Levina and Diem-My T. Bui, 133–46. London: Bloomsbury Academic, 2013.

Chapter 11 was first published as Edward P. Comentale, "Zombie Race," in *The Year's Work at the Zombie Research Center*, ed. Edward P. Comentale and Aaron Jaffe, 276–314. Bloomington: Indiana University Press, 2014. Copyright 2014 Indiana University Press. Reprinted with permission of Indiana University Press.

Chapter 12 was first published as Barry Keith Grant, "Taking Back the *Night of the Living Dead*: George Romero, Feminism, and the Horror Film," in *The Dread of Difference: Gender and the Horror Film*, ed. Barry Keith Grant, 200–212. Austin: University of Texas Press, 1996.

Chapter 13 was first published as Shaka McGlotten, "Dead and Live Life: Zombies, Queers, and Online Sociality," in *Generation Zombie*, ed. Stephanie Boluk and Wylie Lenz, 182–93. Jefferson, N.C.: McFarland, 2011. Copyright 2011. Reprinted by permission of McFarland and Company, Inc., Box 611, Jefferson, NC 28640. http://www .mcfarlandpub.com/.

Chapter 14 was first published as Anna Mae Duane, "The Crawling Dead: Disability and the Zombie's Revenge," http://annamaeduane.com/2014/02/04/the-crawling -dead-disability-and-the-zombies-revenge/.

Chapter 15 was first published as Jon Stratton, "Zombie Trouble: Zombie Texts, Bare Life, and Displaced People," *European Journal of Cultural Studies* 14 (2011): 265–81.

Chapter 16 was first published as Fred Botting, "Zombie London: Unexceptionalities of the New World Order," in *London Gothic: Place, Space, and the Gothic Imagination*, Continuum Literary Series, ed. Lawrence Phillips and Anne Witchard, 153–71. London: Continuum, 2010.

Chapter 17 was first published as Simon Orpana, "Spooks of Biopower: The Uncanny Carnivalesque of Zombie Walks," *TOPIA: Canadian Journal of Cultural Studies* 25 (Spring 2011): 153–76.

Chapter 18 was first published as Tavia Nyong'o, "The Scene of Occupation," *The Drama Review* 56, no. 4 (2012): 136–49.

Chapter 19 was first published as Travis Linnemann, Tyler Wall, and Edward Green, "The Walking Dead and Killing State: Zombification and the Normalization of Police Violence," in *Theoretical Criminology*, published online April 7, 2014, 1–22. Copyright 2014 by SAGE Publications, Ltd. Reprinted by permission of SAGE Publications, Ltd.

Chapter 20 was first published as Eugene Thacker, "Nekros: or, The Poetics of Biopolitics," in *Incognitum Hactenus: Journal of Art, Horror, and Philosophy*, http:// incognitumhactenus.com/nekros-or-the-poetics-of-biopolitics/.

Chapter 21 was first published as Jeffrey Jerome Cohen, "Grey (A Zombie Ecology)," in *Prismatic Ecology: Ecotheory beyond Green*, ed. Jeffrey Jerome Cohen, 270–89. Minneapolis: University of Minnesota Press, 2013.

Chapter 22 was first published as Sarah Juliet Lauro and Karen Embry, "A Zombie Manifesto: The Nonhuman Condition in the Era of Advanced Capitalism," in *boundary 2* 35, no. 1 (2008): 85–108. Copyright 2008 Duke University Press. All rights reserved.

Reprinted by permission of the copyright holder, Duke University Press. http://www.dukeupress.edu/.

Chapter 23 was first published as Gerry Canavan, "'We *Are* the Walking Dead': Race, Time, and Survival in Zombie Narrative," *Extrapolation* 51 (2010): 431–53.

Contributors

FRED BOTTING is professor of English literature and creative writing at Kingston University in London. He has written extensively on gothic fictions and on theory, film, and cultural forms, most recently publishing the books *Gothic Romanced: Consumption, Gender, and Technology in Contemporary Fictions* and *Limits of Horror: Technology, Bodies, Gothic.*

SAMUEL BYRNAND is a research student and teacher at the University of Canberra and is building an archive of legislation and governmental policy regarding Indigenous Australian people for the purposes of analysis. He is a shameless cinephile, screenwriter, and horror genre analyst—and a zombie at heart.

GERRY CANAVAN is assistant professor of English at Marquette University, specializing in science fiction of the twentieth- and twenty-first centuries. He is a coeditor of *Green Planets: Ecology and Science Fiction* and *The Cambridge Companion to American Science Fiction* and the author of *Octavia E. Butler.*

JEFFREY JEROME COHEN is professor of English and director of the Medieval and Early Modern Studies Institute at the George Washington University. He is the author, most recently, of *Stone: An Ecology of the Inhuman* (Minnesota, 2015) and the editor of the collections *Monster Theory: Reading Culture* (Minnesota, 1996), *Prismatic Ecology: Ecotheory beyond Green* (Minnesota, 2013), and *Elemental Ecocriticism: Thinking with Earth, Air, Water, and Fire* (with Lowell Duckert; Minnesota, 2016).

JEAN COMAROFF is the Alfred North Whitehead Professor of African and African American Studies and Anthropology at Harvard University. She is coauthor, with John Comaroff, of *Millennial Capitalism and the Culture of Neoliberalism* and *Thinking through Crime and Policing.*

JOHN COMAROFF is Hugh K. Foster Professor of African and African American Studies and of Anthropology at Harvard University; he is also Oppenheimer Research Fellow in African Studies at Harvard and an Honorary Professor of Anthropology at the University of Cape Town. His most recent books, with Jean Comaroff, include *Theory from the*

South: How Euro-America Is Evolving toward Africa and *The Truth about Crime: Sovereignty, Knowledge, Social Order.*

EDWARD P. COMENTALE is professor of English and associate vice provost of arts and humanities at Indiana University. He is the author of *Sweet Air: Modernism, Regionalism, and American Popular Song* and *Modernism, Cultural Production, and the British Avant-Garde,* as well as a coeditor of *The Year's Work at the Zombie Research Center* (with Aaron Jaffe), *The Year's Work in Lebowski Studies* (with Aaron Jaffe), and *The Cultural Politics of Ian Fleming and 007* (with Stephen Watt and Skip Willman).

ANNA MAE DUANE is associate professor of English at the University of Connecticut. She is the author of *Suffering Childhood in Early America: Violence, Race, and the Making of the Child Victim* and editor of *The Children's Table: Childhood Studies and the Humanities* and (with Katharine Capshaw) *Who Writes for Black Children? African American Children's Literature before 1900* (Minnesota, 2017).

KAREN EMBRY is an instructor of composition and literature at Portland Community College. Her writing has been published in *boundary 2, Symposium,* and *Best New Poets 2014.*

BARRY KEITH GRANT is professor emeritus of film studies and popular culture at Brock University in Ontario, Canada. His many books include *The Dread of Difference: Gender and the Horror Film, 100 Science Fiction Films, Shadows of Doubt: Negotiations of Masculinity in American Genre Films,* and *Invasion of the Body Snatchers.*

EDWARD GREEN is assistant professor of criminal justice at Roosevelt University. His work focuses on the sociology of punishment, prisons, and social justice.

LARS BANG LARSEN is an art historian, independent curator, and writer based in Barcelona and Copenhagen. His publications include *Sture Johannesson,* a monograph about Palle Nielsen's utopian adventure playgrounds; *The Model: A Model for a Qualitative Society*; and the essay series *Kunst er Norm* (Art is norm).

SARAH JULIET LAURO is assistant professor of hemispheric literature at the University of Tampa. She is the author of *The Transatlantic Zombie: Slavery, Rebellion, and Living Death* and a coeditor of *Better Off Dead: The Evolution of the Zombie as Posthuman.*

TRAVIS LINNEMANN is assistant professor of justice studies at Eastern Kentucky University. He is the author of *Meth Wars: Police, Media, Power.*

ELIZABETH McALISTER is professor of religion and African American studies at Wesleyan University in Middletown, Connecticut, and author of *Rara! Vodou, Power, and Performance in Haiti and Its Diaspora* and *Race, Nation, and Religion in the Americas.*

SHAKA McGLOTTEN is associate professor of media, society, and the arts at Purchase College–SUNY. He is the author of *Virtual Intimacies: Media, Affect, and Queer Sociality* and coeditor of *Black Genders and Sexualities* and *Zombie Sexuality.*

DAVID McNALLY is professor of political science at York University in Toronto. He is the author of many books, including *Political Economy and the Rise of Capitalism*; *Against the Market: Political Economy, Market Socialism, and the Marxist Critique*; *Bodies of Meaning: Studies on Language, Labor, and Liberation*; and *Another World Is Possible: Globalization and Anti-Capitalism*.

TAVIA NYONG'O is professor of American studies at Yale University and a coeditor of the journal *Social Text*. He is the author of *The Amalgamation Waltz: Race, Performance, and the Ruses of Memory* (Minnesota, 2009).

SIMON ORPANA is a Social Sciences and Humanities Research Council of Canada postdoctoral fellow at the Department of English and Film Studies, University of Alberta. His writing has appeared in journals such as *TOPIA* and *English Studies in Canada*, and he is a coauthor of the graphic history *Showdown! Making Modern Unions* (with Rob Kristofferson).

STEVEN SHAVIRO is the DeRoy Professor of English at Wayne State University. His books include *Connected, or What It Means to Live in the Network Society* (Minnesota, 2003), *The Universe of Things: On Speculative Realism* (Minnesota, 2014), and *Discognition*.

OLA SIGURDSON is professor of systematic theology at the University of Gothenburg, Sweden. He is the author of *Heavenly Bodies: Incarnation, the Gaze, and Embodiment in Christian Theology* and *Theology and Marxism in Eagleton and Žižek: A Conspiracy of Hope*.

JON STRATTON is adjunct professor of cultural studies in the School of Communication, International Studies, and Languages at the University of South Australia. He has published in cultural studies, Jewish studies, popular music studies, Australian studies, and on race and multiculturalism and is the author or editor of fourteen books, the most recent being *When Music Migrates: Crossing British and European Racial Faultlines 1945–2010* and *Black Popular Music in Britain since 1945* (edited with Nabeel Zuberi).

EUGENE THACKER is professor at the New School in New York City. He is the author of several books, including *In the Dust of This Planet, Biomedia* (Minnesota, 2004), and (with Alexander Galloway) *The Exploit: A Theory of Networks* (Minnesota, 2007).

SHERRYL VINT is professor of English at the University of California at Riverside, where she directs Science Fiction and Technoculture studies. She is the author of *Science Fiction: A Guide for the Perplexed* and *Beyond Cyberpunk* and coeditor of *The Routledge Companion to Science Fiction*.

PRISCILLA WALD is R. Florence Brinkley Professor of English and Margaret Taylor Smith Director of the Program in Gender, Sexuality, and Feminist Studies at Duke University. She is author of *Constituting Americans: Cultural Anxiety and Narrative Form* and *Contagious: Cultures, Carriers, and the Outbreak Narrative* and coeditor of *The American Novel 1870–1940*, vol. 6, *Oxford History of the Novel in English* (with Michael Elliott).

TYLER WALL is associate professor of justice studies at Eastern Kentucky University.

JEN WEBB is Distinguished Professor of Creative Practice and director of the Centre for Creative and Cultural Research at the University of Canberra, Australia. Her most recent book was *Art and Human Rights: Contemporary Asian Contexts.*

JEFFREY ANDREW WEINSTOCK is professor of English at Central Michigan University and an associate editor for the *Journal of the Fantastic in the Arts.* He is an author or editor of twenty books. The most recent include *The Cambridge Companion to the American Gothic, Goth Music: From Sound to Subculture* (with Isabella van Elferen), *Return to Twin Peaks: New Approaches to Materiality, Theory, and Genre on Television* (with Catherine Spooner), and *The Age of Lovecraft* (with Carl Sederholm; Minnesota, 2016).

Index

235n5, 319, 321–25, 356, 407; French, 402; postrevolutionary, 137, 139, 141, 150, 153n19; revolutionary time, 322, 325, 322. *See also* Haiti: revolution of; Industrial age

Rhys, Jean, 252–53

Rieder, John, 356, 416–19

riot, 103, 106, 124–25, 127, 129, 130, 201, 398, 428

ritual, 8, 16, 64, 66–71, 103, 143, 192, 195–96, 253, 322, 335, 363, 367, 402, 405, 409n7, 411n52; murder, 143, 154n35

Romanticism, 91, 273, 278–82, 322, 378

Romero, George, x–xiii, xix–xx, 1–4, 6, 7–19, 21, 24–25, 31, 64, 74–81, 91–94, 99, 101n27, 101n35, 101n39, 103, 106–8, 117, 128, 159–60, 164, 169n14, 172, 184–85, 187, 205, 209, 212–21, 235n4, 241, 247, 250, 252, 254–55, 259–60, 262, 277, 281–82, 294, 309, 313nn1–2, 314n19, 315n62, 315n71, 348, 354, 356–57, 378, 385, 388, 396, 413, 416–17. See also *Crazies, The*; *Dawn of the Dead*; *Day of the Dead*; *Land of the Dead*; *Night of the Living Dead*

Ronell, Avital, 3, 20

rupture, 76, 124, 149, 202, 273, 306, 322–23, 398, 401

rural, 25, 106, 139, 142–46, 149, 153n25, 154n45, 180, 251, 273, 275, 280, 417

Russell, Jaime, xx, 409nn15–16

sacrifice, 14–15, 46, 70, 98, 163, 172, 176–78, 195, 256, 290, 298, 309, 408

Said, Edward, 253, 401

Saint Domingue, xi, 64–65, 401. *See also* Haiti

saints, xv, 39, 76, 197, 321, 373, 379

salt, 68; bath salts, 339–45

SARS, 281, 431n31

Sartre, Jean Paul, 119, 190–91

Savini, Tom, 185, 214, 216

Scarry, Elaine, 259–60

science fiction, 35–36, 41, 43, 50–51, 59n11, 59n14, 171, 215, 313n1, 359, 365, 368, 415–16, 419, 431n35

scientist, 10, 13, 32n15, 33–34, 36, 50, 58, 60n28, 113, 178, 226, 247, 279, 353, 384–85, 409n5. *See also* mad scientist

Seabrook, W. B., xiii, 83n30, 128, 191–93

Searle, John, xiii, 6, 411n54

secularism, 85–86, 260

segregation. *See* desegregation

September 11. *See* 9/11

serial killer, 263, 337, 423

sexism, 7, 93, 160

sexuality, xiii, 46, 61n37, 78, 81, 125, 184–85, 187–88, 224, 424, 430, 314n41; sexual libera-

tion, 227; sex symbol, 300; sex work, 146. *See also* heterosexual; homosexuality

sf. *See* science fiction

Shakespeare, William, 125, 383

Shane (film), 431n18

Shaun of the Dead (film), 103, 108, 173, 236n21, 249, 262, 266, 281, 408n1, 413

Shelley, Mary, 91, 106, 126, 159, 277–78, 380n23, 411n47

Shelley, P. B., 133, 278

Shining, The (film), 280

shoppers, 12, 118

shopping mall, xi, 2, 12, 25, 76, 93–94, 103, 117, 124, 159, 284, 344–45

siege film, 268n69

slavery, x, 3, 45, 64–69, 71, 74, 80–81, 119, 134n9, 137n39, 162–63, 174, 183, 190, 192, 209, 250–54, 356, 402–4, 423, 427, 430n6; slave rebellion, 396–99, 401–2, 407–8; slaves, ix, xi, 1, 3, 64, 69, 72, 75, 78, 83n30, 130–31, 174, 193, 252–54, 261, 399, 402–3; slave trade, xi, 2, 68, 70, 183, 186, 190, 193, 199, 209n3, 253, 410n32. *See also* Africa: Africans, enslaved; enslavement

Smith, Adam, 138, 158

Snyder, Zack, 93, 281, 315n62, 408n1

Sobchack, Vivian, 49–50, 59n11, 415–16

socialism, 130, 141, 153n21

social order, 9, 75, 140, 200, 218, 265, 294, 298, 302, 309–10, 333–34, 346, 348, 416; social collectivity, 126

sociopath, 165, 337, 423

Socrates, 365–67

soldiers, 13–15, 18, 70, 112–14, 129, 160, 174, 200, 262, 286, 290, 365, 407–8. *See also* military

sorcerer, 66, 70, 72, 74, 83n16, 143, 158, 195. *See also* bokor; *houngan*; witch doctor

soul (spiritual principle), ix, 47, 50, 64, 66–67, 70, 74–75, 86, 88, 112, 120, 157, 164–65, 178, 190, 196, 220, 250, 278, 303, 308, 321–22, 328, 353, 364, 369, 373, 379–80n17, 383–84, 388, 393n6, 397, 402, 404, 410n21

South Africa, 5, 44–45, 106, 137–52, 153n25, 154n37, 154n45, 155n48, 155n55, 187, 251, 254, 420

space invaders, 36, 38; space invasion, 39, 48. *See also* alien; outer space

spectacle, 11, 15, 18–19, 144, 160, 186, 198, 213, 218–19, 271, 273, 278, 281, 286, 295, 300, 306, 309, 332–33, 342–44, 346, 348

specter, xi, 85, 103, 139, 144, 150, 158–59, 254, 283, 288, 290, 309, 353, 364, 383, 387, 395–98, 404; spectral subject, 329

speed, 141, 146, 174, 206, 273, 280–82, 328, 354, 388, 411n43